THE CLASSICS OF WESTERN SPIRITUALITY
A Library of the Great Spiritual Masters

President and Publisher
Kevin A. Lynch, C.S.P.

EDITORIAL BOARD

The Classic Midrash
TANNAITIC COMMENTARIES ON THE BIBLE

TRANSLATION, INTRODUCTION AND COMMENTARIES BY
REUVEN HAMMER

PREFACE BY
JUDAH GOLDIN

PAULIST PRESS
NEW YORK • MAHWAH

Cover art: This depiction of Rabban Gamaliel, together with his pupils, is from the famous fourteenth-century Hebrew illuminated manuscript, the *Sarajevo Haggadah.* The text by Cecil Roth that accompanies a facsimile edition of the *Sarajevo Haggadah* states that "apparently, . . .this [depiction] perpetuates the traditional representation of the scribe-teacher which seems to have figured in the early illuminated codices of the Hebrew Bible." The facsimile edition of the *Sarajevo Haggadah* from which this representation comes is used courtesy of Dr. Andre Ungar, Rabbi of Temple Emanuel, Woodcliff Lake, New Jersey.

Excerpts from the TANAKH: The New JPS Translation According to the Traditional Hebrew Text. Copyright 1962 by the Jewish Publication Society. Used by permission.

Library of Congress Cataloging-in-Publication Data

The Classic Midrash: Tannaitic commentaries on the Bible: translation, introduction and commentaries by Reuven Hammer; preface by Judah Goldin.
    p. cm.—(Classics of Western spirituality)
    Includes bibliographical references.
    ISBN 0-8091-0467-9 (cloth)—ISBN 0-8091-3503-5 (pbk.)
    1. Halakhic Midrashim—Translations into English. 2. Bible. O.T. Pentateuch—Commentaries. I. Hammer, Reuven. II. Bible. O.T. Pentateuch. English. Hammer. Selections. 1994. III. Series.
BM512.C56 1994
296.1'40521—dc20   94-35177
                                                  CIP

Published by Paulist Press
997 Macarthur Boulevard
Mahwah, New Jersey 07430

Printed and bound in the
United States of America

CONTENTS

I
SCRIPTURAL INTERPRETATION—AGGADAH

II
INTERPRETATION OF LEGAL PORTIONS—HALAKHA

CONTENTS

Translator of this Volume

REUVEN HAMMER received his rabbinic ordination and a doctorate in theology from the Jewish Theological Seminary and a Ph.D. in Communicative Disorders from Northwestern University. After serving as a chaplain in the U.S. Air Force and a congregational rabbi for fifteen years, he and his family moved to Israel in 1973, where he has taught Jewish studies and special education in various institutions, including the Hebrew University, David Yellin College and Oranim.

As Dean of the Jewish Theological Seminary of America's Jerusalem Campus and founding Director of the Seminary of Judaic Studies, he supervised the training of hundreds of American, Israeli, and South American rabbinic students. He has taught and lectured in the United States, South America, England, and the former Soviet Union.

His articles on both popular and scholarly topics have appeared in numerous periodicals in both Hebrew and English. His book *Sifre: A Tannaitic Commentary on the Book of Deuteronomy* received the National Jewish Book Council award as the outstanding work of scholarship of 1987.

Author of the Preface

JUDAH GOLDIN is Emeritus Professor of Postbiblical Hebrew Literature and Oriental Studies at the University of Pennsylvania. Among his academic positions before joining the University of Pennsylvania were undergraduate Dean and Associate Professor of Aggadah at the Jewish Theological Seminary (1952–1958) and Professor of Classical Judaica at Yale University (1958–1973). He is a Fellow of the American Academy for Jewish Research, a Fellow of the American Academy of Arts and Sciences, and a Guggenheim Fellow. An author, editor, and translator, he has written *The Fathers According to Rabbi Nathan, The Living Talmud,* and *The Song at the Sea.*

To my mother,
Link Hammer,
of blessed memory
whose love and devotion to her husband and her son
were without bound.
PROVERBS 31:28

PREFACE

The contents of midrashic-talmudic literature may be described as the answer to two questions. The first is, How shall we conduct ourselves and our institutions (halakah); the second is, What contemporary significance is there to the inherited records our Teachers designate as *kitbe ha-qodesh*, Sacred Scriptures, and that is haggadah.

During almost five hundred years before the destruction of the second Jerusalem Temple (69–70 C.E.), the Torah of Moses had been subject to interpretation in some form—by translation, by para-Biblical reworking and retelling, by imitation, by epigrammatization, by citation for support of favored views. At Ezra's reading of the Torah (c.458 B.C.E.), Levites and prominent men explained what it proclaimed. So they obviously had studied it. And as books after the Five Books of Moses were gradually added to the corpus of authoritative sources, sometimes after debate and defense, they too were studied and explained, drawn on for instruction and guidance and review.

The contents and implications of law grew out of, or were regarded as growing out of, the Five Books (Pentateuch) of Moses, although there are ad hoc decrees too; but allusions to and endorsements of the laws occur even in a number of the post-Mosaic books. The Teachers do not hesitate to draw on these. And though when they are in the intellectual mood for it, they do not refrain from homiletical and narrative justification of prescribed rules of conduct (see, for many examples, Mekilta, Ba-Hodesh 8, II, 257–259, or M. Baba Qamma 8:6), it is in the field of haggadah, the nonstatutory exhortation-speculation, imaginative and homiletic inventiveness, that the intellectual leaders emerge especially as spokesmen of the tradition that shapes the Jewish mentality, and ideally shapes their behavior too. This gave the Hebrew Scriptures their afterlife, and by that token life to the folk, scholars, and people as a whole. Without it Biblical literature would have been forgotten except perhaps by some antiquarians. And by intertwining all the books with the Torah of Moses, a unity was superimposed on Pentateuch, Prophets, and the Sacred Writings (Ketubim).

1

PREFACE

The activity and products of interpretation are known as Midrash, a noun formed from the verbal root "darash" (drš). That root is not uncommon in Biblical composition (as "seek out"); but post-Biblically it gets to mean "interpret," or "explain," and it may even be used (e.g., in M. Ketubot 4:6 or Pesiqta R. 113B) for one sage interpreting the view of another. Similarly it may be employed for interpretation of a document or a contract (cf. T. Ketubot 4:9). But the overwhelming use of Midrash is for interpretation and enlisting of a verse or verses of Scripture. The term in fact is adopted for classification of one of the three branches of the academic curriculum. (The other two are halakot and aggadot.)

Enlistment of Biblical verses takes place even in halakic exposition. For example (M. Gittin 9:10), in trying to decide what are legitimate grounds for divorce, the School of Shammai objects to it unless the woman has been found guilty of unchastity, as the verse (Deut. 24:1) says, If the husband found her guilty of unchastity. The School of Hillel says, Even if she ruined his supper, as that verse reads, "Anything improper." R. Akiba says, Even if he found someone more attractive, as that very verse reads, "and if it come to pass that in his eyes [his wife] no longer found favor." All three views draw on the same verse but each with its own emphasis of reading. (Cf. Sifre Deut. p. 288.) The orientation is of course patriarchal but the aim is reenforcing domestic stability.

Or more strikingly (slightly condensed): Scripture (Deut. 17:8) prescribes that when in a civil dispute the issue is baffling, it is to be brought to a court "of levitical priests or the magistrate in charge at the time." The Sifre (Deut. 153:206–7) explains this as follows: The ancient Biblical rule applies no less to the court of Jabneh (after 70 C.E.) for that is a legitimate court even if its members include neither priests nor Levites. And since the meaning of "at that time" is obvious—to whom else can you bring your case?—the Midrash summons Ecclesiastes 7:10, "Don't say ... former times were better than these." There are those in every society to whom once upon a time was always superior to the present.

One more example: Exodus 21:5–6 declares that the Hebrew slave who refuses to be freed after six years of servitude is to have his ear pierced and remain in bondage. In this connection Rabban Yohanan ben Zakkai is quoted, "The ear that [at Sinai] heard the command, 'Thou shalt not steal,' but proceeded to steal" (and thus incurred the penalty of bondage) "shall be pierced rather than any other part of the body." The text goes on: The Scripture declares that "the ear should be pierced by an awl" but the halakic interpretation declares that any instrument will do.

What is so special about an awl? (Rabbi maintains that only a metal

2

instrument shall be used.) Even if we wish to say that the halakic interpretation is an amplification or modification of the verbatim Biblical injunction, what is significant is that the Midrash clings to what the verse says, is attentive to it, but decides what it must have meant even at its first publication, and Rabbi therefore strives to get as close as he can to the terminology of the recorded law. For the compiler of the Midrash it is apparently noteworthy that the word *awl* in the verse may be regarded in more than one way. Alternatives are preserved whenever more or less feasible and recalled. But there is forgetting too.

While it is true that even in the course of striving to arrive at precise halakic meaning, a haggadic reflection may be introduced from time to time—for example, on the Exodus 21:18 clause, "When men quarrel," the Midrash (MRS 173) observes, "No good ever comes out of quarreling" and even invokes the example from Genesis 13 of what led to the parting of Lot from Abraham—it is primarily in connection with haggadah that we witness the imaginativeness and spontaneity of the midrashic mind. And this is already true of the compilations of teachings by the Tannaim, the Sages of the first two centuries C.E., on the books of Exodus through Deuteronomy. It has recently been proposed (by A. Mirsky) that once there was even a similar compilation for Genesis, which contains extremely little of what may be regarded as halakah.

In interpretation of haggadah there is greater readiness to welcome expository extensions than in the use of Biblical support for halakic ruling. But even in the former, the midrashic comments attempt to keep to the mood of the verse. Some doubtless are artificial, as wherever imaginativeness is encouraged, or consolation. Deuteronomy 20:1 reassures Israel that when they encounter their enemies "You shall not fear them, for the Lord your God who led you out of the land of Egypt is with you." The brief midrashic comment on that verse (Sifre Deut. 190, p. 232) is "He who led you out of the Land of Egypt is with you whenever you're in distress."

Or again: On Deuteronomy 11:13, "to love the Lord your God," the Midrash (Sifre Deut. 41, p. 87) comments, "Lest you say I shall study Torah, so that I might become rich, so that I may acquire the title 'Rabbi,' so that I might be rewarded in the World to Come, the verse teaches 'to love the Lord your God,' that is, whatever you do, do only out of love for Him." The homiletical spelling-out is certainly not hyperbolic though its concretizing illustrations go beyond the Biblical text.

There is nothing remarkable about these examples and the many more that can be introduced. But probably it is useful to recall the presence of what may be called the "natural homiletical" because of the too frequent appropriation of the term Midrash for varieties of forced and baroque exegesis only. This of course is not to deny that even in the tannaite compilations such meanings do appear. It came to pass when Pharaoh sent out the Israelites (Exod. 13:17) means, When he accompanied them (Mekilta, Be-Shallah, 1, I, 169), though the chapter continues with his hostile pursuit of them. "Fairest of women" (Cant. 1:15) = "superlative one among the prophets" (Sifre Num. 139, p. 186). When you concentrate on a word it suddenly attains independence from what precedes or succeeds. "This was sometime a paradox, but now the time gives it proof."

And sometimes the line between halakah and haggadic interpretation is hard to draw. For example, Exodus 23:7 exhorts, "keep far from falsehood." For the Mekilta (Kaspa 3, III, 168 f.) five interpretations may be applicable: (1) It is a warning not to engage in slander; (2) judges are not to invite ignoramuses, boors, as their judicial colleagues; (3) judges are not to summon (solely) advocates for defense; (4) R. Nathan says, The verse is a warning to keep far from sectarianism, and verses from Ecclesiastes and Psalms are said to bear him out; (5) still another interpretation applies to a scholar: If one heard his colleague expounding a halakah properly and decides to contradict and destroy the interpretation, in order thereupon to revert to its proper meaning, and thus get the reputation for being a superior scholar, he is a speaker of falsehoods.

That the verse does indeed refer to the behavior of judges can be justified by reference to Exodus 23:6–8. That the other interpretations are homiletical need not be denied; but they reflect concerns with second century (C.E.) social problems and dangers at all times, which the Sages as usual seek to relate to the Biblical text. What is especially interesting is the criticism of what may happen in academic establishments, otherwise so often idealized.

The very close attentiveness to the particulars in a Biblical verse makes it possible for the Teachers to create a balance, as it were, where otherwise only extremes would be favored. After speaking of the Passover offering, Deuteronomy 16:8 concludes, "On the seventh day you shall hold a solemn gathering ('ṣrt, 'ṣeret) for the Lord your God." Is this to say (Sifre Deut. 135, p. 191) that a person is to be closeted ('ṣwr, 'aṣur) in the study house (bet ha-midrash) the whole of that day? The verse teaches "an 'ṣeret for the Lord" your God. Meaning what? Devote part of it to the study house and part to the pleasure of eating and drinking.

There are times when the immediate comment on a verse leads the compiler of the Midrash to assemble a number of views and exhortations that create an eloquence apparently felt necessary to rebuke attitudes of superiority over nonnative Israelites. Exodus 22:20 reads, "You shall not wrong a stranger (gr, ger) nor oppress him." In Scripture, ger is a stranger; in post-Biblical language, the ger is a proselyte.

Now, first the Midrash (Mekilta, Neziqin 18, ש, 137 ff.) spells out, *Don't wrong him* by the way you talk; *don't oppress him* in money matters. Observe: The latter is not enlarged upon, as though it were self-evident. The former however is illustrated: Don't say to him, Yesterday you were still worshiping idols and the swine you ate is still snorting from between your teeth; and you dare to argue against me! And how do we know that if you so wrong him, he can in turn retort to you? For the verse continues, "For you were gerim in the land of Egypt." Hence, R. Nathan said, Don't upbraid your fellow for a blemish that disfigures yourself.

From this point on come statements encouraging love of the ger. We are instructed that the vocabulary Scripture uses for gerim, it uses for Israel too. "Precious are the gerim." And not only that, but Abraham and King David were also addressed as gerim. In fact, not until he was ninety-nine years old did Abraham adopt circumcision, so that no stranger should ever be discouraged and say, I am too old to enter the covenant. And the paragraph closes with approval of the "four classes" in Israel: the sinless totally devoted to the Lord, the genuine proselytes, the ones who repent, and those (of the nations) who fear the Lord (sebomenoi ton theon).

Such high-pitched exhortations of course testify to the existence of contrary attitudes, to lack of hospitality to aliens. An extremist like R. Simeon b. Yohai, who had to keep in hiding from the Romans for many years, is violently antagonistic, and the Midrash (Mekilta, Be-Shallah 2, I, 201) will not suppress that. There is condemnation of the behavior of gentiles (especially Israel's enemies) and, as has been remarked, it reads like what gentile moralists say about their own society. But Israel's misconduct also leads to loud and merciless outburst. Polemics seldom are a subdued account of the day-to-day neighborhood relationships. But tensions are certainly present and this accounts for the inconsistency of midrashic views on the subject of Israelites/non-Israelites.

We have seen above (pp. 2–3) how different halakic views are adopted by Sages, all of whom draw on the same Biblical verse but each focusing on a single phrase or clause in that verse. (The reverse is also true: the same halakic conclusion but different prooftexts. Cf. Sifre Z. p 279.) Disagreement on the meaning of a verse occurs often, very vividly in the disagreement between R. Papias and R. Akiba—there may even be a theological issue involved. Thus, R. Papias interprets Canticles 1:9 in almost crass terms: As Pharaoh rode out against the Israelites on a male horse (lssty, lesussati), the Holy One blessed be He revealed Himself against him on a male horse; when Pharaoh rode out on a mare, thus the Holy One revealed Himself to him. (On the other hand, see R. Joshua ben Qorha in ARN 27, p. 83.) Enough out of you, said Akiba to him. How then do *you* interpret that verse, asked Papias. And Akiba replied, It means that just as I rejoiced (śśty) at the destruction of the Egyptians so I virtually rejoiced at My decision to destroy Israel. And what saved them? Their carrying out the commandments "of their right hand and their left." (That is, Israel's carrying out the rite of the mezuzah on their doorposts and the commandment to wear tefillin, phylacteries, on the left arm.)

The compiler of the Mekilta (Be-Shallah 7, I, 247–49) now furnishes three additional exchanges between Papias and Akiba, and each in stereotypical construction characteristic of midrash compilations (and often Mishna too): R. Papias taught and R. Akiba objects each time with, "That's enough out of you." Finally comes Akiba's explanation, after he is challenged.

Several points deserve attention. First, the Exodus verse (14:22) on the waters of the Red (Reed) Sea forming a wall for the Israelites on the right side and left becomes allegorically a reference to the two commandments the homilist wishes to underscore. Are they being neglected? (Notions of "right" and "left" intrigue thinkers in a variety of cultures.) Second, because the Canticles verse has used the imagery of a mare of Pharoah's chariot, the association with the Exodus account attracts Akiba too, but not for theriomorphic motives. Third, a pun (ssty, sussati—the samek [s] and śin [ś] are interchanged, fairly frequent especially in Palestinian sources) leaps to his mind. It is all regular manner and mannerism of midrashic literature; although there can also be objections to it (R. Eleazar ha-Modai in Mekilta Wa-Yassa 1, II, 94). However, for Akiba ssty becomes śśty, for that yields a moral: what all the Sages are on the lookout for.

Now, punning is commonplace in every literary (and oral) tradition, and that it should take place in midrashic teaching is in no way extraordinary. It would be missed if it were completely absent from rhetoric—consider John Donne's "A Hymne to God the Father": "When thou hast done, thou hast not done/For I have more." The word mqwh (miqweh) in Jeremiah 17:23, "hope," can be taken as mqwh, ritual bath, for just as the prescribed bath makes the impure pure, so the mqwh of Israel will purify Israel. Or, Who is like unto Thee among the 'lym (gods, or mighty) can yield, Who is like unto Thee among the 'lmym, the mute ones, beholding His children in distress yet holding His peace.

Taking a hint from dream interpreters, or slip of the tongue, one can split words and make them release special instruction—particularly if the word is something of a problem. The word hskt (hasket) occurs only once in Scripture; break it in two and you derive a lesson of how to proceed in study, that is, hs ktt (has, kattet), in the beginning simply listen, take in what the teacher teaches (has); thereafter (kattet) probe in depth, analyze and raise questions, and argue.

In Leviticus 14:14 we are informed that the priest is to put oil on the lobe (tnwk—root unknown) of the ear of the person to be purified of his leprosy. Tnwk, says the midrash (Sifra 72a) is twk nwk, the middle ridge of the ear (see Rabad ad loc.). And so it goes with a number of expressions that obviously call for some philological or homiletical conjecture. The word zmh (zimmah, "depravity," Lev. 20:14) can be associated with the exclamation, zh *m*h *h*w', "this child, what is it!"

Whether such explanations are mere folk etymologies, or downright playfulness, is beside the point. The rabbis are not embarrassed by them, for even the Biblical authors resort to name and word plays. Tannaite teachers are even prepared to equate Hebrew words with Greek and Roman ones. This makes the *Hebrew* unforgettable to their audience, whose vernacular is often Aramaic and Greek. (The Sages are not out to teach the people Greek!) Such a dialect reveals determination to convey the precise understanding of Biblical vocabulary to the auditors, for Torah study is never to be taken casually or in mechanical repetition. Environment influences speech, and who can say if deliberate witticism was or was not present? So impatient was Leah for Jacob (Gen. 30:16) that she did not give him time to wash his feet (Gen. R. 72:5, 841) on his return from the fields. The way our texts have survived without accompanying notation, one cannot tell whether a smile was on anyone's face, though satire is not wanting.

One can go on and on with examples of this sort, for all kinds of rhetorical acrobatics—in Scripture *qls* = "derision"; in hellenistic Roman times, the Greek word *kalos* leads the Rabbis to equate the root qls with "praise," "hail"—are permissible so long as the lesson derived is not blasphemous, is not an endeavor to undermine the rules and doctrinal assertions the talmudic Sages have set up as normative. Loan words actually contribute a touch of up-to-dateness to literalism, even chic!

A word about "normative," which disturbs a number of contemporary scholars. The rabbis unquestionably put forth their halakic rulings as normative, that is, as the only legitimate course to be adopted by all Jews. But every sect so regarded its own program. What it taught was normative—its calendar, its Sabbath regulations, its marital injunctions were normative. What probably led in the end, and not necessarily the remote end, to the triumph of Pharisaism-Rabbinism (but it was never 100 percent) was the vigor of its propaganda among the folk, its repeated admonitions and promise of reward in the World to Come, its sensitivity to what the majority could bear, its readiness to adapt to inevitable change. And not at all to be underestimated is their determination to remain in the midst of the populace, not withdrawing to isolated settlements, or identifying exclusively with one or other segment of society. Their praise of scholars did not suppress their criticism of scholarly bad behavior.

All groups chose to justify their outlook on what they insisted the Scriptures said. All demanded a degree of strictness of adherence, all adopted homiletical exhortation. And even among separatists, it is specific laws that they argue against, not a generalized philosophy of law or summa of theology, as has recently been demonstrated brilliantly (by Y. Sussmann). Social orientations did differ and there is fixation on ideas of "light and darkness," their side and our side. They set themselves apart from the community as a whole, at least the rabbinic image of community as a whole. For all of them, normative simply means that if you do not accept my teachings, you are deviant, heterodox. The intellectual-spiritual tumult in tannaite-amoraic times (and beyond) was considerable. Midrashic exercise made the vocabulary and figures of speech of the Scriptures the mental lexicon of all in the synagogues, let alone those inside the rabbinic academies.

It is true of course that the tannaite (and post tannaite) midrashim are not logically organized textbooks, syntheses of selected subjects, for example, Handbook on Ritual, Handbook on Civil Law, on Criminal Law, on Ethics, Piety, Charity, Doctrine, and so on. This has been emphasized by all scholars especially since Solomon Schechter's *Some Aspects of Rabbinic Theology*. ("Aspects" was a splendid choice for a title!—let alone "some"—and is not unjust for description even of the contents of the Mishna treatises.)

Kohelet (Ecclesiastes), about to conclude, warns, "My son, beware of composing many books for these are limitless and an exhaustion of the flesh." It may well be that the author of this line had in mind what the rabbis say, that is, that noncanonized books are not to be added to the library of Holy Scriptures (Eccl. R. 12:12, 31b)—although in rabbinic literature on a few occasions we do run into approved citation from Ben Sira (fragments of it have been found also among the Dead Sea sectarians and in the Masada compound). But the fact is that the rabbis were not interested in being authors of *books*. Even a composition like the "Seder Olam" is meant to make comprehensible *Biblical* chronology. What they sought above all was to be teachers, immediate expositors of Scripture, every detail of it. The oral rather than the written (despite private notes) is their vocation. In haggadah especially they recognized that variety of interpretation could and would be present. They delighted in preserving as much of it as they could because that made manifest that everything, literally everything, is in the Torah; "turn it this way, turn it that way, everything is in it": and in the synagogue the congregation included men, women, even children; all listen to these words! Since their biblical texts (in scroll and later in codex form—the same is true of Dead Sea documents) were unvocalized, notwithstanding tradition of proper pronunciation, every word was an invitation to derive an additional lesson from it, so that there are also times when the word itself is left untouched, but listeners are advised to read it as though the accepted pronunciation were superseded ('al tiqre . . . 'el'a) by a more dramatic one. Paronomasia is not scorned by Greeks, or Jews, or any lover of language.

The pattern of organization of exegetical midrashim, then, was the order of the biblical verses. One follows them as they line up, consecutively, in order to make sure that nothing is overlooked, neither prepositions nor conjunctions nor terms for disjunction (one is tempted to say, nor "punctuation" by tone of voice) nor signs of the accusative nor spelling—nothing was empty of meaning. "If it appears senseless, it is you who are senseless."

Nevertheless, it is clear from the way the compilers have arranged the comments that some rudimentary forms of systematization were adopted when the opportunity presented itself. One of the recurrent formulas used for this purpose is kywṣ' bw (ka-yoṣe bo, "similarly," "in like manner") after an interpretation has been offered for a particular expression in one verse. Thus (Mekilta Kaspa 4, III, 184 f.): Exod. 34:23 reads, "Three times a year all your males shall appear before ('et) the Sovereign Lord, the God of Israel." But has it not already been said (in Exod. 23:17), "Three times a year all your males shall appear before ('el) the Sovereign, the Lord"? What then is taught by the additional phrase "God of Israel?" It teaches that to Israel primarily He affixed His Name.

Similarly, Deuteronomy 6:5 reads, "Hear O Israel, the Lord is our God, the Lord alone." But what point is there to the words "the Lord alone?" Has it not already been said, "The Lord is our God?" However, it teaches that to us primarily He affixed His Name.

Similarly, Psalm 50:7 reads, "Pay heed, My people, and I will speak, O Israel . . . I am your God." I am God of all the inhabitants of the world, and yet primarily I affixed My Name only to My people Israel.

There are long units with the introductory formula wkn [we-k'an] 'th mwṣ' (we-ken [we-k'an] 'attah moṣe, "and so too you find"). That by means of the east wind God punishes sinners can be demonstrated by nine plus one examples (Mekilta Be-Shallah, I, 229 f.): the Flood Generation, the Men of the Tower (of Babel), the Egyptians, the tribes of Judah and Benjamin, the

PREFACE

Ten Tribes, the Lawless Empire, the wicked in Gehenna. A number of verses and their message are drawn up to prove this. This seems to be the work of the compiler-redactor. (See also Sifre Num. 19, p. 22.) Nevertheless, another possibility should not be dismissed, namely, that originally these did constitute a unified homily by a preacher to which the Midrash compiler helped himself in his organization of the treatise, because that best served as commentary on the Biblical verse, and simultaneously on still other verses. (A very much longer example of twenty-six interpretations is presented in Mekilta Pisha 12, I, 89–94.)

Be such passages what they may in origin, all exemplify what the tannaite (and other exegetical) midrashim undertake to perform: to make the very shape, size, and substance of the biblical texts intelligible, immediately relevant, stimuli to continued analysis of detail, maximally particular rather than abbreviated summary. That the thrust of many comments is not entirely clear is no surprise. For background is not furnished (many sayings resemble fragmentary inscriptions deprived of context), specific objective has not been provided to us. In their time they were most likely understood; later they take on the appearance of imperative pronouncements. Why, for example, is it emphasized that the Sabbath is a covenantal sign between God and Israel (Exod. 31:17) and *not* between Him and the nations of the world? Is it to underscore that the Jewish Sabbath day is permanently immovable, unaffected by climate, season, economy, anything, unlike the fluctuations of the day of rest among the gentiles? The Jewish week is totally free of planetary domination, is not governed by human fashion or preference—is that the message? Again: That the thirty-nine principal categories of "labor" as, enumerated by the Sages, though not spelled out as such by Scripture, are however the base of Sabbath observance, indeed were at the outset communicated orally to Moses (Mekilta Shabbata 2, III, 206) is stressed. Did anyone insist on another *classification* list? Much remains unclear. That the Israelites borrowed (š' 1, Exod. 12:35) from the Egyptians silver and gold vessels and *garments,* we are told, is proof that the Egyptians cherished their clothing more than everything else (Mekilta Pisha 13, I, 105). To what exactly does this refer? Whom are the rabbis ridiculing?

Regardless of the many puzzles that remain, there is no mistaking the passion behind and within the midrashic exercises. It is to save the Scriptures from becoming archaic, from being treated as though their specific lessons, down to minutest particularities, were only of sentimental historical interest, fossil regulations and narratives no longer compelling. And every facet of life is considered, as the volume before us will demonstrate: Everything is in the Scriptures. So too are allegories, parables, anecdotes, visions,

PREFACE

give-and-take with critical or curious gentiles—in such exchanges the latter initiate the conversation and the Jews respond in self-approbation.

It is this attributed richness that makes understandable a melancholy albeit rabbinically consoling reflection (Sifra 112c) on the verse (Lev. 26: 44), "even . . . when they are in the land of their enemies, I will not reject them or spurn them or deny them." "But what have they been left with? Why, all the precious gifts that had been given to them, were taken away from them! Were it not for the text (sefer) of the Torah which has remained with them, they would in no way differ from the Nations of the World."

The people are unique because their Scriptures are unique, and exegesis (midrash) prevents the uniqueness from passing out of sight.

ABBREVIATIONS

ARN = Abot de-Rabbi Natan, ed. S. Schechter

Gen. R. = Genesis Rabba, ed. Theodor-Albeck

M. = Mishna

Mekilta = Mekilta de-R. Ishmael, ed. J. Z. Lauterbach

MRS = Mekilta de-R. Simeon, ed. Epstein-Melamed

Pesiqta R. = Pesiqta Rabbati, ed. Friedmann

Sifra = Torat Kohanim, ed. I. H. Weiss

Sifre Deut. = Sifre on Deuteronomy, ed. L. Finkelstein

Sifre Num. = Sifre Numbers, ed. H. S. Horovitz

T. = Tosefta

INTRODUCTION

> Do you want to come to know He Who Spoke and the world came into being? Learn *haggada* (rabbinic lore) for by doing that you will come to know He Who Spoke and the world came into being and hold fast to His ways.   —Sifre Deuteronomy 49

Since its creation by the Sages of Israel, midrash*—the simultaneous reach for meaning in Scripture and for the meaning of Scripture—the repository of both *aggadah,* rabbinic lore, and *halakha,* rabbinic law—has seldom been appreciated as much as it is today. There was a time, not so very long ago, when little significance was attached to the works presented here. Both Jews and non-Jews were known to belittle or ignore *aggadah* (from the Hebrew root to tell).[1] Rationalists felt that it was too fantastical and too far removed from philosophical and scientific thinking. Masters of Jewish law devoted their attention to study of Mishna and Talmud and tended to ignore even the nonlegal aspects of the Talmud as appropriate for the common man, for women and children, but not for scholars. Non-Jewish scholars belittled all rabbinic literature and took little interest in these works of midrash, which, they felt, could hardly be taken seriously as Biblical exegesis. Both the form and the content were foreign to the cultural milieu of Western civilization. Since many Midrashim were not even available in translation, they were totally unknown to the general public, including the more cultured and literary sector.

Today, however, this attitude has changed. Scholars like Leopold Zunz at the beginning of the scientific study of Judaism some 150 years ago began to redeem this little-known branch of learning and to study it with the seriousness due the subject.[2] Midrash began to receive serious attention when great scholars such as Louis Ginzberg devoted themselves to it seriously.

---

* Midrash with a capital "M" will designate a volume of Midrash. With a small "m" it will refer to the individual midrashic comment or to midrash as a method of interpretation.

13

INTRODUCTION

Solomon Schechter, Louis Finkelstein, Shalom Spiegel, Yaakov Epstein, Gedalia Alon, Isaac Heineman, and Saul Lieberman were among those whose works demonstrated that here could be found matters of substance. Following them, Judah Goldin, Ephraim Urbach, Max Kadushin, and a host of younger scholars have turned midrash into a major field of Jewish and general religious studies. Ginzberg's monumental *Legends of the Jews*, later abridged and issued with a wonderfully incisive introductory essay by Shalom Spiegel as *Legends of the Bible*, introduced first the German- and then the English-speaking public to this material, while H. N. Bialik and Y. H. Ravnitzky's collection in Hebrew *Sefer HaAggadah (The Book of Legends)* did the same for the general Hebrew-speaking public.

Today all of the major Tannaitic Midrashim containing the works of the early rabbinic masters until the third century C.E., the Tannaim, are available in English translation, as is much of the later midrashic material. Most interesting is the fact that scholars in the field of literature now see in the midrashic methods of interpretation precursors of their own theories of interpretation of text.[3] They are impressed by the ability of midrash to "affirm the integrity and authority of the text while fragmenting it and sowing it endlessly"[4] and are attracted by the "infinite unfolding of textual signification."[5] Scholars involved in religious studies, no matter what their own religious affiliation, recognize in midrash a major contribution to religious thinking while students of Judaism see in it one the basic building blocks—perhaps the major one—in the creation of rabbinic (as opposed to Biblical) Judaism. Thus what was once dismissed and discarded has regained its ancient stature. To use a Biblical phrase, "The stone which the builders rejected has become the chief cornerstone" (Ps. 118:22).

The midrashic works from which this volume draws are but a small part of the corpus of midrashic literature. They are, however, as we shall have occasion to discuss later, the earliest and therefore the fundamental works of the genre, the classic Midrash.

What exactly is "midrash?" Midrash is both a process and a product.[6] It is a method of study and interpretation of the Bible and it is the name given to the literary works that emerge from that study. A midrash is both the individual interpretive comment to a work or a verse and also the book into which these individual pericopes have been incorporated.

Midrash is exegesis, explanation of a Biblical text and a commentary on it. To qualify as midrash, there must be a connection to a text. As we shall see, the Midrashim also contain other types of material, but quantitatively the majority of the material is text-connected. The Sages did not write philosophical treatises on various topics,[7] nor did they compose books about the Bible.[8] They took each verse, indeed each word, of Scripture and explained and commented on it.[9] To these comments were frequently attached other material—legends, sayings, parables, and stories about the Sages themselves. The principle of organization, however, always remained the Biblical phrase.

As a process, midrash began no later than the time of Ezra and, in a certain sense, may be said to continue to this day. As product, the earliest extant works of Midrash were edited in the third century of the Common Era. They may have been compiled orally at least in part in the first century C.E.[10] We have no way of knowing when they were actually written down since the prohibition of writing "Oral Torah" was a strong one, overcome only with the greatest reluctance. Presumably these Midrashim were fixed in writing by the fifth century, although we have no manuscripts earlier than the tenth century.[11] Other Midrashim compiled by the later teachers, the Amoraim, emerged a few centuries thereafter, and collections based on this material were compiled during the Middle Ages. The works contained in this book are the earliest Midrashim and, as such, constitute the classic creations of the midrashic process.

Classicism implies both a flowering of a process and a basic simplicity. That is what is found in these Midrashim. Emerging after a period of some 900 years of productivity, they contain the collective work of generations. They also clearly reflect the time and place of their final composition and compilation. They are the product of the Jewish community of the Land of Israel and were edited in the period of postdestruction Judaism, when Jewish tradition needed to be ordered and regularized to prevent loss and chaos, when Judaism (as opposed to Biblical religion) had already reached its fruition, and when the challenges of both paganism and Christianity were deeply felt. Although the Temple and Jerusalem had been destroyed and many Jews were in exile, a Jewish community existed in the Land of Israel that continued to create and to flourish spiritually under the leadership of the Pharisaic Sages who alone of all the competing groups of religious leaders had survived the destruction.

These Midrashim also evidence the simplicity of classical works. Their language is pure and not overly elaborate and they do not contain the heights of fantasy that later Midrashim came to incorporate. These works of the Tannaim may lack some of the color of the works compiled by the later Sages, the Amoraim, but they make up for it in directness and originality. Everything that will appear in this introduction applies specifically to these early Midrashim, although much of it is equally valid for the later works of midrashic activity, which will not be considered here. Our concern is the "Classic Midrash."

Although written in Hebrew, these works have traditionally been known by Aramaic titles found first either in the Talmud or in the works of the Gaonim in the tenth century.[12] They themselves do not carry titles and we therefore have no way of knowing what they might have been called by their editors. The names ascribed to them are either Mekhilta, meaning a measure or treatise in the sense of a collection of treatises of logic, or simply Sifra (singular) or Sifre (plural) d'bei Rab—Books of the Academy.[13] In much of the current literature they are referred to as Midrash Halakha— "Legal Midrash"—a misnomer first coined in the nineteenth century that was meant to distinguish them from later Midrashim, which these scholars called Midrash Aggadah—"Narrative Midrash." This title was felt to be appropriate since these latter works contain little if any legal material and are sermonic in nature. But while it is true that the early works we are considering have much legal material, some more so than others, that is not their exclusive interest. They represent interpretations by the Sages of four books of the Pentateuch: Exodus, Leviticus, Numbers, and Deuteronomy. If a similar work ever existed to Genesis, we have no knowledge of it, although a great many interpretations of material from Genesis are contained in the Tannaitic midrashim.[14] They make no distinction between legal and narrative material, commenting on both. It has been suggested that they be called "Midrash Torah."[15] The best title for them, in my opinion, would be one that describes their time of origin and identifies their collective authorship. Since they represent the culmination of interpretive activity of the early Sages known as Tannaim (Teachers), why not refer to them as Tannaitic Midrash? In a more general fashion, based on their place as the earliest flowering of the genre, they could also be known as Classic Midrash. The Sages themselves use the term Midrash Hakhamim, the Midrash or interpretation of the Sages (Sifra to Lev. 26:14), although they are probably not referring to a specific compilation but rather to rabbinic understanding and interpretation of the Torah.

What is the origin of midrashic activity? Midrash begins when the writing of Scripture ends. When a work is completed, others can and do begin to comment on it.[16] In regard to the legal portions, the creation of "oral law" by means of reinterpretation was an "unavoidable consequence of the lack of legislative power."[17] The narrative was no less important since it contained the sacred history of the people of Israel and its relationship to

16

God, written by the supreme prophet Moses at the behest of God. Thus the book they accepted is called "The Teaching of Moses with which the Lord had charged Israel" (Neh. 8:7), "the Teaching of God," (Neh. 8:8), and "the Book of Moses" (Neh. 13:1). As such it had supreme authority. Torah became final when it was edited into its present form and accepted by the people of Israel as its sacred constitution after the return from the Exile. Today it is generally accepted that the completion of the redaction of the Five Books of Moses was undertaken by Ezra the Scribe, who was also a Priest, in the fifth century B.C.E. At a great ceremony described in Nehemiah 8–10, this work was officially accepted by the entire people.[18]

The completion of such a book immediately and automatically calls for certain activities. Since it contains laws, these laws must be understood, taught, applied, and interpreted. In addition, they must be applied to new times, circumstances, and situations. If there are contradictions between laws, all of which have equal authority, these contradictions must be resolved. Theoretically, one might have assumed that the legal portions alone required interpretation. Historical works, stories of the ancestors, could stand by themselves. Any work, however, that is considered important immediately calls for comment. The more important the work, the more voluminous the commentaries. Building after building could be filled with books written about Shakespeare's plays. The volume of commentaries far exceeds the works themselves. This was true in the ancient world as well. Homer, whose works attained near canonical status in the Hellenic world, was also the subject of careful scrutiny, although there is no law to be derived from them. Certainly all sacred texts from all ancient religions were studied and commented on. In the case of the Torah, it is easy to understand the impetus for interpretation. The Torah was considered to be Divine. It was the work of God and the word of God. If the grammarians of Alexandria could devote a lifetime of study to Homer, surely Jewish scholars should devote their lives to the study of Torah.[19] This point is reflected in a discussion held centuries later in the Academies of Babylonia. Discussing the question of the way in which Moses dressed Aaron in his sacred garments, one Sage asked: What's the difference? What was, was! One reply was that we will need to know for the Messianic Age when once again such a ceremony will take place. To this the objection was raised that Moses and Aaron will be there then and will be able to tell us. Therefore we need to know because "we must be able understand the Scripture" (Yoma 5b). There are problems and contradictions and even if there is no practical need for the understanding, Scripture must be made clear.

It is not accidental, then, that it is with Ezra that we find the first appearance of the root *d-r-sh* in the meaning it came to have as midrash.[20] Contrast Ezra 7:10 with Genesis 25:22: "But the children struggled in her womb, and she said, "if so, why do I exist?" She went to inquire (lidrosh) of the Lord, and the Lord answered her." In Genesis one goes to "consult" God, possibly through a prophet or an oracle, and receives an answer. See also 1 Kings 22:8. In Ezra, one consults the sacred text: "For Ezra had dedicated himself to study (lidrosh) the Teaching (Torah) of the Lord so as to observe it, and to teach laws and rules to Israel" (Ezra 7:10). Here too, an answer is expected, not to a specific question such as Rebecca's, but as to the meaning of the text, the intent or application of a law. Later rabbinic statements such as "It is not in Heaven," "One does not listen to a Heavenly voice,"[21] "Whatever the latest teacher has to teach was already revealed at Sinai,"[22] "Moses received Torah at Sinai and passed it to Joshua,"[23] are all implicit in these early actions. One is no longer to seek answers from prophets. Revelation comes now not directly from Heaven but through the medium of the Torah. Through it, all knowledge is possible. When the word *midrash* made its appearance as the product of this search is difficult to ascertain. It does appear in 2 Chronicles 13:22 and 24:27 as some sort of a book but in a different sense.[24] Certainly by the time these Midrashim came into being and probably long before, midrash was established as one of the categories of rabbinic teaching, along with mishna, halakha, and aggadah.[25]

The meaning of midrash, then, is to search. Thus the process is one of "searching the Scripture," or, as James Kugel has suggested, "*midrash* might be best translated as 'research.' "[26] The Scribe and later the Sage is the expert in the book, the researcher, if you will. He is its keeper and transmitter. As such, he undoubtedly made marks to indicate difficulties, decided how it was to be divided, gave alternative readings, and even made changes when required. It addition, he may have served as a legal consultant to demonstrate how the laws were to be applied. The early Scribes were, as Bickerman suggests, similar to the "Roman *juris periti* of the same period, who were the legal advisers of the pontifices."[27] Some think that these Scribes were the predecessors of the Sages and eventually, the Rabbis—Masters or teachers of Torah.[28] Other scholars think that the Scribes were of more limited scope and that the class of Hakhamim (Elders, Wise Men, or Sages) such as Ben Sira and those he described were the real ancestors of the rabbinic Sages.[29] Instead of the more worldly wisdom that was the realm of the early Hakhamim of the first Temple period such as the author of Ecclesiastes, during the second Temple period Torah (Divine Teaching), now revealed in a specific text, revered and accepted, becomes their preoccupation because *that* is wisdom.[30] Their task is to understand it, explain it, and teach it.

This task applies to all parts of the Bible. The entire collection of sacred books, the Tanakh or Hebrew Bible, was seen as deriving from One and the same Source. Therefore any part of it could be used to illuminate its most important section, the Torah of Moses, the Pentateuch.

As the class of Hakhamim grows in power and authority, their task becomes to apply the laws to life, including the integration of the laws of the written Torah with the traditions that came down from antiquity and that do not appear in writing.[31] Most important, with the public acceptance of the Torah, the Torah and its interpretation became the property of all. Whereas elsewhere sacred writings were the exclusive possession of priests, in post-Biblical Judaea, it was the possession of all. Any man could study it and thus become a Hakham. The duty of the Hakham was to make it available and understood by any person.

The nature of these commentaries is unique in that the commentaries themselves are seen as part of the work on which they comment.

> Just as the rain comes down upon fruit trees and gives each one its own flavour according to its nature . . . so it is with words of Torah. Although they are basically one, they contain Scripture, Mishna, Talmud, *halakhot* (in some manuscripts "midrash") and *haggadot*. [p. 347]*

One may be Written Torah, the other Oral Torah but both are Torah—Divine Teaching. As Goldin put it, "How are an ancient text and its contents kept relevant? To meet this assignment Judaism adopts not the neutral and descriptive terms of change and adaptation, but a view of revelation which is permanently at work through an activity called 'Midrash.' "[32] Thus the midrash itself is revelation, just as the verse it comments on is revelation. The Sage has authority, stemming from Moses at Sinai, to search these words and to reveal their meaning.[33] Behind this revelation stands the Living God. As a midrash itself puts it, when learning these traditions from anyone it is as if one learns from Moses—indeed from God.[34] If at Sinai the word came to Israel through Moses, so it continues to come to Israel in every generation through the successors of Moses, the Sages. Paradoxically,

---

* This and other numbers in brackets are references to pages in this volume.

everything a Sage teaches is called "an innovation" (hidush)[35] while at the same time it is ascribed to the Sinaiatic revelation.[36]

The aim of all of these works is to present the collective view of Pharisaic Judaism concerning the Scripture. Whereas later commentators on the Bible such as Rashi, Ramban, and Ibn Ezra were authors who gave us their individual views, as had the first-century C.E. commentator Philo of Alexandria, rabbinic Judaism utilized individual authorities and quoted many interpretations, legal and narrative, of some particular Tanna, but the cumulative effect is to present us with the multifaceted approach that represents "the tradition" with all of its complexity. No matter which school of Sages collected and edited the material, viewpoints of other schools were included as well.

Tannaitic Midrash, then, is a collective work. It really has no one author. The resulting impression is that this is not really the work of one person or even of a group effort, but a collective enterprise that, representing everyone, represents no one. Even if different works had different authors and emphasize the viewpoint of one school or another, together they are the product of the collective wisdom of the religious leaders of the nation.[37] These, then, are to be viewed as the collected traditions of Pharisaic Judaism that had their origins at the Sinai revelation, even as did the Written Torah.

Even those books that have the name of a Tanna connected to them, such as "Mekhilta of Rabbi Ishmael," use those names either because that teacher's name appears first in the book or because the work stemmed from the Academy (Bet Midrash) of that teacher. That Tanna is never considered the author of the work.[38]

During the late Tannaitic period the Sages were grouped either into followers of R.* Akiba or followers of R. Ishmael. Each school studied and gathered and eventually "published" the midrashic material that had accumulated until then. Each school followed the methods of its founder, that of Akiba being characterized by the closest possible text study, including the interpretation of textual minutiae, while that of R. Ishmael was centered more around the use of logic and hermeneutical rules such as inferences and analogy.[39] It is probable that each Academy issued its own Midrash on each of the four books mentioned. They did not all survive. What we have today is a commentary on Exodus, *Mekhilta of Rabbi Ishmael*, and one on Num-

---

* R. = Rabbi. Similarly, b. stands for *ben*, "son of." Thus R. Simeon b. Yochai is Rabbi Simeon the son of Yochai.

bers, *Sifre* from the school of R. Ishmael, and commentaries on Leviticus, *Sifra* or *Torat Kohanim*, and one on Deuteronomy, *Sifre*, from the school of R. Akiba, although this latter is a composite work, containing much material from R. Ishmael.[40] In addition, we have reconstructions of some of the lost Midrashim, constructed from sections found in later midrashic compilations and fragments found in the Cairo Geniza.[41] These include the *Mekhilta of Rabbi Simeon b. Yochai*, and Numbers, *Sifre Zuta*, from the school of R. Akiba and, one from R. Ishmael on Deuteronomy, *Midrash Tannaim*. Although the methodology of each school and its technical terminology were different, each school included material from the other and both drew on common material handed down through the generations so that more unites them than separates them.

After the fact, it is common to assume that whatever has come into being had to be. Thus midrash had to emerge the way it did. But we see that the reaction to a revealed book could have gone in other directions. Apocryphal works such as the Genesis Apocryphon indicate another way to deal with received Scriptures. In them the original work is basically retold and rewritten and the result is presented as authoritative.[42] Philo's commentary provides a second model, similar in some ways to midrash but different in others, presented not as accumulated, collective wisdom, but as the workings of the mind of one person, thus changing the nature of its authority. The Dead Sea Scrolls have revealed to us yet another approach to Scriptural interpretation. The "Pesharim" there are expositions of prophetic books and have much in common with midrashic methodology, though they are concerned more with the interpretation and solution of prophetic words. The midrashic approaches to the Song of the Sea and to the Blessing of Moses and Ha-azinu are somewhat similar in seeing specific prophecy of the situation of their time in the ancient words although here too midrash is indeterminate, presenting alternative understandings of the verses, while the Pesharim take the position that this and this alone is the true meaning of the text. Other writings from the Dead Sea Sect incorporate new laws into scriptural text in a way that is reflected in some of the earlier midrashic writing as well and may represent an early form of legal midrash.[43] Surely both the members of the Dead Sea Sect and the Pharisaic Sages believed that theirs was the only authoritative interpretation of Scripture. None of these alternative forms, however, have exactly the qualities that we see in Tannaitic Midrash: (1) collectivity, (2) multiplicity, (3) retention of the original meaning, (4) expansion and openness, (5) text centeredness.

The reason that it is so difficult to trace the development of midrash and of rabbinic traditions in general with any degree of certainty is the paucity of records of the time. So little is really recorded and known that it has been compared to entering a tunnel at the time of Ezra or, at the best, Ben Sira, and not emerging until these Tannaitic midrashim are edited in the third century C.E. Even worse, the knowledge we have from these writings in reference to earlier teachers and to the status of the Sages and the Pharisees is through these later eyes and is therefore somewhat suspect.[44]

Furthermore, the Tannaitic Midrashim themselves have not come down to us in pristine form. The earliest manuscripts we have are from the tenth century.[45] The printed texts come from the sixteenth century.[46] Many marginal glosses became part of the text.[47] What would we not give for a manuscript that went back to the third century or even, for that matter, to the seventh century!

These works form part of the corpus known as "Oral Torah," which was not to be written down. The sacredness of the Torah brought with it the demand that other things not be written down. In that way, for all of its sacredness, it could not compete with the word. From a functional point of view, the oral tradition forced the tradition to remain flexible and made it easier to add, adapt, accumulate, and keep ever fresh and open-ended.[48] Each generation could add its layer while remaining part of an ongoing process. Thus midrash is an oral form that found its way into writing when it was no longer practical to keep it oral. The conditions of the times, the amount of accumulated material, all mandated writing. The first oral work to be committed to writing was the Mishna, Rabbi Judah the Prince's authoritative collection of legal traditions, divorced from their Biblical precedents. Even that was first "published," that is, officially adapted and taught in a fixed form, only orally.[49]

The two main forms of rabbinic teaching in the realm of *halakha* were mishna and midrash. Whereas midrash requires a text, mishna is separate from it and presents legal material without Biblical references and in a logical order rather than as an extension of the Torah codes. In regard to the legal portions of the Tannaitic Midrash, the question must be addressed as to the relationship between these two forms and these two works. We know more about the Mishna than about the Tannaitic Midrashim. The Mishna was edited by Rabbi Judah the Prince around the year 200 C.E., some hundred years prior to the editing of the Tannaitic Midrashim.

Scholars have long debated which form came first—that is, was the rabbinic law formulated first as individual teachings or as commentary on Biblical verses? The current consensus of opinion is that the midrash form, that is, starting with the text and attaching to it new interpretations and even old traditions, is the more ancient and gradually grew and expanded as ever more complicated methods of interpretation evolved, first with Hillel and then with R. Ishmael.[50] Mishna, the apodictic form, was adopted only after the destruction of the Temple (70 C.E.) as a practical measure because of the chaotic conditions of the time and because of the vast quantity of material that made the midrash form clumsy and difficult to sustain. The Tannaitic Midrashim as we have them now, of course, are later editions of the earlier works and now contain excerpts and quotations from the Mishna as well.[51]

Although there may be differences in the editing of the four Midrashim translated here,[52] just as there are differences of terminology between the schools of R. Akiba and R. Ishmael, the basic pattern remains fundamentally the same. A section of a verse is quoted and then a question is posed:

AND ALL THE FIRSTBORN OF THE CATTLE (Ex. 12:29). What could possibly be the sin of cattle? [p. 58]

or a comment is made:

I WILL GRANT YOU RAINS IN THEIR SEASON (Lev. 26: 4). This refers to the evening following the Sabbath. [p. 204]

There are wide variations as to the format after that. The entire midrash could be only a few words, perhaps a philological explanation of the meaning of a word or a phrase:

GET YOU (habu) (Deut. 1:13). *Habu* always indicates asking advice, as it is said WHAT DO YOU ADVISE US (habu) TO DO? (2 Sam. 16:20) [p. 294]

On the other hand it could contrast the verse with other verses and explain the difference:

THE CHOICE FIRST FRUITS OF YOUR SOIL YOU SHALL BRING TO THE HOUSE OF THE LORD YOUR GOD (Ex. 23:19). Why is this section stated? When it says YOU SHALL TAKE SOME OF EVERY FIRST FRUIT OF THE SOIL (Deut. 26:2) I know only about bringing fruit as the offering of first fruits. What about liquids? The verse says YOU SHALL BRING TO THE HOUSE OF THE LORD YOUR GOD (Ex. 23:19)—in any form. (Mekhilta Kaspa 5)

It could include a legend about the Biblical event:

AND MOSES TOOK WITH HIM THE BONES OF JOSEPH (Ex. 13:19). This tells us of the wisdom and piety of Moses, for while all Israel busied itself despoiling Egypt, Moses busied himself fulfilling the mitzvah to care for the bones of Joseph. [p. 72]

or bring a parable:

AS THE CLOUD WITHDREW FROM THE TENT (Num. 12:10). A parable. A human king said to a tutor, "Chastise my son, but chastise him only after I have left," because a father has pity on his son. [p. 260]

It could include a story about the Sages themselves:

AT THAT TIME . . . AS FOLLOWS (Deut. 1:16). In the past you were independent. Now you are the servants of the community. It once happened that R. Johanan b. Nuri and R. Eleazar Hisma were put in charge of the Academy by Rabban Gamliel . . . he said to them, ". . . In the past, you were independent. From now on you are the servants of the community!" [p. 298]

In the case of midrash to a legal section of the Torah, it might explain the exact application of the law:

AND, TAKING SOME OF THE EARTH THAT IS ON THE FLOOR OF THE TABERNACLE (Num. 5:17). Scripture informs us that if there was no earth there, they had to take earth from somewhere else and put it there since the place sanctifies it. [p. 469]

It might utilize one of the hermenutical laws of interpretation, inference from minor to major, inclusion and exclusion, basic rule, and so forth:

A SINGLE WITNESS MAY NOT VALIDATE AGAINST A PERSON ANY GUILT OR BLAME (Deut. 19:15). The only reason this verse says SINGLE is to indicate that this is the basic rule for all verses in which the word *witness* appears: It always means two unless Scripture were to specify SINGLE. [p. 464]

INTRODUCTION

It might also cite a law (a mishna) that was derived from the verse:

TOGETHER WITH THE LEVITE AND THE STRANGER IN YOUR MIDST (Deut. 26:11). This is the source of the teaching: Israelites and bastards may recite the declaration, but converts and freed slaves may not do so since they have no portion in the Land. [p. 512]

Often it will inquire about the source of some practice:

YOU SHALL SURELY REPROVE YOUR NEIGHBOR (Lev. 19:17). What is the source which teaches that if you have reproved someone four or five times, you should do so again? The verse says YOU SHALL SURELY REPROVE. [p. 439]

or will indicate how a verse prevents us from coming to incorrect conclusions:

IF HE GETS UP AND WALKS (Ex. 21:19). I might think that this means inside the house. Therefore the verse says OUTDOORS (Ex. 21:19). [p. 406]

There are also sections that bring together many verses and many interpretations in order to discuss a theme. All of these, however, are attached to the verse at hand:

Beloved are converts for He constantly warns us about mistreating them. YOU SHALL NOT WRONG A STRANGER (Ex. 22:20). YOU MUST LOVE THE STRANGER (Deut. 10:19). YOU SHALL NOT OPPRESS A STRANGER (Ex. 23:9). [p. 412]

Thus the books we call Midrash are termed that because in essence they are commentaries on Biblical words or verses.[53] They do that which the word midrash implies: search the Scripture. On the other hand, incorporated within these Midrashim are various forms of rabbinic literary creations: aggadah (legends), sayings, stories from rabbinic lives, and discourses on moral or theological subjects where the connection to Scripture is at best tenuous.

INTRODUCTION

In order to appreciate this material, certain underlying principles should be understood. As will immediately be obvious, some of the assumptions of the Sages may not be acceptable to everyone today. I make no attempt to argue the correctness of these assumptions, but merely to explain them. The reader need not adopt the assumptions and the world view of the rabbis, but without entering into this view, it will be impossible to understand or appreciate the work. It is best to appreciate what has been created by its own set of beliefs and keep theological problems for another discussion.[54]

1. The Bible in its entirety is the word of God. The Torah (the Pentateuch) is the direct dictation of the Almighty.[55] Just as oracles need interpretation, so the words of Scripture carry meaning other than that which appears on the surface.[56] The other books are also under Divine inspiration, even if written by various individuals and therefore reflective of their own personalities. They are all part of one unit and verses from any book may be used to illuminate verses from other places. See, for example, pages [107–110] where Exodus 15:3 is illuminated by use of verses from Psalms, Isaiah, and 2 Samuel.

2. Chronology is of no importance. Even within the Torah, no chronological order is to be observed [pp. 138–140].

3. Because of the Divine nature of the Torah, meanings may be derived from the Torah through interpretation of letters, dots, diacritical marks, and other grammatical indications and innovations introduced as a kind of "proto-midrash" by the early Scribes.[57] These came to serve as the basis for further midrashic activity by the Sages:

> HE DID NOT KNOW WHEN SHE LAY DOWN OR WHEN SHE ROSE (Gen. 19:33). There is a dot over WHEN SHE LAY DOWN indicating that he did not know when she lay down, but did know when she rose up. [p. 235]

> WHEN THE ARK WAS TO SET OUT (Num. 10:35). There is a sign at the beginning and at the end of this passage indicating that this is not its proper place. [p. 240]

The midrash provides a list of verses in which the Scribes had substituted euphemisms in order to protect God's honor:

26

INTRODUCTION

YOU, O LORD, ARE FROM EVERLASTING; MY HOLY
GOD, WE NEVER DIE (Hab. 1:12). Scripture uses a euphemism. [p. 243]

Any extraneous word could serve as a source of additional information:

YET, EVEN THEN (Lev. 26:44). THEN refers to the sin committed in the wilderness. EVEN THEN refers to the sin of Baal
Peor. [p. 218]

The doubling of a verb, which is common in Biblical Hebrew as a method
of emphasis, was seen by R. Akiba and his followers as indicating some
additional thought:

AND IF THE PEOPLE OF THE LAND SHOULD SURELY
SHUT THEIR EYES (Lev. 20:4). How do we know that if they
shut their eyes to one such thing, they will shut their eyes to many
things? The verse says SURELY SHUT [a double verb]. [p. 444]

Parallel words or phrases, another commonplace of Biblical Hebrew, demanded that each be seen as referring to something different:

A GARDEN LOCKED IS MY OWN, MY BRIDE, A FOUN-
TAIN LOCKED, A SEALED-UP SPRING (Song 4:12). A
GARDEN LOCKED refers to the males and A FOUNTAIN
LOCKED to the females. [p. 54]

AND MAKE KNOWN TO THEM THE WAY IN WHICH
THEY ARE TO GO (Ex. 18:20) This refers to the study of Torah. AND THE PRACTICES THEY ARE TO FOLLOW (Ex.
18:20). This refers to good deeds . . . AND THE PRACTICES—
this refers to strictly following the law. THAT YOU SHALL GO
refers to going beyond the demands of strict law. [p. 135]

Even those Sages who believe that "the Torah uses human language" do not
mean to imply that the words are not to be scrutinized for specific Divine
intent but merely that one may not use certain grammatical forms such as
the doubling of verb forms in order to derive new laws.[58]

4. Punctuation and vocalization may be changed in order to derive new

27

meanings. Since the text is actually neither vocalized nor punctuated except by oral tradition, this presents no problem.

> SO MOSES DIED (vaymat Moshe) THERE—Woe! Moses is dead (vay—met Moshe)! [p. 390]

A word may be interpreted as meaning or indicating another word that is similar in spelling and sound:

> AND WITH ALL YOUR MIGHT (meodecha) (Deut. 6:5) Give thanks (modeh) unto Him. [p. 316]

Letters that have a similar sound may be substituted for one another in a word:

> I WILL PROTECT YOU (Ex. 12:13). R. Josiah says, "Do not read 'pasahti,' I WILL PROTECT, but 'pasa'ti'—I will step over." [p. 57]

Even intonation, changing a verse from a statement into a question or the opposite, can be the source of interpretation. Thus Job 2:10 YOU TALK AS ANY SHAMELESS WOMAN MIGHT TALK! SHOULD WE AC-CEPT ONLY GOOD FROM GOD AND NOT ACCEPT EVIL? is read by R. Akiba as an exhortation to Job's wife to talk like the women of the flood (shameless women):

> TALK AS ONE OF THE SHAMELESS WOMEN TALKS! SHOULD WE ACCEPT ONLY GOOD FROM GOD AND NOT ACCEPT EVIL? (Job 2:10) The people of the generation of the flood were vile during good times, but when punishment came upon them, they accepted it—whether they liked it or not . . . should not we . . . be pleasant when punishment comes upon us? [p. 313]

Varying the punctuation yields new meanings:

> He has been assured that he has a place in the world-to-come. Thus it is said THE LORD SAID TO MOSES: YOU ARE SOON TO LIE WITH YOUR FATHERS AND ARISE (Deut. 31:16). [p. 334]

The words AND ARISE are part of the next verse and have nothing to do with the death of Moses.

5. Verses and words are capable of carrying multiple interpretations. Unlike human speech, the words of God can carry more than one meaning.[59] In Kadushin's term, "indeterminacy of belief" indicates that meaning can shift and that even contradictory interpretations may be presented together without determining if one or the other is "correct."[60] Thus the word *enough* in Deuteronomy 3:26 yields four different interpretations [p. 305]; three explanations are offered as to what Jethro heard that caused him to come to join Moses [p. 130]; ALTHOUGH IT WAS NEAR in Exodus 13:17 is given seven different and even contradictory explanations [p. 67].

Although in legal matters, decisions have to be taken, even there the assumption is "both these and those are the words of the Living God."[61]

6. The Sages are the authoritative interpreters of the Scripture. The rules and methods of interpretation and, in a sense, even the interpretations themselves are therefore all included in the revelation at Sinai and have validity.[62]

> THROUGH MOSES ON MT. SINAI (Lev. 26:46). This teaches that the Torah, its laws, details, and explanations, were all given through Moses at Sinai. [p. 219]

The Sages carried to an extreme the concept that is valid both in human law and in interpretation of literature that once a document leaves the pen of its author, that author can no longer determine its meaning. In this case, it is the Author Himself who has given permission to the interpreters to determine the meaning of the text and He will not and cannot interfere.

> BUT IF YOU DO NOT OBEY ME (Lev. 26:14). If you do not obey the interpretations of the Sages. (Sifra to Lev. 26:14)

> Someone who has not learned, does not obey, despises others, hates the Sages and will not permit others to obey will come to deny that the mitzvot come from Sinai . . . and the existence of God. (Sifra to Lev. 26:15)

> AND HOLDING FAST TO HIM (Deut. 11:22). How is it possible for a person to ascend on high and hold fast to fire? For is it not said elsewhere FOR THE LORD YOUR GOD IS A CON-

SUMING FIRE (Deut. 4:24). . . . Rather—hold fast to the Sages and their disciples and I will consider it as if you had ascended on high and received (the Torah) there. [p. 329]

All of these points are clearly stated by the Sages themselves and constitute the rabbinic understanding of Torah that was developed following the acceptance of the Torah at the time of Ezra. But having seen their methodology and understood their basic world view, it remains for us to see what purposes were served by their Scriptural research.

Rabbinic thinking in general and midrashic creativity specifically are not products of the philosophic mode of thought. Although rabbinic teaching methods had much in common with the methods of the philosophers and of Socrates, the mode of reasoning was different. No Aristotle emerges among the Sages. It remained for later teachers of Judaism, Saadia and eventually the great Maimonides, to incorporate philosophical thinking and reasoning into the Judaic mode. Rabbinic thought has been termed "organismic" thinking.[63] Heineman defines this type of natural or popular thinking as thinking that (1) grows like an organism; it is natural and not revolutionary; (2) is part of an overall entity; emphasizes the importance of the group over the individual; (3) is based on feelings and emotions and not mere intellect.[64] According to Kadushin, the rabbis begin with a set of values that are never debated but always taken for granted. These values or "value-concepts" were derived from the Bible itself and are organically related to one another. They also interplay with one another. The concepts have to do with God, the world, and human life. Kadushin has listed four main ones: Love, Justice, Torah, Israel, each of which has many subconcepts.[65] Thus when interpreting the Biblical verse or discussing a narrative, these value-concepts are utilized in order to explain the verses. Sometimes one value will be stressed, sometimes another. Like threads in a tapestry, they will interweave with one another in order to create the total picture.

Renee Bloch described five characteristics of midrash: (1) includes a meditation on the Bible, (2) is homiletical, (3) uses the Bible to explain the Bible, (4) adapts the message to the times, (5) attempts to find the true significance or the basic legal principles.[66]

One of the main concerns of the Sages was to make the Torah as a whole an intelligible book. It was surely as evident to them as it is to us that there are contradictions between various verses, that there are laws that seem not to agree, that there are repetitions, and that there are chronological difficulties. All of the problems that have led in modern times to theories of higher Biblical criticism and especially to the documentary hypothesis were noted by them as well, but were utilized for totally different purposes. Given their belief and given the fact that must be acknowledged by moderns as well, that the Torah presents itself and demands to be read as one unified work, then, in the words of Daniel Boyarin, these "gaps, repetitions, contradictions, and heterogeneity of the biblical text must be read, as a central part of the system of meaning production of that text."[67] The rough spots, the spare and sparse words, the seeming problems, are all viewed as a literally God-given opportunity and challenge to fill them in, smooth them over, and extract the multileveled meanings the Author has implanted within. Since the Torah is a book to be lived by, whether this be in regard to its legal demands or its general precepts and implied ethical and moral teachings and insights gained through the narrative portions, it must be as thoroughly understood as possible. That work which Ezra began when he not only read the Torah to the people assembled but appointed men who were to read from the scroll of the Teaching of God:

> translating it and giving the sense;
> so they understood the reading (Neh. 8:8)

was carried on by the Sages and codified in their midrashim.

Thus contradictions not only in the Torah but in the entire Bible had to be dealt with. How, for example, explain the fact that speaking of the Temple, God says MY EYES AND MY HEART SHALL EVER BE THERE (1 Kings 9:3) while in Proverbs 15:3 we read THE EYES OF THE LORD ARE EVERYWHERE, OBSERVING THE BAD AND THE GOOD? Their answer is:

> It is—if it were possible to say so—as if His eyes and heart were only there [but because they are there, they are everywhere]. (Sifre D. 40)

At the same time it is obvious that the midrash is stating its value-concept of the importance of Israel. The opportunity is presented by a problematic text to state an axiom of rabbinic belief. But how could it be otherwise, for the verses are being filtered through the accepted cultural values of the interpreters?[68]

Problems of conflicting legal codes were similarly dealt with:

> One verse says SIX DAYS YOU SHALL EAT UNLEAVENED BREAD (Deut. 16:8) and another verse says YOU SHALL EAT

31

INTRODUCTION

UNLEAVENED BREAD FOR SEVEN DAYS (Lev. 23:6). How can both of these verses be upheld? The reference is to a kind of unleavened bread which cannot be eaten for the full seven days. That made from the new wheat can be eaten only six days. [p. 451]

The Sages also attempted to clarify sections of the Torah in which the narrative was unclear or the sequence of events difficult to ascertain. This is true, for example, in the story of the theophany at Sinai in Exodus 19–24. The midrash reconstructs the story on the basis of clues from different words:

TODAY (Ex. 19:10). This refers to the fourth day of the week. AND TOMORROW (Ex. 19:10)—the fifth day of the week. LET THEM BE READY FOR THE THIRD DAY—the sixth day of the week on which the Torah was given. [p. 138]

and transfers sections in order to fill in that which is missing:

What did Moses do on the fifth day of the week? He rose early in the morning, and built an altar at the foot of the mountain, as it is said EARLY IN THE MORNING, HE SET UP AN ALTAR AT THE FOOT OF THE MOUNTAIN (Ex. 24:4). [p. 138]

If vital information is missing, they supply it:

THEN HE TOOK THE RECORD OF THE COVENANT AND READ IT ALOUD TO THE PEOPLE (Ex. 24:7). This does not tell us, however, what portion he read. R. Jose b. R. Judah says, "From the beginning of Genesis to this point." R. Judah the Prince says, "[He read] all of the mitzvot that had been commanded to primal Adam . . . R. Ishmael says . . . "[He read about] sabbatical years, the jubilee and the blessings and curses." [p. 139]

Leviticus 9:6 reads THIS IS WHAT THE LORD HAS COMMANDED YOU TO DO but does not say what it was. The midrash supplies the answer:

Rid your hearts of the evil inclination. Be united together in awe and determination to serve God. As He is unique in the world, so let your service be unique before Him. (Sifra to Lev. 9:6)

32

Passages that they were unable to accept literally were reinterpreted. Thus Moses holding up his hands at the battle against Amalek (Ex. 17:11), the fiery serpent that healed (Num. 21:8), and the blood placed as a sign on the houses in Egypt (Ex. 12:13) were interpreted as ways of having Israel obey and trust God so that:

> the Holy One would have pity upon them. [p. 128]

Similarly, the Sages dealt with the problem of passages that seem to contradict their concept of God as well as contradicting other verses:

> AND LET THEM MAKE ME A SANCTUARY THAT I MAY DWELL AMONG THEM (Ex. 25:8)... Do we not learn elsewhere... THE HEAVEN IS MY THRONE AND THE EARTH IS MY FOOTSTOOL: WHERE COULD YOU BUILD A HOUSE FOR ME, WHAT PLACE COULD SERVE AS MY ABODE (Isa. 66:1)? Why then does it says AND LET THEM MAKE ME A SANCTUARY? So that they may be rewarded. (Mekhilta Pisha 16)

Again, the answers not only provide a solution to a problem, but also reflect a system of values. To complicate matters even more, midrashim such as this probably also served to refute accusations made against the Bible by sectarian Jews, unbelievers, or Christians. The reader will find that in many sections, I have suggested that the midrash is attempting to answer Christian allegations. This is a complicated subject since although there are some instances where the text says "This is a refutation of those who say," making it obvious that a polemic is involved, the opponent is not always specified:

> SEE, THEN, THAT I, I AM HE (Deut. 32:39). This is a refutation of those who claim that there is no Power in heaven. One may refute those who say that there are two Powers in heaven by saying, "Does it not also say THERE IS NO GOD BESIDES ME? " (Deut. 32:39) [p. 374]

In most cases the polemic purpose is not specified and can only be inferred from the text itself and from a knowledge of the Christian and pagan literature of the same period. There is enough evidence, however, to feel on safe ground in asserting that there was significant contact between groups, causing the Sages to want to present their answers, assertions, and refutations to the claims of the fledgling daughter religion.[69] It seems clear, for example, that the discussion of atonement [p. 156], the emphasis on belief in God and Moses:

> THEY HAD FAITH IN THE LORD AND IN HIS SERVANT MOSES (Ex. 14:31) . . . the verse teaches us that if one believes in the shepherd of Israel, it is as if one believes in He Who Spoke and the world came into being. [p. 96]

and the midrash concerning Moses and David that states:

> The entire world could have been sustained by their good deeds, yet they never asked God to grant them anything except as an expression of His grace. [p. 302]

were part of the polemic between Judaism and Christianity. At the same time they were also legitimate Jewish interpretations of Biblical verses.

In dealing with legal matters, the Sages used the midrashic method in order to connect the laws they observed to the Biblical text. The law of the Sotah, the woman suspected of adultery, is a good example of this. Many changes had been made in the Biblical law, but scriptural warrant was found for all of them. Thus the elimination of this practice when the norms of society had broken down could be connected to a few words from a verse:

> Why does it say THE MAN SHALL BE CLEAR OF GUILT; BUT THAT WOMAN SHALL SUFFER FOR HER GUILT (Num. 5:31)? . . . He said to them, "Since you run after prostitution, the water will not test your wives." Therefore it says THE MAN SHALL BE CLEAR OF GUILT—his guilt. [p. 478]

The Sages establish the principle that saving a life takes precedence over the Sabbath by the interpretation of a verse:

> THE ISRAELITE PEOPLE SHALL KEEP THE SABBATH, OBSERVING THE SABBATH THROUGHOUT THE GENERATIONS AS A COVENANT FOR ALL TIME (Ex. 31:16). Desecrate one Sabbath for him so that he may observe many Sabbaths. [p. 421]

Midrash also seeks to invest the observance of the ritual laws with meaning by connecting them to Biblical verses or events. Thus the daily recitation of Biblical portions known as the Shema was connected to events in the life of Jacob [p. 308], the practice of beginning the Sabbath before dark is derived from the pillar of cloud and fire:

> THE PILLAR OF CLOUD BY DAY AND THE PILLAR OF FIRE BY NIGHT DID NOT DEPART (Ex. 13:22). From the Torah we learn proper conduct. On Sabbath eve, the pillar of fire should emerge while the pillar of cloud is still there. [p. 78]

The three meals of the Sabbath come from the story of the manna:

> THEN MOSES SAID, "EAT IT TODAY, FOR TODAY IS A SABBATH TO THE LORD; YOU WILL NOT FIND IT TO-DAY ON THE PLAIN" (Ex. 16:25). R. Zerika says, "This is the source of the three Sabbath meals." [p. 125]

Important as it was for them to explain words and verses and to clarify portions and stories of the Torah, the editors of these works often went far beyond that and constructed lengthy discussions on specific themes. This was usually done by gathering together Biblical verses on one subject and placing them into a literary framework, often complete with repetitive refrains, emphasizing the concept under discussion. Thus sections are created concerning idolatry [p. 264], converts [p. 412], the Land of Israel [p. 319], rebuke [p. 289], and peace:

> Great is peace. For the sake of peace [God] altered
>   Sarah's words . . .
> Great is peace. For the sake of peace the Holy One altered
>   [His words].
> Great is peace. For the sake of peace the Name written
>   in holiness is erased by the water. [p. 229]

The Tannaitic Midrashim are replete with allusions to the present or to recent events and to what will happen in the future. Scripture is not only the story of the past; it is also seen as the key to understanding life today and the assurance of the future. Even the description of Pharoah's method of attack was taken as a lesson to the Romans:

ADVANCING (Ex. 14:10) . . . indicating that they were formed into squadrons which were each like one man. From this did the Empire learn to utilize the formation of squadrons. [p. 80]

Ancient promises were interpreted as valid even now:

THE LORD WILL BATTLE FOR YOU (Ex. 14:14). Not only now, but forever will He battle against your enemies. [p. 85]

Rabbi Akiba combined his reading of Exodus 15:2 I WILL BEAUTIFY HIM with his understanding of the Song of Songs as a dialogue between God and Israel to form a drama in which the nations quiz Israel about God and, when told some of His praise, ask to amalgamate with Israel only to be told:

"You have no portion in Him!" as it is said MY BELOVED IS MINE AND I AM HIS (Song 2:16) [p. 105]

Thus the midrash asserts the continuation of an exclusive relationship then under challenge.

The problem of observing Judaism at the peril of death under the Hadrianic persecution of the second century is read back into a Biblical verse:

OF THOSE WHO LOVE ME AND KEEP MY COMMAND-MENTS (Ex. 20:6) THOSE WHO LOVE ME refers to our father Abraham and those like him. AND KEEP MY COMMAND-MENTS refers to all who dwell in the Land of Israel and give their lives for the sake of the mitzvot. "Why are you being taken out to be executed?" "Because I circumcised my son." [p. 154]

The verse IN EVERY PLACE WHERE I CAUSE MY NAME TO BE MENTIONED, I WILL COME TO YOU AND BLESS YOU (Ex. 20: 21) is the source of the teaching that

whenever ten people enter the synagogue, the Divine Presence enters with them. [p. 168]

The description of Moses and Joshua is the exact description of the Sage and his disciple:

INTRODUCTION

> Give Joshua a spokesman and let him propound questions, expound and convey instructions during your lifetime. . . . He raised him up from the ground and sat him between his knees. Moses and Israel would lift up their heads to hear Joshua's words. What would he say? "Blessed is the Lord who gave Torah to Israel through Moses our teacher." [p. 330]

The Song of Moses (Deut. 42:1–43) was interpreted as referring to the contemporary situation:

> You may well say: How great is this song! It contains references to the present, the past and the future as well as to this world and the world-to-come! [p. 377]

The midrash uses many Latin and Greek terms and applies the verses to the Roman persecutions:

> WHO ATE THE FAT OF THEIR OFFERINGS (Deut. 32: 38)—to whom we used to give *opsonia, donativa,* and *alaria*—LET THEM RISE UP AND HELP YOU (Deut. 32:38). . . . This refers to the wicked Titus, the son of Vespasian's wife, who entered the Holy of Holies, and cut the two curtains with his sword. [p. 373]

Thus reading the Bible became an experience of contemporary events as well as knowledge of the past while the past took on the immediacy of the present.

The Torah also became the source of hope for the future:

> REMEMBER THE DAYS OF OLD (Deut. 32:7) He said to them, "whenever the Holy One brings sufferings upon you, remember all the good things and consolations He is going to grant you in the world-to-come." [p. 357]

Several dialogues that will take place in the future between God and Israel are created as midrashim to Deuteronomy 30:19, the message of which is that all witnesses against Israel will disappear and Israel will remain the bride of the Holy One. [pp. 337–338]

Granted that these particular Midrashim record a process of continual revelation, of uncovering new levels of meaning, of application of ancient texts to new conditions of life, of solving textual difficulties and emphasizing values and concepts that were at the heart of the belief system of the Sages, one must ask both how the comments came about that are recorded here and for whom they were recorded or, better, orally formulated until eventually put into written form. It has been suggested that much of the material comes from sermons (*derashot,* another use of the same root d-r-sh).[70] Indeed, if comments were made on Scripture in the synagogues, which were primarily places for the public reading and teaching of Scripture, it would seem sensible that some would have found their way into these Midrashim. Although some of the tales may seem appropriate for that, much of the material here is either too complex or too fragmentary to have been *derashot.*[71] One suggestion is that these were "textbooks" for the scholars themselves.[72] It may be that these Midrashim are the collection of teachings that were disseminated among the Sages and their disciples in the Academies, which were called *batei (houses of) midrash* (singular: Bet Midrash). They were the material that emerged from the studies and formed the basis for continual study, each generation passing it down to the next. The purpose of such study was not only to learn but also to disseminate.

Much is made in the midrash itself of the importance of teaching Torah to others, with advice given as to how to do it properly [p. 344]. It was the very opposite of ivory tower studies. Therefore the material herein certainly did find its way out to the synagogues and to wherever Torah was studied and taught.

In some of the selections, we learn the way in which the Sages created their comments. Some of them were given in expositions on the Sabbath [p. 61], in informal discussions between Master and students [p. 92], in Sages' answering questions from students, each one giving his opinion [p. 325].

As Judah Goldin has written, "There is always a reason for a midrashic comment."[73] There is always something in the text that provokes the midrash. There is always some reason for them to want to say what they say ever though it may not always be apparent to us. First of all, the problem that bothered them may be unknown to us. Second, the text we have may be corrupt so that we cannot solve it. Third, we may not know exactly how they understood or defined a word.

The Sages had a love affair with Scripture. Their admiration for it emerges from every page:

MAY MY DISCOURSE COME DOWN AS THE RAIN (Deut. 32:2). MY DISCOURSE means words of Torah, as it is said FOR

INTRODUCTION

I HAVE GIVEN YOU GOOD DISCOURSE; DO NOT FOR-
SAKE MY TORAH (Prov. 4:2). And it says ACCEPT MY DIS-
CIPLINE RATHER THAN SILVER (Prov. 8:10) and "disci-
pline" always means words of Torah. [p. 343]

AS THE RAIN (Deut. 32:2). Just as the rain endures forever, so
words of Torah endure forever . . . MY SPEECH DISTILL AS
THE DEW (Deut. 32:2). Just as the entire world rejoices over
dew, thus the entire world rejoices over words of Torah. [p. 344]

LIKE DROPLETS ON THE GRASS (Deut. 32:2). Just as the
droplets are pure and cover everything, so do words of Torah
cover all sin and transgression. [p. 344]

Moses said to Israel, "Perhaps you do not know how much I
suffered for the Torah, how much effort I put into it, how much I
toiled for it. . . . I gave my life for it, I gave my blood for it. Just
as I learned it through suffering, so should you learn it through
suffering." Perhaps just as you learn it by suffering, so you should
teach it by suffering? The verse says MY SPEECH DISTILL (tizzal) AS THE DEW (Deut. 32:2)—think of it as something sold
cheaply (zol). [p. 345]

But this delight is evidenced not only in explicit comments, but in their
method of handling the text. They gather quotations from throughout the
Scripture and pile them on one another. They explain a word by bringing
examples of its use in other verses; they strengthen their arguments and
interpretations by quoting other verses. They create interesting combina-
tions of verses. Often the coda of a section will be nothing more than one
verse after the other, devoid of any comment:

The Temple, which is the highest of all, is of greater excellence,
as it is said YOU SHALL ARISE AND GO UP TO THE PLACE
WHICH THE LORD YOUR GOD HAS CHOSEN (Deut. 17:
8). AND THE MANY PEOPLE SHALL GO AND SHALL
SAY: "COME, LET US GO UP TO THE MOUNT OF THE
LORD" (Isa. 2:3). FOR THE DAY IS COMING WHEN
WATCHMEN SHALL PROCLAIM ON THE HEIGHTS OF
EPHRAIM COME, LET US GO UP TO ZION, TO THE
LORD OUR GOD! (Jer. 31:6). [p. 323]

39

INTRODUCTION

Those of us who depend on a concordance to locate a verse or find where a
root appears stand in awe of these Sages, who could always locate the appropriate verse and knew how to gather together as many examples as they
wanted of the appearance of a particular word or concept.

Their love is also seen in the way in which they use one section of the
Bible to illuminate another and make connections between verses and stories so that an ever richer tapestry is woven. Thus the creation of the Tabernacle is connected to the creation of the world:

> What is meant by AND IT WAS (Lev. 9:1)? This teaches that
> there was rejoicing before Him on high as on the day on which
> the heavens and the earth were created. Concerning the creation
> it says AND THERE WAS (vayehi) EVENING AND MORN-
> ING (Gen. 1:5) and here it says AND IT WAS (vayehi) (Lev.
> 9:1). [p. 179]

Or the story of the splitting of the Sea is connected to that of the binding of
Isaac, so that the two merge into one event:

> When Israel went into the sea, Mount Moriah was uprooted from
> its place and upon it the altar of Isaac and the wood already pre-
> pared and Isaac as if bound upon the altar and Abraham stretching
> out his hand to seize the knife to slaughter his son! . . . God said to
> Moses . . . "LIFT UP YOUR ROD" (Ex. 14:16). [p. 91]

Abraham's knife and Moses' rod merge into one.

Similarly, the story of the life of Joseph and the contents of the Ark of
the Covenant are compared in such a way as to make Joseph a living embodiment of the tablets contained in the Ark:

> He who rests in that coffer fulfilled that which is written upon
> what is contained in the other coffer. [p. 73]

Clearly the Sages viewed themselves not so much as masters of the text,
which they were, but as servants of it. They delighted in a text that could
yield many meanings:

> THE LORD, THE WARRIOR—LORD IS HIS NAME! (Ex.
> 15:3). R. Judah says, "What a rich verse this is, with many ech-
> oes!" [p. 107]

40

That is why any midrash, including this volume, must be read with Bible in hand.

A word about literary style. The main concern of the Sages may have been elucidation of the text, but consciously or subconsciously, they couched much, if not all, of their creation in literary style too rich and sophisticated to be ignored. The legends they told of the Biblical figures are often beautiful examples of narration as well as fanciful examples of the creative imagination. Read the story of the coffin of Joseph that Moses has to locate [p. 72], the legend of Jacob on his death bed [p. 309], the story of the death of Aaron [p. 333], or the many narratives about the death of Moses, especially the tale of Moses and the Angel of Death [p. 333] and you will see that we are dealing with masters of the art of storytelling. If these masterful legends did not form the basis of popular sermons of the day, they should have.

Of equal value are the complex sections, such as that on the Land of Israel [p. 319], that show obvious signs of careful editing and may have emerged in this form only when the work was actually set down in writing.[74] They make use of such rhetorical devices as repetitive phrases and refrains to drive home a point.

One final clue to reading midrash. A midrash, by definition, always starts with a text. It is true that the textual stimulus is not always identical with the value or the message the midrash wishes to teach. Some messages may have been political or theological, forming part of an ongoing polemic. In addition, the Sages utilize textual difficulties in order to present their value-concepts. Nevertheless, most comments are answers to questions raised by the Scripture itself. It is the seriousness with which they took the Scriptural text that caused the Sages to search it for its multiplicity of meanings. The textual stimulus may be an extra word, a peculiar form, an unusual placement of a word, a contrast with another verse, even a contradiction, a logical problem with the text: It cannot possibly mean what it seems to mean![75] The first clue to understanding a midrash, then, is always to look for the textual stimulus.[76] The free associations and unusual methods that sometimes appear far from the text should never be permitted to distract one from the fact that valuable exegesis of the meaning of the text is to be found there.

Are these works really classics of religious thought? Are they important enough to warrant serious study today or do they have mere antiquarian value? Certainly there can be no question that one interested in either the history of religions or comparative religion will find them invaluable. They represent the state of belief of normative Judaism at the conclusion of the period of the Second Temple and during the formative years of Christianity. Some Christians view post-Biblical Judaism as virtually a new religion, so that both Judaism and Christianity are seen as offshoots of the original religion of Israel with Christianity taking the place of the true Israel. Jews tend to see it otherwise, with Christianity as a sectarian branch of Judaism that eventually separated itself from the tree. Whatever the truth, it is obvious that Judaism of the Second Temple period evolved and grew beyond the Biblical religion, basing itself firmly on it but nevertheless changing.[77] The Judaism to which Christianity had to relate, from which it grew and which it challenged (and was challenged by) was this later development. Therefore Christianity cannot possibly be understood without a knowledge of that Judaism and these Midrashim present the most coherent view of the beliefs and values of that Judaism and of its reading of Scripture. Nor can Judaism, in any of its contemporary manifestations, even the most secular, be understood without a knowledge of them. Although there were subsequent developments within Judaism and although the Talmud represents a much more extensive version of rabbinic Judaism, the basis of it is to be found here in its more pristine, classic form. Together with the Mishna, which represents the distillation of legal thinking in its nonmidrashic or apodictic form, these works represent the minimum knowledge needed for an understanding of post-Biblical Judaism.

What of its message? Has it meaning and relevance? Its very method is itself a message of importance. Its approach to a text is in and of itself significant for the reading of any text, and especially for the reading of a fixed Divine text. Midrash is the very enemy of fundamentalism. Simplistic, literalistic interpretation and reading of a text can be its death knell. That is where the letter kills. On the other hand, the method of symbolism or allegory can be equally dangerous, for that is a way of reading a text out of existence and transforming it into something totally different.[78] The Sages could be literal when they wanted to. They spoke of a text meaning *k'mashmao*—exactly what it sounds like. They established the principle that "the verse never abandons its fundamental meaning," although the fundamental meaning they understood might not be the same as ours. They also used symbolism and even allegory from time to time, but through the method of midrash they also managed to establish the possibility of adding meaning, of opening up texts, of probing the depth and the breadth of a text, of investing it with flexibility, of allowing it to fit the times without abandoning truth and simple meaning. "With a combination of reverence and spontaneity, they so open up and arrange and illuminate the individual volumes of the entrusted collection, that they and their contemporaries will discover the reflection of their own features in it, and the response to their own needs and even fantasies."[79] Because of their work, Scripture is never out of date, never abandoned, and never runs dry. When Allan Bloom wrote of texts that form the basis of life,[80] he was describing the way in which the Bible functioned, but it is a functioning in which the text itself grows. The interchange is between the reader and the text, between society and the text, between the word and the meaning. They poured "new wine of the spirit into the old bottles of the letter."[81]

In addition, the concepts and values exemplified by the text are also important enough to render this a classic work. The texts are God-intoxicated. It is the search for "knowing" God that informs them, and "knowing" here is used in the Biblical sense—to be intimate with, to be close to God, to feel His presence in every act and to express it in every deed. The texts bring meaning to religious actions, investing rituals either with specific meaning or with the function of fulfilling the will of God. The texts assert the value of Israel within God's plan, the value of all humanity and the hope for the future when the inconsistencies, the contradictions, and the injustices of the present will vanish. The texts engage in discussion and debate on questions of repentance, the value of deeds, the importance of study, the value of human life and the saving of it, the importance of peace, morality, and honesty as the indications of religious life. And if, here and there, a text may fall beneath the high standards set by the work as a whole, this should not be a matter of astonishment in a work that reflects the ideas of so many individual human Sages, each with his own life experiences.

No student of the Bible should read the Bible without the insights of the classic Sages. No student of religion should neglect the insights of these masters of the spirit. No student of culture and literature should ignore the methods and the products embodied in these creations. No one concerned with the problems of being human in this day and age should ignore the answers to these problems, which are found in these classic works.

Just as these texts cannot be a complete and exhaustive treatment of this major genre of literature, so this introduction too has dealt with some of the qualities of midrash but has hardly exhausted the subject. The best advice that can be given is that of the great Sage Hillel when he was asked to teach the entire Torah while standing on one foot. "Do not do unto others what you would not want done unto you," he replied, giving his midrash on Leviticus 18:18, "Love your neighbor as yourself." He then added, "the rest is commentary—go learn." It is hoped that this volume will provide enough material and sufficient explanation to demonstrate the value of midrash and that this will stimulate many readers to go further into this fascinating subject.

A NOTE ON THE TEXTS

This book represents an attempt to present the essential Tannaitic Midrash within the limited framework of one volume. Since we are dealing basically with four works, each of which is a volume in itself, drastic editing had to be done. The common method of selection found in many collections is to take midrashim that deal with a common theme, let us say God, the creation, good and evil, and put them together. My intent, however, was to attempt to give the reader the feeling of the way in which Tannaitic Midrash is structured and formulated. Therefore I have simply presented as many texts as space allowed, following the structure of the works that is according to the order of the Scriptural verses. The numbering of each individual selection indicates nothing more than that the section is not continuous with the end of the previous section. Thus whenever a considerable amount of text has been eliminated, a new section begins. A section, then, may be relatively brief or, more often, it will be long and will contain the comments on several Biblical verses. In instances where only a few lines have not been translated, three dots (. . .) appear to indicate that there is some omission. Thus the reader will experience the same type of organization that would be found in a complete translation of these works. Midrashim of different types, multiple comments, mixtures of midrash, stories, legends, sayings, and so forth, will appear together. The only exception to this is that the book has been divided into two sections, the first containing selections that are narrative in nature, the second containing selections of rabbinic interpretation of legal texts. This was done for the convenience of the reader who may be interested in one kind of material or the other. Both are presented in order of the Biblical verses they interpret, as they are in the original text. As will be seen, more space is devoted in this volume to the narrative midrash than to the legal midrash. This does not reflect the correct proportion within the original works where, depending on the particular work, the legal is frequently greater than the narrative or equal to it. However, many of the legal sections would be either too complex or too obscure for the purposes of this series. Therefore those presented here are the ones of most interest and most accessible, even though some of them may also be difficult.

Selections were translated from the four main works of Tannaitic Midrash using the following editions:

INTRODUCTION

1. Mekilta de-Rabbi Ishmael, ed. Jacob Z. Lauterbach, Philadelphia, 1949. (Since the title is usually transliterated as Mekhilta, that is the spelling I used in this volume.)

2. Sifra on Leviticus, ed. Louis Finkelstein, New York, 1989. Sifra d'be Rab, ed. Isaac H. Weiss, New York, 1946.

3. Siphre d'be Rab, Siphre to Numbers and Sifre Zutta, ed. H. S. Horovitz, Jerusalem, 1966.

4. Sifre on Deuteronomy, ed. Louis Finkelstein, New York, 1969.

It should be noted that in each case these represent the best available scholarly edition of the work but by no means has the final word been said in regard to the publication of the most ancient and authentic manuscripts of these texts. Even such a highly praised edition as Horovitz's Siphre is far from ideal, as M. Kahana pointed out in his proposal for a new edition based on more recent studies, improved methodology, and a better manuscript.[82]

Since space is limited, I decided not to use selections from the other Tannaitic works mentioned in the introduction, which are reconstructions of lost books created from later Midrashim. The exception to this is that a few important sections from Sifre Zuta have been incorporated into the section on Sifre Numbers.

In such an attempt at condensation, the personal taste and preference of the author is obviously a major factor. I attempted to include portions that deal with Biblical sections of particular importance such as the Song of the Sea, the Ten Commandments, the Shema (Hear, O Israel), and the Song of Moses. I also included those portions that have the greatest literary, religious, and ethical interest and sought to include as many variations of midrashic method as possible. Where the same midrashim appear more than once, I selected that which I felt was the best and most complete version. Those familiar with the entire works will undoubtedly find sections missing that they consider important. I also found it necessary to eliminate passages I think are important, but such are the requirements of an abridged volume.

Sections are identified by the first Biblical verse and by the section and the page in the Hebrew edition. Thus the first selection in the book is marked Exodus 12:3, Mekhilta Pisha 5, I 33, which means that the first verse interpreted is Exodus 12:3 and that it is found in the Mekhilta, the section known as Pisha 5, which is on page 33 of volume I of the edition. In the case of Leviticus, since two editions were used, they are identified by the name of the editor, either Finkelstein or Weiss, and the page in that edition. The Sifre, both to Numbers and to Deuteronomy, is marked first with the number of the selection (called a Piska) and then by the page number.

Transliterations of Hebrew words basically follow the sound rather than the accepted scholarly transliteration in order to permit the general reader to get a sense of the pronunciation. Many midrashim are based on similarities of a word to another word or a variation of meaning of that same Hebrew root. In the current translation, if the Hebrew word appears in transliteration in parentheses, that indicates that it will be compared with another Hebrew word or that there may be a play on words. Although these are not always explained in detail, the resemblance in sound should be sufficient to indicate the mode of interpretation.

The word *Torah*, referring either to the Pentateuch or to the corpus of Jewish learning, is not translated, nor is the word *mitzvot*, meaning the deeds or commandments of God. The common midrashic term for God is HaKadosh Baruch Hu, the Holy One Blessed Is He. In this work, that phrase is translated simply as the Holy One. In order to distinguish between the mitzvot and the ten terms of the Covenant usually called the Ten Commandments, the term Ten Pronouncements is used. That is a more accurate rendering of the Hebrew *Dibrot*, which come from the root d-b-r, to speak declare or pronounce. The technical term *kal va-homer*, an inference from minor to major, is usually translated as "a question of logic." The word *minayin*, which begins a question concerning the origin of a law or interpretation, is sometimes translated "What is the source which tells us," but sometimes merely as "How do we know," or "What about . . ." depending on the context.

Since midrash is so overwhelmingly an interpretation of the text of the Bible, Biblical verses play a major role in this volume and the decision as to which translation to use was a crucial one. I chose to utilize the excellent English translation *Tanakh: The New JPS Translation according to the Traditional Hebrew Text* (Jewish Publication Society, Philadelphia, 1962), since I find it to be the most accurate rendering of the Hebrew Scriptures. I am deeply appreciative of the generous permission that was granted me by the Jewish Publication Society to utilize these quotations. It must be noted, however, that the midrashic understanding of the text occasionally required me to translate a verse differently from the Jewish Publication Society version. Such translations are my responsibility. Since the manuscripts indicate that we are not always certain how much of a particular verse was quoted before a comment was made, I have sometimes included more than appears in the Hebrew text in order to make the comment more understandable.

INTRODUCTION

This volume is intended for the general reader whose knowledge of midrash is limited. I have therefore accompanied the text with a running explanation, which appears at the bottom of each page and should be read together with the text. This explanation provides the minimum information and interpretation needed to understand the text. I have also interspersed other comments into the text itself from time to time wherever I felt that it was important to do so. These appear either at the conclusion of a section or following some part of the text that I felt required a lengthier explanation. These comments discuss the major themes of the midrash, and give some information concerning the historical background or the particular methodology being followed. They attempt to place the particular midrash within a broader context. These too are intended for the general reader and by no means exhaust all that could be said about a text. The limitations of this text would not permit me to go beyond that. The reader who is interested in more technical aspects, in comparisons with other texts or references to parallels, will find additional information in the complete translations of these texts, which are referred to in the Bibliography and in the specialized works mentioned there that give lengthy and detailed commentaries to sections of these Midrashim such as Goldin's work on the Song at the Sea, Kadushin to the Mekhilta, and Fraade to Sifre Deuteronomy.

Finally, I should like to express my loving appreciation to my wife, Raḥel, who patiently read, reread, and corrected these pages and whose valuable questions and comments are reflected throughout this work.

To quote the words usually written by a scribe at the conclusion of a manuscript:

—the end of (this Midrash). Let us be strong and strengthen each other.

NOTES TO INTRODUCTION

1. Daniel Boyarin, *Intertextuality and the Reading of Midrash* (Bloomington, 1990), p. xii.

2. Gary Porton, "Midrash," *Aufsteig und Niedergand II* (Berlin, 1974), p. 104; and Geoffrey H. Hartman and Sanford Budick, *Midrash and Literature* (New Haven, 1986), p. x.

3. Boyarin, *Intertextuality*, p. x.

4. Hartman and Budick, *Midrash and Literature*, p. xiii.

5. Betty Roitman, "Sacred Language and Open Text," in Hartman and Budick, *Midrash and Literature*, p. 159.

6. Haim Z. Dimitrovsky, "Talmud and Midrash," *Encyclopaedia Britannica, 15th Edition* (1974), p. 1006; Porton, "Midrash," p. 108.

7. Max Kadushin, *The Rabbinic Mind* (New York, 1952), p. 6.

8. Steven D. Fraade, "Interpreting Midrash I," *Prooftexts* 7 (1987), p. 179.

9. Boyarin, *Intertextuality*, p. 28.

10. Louis Finkelstein, "Maimonides and the Midrashim," *Sifra on Leviticus, Vol. 5* (New York, 1992), p. 471.

11. M.D. Herr, "Sifra," *Encyclopedia Judaica 14*, p. 1517.

12. B. Kid 49b, Meg 28b, Sanh 86a, Shebu 41b, *Iggerret Sherira Ga'on* (Jerusalem, 1971), p. 39.

13. Dimitrovsky, "Talmud and Midrash," p. 1008.

14. The first Midrash on Genesis is *Genesis Rabba*, dating from the fifth century. It may be that Genesis received less attention either because it contains no legal sections or because it deals with the time prior to the revelation at Sinai and the formation of the people of Israel.

15. Solomon Zeitlin, "Midrash: A Historical Study," *Jewish Quarterly Review 44 N.S.* (1953): 21.

16. Ibid., p. 25.

17. Elias J. Bickerman, *The Jews in the Greek Age* (Cambridge, 1988), p. 192.

18. Michael Fishbane, *The Garments of Torah* (Bloomington, 1989), p. 66.

19. Porton, "Midrash," p. 134.

20. Ibid., p. 105; Bickerman, *Jews in the Greek Age*, p. 172; Fishbane, *Garments of Torah*, p. 66.

21. B.M. 59b.

22. J. Peah 2:4; Judah Goldin, *Studies in Midrash and Related Literature* (Philadelphia, 1988), p. 222.

23. Avot 1:1.

24. Porton, "Midrash," p. 107.

25. Ibid., p. 108.

26. James L. Kugel, "Two Introductions to Midrash," in Hartman and Budick, *Midrash and Literature*, p. 91.

27. Bickerman, *Jews in the Greek Age*, p. 163.

28. Dimitrovsky, "Talmud and Midrash," p. 1007.

29. Bickerman, *Jews in the Greek Age*, p. 166.

30. See page [344] below.

31. Zeitlin, "Midrash," p. 30; and Kadushin, *Rabbinic Mind*, p. 127.

32. Goldin, *Studies in Midrash*, p. 221.

33. Avot 1:1; and Judah Goldin *The Fathers according to Rabbi Nathan* (New Haven, 1955), p. 4.

34. Reuven Hammer, *Sifre on Deuteronomy* (New Haven, 1986), p. 84.

35. J. Peah 2:4.

36. See above, note 22.

37. Porton, "Midrash," p. 8; and Fraade, "Interpreting Midrash I," p. 294.

38. Dimitrovsky, "Talmud and Midrash," p. 1007.

39. Ibid.

40. Finkelstein, "Maimonides," p. 471.

41. Dimitrovsky, "Talmud and Midrash," p. 1008.

42. Steven D. Fraade, *From Tradition to Commentary* (Albany, 1991), p. 2.

43. Judah Goldin, "From Text to Interpretation," *Prooftexts 3* (1983): 158.

44. Fraade, *From Tradition*, p. 72.

45. Herr, "Sifra." *Encyclopedia Judaica*, 14 (Jerusalem, 1972), p. 1519.

46. Louis Finkelstein, "Prolegomena to an Edition of the Sifre on Deuteronomy," *Proceedings of the American Academy of Jewish Research III* (1932): 3.

47. Ibid., p. 26.

48. Goldin, *Studies in Midrash*, p. 235.

49. Saul Lieberman, *Hellenism in Jewish Palestine* (New York, 1962), p. 88.

50. Kadushin, *Rabbinic Mind*, p. 123.

51. David Weiss Halivni, *Midrash, Mishnah, and Gemara* (Cambridge, 1986), p. 61.

52. Judah Goldin, *The Song at the Sea* (New Haven, 1971), p. 12.

53. Kadushin, *Rabbinic Mind*, p. 120; Fraade, *From Tradition*, p. 14.

54. Steven D. Fraade, "Interpreting Midrash 2," *Prooftexts 8* (1988): 291, posits three main traits: indeterminacy of textual meaning; intertextuality (bringing in other texts); free, open-ended, serious play and interplay of the first two principles.

55. Porton, "Midrash," p. 111.

56. Fraade, *From Tradition*, p. 8; Bickerman, *Jews in the Greek Age*, p. 169.

57. Goldin, "From Text," p. 158.

58. Isaac Heineman, *Darkei Agadda* (Jerusalem, 1954), p. 12.

59. Boyarin, *Intertextuality*, p. ix.

60. Kadushin, *Rabbinic Mind*, p. 140.

61. Heineman, *Darkei Agadda*, p. 12.

62. Goldin, *Studies*, p. 221.

63. Kadushin, *Rabbinic Mind*, p. 14.

64. Heineman, *Darkei Agadda*, p. 8.

65. Kadushin, *Rabbinic Mind*, p. 15.

66. Geza Vermes, *Scripture and Tradition in Judaism* (Leiden, 1973), p. 7.

67. Boyarin, *Intertextuality*, p. 40.

68. Ibid., p. 36.

69. See Marc Hirshman, *Mikra and Midrash* Tel Aviv, 1992 (Hebrew).

70. Kadushin, *Rabbinic Mind*, p. 84.

71. Porton, "Midrash," p. 131.

72. Fraade, *Tradition*, p. 18.

73. Goldin, "From Text," p. 161.

74. Reuven Hammer, "Section 38 of Sifre Deuteronomy," *Hebrew Union College Annual 50* (Cincinnati, 1979).

75. Bickerman, *Jews in the Greek Age*, p. 189.

76. Goldin, "From Text," p. 161.

77. Heineman, *Darkei Agadda*, p. 90.

78. Goldin, *Studies*, p. 229.

79. Goldin, "From Text," p. 166.

80. Allan Bloom, *The Closing of the American Mind* (New York, 1987), pp. 45–62. He writes specifically about the impact of the Bible on his grandparents in a way not unconnected, I think, to midrash: "But their home was spiritually rich because all things done in it . . . found their origins in the Bible's commandments, *and their explanation in the Bible's stories and the commentaries on them* and they interpreted their special sufferings with respect to a great and ennobling past" (p. 60; emphasis added).

81. Bickerman, *Jews in the Greek Age*, p. 176.

82. Menachem Kahana, *Akdamot Le'hotz-a hadasha shel Sifre Bamidbar* Jerusalem, 5742.

I.
SCRIPTURAL
INTERPRETATION—
AGGADAH

EXODUS

1. Exodus 12:3, Mekhilta Pisha 5, I 33

SPEAK TO THE WHOLE ASSEMBLY OF ISRAEL AND SAY THAT ON THE TENTH OF THIS MONTH EACH OF THEM SHALL TAKE A LAMB . . . YOU SHALL KEEP WATCH OVER IT UNTIL THE FOURTEENTH DAY OF THIS MONTH (Ex. 12:3, 6). Why did Scripture require that the Paschal lamb be taken four days before it was to be slaughtered?

R. Matya b. Heresh used to say, "It says WHEN I PASSED BY YOU AND SAW THAT YOUR TIME FOR LOVE HAD ARRIVED (Ezek. 16:8). The time had come to fulfill the oath made to our father Abraham to redeem his children, but they had no mitzvot with which to occupy themselves in order to make them worthy of redemption, as it is said, YOUR BREASTS BECAME FIRM AND YOUR HAIR SPROUTED—YOU WERE STILL NAKED AND BARE (Ezek. 16:7)—bare of mitzvot. Therefore the Holy One gave them two mitzvot, the Paschal lamb and circumcision, so that they should fulfill them and be redeemed, as it is said WHEN I PASSED BY YOU AND SAW YOU WALLOWING IN YOUR BLOOD, I SAID TO YOU, 'BY YOUR BLOOD SHALL YOU LIVE,' YEA, I SAID TO YOU, 'BY YOUR BLOOD SHALL YOU LIVE!' (Ezek. 16:6) and it is said YOU FOR YOUR PART HAVE RELEASED YOUR PRISONERS FROM THE DRY PIT, FOR THE SAKE OF THE BLOOD OF YOUR COVENANT (Zech. 9:11)."

---

1. *four days before* In Ex. 12:3 the Israelites are commanded to take a lamb on the tenth day of the month and do nothing but watch over it until the fourteenth of the month.

the oath In Gen. 15:16 God promised Abraham that although his children would be enslaved, after four hundred years they would return to Canaan. The verses from Ezekiel are taken as referring to that time of redemption which had arrived. The oath could not be fulfilled, however, unless the Israelites earned it by the performance of deeds—in Hebrew "mitzvot," usually translated as "commandments."

This explains why Scripture required that the Pascal lamb be taken four days before it was to be slaughtered, since only deeds bring reward.

R. Eleazar ha-Kappar says, "But had not Israel already fulfilled four mitzvot which are of greater worth than the world itself? They were not suspect of sexual misconduct nor of speaking evil, neither had they changed their names or their language."

How do we know that they were not suspect of sexual misconduct? As it is said, THERE CAME OUT AMONG THE ISRAELITES ONE WHOSE MOTHER WAS ISRAELITE AND WHOSE FATHER WAS EGYP-TIAN (Lev. 24:10). This informs us that Israel was praiseworthy in that this was the only case of sexual misconduct among them. That is why Scrip-ture singles it out. This is stated explicitly in the Writings: A GARDEN LOCKED IS MY OWN, MY BRIDE, A FOUNTAIN LOCKED, A SEALED-UP SPRING (Song 4:12). A GARDEN LOCKED refers to the males and A FOUNTAIN LOCKED to the females. R. Nathan says that A GARDEN LOCKED refers to those married and A FOUNTAIN LOCKED to those engaged. Another interpretation: A GARDEN LOCKED and A FOUNTAIN LOCKED refer to two types of intercourse.

How do we know that they were not suspect of speaking evil, but rather loved one another? As it is said, EACH WOMAN SHALL BORROW FROM HER NEIGHBOR . . . (Ex. 3:22). They had known of this for twelve months and yet no one had informed on another.

And how do we know that they had not changed their names? By the fact that just as when they came into Egypt they were recorded as being Reuven, Shimon, Levi, and Yehudah (Gen. 46:8f), so when they leave they are recorded as Reuven, Shimon, Levi, and Yehudah, as it is said WHO WERE REGISTERED BY THE CLANS OF THEIR ANCESTRAL HOUSES . . . (Num. 1:18) and it says THE ANGEL WHO HAS RE-DEEMED ME FROM ALL HARM—BLESS THE LADS. IN THEM MAY MY NAME BE RECALLED . . . (Gen. 48:16).

---

only deeds Keeping watch over the lamb during the four days was considered a deed done in obedience of God's will and thus gave them merit that would warrant their redemption.
four mitzvot—not of a ritual nature, but in the ethical sphere and in the area of loyalty to the tradition.

And how do we know that they did not change their language? As it is said, HE RETORTED, "WHO MADE YOU CHIEF AND RULER OVER US?" (Ex. 2:14). It is clear from this that they were speaking Hebrew. And it says THAT IT IS INDEED MY MOUTH SPEAKING TO YOU (Gen. 45:12). And it says THEY ANSWERED, "THE GOD OF THE HEBREWS HAS MANIFESTED HIMSELF TO US" (Ex. 5:3). And it says A FUGITIVE BROUGHT THE NEWS TO ABRAM THE HEBREW . . . (Gen. 14:13).

If this is so, why did Scripture command that the Paschal lamb be taken four days before it was to be slaughtered? It was because Israel was steeped in idolatry in Egypt, and the prohibition of idolatry is equal to all the other mitzvot of the Torah . . . for just as one who transgresses all of the mitzvot casts off the yoke [of Heaven], annuls the covenant and falsifies the Torah, . . . so one who transgresses this one mitzvah casts off the yoke, annuls the covenant and falsifies the Torah . . . therefore He said to them, "Refrain from idolatry and cling to mitzvot!"

R. Judah b. Beterah says, "It says BUT WHEN MOSES TOLD THIS TO THE ISRAELITES, THEY WOULD NOT LISTEN TO MOSES, THEIR SPIRITS CRUSHED BY CRUEL BONDAGE (Ex. 6:9). Is there anyone who would not rejoice when hearing good news? 'You have a son!' Would he not rejoice? 'Your master has emancipated you!' Would he not rejoice? Considering this, what is the meaning of THEY WOULD NOT LISTEN TO MOSES? It was difficult for them to separate themselves from idolatry. Similarly it states I ALSO SAID TO THEM: CAST AWAY, EVERY ONE OF YOU, THE DETESTABLE THINGS THAT YOU ARE DRAWN TO AND DO NOT DEFILE YOURSELVES WITH THE FETISHES OF EGYPT (Ezek. 20:7) and BUT THEY DEFIED ME AND REFUSED TO LISTEN TO ME. THEY DID NOT CAST AWAY THE DETESTABLE THINGS THAT THEY WERE DRAWN TO, NOR DID THEY GIVE UP THE FETISHES OF EGYPT. THEN I RE-

---

speaking Hebrew The words recorded in Hebrew are the words they were speaking.

If this is so—there was no need for additional mitzvot, such as taking the lamb and watching it for four days. These four mitzvot were sufficient to merit salvation.

cling to mitzvot The task of watching over the lamb means that they will not be able to worship idols. Their minds will be directed instead to obeying God. In addition, the lamb was worshiped in Egypt so that preparing it for slaughter meant denying its divinity.

SOLVED TO POUR OUT MY FURY UPON THEM ... IN THE
LAND OF EGYPT (Ezek. 20:8–9). That is what is meant by the verse
SO THE LORD SPOKE TO MOSES AND AARON COMMANDING
THEM IN REGARD TO THE ISRAELITES (Ex. 6:13). He commanded
that they give up idolatry."

COMMENTARY   *On the surface, this midrash raises the question: What
is the purpose of the command that the Israelites keep watch over a lamb
four days prior to sacrificing it? The first answer given is that there is no
redemption without performance of mitzvot. Since they had not yet been
given mitzvot, God gave them this to make them worthy of redemption.
This is refuted by the tradition that indeed they already had mitzvot—not
ritual ones, but ethical ones, which are much more important. They lived
according to high morality and were true to their heritage. Why then the
command to take the lamb four days early? It was to wean them away from
idolatry, the lamb being one of the idols worshiped in Egypt. It was idolatry
and not lack of deeds that prevented their redemption. The editor uses this
question as a means of bringing together many different comments and creating a discussion of various themes: the importance of deeds in bringing
redemption, the relative merit of ritual and ethical commandments, and the
enticing power of idolatry. The section reflects the argument between Judaism and early Christianity regarding the importance of deeds in achieving
salvation, ironically utilizing the Pascal lamb, which was identified by Christians with Jesus for this purpose.*

2. Exodus 12:13, Mekhilta Pisha 7, I 56

WHEN I SEE THE BLOOD (Ex. 12:13). R. Ishmael used to say, "But is
not everything known to Him? As it is said, HE KNOWS WHAT IS IN
THE DARKNESS, AND LIGHT DWELLS WITH HIM (Dan. 2:22) and
DARKNESS IS NOT DARK FOR YOU; NIGHT IS AS LIGHT AS
DAY; DARKNESS AND LIGHT ARE THE SAME (Ps. 139:12). What
then does WHEN I SEE THE BLOOD mean? Is it not that as a reward for
the mitzvah which you perform I will reveal Myself and protect you? As it
is said I WILL PASS OVER YOU (Ex. 12:13) and PASS OVER always
means to protect as we see from the verse LIKE THE BIRDS THAT FLY,

---

2. *known to Him*—in which case the verse cannot be taken literally. God does not need to see
the blood in order to know in which houses Israelites live.
as a reward for the mitzvah—referring to the slaughtering of the lamb.

EVEN SO WILL THE LORD OF HOSTS SHIELD JERUSALEM, SHIELDING AND SAVING, PASSING OVER AND RESCUING (Isa. 31:5)."

WHEN I SEE THE BLOOD (Ex. 12:13). I see the blood of the binding of Isaac, as it is said AND ABRAHAM NAMED THAT SITE THE LORD WILL SEE (Gen. 22:14). Similarly it says . . . AS HE WAS ABOUT TO WREAK DESTRUCTION, THE LORD SAW AND RENOUNCED FURTHER PUNISHMENT AND SAID TO THE DESTROYING AN-GEL, "ENOUGH! STAY YOUR HAND!" (1 Chron. 21:15). What did He see? He saw the blood of the binding of Isaac as it is said THE LORD HIMSELF WILL SEE THE SHEEP (Gen. 22:8).

I WILL PROTECT YOU (Ex. 12:13). R. Josiah says, "Do not read 'pa-sahti,' I WILL PROTECT but 'pasa'ti'—I will step over—for God leaped over the houses of His children in Egypt, as it says HARK! MY BELOVED! THERE HE COMES, LEAPING OVER MOUNTAINS, BOUNDING OVER HILLS (Song 2:8)."

R. Jonathan says, "I WILL PROTECT YOU. **You,** will I protect, but I will not protect the Egyptians. Thus I might have thought that an Egyptian in the house of an Israelite would be saved because of him, but Scripture says I WILL PASS OVER YOU. **You,** will I protect, but I will not protect the Egyptians. I might have thought that if an Israelite were in the house of an Egyptian, he would be smitten because of him, but Scripture says SO THAT NO PLAGUE WILL DESTROY YOU WHEN I STRIKE THE LAND OF EGYPT (Ex. 12:13) Upon **you** I shall not bring it, but I shall bring it upon Egyptians. Another interpretation: I will not bring it upon you WHEN I STRIKE THE LAND OF EGYPT but I will bring it upon you at a later time."

COMMENTARY   *The Sages emphasize that this verse, like so many others, is not to be taken literally. Obviously God needs no sign in order to*

---

the blood of the binding of Isaac   "Seeing the blood" does not mean literally looking at the blood on the doorposts, but remembering the actions of Abraham and Isaac in the story of the binding of Isaac. The Israelites are protected because of the merit of their ancestors. According to midrashic tradition, the blood of Isaac was actually shed when he was bound.
WILL SEE—usually translated "will provide." The "sheep," in this interpretation, is Isaac himself.

know where the Israelites are. Therefore the verse must mean either that He commanded them to do this in order to give the Israelites an opportunity to earn redemption through performance of mitzvot or, connecting the word blood here with a different blood, namely that of Isaac, since, according to other midrashim, Isaac's blood was actually shed upon the altar. Thus saying that God "sees" the blood means that He recalls the merit of Isaac's sacrifice. Following this, different explanations are offered of the word pasahti (usually translated "pass over" but understood by the Sages as meaning "protect") through a method commonly accepted of suggesting that for purposes of interpretation, it should be read as if one letter were a different one similar in sound, which yields a different meaning to the word. Finally the word you is understood as emphasizing a specific point, namely the contrast between the Israelites and the Egyptians.

3. Exodus 12:29, Mekhilta Pisha 13, I 98

TO THE FIRST BORN OF THE CAPTIVE (Ex. 12:29). But in what way had the captives sinned? Rather this was to prevent them from saying "*Our* god brought this punishment upon them. How mighty is our god who has thus prevailed and who let no punishment come upon us!"

Another interpretation: This teaches us that whenever Pharaoh inflicted his decrees on Israel, the captives rejoiced over them, as it is said HE WHO REJOICES OVER ANOTHER'S MISFORTUNE WILL NOT GO UNPUNISHED (Prov. 17:5) and IF YOUR ENEMY FALLS, DO NOT REJOICE (Prov. 24:17) and O MORTAL, BECAUSE TYRE GLOATED OVER JERUSALEM . . . (Ezek. 26:2). What does it say thereafter? I AM GOING TO DEAL AGAINST YOU, O TYRE! I WILL HURL MANY NATIONS AGAINST YOU, AS THE SEA HURLS ITS WAVES (Ezek. 26:3). And this was true not only of the captives, but also of the male and female slaves, as it is said TO THE FIRST-BORN OF THE SLAVE GIRL (Ex. 11:5).

AND ALL THE FIRSTBORN OF THE CATTLE (Ex. 12:29). What could possibly be the sin of cattle? Rather this was to prevent the Egyptians from saying, "*Our* god brought this punishment upon us. How mighty is our god who has thus prevailed. How mighty is our god who was not affected by this punishment."

COMMENTARY   *The midrash is troubled by the seeming injustice of the suffering of the captives and the cattle. It was axiomatic that God is just and would not punish the innocent. The answers suggested are either that they were really guilty in some way or that they had to be smitten lest the captives believe that their gods were real and powerful and lest the Egyptians believe that cattle, which they worshiped, were indeed divine. Comments such as these may well reflect real challenges to the Scriptures from pagans or questions brought by Jews who sought to avoid moral contradictions between their belief and the Bible.*

4. Exodus 12:39, Mekhilta Pisha 14, I 110

NOR HAD THEY PREPARED ANY PROVISIONS FOR THEMSELVES (Ex. 12:39). This informs us how praiseworthy Israel was, for they did not say to Moses, "How can we go into the wilderness without any provisions?" Rather they believed in Him and followed Moses. Concerning them the tradition says: GO PROCLAIM TO JERUSALEM: THUS SAID THE LORD: I ACCOUNTED TO YOUR FAVOR THE DEVOTION OF YOUR YOUTH, YOUR LOVE AS A BRIDE—HOW YOU FOLLOWED ME IN THE WILDERNESS, IN A LAND NOT SOWN (Jer. 2:2). What reward did they receive for this? ISRAEL WAS HOLY TO THE LORD, THE FIRST FRUITS OF HIS HARVEST. ALL WHO ATE OF IT WERE HELD GUILTY; DISASTER BEFELL THEM (Jer. 2:3). . . .

TO THE VERY DAY, ALL THE RANKS OF THE LORD DEPARTED FROM THE LAND OF EGYPT (Ex. 12:41). This refers to the ministering angels. Thus we find that whenever Israel is enslaved, the Divine Presence, as it were, is enslaved with them, as it is said, AND THEY SAW THE GOD OF ISRAEL: UNDER HIS FEET THERE WAS THE LIKENESS OF A PAVEMENT OF SAPPHIRE . . . (Ex. 24:10) while when they are redeemed what does it say? LIKE THE VERY SKY FOR PURITY (Ex. 24:10).

---

4. *Divine Presence*—or the "Indwelling Presence," the *Shekhina*, literally "that which dwells." This is the quality of God's immanence, His manifestation to man when He is close, as opposed to His transcendence. In Hebrew the term is feminine.

when they are redeemed The first part of the verse, describing a pavement that consists of bricks, is taken to refer to the time of slavery. The last part, THE VERY SKY FOR PURITY, describes the appearance of God after they had attained their freedom. The pavement-bricks, the symbol of slavery, have disappeared.

It says IN ALL THEIR TROUBLES HE WAS TROUBLED (Isa. 63:9). This indicates only that He suffers with the community. What source is there that indicates that He also suffers with the individual? The verse says WHEN HE CALLS ON ME, I WILL ANSWER HIM; I WILL BE WITH HIM IN DISTRESS (Ps. 91:15) and it says SO JOSEPH'S MASTER HAD HIM PUT IN PRISON, WHERE THE KING'S PRISONERS WERE CONFINED. BUT EVEN WHILE HE WAS THERE IN PRISON, THE LORD WAS WITH JOSEPH (Gen. 39:20–21).

Similarly it says ... BEFORE YOUR PEOPLE WHOM YOU REDEEMED FOR YOURSELF FROM EGYPT—A NATION AND ITS GOD (2 Sam. 7:23). R. Eliezer says, "An idol passed through the sea with Israel, as it says A RIVAL PASSED OVER THE SEA (Zech. 10:11). And which idol was it? Micah's."

R. Akiba says, "Were it not explicitly stated in Scripture, one would not dare say it. It is as if Israel said to God, 'You redeemed Yourself.' Thus we find that whenever Israel went into exile, the Divine Presence, as it were, went into exile with them. They went into exile to Egypt—the Divine Presence went into exile with them, as it is said I EXILED MYSELF TO YOUR FATHER'S HOUSE IN EGYPT (1 Sam. 2:27). When they went into exile to Babylonia, the Divine Presence went into exile with them, as it is said FOR YOUR SAKE I WAS SENT TO BABYLON (Isa. 43:14). When they went into exile to Elam, the Divine Presence went into exile with them, as it is said AND I WILL SET MY THRONE IN ELAM (Jer. 49:38). When they went into exile to Edom, the Divine Presence went into exile with them, as it is said WHO IS THIS COMING FROM EDOM IN CRIMSONED GARMENTS FROM BOZRAH ... (Isa. 63:1). And when they return in the future the Divine Presence, as it were, will return with them, as it is said THEN THE LORD YOUR GOD WILL RETURN WITH YOUR CAPTIVITY ... (Deut. 30:3). It does not say *veheshib* 'He will

---

An idol In R. Eliezer's view the word "its god" refers to an idol representing a heathen god and not to the Divine Presence.

Micah's—referring to the story in Judges 17 in which a certain Micah set up an idol in his house.

R. Akiba He disagrees with R. Eliezer. According to him, ITS GOD refers not to an idol but to God Himself. Difficult as it may be to comprehend, the verse depicts God Himself passing through the Sea and experiencing redemption.

Edom—the symbol of Rome in rabbinic literature. The name itself means "red," which was suggestive of the royal Roman purple.

bring back . . .' but *ve-shab* 'He will return.' And it says FROM LEBANON COME WITH ME; FROM LEBANON, MY BRIDE, WITH ME! (Song 4:8). Now was she really coming from Lebanon? Was she not going to Lebanon? What then is the meaning of the verse FROM LEBANON COME WITH ME? It is as if you and I went into exile from Lebanon and you and I will go up to Lebanon."

COMMENTARY   *Seizing upon the phrase "hosts," which probably refers to Israel, the midrash chooses to remind us that the "Hosts of the Lord" could well be the angels. What would angels be doing here? If God Himself were emerging from Egyptian slavery, they would be accompanying Him. Other verses are brought to illustrate the idea that God went into exile in Egypt and was redeemed from it and that wherever there is enslavement of the just individual or of His people, He too is found. God is with those who suffer and not with those who inflict the suffering. He is free only when they are free. The verse from Exodus 24:10 is explained more fully elsewhere in rabbinic literature. What is seen under God's feet, that is, the pavement, are the bricks of slavery. According to some authorities the tools of the slave were also to be seen with Him. When redemption comes, these bricks disappear in token of His freedom. The concept of the Exile of the Divine Presence and of the God who suffers was developed into an extensive theology in later Jewish mysticism. Here it serves to strengthen the identification of God with His people in their time of suffering.*

5. Exodus 13:1, Mekhilta Pisha 16, I 131

Once the disciples spent the Sabbath in Jabneh, but R. Joshua was not with them. When the disciples went to see him, he said to them, "What new thing did you hear at Jabneh?"

Lebanon—a rabbinic term for Jerusalem, especially the Temple. The word means "white" and the Temple was the place where sins were whitened. Hence the verse is taken to mean that God and Israel will go into exile together from Jerusalem and will return there together. The Song of Songs was consistently interpreted as a parable of the love relationship between God and Israel.

---

5. *Jabneh*—a city near the Mediterranean coast in which Rabban Johanan b. Zakkai established a center of learning and of authority when Jerusalem was destroyed in the year 70 C.E.

They said to him, "After you, Master."

He said to them, "Who spent the Sabbath there?"

They said to him, "R. Eleazar b. Azariah."

He said to them, "Is it possible that R. Eleazar b. Azariah spent the Sabbath there and taught you nothing new?"

They said to him, "He expounded this idea: YOU STAND THIS DAY, ALL OF YOU, BEFORE THE LORD YOUR GOD—YOUR TRIBAL HEADS, YOUR ELDERS AND YOUR OFFICIALS, ALL THE MEN OF ISRAEL, YOUR CHILDREN (Deut. 29:9–10). Does an infant have any notion of the distinction between good and evil? Rather it was in order to give the fathers a reward for their children so that those who perform His will may increase their reward. This fulfills the verse THE LORD DESIRES HIS [SERVANT'S] VINDICATION, [THEREFORE] HE ENLARGES AND GLORIFIES HIS TORAH (Isa. 42:21).

He said to them, "This is indeed a new teaching. Behold I am about eighty years old and never had the privilege of hearing it until today. Happy are you, our father Abraham, that Eleazar b. Azariah descended from you. The generation which has Eleazar b. Azariah in its midst is not bereft!"

They said to him, "Master. He taught another interpretation: ASSUREDLY, A TIME IS COMING—DECLARES THE LORD—WHEN IT SHALL NO MORE BE SAID, 'AS THE LORD LIVES, WHO BROUGHT THE ISRAELITES OUT OF THE LAND OF EGYPT,' BUT RATHER, 'AS THE LORD LIVES, WHO BROUGHT OUT AND LED THE OFFSPRING OF THE HOUSE OF ISRAEL FROM THE NORTHLAND AND FROM ALL THE LANDS TO WHICH I HAVE BANISHED THEM' (Jer. 23:7–8). A parable. This may be likened to one who wanted to have sons, but had a daughter. He would swear by the life of the daughter. Then a son was born to him, so he stopped [swearing by] the daughter and would swear by the life of his son."

R. Simeon b. Yohai says, "A parable. It may be likened to a person who was going on a journey and was attacked by a wolf, but was saved from it. He would tell everyone about his encounter with the wolf. Then he was attacked by a lion, but was saved from it and he would tell everyone of his

---

After you, Master   Out of politeness they give him the opportunity either to teach or to continue to question.

it was in order   The command to bring the children had a specific purpose. It was to enable the fathers to receive a reward for bringing them.

THEREFORE HE ENLARGES   Usually translated "That He may magnify and glorify His Teaching." The Midrash takes it to mean that God increases the number of commands in the Torah in order to give an individual an opportunity to vindicate himself and earn reward.

encounter with the lion. He was attacked by a serpent and saved from it, so he forgot about the other two and would tell everyone about his encounter with the serpent. So it is with Israel. Recent difficulties cause us to forget the previous ones."

COMMENTARY   *This section is not connected to an interpretation of a particular passage but tells an incident in the lives of the Sages. Here we can see one of the major ways in which midrashic traditions were created. A Sage was assigned to teach in an Academy during the Shabbat, where he expounded the Scriptual lesson. His ideas then became known to all the others and what he had said became part of the stream of an oral tradition passed on from one to the other and from generation to generation.*

6. Exodus 13:3, Mekhilta Pisha 16, I 135

AND MOSES SAID TO THE PEOPLE, "REMEMBER THIS DAY, ON WHICH YOU WENT FREE FROM EGYPT . . ." (Ex. 13:3). This indicates only that one is to make mention of the Exodus from Egypt during the day. What source teaches that it is to be mentioned at night as well? The verse says SO THAT YOU MAY REMEMBER THE DAY OF YOUR DEPARTURE FROM THE LAND OF EGYPT ALL THE DAYS OF YOUR LIFE (Deut. 16:3). THE DAYS OF YOUR LIFE indicates the days, but the phrase ALL THE DAYS OF YOUR LIFE includes the nights as well. So taught Ben Zoma, while the Sages say, "THE DAYS OF YOUR LIFE indicates this world, while ALL THE DAYS OF YOUR LIFE includes the world to come." Ben Zoma said to them, "Israel will not make mention of the Exodus from Egypt in the future, as it is said ASSUREDLY, A TIME IS COMING—DECLARES THE LORD—WHEN IT SHALL NO MORE BE SAID, 'AS THE LORD LIVES WHO BROUGHT THE

---

6. *during the day*—when reciting the blessings after the daily morning Shema, the recitation of three sections from the Torah, the last of which, Num. 15:36–41, concludes with I THE LORD AM YOUR GOD, WHO BROUGHT YOU OUT OF THE LAND OF EGYPT TO BE YOUR GOD: I THE LORD YOUR GOD. This is the only mention of the Exodus in the Shema. The blessings echo the themes of the sections from the Torah.

at night—after the recitation of the evening Shema when, according to the practice at that time, the third paragraph in which the Exodus is mentioned was not recited. The extra word *ALL* indicates that even then the Exodus is to be included in the blessing.

not make mention—since even greater events will have taken place, i.e., the coming of the Messiah and the final redemption.

in the future   R. Nathan disagrees. Even in the Messianic age, the first redemption, that from Egypt, will not be forgotten, so great is its importance.

ISRAELITES OUT OF THE LAND OF EGYPT,' BUT RATHER, 'AS THE LORD LIVES WHO BROUGHT THE ISRAELITES OUT OF THE NORTHLAND, AND OUT OF ALL THE LANDS TO WHICH HE HAD BANISHED THEM' (Jer. 16:14–15)!" R. Nathan says, "The fact that it states WHO BROUGHT OUT AND LED (Jer. 23:8) indicates that they *will* make mention of the Exodus from Egypt in the future."

What indicates that we should say "Blessed are You O Lord, our God and the God of our Fathers, the God of Abraham, the God of Isaac, and the God of Jacob?" As it is said AND GOD SAID FURTHER TO MOSES, "THUS SHALL YOU SPEAK TO THE ISRAELITES: THE LORD, THE GOD OF YOUR FATHERS, THE GOD OF ABRAHAM, THE GOD OF ISAAC, AND THE GOD OF JACOB, HAS SENT ME TO YOU (Ex. 3:15)."

What indicates that we should say a blessing after eating? It is said WHEN YOU HAVE EATEN YOUR FILL, BLESS THE LORD YOUR GOD FOR THE GOOD LAND HE HAS GIVEN YOU (Deut. 8:10). BLESS refers to the first benediction, FOR THE LAND refers to the second, GOOD refers to the benediction "who builds Jerusalem," as it is said THAT GOOD HILL COUNTRY, AND THE LEBANON (Deut. 3:25). HE HAS GIVEN YOU refers to the benediction concerning all the goodness He has bestowed. R. Hiyya b. Nachmani said in the name of R. Ishmael, "Why add HE HAS GIVEN YOU to the words WHEN YOU HAVE EATEN YOUR FILL, BLESS—? To indicate that one should bless regardless of whether God has been merciful to him or has punished him."

Thus far we know that one is required to bless after eating. What source indicates that one is to bless before eating? R. Ishmael used to say, "It is a

---

Blessed are You   These are the opening words of the Amida, the basic prayer of Judaism, which is recited three times each day.

first benediction—which begins with the word "Blessed."

second   The second blessing in the Grace After Meals concludes with the words "for the Land and for food."

Jerusalem—the third benediction.

the goodness—the subject of the fourth benediction. All of these are the sections of the Grace After Meals, *Birkat HaMazon*, which is recited after any meal at which bread has been consumed.

punished him   The Name of God is to be proclaimed "blessed" under all circumstances. Whatever happens to one is an occasion for proclaiming Him and reaffirming one's belief.

before eating   The Grace After Meals is of Biblical origin. There is, however, a traditional blessing required before eating: Blessed are You, O Lord our God, King of the universe, Who brings forth bread from the earth. Does this blessing also have Biblical origins?

question of logic. If one is required to recite a blessing after eating when satiated, how much more so when wanting to eat?" R. Nathan says that the source is the verse AS SOON AS YOU ENTER THE TOWN, YOU WILL FIND HIM BEFORE HE GOES UP TO THE SHRINE TO EAT; THE PEOPLE WILL NOT EAT UNTIL HE COMES; FOR HE MUST FIRST BLESS THE SACRIFICE AND ONLY THEN WILL THE GUESTS EAT (1 Sam. 9:13). R. Isaac says, "It says YOU SHALL SERVE THE LORD YOUR GOD, AND BLESS YOUR BREAD AND YOUR WATER (Ex. 23:25). When is it YOUR BREAD? Before you have eaten it."

Thus far we know only that one must recite a blessing before and after eating food. What about the study of Torah? R. Ishmael used to say, "It is a question of logic. If food, which sustains us in this brief life, requires a blessing before and after eating it, how much more is a blessing required before and after Torah which is life eternal?" R. Judah b. Beterah says, "Why add the word GOOD to the phrase WHEN YOU HAVE EATEN YOUR FILL BLESS ... (Deut. 8:10)? In order to refer to Torah, as it is said FOR I GIVE YOU GOOD INSTRUCTION; DO NOT FORSAKE MY TORAH (Prov. 4:2)."

R. Hanina the nephew of R. Joshua says, "It says FOR THE NAME OF THE LORD I PROCLAIM; GIVE GLORY TO OUR GOD (Deut. 32:3). FOR THE NAME OF THE LORD I PROCLAIM refers to the one who pronounces the blessing. GIVE GLORY TO OUR GOD refers to those who respond to him. What is their response? 'Blessed is the Lord

---

of logic—but there is no Biblical source.

R. Nathan—finds a Biblical verse on which to base the practice.

have eaten it The usual translation is AND HE WILL BLESS YOUR BREAD AND YOUR WATER. R. Isaac understands it to mean that you should bless your bread when it is yours, namely before eating. After you have eaten it, it is no longer in your possession. Therefore the verse is referring to the blessing before eating.

the study of Torah The public recitation of the Torah at synagogue services has blessings before and after each reading. The blessing after the reading incorporates the words used by R. Ishmael: and has implanted within us life eternal.

to refer to Torah—in which case here too there is a Biblical verse referring to the blessing. R. Judah b. Beterah does not consider logic sufficient and prefers to find a verse on which to base this practice.

the blessing—over Torah. The same practice also came to be used in the leader's call to recite the Shema morning and evening. This is known as the *Barchu*, the word meaning "Let us bless," which are the first words in this blessing.

who is blessed forever.' When he utters the Name of God, they should say 'Blessed is the Name of His glorious Majesty for ever.' Thus David said EXALT THE LORD WITH ME; LET US EXTOL HIS NAME TO-GETHER (Ps. 34:4)."

Rabbi Judah the Prince says, "THE NAME OF THE RIGHTEOUS IS INVOKED IN BLESSING (Prov. 10:7) means that when he mentions 'the righteous one' meaning The Righteous One who lives forever, as it is said THE LORD IS RIGHTEOUS IN ALL HIS WAYS (Ps. 145:17) render unto Him a BLESSING by saying Amen."

COMMENTARY   *A section concerning various practices of prayer has been attached to the comment on this verse. The impetus for this came from the fact that the verse was used to clarify the disputed practice of reciting a blessing after the evening Shema recalling the Exodus although the only section of the Shema that mentions the Exodus (Num. 15:37–41) was not recited in the evening. The midrash then goes on to seek out Biblical sanctions for the opening words of the Amida, Judaism's central prayer, the blessings before and after meals, the blessing of Torah, and the practice of having the congregation respond to that blessing and to any mention of God's name, as well as answering Amen to any blessing. Although R. Ishmael was content with the use of logic, that is, the rule of inference from minor to major that was one of his thirteen methods of interpretation, others preferred to seek some Biblical sanction for these already existing practices.*

7. Exodus 13:17, Mekhilta Beshalah 1, I 169

NOW WHEN PHARAOH LET THE PEOPLE GO (Ex. 13:17). LET . . . GO always means "accompanying," as we see from these verses: ABRAHAM WALKING WITH THEM TO LET THEM GO (Gen. 18:16); ISAAC LET THEM GO, AND THEY DEPARTED FROM HIM IN PEACE (Gen. 26:31).

---

the Name of God—probably referring to the use of the actual name of God, the Tetragrammaton, which was uttered at various times in the Temple such as during the Priestly Benediction (Num. 6:24–26), as opposed to the substitution *Adonai* (Lord) used everywhere else. This response, however, became a part of the recitation of the Shema outside the Temple as well.

7. *accompanying*   Pharoah did not merely let them go, he personally escorted them on the way, a sign of honor and respect.

The mouth that had said NOR WILL I LET ISRAEL GO (Ex. 5:2) now says I WILL LET YOU GO (Ex. 8:24). What reward did he receive for this? YOU SHALL NOT ABHOR AN EGYPTIAN (Deut. 23:8).

The mouth that had said "I DO NOT KNOW THE LORD" (Ex. 5:2) now says, "LET US FLEE FROM THE ISRAELITES, FOR THE LORD IS FIGHTING FOR THEM AGAINST EGYPT" (Ex. 4:25). What reward did he receive for this? IN THAT DAY, THERE SHALL BE AN ALTAR TO THE LORD INSIDE THE LAND OF EGYPT AND A PILLAR TO THE LORD AT ITS BORDER (Isa. 19:19).

The mouth that had said "WHO IS THE LORD THAT I SHOULD HEED HIM?" (Ex. 5:2) now says "THE LORD IS IN THE RIGHT AND I AND MY PEOPLE ARE IN THE WRONG" (Ex. 9:27). What reward did they receive for this? They were granted a burial place as it is said YOU PUT OUT YOUR RIGHT HAND, THE EARTH SWALLOWED THEM (Ex. 15:12).

GOD DID NOT LEAD THEM (Ex. 13:17). "Nihui" (leading) always means to lead as we see from the verses YOU LED YOUR PEOPLE LIKE A FLOCK (Ps. 77:21) and HE LED THEM WITH A CLOUD BY DAY, AND THROUGHOUT THE NIGHT BY THE LIGHT OF FIRE (Ps. 78:14).

GOD DID NOT LEAD THEM BY WAY OF THE LAND OF THE PHILISTINES, ALTHOUGH IT WAS NEAR (Ex. 13:17). The time WAS NEAR to fulfill that which the Holy One had said to Moses: AND WHEN YOU HAVE FREED THE PEOPLE FROM EGYPT, YOU SHALL WORSHIP GOD AT THIS MOUNTAIN (Ex. 3:12).

Another interpretation: ALTHOUGH IT WAS NEAR (Ex. 13:17). The way to return to Egypt WAS NEAR as it is said SO WE MUST GO A DISTANCE OF THREE DAYS INTO THE WILDERNESS (Ex. 8:23).

Another interpretation: ALTHOUGH IT WAS NEAR. The oath which Abraham had sworn to Abimeleh WAS NEAR, as it is said THEREFORE SWEAR TO ME HERE BY GOD THAT YOU WILL NOT DEAL

---

the time WAS NEAR   NEAR refers, then, not to the place where the road was but to the time of fulfillment.

the oath . . . WAS NEAR   Not enough time had elapsed. Therefore they would have to wander a bit before entering the Land.

FALSELY WITH ME OR WITH MY CHILDREN OR CHILDREN'S CHILDREN (Gen. 21:23). His grandson was still alive.

Another interpretation: ALTHOUGH IT WAS NEAR. The first battle was too NEAR to have a second.

Another interpretation: ALTHOUGH IT WAS NEAR. The Canaanites had inherited the land too "recently" as it is said AND THEY SHALL RETURN HERE IN THE FOURTH GENERATION, FOR THE IN-IQUITY OF THE AMORITES WILL NOT BE FULFILLED UNTIL THEN (Gen. 15:16).

Another interpretation: Should not God have brought them in the quickest way? Rather God said, "If I bring Israel into the Land of Israel now, they will immediately set to work in their fields and vineyards and neglect the Torah. Therefore I shall take them round about in the wilderness for forty years, eating manna and drinking from the miraculous well, so that the Torah will be absorbed into their very bodies!" This was the source of R. Simon b. Yohai's teaching, "The only ones who can really interpret the Torah are those who eat manna or *terumah*."

Another interpretation: Should not God have brought them in the quickest way? Rather once the Canaanites heard that Israel was poised to enter the Land, they burned all the seeds, cut down the trees, tore down the buildings, and stopped up the wells. The Holy One then said, "I promised their father Abraham to bring them to a land filled with all good things, as it is said HOUSES FULL OF ALL GOOD THINGS . . . (Deut. 6:11), not to a land which is laid waste! Therefore I shall take them round about in the wilderness for forty years so that the Canaanites will repair what they have destroyed."

---

first battle—possibly referring to the tradition that the story in 1 Chron. 7:20, which is mentioned further on in this midrash, alludes to an earlier, abortive struggle to leave Egypt. This would have caused Israel to fear another defeat if they had to fight again so soon.

"recently"—another meaning of NEAR. Not enough time had elapsed to justify expelling the Canaanites.

forty years—ignoring the fact that here the discussion is of a limited addition of time. The forty years actually came later (Num. 14:33) as a punishment for the actions of the spies who discouraged the people from immediate entry to the Land.

terumah—the priestly dues. The priests could devote themselves to study because they did not have to earn a living. The same was true of the Israelites who ate manna.

COMMENTARY   *The words "it was near" are unclear and can therefore be interpreted in many ways. Exactly what is the "it" referred to? Some interpret it to refer to a specific place, others to a specific time or event. Midrash permits, indeed encourages, multiple meanings. An editor is free to take all the various suggestions that have been made and list them, one after another, leaving the reader free to judge their merits. The suggestion of Simon b. Yohai is particularly interesting because it reflects his general philosophy, which was protested by the other Sages. To bring them in so soon would have denied them the opportunity to study and contemplate the Torah because they would have been immediately burdened with the task of supporting themselves. For his purposes, the decision to have them wander forty years is taken at the very beginning, not after the incident of the spies. He wanted people to be able to devote themselves totally to the study of Torah and neglect all else. Thus for him, those many years in the wilderness were not in any sense a punishment, but a wonderful opportunity for total devotion to the study of God's way.*

FOR GOD SAID, "THE PEOPLE MAY HAVE A CHANGE OF HEART WHEN THEY SEE WAR, AND RETURN TO EGYPT" (Ex. 13:17). This refers to the war of Amalek, as it is said AND THE AMALEKITES AND THE CANAANITES WHO DWELT IN THAT HILL COUNTRY CAME DOWN AND DEALT THEM A SHATTERING BLOW AT HORMAH (Num. 14:45).

Another interpretation: FOR GOD SAID, "THE PEOPLE MAY HAVE A CHANGE OF HEART WHEN THEY SEE WAR, AND RETURN TO EGYPT" (Ex. 13:17). This refers to the war of the children of Ephraim, as it is said THE SONS OF EPHRAIM: SHUTHELAH, HIS SON BERED . . . THE MEN OF GATH, BORN IN THE LAND, KILLED THEM (Chron. 1 7:20–21)—two hundred thousand sons of Ephraim. And it says LIKE THE EPHRAIMITE BOWMEN WHO PLAYED FALSE ON THE DAY OF BATTLE (Ps. 78:9). Why? Because THEY DID NOT KEEP GOD'S COVENANT, THEY REFUSED TO FOLLOW HIS INSTRUCTIONS (Ps. 78:10). They attempted to advance the time of redemption and violated the oath.

---

war of the children of Ephraim—as discussed above, an abortive attempt at an exodus.
violated the oath—God's oath that the redemption would come only after a specific amount of time had passed.

Another interpretation: So that they should not see the bones of their brethren strewn about Philistia and return.

Another interpretation: So that they should not turn and retreat. It is a matter of logic. If they said LET US HEAD BACK FOR EGYPT (Num. 14:4) when He had taken them the long way around, how much more would this have been so had He brought them the quickest way!

SO GOD LED THE PEOPLE ROUNDABOUT, BY THE WAY OF THE WILDERNESS AT THE SEA OF REEDS (Ex. 13:18). For what purpose? In order to perform wonders and miracles for them through the manna, the quail, and the well.

R. Eliezer says, "WAY indicates that He intended to tire them, as in the verse HE DRAINED MY STRENGTH IN THE WAY (Ps. 102:24).

"OF THE WILDERNESS (Ex. 13:18) indicates that He intended to purify them as in the verse WHO LED YOU THROUGH THE GREAT AND TERRIBLE WILDERNESS . . . WHO FED YOU IN THE WILDERNESS . . . IN ORDER TO TEST YOU BY HARDSHIPS ONLY TO BENEFIT YOU IN THE END (Deut. 8:15–16).

"SEA OF REEDS indicates that He intended to test them, as we see in the verse OUR FOREFATHERS IN EGYPT . . . REBELLED AT THE SEA, AT THE SEA OF REEDS . . . THEY WERE SEIZED WITH CRAVING IN THE WILDERNESS, AND PUT GOD TO THE TEST IN THE WASTELAND (Ps. 106:7–14)."

R. Joshua says, "WAY (Ex. 13:18) indicates that He intended to give them the Torah as in the verses FOLLOW ONLY THE WAY THAT THE LORD YOUR GOD HAS ENJOINED UPON YOU (Deut. 5:30) and FOR THE COMMANDMENT IS A LAMP, THE TORAH IS A LIGHT AND THE WAY TO LIFE (Prov. 6:23).

"OF THE WILDERNESS (Ex. 13:18) indicates that He intended to give them manna to eat as in the verse WHO FED YOU IN THE WIL-DERNESS WITH MANNA (Deut. 8:16).

"THE SEA OF REEDS (Ex. 13:18) indicates that He intended to per-form wonders and miracles for them as in the verses WONDROUS

---

the bones of their brethren   The legend was that the children of Ephraim had reached Philistia only to be slaughtered in battle by the inhabitants.

DEEDS IN THE LAND OF HAM, AWESOME DEEDS AT THE SEA OF REEDS (Ps. 106:22) and HE SENT HIS BLAST AGAINST THE SEA OF REEDS; IT BECAME DRY; HE LED THEM THROUGH THE DEEP AS THROUGH A WILDERNESS (Ps. 106:9)"

NOW THE ISRAELITES WENT UP ARMED (Ex. 13:18). "Hamushim" (ARMED) always means "with weapons" as in the verse BUT EVERY ONE OF YOUR FIGHTING MEN SHALL GO ACROSS ARMED IN THE VAN OF YOUR KINSMEN (Josh. 1:14).

Another interpretation: "Hamushim" (ARMED) always means "zealous" as in the verse THE REUBENITES, THE GADITES, AND THE HALF TRIBE OF MANASSEH WENT ACROSS ZEALOUSLY (hamushim) IN THE VAN OF THE ISRAELITES, AS MOSES HAD CHARGED THEM. ABOUT FORTY THOUSAND SHOCK TROOPS WENT ACROSS (Josh. 4:12–13).

Another interpretation: WENT UP ARMED (humashim) (Ex. 13:18). Only one in five (hamesh) left. Some say only one in fifty and others, one in five hundred. R. Nehorai says, "By the Temple Service—not even one in five hundred left, as it says I LET YOU GROW LIKE THE PLANTS OF THE FIELD . . . (Ezek. 16:7) and BUT THE CHILDREN OF ISRAEL WERE FERTILE AND PROLIFIC; THEY MULTIPLIED AND INCREASED VERY GREATLY, SO THAT THE LAND WAS FILLED WITH THEM (Ex. 1:7), indicating that a woman would give birth to six at once! And you say that one in five hundred left? By the Temple Service, not even one in five hundred, for a great number of Israelites died in Egypt. When did they die? During the three days of darkness, as it is said PEOPLE COULD NOT SEE ONE ANOTHER, AND FOR THREE DAYS NO ONE COULD GET UP FROM WHERE HE WAS; BUT ALL THE ISRAELITES ENJOYED LIGHT IN THEIR DWELLINGS (Ex. 10:23). This was so that they could bury their dead, all the while thankful to God that their enemies could not see this and rejoice at their disaster."

---

one in five   The Hebrew word translated "armed" has the same Hebrew root as the word *five* leading to these fanciful interpretations based on the number five.

rejoice at their disaster   The darkness was brought to keep the Egyptians from knowing what had happened. This reflects the tradition that there were Israelites who did not want to leave and thus were unworthy of redemption.

AND MOSES TOOK WITH HIM THE BONES OF JOSEPH (Ex. 13:19). This tells us of the wisdom and piety of Moses, for while all Israel busied itself despoiling Egypt, Moses busied himself fulfilling the mitzvah to care for the bones of Joseph. Of him Scripture says: HE WHOSE HEART IS WISE ACCEPTS COMMANDS (mitzvot) (Prov. 10:8). How did Moses know where Joseph was buried? It was said that Serah, daughter of Asher, remained alive from that generation and showed Moses Joseph's tomb. She said to him, "The Egyptians made him a metal coffin and sank it in the Nile." Moses went and stood on the banks of the Nile, took a tablet of gold and engraved the name of God upon it. He cast it in and cried out, "Joseph son of Jacob! The time has come for the fulfillment of the oath the Holy One swore to Father Abraham that He would redeem his children. If you emerge, it is well, but if not we are free from our obligation to fulfill your oath." Joseph's coffin surfaced immediately and Moses took it.

Now this should not surprise you, for we are told (of a similar incident): AS ONE OF THEM WAS FELLING A TRUNK, THE IRON AX HEAD FELL INTO THE WATER. AND HE CRIED ALOUD, "ALAS, MASTER, IT WAS A BORROWED ONE!" "WHERE DID IT FALL?" ASKED THE MAN OF GOD. HE SHOWED HIM THE SPOT; AND HE CUT OFF A STICK AND THREW IT IN, AND HE MADE THE AX HEAD FLOAT (2 Kings 6:5–6). This is a matter of logic. If Elisha, the disciple of Elijah, could make iron float, surely Moses, the teacher of Elijah, could do so!

R. Nathan says, "They had buried him in the capitol of Egypt in the royal mausoleum, as it is said AND HE WAS EMBALMED AND PLACED IN A COFFIN IN EGYPT (Gen. 50:26). How did Moses know which was the coffin of Joseph? Moses went and stood amidst the coffins and cried out, 'Joseph, Joseph! The time has come for the fulfillment of the oath the Holy One swore to Father Abraham that He would redeem his children. . . .' Immediately Joseph's coffin began to move and Moses took it."

All of this teaches us that the measure a man metes is in turn meted out to him. Miriam waited some time for Moses, as it is said AND HIS SISTER STATIONED HERSELF AT A DISTANCE, TO LEARN WHAT

---

the teacher of Elijah   As the first and greatest of the prophets, Moses was the example Elijah had emulated.
All of this—the story of Moses' fulfillment of the oath to Joseph.

WOULD BEFALL HIM (Ex. 2:4). Therefore God caused the ark, the Divine Presence, the priests, all of Israel, and the seven clouds of glory to pause for her in the wilderness, as it is said SO MIRIAM WAS SHUT OUT OF CAMP SEVEN DAYS; AND THE PEOPLE DID NOT MARCH ON UNTIL MIRIAM WAS READMITTED (Num. 12:15).

Joseph, the greatest of the brothers, took it upon himself to bury his father, as it is said SO JOSEPH WENT UP TO BURY HIS FATHER (Gen. 50:7). How great was Joseph, that no less a person than Moses occupied himself with him.

Moses, the greatest of all Israel, took it upon himself to care for Joseph's bones, as it is said AND MOSES TOOK WITH HIM THE BONES OF JOSEPH (Ex. 13:19). How great was Moses that the Holy One Himself occupied Himself with his burial, as it is said HE BURIED HIM IN THE VALLEY IN THE LAND OF MOAB (Deut. 34:6)!

Furthermore, Jacob was accompanied by the servants of Pharaoh and his elders, while Joseph was accompanied by the ark, the Divine Presence, the priests, the Levites, all Israel, and the seven clouds of glory. Not only that, but the coffer of Joseph went together with the coffer of He Who Lives Forever.

The nations of the world would say to Israel, "What is the nature of these two coffers?" And they would say to them, "This is the coffer of He Who Lives Forever and this is the coffer of one who is dead."

The nations would ask, "What is the nature of the coffer of the dead that it accompanies the coffer of He Who Lives Forever?" They said to them, "He who rests in that coffer fulfilled that which is written upon what is contained in the other coffer."

On that which is in the coffer it is written I THE LORD AM YOUR GOD (Ex. 20:2) and of Joseph it is written AM I A SUBSTITUTE FOR GOD? (Gen. 50:19).

On that which is in the coffer it is written YOU SHALL HAVE NO OTHER GODS BESIDE ME (Ex. 20:3) and of Joseph it is written FOR I AM A GOD-FEARING MAN (Gen. 42:18).

Joseph was accompanied   As a reward for his piety toward his father, his own burial procession was even more honorable.

coffer of He Who Lives Forever—the Ark of Testimony, which contained the tablets of the Ten Pronouncements and scrolls of the Torah. Joseph's life had been a living embodiment of those words, even though he lived prior to the revelation at Sinai.

It is written YOU SHALL NOT SWEAR FALSELY BY THE NAME OF THE LORD YOUR GOD (Ex. 20:7) and of Joseph it is written BY PHAROAH, YOU SHALL NOT DEPART FROM THIS PLACE! (Gen. 42:15).

It is written REMEMBER THE SABBATH DAY AND KEEP IT HOLY (Ex. 20:8) and of Joseph it is written SLAUGHTER AND PREPARE AN ANIMAL (Gen. 43:16). PREPARE always refers to preparation for the Sabbath as it is said, BUT ON THE SIXTH DAY, WHEN THEY PREPARE WHAT THEY HAVE BROUGHT IN . . . (Ex. 16:5).

It is written HONOR YOUR FATHER AND YOUR MOTHER (Ex. 20:12) and of Joseph it is written ISRAEL SAID TO JOSEPH, "YOUR BROTHERS ARE PASTURING AT SCHECHEM. COME, I WILL SEND YOU TO THEM." HE ANSWERED, "I AM READY" (Gen. 37:13). He knew that his brothers hated him, yet he did not want to disobey his father's command.

It is written YOU SHALL NOT MURDER (Ex. 20:13) and Joseph did not murder Potiphera.

It is written YOU SHALL NOT COMMIT ADULTERY (Ex. 20:13). He did not commit adultery with Potiphera's wife.

It is written YOU SHALL NOT STEAL (Ex. 20:13). He did not steal, as in the incident of which it says JOSEPH GATHERED IN ALL THE MONEY THAT WAS TO BE FOUND IN THE LAND OF EGYPT . . . AND JOSEPH BROUGHT THE MONEY INTO PHARAOH'S PALACE (Gen. 47:14).

It is written YOU SHALL NOT BEAR FALSE WITNESS AGAINST YOUR NEIGHBOR (Ex. 20:13). Joseph did not tell his father what his brothers had done to him. It is a matter of logic. If he did not tell his father that which was true, surely he would not tell him what was false!

It is written YOU SHALL NOT COVET . . . (Ex. 20:14). He did not covet Potiphera's wife.

It is written YOU SHALL NOT HATE YOUR KINSMAN IN YOUR HEART (Lev. 19:17). Of Joseph it is written THUS HE REASSURED THEM, SPEAKING KINDLY TO THEM (Gen. 50:21).

It is written YOU SHALL NOT TAKE VENGEANCE OR BEAR A GRUDGE AGAINST YOUR KINFOLK (Lev. 19:18). Of Joseph it is written BESIDES, ALTHOUGH YOU INTENDED ME HARM, GOD INTENDED IT FOR GOOD . . . (Gen. 50:20).

BY PHAROAH Joseph swore by Pharoah and did not invoke the name of the Lord in this oath.

It is written SO THAT YOUR BROTHER MAY LIVE WITH YOU (Lev. 25:36). Of Joseph it is written JOSEPH SUSTAINED HIS FATHER, AND HIS BROTHERS, AND ALL HIS FATHER'S HOUSE-HOLD WITH FOOD, DOWN TO THE LITTLE ONES (Gen. 47:12).

WHO HAD EXACTED AN OATH (Ex. 13:19). He made them take an oath that they would make their children take an oath [to do this.] R. Nathan says, "Why did he make his brothers take an oath rather than his own children? He thought, 'If I make my children take an oath, the Egyptians will not permit them to do this. And if they say to [the Egyptians] "But our father took his father's body up," they will say to them, "Your father was a king!" ' Therefore he made his brothers take an oath rather than his own children."

Another interpretation: Joseph said to them, "My father came down here of his own free will and I brought him up. I came down against my will. I make you take an oath that you will return me to the place from whence you stole me!" And so they did, as it is said THE BONES OF JOSEPH, WHICH THE ISRAELITES HAD BROUGHT UP FROM EGYPT, WERE BURIED AT SHECHEM (Josh. 24:32).

GOD WILL BE SURE TO TAKE NOTICE OF YOU (Ex. 13:19). He will take notice of you in Egypt and He will take notice of you at the sea. After taking notice of you at the sea, He will take notice of you in the wilderness. After He has taken notice of you in the wilderness, He will take notice of you at the rivers of Arnon. After taking notice of you in this world, He will take notice of you in the world to come.

THEN YOU SHALL CARRY UP MY BONES FROM HERE WITH YOU (Ex. 13:19). I might think that this means: immediately! But the verse says WITH YOU—whenever you go up. How do we know that they took

---

EXACTED AN OATH   The Hebrew repeats the root word for "oath" twice, leading the Midrash to say that he made them swear that they would make their children swear, i.e., there were two oaths.

from whence you stole me   Joseph went to seek his brothers in Shechem. When he found them nearby, they cast him into the pit and sold him to the passing Ishmaelites. See Gen. 37:12ff.

TAKE NOTICE   The Hebrew is an emphatic form in which the root word appears twice. This leads to interpretations of each of the words as if each one referred to something different. To "take notice" means to take an action in favor of someone.

rivers of Arnon—referring to the war against Sihon in Num. 21.

the bones of all the tribal founders with them? As it is said FROM HERE WITH YOU.

COMMENTARY   *This remarkable section is an excellent example of a word-by-word, phrase-by-phrase, analysis of the text. Each word is explained and different authorities offer different explanations. Philological midrash is used, in which the meaning of words is determined from their usage in other verses, as are more fanciful interpretations brought on by the similarity of words or their multiple meaning such as hamushim (armed) and hamesh (five). The multiplicity of interpretations, including those that contradict one another, should be noted. Questions are posed concerning the reasons for events and a variety of answers are proposed. They wanted to know things the Biblical text does not tell us. How could Moses have known where Joseph's coffin was? The answers are couched in fanciful legends created to fill out events. A particularly striking one is the juxtaposition of Joseph's coffin with the Ark of the Lord, which is facilitated by the fact that the Hebrew word for both is the same: "aron," a box or coffer. From this springs an analysis of Joseph's life and the way in which he, who lived before the giving of the Torah, nevertheless carried out its moral precepts during his lifetime. These stories also serve to illustrate rabbinic concepts, in this case "measure for measure."*

8. Exodus 13:21, Mekhilta Beshallah 1, I 184

THE LORD WENT BEFORE THEM IN A PILLAR OF CLOUD BY DAY (Ex. 13:21). This teaches you that the measure a man metes out is in turn meted out to him. Abraham accompanied the ministering angels, as it is said ABRAHAM WALKING WITH THEM TO SEE THEM OFF (Gen. 18:16). Therefore God accompanied his children in the wilderness for forty years, as it is said THE LORD WENT BEFORE THEM IN A PILLAR OF CLOUD BY DAY.

Of Abraham it is written LET A LITTLE WATER BE BROUGHT (Gen. 18:4). Therefore the Holy One brought forth the well for his children, as it is said THEN ISRAEL SANG THIS SONG: SPRING UP, O WELL—SING TO IT—(Num. 21:17).

---

tribal founders—the brothers of Joseph.
WITH YOU—i.e., you and I will go together. Therefore the bodies of his brothers must have gone with that of Joseph.

Of Abraham it is written AND LET ME FETCH A MORSEL OF BREAD (Gen. 18:5). Therefore the Holy One caused manna to descend for his children in the wilderness, as it is said I WILL RAIN DOWN BREAD FOR YOU (Ex. 16:4).

Of Abraham it is written THEN ABRAHAM RAN TO THE HERD (Gen. 18:7). Therefore the Holy One brought the quail for his children in the wilderness as it is said A WIND FROM THE LORD STARTED UP, SWEPT QUAIL FROM THE SEA (Num. 11:31).

Of Abraham it is written AND RECLINE UNDER THE TREE (Gen. 18:4). Therefore the Holy One spread out seven clouds of glory for his children, as it is said HE SPREAD A CLOUD FOR COVER (Ps. 105:39).

Of Abraham it is written AND HE WAITED ON THEM (Gen. 18:8). Therefore the Holy One protected the houses of his children in Egypt so that they should not be smitten, as it is said, AND THE LORD WILL PROTECT THE DOOR AND NOT LET THE DESTROYER ENTER AND SMITE YOUR HOME (Ex. 12:23).

THE LORD WENT BEFORE THEM IN A PILLAR OF CLOUD BY DAY (Ex. 13:21). Is it possible to say that? Is it not written elsewhere FOR I FILL BOTH HEAVEN AND EARTH—DECLARES THE LORD (Jer. 23:24)? Similarly it is written HIS PRESENCE FILLS ALL THE EARTH! (Is. 6:3) and AND THERE . . . WAS THE PRESENCE OF THE GOD OF ISRAEL, AND THE EARTH WAS LIT UP BY HIS PRESENCE (Ezek. 43:2). What then can THE LORD WENT BEFORE THEM really mean?

Said Rabbi Judah the Prince, "When Antoninus was holding court upon the dais it would sometimes happen that darkness would descend while his children were still there with him. When he left the dais, he would take a torch and light the way for his children. Now the important members of the Imperial court would approach him and say, 'We will carry the torch to light the way for your children,' but he would say to them, 'It is not that I have no one to carry the torch and light the way for my children, but that thus I can show you how great is my affection for my children—so that you should treat them with honor!' Thus did the Holy One demonstrate His

---

8. *Is it possible*—to speak of God as if He actually accompanied the Israelites and was confined to that spot alone?

Antoninus—a Roman official who held many discussions with Rabbi Judah the Prince.

affection for Israel to the nations of the world, in that He Himself went before them, so that they would treat them with honor."

It is not bad enough that [the nations] do not treat them with honor, but they slay them in cruel and strange ways. Concerning this it says I WILL GATHER ALL THE NATIONS AND BRING THEM DOWN TO THE VALLEY OF JEHOSHAPHAT. THERE I WILL CONTEND WITH THEM (Joel 4:2). One might think that that is because they practice idolatry, live licentiously, and commit murder. Therefore the verse specifies OVER MY VERY OWN PEOPLE, ISRAEL, WHICH THEY SCATTERED AMONG THE NATIONS (Joel 4:2). Furthermore it says EGYPT SHALL BE A DESOLATION, AND EDOM A DESOLATE WASTE, BECAUSE OF THE OUTRAGE TO THE PEOPLE OF JUDAH, IN WHOSE LAND THEY SHED THE BLOOD OF THE INNOCENT (Joel 4:19). At that time BUT JUDAH SHALL BE INHABITED FOREVER, AND JERUSALEM THROUGHOUT THE AGES (Joel 4:20). When will this occur? When THE LORD SHALL DWELL IN ZION (Joel 4:21).

THE PILLAR OF CLOUD BY DAY AND THE PILLAR OF FIRE BY NIGHT DID NOT DEPART FROM BEFORE THE PEOPLE (Ex. 13:22). Scripture tells us that the pillar of fire emerged while the pillar of cloud was still there. Another interpretation: DID NOT DEPART. From the Torah we learn proper conduct. On Sabbath eve, the pillar of fire should emerge while the pillar of cloud is still there.

COMMENTARY   *Rather than using a parable to explain a Biblical text, Rabbi Judah the Prince tells a story from real life that explains God's conduct in personally leading the people. He is not troubled by the anthropomorphism. True, God cannot be limited, but for the sake of His people He*

---

went before them   He does not deny that God actually went before them. Of course God is everywhere, but here He acted contrary to the norm in order to demonstrate His care for Israel.

One might think—that this punishment will come upon the nations because of these various sins, but that is not so.

OVER MY VERY OWN PEOPLE   The punishment is because of the mistreatment of Israel.

On Sabbath eve   The practice is to kindle the Sabbath lights while it is still light, thus adding time from the previous day to the Sabbath. Like the two pillars that overlapped, there is a time when both weekday and Sabbath exists, as it were.

chooses to limit Himself. Thus God's love for Israel is emphasized and He is portrayed as a doting father. The real-life story concerns a Roman who frequently held discussions with R. Judah the Prince. The Antoninus named here may be a lengendary reference to the Emperor Antoninus Pius who was more favorable to the Jews than his predecessors. R. Judah the Prince sees nothing wrong in using this non-Jew as an example of proper conduct. The Midrash also comments that unfortunately the nations did not learn this lesson. Because of this, retribution will come and Israel will triumph. The interpretation of the pillars of fire and cloud adds significance to the practice of kindling the Sabbath lights and inaugurating the Sabbath while it is still daylight by having it refer to the wilderness period and thus echo God's love and protection.

9. Exodus 14:9, Mekhilta Beshallah 3, I 205

AND ALL THE CHARIOT HORSES OF PHARAOH, HIS HORSE-MEN, AND ALL HIS WARRIORS OVERTOOK THEM ENCAMPED BY THE SEA, NEAR PI-HAHIROT, BEFORE BAAL-ZEPHON. AND PHAROAH DREW NEAR (Ex. 14:9–10). He caused his punishment to "draw near."

Another interpretation: Once Pharaoh saw that Israel had encamped upon the sea, he said, "Baal-zephon agrees with my decision. I decided to destroy them in water and Baal-zephon agrees with that." Thereupon he began to offer sacrifice, burn incense, pour libations, and prostrate himself before his idol. That is why it says AND PHARAOH DREW NEAR in order to offer sacrifice and burn incense.

Another interpretation: AND PHARAOH DREW NEAR. The distance that Israel traversed in three days was traversed by the overseers in a day and a half, and what took the overseers a day and a half was traversed by Pharaoh in one day. That is why it says AND PHARAOH DREW NEAR.

THE ISRAELITES LIFTED UP THEIR EYES (Ex. 14:10). Once they had smitten the overseers, they knew that [the overseers] were bound to pursue them.

---

9. *Baal-zephon agrees*—understood here as the name of an idol worshiped by Pharoah rather than a geographical reference. Baal often means a pagan diety.
to offer sacrifice The Hebrew phrase "draw near" also means to offer a sacrifice.

EXODUS

AND THERE WERE THE EGYPTIANS ADVANCING UPON
THEM (Ex. 14:10). "Advancing" (plural) is not written, but ADVANC-
ING (singular) indicating that they were formed into squadrons which were
each like one man. From this did the Empire learn to utilize the formation
of squadrons.

GREATLY FRIGHTENED, THE ISRAELITES CRIED OUT TO
THE LORD (Ex. 14:10). They quickly seized upon the art practiced by
their ancestors, the art of Abraham, Isaac, and Jacob.

What does it say of Abraham? WITH BETHEL ON THE WEST
AND AI ON THE EAST; AND HE BUILT THERE AN ALTAR TO
THE LORD AND INVOKED THE LORD BY NAME (Gen. 12:8). HE
PLANTED A TAMARISK AT BEER-SHEBA, AND INVOKED
THERE THE NAME OF THE LORD, THE EVERLASTING GOD
(Gen. 21:33).

What does it say of Isaac? AND ISAAC WENT OUT TO MEDI-
TATE IN THE FIELD TOWARD EVENING (Gen. 24:63). Meditation
always means prayer, as we see in the verses EVENING, MORNING,
AND NOON, I MEDITATE AND MOAN, AND HE HEARS MY
VOICE (Ps. 55:18). I POUR OUT MY MEDITATION BEFORE HIM
(Ps. 142:3). A PRAYER OF THE LOWLY MAN WHEN HE IS FAINT
AND POURS FORTH HIS MEDITATION BEFORE THE LORD
(Ps. 102:1).

What does it say of Jacob? HE CAME UPON (vayifga') A CERTAIN
PLACE (Gen. 28:11). Coming upon (pegi'ah) always means prayer, as we
see in the verses AS FOR YOU, DO NOT PRAY FOR THIS PEOPLE,
DO NOT RAISE A CRY OF PRAYER ON THEIR BEHALF, DO NOT
PLEAD (tifga') UPON ME (Jer. 7:16). LET THEM INTERCEDE
(yifge'u) WITH THE LORD OF HOSTS (Jer. 27:18).

On this matter it says FEAR NOT, O WORM JACOB, O MEN OF IS-
RAEL (Isa. 41:14). Just as the worm can smite the tree only with its mouth,
so Israel's only [weapon] is its mouth. That is: Israel's only weapon is
prayer. We see this from the verse AND NOW, I GIVE YOU ONE POR-
TION MORE THAN TO YOUR BROTHERS, WHICH I WRESTED
FROM THE AMORITES WITH MY SWORD AND BOW (Gen.

---

the Empire—Rome.
the art practiced by their ancestors—prayer. When confronted by danger they naturally reverted
to prayer, which had been so important to their ancestors.

48:22). Did he really wrest it with sword and bow? Does it not state I DO NOT TRUST IN MY BOW; IT IS NOT MY SWORD THAT GIVES ME VICTORY (Ps. 44:7)? What then is the meaning of WITH MY SWORD AND BOW? It means prayer.

Similarly it says JUDAH IS A LION'S WHELP (Gen. 49:9) and AND THIS HE SAID OF JUDAH: HEAR, O LORD THE VOICE OF JUDAH (Deut. 33:7). Jeremiah said CURSED IS HE WHO TRUSTS IN MAN, WHO MAKES MERE FLESH HIS STRENGTH (Jer. 17:5) while of prayer he says BLESSED IS HE WHO TRUSTS IN THE LORD, WHOSE TRUST IS THE LORD ALONE (Jer. 17:7). Similarly David says YOU COME AGAINST ME WITH SWORD AND SPEAR AND JAVELIN; BUT I COME AGAINST YOU IN THE NAME OF THE LORD OF HOSTS, THE GOD OF THE RANKS OF ISRAEL (1 Sam. 17:45). And it is written THEY [CALL] ON CHARIOTS, THEY CALL ON HORSES, BUT WE CALL ON THE NAME OF THE LORD OUR GOD. THEY COLLAPSE AND LIE FALLEN, BUT WE RALLY AND GATHER STRENGTH. O LORD, GRANT VICTORY! MAY THE KING ANSWER US WHEN WE CALL (Ps. 20:8-10) and ASA CALLED TO THE LORD HIS GOD, AND SAID, "O LORD, IT IS ALL THE SAME TO YOU TO HELP THE NUMEROUS AND THE POWERLESS. HELP US, O LORD OUR GOD, FOR WE RELY ON YOU, AND IN YOUR NAME WE HAVE COME AGAINST THIS GREAT MULTITUDE" (2 Chron. 14:10).

What does it say of Moses? FROM KADESH, MOSES SENT MESSEN-GERS TO THE KING OF EDOM: "THUS SAYS YOUR BROTHER ISRAEL: YOU KNOW ALL THE HARDSHIPS THAT HAVE BE-FALLEN US; THAT OUR ANCESTORS WENT DOWN TO EGYPT, THAT WE DWELT IN EGYPT A LONG TIME, AND THAT THE EGYPTIANS DEALT HARSHLY WITH US AND OUR ANCESTORS. WE CRIED TO THE LORD AND HE HEARD OUR PLEA (Num. 20:14-16)." They said to them, "You are proud of what your father bequeathed to you—THE VOICE IS THE VOICE OF JACOB (Gen. 27:22). AND THE LORD HEARD OUR PLEA (Deut. 26:7) and we are proud of what our father bequeathed to us. BUT THE HANDS ARE THE HANDS OF ESAU (Gen. 27:22) YET BY YOUR SWORD YOU

---

your father bequeathed The Edomites answered Israel by pointing out that although Isaac had granted Jacob the power of prayer, to Esau he had granted physical strength.

81

SHALL LIVE (Gen. 27:40)." Thus it is written BUT EDOM AN-SWERED HIM, "YOU SHALL NOT PASS THROUGH US, ELSE WE WILL GO OUT AGAINST YOU WITH THE SWORD" (Num. 20:18).

So too in this case when it says THE ISRAELITES CRIED OUT TO THE LORD (Ex. 14:10)—they seized upon the art practiced by their fathers, the art of Abraham, Isaac and Jacob.

AND THEY SAID TO MOSES, "WAS IT FOR WANT OF GRAVES IN EGYPT THAT YOU BROUGHT US TO DIE IN THE WILDER-NESS?" (Ex. 14:11). After putting leaven in the dough, they came to Moses and said to him "IS NOT THIS THE VERY THING WE TOLD YOU IN EGYPT (Ex. 14:12)?" What had Israel said to Moses in Egypt? It says THEY CAME UPON MOSES AND AARON STANDING IN THEIR PATH, AND THEY SAID TO THEM, "MAY THE LORD LOOK UPON YOU AND PUNISH YOU FOR MAKING US OBJECTION-ABLE TO PHARAOH AND HIS COURTIERS—PUTTING A SWORD IN THEIR HAND TO SLAY US" (Ex. 5:20–21). "We suffered being enslaved in Egypt, but the death of our brothers during the period of darkness was even worse. We suffered over the death of our brothers during the period of darkness, but our death in the wilderness will be even worse, for at least our brothers were eulogized and buried, whereas we will be carcasses exposed to the heat of the day and the cold of the night!"

BUT MOSES SAID TO THE PEOPLE, "HAVE NO FEAR!" (Ex. 14:13). Moses encouraged them, which shows his wisdom. He stood and pacified those throngs of thousands upon thousands. Of him the Scripture says "WISDOM IS MORE OF A STRONGHOLD TO A WISE MAN THAN TEN MAGNATES THAT A CITY MAY CONTAIN" (Eccl. 7:19).

"STAND BY, AND WITNESS THE DELIVERANCE WHICH THE LORD WILL WORK FOR YOU TODAY" (Ex. 14:13). Israel said to him, "When?" Moses said to them, "Today the Holy Spirit rests upon you!"

---

leaven in the dough—which causes it to ferment. The phrase has negative connotations and frequently refers to the evil inclination (yetzer ha-ra). Here it indicates that they stirred up trouble.
period of darkness—as discussed above p. 71.

For the word *yezibah* (stand by) always refers to the Holy Spirit as we see from the verses I SAW MY LORD STANDING (nezeb) BY THE ALTAR (Amos 9:1). THE LORD CAME AND STOOD (yityazeb) THERE, AND HE CALLED AS BEFORE: "SAMUEL! SAMUEL!" (1 Sam. 3:10). CALL JOSHUA AND STAND (hityazbu) IN THE TENT OF MEETING, THAT I MAY INSTRUCT HIM (Deut. 31:14).

To what may Israel be likened at that time? To a dove who flees from a hawk by going into a cleft in the rock only to encounter a hissing serpent. If she goes in, the serpent is there! If she flies out, the hawk is there! That was Israel's situation at that time. The sea cuts her off and the enemy pursues her. Prayer was their only hope. Of them the Scripture says O MY DOVE, IN THE CRANNY OF THE ROCKS (Song 2:14). And it says FOR YOUR VOICE IS SWEET (Song 2:14) in prayer AND YOUR FACE IS COMELY (Song 2:14) in the study of Torah. Another interpretation: FOR YOUR VOICE IS SWEET (Song 2:14) in prayer AND YOUR FACE IS COMELY (Song 2:14) in good deeds.

Another interpretation: STAND BY, AND WITNESS (Ex. 14:13). They said to him, "When?"

He said to them, "Tomorrow."

Israel then said to Moses, "Our teacher Moses! We do not have the strength to endure this!"

Moses prayed and God immediately showed them squadrons upon squadrons of ministering angels standing before them.

Similarly it is said WHEN THE ATTENDANT OF THE MAN OF GOD ROSE EARLY AND WENT OUTSIDE, HE SAW A FORCE, WITH HORSES AND CHARIOTS, SURROUNDING THE TOWN. "ALAS, MASTER, WHAT SHALL WE DO?" HIS SERVANT ASKED HIM. "HAVE NO FEAR," HE REPLIED. "THERE ARE MORE ON OUR SIDE THAN ON THEIRS." THEN ELISHA PRAYED: "LORD, OPEN HIS EYES AND LET HIM SEE." AND THE LORD OPENED THE SERVANT'S EYES AND HE SAW THE HILLS ALL AROUND ELISHA COVERED WITH HORSES AND CHARIOTS OF FIRE (2 Kings 6:15–17).

Thus when Moses prayed, God revealed to them squadrons upon squadrons of angels standing before them. Concerning this it says OUT

OF THE BRILLIANCE BEFORE HIM, HAIL AND COALS OF FIRE
PIERCED HIS CLOUDS (Ps. 18:13).
HIS CLOUDS—against their squadrons
HAIL—against their catapults
COALS—against their missiles
FIRE—against their burning oil
THEN THE LORD THUNDERED FROM HEAVEN (Ps.
18:14)—against their clashing shields and tramping boots
THE MOST HIGH GAVE FORTH HIS VOICE (Ps. 18:14)—
against the whetting of their swords
HE LET FLY HIS SHAFTS AND SCATTERED THEM ... (Ps.
18:15)—against their arrows
HE DISCHARGED LIGHTNING AND ROUTED THEM (Ps.
18:15)—against their shouting

Another interpretation: HE LET FLY HIS SHAFTS AND SCATTERED
THEM, HE DISCHARGED LIGHTNING AND ROUTED THEM—
the arrows would scatter them and the lightning would cause them to huddle
together.
AND ROUTED THEM—He confounded and confused them and
took away their signals so that they did not know what they were doing.

Another interpretation: AND ROUTED THEM—routing always refers to
a plague, as in the verse ROUTING THEM UTTERLY UNTIL THEY
ARE WIPED OUT (Deut. 7:23).

COMMENTARY   *This section becomes a running commentary on the
story, heightening its drama as the plight of the Israelites is described.
Rather than providing an analysis of the words and phrases, as is done in
other sections, legends are woven together with the verses to heighten the
story and parables are told to shed light on the situation. The opportunity is
also taken for an excursus on the value of prayer, which is traced back to the
earliest ancestors of Israel. The tradition teaches that the three basic prayers
of the day originated with the three Fathers, Abraham—the morning prayer,
Isaac—the afternoon, and Jacob—the evening prayer. When faced with
danger, the Israelites utilized the weapon of prayer against their enemies.
Describing God's battle against the foe, the midrash takes Psalm 18 as a
description of His weapons, again invoking the principle of "measure for
measure." Thus there is thunder against noise and fire against burning oil.*

There were four groups among the Israelites at the sea.

One said, "Let us throw ourselves into the sea."

One said, "Let us return to Egypt."

One said, "Let us make war against them."

One said, "Let us yell at them."

To the group that said "Let us throw ourselves into the sea," it was said STAND BY, AND WITNESS THE DELIVERANCE WHICH THE LORD WILL WORK FOR YOU TODAY (Ex. 14:13).

To the group that said "Let us return to Egypt," it was said FOR THE EGYPTIANS WHOM YOU SEE TODAY YOU WILL NEVER SEE AGAIN (Ex. 14:13).

To the group that said "Let us make war against them," it was said THE LORD WILL BATTLE FOR YOU (Ex. 14:14).

To the group that said "Let us yell at them," it was said YOU HOLD YOUR PEACE (Ex. 14:14).

THE LORD WILL BATTLE FOR YOU (Ex. 14:14). Not only now, but forever will He battle against your enemies.

R. Meir says, "THE LORD WILL BATTLE FOR YOU. If THE LORD WILL BATTLE FOR YOU when you remain silent, how much more will He do so when you praise Him!"

R. Judah the Prince says, "THE LORD WILL BATTLE FOR YOU— Shall you remain silent while God performs miracles and wonders for you? Israel said to Moses, 'Our teacher Moses, what should we do?' He said to them, 'You should exalt, glorify, praise, utter song and praise, greatness and glorification to Him who is the Master of war,' as it is said WITH PAEANS TO GOD IN THEIR THROATS AND TWO-EDGED SWORDS IN THEIR HANDS (Ps. 149:6). EXALT YOURSELF OVER THE HEAVENS, O GOD, LET YOUR GLORY BE OVER ALL THE EARTH! (Ps. 57:12). O LORD, YOU ARE MY GOD; I WILL EXTOL YOU, I WILL PRAISE YOUR NAME (Isa. 25:1). At that moment Israel opened its mouth and recited the Song I WILL SING TO THE LORD, FOR HE HAS TRIUMPHED GLORIOUSLY (Ex. 15:1)."

---

four groups   Each phrase of these verses is understood as an answer given to a specific suggestion made by a group of Israelites.

COMMENTARY   *The midrash will often take different verses and ascribe them to different individuals and groups. Here parts of verses 14:13–14 are viewed as answers to four different groups of Israelites. Then different views are taken concerning the meaning of one of those phrases. Rabbi Judah the Prince creates yet another legend based on it in which liturgical phrases of his day become the words of Moses urging the people to praise God as a response to His wonders.*

10. Exodus 14:15, Mekhilta Beshallah 4, I 216

THEN THE LORD SAID TO MOSES, "WHY DO YOU CRY OUT TO ME? TELL THE ISRAELITES TO GO FORWARD" (Ex. 14:15). R. Joshua says, "The Holy One said to Moses, 'Moses, all Israel has to do is to go forward!' "

R. Eliezer says, "The Holy One said to Moses, 'Moses, My children are in distress. The sea cuts them off and the enemy pursues them—and all you can do is utter lengthy prayers? WHY DO YOU CRY OUT TO ME?' "

He used to say, "There is a time to shorten prayer and a time to lengthen it. O GOD, PRAY HEAL HER! (Num. 12:13) was a time to shorten prayer and I THREW MYSELF DOWN BEFORE THE LORD—EATING NO BREAD AND DRINKING NO WATER FORTY DAYS AND FORTY NIGHTS, AS BEFORE—(Deut. 9:18) was a time to lengthen it."

R. Meir says, "[Said the Holy One,] 'If I created dry land for the sake of primal Adam, who was only one man, as it is said GOD SAID, "LET THE WATER BELOW THE SKY BE GATHERED INTO ONE AREA, THAT THE DRY LAND MAY APPEAR" (Gen. 1:9), will I not make the sea into dry land for the sake of this holy congregation?! WHY DO YOU CRY OUT TO ME? . . . LIFT UP YOUR ROD AND HOLD OUT YOUR ARM OVER THE SEA AND SPLIT IT, SO THAT THE ISRA-ELITES MAY MARCH INTO THE SEA ON DRY LAND (Ex. 14:15–16).' "

R. Ishmael says, "[Said the Holy One,] 'Because of the merit of Jerusalem I shall split the sea for them,' as it is said AWAKE, AWAKE, O ZION! CLOTHE YOURSELF IN SPLENDOR; PUT ON YOUR ROBES OF MAJESTY, JERUSALEM, HOLY CITY (Isa. 52:1)! AWAKE, AWAKE, CLOTHE YOURSELF WITH SPLENDOR, O ARM OF THE LORD! AWAKE AS IN DAYS OF OLD, AS IN FORMER AGES! IT WAS YOU

THAT HACKED RAHAM IN PIECES, THAT PIERCED THE
DRAGON. IT WAS YOU THAT DRIED UP THE SEA, THE WA-
TERS OF THE GREAT DEEP; THAT MADE THE ABYSSES OF THE
SEA A ROAD THE REDEEMED MIGHT WALK (Isa. 51:9–10)."

Another interpretation: "By splitting the sea I am fulfilling the promise I
made to your fathers," as it is said YOUR DESCENDANTS SHALL BE
AS THE DUST OF THE EARTH; YOU SHALL SPREAD OUT TO
THE SEA, TO THE EAST, TO THE NORTH AND TO THE SOUTH
(Gen. 28:14). Thus He intimated that He would break through the sea.

R. Judah b. Beterah says, "The Holy One said to him, 'I have already fulfilled
the promise I made to their fathers,' as it is said AND TURNED THE SEA
INTO DRY LAND (Ex. 14:21) BUT THE ISRAELITES MARCHED
THROUGH THE SEA ON DRY GROUND (Ex. 14:29)."

R. Simeon b. Yohai says, "The sun and the moon already testify to this, as it
is said THUS SAID THE LORD, WHO ESTABLISHED THE SUN
FOR LIGHT BY DAY, THE LAWS OF MOON AND STARS FOR
LIGHT BY NIGHT, WHO STIRS UP THE SEA INTO ROARING
WAVES, WHOSE NAME IS LORD OF HOSTS: IF THESE LAWS
SHOULD EVER BE ANNULLED BY ME—DECLARES THE
LORD—ONLY THEN WOULD THE OFFSPRING OF ISRAEL
CEASE TO BE A NATION BEFORE ME FOR ALL TIME (Jer.
31:35–36)."

R. Bana'ah says, "[Said the Holy One], 'Because of the merit of the mitzvah
which their father Abraham performed, I shall split the sea for them,' as it is
said HE SPLIT THE WOOD (Gen. 22:3) while here it is said THE WA-
TERS WERE SPLIT (Ex. 14:21)."

Simeon of Timneh says, "[Said the Holy One], 'Because of the merit of
circumcision, I shall split the sea for them,' as it is said THUS SAITH THE
LORD: AS SURELY AS I HAVE ESTABLISHED MY COVENANT
WITH DAY AND NIGHT—THE LAWS OF HEAVEN AND

---

10. *SPREAD OUT TO THE SEA*—usually translated "to the west." The word *yama*, "west-
ward," is actually the same as the word *yam*—"the sea," since the sea is west of the Land of
Israel.
their father Abraham performed—suggested by the fact that the word *bokea*, used in SPLIT
THE WOOD in the story of the binding of Isaac, is also used in the phrase THE WATERS
WERE SPLIT.

EARTH—(Jer. 34:25). Let us see which covenant it is that is observed day and night. Certainly it is the mitzvah of circumcision."

R. Absalom the Elder says, "A parable. To what may this be likened? A man was angry with his son and drove him from his home. His friend came in to entreat him to take him back. [The father] said to him, 'What you are asking is only for the sake of my son. I am already reconciled to my son!' Thus the Holy One said to Moses 'WHY DO YOU CRY OUT TO ME? (Ex. 14:15). Is it not only for my sons? I am already reconciled to My sons! TELL THE ISRAELITES TO GO FORWARD (Ex. 14:15)!' "

R. Judah the Prince says, "[The Lord said,] 'Only the other day you were saying EVER SINCE I CAME TO PHAROAH TO SPEAK IN YOUR NAME, IT HAS GONE WORSE WITH THIS PEOPLE (Ex. 5:23) and now you come and lengthen your prayers? WHY DO YOU CRY OUT TO ME? TELL THE ISRAELITES TO GO FORWARD (Ex. 14:15)!' "

Another interpretation: Rabbi Judah the Prince says, "[The Lord said,] 'TELL THE ISRAELITES TO GO FORWARD (vayisau) (Ex. 14:15). Let them remove (yasiu) from their hearts those words they spoke. Only the other day they were saying WAS IT FOR WANT OF GRAVES IN EGYPT THAT YOU BROUGHT US TO DIE IN THE WILDERNESS? (Ex. 14:11) and now you come and lengthen prayers? WHY DO YOU CRY OUT TO ME? TELL THE ISRAELITES to remove those words from their hearts.' "

The Sages say, "He did this for them for the sake of His own name, as it is said FOR MY SAKE, MY OWN SAKE, DO I ACT—LEST MY NAME BE DISHONORED! (Isa. 48:11) and it is written WHO MADE HIS GLORIOUS ARM MARCH AT THE RIGHT HAND OF MOSES, WHO DIVIDED THE WATERS BEFORE THEM (Isa. 63:12). Why? TO MAKE HIMSELF A NAME FOR ALL TIME (Isa. 63:12)."

Rabbi Judah the Prince says, "[Said the Holy One], 'Their belief in Me is sufficient to cause Me to split the sea for them,' as it is said TELL THE ISRAELITES TO TURN BACK AND ENCAMP BEFORE PI-HAHIROTH (Ex. 14:2)."

PI-HAHIROTH   According to verse Ex. 14:9, when God commanded them to do this, they obeyed Him, a demonstration of their belief that was sufficient to cause Him to split the sea for them.

R. Eleazar b. Azariah says, "[Said the Holy One], 'Because of the merit of their father Abraham I will split the sea for them,' as it is said MINDFUL OF HIS SACRED PROMISE TO HIS SERVANT ABRAHAM, HE LED HIS PEOPLE OUT IN GLADNESS, HIS CHOSEN ONES WITH JOYOUS SONG (Ps. 105:42–43)."

R. Eleazar b. Judah of Kfar Tota says, "[Said the Holy One], 'Because of the merit of the tribes, I will split the sea for them,' as it is said WITH HIS TRIBES YOU SMITE HIS SKULL . . . YOU WILL MAKE YOUR STEEDS TREAD THE SEA, STIRRING THE MIGHTY WATERS (Hab. 3:14–15) and thus it says WHO SPLIT APART THE SEA OF REEDS (Ps. 136:13)."

Shemaya says, "[Said the Holy One], 'Their father Abraham's belief in Me is sufficient to cause Me to split the sea for them,' as it is said AND BECAUSE HE BELIEVED IN THE LORD, HE RECKONED IT TO HIS MERIT (Gen. 15:6)."

Abtalyon says, "[Said the Holy One], 'Their belief in Me is sufficient to cause Me to split the sea for them,' as it is said AND THE PEOPLE BELIEVED (Ex. 4:31)."

Simeon of Kitron says, "[Said the Holy One], 'For the Sake of the bones of Joseph, I will split the sea for them,' as it is said BUT HE LEFT HIS COAT IN HER HAND AND GOT AWAY AND FLED OUTSIDE (Gen. 39:12) and it says THE SEA SAW THEM AND FLED (Ps. 114:3)."

R. Nathan says in the name of Abba Joseph of Mahoz, "[Said the Holy One], 'Have I not written elsewhere NOT SO WITH MY SERVANT MOSES, HE IS TRUSTED THROUGHOUT MY HOUSEHOLD? (Num. 12:7). You are under My command and the sea is under My command. I give you authority over it.' "

R. Hanania b. Halnisi says, "[Said the Holy One], 'Have I not written elsewhere A FRIEND IS DEVOTED AT ALL TIMES; A BROTHER IS BORN TO SHARE ADVERSITY (Prov. 17:17)? I am a brother to Israel

---

HIS TRIBES The usual translation is "bludgeon." The Hebrew word means both a staff and a tribe.

at their time of trouble.' 'Brothers' is a designation for Israel, as it is said FOR THE SAKE OF MY BROTHERS AND FRIENDS (Ps. 122:8)."

R. Simeon b. Judah says, "WHY DO YOU CRY OUT TO ME? (Ex. 14:15) Their cry has preceded yours! As it is said THE ISRAELITES CRIED OUT TO THE LORD (Ex. 14:10)."

R. Aha says, "WHY DO YOU CRY OUT TO ME? For your sake am I doing this. Said the Holy One, 'Were it not for your cry, I would already have obliterated them from the world,' as it is said HE WOULD HAVE DESTROYED THEM HAD NOT MOSES HIS CHOSEN ONE CON-FRONTED HIM IN THE BREACH TO AVERT HIS DESTRUCTIVE WRATH (Ps. 106:23). This is the meaning of WHY DO YOU CRY OUT TO ME? TELL THE ISRAELITES TO GO FORWARD (Ex. 14:15) They can only go forward because of your cry."

R. Eleazar of Modi'in says, "WHY DO YOU CRY OUT TO ME? Do I need to be commanded about My own children? As it is said, WILL YOU QUESTION ME ON THE DESTINY OF MY CHILDREN, WILL YOU INSTRUCT ME ABOUT THE WORK OF MY HANDS? (Isa. 45:11). Have they not been designated as Mine from the six days of creation? As it is said IF THESE LAWS SHOULD EVER BE ANNULLED BY ME—DECLARES THE LORD—ONLY THEN WOULD THE OFFSPRING OF ISRAEL CEASE TO BE A NATION BEFORE ME FOR ALL TIME (Jer. 31:36)."

Others say, "Their belief in Me is sufficient to cause Me to split the sea for them, for they did not say to Moses, 'How can we go into the wilderness without any provisions for the journey?' Rather they believed and followed Moses. Of them it is written GO PROCLAIM TO JERUSALEM: THUS SAID THE LORD: I ACCOUNTED TO YOUR FAVOR THE DEVO-

---

Their cry has preceded yours   Since the Israelites had already cried out, i.e., prayed, to God, there was no need for Moses to do so.

Were it not for your cry   R. Aha disagrees with the previous interpretation. The cry of the Israelites would not have been heeded by God. He will save them only because of the intercession of Moses. R. Aha may be reading the verse not as a question, but an exclamation: How do you cry out to Me! The Hebrew word *ma* translated here as "why" frequently means "how" and introduces an exclamation. Thus Moses is really being told to cry out to God. Although the verse from Psalms actually refers to the incident of the golden calf, the previous verse (Ps. 106:22) concludes with THE SEA OF REEDS, which would permit this interpretation.

TION OF YOUR YOUTH, YOUR LOVE AS A BRIDE—HOW YOU FOLLOWED ME IN THE WILDERNESS IN A LAND NOT SOWN (Jer. 2:2). What reward did they receive for this? ISRAEL WAS HOLY TO THE LORD (Jer. 2:3)."

R. Jose the Galilean says, "When Israel went into the sea, Mount Moriah was uprooted from its place and upon it the altar of Isaac and the wood already prepared and Isaac as if bound upon the altar and Abraham stretching out his hand to seize the knife to slaughter his son!

"God said to Moses, 'Moses! My children are in distress. The sea cuts them off and the enemy pursues them and you stand and lengthen prayers?'

"Moses said to Him, 'What should I do?'

"He said to him, 'LIFT UP YOUR ROD (Ex. 14:16). Lift up—glorify, praise, utter song and praise, greatness and glorification to Him who is the Master of War.' "

COMMENTARY   *This extraordinary section displays rabbinic virtuosity at its best. One notes with wonder the agility with which verses are plucked from all the books of Scripture, always with the apposite words and correct ideas needed to bolster the desired interpretation. Gathered together here are comments from Sages who lived at different times over a stretch of several centuries, who attached various meanings to one brief verse. They all address the question, which must have had relevance to their times as well, "What caused God to save Israel at the Sea?" Were they worthy or not? Was it their own actions—if so, which ones? Was it the merit of their ancestors? Did God need to be convinced to save them? Does He do it for His own glory, for the sake of Moses, Abraham, Joseph, or others—or because of His great love of His own children? The editor lays all of this out for us, leaving the determination to each reader. The discussion is brought to a powerful conclusion with the vivid picture painted by R. Jose the Galilean based on the doctrine of the merit that the Binding of Isaac was held to have in saving the people of Israel throughout the ages. This doctrine is emphasized in Jewish liturgy during the High Holy Days. Depicting it as a kind of deus ex machina in some epic play, he brings to the stage the mountain on which the scene is being played, uprooting it from Canaan to the Sea or the Throne of God, juxtaposing it to the equally dramatic scene of Israel fleeing the enemy and plunging into the sea. In our imaginations the uplifted hand of Abraham merges with the uplifted hand of Moses, the knife becomes the rod of Moses, and the battle is won. All Moses need do now is sing with Israel the praises of the Holy One.*

91

11. Exodus 14:21, Mekhilta Beshallach 6, I 234

R. Judah says, "When Israel stood at the sea, this one said 'I will not be the first to plunge into the sea,' and this one said, 'I will not be the first to plunge into the sea,' as it is said EPHRAIM SURROUNDS ME WITH DECEIT, THE HOUSE OF ISRAEL WITH GUILE (Hos. 12:1)."

While they were debating the issue, Nahshon the son of Amminadab jumped up and plunged first into the sea, falling into the waves. Of him it is said DELIVER ME, O GOD, FOR THE WATERS HAVE REACHED MY NECK; I AM SINKING INTO THE SLIMY DEEP AND FIND NO FOOTHOLD; I HAVE COME INTO THE WATERY DEPTHS; THE FLOOD SWEEPS ME AWAY (Ps. 69:2–3). And it is said LET THE FLOODWATERS NOT SWEEP ME AWAY; LET THE DEEP NOT SWALLOW ME; LET THE MOUTH OF THE PIT NOT CLOSE OVER ME (Ps. 69:16). At the very same time Moses was standing and reciting lengthy prayers before the Holy One. The Holy One said to him, 'Moses, My dear one is sinking in the sea, the sea is encompassing him, the enemy is pursuing and you stand and utter lengthy prayers?' [Moses] said to Him, 'Master of the universe, what else can I do?' He said to him, AND YOU LIFT UP YOUR ROD AND HOLD OUT YOUR ARM OVER THE SEA AND SPLIT IT (Ex. 14:16).

"What did Israel say at the sea? THE LORD WILL REIGN FOR EVER AND EVER (Ex. 15:18). Said the Holy One, 'He who caused Me to be proclaimed king at the sea, him shall I cause to be king over Israel.' "

R. Tarphon and the elders were once sitting in the shade of a dovecote in Jabneh and this question was under discussion: THEIR CAMELS BEARING GUM, BALM, AND LADANUM TO BE TAKEN TO EGYPT (Gen. 37:25).
"This tells us how great is the merit of the righteous and how much it comes to their aid. Had the beloved friend [of God] been taken down there by Arabs, would not the smell of the camels and their *itran* have killed him? Therefore the Holy One caused these to have with them sacks filled with

---

11. *to be king over Israel* Kingship will be granted to the tribe of Judah because one of their members, Nahshon, was the first to plunge into the Sea of Reeds.
beloved friend [of God]—Joseph.
itran—a foul-smelling resin that they transport.

spices, with delicious fragrance so that he would not die from the smell of the camels and their *itran*."

They said to him, "You have instructed us, our Master."

They continued, "Our Master, teach us: If one drinks water to quench his thirst, what blessing should be recited?"

He said to them, "... Who creates multitudes of creatures and fills their needs."

They said to him, "You have instructed us, our Master."

They continued, "Our master, teach us by what merit Judah attained the kingship."

He said to them, "You tell me."

They said, "It was because he said WHAT DO WE GAIN BY KILLING OUR BROTHER AND COVERING UP HIS BLOOD? (Gen. 37:26)."

He said to them, "The merit of saving him was only sufficient to atone for selling him."

"Perhaps it was because he said SHE IS MORE IN THE RIGHT THAN I (Gen. 38:26)."

He said to them, "The merit of acknowledging [his sin] was only sufficient to atone for the illicit relations."

"Perhaps it was because he said THEREFORE, PLEASE LET YOUR SERVANT REMAIN AS A SLAVE TO MY LORD INSTEAD OF THE BOY AND LET THE BOY GO BACK WITH HIS BROTHERS. (Gen. 44:33)."

He said to them, "In every instance we find that the guarantor pays!"

They said to him, "Teach us, our Master. By what merit did Judah attain the kingship?"

He said to them, "When the tribes stood at the sea, this one said, 'I will plunge in first,' and this one said, 'I will plunge in first,' as it is said EPHRAIM SURROUNDS ME WITH DECEIT, THE HOUSE OF IS-

---

selling him   It was Judah who suggested that Joseph be sold into slavery. See Gen. 37:27.

IN THE RIGHT—referring to Tamar who had been accused of being a prostitute.

illicit relations   Judah had had sexual relations with his widowed and childless daughter-in-law Tamar when she disguised herself as a harlot after he had refused to permit another son to marry her.

THE BOY—Benjamin. Judah offers to remain in his place.

the guarantor pays   Judah had promised his father that Benjamin would not be harmed. See Gen. 43:9. Therefore his offer was only to be expected and had no special merit.

this one said—but they were only procrastinating.

RAEL WITH GUILE (Hos. 12:1). And while they were standing and discussing the matter with one another, Nahshon the son of Amminadab and his tribe plunged into the waves of the sea. Therefore [that tribe] merited the kingship, as it is said WHEN ISRAEL WENT FORTH FROM EGYPT, THE HOUSE OF JACOB FROM A PEOPLE OF STRANGE SPEECH, JUDAH SANCTIFIED HIM (Ps. 114:1–2) and therefore ISRAEL IS HIS KINGDOM (Ps. 114:2). Said God, 'He who sanctified My Name upon the sea shall come to rule over Israel.' "

COMMENTARY   *The way in which the Master and his disciples engaged in discussion is illustrated in this section. Using the Socratic method, the Master encouraged his students to suggest their ideas and their answers to questions that they themselves had raised. However, it was usually the Master who gave the correct answer to the question. This illustrates another way in which the traditions were created. These discussions and the interpretations taught in them were passed on from one disciple to another through the generations until finally put into written form. The legend that appears at the beginning of the section is a slightly altered version of Rabbi Tarphon's tale.*

12. Exodus 14:27, Mekhilta Beshallah 7, I 245

THE SEA RETURNED TO ITS NORMAL STATE AND THE EGYPTIANS FLED AT ITS APPROACH (Ex. 14:27). This teaches that wherever an Egyptian ran, the sea would rush to catch him.

A parable. This may be likened to a dove fleeing from a hawk who entered the palace of a king. The king opened a window for her to the east and she flew out and went her way. When the hawk entered in pursuit of her, the king shut all the windows and began to shoot arrows at it.

Thus when the last of the Israelites emerged from the sea and the last of the Egyptians plunged into it, the ministering angels started to hurl their arrows, hailstones, fire, and brimstone against them as it is said I WILL PUNISH HIM WITH PESTILENCE AND WITH BLOODSHED,

---

Nahshon—the head of the tribe of Judah according to Num. 2:3. The story of Nahshon was a well-known rabbinic legend.
JUDAH SANCTIFIED HIM—by showing belief in God's word and doing the seemingly foolhardy act of plunging into the waters of the sea. This is usually translated "Judah became His holy one."

AND I WILL POUR TORRENTIAL RAIN, HAILSTONES, AND
SULFUROUS FIRE UPON HIM (Ezek. 38:22).

COMMENTARY   *Parables are used frequently throughout the midrash to
explain the events under discussion, as they were used throughout the ancient world. The figure of a dove, a much beloved bird, is frequently used to
represent Israel. The enemy, here the hawk, is pursued by God, Who uses
the sea as one uses arrows to kill the enemy.*

13. Exodus 14:29, Mekhilta Beshallach 7, I 247

R. Pappias expounded "TO A MARE IN PHARAOH'S CHARIOTS
(Song 1:9). When Pharaoh rode upon a stallion, the Holy One, as it were,
was revealed to him riding upon a stallion, as it is said YOU WILL MAKE
YOUR STEEDS TREAD THE SEA (Hab. 3:15). When Pharaoh rode
upon a mare, the Holy One was revealed to him, as it were, riding
upon a mare, as it is said TO A MARE IN PHARAOH'S CHARIOTS
(Song 1:9)."

R. Akiba said to him, "Pappias, enough!"

He said to him, "Well how do you interpret TO A MARE IN PHA-
RAOH'S CHARIOTS?"

He said to him, "[The word 'mare'] is written 'lesasti' (I rejoiced). The
Holy One said, 'Just as I rejoiced (sasti) to destroy the Egyptians, so did I
nearly rejoice to destroy the Israelites. What was it that saved them? ON
THEIR RIGHT AND ON THEIR LEFT (Ex. 14:22) (ON THEIR
RIGHT was the merit of the Torah they were to receive, as it is said AT
HIS RIGHT A FIERY LAW [Deut. 33:2] AND ON THEIR LEFT was
prayer.)"

R. Pappias expounded, "HE IS ONE; WHO CAN DISSUADE HIM? (Job
23:13) He is the sole Judge of all creatures of the world and there is no one
who can contradict His decisions."

R. Akiba said to him, "Pappias, enough!"

He said to him, "So how do you explain HE IS ONE; WHO CAN
DISSUADE HIM?"

---

13. *to destroy the Israelites*—referring to the story of the golden calf. See Ex. 32:10.
(ON THEIR RIGHT)   The section is parenthesis is taken from the previous section of this
midrash (I, p. 247).

He said to him, "There is no contradicting the decisions of He Who Spoke and the world came into being, rather they are all true and just."

R. Pappias expounded, "MAN HAS BECOME LIKE ONE OF US (Gen. 3:22)—like one of the ministering angels."

R. Akiba said to him, "Pappias, enough!"

He said to him, "So how do you explain MAN HAS BECOME LIKE ONE OF US?"

He said to him, "Not like one of the ministering angels. Rather: God placed before him two paths, the path of life and the path of death, and [man] chose for himself the path of death."

R. Pappias expounded, "THEY EXCHANGED THEIR GLORY FOR THE IMAGE OF A BULL WHO FEEDS ON GRASS (Ps. 106:20). Since I might have thought it referred to the bull in the heavens, the verse says WHO FEEDS ON GRASS."

R. Akiba said to him, "Pappias, enough!"

He said to him, "So how do you expound THEY EXCHANGED THEIR GLORY FOR THE IMAGE OF A BULL WHO FEEDS ON GRASS?"

"An actual bull. Since I might have thought it was the bull of the zodiac, the verse says WHO FEEDS ON GRASS. There is nothing more disgusting and abominable than the bull when he is eating grass."

COMMENTARY   *Discussions were held not only between a Master and disciples, but among the Sages themselves. Although there was great freedom of interpretation and flexibility of understanding, disputes could arise and, as here, there might even be a point where one Sage would rebuke another. Here the problem seems to be that Akiba fears that these interpretations, or rather misinterpretations, border on the dangerous and the heretical.*

14. Exodus 14:31, Mekhilta Beshallah 7, I 252

THEY HAD FAITH IN THE LORD AND IN HIS SERVANT MOSES (Ex. 14:31). If they believed in Moses, certainly they must have believed in

---

chose for himself   Akiba reads the verse as if it meant: Man has become one who must know good from bad.

the bull in the heavens—the bull in Ezekiel's vision, Ezek. 1:10.

the Lord! Rather the verse teaches us that if one believes in the shepherd of Israel, it is as if one believes in He Who Spoke and the world came into being.

Similarly we interpret the verse AND THE PEOPLE SPOKE AGAINST GOD AND AGAINST MOSES (Num. 21:5). If they spoke against God, certainly they spoke against Moses! Rather the verse teaches that if one speaks against the shepherd of Israel it is as if one spoke against He Who Spoke and the world came into being.

He Who Spoke and the world came into being ascribes great importance to belief, for it is as a reward for the belief which Israel had in the Lord that the Holy Spirit rested upon them and they proclaimed the Song, as it is said THEY BELIEVED IN THE LORD AND IN HIS SERVANT MOSES. THEN MOSES AND THE ISRAELITES SANG THIS SONG TO THE LORD (Ex. 14:31–15:1).

R. Nehemiah said, "What is the source which teaches that one who accepts upon himself one mitzvah in perfect faith is worthy of having the Holy Spirit rest upon him? We see that this was so in the case of our ancestors for as a reward for their belief they merited having the Holy Spirit rest upon them and they proclaimed the Song, as it is said THEY BELIEVED IN THE LORD AND IN HIS SERVANT MOSES. THEN MOSES AND THE ISRAELITES SANG THIS SONG TO THE LORD (Ex. 14:31–15:1).

Similarly we find that it was only as a reward for his faith that our father Abraham inherited this world and the world to come, as it is said AND BECAUSE HE BELIEVED IN THE LORD, HE RECKONED IT TO HIS MERIT (Gen. 15:6).

Similarly we find that it was only as a reward for their faith that Israel was redeemed from Egypt, as it is said AND THE PEOPLE BELIEVED (Ex. 4:31). And it is said THE LORD GUARDS THOSE WHO BE- LIEVE (Ps. 31:24). He remembers the faithfulness of the fathers WHILE AARON AND HUR, ONE ON EACH SIDE AND HIS HANDS WERE "FAITHFUL" (Ex. 17:12).

---

14. *HIS HANDS WERE "FAITHFUL"*—usually translated "steady." The Hebrew is the same. To be steadfast and to have faith in God's steadfastness are one and the same.

THIS IS THE GATEWAY TO THE LORD—THE RIGHTEOUS SHALL ENTER THROUGH IT (Ps. 118:20). But concerning those faithful believers, what does it say? OPEN THE GATES AND LET A RIGHTEOUS NATION ENTER, THOSE THAT KEEP FAITH (Isa. 26:2). Into this gate, all who believe may enter. Thus it says IT IS GOOD TO PRAISE THE LORD, TO SING HYMNS TO YOUR NAME, O MOST HIGH, TO PROCLAIM YOUR STEADFAST LOVE AT DAYBREAK, AND FAITH IN YOU EVERY NIGHT (Ps. 92:2–3). YOU HAVE GLADDENED ME BY YOUR DEEDS, O LORD; I SHOUT FOR JOY AT YOUR HANDIWORK (Ps. 92:5). What enabled us to attain this joy? This was a reward for the faith of our ancestors in this world which is nothing but night. Thus it says TO PROCLAIM YOUR STEADFAST LOVE AT DAYBREAK, AND FAITH IN YOU EVERY NIGHT (Ps. 92:3). Thus Jehoshaphat said to the people TRUST FIRMLY IN THE LORD YOUR GOD AND YOU WILL STAND FIRM; TRUST FIRMLY IN HIS PROPHETS AND YOU WILL SUCCEED (2 Chron. 20:20) and it is written O LORD YOUR EYES LOOK FOR BELIEF (Jer. 5:3). THE RIGHTEOUS MAN SHALL LIVE BY HIS FAITH (Hab. 2:4). THEY ARE RENEWED EVERY MORNING; GREAT IS YOUR FAITHFULNESS! (Lam. 3:23).

Thus too you find that it is only as a reward for belief (emunah) that the dispersed will be gathered together in the future, as it is said FROM LEBANON COME WITH ME; FROM LEBANON, MY BRIDE, WITH ME! TRIP DOWN FROM THE PEAK OF FAITH (AMANA) (Song 4:8) and it is written AND I WILL ESPOUSE YOU FOREVER: I WILL ESPOUSE YOU WITH RIGHTEOUSNESS AND JUSTICE, AND WITH GOODNESS AND MERCY, AND I WILL ESPOUSE YOU WITH FAITHFULNESS (Hos. 2:21–22).

How great is belief unto He Who Spoke and the world came into being! It is only as a reward for their belief that the Holy Spirit rested upon them and they proclaimed the Song, as it is said THEY BELIEVED IN THE LORD AND IN HIS SERVANT MOSES. THEN MOSES AND THE ISRAELITES SANG THIS SONG TO THE LORD (Ex. 14:31–15:1) and it says THEN THEY BELIEVED HIS PROMISE, AND SANG HIS PRAISES (Ps. 106:12).

PEAK OF FAITH   The name of a mountain, Amana, is understood by the midrash as meaning "faith" because it comes from the Hebrew root meaning faith or belief, "emunah." Thus because of their faith they will be enabled to come back from Lebanon, i.e., exile.

COMMENTARY   *The Midrash has created a section emphasizing the importance of belief. The Hebrew word that appears here time and time again is "emunah," sometimes translated "faith" or "faithfulness" and sometimes "belief." In the original, it is all one. The method of the midrash is to emphasize different values at different times. Thus, although there may be times when deeds are extolled as even more important than faith, here the emphasis is on faith or belief with no discussion of deeds at all. Similarly a previous section had denigrated the role of Moses, while here it is emphasized, possibly in order to combat those who said that the teaching of Moses was inferior to that of other religious leaders. Midrash need not take a consistent position or always stress the same value. It utilizes a constellation of values and weaves interpretations about them, giving pride of place at times to one while other times a different value takes center stage. The verse that connects the Song with their belief provided an excellent opportunity for gathering together many different midrashim on belief and collecting Biblical verses that stress that idea as well.*

15. Exodus 15:1, Mekhilta Shirata 1, II 8

I WILL SING TO THE LORD, FOR HE HAS TRIUMPHED GLORIOUSLY (Ex. 15:1). It is becoming to ascribe greatness to the Lord. It is becoming to ascribe might to the Lord. It is becoming to ascribe splendor, triumph, and majesty to the Lord. Thus David says, YOURS, LORD, ARE GREATNESS, MIGHT, SPLENDOR, TRIUMPH, AND MAJESTY (1 Chron. 29:11).

I WILL SING TO THE LORD, FOR HE HAS TRIUMPHED GLORIOUSLY (Ex. 15:1). When a human king makes his entry into a city, it often happens that the multitude will shout his praises, saying that he is mighty when in truth he is weak; that he is wealthy, when he is poor; that he is wise, when he is foolish; that he is merciful, when he is cruel; that he is an honest judge or that he is faithful, when he has none of these qualities. People are merely flattering him.

This is not the case, however, with He Who Spoke and the world came into being. Rather I WILL SING TO THE LORD that He is mighty, as it is said THE GREAT, THE MIGHTY, AND THE AWESOME GOD (Deut. 10:17) and it says THE LORD, MIGHTY AND VALIANT, THE LORD VALIANT IN BATTLE (Ps. 24:8). THE LORD GOES FORTH LIKE A MIGHTY MAN (Isa. 42:13). O LORD, THERE IS NONE LIKE

YOU! YOU ARE GREAT AND YOUR NAME IS GREAT IN POWER (Jer. 10:6).

I WILL SING TO THE LORD that He is wealthy, as it is said MARK, THE HEAVENS AND THE HEAVENS OF HEAVENS BE-LONG TO THE LORD YOUR GOD, THE EARTH AND ALL THAT IS ON IT (Deut. 10:14)! THE EARTH IS THE LORD'S AND ALL THAT IT HOLDS, THE WORLD AND ITS INHABITANTS (Ps. 24:1). HIS IS THE SEA, HE MADE IT; AND THE LAND, WHICH HIS HANDS FASHIONED (Ps. 95:5). SILVER IS MINE AND GOLD IS MINE—SAYS THE LORD OF HOSTS (Hag. 2:8). CONSIDER, ALL LIVES ARE MINE (Ezek. 18:4).

I WILL SING TO THE LORD that He is wise, as it is said THE LORD FOUNDED THE EARTH BY WISDOM; HE ESTABLISHED THE HEAVENS BY UNDERSTANDING (Prov. 3:19). WITH HIM ARE WISDOM AND COURAGE; HIS ARE COUNSEL AND UN-DERSTANDING (Job 12:13). FOR THE LORD GRANTS WISDOM; KNOWLEDGE AND DISCERNMENT ARE BY HIS DECREE (Prov. 2:6). HE GAVE THE WISE THEIR WISDOM AND KNOWLEDGE TO THOSE WHO KNOW (Dan. 2:21). WHO WOULD NOT RE-VERE YOU, O KING OF THE NATIONS? FOR THAT IS YOUR DUE, SINCE AMONG ALL THE WISE OF THE NATIONS AND AMONG ALL THEIR ROYALTY THERE IS NONE LIKE YOU (Jer. 10:7).

I WILL SING TO THE LORD that He is merciful, as it is said THE LORD! THE LORD! A GOD MERCIFUL AND GRACIOUS (Ex. 34:6). FOR THE LORD YOUR GOD IS A MERCIFUL GOD (Deut. 4:31). THE LORD IS GOOD TO ALL AND HIS MERCY IS UPON HIS WORKS (Ps. 145:9). TO THE LORD OUR GOD BELONG MERCY AND FORGIVENESS (Dan. 9:9).

I WILL SING UNTO THE LORD that He is an honest judge, as it is said FOR JUDGMENT IS GOD'S (Deut. 1:17). GOD STANDS IN THE DIVINE ASSEMBLY; AMONG THE DIVINE BEINGS HE PRO-NOUNCES JUDGMENT (Ps. 82:1). THE ROCK—HIS DEEDS ARE PERFECT, YEA, ALL HIS WAYS ARE JUST (Deut. 32:4).

I WILL SING TO THE LORD that He is faithful, as it is said THE FAITHFUL GOD (Deut. 7:9). A FAITHFUL GOD, NEVER FALSE, TRUE AND UPRIGHT IS HE (Deut. 32:4).

Thus it is becoming to ascribe unto the Lord might, splendor, triumph, and majesty.

COMMENTARY   *There is no organized theological discussion of God in rabbinic writings, but various qualities are ascribed to Him, as they are in the Bible. Here we see how Biblical verses are used in order to describe and emphasize those qualities, prime among them His might, mercy, righteousness, and dependability. These qualities are those that are stressed in the liturgy created by these same rabbis. Although the rabbis were reticent in their usage of praise and description of God in the liturgy, they felt no such compunctions in the freer media of the midrash. This is especially true in their discussion of the Song of the Sea, which was considered the song of praise par excellence.*

16. Exodus 15:1, Mekhilta Shirata 2, II 21

HORSE AND HIS DRIVER (Ex. 15:1). The Holy One brings both the horse and his driver [before Him] to stand trial.

To the horse He says, "Why did you run after My children?"

He replies, "An Egyptian forced me to run against my will," as it is said THE EGYPTIANS GAVE CHASE TO THEM (Ex. 14:9).

He says to the Egyptian, "Why did you run after My children?"

He says, "The horse carried me along against my will," as it is said FOR THE HORSES OF PHARAOH, WITH HIS CHARIOTS AND HORSEMEN, WENT INTO THE SEA (Ex. 15:19).

What did God do? He placed the man upon the horse and judged them together, as it is said HORSE AND HIS DRIVER HE HAS HURLED INTO THE SEA (Ex. 15:1).

Antoninus asked our Holy Master (R. Judah the Prince), "When a person dies and the body ceases to exist, does the Holy One make it stand trial?"

He said to him, "Rather than asking me about the body which is impure, ask me about the soul which is pure. A parable will explain it. It may be likened to a human king who had a beautiful orchard. The king placed two guards within it, one of whom was lame and the other blind. [The lame guard said to the blind one, 'I see beautiful choice figs in the orchard. Come and carry me on your shoulders so that we can take them and eat them!' The lame guard rode upon the shoulders of the blind one and they took the figs and ate them. After a few days the owner of the orchard came and said to them, 'My beautiful choice figs—where are they?' The lame guard said, 'Do

---

16. *Antoninus*   A Roman official identified with the emperor Antoninus Pius (ruled 138–161 C.E.).

I have legs that would enable me to reach them?' The blind guard said, 'Do I have eyes that would enable me to see them?' What did the owner do? He placed the lame guard on the blind one and judged them as one. So the Holy One brings the soul and implants it in the body and judges them as one as it is said HE SUMMONED THE HEAVENS ABOVE, AND THE EARTH, FOR THE TRIAL OF HIS PEOPLE (Ps. 50:4). HE SUMMONED THE HEAVENS ABOVE refers to the soul AND THE EARTH, FOR THE TRIAL OF HIS PEOPLE refers to the body." (Talmud Sanhedrin 91b)]

COMMENTARY   *Many conversations are reported between the Roman Antoninus and Rabbi Judah the Prince. The text of the Midrash quotes only the beginning of this one, assuming that the reader knows the story, which is recorded in the Talmudic tractate Sanhedrin where many other such conversations are also found. The question of body and soul was one that concerned the ancients. What was the relationship between the two? Were they of equal value and importance? Was one pure and the other impure? The Greeks tended to exalt the soul at the expense of the body even though Greek civilization glorified the body and its beauty. Judaism was ambiguous about this. The idea of the purity of the soul, as expressed here by R. Judah the Prince, is often mentioned, but the divine origin and therefore ultimate worth of the body is also expressed. The body was thought by the rabbis to be literally the "image of God" in which man was created, to the extent that Hillel said that keeping the body clean was equivalent to washing the image of the Divine, as it were, just as pagans keep the statues of their gods clean. This concept of the importance of both body and soul is expressed in the parable here and in the basic Jewish doctrine of the resurrection of the dead in which the body and soul are reunited so that they may stand trial before God. This also explains the Jewish prohibition of cremation or destruction of the body in any way.*

17. Exodus 15:2, Mekhilta Shirata 3, II 23

THE LORD IS MY STRENGTH (ozi) (Ex. 15:2). You are the Helper (ozer) and the Stay of all human beings, but particularly so to me.

AND MY SONG (Ex. 15:2). You are the subject of song for all human beings, but particularly so for me. I have proclaimed His fame and He has

---

implants it in the body—at the time of the resurrection of the dead. The section in brackets is supplied from the Talmud, Sanhedrin 91b.

proclaimed my fame, as it is written AND THE LORD HAS PRO-
CLAIMED THIS DAY THAT YOU ARE, AS HE PROMISED YOU,
HIS TREASURED PEOPLE (Deut. 26:18) and I have proclaimed His
fame, as it is said YOU HAVE PROCLAIMED THIS DAY THAT THE
LORD IS YOUR GOD (Deut. 26:17). For all the nations of the world
proclaim the glory of He Who Spoke and the world came into being, but
mine is particularly pleasing to Him, as it is said PLEASANT ARE THE
SONGS OF ISRAEL (2 Sam. 23:1).

Israel says HEAR, O ISRAEL! THE LORD IS OUR GOD, THE
LORD IS ONE (Deut. 6:4) and the Holy Spirit exclaims from heaven AND
WHO IS LIKE YOUR PEOPLE ISRAEL, ONE NATION ON EARTH
(1 Chron. 17:21).

Israel says WHO IS LIKE YOU, O LORD, AMONG THE CELES-
TIALS (Ex. 15:11) and the Holy Spirit exclaims from heaven O HAPPY
ISRAEL! WHO IS LIKE YOU (Deut. 33:29).

Israel says (WHAT GREAT NATION IS THERE THAT HAS A
GOD SO CLOSE AT HAND) AS IS THE LORD OUR GOD WHEN-
EVER WE CALL UPON HIM (Deut. 4:7) and the Holy Spirit exclaims
from heaven (OR WHAT GREAT NATION) HAS LAWS AND
NORMS AS PERFECT (AS ALL THIS TEACHING) (Deut. 4:8).

Israel says FOR YOU ARE THEIR STRENGTH IN WHICH
THEY GLORY (Ps. 89:18) and the Holy Spirit exclaims from heaven YOU
ARE MY SERVANT ISRAEL IN WHOM I GLORY (Isa. 49:3).

HE IS BECOME MY SALVATION (Ex. 15:2). You are the salvation of
all human beings, but particularly so for me. Another interpretation: He was
mine and will be mine. He was mine in the past and will be mine in the time
to come.

COMMENTARY   *The fact that the verse speaks of "my strength" is interpreted as stressing the particular relationship between God and Israel, the
"me" referred to. Thus although God governs and helps the entire world
and all nations, His connection to Israel is unique. This section is particularly illustrative of the rabbinic emphasis on the mutual relationship between
God and Israel. Never denying God's love and concern for all humanity,
they nevertheless maintained that His relationship with Israel is unique.
Drawing on their wealth of knowledge of the Scriptures, they found verses
that could be juxtaposed and that echoed one another in vocabulary and idea
and put them into the mouths of God and Israel, creating a dialogue of
mutual love and admiration. It is this concept that stands behind the doctrine*

of the so-called chosen people. In Hebrew, to choose is to love. The ritual expression of this is seen most clearly in the Shema, where the recitation of the command "you shall love the Lord your God" is preceded by the assertion that God loves Israel with great or everlasting love. The relationship is mutual and reciprocal.

THIS IS MY GOD AND I WILL BEAUTIFY HIM (Ex. 15:2). R. Eliezer says, "How do we know that a maidservant at the sea beheld that which even the prophets—including Isaiah and Ezekiel—never saw? As it is said WHEN I SPOKE TO THE PROPHETS; FOR I GRANTED MANY VISIONS, AND SPOKE PARABLES THROUGH THE PROPHETS (Hos. 12:11). And it is written THE HEAVENS OPENED AND I SAW VISIONS OF GOD (Ezek. 1:1)."

A parable. This may be likened to a human king who makes an entry into a city surrounded by bodyguards, with warriors to his right and left and troops before him and behind him. Since he is only human like the rest of them, the multitudes ask, "Which one is the king?" But when The Holy One revealed Himself at the Sea there was no need to ask which one was the King. Rather as soon as they saw Him they recognized Him and all opened their mouths and proclaimed THIS IS MY GOD (Ex. 15:2).

I WILL BEAUTIFY HIM (Ex. 15:2). R. Ishmael says, "How is it possible for a human being to beautify his Creator? Rather it means 'I will beautify Him' through mitzvot. I will use a beautiful *lulav* before Him, a beautiful *sukkah*, beautiful fringes, beautiful phylacteries."

Abba Saul says, "It means that one should imitate Him. As He is gracious and merciful, so should you be gracious and merciful."

---

17. *including Isaiah and Ezekiel* These prophets are singled out since they both record seeing visions of God Himself. Even their visions were less direct than that of the most ordinary person at the Sea.
VISIONS OF GOD They saw only visions, while all the Israelites, from the highest to the humblest maidservant, could point to Him and say THIS IS MY GOD.
no need to ask—since God is not like any other being, human or divine. He is sui generis.
BEAUTIFY The word usually translated "glorify" also means to make beautiful.
lulav—the palm branch, willows, and myrtles used on the Feast of Tabernacles.
sukkah—the temporary hut or tabernacle erected for that Feast.
phylacteries—or *tefillin*. Small leather containers holding parchments with Biblical texts that are bound to the arm and the head by straps, usually worn during daily morning prayers.

R. Jose says, "I will speak unto all the nations of the world of the beauty and praise of He Who Spoke and the world came into being."

R. Jose the son of a woman from Damascus says, "I will build for Him a beautiful Sanctuary. The word "naveh" (beautiful) always refers to the Sanctuary as it is said FOR THEY HAVE DEVOURED JACOB AND DESOLATED HIS HOME (navehu) (Ps. 79:7). And it also says WHEN YOU GAZE UPON ZION, OUR CITY OF ASSEMBLY, YOUR EYES SHALL BEHOLD JERUSALEM AS A SECURE HOMESTEAD (naveh) (Isa. 33:20)."

R. Akiba says, "I will speak unto all the nations of the world of the beauty and praise of He Who spoke and the world came into being.

For the nations of the world ask Israel, 'HOW IS YOUR BELOVED BETTER THAN ANOTHER, O FAIREST OF WOMEN? HOW IS YOUR BELOVED BETTER THAN ANOTHER THAT YOU ADJURE US SO? (Song 5:9)—that you are willing to die for Him and are slaughtered for His sake, as it is said THEREFORE DO MAIDENS (alamot) LOVE YOU (Song 1:3), that is, they love you even unto death (ad mavet) and it is written IT IS FOR YOUR SAKE WE ARE SLAIN ALL DAY LONG (Ps. 44:23). You are handsome and mighty. Come and join with us.'

"Israel says to the nations of the world, 'Do you indeed recognize Him? Let us tell you a modicum of His praise. MY BELOVED IS CLEAR-SKINNED AND RUDDY, PREEMINENT AMONG TEN THOUSAND (Song 5:10).'

"Once the nations of the world hear this, they say to Israel, 'We will go with you' as it is said WHITHER HAS YOUR BELOVED GONE, O FAIREST OF WOMEN? WHITHER HAS YOUR BELOVED TURNED? LET US SEEK HIM WITH YOU (Song 6:1).'

"But Israel says to the nations of the world, 'You have no portion in Him!' as it is said MY BELOVED IS MINE AND I AM HIS (Song 2:16); I AM MY BELOVED'S AND MY BELOVED IS MINE (Song 6:3)."

The Sages say, "I will accompany (alavenu) Him until I come with Him to the Temple." A parable. A king had a son who went to a far-off land, and

---

speak unto all the nations—and thus I will beautify and glorify Him by making others recognize His qualities.
Sanctuary—referring to the Temple in Jerusalem.
accompany (alavenu)—another interpretation of the word *beautify* (anvehu).

[the king] went with him and stayed with him. He then went to another land, and he went with him and stayed with him. Thus when Israel went down to Egypt, the Divine Presence went down with them, as it is said I MYSELF WILL GO DOWN WITH YOU TO EGYPT (Gen. 46:4). When they went up from there, the Divine Presence went up with them, as it is said AND I MYSELF WILL ALSO BRING YOU BACK (Gen. 46:4). They plunged into the sea, the Divine Presence was with them as it is said THE ANGEL OF GOD, WHO HAD BEEN GOING AHEAD OF THE ISRAELITE ARMY, NOW MOVED AND FOLLOWED BEHIND THEM (Ex. 14:19). They went into the wilderness, the Divine Presence was with them, as it is said THE LORD WENT BEFORE THEM IN A PILLAR OF CLOUD BY DAY (Ex. 13:21) until they brought Him to the Temple. Thus it is said SCARCELY HAD I PASSED THEM WHEN I FOUND THE ONE I LOVE. I HELD HIM FAST, I WOULD NOT LET HIM GO TILL I BROUGHT HIM TO MY MOTHER'S HOUSE (Song 3:4).

COMMENTARY   *The phrase I WILL BEAUTIFY HIM (usually translated "I will glorify Him") puzzled the Sages. Can one actually add anything to God? Can you add to His beauty? Therefore the rabbis offered a multitude of alternative meanings of the phrase, one of which is the source of the idea of imitating God and another of the concept of adding an esthetic dimension to the observance of the mitzvot. These interpretations also lead to two very interesting literary creations: Akiba's dramatic dialogue between Israel and the nations and the parable of the Sages. Akiba consistently interpreted the Song of Songs as the song of love between Israel and God. The section he uses here becomes a discussion with the nations who seek to take God's love or at least share in it. Akiba is not willing for them to do this, an attitude most understandable considering the times in which Akiba lived, times of destruction and martyrdom culminating in the Hadrianic persecution. The parable of the Sages is one of a series of teachings in which God is depicted, through His indwelling presence, called the Shekhina, as participating in the trouble and suffering both of individuals and, as here, of the people Israel. Thus those who say to Israel, "God has deserted you, abandoned you, or even works against you" are told that on the contrary, God is with us, suffers with us and sustains us in our suffering. Another example of this idea can be found above in selection 4.*

18. Exodus 15:3, Mekhilta Shirata 4, II 30

THE LORD, THE WARRIOR—LORD IS HIS NAME! (Ex. 15:3). R. Judah says, "What a rich verse this is, with many echoes. It tells us that He appeared to them with all the implements of war."

He appeared to them as a hero girded with a sword, as it is said GIRD YOUR SWORD UPON YOUR THIGH, O HERO (Ps. 45:4).

He appeared to them as a rider, as it is said HE MOUNTED A CHERUB AND FLEW, GLIDING ON THE WINGS OF THE WIND (Ps. 18:11).

He appeared to them as an armed warrior with armor and helmet, as it is said HE DONNED VICTORY LIKE A COAT OF MAIL, WITH A HELMET OF TRIUMPH ON HIS HEAD (Isa. 59:17).

He appeared to them with a spear, as it is said AS YOUR ARROWS FLY IN BRIGHTNESS, YOUR FLASHING SPEAR IN BRILLIANCE (Hab. 3:11). And it says READY THE SPEAR AND JAVELIN AGAINST MY PURSUERS (Ps. 35:3).

He appeared to them with bow and arrow, as it is said ALL BARED AND READY IS YOUR BOW (Hab. 3:9) and it says HE LET LOOSE ARROWS AND SCATTERED THEM (2 Sam. 22:15).

He appeared to them with shield and buckler, as it is said HIS FIDEL-ITY IS AN ENCIRCLING SHIELD (Ps. 91:4) and it says TAKE UP SHIELD AND BUCKLER AND COME TO MY DEFENSE (Ps. 35:2).

I might think that He is in need of these implements, therefore the verse says THE LORD, THE WARRIOR—LORD IS HIS NAME—He fights with His name and is in no need of any of these implements. If that is so, why does the Scripture bother to mention each of these specifically and individually? To emphasize that should it be necessary, God will make war for Israel and woe unto the nations of the world! Let them heed carefully with their own ears that He Who Spoke and the world came into being will yet fight against them.

THE LORD, THE WARRIOR—LORD IS HIS NAME. Why state [LORD IS HIS NAME]? Since He appeared at the Sea as a heroic warrior, as it is said THE LORD, THE WARRIOR, at Sinai as a merciful elder, as it is said AND THEY SAW THE GOD OF ISRAEL: UNDER HIS FEET THERE WAS THE LIKENESS OF A PAVEMENT OF SAPPHIRE (Ex.

24:10), and when they were redeemed, what does it say? LIKE THE VERY SKY FOR PURITY (Ex. 24:10) and it says THRONES WERE SET IN PLACE, AND THE ANCIENT OF DAYS TOOK HIS SEAT. HIS GARMENT WAS LIKE WHITE SNOW, AND THE HAIR OF HIS HEAD WAS LIKE LAMB'S WOOL (Dan. 7:9). And it says A RIVER OF FIRE STREAMED FORTH BEFORE HIM; THOUSANDS UPON THOUSANDS SERVED HIM; MYRIADS UPON MYRIADS ATTENDED HIM (Dan. 7:10)). It was important not to give the nations of the world any excuse to say that there are two divine powers. Therefore it says THE LORD, THE WARRIOR—LORD IS HIS NAME! (Ex. 15:3).

> He was in Egypt
> He was at the Sea
> He was there in the past
> He will be there in the future
> He is in this world
> He will be in the world to come

as it is said SEE, THEN, THAT I, I AM HE; THERE IS NO GOD BESIDE ME (Deut. 32:39). And it says I, THE LORD, WHO WAS FIRST AND WILL BE WITH THE LAST AS WELL (Isa. 41:4).

There may be a warrior in a city who has all the weapons of war but does not have strength, courage, tactics, or knowledge of warfare. But He Who Spoke and the world came into being is not like that. He has strength and courage, tactics and knowledge of war, as it is said THE LORD CAN GIVE VICTORY WITHOUT SWORD OR SPEAR. FOR THE BATTLE IS THE LORD'S (1 Sam. 17:47). And it is written BLESSED IS THE LORD, MY ROCK, WHO TRAINS MY HANDS FOR BATTLE, MY FINGERS FOR WARFARE (Ps. 144:1).

There may be a warrior in a city whose strength at sixty is not what it was at forty, and at seventy not what it was at sixty, for as he grows older his strength is constantly diminishing. But He Who Spoke and the world came

---

18. *when they were redeemed*—a reference to the midrash above (p. 60) in which the appearance of God before and after the Exodus is described.

two divine powers—the popular dualist conception. Had Scripture described God differently without specifying that all of these are merely manifestations of the One God, it would have strengthened this dualist argument.

into being is not like that. Rather FOR I AM THE LORD—I HAVE NOT CHANGED (Mal. 3:6).

There may be a warrior in a city who, when overcome with wrath and fury, will smite even his father and mother and other relatives, but He Who Spoke and the world came into being is not like that. Rather THE LORD, WARRIOR—LORD IS HIS NAME! (Ex. 15:3). THE LORD, WARRIOR is the One Who fought against Egypt. LORD IS HIS NAME—He is the One Who has pity on His creatures, as it is said THE LORD! THE LORD! A GOD COMPASSIONATE AND GRACIOUS, SLOW TO ANGER, RICH IN STEADFAST KINDNESS, EXTENDING KINDNESS TO THE THOUSANDTH GENERATION (Ex. 34:6).

There may be a warrior in a city who can shoot an arrow but cannot call it back to him. He Who Spoke and the world came into being is not like that. Rather when Israel disobeys God's will, as it were, He issues a decree against her, as it says, WHEN I WHET MY FLASHING BLADE (Deut. 32:41), but if Israel repents He immediately rescinds [the decree,] as it is said AND MY HAND LAYS HOLD ON JUDGMENT (Deut. 32:41). Might this verse be taken to mean that He withholds justice? The verse says RETRIBUTION I'LL DEAL TO MY FOES (Deut. 32:41). Upon whom does He turn His judgment? Upon the nations of the world as it is said METE OUT TO THOSE WHO REJECT ME (Deut. 32:41)

When a human king goes out to war, if other cities nearby come and ask for his help with their needs, they are told that he is preoccupied with war, and they should come and ask again when he returns. But this is not so with He Who Spoke and the world came into being. Rather THE LORD, THE WARRIOR (Ex. 15:3)—fighting against the Egyptians, LORD IS HIS NAME (Ex. 15:3)—yet giving heed to the petitions of all creatures, as it is said ALL MANKIND COMES TO YOU, YOU WHO HEAR PRAYER (Ps. 65:3).

A human king engaged in war cannot provide food for his soldiers and supply all their needs, but He Who Spoke and the world came into being is not like that. Rather THE LORD, THE WARRIOR—(Ex. 15:3) fighting

---

has pity   His prowess as a warrior does not obliterate His basic quality, which is the Quality of Mercy.

against the Egyptians, LORD IS HIS NAME—(Ex. 15:3) feeding and providing for all His creatures as it is said WHO SPLIT APART THE SEA OF REEDS (Ps. 136:13) after which it says WHO GIVES FOOD TO ALL FLESH (Ps. 136:25).

THE LORD, THE WARRIOR (Ex. 15:3). Can this really be said? Has it not been said FOR I FILL BOTH HEAVEN AND EARTH—DECLARES THE LORD (Jer. 23:24) and it is written AND ONE WOULD CALL TO THE OTHER, "HOLY, HOLY, HOLY! THE LORD OF HOSTS! HIS PRESENCE FILLS ALL THE EARTH!" (Isa. 6:3) and it is written AND THERE, COMING FROM THE EAST WITH A ROAR LIKE THE ROAR OF MIGHTY WATERS, WAS THE PRESENCE OF THE GOD OF ISRAEL, AND THE EARTH WAS LIT UP BY HIS PRESENCE (Ezek. 43:2). What then can be the meaning of the verse THE LORD, THE WARRIOR? "Because of the great love I bear you and because of your holiness, I shall hallow My name through you." Thus it says FOR I AM GOD, NOT MAN, THE HOLY ONE (Hos. 11:9)—"I shall hallow My name through you."

COMMENTARY   *This section makes it abundantly clear that anthropomorphism was not anathema to the Sages. When the verse describes God as a warrior, what disturbs them is not the usage of human terms to depict God but the implied limitation on Him. They are willing to accept all the various descriptions as real possibilities so long as one realizes that it is the same God using various forms and that none of those forms is to be taken as a description of His reality, which fills the universe and is beyond the ability of man to describe. This particular verse, divided into two, is particularly useful in providing a contrast between God's various manifestations in the world and the reality beyond understanding that is implied in the statement LORD IS HIS NAME. The universalist concept of God is also stressed in many of these interpretations. He may be fighting against the Egyptians, but at the same time it is He who hears the prayers of all mankind and fulfills the needs of all human beings.*

---

hallow My Name   By acting as a warrior against Egypt and saving Israel God causes the nations to praise and recognize Him.

19. Exodus 15:6, Mekhilta Shirata 5, II 39

GLORIOUS IN POWER (Ex. 15:6). You are lovely and glorious in power in that You granted time to the generation of the flood to repent, but they did not do so as it is said MY SPIRIT SHALL NOT SHIELD MAN FOREVER (Gen. 6:3). Nor did You decree their destruction until they had demonstrated to You their utter wickedness.

Thus too we find with the generation of the Tower [of Babel] that You granted them time to repent, but they did not do so, as it is said AND THE LORD SAID, "IF, AS ONE PEOPLE WITH ONE LANGUAGE FOR ALL, THIS IS HOW THEY HAVE BEGUN TO ACT, AND NOW . . . (Gen. 11:6)." NOW always refers to repentance, as in the passage AND NOW, O ISRAEL, WHAT IS IT THAT THE LORD YOUR GOD DEMANDS OF YOU? IT IS TO REVERE THE LORD YOUR GOD, TO WALK ONLY IN HIS PATHS, TO LOVE HIM, AND TO SERVE THE LORD YOUR GOD WITH ALL YOUR HEART AND SOUL (Deut. 10:12). Nor did You decree their destruction until they had demonstrated to You their utter wickedness.

Thus too we find with the people of Sodom that You granted them time to repent, but they did not do so, as it is said THEN THE LORD SAID, "THE OUTRAGE OF SODOM AND GOMORRAH IS SO GREAT, AND THEIR SIN SO GRAVE! I WILL GO DOWN AND SEE (Gen. 18:20–21)." What does it say there? THE LORD RAINED UPON SODOM AND GOMORRAH SULFUROUS FIRE FROM THE LORD OUT OF HEAVEN (Gen. 19:24). That is: If they repent they will receive rain, but if not—SULFUROUS FIRE. Nor did You decree their destruction until they had demonstrated to You their utter wickedness.

You brought ten plagues upon the Egyptians in Egypt but did not decree their destruction until they had demonstrated to You their utter wickedness.

---

19. *glorious in power* Your power is limitless but You hold it back in order to allow for repentance. Your restraint demonstrates Your power.

FOREVER There is a limit to the time You will wait, but You do grant them time enough to repent.

GO DOWN AND SEE—giving them time to repent. Only when He sees that there is no hope will He destroy them.

COMMENTARY   *Ingeniously the Sages inserted missing elements into Biblical stories, in this case the concept of repentance, which is central to later Biblical Judaism and to rabbinic Judaism, but does not appear in Genesis. It was inconceivable to them that God would not be willing to offer even the worst sinners an opportunity to repent and would destroy them, unless there was clearly no hope for their salvation. Thus verses were interpreted to indicate that in all these instances, repentance was offered and rejected.*

20. Exodus 15:9, Mekhilta Shirata 7, II 54

THE FOE SAID (Ex. 15:9). This occurred at the beginning of the incident. Why was it written here? Because the Torah does not observe chronological order. Similarly ON THE EIGHTH DAY MOSES CALLED AARON AND HIS SONS (Lev. 9:1). This occurred at the beginning of the incident. Why was it written here? Because the Torah does not observe chronological order.

Similarly IN THE YEAR THAT KING UZZIAH DIED (Isa. 6:1) should be the beginning of the book. Why is it written here? Because the Torah does not observe chronological order.

Similarly AND HE SAID TO ME, "O MORTAL, STAND UP ON YOUR FEET THAT I MAY SPEAK TO YOU" (Ezek. 2:1)"—some say O MORTAL, PROPOUND A RIDDLE (Ezek. 17:2)—should be the beginning of the book. Why is it written here? Because the Torah does not observe chronological order.

Similarly GO PROCLAIM TO JERUSALEM (Jer. 2:2) should be the beginning of the book. Why is it written here? Because the Torah does not observe chronological order.

Similarly ISRAEL IS A RAVAGED VINE (Hos. 10:1) should be the beginning of the book. Why is it written here? Because the Torah does not observe chronological order.

Similarly I, KOHELETH, WAS KING IN JERUSALEM OVER ISRAEL (Eccl. 1:12) should be the beginning of the book. Why is it written here? Because the Torah does not observe chronological order.

---

20. *at the beginning of the incident*   In the Song of the Sea (Ex. 15) there is a description of the defeat of the Egyptians after which this verse describes how they had threatened Israel before the battle.

COMMENTARY   *Although Scripture is the word of God, the regulations for its interpretation which the Sages formulated permitted great flexibility and did not confine them to a fundamentalistic conception. Chronological order, for example, did not exist for them. Events, verses, chapters, could then be moved around in interpretation, although never in the actual text, in order to create a more logical order.*

THE FOE SAID (Ex. 15:9). It was Pharaoh. But how could Israel know what Pharaoh was thinking about them in Egypt? The Holy Spirit descended upon them and thus they knew what Pharaoh was thinking about them in Egypt. When Pharaoh was aware that Israel had departed he said, "It would not be worth our while to pursue the Israelites except for the silver and gold that they have taken." But those Egyptians who had lost but a little money said, "We are willing to forgo it and not pursue the Israelites." When Pharaoh realized this he said, "We shall all be equal in the spoil," as it is said I WILL DIVIDE THE SPOIL (Ex. 15:9). "Furthermore I shall open my store of silver and gold and hand out precious gems and pearls to you!"

Another interpretation: THE FOE SAID (Ex. 15:9). It was Pharaoh, but he did not understand the meaning of what he said. A MAN MAY ARRANGE HIS THOUGHTS, BUT WHAT HE SAYS DEPENDS ON THE LORD (Prov. 16:1).
    It does not say "We will pursue, we will overtake, we will divide . . ." but I WILL PURSUE, I WILL OVERTAKE, I WILL DIVIDE (Ex. 15:9), which means "I will be pursued and overtaken by them. My spoil and my wealth will be divided among them."
    It does not say "My desire shall have its fill of them" but "MY DESIRE SHALL FILL HIM" (Ex. 15:9), which means "they will fill themselves up upon me!"
    It does not say "My hand shall possess them" but "MY HAND SHALL POSSESS HIM" (Ex. 15:9), which means "I will give them possession of my wealth and substance."

Pharaoh   They understand FOE not as a poetic personification, but as a reference to the supreme enemy, Pharaoh himself.
MY DESIRE SHALL FILL HIM—which seems to refer to Israel but viewed by this midrash as a peculiar usage subject to interpretation. It should be the plural "them." The conclusion is that in all these phrases where the singular is used it refers it back to him himself, thus making Pharaoh an unwitting prophet of his own doom.

[Said Pharoah to his people,] "Previously you would despoil [the Israelites] and I would prosecute you under royal law. But now I WILL DIVIDE THE SPOIL (Ex. 15:9).

"Previously you would kill them and I would prosecute you under royal law, but now I WILL EMPTY MY SWORD (Ex. 15:9).

"Previously you would rape their wives, their sons and their daughters, and I would prosecute you under royal law, but now MY HAND SHALL POSSESS THEM" (Ex. 15:9).

Others say, "It does not say 'I will use my sword' but I WILL EMPTY MY SWORD, which means that he intended to ravish the males, as we find in the verse I SWEAR I WILL BRING AGAINST YOU STRANGERS, THE MOST RUTHLESS OF NATIONS. THEY SHALL EMPTY THEIR SWORDS AGAINST THE MOST BEAUTIFUL OF YOUR WISE ONES AND DESECRATE YOUR SPLENDID ONES (Ezek. 28:7). Here too it does not say, 'they will use their swords' but THEY SHALL EMPTY THEIR SWORDS AGAINST THE MOST BEAUTIFUL OF YOUR WISE ONES."

Because his heart was so proud and haughty God humbled him and all the nations of the world despoiled him.

The Egyptians were divided into three groups in regard to the Israelites at the Sea.

One said, "Let us take their money and take back our money, but not kill them."

One said, "Let us kill them but not take their money."

The third said, "Let us kill them and take their money."

I WILL DIVIDE THE SPOIL (Ex. 15:9) refers to the group that said "Let us take their money, but not kill them."

MY DESIRE SHALL HAVE ITS FILL OF THEM (Ex. 15:9) refers to the group that said, "Let us kill them but not take their money."

MY HAND SHALL POSSESS THEM (Ex. 15:9) refers to the group that said, "Let us kill them and take their money."

EMPTY MY SWORD—understood in all these verses as a euphemism for homosexual intercourse.

kill them—connected to the fact that the Hebrew word translated here "desire" usually means "soul" in the sense of "life."

EXODUS

In the Land of Egypt Pharaoh made five defiant boasts:

> THE FOE SAID,
>   "I WILL PURSUE,
>   I WILL OVERTAKE,
>   I WILL DIVIDE THE SPOIL;
>   MY DESIRE SHALL HAVE ITS FILL OF THEM.
>   I WILL EMPTY MY SWORD;
>   MY HAND SHALL POSSESS THEM" (Ex. 15:9).

The Spirit of Holiness in turn uttered these [five] statements:

YOU MADE THE WIND BLOW, THE SEA COVERED THEM
  (Ex. 15:10).
YOUR RIGHT HAND, O LORD, SHATTERS THE FOE! (Ex. 15:6).
IN YOUR GREAT TRIUMPH YOU BREAK YOUR OPPONENTS
  (Ex. 15:7).
YOU SEND FORTH YOUR FURY, IT CONSUMES THEM LIKE
  STUBBLE (Ex. 15:7).
YOU PUT OUT YOUR RIGHT HAND, THE EARTH
  SWALLOWED THEM (Ex. 15:12).

A parable. This may be likened to a robber who stood behind the king's palace and defiantly boasted, "If I find the king's son I will seize him, slay him, crucify him, and subject him to terrible deaths." Thus did Pharaoh make five defiant boasts in the Land of Egypt: THE FOE SAID, "I WILL PURSUE, I WILL OVERTAKE, I WILL DIVIDE THE SPOIL; MY DESIRE SHALL HAVE ITS FILL OF THEM. I WILL EMPTY MY SWORD; MY HAND SHALL POSSESS THEM" (Ex. 15:9) while the Holy Spirit mocked him saying YOU MADE THE WIND BLOW (Ex. 15:10) and it says YOU PUT OUT YOUR RIGHT HAND (Ex. 15:12).

Similarly it says WHY DO THE NATIONS ASSEMBLE, AND PEOPLE PLOT VAIN THINGS; KINGS OF THE EARTH TAKE THEIR STAND, AND REGENTS INTRIGUE TOGETHER AGAINST THE LORD AND AGAINST HIS ANOINTED? LET US BREAK THE CORDS OF THEIR YOKE, SHAKE OFF THEIR ROPES FROM US!" HE WHO IS ENTHRONED IN HEAVEN LAUGHS; THE LORD MOCKS AT THEM (Ps. 2:1–4). And it says THEY RAVE WITH THEIR MOUTHS, SHARP WORDS ARE ON THEIR LIPS; [THEY THINK] "WHO HEARS?" (Ps. 59:8). What is written after that?

BUT YOU, O LORD, LAUGH AT THEM; YOU MOCK ALL THE NATIONS (Ps. 59:9).

So too it says SHEBA AND DEDAN, AND THE MERCHANTS AND ALL THE MAGNATES OF TARSHISH WILL SAY TO YOU, "HAVE YOU COME TO TAKE SPOIL? (Ezek. 38:13). And it says ON THAT DAY, WHEN GOG SETS FOOT ON THE SOIL OF ISRAEL— DECLARES THE LORD GOD—MY RAGING ANGER SHALL FLAIR UP . . . AND EVERY HUMAN BEING ON EARTH SHALL QUAKE BEFORE ME (Ezek. 38:18–20)."

Thus because of the boasts of one man, all of those thousands and those myriads SANK LIKE LEAD (Ex. 15:10)!

Another interpretation: SANK LIKE LEAD (Ex. 15:10). Four are called mighty:

- The Holy One is called mighty, as it is said THE LORD IS MIGHTY ON HIGH (Ps. 93:4).
- Israel is called mighty, as it is said THEY ARE HOLY AND MIGHTY, IN WHOM IS ALL MY DELIGHT (Ps. 16:3).
- Egypt is called mighty, as it is said O MORTAL, WAIL—ALONG WITH THE WOMEN OF THE MIGHTY NATIONS—OVER THE MASSES OF EGYPT (Ezek. 32:18).
- The waters are called mighty, as it is said ABOVE THE THUNDER OF THE MIGHTY WATERS (Ps. 93:4).

The Holy One, Who is mighty, revealed Himself to Israel who is called mighty in order to requite punishment from the Egyptians who are called mighty in the waters that are called mighty, as it is said THEY SANK LIKE LEAD IN THE MIGHTY WATERS (Ex. 15:10).

COMMENTARY   *The fundamental principle of Biblical poetry is repetition of the same idea in different words. The Sages, on the other hand, looked for different meaning in every phrase. Thus the Song of the Sea is a particularly rich source of material for them. Every phrase uttered by the foe, Pharaoh, is turned into a specific reference to what he wishes to accomplish. In this way rich legends are created about the actions of the Egyptians and their attitudes toward the people of Israel. The list of "four called mighty" is another typical method of the Sages. They find several verses using the same word, make a list of them, and then connect then ideationally.*

21. Exodus 15:11, Mekhilta Shirata 8, II 60

WHO IS LIKE YOU, O LORD, AMONG THE CELESTIALS (elim) (Ex. 15:11). It is written *ba-alm* "powerful." WHO IS LIKE YOU . . . AMONG the powerful. Who is like You in the miracles and mighty wonders which You performed at the sea, as it is said AWESOME DEEDS AT THE SEA OF REEDS (Ps. 106:22). HE SENT HIS BLAST AGAINST THE SEA OF REEDS; IT BECAME DRY; HE LED THEM THROUGH THE DEEP AS THROUGH A WILDERNESS (Ps. 106:9).

WHO IS LIKE YOU, O LORD, AMONG THE CELESTIALS (elim) (Ex. 15:11). WHO IS LIKE YOU . . . AMONG the silent (ilmim), O LORD. Who is like You—seeing the shame suffered by Your children and remaining silent, as it is said "I HAVE KEPT SILENT FAR TOO LONG, KEPT STILL AND RESTRAINED MYSELF; NOW I WILL SCREAM LIKE A WOMAN IN LABOR, I WILL PANT AND I WILL GASP" (Isa. 42:14–15). "In the past I KEPT STILL AND RESTRAINED MYSELF but from now on I WILL SCREAM LIKE A WOMAN IN LABOR, I WILL PANT AND I WILL GASP."

Another interpretation: WHO IS LIKE YOU, O LORD, AMONG THE CELESTIALS (Ex. 15:11). Who is like You among those who serve You on high, as it is said FOR WHO IN THE SKIES CAN EQUAL THE LORD, CAN COMPARE WITH THE LORD AMONG THE DIVINE BEINGS, A GOD GREATLY DREADED IN THE COUNCIL OF HOLY BEINGS, HELD IN AWE BY ALL AROUND HIM? (Ps. 89:7–8).

WHO IS LIKE YOU, O LORD, AMONG THE CELESTIALS (Ex. 15:11). Who is like You among those who ascribe divinity to themselves?
 Pharaoh called himself a god, as it is said HE BOASTED, "THE NILE IS MINE AND I MADE IT (Ezek. 29:9)." I AM GOING TO DEAL WITH YOU, O PHARAOH KING OF EGYPT . . . WHO SAID, MY NILE IS MY OWN; I MADE IT FOR MYSELF (Ez. 29:3).
 Sennacherib called himself a god, as it is said WHICH AMONG ALL

---

21. *CELESTIALS* The Hebrew word is "elim," which can mean "gods," "powerful beings," or "celestial beings."
ascribe divinity—taking the word in its meaning of "gods." These gods, however, are not real.

THE GODS OF THOSE COUNTRIES SAVED THEIR COUNTRIES FROM ME (Isa. 36:20).

Nebuchadnezzar called himself a god, as it is said I WILL MOUNT THE BACK OF A CLOUD—I WILL MATCH THE MOST HIGH (Isa. 14:14).

The ruler of Tyre called himself a god, as it is said O MORTAL, SAY TO THE PRINCE OF TYRE: THUS SAID THE LORD GOD: BECAUSE YOU HAVE BEEN SO HAUGHTY AND HAVE SAID, "I AM A GOD; I SIT ENTHRONED LIKE A GOD IN THE HEART OF THE SEAS" (Ezek. 28:2).

WHO IS LIKE YOU, O LORD, AMONG THE CELESTIALS (Ex. 15:11). Who is like You among those to whom others ascribe divinity, but in whom there is no substance. Of them is it said THEY HAVE MOUTHS, BUT CANNOT SPEAK (Ps. 115:5). Those have mouths but cannot speak, but He Who Spoke and the world came into being is not like that. Rather He can even say two things in one, which humans cannot do, as it is said ONE THING GOD HAS SPOKEN; TWO THINGS HAVE I HEARD (Ps. 62:12). BEHOLD MY WORD IS LIKE FIRE—DECLARES THE LORD—AND LIKE A HAMMER THAT SHATTERS ROCK! (Jer. 23:29) and it is written JUST LISTEN TO THE NOISE OF HIS RUMBLING, TO THE SOUND THAT COMES OUT OF HIS MOUTH (Job 37:2).

COMMENTARY   *If the word "elim" (celestials) is taken in its common and fundamental meaning, "gods," it is problematic in implying that many gods exist. The interpretations here offer various alternatives. Some read the word slightly differently, which is made possible by the fact that it is written without the letter "yod," which usually is there, and therefore can easily be vocalized in different ways. Others point out that it may mean angels who are often termed "elim" or may mean those who are called or call themselves gods, but are obviously not. In view of the fact that Roman emperors were often deified, this interpretation had contemporary implications. The most daring of the interpretations is to read it as "silent"—the Hebrew letters are the same for both meanings—and then ask that most painful of all questions: Why are You silent, O Lord? The answer is less than satisfactory but at least holds out hope for the future: I was silent in the past, but now I will not be so.*

22. Exodus 15:11, Mekhilta Shirata 8, II 63

AWESOME IN SPLENDOR (Ex. 15:11). Human beings are held in awe more by those far from them than by those close to them. But this is not so in the case of He Who Spoke and the world came into being. Rather those closest to Him hold Him in awe more than those far from Him, as it is said, THROUGH THOSE NEAR TO ME I SHOW MYSELF HOLY (Lev. 10:3) and it is written AROUND HIM IT STORMED FIERCELY (Ps. 50:3). It is written A GOD GREATLY DREADED IN THE COUNCIL OF HOLY BEINGS, HELD IN AWE BY ALL AROUND HIM. O LORD, GOD OF HOSTS, WHO IS MIGHTY LIKE YOU, O LORD? YOUR FAITHFULNESS SURROUNDS YOU (Ps. 89:8–9).

With human beings, if one works for an employer, ploughing, sowing, weeding, hoeing for him, he gives him one coin and [the worker] goes on his way. But this is not so in the case of He Who Spoke and the world came into being. Rather if a man desires children, He grants them to him, as it is said SONS ARE THE PROVISION OF THE LORD; THE FRUIT OF THE WOMB, HIS REWARD (Ps. 127:3). If he desires wisdom, He grants it to him, as it is said FOR THE LORD GRANTS WISDOM (Prov. 2:6). If he desires possessions, He grants it to him, as it is said RICHES AND HONOR ARE YOURS TO DISPENSE (1 Chron. 29:12).

With human beings, one builds the lower floor first and then the upper. But this is not so in the case of He Who Spoke and the world came into being. He built the upper part first and then the lower as it is said, IN THE BEGINNING GOD CREATED THE HEAVENS and then AND THE EARTH (Gen. 1:1).

With human beings, if one builds a roof he builds it with wood, stones, earth, and water. But this is not so in the case of He Who Spoke and the world came into being. He covered His world with water, as it is said HE SETS THE RAFTERS OF HIS LOFTS IN THE WATERS (Ps. 104:3).

---

22. *SHOW MYSELF HOLY* Perceiving God's holiness is part of the feeling of awe.
one coin No matter what the work, the payment is in the same coin.

With human beings, it is impossible to make shapes out of water, but this is not so in the case of He Who Spoke and the world came into being. Rather He creates forms with water, as it is said LET THE WATERS BRING FORTH SWARMS OF LIVING CREATURES (Gen. 1:20).

With human beings, it is impossible to make shapes within the earth but this is not so in the case of He Who Spoke and the world came into being. He created shapes within the earth, as it is said WHEN I WAS SHAPED IN A HIDDEN PLACE, KNIT TOGETHER IN THE RECESSES OF THE EARTH (Ps. 139:15).

With human beings, one who shapes a figure begins with the head or one of the limbs and then completes it. But this is not the case with He Who Spoke and the world came into being. He creates the entire figure as a whole, as it is said FOR HE FORMS IT ALL (Jer. 10:16) and it says THERE IS NO ROCK (tzur) LIKE OUR GOD (1 Sam. 2:2)—there is no shaper (tzayar) like our God.

With human beings, one goes to an image maker and says to him, "Make me an image of my father," and he replies, "Bring your father and let him stand before me or bring me a likeness of him and I will make you an image of him." But this is not the case with He Who Spoke and the world came into being. Rather He creates a son for a man from a drop of fluid and he is just like the image of his father.

COMMENTARY   *Rabbinic theology is couched not in philosophical terms but in more concrete descriptions of God's abilities such as these in which He is compared to human beings. Humans are limited in what they can do and how they can create. What He does is beyond all comparison. God's creativity is seen in the creation of the world and of human beings. Even that most common and natural of all processes, human reproduction, is seen as an extraordinary example of the Divine powers of creativity.*

23. Exodus 15:16, Mekhilta Shirata 9, II 75

TILL YOUR PEOPLE PASS BY, O LORD, TILL THE PEOPLE PASS (Ex. 15:16). TILL YOUR PEOPLE PASS BY the Sea. TILL THE PEOPLE PASS the rivers of Arnon.

---

23. *rivers of Arnon*—at the time of war with Sihon. See Num. 21.

THE PEOPLE WHOM YOU HAVE ACQUIRED (kanita) (Ex. 15:16). For although all the world is Yours, You have no people other than Israel, as it is said THE PEOPLE I FORMED FOR MYSELF THAT THEY MIGHT DECLARE MY PRAISE (Isa. 43:21).

Four are called "kinyan" (an acquisition).

Israel is called "acquisition" as it is said . . . THE PEOPLE WHOM YOU HAVE ACQUIRED (kanita) (Ex. 15:16).

The Land of Israel is called "acquisition" as it is said ACQUIRER (koneh) OF HEAVEN AND THE LAND (Gen. 14:22).

The Temple is called "acquisition" as it is said HE BROUGHT THEM TO HIS HOLY REALM, THE MOUNTAIN HIS RIGHT HAND HAD ACQUIRED (kanta) (Ps. 78:54).

The Torah is called "acquisition," as it is said THE LORD ACQUIRED ME (kannani) AT THE BEGINNING OF HIS COURSE, AS THE FIRST OF HIS WORKS OF OLD (Prov. 8:22).

Let Israel which is called "acquisition" come to the land which is called "acquisition" and build the Temple which is called "acquisition" because of the merit of the Torah which is called "acquisition." Therefore it is said THE PEOPLE . . . WHOM YOU HAVE ACQUIRED.

24. Exodus 15:17, Mekhilta Shirata 10, II 77

THE MOUNTAIN OF YOUR INHERITANCE (Ex. 15:17). Four are called "nahalah" (an inheritance).

Israel is called "inheritance" as it is said YET THEY ARE YOUR PEOPLE AND YOUR INHERITANCE (Deut. 9:29).

The Land of Israel is called "inheritance" as it is said IN THE LAND THAT THE LORD YOUR GOD IS GIVING YOU AS AN INHERITANCE (Deut. 15:4).

The Temple is called "inheritance" as it is said THE MOUNTAIN OF YOUR INHERITANCE (Ex. 15:17).

The Torah is called "inheritance" as it is said AND FROM MATTANAH TO NAHALIEL (Num. 21:19).

---

24. *MATTANAH* The literal meaning of the name is "a gift," i.e., something that is given. This is then taken to refer to the Torah, which was given to Israel.

Let Israel which is called "inheritance" come to the land which is called "inheritance" and build the Temple which is called "inheritance" because of the merit of the Torah which is called "inheritance." Therefore it is said THE MOUNTAIN OF YOUR INHERITANCE (Ex. 15:17).

25. Exodus 15:20, Mekhilta Shirata 10, II 81

THEN MIRIAM THE PROPHETESS TOOK (Ex. 15:20). Where do we find that Miriam prophesied? She told her father, "You are destined to sire a son who will arise and save Israel from the Egyptians." Immediately A CERTAIN MAN OF THE HOUSE OF LEVI WENT AND MARRIED A LEVITE WOMAN. THE WOMAN CONCEIVED AND BORE A SON; AND WHEN SHE SAW HOW BEAUTIFUL HE WAS, SHE HID HIM FOR THREE MONTHS. WHEN SHE COULD HIDE HIM NO LONGER (Ex. 2:1–3). Her father rebuked her. He said to her, "Miriam, what has become of your prophecies?" But she held fast by her prophecy, as it is said AND HIS SISTER STOOD HERSELF AT A DISTANCE TO LEARN WHAT WOULD BEFALL HIM (Ex. 2:4). And "standing" always implies the presence of the Holy Spirit, as in the passages I SAW MY LORD STANDING BY THE ALTAR (Amos 9:1); THE LORD CAME AND STOOD THERE (1 Sam. 3:10) and CALL JOSHUA AND STAND YOURSELVES IN THE TENT OF MEETING THAT I MAY INSTRUCT HIM (Deut. 31:14).

AT A DISTANCE (Ex. 2:4). "Distance" always implies the presence of the Holy Spirit as it is said FROM A DISTANCE THE LORD REVEALED HIMSELF TO ME (Jer. 31:3).

TO LEARN (Ex. 2:4). "Learning" always suggests the presence of the Holy Spirit, as it is said FOR THE LAND SHALL BE FILLED WITH THE KNOWLEDGE OF THE LORD (Isa. 11:9) and FOR THE EARTH SHALL BE FILLED WITH KNOWLEDGE OF THE GLORY OF THE LORD (Hab. 2:14).

AARON'S SISTER (Ex. 15:20). Was she not the sister of both of them? Why then does the verse state AARON'S SISTER? Since he was totally

---

25. *Miriam prophesied* If she is given the title "prophet" one would expect her prophecies to be recorded, yet there are none in the Scriptural text. The midrash provides some prophecies that will justify her title.

devoted to her she is referred to by his name. We see the same thing in the passage SIMON AND LEVI, TWO OF JACOB'S SONS, BROTHERS OF DINAH (Gen. 34:25). Was she not the sister of all the brothers? Why then does the verse say BROTHERS OF DINAH? Since they were totally devoted to her she is referred to by their names . . .

TOOK A TIMBREL IN HER HAND (Ex. 15:20). Where did Israel get timbrels and flutes in the wilderness? This shows that they were righteous and utterly convinced that God would perform miracles and wonders for them when they would leave Egypt. Therefore they prepared timbrels and flutes for themselves.

AND MIRIAM CHANTED FOR THEM (Ex. 15:21). This verse indicates that just as Moses proclaimed the Song for the men, Miriam did so for the women. "SING TO THE LORD, FOR HE HAS TRIUMPHED GLORIOUSLY" (Ex. 15:21).

26. Exodus 15:25, Mekhilta Vayassa 1, II 91

SO HE CRIED OUT TO THE LORD (Ex. 15:25). From this we learn that the righteous are not hard to persuade. Incidentally you learn that the prayer of the righteous is brief. It once happened that a disciple led the service in the presence of R. Eliezer and was very brief in his blessings. [R. Eliezer's] disciples said to him, "Our master, did you note how very brief so-and-so was in his blessings?" They used to refer to him as "the disciple of the wise who is brief." [R. Eliezer] said to them, "He did not abbreviate more than Moses who prayed O GOD, PRAY HEAL HER! (Num. 12:13)."

Another time a disciple led the service in the presence of R. Eliezer and was very lengthy in his blessings. His disciples said to him, "Our master,

---

prepared timbrels and flutes—while in Egypt for the purpose of accompanying their song of thanksgiving.

---

26. *not hard to persuade*   The Israelites grumbled about the water (Ex. 15:24) and yet immediately Moses prays to God to help them.
the prayer of the righteous is brief   This is inferred from the fact that no words of Moses are mentioned. Perhaps all he did was to utter a cry.
brief in his blessings   The exact wording of the blessings may not yet have been fixed and those who led the prayers, although keeping to certain ideas and general formulas, had latitude in what they said and could lengthen or shorten the blessings.

did you note how very lengthy so-and-so was in his blessings?" They used to refer to him as "the disciple of the wise who is lengthy." [R. Eliezer] said to them, "He is no lengthier than Moses, as it is said WHEN I LAY PROSTRATE BEFORE THE LORD THOSE FORTY DAYS AND FORTY NIGHTS (Deut. 9:25)." He used to say, "There is a time to be brief and there is a time to be lengthy."

27. Exodus 16:4, Mekhilta Vayassa 3, II 103

EACH DAY THAT DAY'S PORTION (Ex. 16:4). R. Joshua says, "This indicates that a person would gather enough one day for the next, as one [prepares] for the Sabbath on Sabbath eve." R. Eleazar of Modi'in says, "This indicates that a person was not to gather enough on one day for the next, as one [prepares] for the Sabbath on Sabbath eve, as it is said EACH DAY THAT DAY'S PORTION. He who created the day created its provisions." This was the source of R. Eliezer's saying, "Anyone who has enough to eat today and says, 'What will I eat tomorrow?' is one of little faith, as it is said THUS I MAY TEST THEM TO SEE WHETHER THEY WILL FOLLOW (yelech) MY INSTRUCTIONS OR NOT (Ex. 16:4).

R. Joshua says, "If a man studies two *halachot* each morning, and two *halachot* in the evening and engages in business all day long, he is considered to have fulfilled the entire Torah."

This was the source of R. Simeon b. Yohai's saying, "The Torah can be expounded only by those who eat manna." Why is this? Can one sit and expound the Torah if he does not know how he will obtain food and drink, or how he will obtain clothing and coverings? Thus the Torah can be expounded only by those who eat manna or, similarly, by those who eat terumah.

COMMENTARY   *The rabbis tended to see the manna either as a test of faith or as a special gift to allow the Israelites time to learn the Torah without worrying about their provisions. Since they were to collect a limited*

---

27. *halachot*—laws, legal material as promulgated by the Sages. The root of the word is the same as that in the word *follow*.
terumah—the priestly dues.

amount each day, it was a trial of faith. It inculcated the concept that God was dependable and would give food each day just as one could count on the sun to rise each day. From this they extrapolated to their lives: A man of faith will not worry about tomorrow's food. He Who made the day will make provisions of that day.

28. Exodus 16:25, Mekhilta Vayassa 5, II 119

THEN MOSES SAID, "EAT IT TODAY, FOR TODAY IS A SABBATH TO THE LORD; YOU WILL NOT FIND IT TODAY ON THE PLAIN" (Ex. 16:25). R. Zerika says, "This is the source of the three Sabbath meals."

Since Israel was accustomed to going out in the morning [to gather manna] they said to him, "Our teacher Moses, shall we go out in the morning?"
He said to them, "There is none today."
They said to him, "Since we did not go out in the morning, should we go out toward evening?"
He said to them FOR TODAY IS A SABBATH TO THE LORD (Ex. 16:25).

And what is the meaning of the verse YOU WILL NOT FIND IT TODAY ON THE PLAIN (Ex. 16:25)? [The Sages] said, "The hearts of our ancestors were shattered at that moment, for they said, 'Since we have not found it today, we may not find it tomorrow either!'
"He said to them, 'This day you will not find it, but tomorrow you will find it.' "

R. Eleazar Hisma says, "You will not find it in this world, but you will find it in the world to come."

---

28. *three Sabbath meals* The word *day* is repeated three times in regard to not finding the manna on the Sabbath, indicating that three meals are to be eaten on the Sabbath instead of the normal quota of two: one at midday and one in the evening. This is done by eating the first on the Sabbath eve, the second on Sabbath midday, and the third before dark on the Sabbath.
this world—referred to as "today." He reinterprets the verse to be a reference to the difference between our world in which one labors for food and paradise where we will eat the heavenly bread, manna.

THEN MOSES SAID "EAT IT TODAY" (Ex. 16:25). R. Joshua says, "[Moses said,] 'If you observe the Sabbath, later the Holy One will give you three festivals, Passover, Pentecost, and Tabernacles.' This is why it says EAT IT TODAY, FOR TODAY IS A SABBATH TO THE LORD; YOU WILL NOT FIND IT TODAY ON THE PLAIN."

R. Eleazar of Modi'in says, "If you observe the Sabbath, later the Holy One will give you six precious things: the Land of Israel, the world to come, a new world, the Davidic kingship, the Priesthood, and the Levitical order. This is why it says EAT IT TODAY."

R. Eliezer says, "If you observe the Sabbath, the Holy One will save you from three times of suffering: the day of Gog, the pangs of the Messiah, and the great Day of Judgment. This is why it says EAT IT TODAY." . . .

YET SOME OF THE PEOPLE WENT OUT ON THE SEVENTH DAY TO GATHER (Ex. 16:27). Those were the people of little faith among the Israelites.

AND THE LORD SAID TO MOSES, "HOW LONG WILL YOU MEN REFUSE TO FOLLOW MY COMMANDMENTS AND MY TEACH-INGS?" (Ex. 16:28). R. Joshua says, " 'The Holy One said to Moses, "Say to Israel: I brought you out of Egypt, split the sea, brought down the manna, created the well, brought the quail and fought the war of Amalek. How long will you go on refusing TO FOLLOW MY COMMANDMENTS AND MY TEACHINGS? If you say that I imposed many mitzvot upon you, what about the Sabbath which I gave you at Marah? You did not observe it either." If you say, "If one observes the Sabbath and then dies anyway, what reward has he received for it?" The verse says "HAPPY IS THE MAN WHO DOES THIS, THE MAN WHO HOLDS FAST TO IT: WHO KEEPS THE SABBATH AND DOES NOT PROFANE IT, AND STAYS HIS HAND FROM DOING ANY EVIL (Isa. 56:2)." ' Thus we learn that one who observes the Sabbath is kept far from transgression."

---

three festivals Each mention of "today" hints at a festival. These are the three pilgrimage festivals when people came to the Temple in Jerusalem.
six precious things The number six may be derived from the six days of gathering manna mentioned in the next verse, Ex. 16:26.
Marah before you had a large number of mitzvot.

COMMENTARY   *The Sabbath is a central pillar of rabbinic Judaism as it was of Biblical religion. Therefore the Sages emphasize its importance whenever the opportunity presents itself. This verse, which seems to be overly wordy and repeats the word today three times, led to all of these various comments. Obviously the implication was not only that if the Israelites in the wilderness observed the Sabbath as Moses commanded they would receive numerous rewards, but that if anyone observes it properly it will bring great benefits.*

29. Exodus 16:34, Mekhilta Vayassa 6, II 124

This [the Ark] was one of ten things created on the Sabbath eve at twilight. Namely:

the rainbow,
the manna,
the rod,
the writing,
the *shamir*,
the tablets,
the opening of the mouth of the earth which swallowed the wicked,
the mouth of the evil Balaam's ass,
the burial place of Moses,
the cave in which Moses and Elijah stood.
   Some add:
Adam's garments and the rod of Aaron with its almonds and blossoms.

Seven things are hidden from men. Namely:

the day of death,
the day of comfort,
the depth of judgment,
the knowledge of what brings reward,
what is in another person's heart,
when the kingship will return to the line of David,
when the guilty kingdom will be uprooted.

COMMENTARY   *Numerical lists of special things were a commonplace among the Sages. The ten things enumerated here were matters of mystic speculation, unusual, special events that are seen as supernatural creations by God during that time which seems to be suspended between the world of active creation and the world that follows the laws God established, as they put it, "the world goes on in its natural way." Thus supernatural events are actually made part of the natural order of the world. Those things hidden from human knowledge include many of the questions that are cause for speculation in religious thinking and that are also challenges to religious belief.*

30. Exodus 17:11, Mekhilta Amalek 1, II 143

THEN WHENEVER MOSES HELD UP HIS HAND, ISRAEL PREVAILED; BUT WHENEVER HE LET DOWN HIS HAND, AMALEK PREVAILED (Ex. 17:11). Could the hands of Moses strengthen Israel or destroy Amalek? Rather whenever Moses raised his hands toward heaven, Israel would look at him and believe in He Who Commanded Moses to do so and God would then perform miracles and wonders for them.

Similarly THEN THE LORD SAID TO MOSES, "MAKE A FIERY SERPENT AND MOUNT IT ON A STANDARD. AND IF ANYONE WHO IS BITTEN LOOKS AT IT, HE SHALL RECOVER" (Num. 21:8). Could the serpent kill or restore life? Rather when Moses did this, Israel would look at him and believe in He Who Commanded Moses to do so and God would send them healing.

Similarly AND THE BLOOD ON THE HOUSES IN WHICH YOU DWELL SHALL BE A SIGN FOR YOU: WHEN I SEE THE BLOOD I WILL PASS OVER YOU SO THAT NO PLAGUE WILL DESTROY YOU (Ex. 12:13). Could the blood be of any use to an angel or to Israel? Rather when Israel did this, putting the blood on their doors, the Holy One would have pity upon them as it is said I WILL PASS OVER YOU SO THAT NO PLAGUE WILL DESTROY YOU.

COMMENTARY   *Miracles, God's active intervention in men's affairs, were not really a problem to the Sages. Sympathetic magic, that is an action that causes an automatic effect or any implication that God was limited, was not acceptable. Signs of blood, images of serpents, raising of hands—none of these could be seen by them as having any effect. These few vestiges of more primitive forms that remain in the Bible seemed too close to pagan ways for the Sages to permit them to be taken literally. They explain them, therefore, as actions that were commanded in order to permit the people to do something that would move God to help them. God, and God alone, can interfere and cause an effect.*

31. Exodus 17:14, Mekhilta Amalek 2, II 158

I WILL UTTERLY BLOT OUT THE MEMORY OF AMALEK FROM UNDER THE HEAVEN (Ex. 17:14)—so that there shall be no descendants at all of Amalek anywhere under the entire heavens.

R. Joshua says, "When Amalek came to harm Israel under the very wings of their Father in Heaven, Moses said to the Holy One, 'Lord of the universe, this evil man has come to destroy Your children from under Your wings. Who will be left to read the scroll of the Torah which You gave them?' "

R. Eleazar of Modi'in says, "When Amalek came to harm Israel under the very wings of their Father in Heaven, Moses said to the Holy One, 'Lord of the universe, Your children whom You intend to scatter in the future to the four winds of heaven, as it is said THOUGH I SWEPT YOU [THERE] LIKE THE FOUR WINDS OF HEAVEN (Zech. 2:10), this evil man has come to destroy them from under Your wings. Who will be left to read the scroll of the Torah which You gave them?' "

R. Eliezer says, "When will their name be blotted out? At the time that idolatry will be uprooted together with idolaters and God alone will [be worshiped] in the world and His kingship will be established for all eternity. At that time THEN THE LORD WILL COME FORTH AND MAKE WAR ON THOSE NATIONS AS HE IS WONT TO MAKE WAR ON A DAY OF BATTLE (Zech. 14:3) AND THE LORD SHALL BE KING OVER ALL THE EARTH; IN THAT DAY THERE SHALL BE ONE LORD WITH ONE NAME (Zech. 14:9). And it says OH, PURSUE THEM IN WRATH AND DESTROY THEM FROM UNDER THE HEAVENS OF THE LORD! (Lam. 3:66)."

R. Nathan says, "Haman came only to serve as a reminder for all generations, as it is said AND THESE DAYS OF PURIM SHALL NEVER

---

31. *a reminder*—of the need to continually fight against Amalek.
THESE DAYS OF PURIM—when a descendant of Amalek, Hamam, attempted to eradicate the Jews and was himself defeated, as recounted in the Book of Esther.

CEASE AMONG THE JEWS, AND THE MEMORY OF THEM SHALL NEVER PERISH AMONG THEIR DESCENDANTS (Esther 9:28)."

COMMENTARY   *Amalek is the perpetual enemy, the very embodiment of evil, which must be destroyed. Although God promises to destroy Amalek, Amalek continued to exist. By connecting the phrase UNDER THE HEAVEN in Exodus 17:14 to the same phrase in Lamentations 3:66, R. Eliezer is able to answer the question as to when the promise of utterly destroying Amalek will be fulfilled: at the end of days when all idolatry will perish. R. Nathan explains that one descendant of Amalek, Haman, served the purpose of establishing the everlasting reminder of the need to eradicate Amalek.*

32. Exodus 18:1, Mekhilta Amalek 3, II 162

JETHRO PRIEST OF MIDIAN, MOSES' FATHER-IN-LAW, HEARD (Ex. 18:1). What news had he heard that caused him to come? He came when he heard about the war against Amalek, for that is what is written immediately before [this verse]. So taught R. Joshua.

R. Eleazar of Modi'in says, "He came when he heard about the giving of the Torah, for when the Torah was given to Israel all the kings of the world trembled in their palaces, as it is said WHILE IN HIS TEMPLE ALL SAY 'GLORY!' (Ps. 29:9). At that time the kings of all the nations of the world gathered together and went to the wicked Balaam. They said to him, 'Balaam, may it not be that God is planning to do to us what He did to the generation of the flood, as it is said THE LORD SAT ENTHRONED AT THE FLOOD (Ps. 29:10)?'

"He said to them, 'Fools! The Holy One has already sworn to Noah that He will not bring another flood, as it is said FOR THIS TO ME IS LIKE THE WATERS OF NOAH: AS I SWORE THAT THE

---

32. *immediately before*   The account of the war against Amalek concludes chap. 17 of Exodus and is followed in Ex. 18:1 by JETHRO HEARD.

the giving of the Torah—in which case this story would take place after the revelation of Sinai, although in the Bible it precedes it. This accords with the rabbinic principle that there is no chronological order in the Torah.

Balaam—the most outstanding prophet or seer of the nations. See Num. 22.

WATERS OF NOAH NEVERMORE WOULD FLOOD THE EARTH
(Isa. 54:9).'

"They said to him, 'Perhaps even if He will not bring a flood of water,
He will bring a flood of fire?'

"He said to them, 'He is not bringing a flood of water or of fire. He is
giving the Torah to His people, as it is said MAY THE LORD GRANT
STRENGTH TO HIS PEOPLE (Ps. 29:11).' When they heard this from
him, they all returned, each man to his place."

COMMENTARY   *Many legends grew up about the revelation at Sinai.
This one interprets Psalm 29 as a comment on that event. The supernatural
sights and sounds that accompanied it frightened the rulers of the nations,
who mistakenly thought that it was the beginning of some cataclysm. Balaam, the supreme prophet of the nations, explains the event to them, to
which they can only proclaim, "Glory!" This legend and the others that
follow are based on the fact that the Bible says that Jethro came when he
heard, but does not tell us what it was that he heard. The Sages supply
some possible answers and also take the opportunity to praise Jethro, who
generally plays a positive role in rabbinic tradition.*

R. Eliezer says, "[Jethro] came when he heard about the splitting of the Sea
of Reeds, for when He split the Sea for Israel, it was heard from one end of
the world to the other, as it is said WHEN ALL THE KINGS OF THE
AMORITES ON THE WESTERN SIDE OF THE JORDAN, AND ALL
THE KINGS OF THE CANAANITES NEAR THE SEA, HEARD
HOW THE LORD HAD DRIED UP THE WATERS (Josh. 5:1). Sim-
ilarly Rahab the harlot said to the messengers of Joshua FOR WE HAVE
HEARD HOW THE LORD DRIED UP THE WATERS OF THE SEA
OF REEDS FOR YOU WHEN YOU LEFT EGYPT... WHEN WE
HEARD ABOUT IT, WE LOST HEART, AND NO MAN HAD ANY
MORE SPIRIT LEFT BECAUSE OF YOU (Josh. 2:10–11)."
They say that Rahab was ten years old when Israel went out of Egypt
and was a harlot for the forty years that Israel was in the wilderness. When
she was fifty, she converted, saying to the Holy One, "Master of the Uni-
verse, I have sinned in three things. Forgive me because of three things: the

---

three things—not specified. Some printed texts, however, add: the laws of menstrual purity,
setting aside a portion of the dough, and the lighting of Sabbath lights, which are the three
principle mitzvot specified for women alone.

rope, the window, and the wall," as it is said THEN SHE LET THEM DOWN BY A ROPE THROUGH THE WINDOW—FOR HER DWELLING WAS AT THE OUTER SIDE OF THE CITY WALL (Josh. 2:15).

JETHRO ... HEARD (Ex. 18:1). He had eight names: Yeter, Jethro, Hever, Hovav, Ben, Reuel, Potiel, and Keni.
> Yeter because he caused the addition (hotir) of a section to the Torah;
> Jethro (Yitro) because he multiplied (hotir) good deeds;
> Hever because he bound himself (nithaber) to God;
> Hovav because he was precious (haviv) to God;
> Ben because he was like a son (ben) to God;
> Reuel because he was like a friend (rea) to God (el);
> Potiel because he desisted (niftar) from idolatry;
> Keni because he was zealous (kan'a) for Heaven and acquired (kana) the
Torah for himself.

Another interpretation: JETHRO ... HEARD. At first he was called only Yeter, as it is said MOSES WENT BACK TO HIS FATHER-IN-LAW YETER (Ex. 4:18). When he performed good deeds a letter was added to his name and he was called Yitro (Jethro).
> Similarly we find that at first Abraham was called Abram. When he performed good deeds a letter was added and he was called Abraham.
> Similarly we find that at first Sarah was called Sarai. When she performed good deeds an important letter was added and she was called Sarah.
> Similarly we find that at first Joshua was called Hoshea. When he performed good deeds a letter was added and he was called Yehoshua (Joshua), as it is said BUT MOSES CHANGED THE NAME OF HOSHEA SON OF NUN TO YEHOSHUA (Num. 13:16).

There are others from whose names a letter was taken.
> We see this in the case of Ephron. At first he was called Ephron. When he extorted the money from our father Abraham a letter was taken

---

the rope   The Hebrew words for these three things all begin with the same letter, "het."
a letter was added to his name   Yeter has three Hebrew letters. Yitro has four.
Abraham   In Hebrew this change requires the addition of only one letter, "hey."
important—or big. Unlike the other instances, the number of letters in her name remained the same, three. Therefore the midrash has to change the format and indicate that the new letter was more important possibly because it appears twice in God's name. Physically the "hey" is also a larger letter than the "yod" it replaced.

away and he was called Ephrn, as it is said ABRAHAM ACCEPTED EPHRON'S TERMS. ABRAHAM PAID OUT TO EPHRN THE MONEY (Gen. 23:16).

Similarly we find that at first Yonadav was called Yehonadav. When he did that deed a letter was taken away and he was called Yonadav. Because of this the Sages said, "One should not associate with the wicked, even to bring him close to the Torah."

33. Exodus 18:3, Mekhilta Amalek 3, II 168

AND HER TWO SONS—OF WHOM ONE WAS NAMED GER-SHOM, THAT IS TO SAY, "I HAVE BEEN A STRANGER IN A FOR-EIGN LAND" (Ex. 18:3). R. Joshua says, "It was indeed a strange land to him." R. Eleazar of Modi'in says, " 'Strange' (nochriya) means estranged from God (necher—Ya)."

Moses said, "When the whole world is worshiping idols, whom shall I worship? He Who Spoke and the world came into being!" For when Moses said to Jethro, "Give me your daughter Zipporah as my wife," Jethro said to him, "I will give her to you as a wife if you accept one condition."

He said to him, "What is it?"

He said to him, "The first son born unto you shall be an idol worshiper. The others may be devoted to Heaven," and [Moses] accepted that.

He said to him, "Swear it unto me," and he did so as it is said MOSES CONSENTED (Ex. 2:21). . . .

That is why the angel intended to kill Moses. Immediately SO ZIP-PORAH TOOK A FLINT AND CUT OFF HER SON'S FORESKIN, AND TOUCHED HIS LEGS WITH IT, SAYING, "YOU ARE TRULY A BRIDEGROOM OF BLOOD TO ME" AND HE LET HIM ALONE (Ex. 4:25–26).

R. Eleazar b. Azariah says, "Detestable is uncircumcision for the wicked

---

that deed   Yonadav (Jonadab), the friend of Amnon, told him how to trick his half-sister Tamar, enabling Amnon to rape her. See 2 Sam. 13.

Because of this—referring to the story of Yonadav. This principle was not accepted by all. On the contrary, Aaron is held in great esteem by the Sages for going out of his way to associate with the wicked and bring them to the Torah.

---

33. *a strange land*   He was not at home there because of the idolatry, as illustrated below.

an idol worshiper   Therefore the child was not circumcised.

uncircumcision   The mention of Zipporah and their two sons in Ex. 18:6 leads the midrash to

are reproached with it, as it is said FOR ALL THOSE NATIONS ARE UNCIRCUMCISED (Jer. 9:25)."

R. Ishmael says, "Great is circumcision for thirteen covenants were made concerning it."

R. Jose the Galilean says, "Great is circumcision for it takes precedence over the Sabbath which is itself of such importance that violating it is punishable by extinction."

R. Joshua b. Korha says, "Great is circumcision for even the merit of Moses could not suspend punishment for its neglect for even a moment."

R. Nehemiah says, "Great is circumcision for it takes precedence over the laws of plagues."

Rabbi Judah the Prince says, "Great is circumcision for all of Moses's many merits could not help him at the time of crises. Here he was going to take Israel out of Egypt, but because he had neglected circumcision for a moment the angel sought to kill him, as it is said AT A NIGHT EN-CAMPMENT ON THE WAY, THE LORD ENCOUNTERED HIM AND SOUGHT TO KILL HIM (Ex. 4:24)."

R. Jose says, "Heaven forbid that [we should say] that that righteous man would neglect circumcision for even a moment! Rather he [faced a dilemma]. To circumcise and then set out would be to place life in jeopardy. Yet how could he tarry and circumcise when God had said to him, 'Go and bring Israel out of Egypt?' Since he tarried, stopping to lodge before performing the circumcision, the angel sought to kill him, as it is said AT A NIGHT ENCAMPMENT ON THE WAY (Ex. 4:24)."

Rabban Simeon b. Gamliel says, "The angel did not seek to kill Moses but to kill the child, as it is said YOU ARE TRULY A BRIDEGROOM OF

---

a discussion of the story related earlier in Ex. 4:24–26 concerning the circumcision of their child and to the merits of circumcision.

thirteen covenants Circumcision is mentioned thirteen times in the Torah and called a covenant.

over the Sabbath The circumcision ceremony must be held on the eighth day of the child's life, even if that day is the Sabbath.

extinction—death at the hands of Heaven and not by a human court.

punishment—the threatened death of the child in the story referred to below.

the law of plaques If the foreskin has discolorations that would normally call for the priest to decide what was to be done, the circumcision is still to take place on the eighth day.

kill Moses The Biblical text is ambiguous as to whom the angel is attempting to kill. Some say it was Moses, others the child.

BLOOD TO ME! (Ex. 4:25). Now who could be called a 'bridegroom,' Moses or the child? You must say—the child."

COMMENTARY   *The mitzvah of circumcision was one of the most problematic aspects of Judaism for non-Jews. During the Hellenistic period it was considered an act of mutilation that desecrated the perfection and beauty of the body. Some Hellenistic Jews attempted to surgically obliterate it. At various times it was prohibited by the Romans and it became one of the significant controversies between Judaism and certain elements of early Christianity who claimed that it need not be observed by those who wished to enter the "new Israel," that is, the Christian faith. Here the Sages explain a difficult story in which circumcision plays an unusual role and interpret it in such a way as to emphasize that no one, not even Moses, could be excused for neglecting it—no matter what the reason. The editor then takes the opportunity to create a collection of sayings that emphasize the centrality of circumcision to Judaism.*

34. Exodus 18:20, Mekhilta Amalek 4, II 182

AND ENJOIN UPON THEM THE LAWS (Ex. 18:20). These are the interpretations. AND THE TEACHINGS (Ex. 18:20). These are the decisions. So taught R. Joshua. R. Eleazar of Modi'in says, "THE LAWS refers to the injunctions concerning sexual relations, as it is said NOT TO ENGAGE IN ANY OF THE ABHORRENT LAWS THAT WERE CARRIED ON BEFORE YOU (Lev. 18:30). AND THE TEACHINGS refers to the decisions."

AND MAKE KNOWN TO THEM THE WAY IN WHICH THEY ARE TO GO (Ex. 18:20). This refers to the study of Torah. AND THE PRACTICES THEY ARE TO FOLLOW (Ex. 18:20). This refers to good deeds. So taught R. Joshua. R. Eleazar of Modi'in says "AND MAKE KNOWN TO THEM—make known to them how they are to live. THE WAY refers to visiting the sick. THEY ARE TO GO refers to burying the dead. IN WHICH refers to acts of lovingkindness. AND THE PRACTICES—this refers to strictly following the law. THAT YOU SHALL GO refers to going beyond the demands of strict law."

---

bridegroom   This designation is reserved for an unmarried male.

---

34. *interpretations*—the rabbinic explanations of Scripture.
decisions of the Sages concerning the various laws.

COMMENTARY   *This brief passage, which is echoed in many places in rabbinic literature, emphasizes the all-encompassing nature of religious observance in rabbinic Judaism. The Israelites are being told not merely to observe the specific laws that are mentioned in the Scripture or even rabbinic law but to mold their lives in the way of goodness, ways that often cannot be specified. Whatever they do must be judged by the standard of the good way, which is based on the principle of lovingkindness and includes acts that go far beyond the strict demands of specific laws. They must perform acts of lovingkindness (hesed, often translated charity), acts of selflessness such as helping the sick and burying the dead and, most importantly, they are told that in addition to observing the laws, they must go beyond them, doing things that are not prescribed and seeking that which is right even if the "law" does not require it. This is the way of Piety (Hasidut).*

35. Exodus 19:2, Mekhilta Bahodesh 1, II 198

ENCAMPED IN THE WILDERNESS (Ex. 19:2). Torah was given openly, in public, in a place belonging to no one, for had Torah been given in the Land of Israel they would have said to the nations of the world, "You have no portion in it!" Since it was given openly, in public, in a place belonging to no one, anyone who wants can come and receive it.

Is it possible that it was given at night? The verse states ON THE THIRD DAY, AS THE MORNING DAWNED (Ex. 19:16). Is it possible that it was given silently? The verse states THERE WAS THUNDER, AND LIGHTNING (Ex. 19:16). Is it possible that the voice was not heard? The verse states THE VOICE OF THE LORD IS POWER; THE VOICE OF THE LORD IS MAJESTY (Ps. 29:4); THE LORD SAT ENTHRONED AT THE FLOOD; THE LORD SITS ENTHRONED, KING FOREVER (Ps. 29:10).

Balaam said to those who stood around him MAY THE LORD GRANT STRENGTH TO HIS PEOPLE and they all proclaimed MAY THE LORD BESTOW ON HIS PEOPLE WELL-BEING (Ps. 29:11).

---

35. *Balaam*   See above, page 130.
STRENGTH—interpreted by the Sages as a reference to Torah.

R. Jose says, "It says I DID NOT SPEAK IN SECRET, AT A SITE IN A LAND OF DARKNESS (Isa. 45:19). From the very beginning I gave it not in a place of darkness, nor in a secret place, nor in an obscure place. I DID NOT SAY [IT IS FOR] THE STOCK OF JACOB (Isa. 45:19)—to them do I give it. SEEK ME OUT IN A WASTELAND (Isa. 45:19)—did I not give it openly? Thus it says I THE LORD, WHO FORETELL RELIABLY, WHO ANNOUNCE WHAT IS TRUE (Isa. 45:19). Before I even gave them the mitzvot I had already given them a reward for them, as it is said BUT ON THE SIXTH DAY, WHEN THEY APPORTION WHAT THEY HAVE BROUGHT IN, IT SHALL PROVE TO BE DOUBLE THE AMOUNT THEY GATHER EACH DAY (Ex. 16:5). And it is written I WILL ORDAIN MY BLESSING FOR YOU IN THE SIXTH YEAR, SO THAT IT SHALL YIELD A CROP SUFFICIENT FOR THREE YEARS (Lev. 25:21). Was it only for those specific mitzvot? The verse says HE GAVE THEM THE LANDS OF NATIONS; THEY INHERITED THE WEALTH OF PEOPLES (Ps. 105:44). Why? THAT THEY MIGHT KEEP HIS LAWS AND OBSERVE HIS TEACHINGS (Ps. 105:45).

R. Eleazar b. R. Jose the Galilean says, "It says HE ISSUED HIS COMMANDS TO JACOB, HIS STATUTES AND RULES TO ISRAEL. HE DID NOT DO SO FOR ANY OTHER NATION (Ps. 147:19–20). What had those wretched nations done that He did not want to give them the Torah? OF SUCH RULES THEY KNOW NOTHING (Ps. 147:20). They themselves did not want to take it, as it is said GOD IS COMING FROM TEMAN, THE HOLY ONE FROM MOUNT PARAN. HIS MAJESTY COVERS THE SKIES, HIS SPLENDOR FILLS THE EARTH: IT IS A BRILLIANT LIGHT WHICH GIVES OFF RAYS ON EVERY SIDE—AND THEREIN HIS GLORY IS ENVELOPED. PESTILENCE MARCHES BEFORE HIM AND PLAGUE AT HIS HEELS. WHEN HE STANDS, HE MAKES THE EARTH SHAKE; WHEN HE GLANCES, HE MAKES NATIONS TREMBLE (Hab. 3:3–6).

AND ENCAMPED IN THE WILDERNESS (Ex. 19:2). Wherever it uses the plural, "they journeyed," "they encamped," it means that they quarreled

---

FROM TEMAN   God is coming to Sinai from the various places where He had offered the Torah to the nations. They, however, had rejected it.

when journeying or encamping. But here it says "vayyihan"—"encamped" (in the singular)—indicating that they were of one heart.

COMMENTARY   *Two streams of thought existed in regard to the question of the nations and the giving of Torah, and sometimes they intermingle. One emphasized that it was open to all and that therefore anyone could take it at any time. The other bitterly castigates the nations for refusing it. Other, more detailed midrashim on this refusal are referred to here but are not made explicit. The nations are mocked. They were so steeped in immorality that they would not even consider these laws demanding ethical conduct.*

36. Exodus 19:10, Mekhilta Bahodesh 3, II 210

AND THE LORD SAID TO MOSES, "GO TO THE PEOPLE AND WARN THEM TO STAY PURE TODAY" (Ex. 19:10). This refers to the fourth day of the week. AND TOMORROW (Ex. 19:10)—the fifth day of the week. LET THEM BE READY FOR THE THIRD DAY (Ex. 19:11)—the sixth day of the week on which the Torah was given.

What did Moses do on the fifth day of the week? He rose early in the morning, and built an altar at the foot of the mountain, as it is said EARLY IN THE MORNING, HE SET UP AN ALTAR AT THE FOOT OF THE MOUNTAIN (Ex. 24:4) and erected TWELVE PILLARS FOR THE TWELVE TRIBES OF ISRAEL (Ex. 24:4). This is the teaching of R. Judah. The Sages say that he erected twelve pillars for each one of the tribes. He built an altar and offered upon it a burnt offering and a peace offering. From the burnt offering he took blood in two cups, a portion for God and a portion for the congregation. From the peace offering he [also] took blood in two cups, a portion for God and a portion for the congregation, as it is said MOSES TOOK ONE PART OF THE BLOOD AND PUT IT IN BASINS (Ex. 24:6). This is the portion for God. AND THE OTHER PART OF THE BLOOD HE DASHED AGAINST THE ALTAR (Ex. 24:6). This is the portion for the congregation.

---

36. *fourth day* Wednesday. Sunday is the first day of the Jewish week, following the pattern of the story of creation.
built an altar In the Biblical account, all of these events occur after the revelation at Sinai.

THEN HE TOOK THE RECORD OF THE COVENANT AND READ IT ALOUD TO THE PEOPLE (Ex. 24:7). This does not tell us, however, what portion he read.

R. Jose b. R. Judah says, "From the beginning of Genesis to this point."

Rabbi Judah the Prince says, "[He read] all of the mitzvot that had been commanded to primal Adam, to the children of Noah, [to Israel] in Egypt and at Marah and all the other mitzvot."

R. Ishmael says, "What was said at the beginning of the section? THE LORD SPOKE TO MOSES ON MOUNT SINAI: SPEAK TO THE ISRAELITE PEOPLE AND SAY TO THEM: WHEN YOU ENTER THE LAND THAT I GIVE YOU, THE LAND SHALL OBSERVE A SABBATH OF THE LORD. SIX YEARS YOU MAY SOW YOUR FIELD (Lev. 25:1–3). [He read about] sabbatical years, the jubilee and the blessings and curses. What was said at the end of the section? THESE ARE THE LAWS, NORMS, AND DIRECTIONS THAT THE LORD ESTABLISHED, THROUGH MOSES ON MOUNT SINAI, BETWEEN HIMSELF AND THE ISRAELITE PEOPLE (Lev. 26:46). They said, 'We accept these laws upon ourselves.' When [Moses] saw that they accepted this upon themselves he took the blood and sprinkled it upon the people, as it is said MOSES TOOK THE BLOOD AND DASHED IT ON THE PEOPLE AND SAID, 'THIS IS THE BLOOD OF THE COVENANT WHICH THE LORD NOW MAKES WITH YOU CONCERNING ALL THESE COMMANDS' (Ex. 24:8). He said to them, 'Now you are tied, held, and bound [to the covenant]. Tomorrow you shall come and accept upon yourselves all of the mitzvot.' "

COMMENTARY   *The chronology of the account of the encampment at Sinai is difficult to understand. Scholars and commentators have long puzzled over exactly what happened and in what sequence. The Sages attempted to give a day-by-day account, identifying the day of the week of the revelation as Friday and working backward from there. They also employed the rabbinic principle that "there is no chronological sequence in the Torah," that is, that portions may have taken place earlier or later. Thus they assume here that the description in Exodus 24:4 occurred not after the revelation*

---

we accept these laws upon ourselves   Prior to the giving of the Torah the Israelites already accepted some of the laws. This proved that they were worthy and prepared to receive the entire Torah.

but during the otherwise unclear days before it. R. Ishmael assumes that the "book of the covenant" referred to there was chapters 25 and 26 of Leviticus. Indeed those chapters do seem to form a unit of their own and specify that they were given at Sinai. When were they spoken at Sinai? R. Ishmael answers: as a prelude to the revelation, serving as a test of the people's willingness to abide by God's mitzvot. Once they accepted these rather difficult ones, Moses was ready to have them accept the rest. R. Judah, however, cannot conceive of the Torah in any other form and says that Moses read them the Torah from the beginning until that point in their history. Others assume that the mitzvot were the main point and were separated from the narrative.

37. Exodus 19:16, Mekhilta Bahodesh 3, II 217

ON THE THIRD DAY, AS MORNING DAWNED (Ex. 19:16). This teaches that God arrived early, thus fulfilling what is said in the verse WHILE THE KING WAS ON HIS COUCH, MY NARD GAVE FORTH ITS FRAGRANCE (Song 1:12).

THERE WAS THUNDER (Ex. 19:16)—thunders upon thunders and all kinds of thunderous noises, different from one another.
AND LIGHTNING (Ex. 19:16)—lightnings upon lightnings and all kinds of lightnings, different from one another.

AND A DENSE CLOUD UPON THE MOUNTAIN (Ex. 19:16). This was the thick darkness, as it is said AND MOSES APPROACHED THE THICK DARKNESS (Ex. 20:18).

AND A VERY LOUD BLAST OF THE HORN (Ex. 19:16). The usual order of things is that the sound grows weaker the longer it is held, but here it grows louder and louder. Why was it soft at the beginning? In order to accustom the ear to hearing it.

---

37. *God arrived early* The sequence indicates that the signs of God's presence upon the mountain, thunder and lightning, preceded the approach of Moses or the people to the mountain. God, as a sign of love, awaits the people, the bride, rather than the other way around.
louder and louder—as indicated by Ex. 19:19.
to accustom the ear—to lead the people gradually toward being able to accept the full force of a Divine revelation.

AND ALL THE PEOPLE WHO WERE IN THE CAMP TREMBLED (Ex. 19:16). This teaches that they were shocked.

MOSES LED THE PEOPLE OUT OF THE CAMP TOWARD GOD (Ex. 19:17). Said R. Jose, "Thus did Judah expound the text THE LORD CAME FROM SINAI (Deut. 33:2): Do not read it thus but rather 'The Lord came *to* Sinai' to give Torah to Israel. But I say that THE LORD CAME FROM SINAI is correct—He came to receive Israel as a bridegroom goes out to meet the bride."

AND THEY TOOK THEIR PLACES (Ex. 19:17). They crowded together. This teaches that they were afraid of the wind, the quaking, the thunder, and the lightning that inundated them.

AT THE FOOT OF THE MOUNTAIN (Ex. 19:17). This teaches that the mountain was uprooted from its place and they drew near and stood underneath it, as it is said AND STOOD UNDER THE MOUNTAIN (Deut. 4:11). Of them it is said in the writings O MY DOVE, IN THE CRANNY OF THE ROCKS, HIDDEN BY THE CLIFF, LET ME SEE YOUR FACE (Song 2:14)—this refers to the twelve pillars representing the twelve tribes. LET ME HEAR YOUR VOICE (Song 2:14)—this refers to the Ten Pronouncements. FOR YOUR VOICE IS SWEET (Song 2:14)—after the Ten Pronouncements. AND YOUR FACE IS COMELY (Song 2:14)—when THE WHOLE COMMUNITY CAME FORWARD AND STOOD BEFORE THE LORD (Lev. 9:5).

R. Eliezer said, "These verses refer to what happened at the Sea of Reeds. LET ME SEE YOUR FACE (Song 2:14)—refers to [that which Moses said] STAND BY, AND WITNESS THE DELIVERANCE WHICH THE LORD WILL WORK FOR YOU TODAY (Ex. 14:13). LET ME HEAR YOUR VOICE (Song 2:14) refers to GREATLY FRIGHTENED, THE ISRAELITES CRIED OUT TO THE LORD (Ex. 14:10). FOR YOUR VOICE IS SWEET (Song 2:14) refers to AND THEY CRIED OUT AND THEIR CRY FOR HELP FROM THE BONDAGE ROSE

---

as a bridegroom At a wedding the custom is for the groom to leave the bridal canopy and walk toward the bride and then bring her under it with him. Thus God is indeed coming *from* Sinai, the bridal canopy (see below), to meet Israel the bride.

underneath it—understanding *tachtit*, usually translated "at the foot of," in a literal fashion as "underneath." Thus in this image the people are standing not at the foot at Sinai but actually underneath the mountain, which is held above them as a bridal canopy.

UP TO GOD (Ex. 2:23). AND YOUR FACE IS COMELY (Song 2:14) when HE PERFORMED THE SIGNS IN THE SIGHT OF ALL THE PEOPLE, AND THE PEOPLE WERE CONVINCED (Ex. 4:30–31)."

Another interpretation: FOR YOUR VOICE IS SWEET (Song 2:14)—at the Sea when I WILL SING TO THE LORD, FOR HE HAS TRIUMPHED GLORIOUSLY (Ex. 15:1). AND YOUR FACE IS COMELY (Song 2:14)—when FROM THE MOUTHS OF INFANTS AND SUCKLINGS YOU HAVE FOUNDED STRENGTH (Ps. 8:3).

COMMENTARY   *Once again the allegorical interpretation of the Song of Songs is utilized in connection with events in the history of Israel. The revelation at Sinai or, alternatively, the splitting of the Sea, is the occasion for those verses. God is pictured as the bridegroom who follows the custom of leaving his place to greet the bride and bring her beneath the marriage canopy. By an ingenious interpretation of the word tachtit (AT THE FOOT) to mean not the foot of the mountain but literally "underneath it," Sinai itself is transformed into the wedding canopy, which hovers over the heads of the people Israel as they receive the Ten Pronouncements, the text of the wedding agreement. Thus the covenant is really a marriage. The Ten Pronouncements (a more literal translation of "the Ten Commandments") are the terms of the Ketubah, the marriage contract.*

38. Exodus 19:20, Mekhilta Bahodesh 4, II 224

THE LORD CAME DOWN UPON MOUNT SINAI (Ex. 19:20). I might have thought that [He came down] upon the entire [mountain], therefore the verse states ON THE TOP OF THE MOUNTAIN (Ex. 19:20). Could this mean that His Glory actually descended and rested upon Mt. Sinai? The verse says I SPOKE TO YOU FROM THE VERY HEAVENS (Ex. 20:19), thus teaching that the Holy One bent the lower heavens and the upper heavens onto the mountain and His Glory descended and rested upon the top of Mt. Sinai. It would be similar to a man who places a mattress upon a bed and speaks from on top of the mattress. . . .

---

38. *thus teaching* Since the verse states explicitly that He spoke from Heaven, He could not have been on the mountain. What then does it mean when it says that He came down on the mountain?

speaks from on top of the mattress—but it would be equally correct to say that he spoke from on top of the bed. Thus it can say of God that He spoke from the mountain even though He remained in Heaven and really spoke from there.

R. Jose says, "It says THE HEAVENS BELONG TO THE LORD, BUT THE EARTH HE GAVE OVER TO MAN (Ps. 115:16). Neither Moses nor Elijah ascended to Heaven nor did the Glory of God descend [to earth]. Rather [these verses] teach that God said to Moses, 'I shall call to you from the top of the mountain and you will go up it,' as it is said AND THE LORD CALLED MOSES TO THE TOP OF THE MOUNTAIN AND MOSES WENT UP (Ex. 19:20)."

COMMENTARY   *The difficulty these midrashim seek to overcome is the implication in the text that God actually descended onto earth. Paganism blurred the boundaries between man and the gods, between heaven and earth. To the rabbis, the idea of God descending or man ascending to heaven was not acceptable. This may be seen both as an extension of the Biblical concept of God as totally other and as a reaction to other religions. God does not become man, nor man God. If God coming down on a mountain top were to be thus understood, it would contradict the basic concept of God held by the religion of Israel.*

39. Exodus 20:1, Mekhilta Bahodesh 4, II 227

GOD SPOKE (Ex. 20:1). Whenever the term "God" is used it always refers to God as judge. He is a judge who will faithfully exact punishment and dispense reward. Since there are sections of the Torah the observance of which brings reward but whose neglect does not exact punishment, I might have thought that this was so in regard to the Ten Pronouncements. Therefore the verse states GOD SPOKE and "God" always refers to God as judge. He is a judge who will exact punishment and dispense reward.

ALL THESE WORDS (Ex. 20:1). This teaches that God uttered the Ten Pronouncements in one utterance, something that no human being can do, as it is said GOD SPOKE ALL THESE WORDS SAYING. If so, why

---

nor Elijah   Regardless of the fact that the Scripture states that he went up to Heaven (2 Kings 2:11), this must not be taken literally.

from the top—but He will be above the mountain. Moses will ascend the mountain, but will not go into Heaven.

---

39. *the term God*   The rabbis established the principle that the two names of God had different connotations. *Elohim* (God) indicated justice since the same word is used for human judges, while *adonai* (Lord) referred to mercy, since this is the name used in the verse delineating His qualities: The Lord! the Lord! a God compassionate and gracious (Ex. 34:6).

does the verse state I THE LORD AM YOUR GOD ... YOU SHALL HAVE NO OTHER GOD BESIDE ME ... (Ex. 20:2-3)? This teaches that the Holy One said the Ten Pronouncements in one utterance but then repeated and spelled them out one by one individually. I might have thought that this was so concerning all the other pronouncements in the Torah as well, that they too were said in one utterance, therefore the verse says ALL THESE WORDS—these words were said in one utterance while all the other pronouncements in the Torah were uttered individually.

SAYING (Ex. 20:1). This teaches that they said "yes" to each positive one and "no" to each negative one, so taught R. Ishmael. R. Akiba says, "They answered yes to the positive and yes to the negative."

Another interpretation: SAYING—"Go out and say [this] to them and let Me know what they reply." How do we know that Moses repeated their words to the Almighty? It is said, AND MOSES BROUGHT BACK THE PEOPLE'S WORD TO THE LORD (Ex. 19:8). What were the words of the people which he repeated? ALL THAT THE LORD HAS SPOKEN WE WILL FAITHFULLY DO (Ex. 24:7)! And how do we know that God was pleased with their words? As it is said AND THE LORD SAID TO ME ... THEY DID WELL TO SPEAK THUS (Deut. 5:25).

I THE LORD AM YOUR GOD (Ex. 20:2). Why were the Ten Pronouncements not said at the beginning of the Torah? A parable. It may be likened to a king who entered a city. He said to [the people], "I shall rule over you," but they said to him, "Have you brought us any benefits at all that [give you the right] to rule over us?" What did he do? He built them a wall, brought water within for them, and waged war for them. Then he said to them, "I shall rule over you." They said, "Yes, Oh, yes." Thus God brought Israel out of Egypt, split the Sea for them, brought down manna for them, caused the well to spring up for them, brought the quail for them, and

---

in one utterance   The word *all* is taken literally, indicating that He said them all at once.

they said "yes"   The word *saying* is superfluous and indicates something additional. It teaches that the Israelites said something, answering after hearing each Pronouncement.

beginning of the Torah   What need was there for them to receive all the historical material before hearing the Ten Pronouncements?

water within—the walls. Not having a source of water within the walls would render the city vulnerable to siege.

the well   On the miraculous well see Num. 21:17.

waged war for them against Amalek. [Then] He said to them, "I shall rule over you," and they replied, "Yes, Oh, yes."

R. Judah the Prince says, "This informs us how praiseworthy Israel was, for when they all stood before Mt. Sinai to receive the Torah, all of them were united as one to accept the kingship of God with joy. Not only that, but they stood surety for each other. God wanted to make a covenant with them concerning not only those deeds which are done in public, but also those which are hidden, as it is said CONCEALED ACTS CONCERN THE LORD OUR GOD; AND OVERT ACTS (Deut. 29:28)." They said to Him, "We will make a covenant with You concerning those deeds which are done in public, but not those which are hidden lest one of us sin secretly and the entire congregation be responsible for him!"

I THE LORD AM YOUR GOD (Ex. 20:2). R. Nathan said, "This is a refutation of the heretics who contend that there are two divine powers, for when the Holy One stood and proclaimed I THE LORD AM YOUR GOD, who arose to contradict Him? If you say that this was done in secret, is it not stated I DID NOT SPEAK IN SECRET, AT A SITE IN A LAND OF DARKNESS (Isa. 45:19). I DID NOT SAY TO THE STOCK OF JACOB (Isa. 45:19) that I am giving it only to them, but SEEK ME OUT IN A WASTELAND (Isa. 45:19). Nor did I give it only as a pledge. Thus it says I THE LORD, WHO FORETELL RELIABLY, WHO AN-NOUNCE WHAT IS TRUE (Isa. 45:19)."

Another interpretation: I THE LORD AM YOUR GOD (Ex. 20:2). When the Holy One stood and said I THE LORD AM YOUR GOD the mountains quaked and the hills collapsed. Tabor came from Bet Elim and Carmel from Aspamea, as it is said AS I LIVE—DECLARED THE KING, WHOSE NAME IS LORD OF HOSTS—AS SURELY AS TABOR AMONG THE MOUNTAINS AND CARMEL BY THE SEA WILL COME (Jer. 46:18). This one said, "I have been summoned," and that one said, "I have been summoned!" When they heard from His mouth WHO BROUGHT YOU OUT OF THE LAND OF EGYPT (Ex. 20:2) they stood again at their own places saying, "He is only dealing with those He brought out of Egypt."

---

to contradict Him   Since no other divine power proclaimed its existence then, this proves that there is only one God.

Another interpretation: I THE LORD AM YOUR GOD (Ex. 20:2). When the Holy One stood and said I THE LORD AM YOUR GOD the earth trembled, as it is said O LORD, WHEN YOU CAME FORTH FROM SEIR, ADVANCED FROM THE COUNTRY OF EDOM, THE EARTH TREMBLED (Judges 5:4). Then it goes on THE MOUNTAINS QUAKED BEFORE THE LORD (Judges 5:5). And it says THE VOICE OF THE LORD IS POWER; THE VOICE OF THE LORD IS MAJESTY (Ps. 29:4) until WHILE IN HIS TEMPLE ALL SAY "GLORY!" (Ps. 29:9), until their houses were filled with the brightness of the Divine Presence. . . .

The nations of the world were offered [the Torah] so that they should have no excuse to say, "Had we been offered it, we would have accepted it." They were offered it and they did not accept it, as it is said THE LORD CAME FROM SINAI; HE SHONE UPON THEM FROM SEIR (Deut. 33:2). He revealed Himself to the children of the wicked Esau and said to them, "Will you accept upon yourselves the Torah" They said to Him, "What is written in it?" He said to them, "YOU SHALL NOT MURDER" (Ex. 20:13). They said to Him, "But this is the very inheritance bequeathed us by our father YET BY YOUR SWORD YOU SHALL LIVE (Gen. 27:40)."

He revealed Himself to the Ammonites and the Moabites and said to them, "Will you accept the Torah?" They said to Him, "What is written in it?" He said to them, "YOU SHALL NOT COMMIT ADULTERY" (Ex. 20:13). They said to Him that they were all the offspring of adultery, as it is said THUS THE TWO DAUGHTERS OF LOT CAME TO BE WITH CHILD BY THEIR FATHER. THE OLDER ONE BORE A SON AND NAMED HIM MOAB; HE IS THE FATHER OF THE MOABITES OF TODAY. AND THE YOUNGER ALSO BORE A SON, AND SHE CALLED HIM BEN-AMMI; HE IS THE FATHER OF THE AMMONITES OF TODAY (Gen. 19:36–38).

He revealed Himself to the Ishmaelites and said to them, "Will you accept the Torah?" They said to Him, "What is written in it?" He said to them, "YOU SHALL NOT STEAL" (Ex. 20:13). They said to Him, "But this is the very blessing which was bestowed upon our father HE SHALL BE A WILD ASS OF A MAN; HIS HAND AGAINST EVERYONE

---

wicked Esau—always understood as a reference to Rome.
NOT STEAL This was understood by the Sages to refer to the stealing of persons, kidnapping. The Ishmaelites had kidnapped Joseph.

(Gen. 16:12) and it is written FOR IN TRUTH I WAS STOLEN FROM THE LAND OF THE HEBREWS . . . (Gen. 40:15)."

But when He came to Israel AT HIS RIGHT HAND A FIERY LAW FOR THEM (Deut. 33:2), they all opened their mouths and said, ALL THAT THE LORD HAS SPOKEN WE WILL FAITHFULLY DO! (Ex. 24:7). That is what is said: WHEN HE STANDS, HE MAKES THE EARTH SHAKE; WHEN HE GLANCES, HE MAKES NATIONS TREMBLE (Hab. 3:6).

R. Simon b. Eleazar says, "If [the nations] could not manage to observe the seven mitzvot commanded to the children of Noah, how would they possibly observe all the mitzvot of the Torah? A parable. A king appointed two overseers, one responsible for the treasury of grain and the other for the treasury of silver and gold. The one responsible for grain was under suspicion, but complained that he had not been placed in charge of silver and gold. They said to him, 'Fool! If you could not be trusted with the grain, do you suppose they would put you in charge of the silver and gold?' This is a matter of logical inference. If they could not manage to observe the seven mitzvot commanded to the children of Noah, how would they possibly observe all the mitzvot of the Torah?"

Why was the Torah not given in the Land of Israel? In order not to give an excuse to the nations of the world to say, "We did not accept it because it was given in their land." Another answer: So that there should be no quarrel among the tribes, for this one would then say, "In my territory was the Torah given" and that one would say, "In my territory was the Torah given." Therefore it was given in the wilderness, openly, in public in a place belonging to no one.

The Torah is compared to three things: the wilderness, fire, and water, indicating that just as these things are free for all creatures of the world, so the teachings of Torah are free for all the creatures of the world.

---

seven mitzvot Tradition elaborated on the Biblical account of mankind after the flood and said that at that time a new covenant was made requiring humans to observe seven rules: courts of justice; prohibition of blasphemy, of idolatry, of incest, of bloodshed, of theft, of eating flesh cut from a living animal. See Gen. 9. Rabbinic tradition frequently states that the nations had never abided by these seven. What right did they have to complain, therefore, that they were not to be trusted with 613 mitzvot of the Torah?

free for all creatures The Torah remains openly available to all humankind.

WHO BROUGHT YOU OUT OF THE LAND OF EGYPT, THE
HOUSE OF BONDAGE (avadim) (Ex. 20:2). They were slaves to kings.
You say that they were slaves to kings—were they not rather slaves to slaves
(avadim)? When it says RESCUED YOU FROM THE HOUSE OF
BONDAGE, FROM THE POWER OF PHARAOH KING OF EGYPT
(Deut. 7:8) it makes it clear that they were slaves to kings and not slaves to
slaves.

Another interpretation: THE HOUSE OF BONDAGE (avadim) the house
of worshipers (ovdim) for they were worshipers of idolatry.

YOU SHALL HAVE NO OTHER GODS BESIDES ME (Ex. 20:3). Why
is this said? Because of the verse I THE LORD AM YOUR GOD (Ex.
20:2). A parable. A human king entered a town and his servants said to him,
"Proclaim your edicts to them!" He said to them, "No. When they have
accepted my kingship I will proclaim my edicts, for if they do not accept my
kingship, how will they observe my edicts?" Thus God said to Israel, "I
THE LORD AM YOUR GOD—I am He whose kingship you accepted
upon yourselves in Egypt." They said to Him, "Yes, oh, yes." "You accepted My kingship, accept now My edicts: YOU SHALL HAVE NO
OTHER GODS BESIDES ME."

R. Simon b. Yohai says, "That is indeed the meaning of what is said later I
THE LORD AM YOUR GOD (Lev. 18:2)"—"I am He whose kingship
you accepted at Sinai." They said to Him, "Yes, Oh, yes." "You accepted
My kingship, accept now My edicts: YOU SHALL NOT COPY THE
PRACTICES OF THE LAND OF EGYPT (Lev. 18:3)."

That is the meaning of what is said here. I THE LORD AM YOUR GOD
WHO BROUGHT YOU OUT OF THE LAND OF EGYPT (Ex.
20:2)—"I am He whose kingship you accepted." They said to Him, "Yes,
oh, yes." "You accepted My kingship, accept now My edicts: YOU SHALL
HAVE NO OTHER GODS BESIDES ME."

---

slaves to slaves   THE HOUSE OF BONDAGE could be translated "the house of slaves,"
implying that their masters were themselves slaves.
accept now My edicts   The second Pronouncement could not be uttered until it was clear that
Israel had accepted the Kingship of God as proclaimed in the first Pronouncement.

COMMENTARY   *The Sages taught that there are two "yokes" that the Jew must accept on himself: the yoke of God's kingship and the yoke of His mitzvot. This concept is the basis of these midrashim. The people of Israel had first to freely accept God as their ruler and pledge their loyalty to Him. Once they have done this, He can proclaim the rules and regulations they must follow. If He is indeed their king, they will readily accept His decrees. Thus the opening statement of the Ten Pronouncements is not a decree or command but a statement reminding them that He is their ruler whom they have accepted. The first of His regulations is that they are not to worship other so-called gods. The twice daily recitation of the Shema (Hear, O Israel) in Jewish worship repeats this pattern. The first paragraph is considered the acceptance of God's kingship and the second, the acceptance of His mitzvot.*

YOU SHALL HAVE NO OTHER GODS BESIDES ME (Ex. 20:3). Why is this said? When it says YOU SHALL NOT MAKE FOR YOURSELVES A SCULPTURED IMAGE (Ex. 20:4) this only prohibits the making of idols. What prohibits me from keeping those that were already made? Therefore the verse says YOU SHALL HAVE NO OTHER GODS.

OTHER GODS (Ex. 20:3). Are they really divine? Does it not say AND HAVE COMMITTED THEIR GODS TO THE FLAMES AND HAVE DESTROYED THEM; FOR THEY ARE NOT GODS (Isa. 37:19)? What then is the meaning of OTHER GODS? Others ascribe to them divinity. Another interpretation: OTHER (aherim) GODS—they delay (maherim) the coming of goodness into the world. Another interpretation: OTHER GODS—They cause those who worship them to be other. Another interpretation: OTHER GODS. They are other [strangers] to those who worship them. Thus it says IF THEY CRY OUT TO IT, IT DOES NOT ANSWER; IT CANNOT SAVE THEM FROM THEIR DISTRESS (Isa. 46:7).

R. Jose says, "Why does it say OTHER GODS (Ex. 20:3)? In order not to give the nations of the world an excuse to say, 'Were they to be called by

---

to be other—to be estranged from the true God. The word *other* (aher) denotes a heretic.

the proper name, they would be useful.' Here they are called by the proper name and nevertheless they are useless. When [else] were they called by the proper name? In the days of Enosh son of Seth, as it is said IT WAS THEN THAT MEN BEGAN TO INVOKE BY THE NAME OF THE LORD (Gen. 4:26). At that time the ocean rose and inundated a third of the world. God said to them, 'You have done a new thing, calling yourselves divine. I too shall do a new thing and will call Myself LORD,' thus it says WHO SUMMONS THE WATERS OF THE SEA AND POURS THEM OUT UPON THE EARTH—HIS NAME IS THE LORD! (Amos 5:8)."

R. Eliezer says, "OTHER GODS (Ex. 20:3). They change their gods every day. How so? He had an idol of gold but needed the gold, so he made an idol of silver. He had an idol of silver but needed the silver, so he made one of bronze. He had one of bronze but needed the bronze so he made one of iron. And so on with tin and lead, as it is says GODS THEY HAD NOT KNOWN, NEW ONES, WHO CAME BUT LATELY (Deut. 32:17)."

R. Isaac says, "All the parchment in the world would not be sufficient to list the names of all the idols."

R. Hananya b. Antigonos says, "Come and see the language the Torah uses—TO MOLECH (Lev. 18:21)—anything that you accept as ruling (tamlichuhu) over you, even a piece of dust or a shard."

Rabbi Judah the Prince says, "OTHER (aherim) GODS (Ex. 20:3). The last (aharonim), for they came after the very last of all creations. Who was the last of all creations? The one who calls them divinities!"

BESIDE ME (Ex. 20:3). Why is this said? So as not to give Israel an excuse to say: Only those who left Egypt were commanded concerning idolatry. Therefore it says BESIDE ME meaning that "Just as I live and endure forever, so you, your child and your child's child shall not worship idols until the end of all generations."

---

proper name They are referred to as "elohim," the same word used to refer to the Lord. Therefore their powerlessness does not come from the lack of appropriate nomenclature but from their nonexistence.

they change their gods—therefore they are referred to as "other gods" since there are constantly other ones.

the last Unlike God, who existed before all else, these so-called gods came into being, i.e., were invented, after all else by humans, the last of God's creations.

YOU SHALL NOT MAKE FOR YOURSELF A SCULPTURED IM-
AGE (Ex. 20:4). He may not make himself an engraving, but perhaps he
may make one which is solid? The verse says OR ANY LIKENESS
(Ex. 20:4).

He may not make himself one which is solid, but perhaps he may plant
a sacred tree? The verse says YOU SHALL NOT PLANT A POLE
(Deut. 16:21).

He may not plant a sacred tree, but perhaps he may make an idol of
wood? The verse says OF ANY KIND OF WOOD (Deut. 16:21).

He may not make one of wood, but perhaps he may make one of stone?
The verse says OR PLACE FIGURED STONES (Lev. 26:1). He may not
make one of stone, but perhaps he may make one of silver or gold? The
verse says YOU SHALL NOT MAKE ANY GODS OF SILVER, NOR
SHALL YOU MAKE FOR YOURSELVES ANY GODS OF GOLD
(Ex. 20:20).

He may not make one of silver or gold, but perhaps he may make one
of bronze, iron, or tin? The verse says DO NOT TURN TO IDOLS OR
MAKE MOLTEN GODS FOR YOURSELVES (Lev. 19:4).

He may not make an image of any of these, but perhaps he may make
an image of a figure? The verse says NOT TO ACT WICKEDLY AND
MAKE FOR YOURSELVES A SCULPTURED IMAGE IN ANY LIKE-
NESS WHATSOEVER (Deut. 4:16).

He may not make an image of a figure, but perhaps he may make an
image of cattle or fowl? The verse says, THE FORM OF ANY BEAST
ON EARTH, THE FORM OF ANY WINGED BIRD THAT FLIES IN
THE SKY (Deut. 4:17).

He may not make an image of any of these, but perhaps he may make
an image of fish, locust, unclean animals, and crawling things? The verse
says THE FORM OF ANYTHING THAT CREEPS ON THE
GROUND, THE FORM OF ANY FISH THAT IS IN THE WATERS
BELOW THE EARTH (Deut. 4:18).

He may not make an image of all those, but perhaps he may make an
image of the sun, the moon, the stars, and the planets? The verse says AND
WHEN YOU LOOK UP TO THE SKY AND BEHOLD THE SUN
AND THE MOON AND THE STARS, THE WHOLE HEAVENLY
HOST (Deut. 4:19).

He may not make an image of those, but perhaps he may make an image
of angels, cherubim, and ophanim? The verse says WHAT IS IN THE

---

ophanim   Heavenly creatures such as those described in the first chapter of Ezekiel.

HEAVENS ABOVE (Ex. 20:4). One might think that IN THE HEAVENS refers to images of the sun, the moon, the stars, and the planets. Therefore the verse says OF WHAT IS IN THE HEAVENS ABOVE (Ex. 20:4)—not the image of angels, not the image of cherubim, and not the image of ophanim.

He may not make an image of any of these, but perhaps he may make an image of the deep or the darkness? The verse says OR IN THE WATERS UNDER THE EARTH (Ex. 20:4)—which includes reflected images. So taught R. Akiba. There are those who say that it means to include the sha-briri (demons).

The Scripture certainly goes out of its way to pursue the evil inclination in order to eliminate any possibility of one finding the least excuse to permit [idolatry]!

YOU SHALL NOT BOW DOWN TO THEM OR SERVE THEM (Ex. 20:5). Why is this said? When it states TURNING TO THE WORSHIP OF OTHER GODS AND BOWING DOWN TO THEM (Deut. 17:3) we learn that one is liable for worshiping by itself and one is liable for bowing down by itself.

This is your contention, but perhaps one is not liable unless he both worships and bows down?

The verse says YOU SHALL NOT BOW DOWN TO THEM OR SERVE THEM, clearly indicating that one is liable for worshiping by itself and for bowing down by itself.

Another interpretation: YOU SHALL NOT BOW DOWN TO THEM (Ex. 20:5). Why is this said? When it states WHOEVER SACRIFICES TO A GOD OTHER THAN THE LORD ALONE SHALL BE PRO-SCRIBED (Ex. 22:19) it indicates the punishment, but where do we find the warning? The verse states YOU SHALL NOT BOW DOWN TO THEM and it also says FOR YOU MUST NOT BOW DOWN TO ANY OTHER GOD (Ex. 34:14).

---

reflected images—often worshiped in the ancient world and considered to have independent existence.

the warning According to the Sages, there must be both a prohibition and a warning against violating the prohibition.

EXODUS

FOR I THE LORD YOUR GOD AM A JEALOUS GOD (Ex. 20:5). Rabbi Judah the Prince says, "I am the God over jealousy. I rule over jealousy and jealousy does not rule over Me. I rule over slumber and slumber does not rule over Me. Thus it says SEE, THE GUARDIAN OF ISRAEL NEITHER SLUMBERS NOR SLEEPS! (Ps. 121:4)."

Another interpretation: FOR I THE LORD YOUR GOD AM A JEALOUS GOD (Ex. 20:5). Jealously I exact punishment upon idolatry but I am gracious and merciful in all other matters.

A philosopher asked Rabban Gamliel, "In your Torah it is written FOR I THE LORD YOUR GOD AM A JEALOUS GOD. Does an idol have enough power to arouse jealousy? A hero is jealous of another hero. A sage is jealous of another sage. A wealthy man is jealous of another wealthy man. Does then an idol have enough power to arouse jealousy?"

He said to him, "If a man were to give his dog his father's name and then swear by the life of that dog, of whom would the father be jealous, the son or the dog?"

[The philosopher] said to him, "Some of them are useful."

He said to him, "What have you seen to indicate that?"

He said to him, "There was once a fire in a certain city and the temple of idolatry was saved. Was it not because it had some power of its own?"

[Rabban Gamliel] said to him, "Let me tell you a parable. It may be likened to a human king who went to war. Against whom does he fight? The living or the dead?"

---

over jealousy   The word *jealous* does not describe God, i.e., "a jealous God," but is understood as "the God *of* jealousy," the God who controls jealousy.

jealously   The Hebrew word *kana* means to be extreme. The translation and understanding of the verb therefore vacillates between "jealous" and "zealous."

philosopher—a non-Jew.

to arouse jealousy   Does this not mean that idols are real? Otherwise why would God be jealous of them?

or the dog   There is nothing in the idol that arouses jealousy. Idols are no more important than the dog in this story. But if a human being calls this idol "god," God will be jealous not of the idol but of His honor.

are useful   They seem to have power or utilitarian effect.

the living   Since the idol has no life, no importance, why bother to destroy it?

He said to him, "The living." Then he said, "But if they have no usefulness at all why does He not simply do away with them?"

He said to him, "Do you worship only one type of thing? Do you not worship the sun, the moon, the stars, and the planets, mountains, hills, springs, and valleys and even human beings? Shall He destroy His world because of fools? [SHALL] I SWEEP EVERYTHING AWAY FROM THE FACE OF THE EARTH—DECLARES THE LORD (Zeph. 1:2).

(The philosopher) said, "But if they indeed cause the wicked to stumble, should He not remove them from the world?"

He said to him, "Because of fools? Because (they worship) humans (SHALL) I DESTROY MANKIND FROM THE FACE OF THE EARTH?—DECLARES THE LORD (Zeph. 1:3)?"

VISITING THE GUILT OF THE FATHERS UPON THE CHILDREN (Ex. 20:5)—when there is no break but not when there is a break. What does this mean? When he is the wicked son of a wicked son of a wicked person. R. Nathan says, "A destroyer the son of a destroyer the son of a destroyer." When Moses heard this MOSES HASTENED TO BOW LOW TO THE GROUND IN HOMAGE (Ex. 34:8). He said, "Heaven forbid. There is no such thing among the people Israel as a wicked son of a wicked son of a wicked person!"

Is it possible that just as the Quality of Punishment extends for four generations, so the Quality of Goodness extends only for four generations? The verse states TO THE THOUSANDTH (Ex. 20:6). Since it says TO THE THOUSANDTH I might think that it is limited to two thousand years. The verse says TO THE THOUSANDTH GENERATION (Deut. 7:9) indicating that there is absolutely no boundary or limit.

OF THOSE WHO LOVE ME AND KEEP MY COMMANDMENTS (Ex. 20:6). THOSE WHO LOVE ME refers to our father Abraham and those like him. AND KEEP MY COMMANDMENTS—this refers to all

---

no break—in the genealogical chain of evildoers. Those who carry the burden of the sins of the fathers are only those who directly follow in that path of wickedness which is passed on for at least three generations running.

When Moses heard—he bowed in thankfulness. He was overjoyed because there were none among the people of Israel to whom this could possibly apply.

two thousand years Since the Hebrew word is the plural "thousands," it implies at least two thousand, but could refer to years and not generations. The verse in Deuteronomy, however, adds the word *generation*, thus making it explicit.

who dwell in the Land of Israel and give their lives for the sake of the mitzvot.

"Why are you being taken out to be executed?" "Because I circumcised my son."

"Why are you being taken out to be burned?" "Because I read the Torah."

"Why are you being taken out to be crucified?" "Because I ate the *matzah*."

"Why are you being punished with a hundred lashes?" "Because I waved the *lulab*."

It is said FROM BEING BEATEN IN THE HOMES OF MY FRIENDS (Zech. 13:6). These wounds cause me to be beloved to my Father Who is in Heaven.

COMMENTARY   *Rabbinic literature defines God, as it were, by ascribing to Him two qualities (middot), the qualities of mercy and justice, sometimes called as they are here, the qualities of goodness and punishment or suffering. Whenever a comparison is drawn between the two, it is invariably in favor of the quality of mercy. Punishment and strict justice may exist in the world, but God's mercies outweigh them, as we see here, by a ratio of four to infinity. The reality of life in the Land of Israel during the Tannaitic period, however, was of death and suffering under the rule of the Romans. This was especially so during the years of the Hadrianic persecutions when performance of the rites of Judaism was forbidden and punishable by death. Thus the examples given here are drawn from life and are not mere imaginings. The assertion of this midrash, however, is that these sufferings are not to be interpreted as punishments from Heaven, but as wounds inflicted by an enemy that will cause God, the Friend of Israel, to love Israel even more.*

40. Exodus 20:7, Mekhilta Bahodesh 7, II 248

YOU SHALL NOT SWEAR FALSELY BY THE NAME OF THE LORD YOUR GOD (Ex. 20:7). Why is this said? When it says YOU SHALL NOT SWEAR FALSELY BY MY NAME (Lev. 19:12) I know

---

for the sake of the mitzvot   They are willing to be executed rather than abandon God's ways.
matzah—the unleavened bread eaten at Passover.
lulab—the palm branch used at Tabernacles.
MY FRIENDS—referring to God.

that swearing is not allowed, but what teaches that one should not even take it upon himself to swear? The verse states YOU SHALL NOT SWEAR FALSELY BY THE NAME OF THE LORD YOUR GOD (Ex. 20:7). Before you take it upon yourself to swear, I am God to you, but once you take it upon yourself to swear I am your judge. Thus it says FOR THE LORD WILL NOT CLEAR ONE WHO SWEARS FALSELY BY HIS NAME (Ex. 20:7).

R. Eliezer says, "It is impossible to say WILL NOT CLEAR (Ex. 20:7) when elsewhere it says WILL CLEAR (Ex. 34:7) nor can it say WILL CLEAR when elsewhere it says WILL NOT CLEAR! Therefore we must understand that it means that HE WILL CLEAR those who repent and HE WILL NOT CLEAR those who do not repent."

R. Matya b. Heresh went to R. Eleazar ha-Kappar at Laodicea to clarify a teaching concerning four things. He said to him, "My master, have you heard the teaching of R. Ishmael concerning four types of atonement?"

He said to him, "One verse says TURN BACK, REBELLIOUS CHILDREN—DECLARES THE LORD. THOUGH I HAVE RE-JECTED YOU, I WILL TAKE YOU, ONE FROM A TOWN AND TWO FROM A CLAN, AND BRING YOU TO ZION (Jer. 3:14), which teaches that repentance brings atonement.

"A second verse says FOR ON THIS DAY ATONEMENT SHALL BE MADE FOR YOU TO CLEANSE YOU OF ALL YOUR SINS (Lev. 16:30), which teaches that the Day of Atonement brings atonement.

"Yet a third verse says THIS INIQUITY SHALL NEVER BE FOR-GIVEN YOU UNTIL YOU DIE (Isa. 22:14), which teaches that death brings atonement.

"A fourth verse says I WILL PUNISH THEIR TRANSGRESSION WITH THE ROD, AND THEIR INIQUITY WITH PLAGUES (Ps. 89:33), which teaches that suffering brings atonement. How can these four verses be reconciled?

"If one transgresses a positive commandment and then repents, he is forgiven before he can even move! It is this case to which the verse TURN BACK REBELLIOUS CHILDREN (Jer. 3:14) refers.

---

40. *take it upon himself*—take an oath to take an oath.
God to you—indicated by the phrase YOUR GOD.
impossible to say WILL NOT CLEAR That expression cannot be understood literally since the opposite is stated elsewhere and vice versa. It is therefore interpreted to mean that He will not clear—if there is no repentance—but will if there is.

"If one transgresses a negative commandment and then repents, repentance is not powerful enough to effect atonement. Rather repentance suspends punishment and the Day of Atonement brings atonement. It is this case to which the verse FOR ON THIS DAY ATONEMENT SHALL BE MADE FOR YOU (Lev. 16:30) refers.

"If one deliberately commits an offense punishable by extinction or by execution by the court and then repents, repentance does not have the power to suspend [punishment] nor does the Day of Atonement effect atonement, but repentance and the Day of Atonement cause half of the atonement and suffering will effect the other half. This is the case to which the verse I WILL PUNISH THEIR TRANSGRESSION WITH THE ROD (Ps. 89:33) refers.

"If one desecrates the Name of Heaven and repents, repentance does not have the power to suspend [punishment], the Day of Atonement does not atone nor does suffering wipe away [the offense], but repentance and the Day of Atonement suspend [punishment] and the day of death together with suffering wipes it away. This is the case to which the verse THIS INIQUITY SHALL NEVER BE FORGIVEN YOU UNTIL YOU DIE (Isa. 22:14) refers."

Similarly it says THE INIQUITY OF THE HOUSE OF ELI WILL NEVER BE EXPIATED BY SACRIFICE OR OFFERING (1 Sam. 3:14) meaning sacrifice and offerings will not atone but death will atone. Rabbi Judah the Prince says, "I might have thought that the day of death does not bring atonement, but when it says YOU SHALL KNOW, O MY PEOPLE, THAT I AM THE LORD WHEN I HAVE OPENED YOUR GRAVES AND LIFTED YOU OUT OF YOUR GRAVES (Ezek. 37:13) we learn that the day of death *does* bring atonement."

COMMENTARY   *The concept of atonement is a major component of Jewish belief. Atonement indicates being received and accepted again by God. Having sinned, how does one effect this reconciliation? Judaism affirms that no matter what the sin, reconciliation with God is always possible. This does not mean that sin does not bring punishment. As this midrash makes clear, different types of transgression demand different actions in order to achieve atonement. In some cases it cannot be achieved until after death. In all cases, repentance is a prerequisite. Sometimes that act itself is enough,*

---

extinction—death at the hands of Heaven and not by a human court.

*sometimes not, but a human being is never to feel that he or she is beyond
the pale and cannot achieve reconciliation with God. It is always possible.
This assertion was particularly important following the destruction of the
Temple since the sacrificial system had been considered a requirement for
atonement. Now repentance, the Day of Atonement, suffering, and death
are stressed instead.*

REMEMBER THE SABBATH DAY AND KEEP IT HOLY (Ex. 20:8).
Both REMEMBER and OBSERVE (Deut. 5:12) were spoken in one
utterance.

Both HE WHO PROFANES IT SHALL BE PUT TO DEATH
(Ex. 31:14) and ON THE SABBATH DAY: TWO YEARLING LAMBS
WITHOUT BLEMISH (Num. 28:9) were spoken in one utterance.

Both DO NOT UNCOVER THE NAKEDNESS OF YOUR
BROTHER'S WIFE (Lev. 18:16) and HER HUSBAND'S BROTHER
SHALL UNITE WITH HER AND TAKE HER AS A WIFE (Deut.
25:5) were spoken in one utterance.

Both YOU SHALL NOT WEAR CLOTH COMBINING WOOL
AND LINEN (Deut. 22:11) and YOU SHALL MAKE TASSELS ON
THE FOUR CORNERS OF THE GARMENT WITH WHICH YOU
COVER YOURSELF (Deut. 22:12) were spoken in one utterance.

This is something no human could do, as it is said ONE THING GOD
HAS SPOKEN; TWO THINGS HAVE I HEARD (Ps. 62:12) and it says
BEHOLD MY WORD IS LIKE FIRE—DECLARES THE LORD—
AND LIKE A HAMMER THAT SHATTERS ROCK (Jer. 23:29).

REMEMBER (Ex. 20:8) and OBSERVE (Deut. 5:12). REMEMBER it before [the Sabbath] and OBSERVE it afterward. This is the source of the
teaching: One adds from the weekday to the holy day. This is like a wolf
which prowls back and forth.

---

in one utterance The two versions of the Ten Pronouncements, one in Exodus and one in
Deuteronomy, have some differences in wording. In the Sabbath commandment, Exodus reads
"remember" and Deuteronomy reads "observe." How is this possible? The answer is that God
said them both in one utterance. Other verses the Sages thought were uttered together are then
discussed. Each set seems to contain a contradiction, but in each case, both are valid.

TWO YEARLING LAMBS The slaughter and burning of the animals would be a profanation
of the Sabbath, but not when it is commanded to be done in the Temple.

THE GARMENT Even if the garment is linen and the fringes are wool.

adds from the weekday The Sabbath is extended by including some time prior to sunset at the
beginning and until dark at the end, thus both back and forth it extends itself.

Eleazar b. Hananya b. Hizkiya b. Garon says, "REMEMBER THE SAB-BATH DAY AND KEEP IT HOLY (Ex. 20:8)—remember it from the first day of the week, for should you find something particularly nice, set it aside for use on the Sabbath." R. Isaac says, "Do not count [the days of the week] as others do, but count them in reference to the Sabbath."

AND KEEP IT HOLY (Ex. 20:8). Sanctify it through reciting a blessing. This is the source of the teaching: Sanctify it over wine when it begins. [SABBATH DAY] (Ex. 20:8) would teach me only about reciting the sanctification prayer during the day. What about reciting it in the evening? [We learn this from] the verse YOU SHALL KEEP THE SABBATH (Ex. 31:14). This teaches only about [reciting the sanctification prayer] on the Sabbath. What about the festivals? The verse says THESE ARE THE SET TIMES OF THE LORD, THE SACRED OCCASIONS (Lev. 23:4).

SIX DAYS YOU SHALL LABOR AND DO ALL YOUR WORK (Ex. 20:9). Can a human being possibly complete all his work in six days? Rather cease from work as if it had all been completed. Another interpretation: Cease from even thinking about work. Thus it says IF YOU REFRAIN FROM TRAMPLING THE SABBATH, FROM PURSUING YOUR AFFAIRS ON MY HOLY DAY; IF YOU CALL THE SABBATH "DE-LIGHT," THE LORD'S HOLY DAY "HONORED"; AND YOU HONOR IT AND GO NOT YOUR WAYS NOR LOOK TO YOUR AFFAIRS, NOR STRIKE BARGAINS—(Isa. 58:13) and THEN YOU CAN SEEK THE FAVOR OF THE LORD (Isa. 58:14).

BUT THE SEVENTH DAY IS A SABBATH OF THE LORD YOUR GOD (Ex. 20:10). Why is this said? When it says WHOEVER DOES WORK ON THE SABBATH DAY SHALL BE PUT TO DEATH (Ex. 31:15) we are told of the punishment but not given a warning. Therefore the verse says BUT THE SEVENTH DAY IS A SABBATH OF THE LORD YOUR GOD (Ex. 20:10). Now we have both the punishment and the warning concerning work done on the day of the Sabbath. Where are the punishment and the warning for that done at night? The verse says HE WHO PROFANES IT SHALL BE PUT TO DEATH (Ex. 31:14). This

---

sanctification prayer—known as the *kiddush,* from the root k-d-sh meaning sanctified. The prayer declares the sanctity of the Sabbath day. The prayer is recited both in the evening and during the day.

the festivals These too are declared holy through recitation of the blessing over wine.

tells us of the punishment but we have not heard a warning. Therefore the verse says BUT THE SEVENTH DAY IS A SABBATH OF THE LORD YOUR GOD (Ex. 20:10). The word SABBATH is there only in order to include the night in the warning. So taught R. Ahai b. Josiah.

YOU, YOUR SON OR DAUGHTER (Ex. 20:10). This refers to minors. Perhaps it refers to adults. Are [adults] not already warned? What, therefore, is the meaning of the verse YOU, YOUR SON OR DAUGHTER? It refers to minors.

YOUR MALE OR FEMALE SLAVE (Ex. 20:10). This refers to those who are members of the covenant. Perhaps it refers to uncircumcised slaves? When it states THAT YOUR BONDMAN AND THE STRANGER MAY BE REFRESHED (Ex. 23:12) it clearly refers to the uncircumcised slave. What, therefore, is the meaning of the verse YOUR MALE OR FE-MALE SLAVE? It refers to those who are members of the covenant.

OR THE STRANGER (ger) (Ex. 20:10). This refers to the righteous convert (ger zedek). Perhaps it refers to the resident alien (ger toshav)? When it states AND THE STRANGER (Ex. 23:12) it refers to the resident alien. What, therefore, is the meaning of the verse OR THE STRANGER? It refers to the righteous convert.

FOR IN SIX DAYS THE LORD MADE HEAVEN AND EARTH, THE SEA AND ALL THAT IS IN THEM (Ex. 20:11). This informs us that the sea is considered as important as all the rest of the creation.

AND HE RESTED ON THE SEVENTH DAY (Ex. 20:11). Is He ever weary? Does it not say HE NEVER GROWS FAINT AND WEARY (Isa. 40:28)? And it says HE GIVES STRENGTH TO THE WEARY, FRESH VIGOR TO THE SPENT (Isa. 40:29). And it says BY THE WORD OF

---

minors   Your minor children are also to rest on the Sabbath day.

members of the covenant—part of the people of Israel, the *eved ivri* or Hebrew slave.

uncircumcised slaves   Non-Jewish slaves were also to be given rest, but the Biblical source is found in a different verse.

righteous convert   While *ger* in the Torah means a stranger who lives in your land, by Rabbinic times it meant a convert. Two terms were developed: *ger zedek*—the convert, and *ger toshav*—the alien who lives with you but has not converted. Both are to be given rest, but for each there is a separate Biblical verse.

THE LORD THE HEAVENS WERE MADE, BY THE BREATH OF HIS MOUTH, ALL THEIR HOST (Ps. 33:6). Rather it is as if He had it written of Himself that He created His world in six days and rested on the seventh [in order] to permit the logical inference that if He who is never weary had it written of Himself that He created the world in six days and rested on the seventh, how much more must man—of whom it is written FOR MAN IS BORN TO TOIL (Job 5:7)—rest thereon!

COMMENTARY   *Since the approach of the Sages to the interpretation of Scripture was not fundamentalistic, they had no difficulty in asserting that the description of God "resting" after the creation was not to be understood literally. Since such an idea was absurd, they asserted that the verse is simply a manner of speaking to impress on human beings the importance of rest.*

THEREFORE THE LORD BLESSED THE SEVENTH DAY AND HALLOWED IT (Ex. 20:11). He blessed it with manna and sanctified it with manna. So taught R. Ishmael.

    R. Akiba says, "He blessed it with manna and sanctified it with the blessing."

    R. Isaac says, "He blessed it with the manna and sanctified it by [punishing] the one who gathered sticks [on the Sabbath]."

    R. Simeon b. Yohai says, "He blessed it with the manna and sanctified it with the lights."

    R. Simeon b. Judah of Kfar Akko says in the name of R. Simon, "He blessed it with the manna and sanctified it with the light of man's countenance. Thus it says THEREFORE THE LORD BLESSED THE SEVENTH DAY AND HALLOWED IT."

HONOR YOUR FATHER AND YOUR MOTHER (Ex. 20:12). I might think that this means [to honor them] with words. The verse says HONOR THE LORD WITH YOUR WEALTH, WITH THE BEST OF ALL YOUR INCOME (Prov. 3:9) [indicating that it means honor them] with food, drink, and clean garments.

---

the blessing—recited over wine, the *kiddush*.

gathered sticks   See Num. 15:32.

the lights—which are kindled at the beginning of the Sabbath.

clean garments   It is the duty of children to supply their parents with their basic needs, thus they fulfill the mitzva of honoring parents.

Another interpretation: HONOR YOUR FATHER AND YOUR MOTHER. Why is this said? Since the verse IF ANY MAN REVILES HIS FATHER OR HIS MOTHER, HE SHALL BE PUT TO DEATH (Lev. 20:9) teaches us only about a man, what is the source which teaches about a woman, a person of doubtful sex or an *androgynous?* The verse says HONOR YOUR FATHER AND YOUR MOTHER—thus including everyone.

Just as in regard to "honor," no distinction is made between man and woman, so in regard to "reverence" no distinction is made between man and woman. So taught R. Ishmael. R. Judah b. Beterah says, "It says YOU SHALL EACH REVERE HIS MOTHER AND HIS FATHER, AND KEEP MY SABBATHS (Lev. 19:3). Just as no distinction is made between man, woman, a person of doubtful sex or an *androgynous* in regard to the Sabbath, so none is made in regard to reverence [of parents]."

Rabbi Judah the Prince says, "How precious to He Who Spoke and the world came into being is the honor due to parents, for He equates their honor to His own, their reverence to His own, and cursing them to cursing Him. It is written HONOR YOUR FATHER AND YOUR MOTHER (Ex. 20:12) and correspondingly it is written HONOR THE LORD WITH YOUR WEALTH (Prov. 3:9), thus connecting the honor due parents to that due to God.

"It is written YOU SHALL EACH REVERE HIS MOTHER AND HIS FATHER (Lev. 19:3) and correspondingly it is written REVERE THE LORD YOUR GOD (Deut. 6:13), thus connecting the reverence of parents to the reverence of God.

"It is written HE WHO REVILES HIS FATHER OR HIS MOTHER SHALL BE PUT TO DEATH (Ex. 21:17) and correspondingly it is written ANYONE WHO REVILES HIS GOD SHALL BE PUT TO DEATH (Lev. 24:15) thus connecting reviling parents to reviling God."

Let us see what reward is forthcoming. It says HONOR THE LORD WITH YOUR WEALTH, WITH THE BEST OF ALL YOUR IN-COME, AND YOUR BARNS WILL BE FILLED WITH GRAIN,

---

androgynous—having sexual features of both male and female.

YOUR VATS WILL BURST WITH NEW WINE (Prov. 3:9–10) and it says HONOR YOUR FATHER AND YOUR MOTHER, THAT YOU MAY LONG ENDURE ON THE LAND WHICH THE LORD YOUR GOD IS GIVING YOU (Ex. 20:12).

REVERE THE LORD YOUR GOD (Deut. 6:13) [is rewarded by] BUT FOR YOU WHO REVERE MY NAME A SUN OF VICTORY SHALL RISE TO BRING HEALING (Mal. 3:20). It says YOU SHALL EACH REVERE HIS MOTHER AND HIS FATHER, AND KEEP MY SABBATHS (Lev. 19:3). What does it say concerning the Sabbath? IF YOU REFRAIN FROM TRAMPLING THE SABBATH, FROM PURSUING YOUR AFFAIRS ON MY HOLY DAY . . . THEN YOU CAN SEEK THE FAVOR OF THE LORD. I WILL SET YOU ASTRIDE THE HEIGHTS OF THE EARTH, AND LET YOU ENJOY THE HERI-TAGE OF YOUR FATHER JACOB (Isa. 58:13–14).

Rabbi Judah the Prince says, "He Who Spoke and the world came into being was well aware that one honors his mother more than his father because she uses words to persuade him, therefore He placed father before mother in regard to honor. He Who Spoke and the world came into being was well aware that a person reveres his father more than his mother because he teaches him Torah, therefore He placed mother before father in regard to reverence. He completed that which was lacking. One might think that that which takes precedence in Scripture is to take precedence in practice as well, therefore the verse states YOU SHALL EACH REVERE HIS MOTHER AND HIS FATHER (Lev. 19:3) indicating that both parents are to be equal in all things.

HONOR YOUR FATHER AND YOUR MOTHER, THAT YOU MAY LONG ENDURE (Ex. 20:12). If you honor them, THAT YOU MAY LONG ENDURE and if not "that you may endure only briefly," for the words of the Torah are *notorikan*, that is, the words of Torah are interpreted in such a way that one infers the negative from the positive and the positive from the negative.

---

equal in all things The two verses in one of which father comes first and in the other, mother, indicate that there is no preference of one over the other.

notorikan—shorthand, in this case meaning that the negative was not written out since it can be inferred.

ON THE LAND WHICH THE LORD YOUR GOD IS GIVING YOU (Ex. 20:12). This was the source of the teaching: If the reward of a mitzvah is specified, the court does not have to enforce it.

YOU SHALL NOT MURDER (Ex. 20:13). Why is this said? When it says WHOEVER SHEDS THE BLOOD OF MAN, BY MAN SHALL HIS BLOOD BE SHED (Gen. 9:6) we have the punishment but not the warning. Therefore the verse says YOU SHALL NOT MURDER (Ex. 20:13).

YOU SHALL NOT COMMIT ADULTERY (Ex. 20:13). Why is this said? When it says IF A MAN COMMITS ADULTERY WITH A MAR-RIED WOMAN, COMMITTING ADULTERY WITH HIS NEIGH-BOR'S WIFE, THE ADULTERER AND THE ADULTERESS SHALL BE PUT TO DEATH (Lev. 20:10) we have the punishment but not the warning. Therefore the verse says YOU SHALL NOT COMMIT ADUL-TERY (Ex. 20:13).

YOU SHALL NOT STEAL (Ex. 20:13). Why is this said? When it says HE WHO STEALS A MAN—WHETHER HE HAS SOLD HIM OR IS STILL HOLDING HIM—SHALL BE PUT TO DEATH (Ex. 21:16) we have the punishment but not the warning. Therefore the verse says YOU SHALL NOT STEAL (Ex. 20:13). Thus this is a warning concerning steal-ing persons (i.e., kidnaping). You say that this is a warning concerning steal-ing persons. May it not be a warning concerning stealing money? When it says YOU SHALL NOT STEAL (Lev. 19:11) we have a warning concern-ing stealing money. What, therefore, is the meaning of the verse YOU SHALL NOT STEAL (Ex. 20:13)? Scripture is speaking of stealing persons. . . .

YOU SHALL NOT BEAR FALSE WITNESS AGAINST YOUR NEIGHBOR (Ex. 20:13). Why is this said? When it says IF THE MAN WHO TESTIFIED IS A FALSE WITNESS, IF HE HAS TESTIFIED FALSELY AGAINST HIS FELLOW MAN, YOU SHALL DO TO HIM AS HE SCHEMED TO DO TO HIS FELLOW (Deut. 19:18–19) we have the punishment but not the warning. Therefore the verse says YOU SHALL NOT BEAR FALSE WITNESS (Ex. 20:13).

---

stealing persons Rabbinic teaching was that the verse YOU SHALL NOT STEAL was a prohibition of kidnapping and not of general theft, which was prohibited elsewhere.

How were the Ten Pronouncements given? There were five on each tablet. I THE LORD AM YOUR GOD (Ex. 20:2) was written on one tablet and opposite it on the other was written YOU SHALL NOT MURDER (Ex. 20:13) indicating that if one sheds blood he is considered to have diminished the Divine Image. A parable. A human king entered a city and images of him were hung, likenesses erected, and coins were struck. After a while they upset the images, broke the likenesses, and defaced the coins, diminishing the image of the king. Thus if one sheds blood he is considered to have diminished the Divine Image, as it is said WHOEVER SHEDS THE BLOOD OF MAN, BY MAN SHALL HIS BLOOD BE SHED; FOR IN THE IMAGE OF GOD WAS MAN CREATED (Gen. 9:6).

It was written YOU SHALL HAVE NO OTHER GODS BESIDES ME (Ex. 20:3) and opposite it was written YOU SHALL NOT COMMIT ADULTERY (Ex. 21:13) indicating that if one worships idols it is considered as if he had committed adultery in reference to God, as it is said [YOU WERE LIKE] THE ADULTEROUS WIFE WHO WELCOMES STRANGERS INSTEAD OF HER HUSBAND (Ezek. 16:32) and it is written THE LORD SAID TO ME FURTHER, "GO, BEFRIEND A WOMAN WHO, WHILE BEFRIENDED BY A COMPANION, COMMITS ADULTERY WITH OTHERS, JUST AS THE LORD BEFRIENDS THE ISRAELITES, BUT THEY TURN TO OTHER GODS (Hos. 3:1)."

It was written YOU SHALL NOT SWEAR FALSELY (Ex. 20:7) and opposite it was written YOU SHALL NOT STEAL (Ex. 20:13) indicating that if one steals he will eventually come to swear falsely as it is said WILL YOU STEAL AND MURDER AND COMMIT ADULTERY AND SWEAR FALSELY (Jer. 7:9) and it is written [FALSE] SWEARING, DISHONESTY, AND MURDER, AND THEFT AND ADULTERY ARE RIFE (Hos. 4:2).

It was written REMEMBER THE SABBATH DAY AND KEEP IT HOLY (Ex. 20:8) and opposite it was written YOU SHALL NOT BEAR FALSE WITNESS (Ex. 20:13) indicating that if one desecrates the Sabbath it is as if he testifies before He Who Spoke and the world came into being

---

the Divine Image　　Man was created in the image of God and therefore may be said to represent God, as it were. For this reason humans were not to disfigure themselves and an unburied corpse was considered an insult to God. Killing a human being thus diminishes the Image.

committed adultery　　Since God demands absolute fidelity, idol worship is tantamount to breaking the marriage vow, as the imagery of prophets such as Ezekiel, Hosea, and Jeremiah makes clear.

that He did *not* create His world in six days nor did He rest on the seventh. If one observes the Sabbath it is as if he gives testimony before He Who Spoke and the world came into being that He *did* create His world in six days and rested on the seventh, as it is said MY WITNESSES ARE YOU— DECLARES THE LORD (Isa. 43:10).

It was written HONOR YOUR FATHER AND YOUR MOTHER (Ex. 20:12) and opposite it was written YOU SHALL NOT COVET (Ex. 20:14) indicating that if one covets he will sire a son who will curse his own father and give honor to one who is not his father.

For this reason the Ten Pronouncements were given five on one tablet and five on another. This is the teaching of R. Hananya b. Gamliel.

The Sages say, "There were ten on each of the tablets, as it is said THE LORD SPOKE THESE WORDS . . . HE INSCRIBED THEM ON TWO TABLES OF STONE (Deut. 5:19) and it says YOUR BREASTS ARE LIKE TWO FAWNS, TWINS OF A GAZELLE (Song 4:5) and HIS HANDS ARE RODS OF GOLD STUDDED WITH BERYL (Song 5:14)."

COMMENTARY *The exact format of the Tablets of the Testimony is never established in the Biblical narrative. It is emphasized that there were two, but nowhere are we told what was written on each tablet. This has led to many different traditions reflected in the way they are depicted in Christian and Jewish art. The majority opinion expressed in this Midrash is one that is never utilized, namely that all ten were written on each of the two tablets. The most common assumption is that cited here in the name of one of the Sages, R. Hananya b. Gamliel, that, regardless of the fact that the first five are much longer than the last, the division was an even one, five and five. His reasoning, however, has nothing to do with physical properties but with an attempt to connect the various pronouncements to one another. By reading them across the face of the two tablets, we arrive at some very revealing and unexpected connections.*

---

sire a son   Coveting will lead to adultery and the birth of children who do not know who their father is.

ten on each of the tablets   Each tablet of stone contained a complete set of the ten. This is based on verse Deut. 5:19, which states that HE INSCRIBED THEM—i.e., *all* of them, on each of the TWO TABLETS. No explanation is offered for this duplication.

41. Exodus 20:15, Mekhilta Bahodesh 9, II 266

ALL THE PEOPLE SAW THE THUNDER AND LIGHTNING (Ex. 20:15). They see what can be seen and hear what can be heard. So taught R. Ishmael. R. Akiba says, "They see and hear what can be seen. They saw a word of fire going out of the mouth of the Almighty and inscribing itself into the tablets, as it is said THE VOICE OF THE LORD HEWED OUT FLAMES OF FIRE (Ps. 29:7)."

ALL THE PEOPLE SAW THE THUNDER AND LIGHTNING (Ex. 20:15)—thunder of thunders of thunder and lightning of lightnings of lightning. How many thunders and lightnings were there? Rather [the plural] indicates that each person heard whatever was in his power to absorb, as it is said THE VOICE OF THE LORD ACCORDING TO HIS POWER (Ps. 29:4).

R. Judah the Prince says, "This indicates how praiseworthy was Israel, for when they stood at Mt. Sinai to receive the Torah, they would hear the Pronouncement and understand it immediately, as it is said HE EN-GIRDED HIM, HE MADE HIM UNDERSTAND (Deut. 32:10), indicating that as soon as they heard the Pronouncement they would under-stand it."

Another interpretation: This indicates how praiseworthy was Israel, for when they stood at Mt. Sinai to receive the Torah we are told that there were no blind ones among them, as it is said AND ALL THE PEOPLE SAW (Ex. 20:15) and we are told that there were no mutes among them, as it is said ALL THE PEOPLE ANSWERED AS ONE (Ex. 19:8). The verse teaches that there were no deaf among them, as it is said ALL THAT THE LORD HAS SPOKEN WE WILL DO AND LISTEN TO (Ex. 24:7) and no lame as it is said AND THEY TOOK THEIR PLACES AT THE FOOT OF THE MOUNTAIN (Ex. 19:17). It also teaches that there were none lacking intelligence, as it is said YOU HAVE BEEN MADE TO KNOW (Deut. 4:35).

---

41. *see and hear what can be seen* R. Akiba believes that at this miraculous time people heard things that are usually seen and saw things that are usually heard such as the Divine word.
each person heard The plural indicates that the same phenomenon was perceived differently by each person in accord with his abilities and understanding.
UNDERSTAND Usually translated "watched over him" but understood here as coming from the root b-y-n, to understand.

COMMENTARY   *Here again we see the different approaches of R. Akiba and R. Ishmael. Paradoxically, R. Akiba, the mystic, whose interpretations frequently range far beyond the literal, here takes the verse literally. They saw both lightning and thunder, thus rendering the event beyond the norm. R. Ishmael, the literalist but also the rationalist, simply sees this as a manner of speaking. To "see" is to experience, however that is usually done.*

42. Exodus 20:21, Mekhilta Bahodesh 11, II 287

IN EVERY PLACE (Ex. 20:21) where I reveal Myself to you—in the Chosen House. This is the source of the teaching: It is forbidden to pronounce the Name of God outside of the Temple.

R. Eliezer b. Jacob says, "If you come to My House I will come to your house, but if you do not come to My House I will not come to your house. My feet lead Me to the place My heart loves."

This was the source of the teaching: Whenever ten people enter the synagogue, the Divine Presence enters with them, as it is said GOD STANDS IN THE DIVINE ASSEMBLY (Ps. 82:1). What is the source which teaches that when three judges come together [the Divine Presence] is with them? As it is said AMONG THE JUDGES HE PRONOUNCES JUDGMENT (Ps. 82:1). And what about two? As it is said THOSE WHO REVERE THE LORD HAVE BEEN TALKING TO ONE ANOTHER (Mal. 3:16). [And is He present with even] one person? As it is said IN EVERY PLACE WHERE I CAUSE MY NAME TO BE MENTIONED, I WILL COME TO YOU AND BLESS YOU (Ex. 20:21).

43. Exodus 20:22, Mekhilta Bahodesh 11, II 290

FOR BY WIELDING YOUR SWORD UPON THEM YOU HAVE PROFANED THEM (Ex. 20:22). This was the basis of R. Simeon b. Eleazar's saying: The altar was created to lengthen man's life and iron was

---

42. *Name of God*   During the Second Temple period the Tetragrammaton was pronounced during the ceremony of blessing the people by the priests and in other prayers, but only in the Temple. Outside of it the substitution *Adonai*, "Lord," was always used.

ten people—the minimum quorum for public prayer, a *minyan*.

---

43. *lengthen man's life*   The altar prolongs life by bringing peace between man and God. See 1 Chron. 22:7 for the story of David who, as a man of war, could not build the Temple.

created to shorten it. It is not proper to wield that which shortens life over that which lengthens it.

R. Johanan b. Zakkai says, "It says YOU MUST BUILD THE ALTAR OF THE LORD YOUR GOD OF WHOLE (shelemim) STONES (Deut. 27:6)—stones which bring peace (shalom). It is a matter of logical inference. If the Holy One prohibited wielding the sword above stones—which cannot see or hear or speak—because they bring peace between Israel and their Father in Heaven, certainly suffering will not come to anyone who brings peace between one man and another, between man and wife, between one city and another, between one nation and another, between one family and another, between one government and another!"

COMMENTARY   *In explaining the prohibition of using metal instruments for building the altar, the Sages contrast the purpose of metal instruments such as swords with their understanding of the Temple service. One kills, the other prolongs life. The verse in Deuteronomy strengthens this thought since the root of the word whole is the same as the word shalom, peace. Thus an explanation is offered that is new and meaningful but totally in consonance with the Biblical view.*

44. Exodus 22:22, Mekhilta Nezikin 18, III 141

IF YOU DO MISTREAT THEM, I WILL HEED THEIR OUTCRY (Ex. 22:22). It matters not if the mistreatment be great or small. . . . When R. Simeon and R. Ishmael were being led forth to be executed, R. Simeon said to R. Ishmael, "My master, my heart is disturbed that I do not know what offense I have committed which would cause me to be executed."

R. Ishmael said to him, "Has it never happened that a person came to you with a case or with a question and you kept him waiting until you finished your drink, or until you put on your sandal or wrapped yourself in your

---

44. *to be executed*   They were martyred during the Hadrianic persecutions of the second century C.E.

what offense I have committed—which would have caused God to permit me to be executed by the Romans.

with a case   The Sages were judges to whom people came with their cases.

cloak? For the Torah says IF YOU DO MISTREAT THEM ... (Ex. 22:22)—it matters not if the mistreatment be great or small."

Upon hearing that, [R. Simeon] said, "You have comforted me, my Master."

When R. Simeon and R. Ishmael were executed, R. Akiba said to his disciples, "Prepare yourself for suffering, for if any good were to be in store for our generation, it would have come upon R. Simeon and R. Ishmael. It must therefore be known to He Who Spoke and the world came into being that for our generation there will only be terrible suffering, and therefore have these two been taken away from our midst, thus fulfilling what is said THE RIGHTEOUS MAN PERISHES, AND NO ONE CONSIDERS; PIOUS MEN ARE TAKEN AWAY, AND NO ONE GIVES THOUGHT THAT BECAUSE OF EVIL THE RIGHTEOUS WAS TAKEN AWAY (Isa. 57:1). And it says YET HE SHALL COME TO PEACE, HE SHALL HAVE REST ON HIS COUCH WHO WALKED STRAIGHTFORWARD (Isa. 57:2) and finally BUT AS FOR YOU, COME CLOSER, YOU SONS OF A SORCERESS, YOU OFFSPRING OF AN ADULTERER AND A HARLOT! (Isa. 57:3)."

COMMENTARY   *Since all the actions and words of the Masters were important as examples of how to live and as interpretations of the way to understand the word of God, stories of incidents in their lives were preserved as part of the oral tradition. This is one of many stories of the martyrdom of the Sages during the period of the Hadrianic persecutions (c. 135 C.E.). The conversation between the two martyrs, whether actual or fictitious, indicates the high degree of sensitivity the Sages had toward their duty as teachers, counselors, and judges of the people and how strictly they held themselves accountable. Note, however, that Akiba does not fault them but explains their deaths as a Divine decree to spare them even worse suffering which was to come.*

MISTREAT THEM   In Hebrew the verb *mistreat* is repeated, thus indicating any mistreatment whatsoever, even the most minor.
taken away from our midst   God is permitting their execution to spare them further suffering. The verses then indicate that they will have rest in the world-to-come, but the wicked who cause this agony will be punished.

LEVITICUS

1. Leviticus 1:1, Sifra Finkelstein 16

THE LORD CALLED TO MOSES AND SPOKE TO HIM FROM THE
TENT OF MEETING (Lev. 1:1). This teaches that the Voice would ter-
minate there and not emerge from the Tent of Meeting. Could this have
been because the Voice was low? The verse says HE WOULD HEAR
THE VOICE (Num. 7:89). The verse does not say "Voice" but THE
VOICE—namely that Voice described in the Writings. What voice is de-
scribed in the Writings? THE VOICE OF THE LORD IS POWER; THE
VOICE OF THE LORD IS MAJESTY; THE VOICE OF THE LORD
BREAKS CEDARS . . . THE VOICE OF THE LORD KINDLES FIRE
(Ps. 29:4–7). If that is so, why does it say FROM THE TENT OF MEET-
ING? This teaches that the Voice would terminate there and not emerge
from the Tent of Meeting.

Similarly it says THE SOUND OF THE CHERUB'S WINGS COULD
BE HEARD AS FAR AS THE OUTER COURT (Ezek. 10:5). Could this
have been because the sound was low? The verse says LIKE THE VOICE
OF EL SHADDAI WHEN HE SPEAKS (Ezek. 10:5). If that is so, why
does it say AS FAR AS THE OUTER COURT? This teaches that when
the sound reached the outer court it would terminate.

FROM THE TENT OF MEETING (Lev. 1:1). Could this mean that [the
Voice] came from anywhere in the structure? The verse says FROM
ABOVE THE COVER (Num. 7:89). Could this mean from anywhere

---

1. *would terminate there* Miraculously the voice of God could be heard only within the Tent.
It stopped there and could not be heard without.
THE COVER—which was upon the Ark.

above the cover? The verse says BETWEEN THE TWO CHERUBIM (Num. 7:89). So taught R. Akiba. R. Simeon b. Azzai said, "I am not contradicting the teaching of my Master, but adding to it. In regard to the Glory, it is said FOR I FILL BOTH HEAVEN AND EARTH—DECLARES THE LORD (Jer. 23:24). See how greatly beloved is Israel. It goes so far as to cause this Glory to contract and appear to be speaking FROM ABOVE THE COVER . . . BETWEEN THE TWO CHERUBIM (Num. 7:89)!"

R. Dosa says, "It says FOR MAN MAY NOT SEE ME AND LIVE (Ex. 33:20). During their lives they may not see Him, but at the hour of their death they can see Him." R. Akiba says, "It says FOR MAN MAY NOT SEE ME AND LIVE but even the creatures that carry [His throne] do not see the Glory." R. Simeon b. Azzai said, "I am not contradicting the teaching of my Master, but adding to it. FOR MAN MAY NOT SEE ME AND LIVE. Even the ministering angels who live forever do not see the Glory."

SAYING (Lev. 1:1). Go and speak words which will be convincing to them. "It is for your sakes that He speaks with me." For thus we find that during the entire thirty-eight years that Israel was wandering, He did not speak to Moses, as it is said WHEN ALL THE WARRIORS AMONG THE PEOPLE HAD DIED, THE LORD SPOKE TO ME, SAYING (Deut. 2:16).

Another interpretation: SAYING. Go and speak to them and inform Me [of their response]. What is the source which teaches that Moses would go out and speak to them? As it is said AND WHEN HE CAME OUT AND TOLD THE ISRAELITES WHAT HE HAD BEEN COMMANDED (Ex. 34:34). What is the source which teaches that Moses would inform God of their response? The verse says AND MOSES BROUGHT BACK THE PEOPLE'S WORDS TO THE LORD (Ex. 19:8). Eleazar b. Ahbai says, "Is it possible that he spoke with him of his own needs? The verse says

---

my Master—R. Akiba, his teacher.
SAYING SAYING is considered a superfluous word. Two explanations of it are offered. The first is that Moses was to tell them that God spoke to him only for the sake of Israel. He does not speak to Moses when He has nothing to say to Israel.
inform Me—the second explanation of the world *saying*. Moses must say these things to Israel and then come and report their response to God.
of his own needs Some manuscripts read exactly the opposite: He did speak to Moses of his own needs.

SAYING—to say to Israel. He spoke to him for Israel. He did not speak to him of his own needs."

COMMENTARY   *Although much of the legendary material in the Sifra is not as highly developed as that of the Mekhilta, it still reflects the same basic rabbinic concepts. The contrast between seemingly contradictory verses is dealt with here. The greatness of God as manifested in His voice, for example, is restricted by God Himself for purposes of emphasizing the importance of Israel and its cult.*

2. Leviticus 3:1, Sifra Finkelstein 98

IF HIS OFFERING IS AN OFFERING OF WELL-BEING (sh'lamim) (Lev. 3:1). R. Judah says, "Whoever brings an offering of well-being, brings peace (shalom) into the world." I know this only concerning the offering of well-being. What about applying this to the Thanksgiving offering as well? I can include the Thanksgiving offering since it is a type of well-being offering, but what about the *olah* offering? I can include the *olah* offering since it is brought as a result of a vow or as a votive offering, but what about the firstborn, the tithe, and the Passover offering? I can include the firstborn, the tithe, and the Passover offering since they are not brought as a result of sin, but what about the sin offering and the guilt offering? The verse says OFFERING. What about fowl, meal offerings, wine, incense, and the wood? The verse says HIS OFFERING IS AN OFFERING OF WELL-BEING. Thus whoever brings an offering of well-being brings peace to the world.

Another interpretation: WELL-BEING (sh'lamim) (Lev. 3:1). Everything in it is to be used (shalum), the blood and the *emurim* (devoted portions) are offered on the altar. The chest and the thigh go to the priests and the skin and flesh to the owners.

R. Simeon says, "He who is at peace (shalom) brings an offering of well-being (sh'lamim). A mourner does not bring an offering of well-being." I

---

2. *olah*—an offering totally consumed on the altar.
OFFERING   Just as the well-being sacrifice is called an offering, so all sacrifices are called offerings. Therefore like the well-being offering (sh'lamim), whose very name includes the word peace (shalom), all of them bring peace to the world.
mourner   A person in a state of mourning is not at peace with himself and therefore should not bring such an offering.

know this only about offerings of well-being since they are expressions of joy. What about applying this to the Thanksgiving offering? I can include the Thanksgiving offering since it, like the offering of well-being, is an expression of joy. What about the *olah* offering? I can include the *olah* offering since it is brought as a result of a vow or as a votive offering, but what about the firstborn, the tithe, and the Passover offering? I can include the firstborn, the tithe, and the Passover offering since they are not brought as a result of sin, but what about the sin offering and the guilt offering? The verse says OFFERING. What about including fowl, meal offerings, wine, incense, and the wood? The verse says HIS OFFERING ... WELL-BEING. Whatever offering he brings, if he is at peace, he may bring it. If he is in mourning, he may not bring it.

COMMENTARY   *The Sages stress that, like the Temple itself, all the offerings, no matter what the reason for bringing them, are a means of bringing peace to the world. The mourner, who suffers the ultimate sadness, whose soul cannot possibly be at peace, may not participate in such a ceremony.*

3. Leviticus 8:1, Weiss 40b

THE LORD SPOKE TO MOSES SAYING: TAKE AARON AND HIS SONS (Lev. 8:1–2). Why is this said? When it says THEN THE LORD SENT A PLAGUE UPON THE PEOPLE, FOR WHAT THEY DID WITH THE CALF THAT AARON MADE (Ex. 32:35) it indicates that Aaron was being shunted away. When it says TAKE AARON AND HIS SONS WITH HIM (Lev. 8:1–2) it indicates that Aaron is now being brought close. How do we know that Moses was aware that Aaron had been shunted away? As it is said MOREOVER, THE LORD WAS ANGRY ENOUGH WITH AARON TO HAVE DESTROYED HIM; SO I ALSO INTERCEDED FOR AARON AT THAT TIME (Deut. 9:20). But it does

---

expressions of joy—which would be inappropriate for a mourner. Perhaps, however, a mourner could bring other offerings.

include—in the prohibition of a mourner bringing the offering. A way is found to include all of them in the prohibition.

not say "and that time too, the Lord gave heed to me." But when it says TAKE AARON AND HIS SONS WITH HIM (Lev. 8:2) Moses was aware that Aaron had been brought close. How do we know that Aaron knew in his heart that he had been shunted away? At the conclusion of this incident it says COME CLOSE TO THE ALTAR (Lev. 9:7). Now Moses had already instructed him regarding the entire service. Therefore this was said so that he should not be wary, for when He said COME CLOSE, Aaron knew that he had been brought close.

Another interpretation: TAKE AARON AND HIS SONS WITH HIM (Lev. 8:2). Why is this said? There are many places where the expression "take" is used in regard to various people. As it is said AND TAKE THE LEVITES FOR ME, THE LORD (Num. 3:41); AND TAKE THEM TO THE TENT OF MEETING (Num. 11:16); AND MOSES AND AARON TOOK THOSE MEN, WHO WERE DESIGNATED BY NAME (Num. 1:17); TAKE JOSHUA SON OF NUN (Num. 27:18). Now what did Moses do? Tie them up and drag them behind him? Rather the Holy One said to him, "Take them with words so that they should not be wary."

THE VESTMENTS (Lev. 8:2). These are the vestments concerning which I have already commanded you as it is said THESE ARE THE VEST-MENTS THEY ARE TO MAKE: A BREASTPLATE, AN EPHOD (Ex. 28:4).

THE ANOINTING OIL (Lev. 8:2). This is the anointing oil concerning which I have already commanded you as it is said MAKE OF THIS A SA-CRED ANOINTING OIL (Ex. 30:25). . . .

---

3. *and that time too*   This is what is said in Deut. 9:19 indicating that God had forgiven the people. This was *not* said in regard to Aaron, indicating that Aaron was shunted aside and not forgiven until now. At the dedication of the Sanctuary and the priesthood Aaron is accepted back and brought close to God once more.

COME CLOSE   Even though Aaron knew exactly what he had to do, he still felt that he had been rejected and was reluctant to approach the altar. Therefore Moses had to tell him to do so. At the end, the printed text again quotes the verse from the beginning of the section TAKE AARON AND HIS SONS WITH HIM but it is more likely that the interpretation is of the verse COME CLOSE, on which the remark is based.

not be wary   By soothing words Moses can convince them not to be distraught.

AND ASSEMBLE THE WHOLE COMMUNITY (Lev. 8:3). This was done in the presence of the entire community so that they should respect the holiness of the priests.

MOSES DID AS THE LORD COMMANDED HIM (Lev. 8:4). Just as Moses arranged the service of the Sanctuary, so did he arrange the service of the priests, the Levites, and the garments needed for the various sacrifices.

THEN MOSES BROUGHT AARON AND HIS SONS FORWARD AND WASHED THEM WITH WATER (Lev. 8:6). At that time they were given the honor of sanctifying hands and feet. At that time they were given the honor of the immersions of the Day of Atonement.

HE PUT THE TUNIC ON HIM, GIRDED HIM WITH THE SASH (Lev. 8:7). This teaches that Moses became Aaron's assistant priest, undressing and dressing him. Just as during his life, he served him as an assistant, so at his death did he serve him, as it is said DIVEST AARON OF HIS GARMENTS AND PUT THEM ON HIS SON ELEAZAR (Num. 20:26). And how do we know that Moses did so? As it is said MOSES DID AS THE LORD HAD COMMANDED. THEY ASCENDED MOUNT HOR IN THE SIGHT OF THE WHOLE COMMUNITY. MOSES DIVESTED AARON OF HIS GARMENTS AND PUT THEM ON HIS SON ELEAZAR (Num. 20:27–28). How was Moses able to divest him of the garments according to the proper order, keeping the upper garments always above and the lower garments always below? These were miraculous deeds which Moses performed, and at [Aaron's] death God performed even greater miracles. Moses stood him upon the rock and divested him of his priestly garments and the garments of the Divine Presence were underneath them. AND PUT THEM ON HIS SON ELEAZAR (Num. 20:28). And how was Moses able to clothe Eleazar according to the proper order? God honored Aaron greatly at the time of his death, more than during his life, for

---

ALL THAT THE LORD COMMANDED HIM   The word *ALL* includes more than the specific things mentioned in the text. He arranged all that had to be done.

proper order   Aaron died after the garments had been put on his son (Num. 20:28), but it would not have been appropriate for Aaron to be divested of all his garments and stand there naked so that they could be put on his son in the correct order. The legend has it that this was accomplished miraculously with the use of special Divine garments that were underneath the regular ones.

He clothed him with garments of the Divine Presence underneath, after which Moses divested Aaron of his garments according to the proper order and clothed Eleazar according to the proper order.

HE PUT THE BREASTPLATE ON HIM, AND PUT INTO THE BREASTPIECE THE URIM AND THUMMIM (Lev. 8:8). This section was applicable to that particular time and for all time. It is applicable to the daily service and to the Day of Atonement. Daily he wears golden vestments and on the Day of Atonement, white ones.

AND HE SET THE HEADRESS ON HIS HEAD (Lev. 8:9). This is not the same order as that found elsewhere (Ex. 29:5). Elsewhere it gives the correct order for the offering of sacrifices (Ex. 29:1ff) and here it gives the correct order for donning the garments. Elsewhere it gives the order of the sacrifices first (Ex. 29:1ff) and then the garments. Here it gives the order of the garments first and then the sacrifices.

MOSES TOOK THE ANOINTING OIL (Lev. 8:10). R. Judah says, "The anointing oil which Moses made in the wilderness was a miraculous creation from beginning to end. At first there were no more than twelve *log* of olive oil, not enough to anoint the wood. And think how much was burnt by the fire, how much the wood absorbed, how much the pot absorbed! Yet from it Aaron and his sons were anointed for seven days of the investure ceremony. From it High Priests and kings were anointed!"

A High Priest whose father was High Priest must be anointed. A king whose father was king is not anointed. Why then was Solomon anointed? Because of the controversy with Adonijah. And Joash was anointed because

---

for all time   This order and procedure in dressing the High Priest was not only for this first investiture, but applied whenever the High Priest was to be dressed.

order of the sacrifices   In Exodus the sacrifices are described first while here the investiture of the garments is described first. In each case, the correct order is according to that which comes first: the sacrifices from Exodus and the garments here in Leviticus.

kings   The oil prepared by Moses was used later for the anointing of all the High Priests and the kings.

Adonijah—who had himself proclaimed king. See 1 Kings 1:3–10. Therefore in order to affirm that Solomon was the true king, Zadok anointed him (1 Kings 1:39.)

Joash—who was secreted away from Queen Athaliah who killed all the royal stock. After six years he was anointed and she was put to death. See 2 Kings 11.

of the controversy with Athaliah, and Jehoahaz because of the controversy with Jehoaikim who was two years older than he.

"And all of it remains for the future, as it is said THIS SHALL BE FOR AN ANOINTING OIL SACRED TO ME THROUGHOUT THE GENERATIONS (Ex. 30:31)!"

AND ANOINTED THE TABERNACLE AND ALL THAT WAS IN IT (Lev. 8:10). This was not done the same way as the anointing of Aaron and his sons. After he dressed them, he anointed them, as it is said IT IS LIKE FINE OIL ON THE HEAD (Ps. 133:2). Is it possible that he anointed them before dressing them? The verse says THAT COMES DOWN OVER THE COLLAR OF HIS ROBE (Ps. 133:2).

In regard to the utensils, each one had to be individually anointed, as it is said ANOINTING THE ALTAR, ALL ITS UTENSILS, AND THE LAVER WITH ITS STAND, TO CONSECRATE THEM (Lev. 8:11). Thus you learn that each one had to be individually anointed. . . .

AND IT WAS SLAUGHTERED. MOSES TOOK THE BLOOD . . . THUS HE CONSECRATED IT AND MADE ATONEMENT FOR IT (Lev. 8:15). I do not know the purpose of this atonement. This atonement was because Moses said, "When the Master of the universe commanded that donations be given to erect the Tabernacle, people were pressured into giving and they brought things grudgingly. This atonement was made lest someone had donated something which had been stolen." Thus it says FOR I THE LORD LOVE JUSTICE, I HATE ROBBERY WITH A BURNT OFFERING (Isa. 61:8).

COMMENTARY   *Regardless of the conflict between the Pharisaic Sages and the Sadducean Priests over the question of authority, the Temple and the priesthood as a divine institution were held in great respect by the Sages. This is expressed in their elaboration of these sections describing the initial consecration of the priesthood. Thus the ceremony itself takes on a mirac-*

Jehoahaz See 2 Kings 23:30. Jehoiakim was twenty-five (2 Kings 23:36) and Jehoahaz only twenty-three (2 Kings 23:31). He too required anointing to demonstrate his legitimacy.

And all of it—the oil prepared by Moses, continuing R. Judah's statement, which was interrupted by the discussion of the anointing of High Priests and kings.

the purpose of this atonement One does not make atonement unless there has been a transgression. What transgression could there have been in regard to the Tabernacle?

ulous nature, as witness the story of the consecrating oil. This may well
have served as the prototype for the more famous tale of miraculous oil
associated with the feast of Hanukkah. For the same reason, the person of
Aaron is accorded great respect. His sin in connection with the golden calf
is expressly forgiven and, for purposes of consecrating him in his holy
office, Moses himself becomes his servant. By the time these interpretations
were recorded in their final form the Temple was long destroyed. The Ro-
mans had demonstrated their contempt for it, and early Christianity had
condemned it and interpreted its destruction as part of God's rejection of
Judaism and punishment of the Jews. Thus the Sages stressed the impor-
tance of the Temple Service.

4. Leviticus 9:1, Sifra Weiss 44b

AND IT WAS ON THE EIGHTH DAY (Lev. 9:1). This was the eighth
day of the sanctification ceremony for Aaron and his sons. Perhaps it was
the eighth day of the month? When it says IN THE FIRST MONTH OF
THE SECOND YEAR, ON THE FIRST OF THE MONTH, THE
TABERNACLE WAS SET UP (Ex. 40:17) we know that the Tabernacle
was erected on the first day of the month. It could have been that it was
erected on the first of the month, but the Divine Presence did not rest upon
it until the eighth day of the month. The verse says ON THE DAY THAT
THE TABERNACLE WAS SET UP, THE CLOUD COVERED THE
TABERNACLE (Num. 9:15). This indicates that on the same day that the
Tabernacle was erected, the Presence of God rested upon the work of
Aaron's hands. During the seven days of the investiture ceremony, while
Moses was serving, the Divine Presence did not rest there. Only when
Aaron came and served in the vestments of the High Priest did the Divine
Presence rest thereon as it is said FOR TODAY THE LORD WILL AP-
PEAR TO YOU (Lev. 9:4).

What is meant by AND IT WAS (Lev. 9:1)? This teaches that there was
rejoicing before Him on high as on the day on which the heavens and the

---

4. *eighth day of the month*   Is it possible that the eighth day referred to here is the eighth day
of the month rather than the eighth day of the ceremony? Exodus 40:17 indicates clearly that
the dedication was completed on the first of the month. The eighth day here, then, is the eighth
day of the dedication ceremony.
Moses was serving   During the ceremony of the dedication and investiture Moses acted as
priest.

earth were created. Concerning the creation it says AND THERE WAS (vayehi) EVENING AND MORNING (Gen. 1:5) and here it says AND IT WAS (veyehi) (Lev. 9:1). And when Israel completed the work of erecting the Tabernacle, Moses came and blessed them as it is said AND WHEN MOSES SAW THAT THEY HAD PERFORMED ALL THE TASKS— AS THE LORD HAD COMMANDED, SO THEY HAD DONE— MOSES BLESSED THEM (Ex. 39:43). What blessing did he give them? He said to them, "May the Divine Presence rest upon the work of your hands."

R. Meir says, "Thus did he bless them: MAY THE LORD THE GOD OF YOUR FATHERS, INCREASE YOUR NUMBERS A THOUSANDFOLD (Deut. 1:11) and they said to him: MAY THE FAVOR OF THE LORD, OUR GOD, BE UPON US; LET THE WORK OF OUR HANDS PROSPER, OH, PROSPER THE WORK OF OUR HANDS! (Ps. 90:17)."

Concerning that time it says GO FORTH AND GAZE, O MAIDENS OF ZION (tzion) (Song 3:11)—wonderful (metzuyanim) children—UPON KING SOLOMON (shelomo) (Song 3:11)—the King of Peace (shalom) WEARING THE CROWN THAT HIS MOTHER GAVE HIM (Song 3:11) referring to the Tent of Meeting which was decorated IN BLUE, PURPLE, CRIMSON YARNS, AND IN FINE LINEN (Ex. 35:35). HIS MOTHER (imo) always refers to Israel as it is said HARKEN TO ME, MY PEOPLE (l'umi), AND GIVE EAR TO ME, O MY NATION (Isa. 51:4). ON HIS WEDDING DAY (Song 3:11)—on the day upon which the Divine Presence rested upon the House. ON HIS DAY OF BLISS (Song 3:11)—on the day when new fire came down from above and consumed THE BURNT OFFERING AND THE FAT PARTS ON THE ALTAR (Lev. 9:24).

COMMENTARY   *The story of the dedication of the Sanctuary is one of both triumph and tragedy. The Midrash enhances both. It depicts the day of the dedication as being as great as that of creation itself. It is as if the Sanctuary and its successor the Temple represent the universe in miniature and serve as the basis for the world's existence. Once again the Song of Songs is*

---

the King of Peace   Following the allegorical interpretation of the Song of Songs, the king referred to there is not Solomon, whose name derives from the word *peace*, but God, whose title is King of Peace.

utilized to create a wedding picture. This time the wedding takes place at the ceremony of dedication where once again God is the groom and Israel the bride.

AARON LIFTED HIS HANDS TOWARD THE PEOPLE AND BLESSED THEM (Lev. 9:22). At that moment he was given the privilege of receiving the priestly gifts and of lifting his arms in bestowing the Priestly Blessing—for him and his descendants until the resurrection of the dead.

AARON LIFTED HIS HANDS TOWARD THE PEOPLE AND BLESSED THEM (Lev. 9:22). This verse is out of order. It should have said "He stepped down after offering the sin offering, the burnt offering and the offering of well-being and Aaron lifted his hands toward the people and blessed them." For he blessed the people when he came down.

AND BLESSED THEM (Lev. 9:22) [Is the blessing performed] while standing and also while not standing? The verse says TO STAND IN SERVICE UPON THE LORD, AND TO BLESS IN HIS NAME (Deut. 10:8). The service and the blessing are juxtaposed. Just as the service is performed while standing, so the blessing is given while standing. So too it says THE LEVITE PRIESTS ROSE AND BLESSED THE PEOPLE, AND THEIR VOICE WAS HEARD AND THEIR PRAYER WENT UP TO HIS HOLY ABODE, TO HEAVEN (2 Chron. 30:27).

In the generation of Hezekiah the King of Judah, when they busied themselves with Torah, what does it say? AND THEIR PRAYER WENT UP TO HIS HOLY ABODE, TO HEAVEN (2 Chron. 30:27). In later generations, when they worshiped idols, what does it say of them? AND WHEN

---

lifting his arms Whenever a priest blesses Israel as part of an official ceremony, he lifts up his arms toward the people. The ceremony is thus called "lifting the hands."

out of order—or "cut up." The verse reads as if he blessed them first and then stepped down. The midrash believes that the correct order would have been the opposite and that that is what the verse really means.

the blessing—the priestly blessing found in Num. 6:23–26.

the service—of offering sacrifices in the Tabernacle.

generation of Hezekiah At that time, the blessing of the priests was accepted by God and fulfilled. Later, however, when they worshiped idols, God did not bless the people when the priests lifted up their hands in blessing. The blessing does not have automatic, magical effect. No ritual in Judaism does.

YOU LIFT UP YOUR HANDS, I WILL TURN MY EYES AWAY
FROM YOU (Isa. 1:15).

AND BLESSED THEM (Lev. 9:22). This blessing is not made explicit, but
later Scripture explains THUS SHALL YOU BLESS THE PEOPLE OF
ISRAEL. SAY TO THEM: THE LORD BLESS YOU AND KEEP YOU
(Num. 6:23–24) until AND GRANT YOU PEACE (Num. 6:26).

AND HE STEPPED DOWN AFTER OFFERING THE SIN OFFER-
ING, THE BURNT OFFERING, AND THE OFFERING OF WELL-
BEING (Lev. 9:22). When he finished his offerings, he went down from
the altar rejoicing.

MOSES AND AARON THEN WENT INSIDE THE TENT OF
MEETING (Lev. 9:23). When Aaron saw that he had offered all the offerings and performed all his duties, but the Divine Presence had not descended upon Israel, he was desolate. He said, "I know that God is angry
because of me and therefore the Divine Presence has not descended on
Israel. My brother Moses has done this in encouraging me to enter although
I was ashamed—and the Divine Presence has not come down." Moses im-
mediately went in with him and they begged for mercy and the Divine Presence descended upon Israel. Thus it is said MOSES AND AARON THEN
WENT INSIDE THE TENT OF MEETING . . . AND THE PRES-
ENCE OF THE LORD APPEARED TO ALL THE PEOPLE
(Lev. 9:23).

MOSES AND AARON THEN WENT INSIDE THE TENT OF
MEETING (Lev. 9:23). Why did Moses and Aaron go in together? So that
Moses could teach him about the incense. . . .

At that moment the fate of Nadab and Abihu was decided. Some say that it
occurred at Sinai. They saw Moses and Aaron walking at the head of the
procession while they followed after them and all Israel after them. Nadab

---

had not descended There was as yet no special sign from Heaven indicating that the Presence
of God was in the Tabernacle.
at that moment When Moses and Aaron went inside, before fire had descended, they decided
to offer fire on their own.
at Sinai—when they came after Moses and Aaron (Ex. 24:1) They envied them their position,
causing God to decree their death.

said to Abihu, "When those two old men die we will lead the congregation!" Said the Holy One, "We will see who will bury who. They will bury you and continue to lead the congregation!"

Another interpretation: When the sons of Aaron saw that all the offerings had been offered and all the duties performed and yet the Divine Presence had not descended upon Israel, Nadab said to Abihu, "Can anyone cook up a dish without fire?" Immediately they took strange fire and went into the Holy of Holies, as it is said NOW AARON'S SONS, NADAB AND ABIHU, EACH TOOK HIS FIRE PAN, PUT FIRE IN IT (Lev. 10:1). Said the Holy One to them, "I honor you more than you honored Me. You brought impure fire before Me. I shall burn you with pure fire!"

How did they die? Two threads of fire emerged from the Holy of Holies and split into four. Two entered the nostrils of this one, and two entered the nostrils of the other one. Their bodies were consumed by fire, but their vestments remained, as it is said AND FIRE CAME FORTH FROM THE LORD AND CONSUMED THEM (Lev. 10:2).

FIRE CAME FORTH FROM BEFORE THE LORD (Lev. 9:24). When they saw new fire descend from heaven and consume THE BURNT OFFERING AND THE FAT PARTS ON THE ALTAR (Lev. 9:24) they fell on their faces and praised Heaven. Similarly in the days of Solomon, they fell on their faces as it is said ALL THE ISRAELITES WITNESSED THE DESCENT OF THE FIRE AND THE GLORY OF THE LORD ON THE HOUSE; THEY KNELT WITH THEIR FACES TO THE GROUND AND PROSTRATED THEMSELVES, PRAISING THE LORD, "FOR HE IS GOOD, FOR HIS STEADFAST LOVE IS ETERNAL" (2 Chron. 7:3). Of that time it is written THEN THE OFFERINGS OF JUDAH AND JERUSALEM SHALL BE PLEASING TO THE LORD AS IN THE DAYS OF YORE AND IN THE YEARS OF OLD (Mal. 3:4). THE DAYS OF YORE—like the days of Moses. THE YEARS OF OLD—like the years of Solomon. Rabbi Judah the Prince says, "THE DAYS OF YORE—like the days of Noah. THE YEARS OF OLD—as the years of Abel when there was no idolatry in the world."

When they saw—the people of Israel.
days of Noah—when God accepted Noah's sacrifice (Gen. 8:31) and made a Covenant with mankind.
years of Abel—whose offering was pleasing to the Lord (Gen. 4:4).

FIRE CAME FORTH FROM BEFORE THE LORD (Lev. 9:24). When they saw the new fire descend from on high to consume THE BURNT OFFERING AND THE FAT PARTS ON THE ALTAR (Lev. 9:24) they opened their mouths and proclaimed songs of praise. Of that time it is written SING FORTH, O YOU RIGHTEOUS, TO THE LORD; IT IS FIT THAT THE UPRIGHT ACCLAIM HIM (Ps. 33:1).

NOW AARON'S SONS, NADAB AND ABIHU, EACH TOOK HIS FIRE PAN (Lev. 10:1). They were also rejoicing. When they saw the new fire, they wanted to add love upon love. EACH TOOK. "Taking" always indicates rejoicing.

NADAB AND ABIHU (Lev. 10:1). Why does the verse say AARON'S SONS (Lev. 10:1)? Because they did not give honor to Aaron. NADAB AND ABIHU—they did not take council of Moses. EACH TOOK HIS FIRE PAN (Lev. 10:1). Each one acted on his own and did not take council with one another.

AND THEY OFFERED BEFORE THE LORD ALIEN FIRE, WHICH HE HAD NOT ENJOINED UPON THEM (Lev. 10:1). R. Ishmael says, "Could it have been actual alien fire? The verse says WHICH HE HAD NOT ENJOINED UPON THEM. They brought it in without asking advice."

R. Akiba says, "They brought it in from the oven as it is said AND THEY OFFERED BEFORE THE LORD ALIEN FIRE. If so, why does it say WHICH HE HAD NOT ENJOINED UPON THEM? They had not consulted with their teacher Moses."

R. Eliezer says, "They were condemned because they dared to instruct law in the presence of Moses, their teacher. Anyone who instructs law in the presence of his teacher is liable to death."

It once happened that a disciple instructed law in the presence of his teacher. [R. Eliezer] said to his wife, Ima Shalom, "He will not last through the Sabbath." He died. After the Sabbath, the Sages came to him and said to him, "Master, are you a prophet?" He said to them, "I am neither a prophet

---

love upon love   This interprets their action as sincere albeit mistaken.

give honor to Aaron   The verse stresses the relationship to Aaron to underscore that their sin was in not honoring their father.

actual alien fire—fire associated with idolatrous worship. This is unlikely. Rather it was fire about which they had not consulted their elders.

nor the son of a prophet, but thus have learned from my teachers: Anyone who instructs law in the presence of his teacher is liable to death."

AND FIRE CAME FORTH FROM THE LORD (Lev. 10:2). This teaches that fire came forth from the Holy of Holies and consumed their souls. Abba Jose b. Dostai says, "Two threads of fire came forth from the Holy of Holies and split into four. Two entered the nostrils of this one and two entered the nostrils of that one. AND CONSUMED THEM (Lev. 10:2). Their souls were consumed but not their garments, as it is said THEY CAME FORWARD AND CARRIED THEM OUT OF THE CAMP BY THEIR TUNICS (Lev. 10:5). BY THEIR TUNICS—the tunics of those who were carried. Perhaps it means the tunics of those who carried them? The verse says AND CONSUMED THEM (Lev. 10:2)—them and not their garments. And it says AND FOR AARON'S SONS ALSO YOU SHALL MAKE TUNICS (Ex. 28:40)—tunics for the priests and not for the Levites."

THUS THEY DIED BEFORE THE LORD (Lev. 10:2). R. Eliezer says, "Actually they died outside—in a place where Levites were permitted to come as it is said THEY CAME FORWARD AND CARRIED THEM OUT OF THE CAMP BY THEIR TUNICS (Lev. 10:5). Why then does it say THUS THEY DIED BEFORE THE LORD? An angel came and pushed them outside."

R. Akiba says, "They did indeed die within, as it says THUS THEY DIED BEFORE THE LORD. If so, why does it say THEY CAME FORWARD AND CARRIED THEM OUT OF THE CAMP BY THEIR TUNICS? This teaches that they took an iron spear and pulled them out in order to take them out."

THEN MOSES SAID TO AARON, "THIS IS WHAT THE LORD MEANT WHEN HE SAID: THROUGH THOSE NEAR TO ME I SHOW MYSELF HOLY" (Lev. 10:3). This had been said to Moses at Sinai, but he did not understand its meaning until this incident took place. Once the incident took place, Moses said to Aaron, "My brother, your sons died only in order to sanctify the name of the Holy One, Blessed is He, as it

---

their souls—their lives were extinguished, their bodies were burnt, but their garments remained untouched.
they died outside—and not within the Tabernacle, which is what BEFORE THE LORD usually implies.

is said AND THERE I WILL MEET WITH THE ISRAELITES, AND IT SHALL BE SANCTIFIED BY MY PRESENCE (Ex. 29:43)." Once Aaron knew that his sons were known by God, he was silent and received a reward for his silence. This is the source of the saying: If one accepts [what happens] upon oneself and is silent, it is a good sign for him. David said BE SILENT AND WAIT FOR THE LORD (Ps. 37:7). Solomon said A TIME FOR SILENCE AND A TIME FOR SPEAKING (Eccl. 3:7). There is a time for everything. A time for a man to keep silent and a time for a man to speak.

[Another interpretation:] Aaron stood confounded and said, "Woe unto me that such sins are upon me and my sons—that this has happened to me." Moses went to him and tried to quiet him. He said, "Aaron my brother, at Sinai I was told that in the future I would sanctify this house and that I would sanctify it through a great man. I thought that it would be sanctified either through me or you. Now we see that your sons are greater that either of us, for it is through them that the house is sanctified." When Aaron heard that, he accepted God's judgment upon himself as it is said AND AARON WAS SILENT (Lev. 10:3).

We see how the righteous accept God's judgment upon themselves. Abraham accepted God's judgment upon himself as it is said I AM BUT DUST AND ASHES (Gen. 18:27).

Jacob accepted God's judgment upon himself as it is said I AM UNWORTHY OF ALL THE KINDNESS THAT YOU HAVE SO STEADFASTLY SHOWN YOUR SERVANT (Gen. 32:11).

David accepted God's judgment upon himself as it is said MY WOUNDS STINK AND FESTER BECAUSE OF MY FOLLY (Ps. 38:6).

---

sanctify it through a great man—referring again to Ex. 29:43. It was sanctified by bringing glory or sanctity to God's Name as mentioned in Lev. 10:3. The great man was either of the two sons of Aaron whose deaths demonstrated that the greater one's sanctity, the greater the responsibility and the more severe the punishment for any infraction.

Abraham accepted God's judgment—in the case of the binding of Isaac. He remains silent and does not question God. See Gen. 22. His unquestioning obedience to God is similar to that of Aaron, who also remains silent.

MOSES CALLED MISHAEL AND ELZAPHAN, SONS OF UZZIEL THE UNCLE OF AARON, AND SAID TO THEM, "COME FORWARD AND CARRY YOUR KINSMEN..." (Lev. 10:4). From this it was said: [Priests] do not make themselves impure for the dead, for Eleazar and Ithamar were priests and did not make themselves impure for the dead. Who did make themselves impure? The Levites.

THEY CAME FORWARD AND CARRIED THEM OUT OF THE CAMP BY THEIR TUNICS (Lev. 10:5). This teaches that God was more merciful toward them in their death than in their life, for had their bodies been burnt and their garments had not remained, they would have been talked about and disgraced, but their bodies were burnt while their garments remained. This is a matter of logic: If God does this for those who came before Him in defiance of His will, how much more will He do so for the righteous!

COMMENTARY   *The Sages elaborate on the tragic death of the sons of Aaron. Various explanations are offered to explain this troubling event. Some see the bringing of "strange fire" as a fairly innocent act. Aaron's sons brought fire when they saw that none descended from heaven. Others see it as an act of rebellion, connected to their jealousy of their father and Moses and their desire to quickly succeed them as leaders of Israel. The truly tragic figure is Aaron, who is comforted by Moses, who explains that Aaron's sons participated in an act of the Sanctification of the Name of God. Aaron's agreement to keep silent is another act of great faith, the archetype of acceptance of God's decrees, "the justification of God's judgment" (tzidduk ha-din), which is a part of Jewish ritual, performed when there is a death or tragedy by declaring God to be a "true Judge." A few paragraphs in the original have been transposed for greater clarity.*

MOSES CALLED MISHAEL AND ELZAPHAN, SONS OF UZZIEL THE UNCLE OF AARON, AND SAID TO THEM (Lev. 10:4). Since it says THE SONS OF KOHATH BY CLAN: AMRAM AND IZHAR, HEBRON AND UZZIEL (Num. 3:19) would I not know that Uzziel was the uncle of Aaron? Why does the verse say THE UNCLE OF AARON?

Eleazar and Ithamar   The other sons of Aaron, who were themselves priests, do not tend to the burial of their brothers. It is done by other members of the family who were Levites and not priests.

LEVITICUS

It juxtaposes the actions of Uzziel with the actions of Aaron. Just as Aaron pursued peace in Israel, so Uzziel pursued peace in Israel. How do we know that Aaron pursued peace in Israel? As it is said THE WHOLE COMMUNITY KNEW THAT AARON HAD BREATHED HIS LAST. ALL THE HOUSE OF ISRAEL BEWAILED AARON THIRTY DAYS (Num. 20:29). And concerning Moses it says AND THE ISRAELITES BEWAILED MOSES IN THE STEPS OF MOAB FOR THIRTY DAYS (Deut. 34:8). Why did ALL THE HOUSE OF ISRAEL bewail Aaron for thirty days while only THE ISRAELITES bewailed Moses for thirty days and not all the house of Israel? Because Aaron had never said to either a man or a woman: You have corrupted your ways. But in the case of Moses, since he was constantly chiding them, it is said THE ISRAELITES BEWAILED MOSES. And so too is it stated explicitly of Aaron in Scripture I HAD WITH HIM A COVENANT OF LIFE AND PEACE (Mal. 2:5)—for he was a pursuer of peace in Israel. WHICH I GAVE TO HIM, AND OF REVERENCE, WHICH HE SHOWED ME (Mal. 2:5)—for he accepted all the words of the Torah upon himself in reverence, in fear and trembling. What does the verse say? FOR HE STOOD IN AWE OF MY NAME (Mal. 2:5).

It is said that when Moses poured the anointing oil upon Aaron's head, it dripped and fell behind him. He said, "Woe unto me that I have misused the anointing oil." The Holy Spirit answered him, "HOW GOOD AND HOW PLEASANT IT IS THAT BROTHERS DWELL TOGETHER. IT IS LIKE FINE OIL ON THE HEAD RUNNING DOWN ONTO THE BEARD, THE BEARD OF AARON, THAT COMES DOWN OVER THE COLLAR OF HIS ROBE; LIKE THE DEW OF HERMON THAT FALLS UPON THE MOUNTAINS OF ZION (Ps. 133:1-3). Just as the dew is not subject to misuse, so the anointing oil is not subject to misuse."

THE TORAH OF TRUTH WAS IN HIS MOUTH (Mal. 2:6)—in that he did not declare the pure impure or the impure, pure. AND NOTHING PERVERSE WAS ON HIS LIPS (Mal. 2:6)—in that he did not prohibit

---

only the ISRAELITES   Only the male Israelites mourned for Moses, while everyone, women and children included, mourned Aaron. The Hebrew literally means "the sons of Israel."
misused the anointing oil   "Misused" is a technical term meaning to desecrate something that is holy by using it for other purposes.
impure—referring to ritual impurity, such as in the realm of permitted foods.

the permitted or permit the prohibited. HE SERVED ME WITH COMPLETE LOYALTY (Mal. 2:6)—in that he did not question God, just as Abraham did not question God. AND HELD THE MANY BACK FROM INIQUITY (Mal. 2:6)—for he caused transgressors to return to the Torah. And it says THE UPRIGHT LOVE YOU (Song 1:4).

AND MOSES SAID TO AARON AND TO HIS SONS, ELEAZAR AND ITHAMAR, "DO NOT DISHEVEL YOUR HAIR AND DO NOT REND YOUR CLOTHES" (Lev. 10:6). This is the source of the teaching: One does not observe mourning for those executed by the court. [Moses said] "Perhaps you will say, 'We shall go to our homes and mourn and weep'—God has commanded that we not leave the Sanctuary as it is said YOU MUST NOT GO OUTSIDE THE ENTRANCE OF THE TENT OF MEETING (Lev. 10:7)." This was the source of the teaching: If someone has died in his family, a High Priest may not follow the bier. He may appear only when they are hidden. When they appear, he must be hidden. AND THEY DID AS MOSES HAD BIDDEN (Lev. 10:7). They accepted God's judgment upon themselves.

AND MOSES SAID TO AARON AND TO HIS SONS, ELEAZAR AND ITHAMAR (Lev. 10:6). Rabbi Judah the Prince says, "In matters of greatness we begin with the greatest. In matters of corruption, with the smallest." How do we know this? As it is said AND THE LORD GOD SAID TO THE SERPENT, "BECAUSE YOU DID THIS, BANNED SHALL YOU BE FROM ALL WILD BEASTS . . . I WILL PUT ENMITY BETWEEN YOU AND THE WOMAN . . . AND TO THE WOMAN HE SAID (Gen. 3:14–16)." He began by cursing the serpent, then He cursed Eve and then He cursed Adam.

COMMENTARY   *This section brings to the fore the picture of Aaron as the peacemaker, a role he plays throughout rabbinic literature. In opposition to Moses, the strict judge, Aaron is the gentle man of peace who never reproves but only tries to bring people to God through love and kindness. This concept was best articulated and possibly originated by Hillel in his statement, "Be of the disciples of Aaron, loving peace and pursuing peace; loving humankind and bringing them to the Torah."*

---

permitted—concerning actions such as observance of Holy Days or the Sabbath or laws of marriage or commerce.

they are hidden   When the funeral procession is in a place where he cannot see it, the High Priest may appear.

5. Leviticus 16:1, Sifra Weiss 89b

THE LORD SPOKE TO MOSES AFTER THE DEATH OF THE
TWO SONS OF AARON WHO DIED WHEN THEY DREW TOO
CLOSE TO THE PRESENCE OF THE LORD. (Lev. 16:1). R. Jose the
Galilean says, "They died because of drawing too close and not because of
the offering." R. Akiba says, "The verse says WHO DIED WHEN THEY
DREW TOO CLOSE TO THE PRESENCE OF THE LORD (Lev.
16:1). Another verse says AND THEY OFFERED BEFORE THE LORD
ALIEN FIRE (Lev. 10:1). A third verse decides the matter: NADAB AND
ABIHU DIED WHEN THEY OFFERED ALIEN FIRE BEFORE THE
LORD (Num. 26:61)—it was because of the offering that they died."
R. Eleazar b. Azariah says, "The offering itself warranted death and the
drawing close itself warranted death."

THE LORD SAID TO MOSES: TELL YOUR BROTHER AARON
THAT HE IS NOT TO COME AT ANY TIME (Lev. 16:2). We do not
know what He said to [Moses] the first time He spoke.

      R. Eleazar b. Azariah says, "A parable. It may be likened to a sick man
going to a doctor. He says to him: Do not drink anything cold and do not lie
on damp ground. Another patient came and he said to him: Do not drink
anything cold and do not lie on damp ground so that you should not
die as so-and-so did. This certainly convinced him more than anything
else. That is why it says AFTER THE DEATH OF THE TWO
SONS OF AARON . . . THE LORD SAID TO MOSES: TELL YOUR
BROTHER AARON THAT HE IS NOT TO COME AT ANY TIME
(Lev. 16:1–2)."

If he does come, he will die as it is said HE IS NOT TO COME . . . LEST
HE DIE (Lev. 16:2). If he comes, he will die as did his sons. That is why it

---

5. *drawing too close*—inappropriately entering the sacred precinct, possibly referring to the
tradition that they were intoxicated.

offering—of strange or alien fire.

a third verse R. Akiba follows the principle that when there are two verses that contradict one
another, a third verse will explain which is correct.

The offering itself R. Eleazar believes that both verses were correct. They committed two
transgressions and would have been killed for either.

the first time He spoke In the previous verse it says THE LORD SPOKE TO MOSES (Lev.
16:1) but does not say what He said. The assumption is that it was something different from
the speaking referred to in Lev. 16:2.

says AFTER THE DEATH OF THE TWO SONS OF AARON . . . THE LORD SAID TO MOSES: TELL YOUR BROTHER AARON THAT HE IS NOT TO COME AT ANY TIME.

They said in the name of R. Ishmael, "Since two pronouncements were made next to one another, one revealed and the other hidden, let the revealed one shed light on the hidden one. Just as the revealed one was that Moses should tell Aaron something about entering the sacred place, so the hidden one was that Moses should tell Aaron something about entering the sacred place. And what was the message? It concerned wine and ale, as it is said, BUT YOUR KINSMEN, ALL THE HOUSE OF ISRAEL, SHALL BE-WAIL THE BURNING THAT THE LORD HAS WROUGHT (Lev. 10:6) . . . AND THE LORD SPOKE TO AARON, SAYING: DRINK NO WINE OR ALE (Lev. 10:8–9)."

YOUR BROTHER (Lev. 16:2). The command not to enter [the sacred place] applies to him but not to Moses. Perhaps the command not to enter [the sacred place] applies to YOUR BROTHER but not to his sons. R. Eliezer says, "It is a matter of logic. If he who is commanded to enter it is also commanded not to enter it [at certain times], certainly he who is not commanded to enter it is commanded not to enter it!" The case of the unblemished priests will prove otherwise for they are commanded to enter but are also commanded not to enter it after drinking wine or ale. Priests with blemishes, however, who are not commanded to enter are also not commanded not to enter it after drinking wine or ale. Nevertheless [the sons] were so commanded, for the verse says TELL YOUR BROTHER AARON when there was no need to say YOUR BROTHER. What does YOUR BROTHER teach? That his sons were included in this.

---

two pronouncements—the two times it says that God spoke to Moses in Lev. 16:1 and Lev. 16:2. The first time is hidden because the contents are not recorded; the second time is revealed.

wine and ale　Aaron was told not to enter after having consumed alcoholic beverages.

commanded to enter it　Aaron is positively commanded to come into the inner sanctuary in Lev. 16:11, but is prohibited from entering except for then. His sons are *never* commanded to enter it.

commanded to enter—the Tent of Meeting. See Lev. 10:9.

Nevertheless　Even if by logical means we cannot prove that they were commanded not to enter it, we can do so by the words of the verse.

THAT HE IS NOT TO COME AT ANY TIME (Lev. 16:2). This refers
to the Day of Atonement. INTO THE SHRINE (Lev. 16:2)—including all
the other days of the year. R. Eliezer says, "It is a matter of logic. If on the
day when he is commanded to enter it, he is also commanded not to enter it,
certainly on all the other days when he is not commanded to enter it, he is
commanded not to enter it!" The case of the Israelites will prove otherwise
for they are commanded to come [to the sanctuary] on the festivals and they
are commanded not to come empty-handed. Whereas on the other days of
the year they are not commanded to come and they are not commanded not
to come empty-handed! So too here. On the day that he is commanded [to
enter it] he is also commanded [not to enter it]. The verse, however, states
INTO THE SHRINE in order to teach that he is also commanded [not to
come] on all the other days of the year.

BEHIND (mibet) THE CURTAIN (Lev. 16:2). This is a warning concerning the entire structure (bayit). Is it possible that the death penalty applies
to entering anywhere in the structure? The verse says IN FRONT OF THE
COVER THAT IS UPON THE ARK, LEST HE DIE (Lev. 16:2). What
does this mean? That IN FRONT OF THE COVER carries the death
penalty. The rest of the structure is merely under a warning.

IN FRONT OF THE COVER THAT IS UPON THE ARK (Lev. 16:2).
Why is this stated? Since it said THE CURTAIN (Lev. 16:2), one might
have thought that it was referring to a covering for the ark. Therefore the
verse says IN FRONT OF THE COVER. It means the cover on the ark
and not some covering for the ark. Could it be that while there was no
covering for the ark, there was something separating the cover from the
Ark of the Pact? The verse says SO THAT THE CLOUD FROM THE
INCENSE SCREENS THE COVER THAT IS OVER [THE ARK OF]
THE PACT, LEST HE DIE (Lev. 16:13).

BEHIND   Since this word also means "a house," it is taken as a warning against entering
anywhere within "the house," i.e., the Sanctuary or the Temple, frequently called simply
"The House."

the cover   This was not merely any kind of covering, but a specific part of the Ark. It is
described in Ex. 37:6—HE MADE A COVER OF PURE GOLD, TWO AND A HALF
CUBITS LONG AND A CUBIT AND A HALF WIDE. On it were the cherubim.

LEST HE DIE (Lev. 16:2). This announces the punishment. FOR I AP-PEAR IN THE CLOUD OVER THE COVER (Lev. 16:2). This is the warning. R. Eliezer says, "Is it possible that the punishment and the warning were given before the death of the two sons of Aaron? The verse says AF-TER THE DEATH OF THE TWO SONS OF AARON (Lev. 16:1). Is it possible that they were both given after the death of the two sons of Aaron? The verse says FOR I APPEAR IN THE CLOUD OVER THE COVER (Lev. 16:2). What does this mean? The warning was given before the death of the two sons of Aaron and the punishment was announced after the death of the two sons of Aaron.

COMMENTARY   *Several concerns of the midrash can be seen here. One is to base as much as possible upon the Biblical text. The use of logic and rules of interpretation are less convincing than the text itself. Therefore wherever possible, they attempt to show that it is the text itself that mandates a particular interpretation. Another tendency is to specify the meaning of the Biblical phrases. Where they might be taken to mean something other than what the Sages thought they meant, they will attempt to prove the specific meaning and eliminate other possibilities. Finally, R. Eliezer is concerned lest it appear that the death of Aaron's sons was not according to the rules of justice, which specified that there be a warning concerning a possible transgression. Thus, even though the text does not seem to say so, he interprets verse Leviticus 16:2 to mean just that.*

6. Leviticus 16:6, Sifra Weiss 80b

AARON IS TO OFFER HIS OWN BULL OF SIN OFFERING, TO MAKE EXPIATION FOR HIMSELF AND FOR HIS HOUSEHOLD (Lev. 16:6). This indicates that he made a verbal confession. Perhaps it

---

the warning—i.e., the prohibition, while the exact penalty (the punishment) is stated separately.
before the death   The prohibition here is of not putting in the proper ingredient to make the smoke rise properly. Had this prohibition been in effect prior to their death, we might have assumed that this was what they violated. Since it was not announced until after their death, that could not have been the cause.
FOR I APPEAR—i.e., I will appear. God had not yet done so, but on the day of their death it says THE PRESENCE OF THE LORD APPEARED TO ALL THE PEOPLE (Lev. 9:23). These words, then, constituting the warning, must have been given prior to that time.

---

6. *a verbal confession*   The expiation spoken of in the verse means a verbal confession.

means expiation through blood. Let us reason thus: "Expiation" is mentioned in connection to the bull and "expiation" is mentioned in connection to the goat (Lev. 16:10). Just as the expiation mentioned in connection to the goat is a verbal confession aside from blood, so the expiation mentioned in connection to the bull is a verbal confession aside from blood. Or you may demonstrate it from the verse: AARON IS TO OFFER HIS OWN BULL OF SIN OFFERING, TO MAKE EXPIATION FOR HIMSELF AND FOR HIS HOUSEHOLD—it has not yet been slaughtered!

How did he confess? [He said]: O Lord, I have committed iniquity, I have transgressed, I have sinned before You, I and my household. Atone, O Lord, for the iniquities, the transgressions, and the sins wherein I have committed iniquity, transgressed, and sinned before You, I and my household, as it says in the Torah of Moses Your servant FOR ON THIS DAY ATONEMENT SHALL BE MADE FOR YOU TO CLEANSE YOU OF ALL YOUR SINS; YOU SHALL BE CLEAN BEFORE THE LORD (Lev. 16:30). And it says AND CONFESS OVER IT ALL THE INIQUITIES AND TRANSGRESSIONS OF THE ISRAELITES, WHATEVER THEIR SINS (Lev. 16:21). So taught R. Meir.

The Sages say, "Iniquities are those sins committed willfully. Transgressions are those committed rebelliously. Sins are those committed unintentionally. Does it make sense that after confessing the willful and rebellious acts, he will confess the unintentional ones? Rather thus did he confess: O Lord, I have sinned, I have committed iniquity, I have transgressed before You, I and my household. Atone, O Lord, for the sins, the iniquities, and the transgressions wherein I have sinned, committed iniquity, and transgressed before You, I and my household, as it says in the Torah of Moses Your servant FOR ON THIS DAY ATONEMENT SHALL BE MADE FOR YOU TO CLEANSE YOU OF ALL YOUR SINS; YOU SHALL BE CLEAN BEFORE THE LORD (Lev. 16:30)." And they responded to him by saying "Blessed be the name of His glorious Majesty forever!"

---

the goat   In Lev. 16:21 it is clear that the expiation made by the goat is a verbal confession. Therefore this must be true of the expiation made through the bull as well. Wherever expiation is mentioned, the Sages interpreted it to mean a verbal confession.

willfully—because of a passion the person wishes to gratify.

rebelliously—deliberately in order to rebel against God's will.

And we find that this is the way in which confession was made by all those who confessed. David said WE HAVE SINNED LIKE OUR FOREFATHERS; WE HAVE GONE ASTRAY, ACTED WICKEDLY (Ps. 106:6). Solomon his son said WE HAVE SINNED, WE HAVE GONE ASTRAY WE HAVE ACTED WICKEDLY (1 Kings 8:47; 2 Chron. 6:37). Daniel said WE HAVE SINNED; WE HAVE GONE ASTRAY; WE HAVE ACTED WICKEDLY (Dan. 9:5). So too did Aaron say: I have sinned, I have committed iniquity, I have transgressed. Why then did Moses say FORGIVING INIQUITY, TRANSGRESSION, AND SIN (Ex. 34:7) and AND CONFESS OVER IT ALL THE INIQUITIES AND TRANSGRESSIONS OF THE ISRAELITES, WHATEVER THEIR SINS (Lev. 16:21)? It means: Once confession has been made, may the iniquities and transgression be no more than sins before You!

AND HE SHALL TAKE THE TWO HE-GOATS (Lev. 16:7). This teaches that the lack of either one impedes the fulfillment of the mitzvah. AND LET THEM STAND BEFORE THE LORD AT THE ENTRANCE OF THE TENT OF MEETING (Lev. 16:7). He places them with the Nicanor Gate behind them to the east while they face west. AND HE SHALL PLACE LOTS UPON THE TWO GOATS (Lev. 16:8). Of any matter. May two be placed on each of them? The verse says ONE MARKED FOR THE LORD AND THE OTHER MARKED FOR AZAZEL (Lev. 16:8). May both lots FOR THE LORD AND . . . FOR AZAZEL be placed on both of them? The verse says ONE MARKED FOR THE LORD AND THE OTHER MARKED FOR AZAZEL—there is only one which says FOR AZAZEL. What then is the implication of LOTS? That they are to be equal. One is not to be large and the other small; one of silver and one of gold; one of marble and one of box wood.

---

this is the way—that confession was always made, beginning with the less serious, unintentional sins and then mentioning the more serious, intentional ones.

AND SIN—putting the least serious sin last and the more serious ones first.

no more than sins He was not listing them in order of severity but meant—May the serious transgressions be of no more importance than the light ones.

Nicanor Gate In Herod's Temple, this gate was directly opposite the entrance to the Holy of Holies. This would be equivalent to the Biblical description that at the Tabernacle, they stood BEFORE THE LORD AT THE ENTRANCE OF THE TENT OF MEETING.

any matter There is no description of how the lots were to be made and there are no specifications for them.

AARON SHALL BRING FORWARD THE GOAT DESIGNATED BY
LOT FOR THE LORD (Lev. 16:9). Should he put the lot on its back? The
verse says DESIGNATED BY LOT—it was designated for it from within
the lottery-box.

WHICH HE IS TO OFFER (Lev. 16:9). If one of them dies after the lots
have been cast, two new ones are brought and the lots are cast again. If the
one designated for the Lord died, [the priest] shall proclaim: That which is
designated now by the lot for the Lord will take its place. If the one designated for Azazel dies, he shall proclaim: That which is designated now by
the lot for Azazel will take its place. The other one shall be allowed to die.
So taught R. Judah. The Sages say, "It shall be put to pasture until a blemish
appears, after which it shall be sold and the purchase price given to the
Temple."

WHICH HE IS TO OFFER AS A SIN OFFERING (Lev. 16:9). He is to
say, "To the Lord: a sin offering!" R. Ishmael says, "He need not say 'a sin
offering,' but merely 'To the Lord!' "

WHILE THE GOAT DESIGNATED BY LOT FOR AZAZEL (Lev.
16:10). Should he put the lot on its back? The verse says DESIGNATED
BY LOT—it was designated for it from within the lottery-box.

SHALL BE LEFT STANDING ALIVE BEFORE THE LORD (Lev.
16:10). Why is this stated? Since it says TO SEND IT OFF (Lev. 16:10)—
it is to be sent to die. Perhaps it is to be sent to live? The verse says SHALL
BE LEFT STANDING ALIVE BEFORE THE LORD TO MAKE EXPI-
ATION WITH IT (Lev. 16:10). How is this to be done? It stands alive
before the Lord and is killed at the rocky cliff. How long need it be kept
alive? TO MAKE EXPIATION (Lev. 16:10)—until the expiation, as it is
said WHEN HE HAS FINISHED PURGING THE SHRINE, THE
TENT OF MEETING AND THE ALTAR (Lev. 16:20). So taught R.
Judah. R. Simeon says, "TO MAKE EXPIATION—expiation by its body.

---

the lot on its back—placing the lot on the back of the goat means nothing. The lots were to be
cast from the box and however it came up determined which goat was for which purpose.
the other one—of the second pair that was not designated to replace the dead goat.
How is this to be done? Since one verse speaks of it standing alive and the other of sending it
away to die, exactly what is to be done?

TO SEND IT OFF (Lev. 16:10)—if its blood was spilt, the goat that is to be sent away is left to die. If the one to be sent away dies, the blood of the other is spilt.

FOR AZAZEL (Lev. 16:10). To a hard place in the mountains. Might it be somewhere inhabited? The verse says TO THE WILDERNESS (Lev. 16:10). And how do we know that it must be to a rocky cliff? The verse says TO AN INACCESSIBLE REGION (Lev. 16:22).

AARON SHALL THEN OFFER HIS BULL OF SIN OFFERING (Lev. 16:11). This is what was meant when they said: It must not come from the funds of the public. TO MAKE EXPIATION FOR HIMSELF AND HIS HOUSEHOLD (Lev. 16:11). This refers to the verbal confession. How did he confess? "O Lord, I have sinned, committed iniquity, and transgressed before You. I, my household and the sons of Aaron your holy people, as it is said in the Torah of your servant Moses FOR ON THIS DAY SHALL ATONEMENT BE MADE FOR YOU (Lev. 16:30)." And they responded: Blessed be the Name of His Glorious Majesty forever and ever!

COMMENTARY   *Through their interpretations the Sages establish the correct procedure for the Temple ceremonies of the Day of Atonement. At the time these interpretations were set down, obviously there was no Temple, but the expectation of rebuilding and renewal was constant. Not content with whatever historical memories there were of what had been done in the Temple, they attempted to determine the correct wording of the confession and the correct actions for the ceremonies on the basis of the text and their understanding of it. The ceremonies of the rebuilt Temple would then be conducted according to these rules.*

7. Leviticus 16:12, Sifra Weiss 81:a

AND HE SHALL TAKE A PANFUL OF GLOWING COALS SCOOPED FROM THE ALTAR BEFORE THE LORD, AND TWO HANDFULS OF FINELY GROUND AROMATIC INCENSE, AND BRING THIS BEHIND THE CURTAIN. HE SHALL PUT THE IN-

---

blood was spilt   If either goat died before the proper ceremony was completed, the other is left to die and two new goats are brought in and a new lottery held. According to the Mishna, this is the opinion of R. Judah.

of the public   It must be paid for by the priest since the verse specifies that it is to be his.

CENSE ON THE FIRE BEFORE THE LORD (Lev. 16:12–13). He may not set it up thus outside [the curtain] and then go within. For the Sadducees say "He should set it up outside and then go within. If this is how it is done before flesh and blood, certainly that is how it should be done before God! And it says FOR I APPEAR IN THE CLOUD OVER THE COVER (Lev. 16:2)." The Sages said to them, "Does it not say HE SHALL PUT THE INCENSE ON THE FIRE BEFORE THE LORD (Lev. 16:13)? He does it only when he is within! What then is the meaning of FOR I APPEAR IN THE CLOUD OVER THE COVER? It means that he must include a plant which raises a great deal of smoke. What is the source which teaches us that he must include such a plant? The verse says SO THAT THE CLOUD FROM THE INCENSE SCREENS THE COVER THAT IS OVER [THE ARK OF] THE PACT, LEST HE DIE (Lev. 16:13). Thus we learn that if he does not include a plant which raises a great deal of smoke or any other of the ingredients required, he is liable to death."

COMMENTARY   *The dispute here was more than theoretical. It records an argument between the Pharisees and the Sadducees prior to the destruction of the Temple. Although the priests who conducted the rites were mostly Sadducees, the Pharisaic group held sway over the majority of the population and were able to force their will on this matter. It has been suggested by L. Finkelstein that the matter was more than a question of the understanding of Scripture, but reflected the superstitions and fears of the priests who would not walk into the Holy of Holies unless they already had the incense burning, lest they behold the Presence of God.*

8. Leviticus 19:1, Sifra Weiss 86b

THE LORD SPOKE TO MOSES, SAYING: SPEAK TO THE WHOLE ISRAELITE COMMUNITY AND SAY TO THEM: YOU SHALL BE HOLY, FOR I, THE LORD YOUR GOD, AM HOLY (Lev. 19:1–2). This indicates that this section was said to the entire group in assembly.

---

7. *and then go within*   He may not place the incense on burning coals outside the Holy of Holies and then go inside it.
before flesh and blood   This was the practice before kings.
when he is within   Since it says BEFORE THE LORD, it means that this must be done within the Holy of Holies.

Why was it said to the entire group in assembly? Because most of the basic laws of the Torah are dependent upon it.

YOU SHALL BE HOLY (Lev. 19:2) You shall be separated. YOU SHALL BE HOLY, FOR I, THE LORD YOUR GOD, AM HOLY (Lev. 19:2). That is to say, if you sanctify yourselves, I shall account it to you as if you had sanctified Me. And if you do not sanctify yourselves, I shall account it to you as if you did not sanctify Me. Perhaps it means that if you sanctify Me I am sanctified, but if not, I am not sanctified? The verse says FOR I . . . AM HOLY. I am sanctified whether you sanctify Me or not. Abba Saul says, "They are the royal escort whose duty it is to follow the king exactly."

A MAN SHALL REVERE HIS MOTHER AND HIS FATHER (Lev. 19:3). This teaches me only about a man. What about a woman? The verse says SHALL REVERE [in the plural] teaching me about both. In that case, why does it say A MAN? Because a man has the means at hand and a woman does not since there are others who have control over her. It says A MAN SHALL REVERE HIS MOTHER AND HIS FATHER and it says YOU MUST REVERE THE LORD YOUR GOD (Deut. 10:20) thus connecting the reverence for God with the reverence for father and mother.

It says HONOR YOUR FATHER AND YOUR MOTHER (Ex. 20:12) and it says HONOR THE LORD WITH YOUR WEALTH (Prov. 3:9) thus connecting honoring father and mother with honoring God.

It says IF A MAN CURSES HIS FATHER OR HIS MOTHER HE SHALL BE PUT TO DEATH (Lev. 20:9) and it says ANYONE WHO CURSES HIS GOD SHALL BEAR HIS GUILT (Lev. 24:15) thus connecting cursing father and mother to cursing God.

It is impossible to speak of striking God (as it does of father and mother in Ex. 21:15), but the analogy holds since the three of them are partners in the human being.

---

8. *basic laws* The concept of holiness requiring separation from immorality and from ritual impurity underlies most of the regulations of the Torah. Because of its importance, the entire people was called together to hear this message.

sanctified Me—performed the act of the sanctification of the Name of God, which involves bringing others—Jews as well as non-Jews—to recognize His greatness.

follow the king—to imitate his actions. Another instance of "imitatio dei," the imitation of God.

control over her In the society of that time, when a woman left her parents' home and married, her husband had control over her actions as well as her material goods.

R. Simeon says, "Sheep always precede goats wherever they are mentioned. Is this because they are better? The verse says IF THE OFFERING HE BRINGS AS A SIN OFFERING IS A SHEEP (Lev. 4:32), which teaches that they are equal. Pigeons always precede turtledoves wherever they are mentioned. Is this because they are better? The verse says AND A PIGEON OR A TURTLEDOVE FOR A SIN OFFERING (Lev. 12:6), which teaches that they are equal. The father always precedes the mother wherever they are mentioned. Does this mean that the honor due a father has preference to that due a mother? The verse says A MAN SHALL REVERE HIS MOTHER AND HIS FATHER (Lev. 19:3), which teaches that they are equal. But the Sages said, 'The father precedes the mother for both the child and the mother are required to honor the father.' "

What is meant by "reverence?" Do not sit in his place. Do not speak in his place and do not contradict his word. What is meant by "honoring?" Giving food and drink. Dressing and covering. Taking out and bringing back. Could A MAN SHALL REVERE HIS MOTHER AND HIS FATHER (Lev. 19:3) mean that if his father or mother told him to transgress one of the mitzvot of the Torah, he should do so? The verse says AND KEEP MY SABBATHS (Lev. 19:3). All of you are required to honor Me.

DO NOT TURN TO IDOLS (Lev. 19:4). Do not turn in order to worship them. R. Judah says, "Do not turn to look at them. That is bad enough!"

IDOLS. This is one of the ten contemptuous names ascribed to idols because of what they do.

They are called IDOLS (elilim) because they are empty (halulim).
"Sculptured image" (pesel) (Ex. 20:4) because they are disqualified (nifsalim).
"Molten image" (masecha) (2 Chron. 34:3) because they are poured out (nesuchim).

---

they are equal   Since the mother comes first in this verse it indicates that the father coming first elsewhere does not mean that he is more important. The child must give equal honor and reverence to both of them.
All of you   The parents are also required to honor God and obey His laws. Should they tell a child not to do so, the child should not follow them.
ten contemptuous names   Another list in the Fathers According to Rabbi Nathan, Chapter 34, lists one not found here, "wickedness," and omits "pillar."

"Pillar" (matzeva) (Gen. 28:18) because they stand still.

"Shapes" (atzabim) (2 Chron. 24:18) because they are made section by section.

"Teraphim" (Gen. 31:19) because they putrefy.

"Fetishes" (gelulim) (Ezek. 22:3) because they are disgusting (megoalim).

"Abominations" (2 Kings 23:24) because they are abominable.

"Sun images" (hamanim) (Isa. 27:9) because they stand under wrath (hemah).

"Asherim" (Isa. 27:9) because they become wealthy (mitashrim) from others.

DO NOT TURN TO IDOLS OR MAKE MOLTEN GODS (Lev. 19:4). At first they are merely idols. If you turn to them, you make them into divinities.

OR MAKE MOLTEN GODS (Lev. 19:4). Perhaps others are permitted to make them for them? The verse says FOR YOURSELVES (Lev. 19:4). Perhaps NOT . . . FOR YOURSELVES but you may make them for others? The verse says both DO NOT MAKE and NOT . . . FOR YOURSELVES. This is the source of the teaching: One who makes an idol violates two warnings: DO NOT MAKE and NOT . . . FOR YOURSELVES. R. Jose says, "He violates three: DO NOT MAKE, NOT . . . FOR YOURSELVES and YOU SHALL HAVE NO OTHER GODS (Ex. 20:3)."

COMMENTARY   *Chapter 19 of Leviticus stresses the concept of holiness or sanctity. The Sages define this as being separated from impurity and abomination, moral or ritual. The word they use for this—"perushim" (separated)—became the name of the group from which rabbinic Judaism springs, "Perushim"—Pharisees. Their separateness did not mean isolation from the masses of people, which did characterize the Essene group, but an attempt to observe carefully the laws of holiness that the Torah prescribes. Among these laws were such ethical precepts as the treatment due to parents, who are compared to God Himself. In these matters mother and father*

---

stand still   The Hebrew for pillar is derived from a root meaning to stand.

section by section   The Hebrew means to shape something. In the Mishnah it also means to straighten out limbs, thus to move sections.

divinities   The only reason the verse calls them "gods" is because when people worship them, they attribute divinity to them. In reality, they are not gods at all.

*are equal. Another matter of holiness is separateness from all forms of idol-
atry. Although during the period of the Second Temple, as opposed to the
time of the First Temple, Jews themselves were not considered to be attracted by idolatrous worship, they were surrounded by an idolatrous world.
Sages frequently have good words to say about pagans, but they have nothing
but contempt for paganism. Here they gather together every term used in
the Bible to refer to idols and explain them in contemptuous ways.*

9. Leviticus 20:22, Sifra Weiss 93a

YOU SHALL FAITHFULLY OBSERVE MY LAWS AND ALL MY
REGULATIONS, LEST THE LAND TO WHICH I BRING YOU TO
SETTLE IN SPEW YOU OUT (Lev. 20:22). The Land of Israel is not
like the other lands. It does not suffer transgressors. A parable. It may be
compared to a prince who was given something to eat which he could not
digest. Therefor he spewed it out. So too the Land of Israel does not suffer
transgressors. Thus it says SO LET NOT THE LAND SPEW YOU OUT
FOR DEFILING IT, AS IT SPEWED OUT THE NATION THAT
CAME BEFORE YOU (Lev. 18:28). . . .

LEST THE LAND TO WHICH I BRING YOU TO SETTLE IN SPEW
YOU OUT (Lev. 20:22). I bring you there in order to settle there,
unlike the Canaanites who were there only in order to guard it until you
could come.

YOU SHALL NOT FOLLOW THE PRACTICES OF THE NATION
(Lev. 20:23). This refers to the Egyptians. THAT I AM DRIVING OUT
BEFORE YOU (Lev. 20:23). This refers to the Canaanites. FOR IT IS
BECAUSE THEY DID ALL THESE THINGS (Lev. 20:23). This teaches
that the Canaanites were steeped in all these practices. It is because of these
practices that I am exiling them. THAT I ABHORRED THEM (Lev.
20:23). Like a man who abhors his food. AND SAID TO YOU: YOU
SHALL POSSESS THEIR LAND (Lev. 20:23–24). You are pleasant. You
shall inherit them, for you were the first to open yourselves [to Me] as it is
said A GARDEN LOCKED IS MY OWN, MY BRIDE, A FOUNTAIN

---

9. *who abhors his food*—and therefore spews it out.

open yourselves The description in Song of Songs, always interpreted as referring to Israel,
indicates that Israel was the first of the nations to open itself to God and had not been open
to idols.

LOCKED, A SEALED-UP SPRING (Song 4:12). FOR I WILL GIVE IT
TO YOU TO POSSESS (Lev. 20:24). In the future I shall give it to you as
an everlasting possession. Should you say, "But it is not Yours to give for it
belongs to others," I tell you that it belongs to you. It is the portion of the
children of Shem and you are the children of Shem, while they are the children of Ham. Why then are they there? Only in order to guard it until you
could come.

I THE LORD AM YOUR GOD WHO HAS SET YOU APART FROM
OTHER PEOPLES (Lev. 20:24). Look at the difference between you and
the other peoples! Among the peoples a man adorns his wife and then delivers her to another man. A man adorns himself and delivers himself to
another man. SO YOU SHALL SET APART THE CLEAN BEAST
FROM THE UNCLEAN (Lev. 20:25). Should it not mention "between
the cow and the ass?" All of this has already been explained. If so why does
it say SO YOU SHALL SET APART THE CLEAN BEAST FROM THE
UNCLEAN? It means that you shall differentiate between that which is
clean for you and that which is unclean for you, between that whose windpipe was cut sufficiently and that which was not cut sufficiently. What is the
difference? No more than a hair's breadth. YOU SHALL NOT DRAW
ABOMINATION UPON YOURSELVES THROUGH BEAST OR
BIRD OR ANYTHING WITH WHICH THE GROUND IS ALIVE,
WHICH I HAVE SET APART FOR YOU TO TREAT AS UNCLEAN
(Lev. 20:25)—making it forbidden.

YOU SHALL BE HOLY TO ME, FOR I THE LORD AM HOLY (Lev.
20:26). As I am holy, so shall you be holy. As I am separated, so shall you be
separated. AND I HAVE SET YOU APART FROM OTHER PEOPLES
TO BE MINE (Lev. 20:26). If you are apart from the other peoples, you are
Mine. If not, you belong to Nebuchadnezzar, King of Babylonia, and his
cohorts.

---

in the future—at the end of your wandering in the wilderness.
children of Ham In Gen. 10:6 Canaan is listed as a descendant of Ham. Rabbinic legend,
found also in the Book of Jubilees 8, describes the division of the earth among Noah's children
(see Gen. 10). The section containing the Land of Canaan went to Shem and not to Ham.
windpipe The accepted method of slaughter that renders an animal fit for consumption according to Jewish law involves the severing of the windpipe.
all of this The description of which animals are clean and which are not was given in detail in
Lev. 11. Therefore the reference here is to something else: those that are rendered fit or unfit
for you to eat by the method of slaughter.

R. Eleazar b. Azariah says, "What is the source which teaches that a person should not say: It is impossible for me to wear a mixture of wool and linen; it is impossible for me to eat the flesh of swine; it is impossible for me to have sexual relations with close relatives. Rather it is possible, but what shall I do when my Father in Heaven has forbidden me to do so? The verse says AND I HAVE SET YOU APART FROM OTHER PEOPLE TO BE MINE—to separate from sin and accept upon himself the yoke of God's Kingship."

COMMENTARY   *Holiness is expressed through separation. This idea is fundamental to the Bible and is extended and made implicit by the Sages. The dietary restrictions are one ritual form of expressing this and of achieving a feeling of dedication to God and His service. The observance of these and so many other similar laws is explained here as a method of training the individual to obedience to God. These matters are effective not when the person feels that he or she could not possibly do them, but when even though natural inclination leads to doing them, obedience to God prevents it. It is this separation that then makes possible the acceptance of God's kingship, embodied in the rabbinic value-concept "the yoke of God's Kingship."*

10. Leviticus 26:3, Sifra Weiss 110b

IF YOU FOLLOW MY LAWS AND FAITHFULLY OBSERVE MY COMMANDMENTS (Lev. 26:3). One must learn in order to observe and not in order not to observe. For it were better for one who learns in order not to observe had he not been created!

I WILL GRANT YOUR RAINS IN THEIR SEASON (Lev. 26:4). This refers to the fourth day of the week. You say "the fourth day of the week," but perhaps it means the eve of the Sabbath? They said, "Even in years that

---

impossible for me   I could not do this because it is inherently abhorrent and disgusting to me.
it is possible   Nothing inherent in these things or in me keeps me from doing them, only God's decree.

---

10. *in order not to observe*   In other places the statement is made in reference to learning "not for its own sake," i.e., for an impure motive. The pure motive for learning Torah is to be able to carry it out. Studying with no intention of observing is condemned.
fourth day of the week—probably "until the fourth day . . . ," i.e., rain at the beginning of the week is good. After that it interferes with preparations for the Sabbath.

are like those of Elijah, if the rain falls on the eve of the Sabbath, it must be seen as a curse." How then should I understand I WILL GRANT YOUR RAINS IN THEIR SEASON? On the fourth day of the week.

It once happened during the days of Herod that the rains would come at night. In the morning, the sun would shine and the wind would blow and dry off the earth so that laborers could go to their work. Thus all knew that they were engaged in the work of Heaven.

I WILL GRANT YOUR RAINS IN THEIR SEASON (Lev. 26:4). This refers to the evening following the Sabbath. It once happened in the days of Simeon b. Shetah and Queen Salome Alexandra that the rains would come down from the evening following the Sabbath until the eve of the Sabbath so that wheat grains were as large as kidneys, barley was as large as olive pits, and lentils were as large as golden dinarii. The Sages stored them away for future generations to see to demonstrate how powerful are the effects of sin, fulfilling the verse IT IS YOUR INIQUITIES WHICH HAVE DIVERTED THESE THINGS, YOUR SINS THAT HAVE WITH-HELD THE BOUNTY FROM YOU (Jer. 5:25).

I WILL GRANT YOUR RAINS IN THEIR SEASON (Lev. 26:4). Not the rains of other lands. How than shall I understand the verse ALL THE FAMILIES OF THE EARTH SHALL BLESS THEMSELVES BY YOU AND YOUR DESCENDANTS (Gen. 28:14)? It means that there will be plenty in the Land of Israel and famine in other lands so that they will come and purchase food from them, thus enriching them in the same way that is described in the verse JOSEPH GATHERED IN ALL THE MONEY THAT WAS TO BE FOUND IN THE LAND OF EGYPT AND IN THE LAND OF CANAAN, AS PAYMENT FOR THE RATIONS THAT WERE BEING PROCURED (Gen. 47:14). Thus it says AND

---

those of Elijah—a time of famine when no rain fell as a punishment for the actions of the wicked Ahab. See 1 Kings 17:1. Even then, when rain is badly needed, if it interferes with the Sabbath, it is a curse and not a blessing.

days of Herod—when the Temple was being built. This was a pious act that deserved the blessing of having it rain only at night when it would not interfere with their work.

Queen Salome Alexandra—a pious queen who reigned from 76 B.C.E. to 67 B.C.E. Then too the rains came as a blessing. She granted great power to the leader of the Pharisees, Simeon b. Shetah.

fulfilling the verse These large vegetables would prove that if such produce is not forthcoming it is a punishment as described in the verse.

YOUR SECURITY (dav'echa) LAST ALL YOUR DAYS (Deut. 33:25)—
all the lands should melt (dov'ot) their gold and bring it to the Land of Israel.

SO THAT THE EARTH SHALL YIELD ITS PRODUCE (Lev. 26:4).
Not as the earth does now, but as it did in the days of primal Adam. How do
we know that in the future the earth will be sown and yield fruit the very
same day? The verse says HE HAS MADE A REMEMBRANCE OF HIS
WONDERS (Ps. 111:4) and it says LET THE EARTH SPROUT VEG-
ETATION: SEED-BEARING PLANTS (Gen. 1:11) indicating that on the
very same day it was sown, the earth yielded fruit.

AND THE TREES OF THE FIELD WILL YIELD THEIR FRUIT (Lev.
26:4). Not as the trees do now, but as they did in the days of primal Adam.
How do we know that in the future trees will be planted and yield their fruit
on the very same day? The verse says HE HAS MADE A REMEM-
BRANCE OF HIS WONDERS (Ps. 111:4) and it says FRUIT TREES OF
EVERY KIND ON EARTH BEARING FRUIT WITH THE SEED IN
IT (Gen. 1:11) indicating that on the very same day they were planted, they
yielded their fruit. How do we know that in the future the tree itself will be
edible? The verse says FRUIT TREES (Gen. 1:11). If this was meant to
teach you that the tree bears fruit, this is said elsewhere: THAT BEAR
FRUIT (Gen. 1:11). Why then does it say FRUIT TREES? It means that
just as the fruit could be eaten, so the tree could be eaten. How do we know
that in the future, even fruitless trees will bear fruit? It says AND THE
TREES OF THE FIELD SHALL YIELD THEIR FRUIT (Lev. 26:4).

YOUR THRESHING SHALL OVERTAKE THE VINTAGE (Lev.
26:5). You will still be threshing when the vintage comes. AND YOUR
VINTAGE SHALL OVERTAKE THE SOWING (Lev. 26:5). You will
still be harvesting the vintage when the time for sowing comes. YOU
SHALL EAT YOUR FILL OF BREAD (Lev. 26:5). One need not state
that if you eat a lot you will be satisfied. Rather it means that you will eat a
small amount and feel contented within, as it is said YOU SHALL SERVE
THE LORD YOUR GOD, AND HE WILL BLESS YOUR BREAD

---

the days of primal Adam Prior to Adam's sin, which resulted in God's cursing the earth, fruit
was sown and harvested the same day. This will happen again in the Messianic era.
REMEMBRANCE OF HIS WONDERS—in that there will be a repetition of the wondrous
conditions under which Adam lived.
FRUIT TREES—trees that were themselves fruit.

AND YOUR WATER (Ex. 23:25). AND DWELL SECURELY IN YOUR LAND (Lev. 26:5) but you shall not dwell securely outside of it.

You may say: What does it matter if there is food and drink if there is no peace? The verse says I WILL GRANT PEACE IN THE LAND (Lev. 26:6). This indicates that peace is as important as all the rest. Thus it says I MAKE PEACE AND CREATE WOE (Isa. 45:7) indicating that peace is as important as all the rest.

AND YOU SHALL LIE DOWN UNTROUBLED BY ANYONE (Lev. 26:6) unafraid of any creature. AND I WILL GIVE THE LAND RE-SPITE FROM VICIOUS BEASTS (Lev. 26:6). R. Judah says, "I will elim-inate them from the world." R. Simeon says, "I will prevent them from doing harm." R. Simeon explained, "When is God praised, when there are no harmful creatures, or when there are, but they can do no harm? One must say that it is when there are harmful creatures but they can do no harm. Thus it says A PSALM. A SONG; FOR THE SABBATH (ha-shabbat) DAY (Ps. 92:1)—for He who prevents (mashbit) harmful creatures from doing harm in the world. He prevents them from doing harm." Thus it says THE WOLF SHALL DWELL WITH THE LAMB, THE LEOPARD LIE DOWN WITH THE KID; THE CALF, THE BEAST OF PREY, AND THE FATLING TOGETHER, WITH A LITTLE BOY TO HERD THEM. THE COW AND THE BEAR SHALL GRAZE, THEIR YOUNG SHALL LIE DOWN TOGETHER; AND THE LION, LIKE THE OX, SHALL EAT STRAW. A BABE SHALL PLAY OVER A VI-PER'S HOLE, AND AN INFANT PASS HIS HAND OVER AN AD-DER'S DEN (Isa. 11:6–8). This teaches that in the future an Israelite babe will be able to stretch out his hand into the very eye of an adder or extract poison from its mouth. He will say, "Look what is in my hand. This is something which usually kills people!"

AND NO SWORD SHALL CROSS YOUR LAND (Lev. 26:6). One need not state that none shall make war against you. What it means is that those who are passing from one place to another to make war will not pass through [your land] as they did in the days of Josiah.

---

all the rest   This comment reflects the fact that when they included this verse in the morning prayers the Sages changed it to read: I make peace and create everything. Thus MAKE PEACE is in apposition to "create everything."

in the days of Josiah—who was slain when he attempted to prevent Pharaoh Neco of Egypt from passing through the Land of Israel to do battle with the Assyrians. See 2 Kings 23:29–30.

YOU SHALL GIVE CHASE TO YOUR ENEMIES, AND THEY
SHALL FALL BEFORE YOU BY THE SWORD (Lev. 26:7). They shall
fall before you, each one smitten by the sword of his fellow.

FIVE OF YOU SHALL GIVE CHASE TO A HUNDRED, AND A
HUNDRED OF YOU SHALL GIVE CHASE TO TEN THOUSAND
(Lev. 26:8). OF YOU—the weakest of you and not the strongest! AND A
HUNDRED OF YOU SHALL GIVE CHASE TO TEN THOUSAND.
Is this the correct sum? Should it not have said "a hundred of you shall give
chase to two thousand?" One cannot compare a small number who obey the
Torah to a multitude who do so. YOUR ENEMIES SHALL FALL BE-
FORE YOU BY THE SWORD (Lev. 26:8). They will simply fall before
you—not in the usual way.

I WILL TURN TOWARD YOU (Lev. 26:9). A parable. It may be likened
to a king who hired many workers but there was one worker who did a great
deal of work for him for many days. The workers went in to receive their
wages, as did that one worker. The king said to that worker, "My son, I will
turn to you. This multitude did very little work for me and they will receive
a small salary. But I have a large sum that I will settle on you in the future."
Thus when Israel asked God for its wages in this world and the nations of
the world also asked God for their wages, God says to Israel, "My children,
I will turn to you. These nations of the world did very little work for Me
and they will receive a small salary. But I have a large sum that I will settle
on you in the future." Therefore it says I WILL TURN TOWARD YOU.

I WILL TURN TOWARD YOU—in graciousness. AND MAKE YOU
FERTILE (Lev. 26:9) in reproduction. AND MULTIPLY YOU (Lev.
26:9) in stature. AND I WILL MAINTAIN MY COVENANT WITH
YOU (Lev. 26:9). This will not be like the first covenant which you broke,
as it is said, A COVENANT WHICH THEY BROKE, SO THAT I RE-
JECTED THEM—DECLARES THE LORD (Jer. 31:32) but a new cov-

---

of his fellow　The verse means not that you will kill them by the sword, but that they will kill
each other and fall before you.
the correct sum　It seems disproportionally large. The answer is that the larger the number of
those who obey the Torah, the greater their power, which does not simply increase propor-
tionately because the multitude has an effect of its own.
not in the usual way　They will not be killed by you, but miraculously fall before you without
your having to do anything to bring it about.
the first covenant—made at Sinai.

enant which will not be broken, as it is said, SEE, A TIME IS COMING—DECLARES THE LORD—WHEN I WILL MAKE A NEW COVENANT WITH THE HOUSE OF ISRAEL AND THE HOUSE OF JUDAH (Jer. 31:31).

YOU SHALL EAT THAT WHICH IS OLD, LONG STORED (Lev. 26:10). This teaches that whatever is older is better. OLD. This teaches me only about wine whose nature it is [to improve with age]. What about everything which ages? The verse says OLD, LONG STORED.

AND YOU SHALL HAVE TO CLEAR OUT THE OLD TO MAKE ROOM FOR THE NEW (Lev. 26:10). The threshing floors will be filled with new produce while the storehouses will still be filled with the old. You will have to worry about taking out the old to make room for the new!

I WILL ESTABLISH MY ABODE IN YOUR MIDST (Lev. 26:11). This refers to the Temple. AND I WILL NOT SPURN YOU (Lev. 26:11). Once I have redeemed you, I will no longer be disgusted by you. I WILL BE EVER PRESENT IN YOUR MIDST (Lev. 26:12). A parable. This may be likened to a king who went out into the orchard with his tenant. The tenant attempted to hide, and the king said to the tenant, "Why do you hide from me? I am just like you." So too the Holy One said to the righteous, "Why should you be frightened of Me?" In the future the Holy One will stroll with the righteous in the Garden of Eden. The righteous will see Him and be frightened, but He will say to them, "I am just like you." Will they then not be in awe of Me? The verse says I WILL BE YOUR GOD AND YOU SHALL BE MY PEOPLE (Lev. 26:12). "And if you do not believe Me about all this I THE LORD AM YOUR GOD WHO BROUGHT YOU OUT OF THE LAND OF THE EGYPTIANS (Lev. 26:13)—I am He who performed miracles for you in Egypt. I am He who will perform all of these miracles in the future."

TO BE THEIR SLAVES NO MORE (Lev. 26:13). Why is this said? Since it says AND RESCUED YOU FROM THE HOUSE OF BONDAGE (Deut. 7:8). One might have thought that they were slaves to slaves, therefore the verse says THEIR (Lev. 26:13)—they were slaves to kings and not slaves to slaves.

---

once I have redeemed you—in the future Messianic age.

in awe of Me   If God makes them feel so comfortable with Him, will they not lose the feeling of awe and reverence for Him?

WHO BROKE THE BARS OF YOUR YOKE (Lev. 26:13). A parable. It may be likened to a householder who had a heifer for ploughing which he lent to someone else for ploughing. That person had ten sons, each of whom would plough and then rest, plough and then rest, until the heifer was worn out and collapsed. All of the other heifers came back, but that one did not. The owner was not satisfied to receive an apology from the borrower but immediately went and smashed the yoke and snapped the cords. So it is with Israel in this world—one nation enslaves her and vanishes after which another comes, enslaves her and vanishes and the furrow is long, as it is said PLOWMEN PLOWED ACROSS MY BACK; THEY MADE LONG FURROWS (Ps. 129:3). Tomorrow when the end comes, the Holy One will not say to the nations, "What is this that you have done to My children—" but He will go immediately and smash the yoke and snap the cords, as it is said, WHO BROKE THE BARS OF THE YOKE (Lev. 26:13) and so too it says THE LORD, THE RIGHTEOUS ONE, HAS SNAPPED THE CORDS OF THE WICKED (Ps. 129:4).

AND MADE YOU WALK ERECT (Lev. 26:13). R. Simeon says, "Two hundred cubits high." R. Judah says, "One hundred cubits, the height of primal Adam as it says FOR OUR SONS ARE LIKE SAPLINGS, WELL TENDED IN THEIR YOUTH (Ps. 144:12)." This teaches me only about men. What about women? The verse says OUR DAUGHTERS ARE LIKE CORNERSTONES TRIMMED TO THE FORM OF THE TEMPLE (Ps. 144:12). What are the dimensions of THE FORM OF THE TEMPLE? One hundred cubits. Another interpretation: AND MADE YOU WALK ERECT (Lev. 26:13). With prideful posture, unafraid of any creature.

COMMENTARY   *The Sages interpreted the blessings and curses in the Torah to refer to events in the past, to events of their own period, and to the promised time of redemption that was to come. Thus these descriptions of great blessing are sometimes illustrated by what happened during the time of the building of Herod's Temple or during the time of the good queen, Salome Alexandra, but frequently they describe that time of peace and of triumph which was yet to come. It must have been a source of consolation to the defeated people of Judaea to know that the nations who had so despoiled them were to be punished while they would walk proud and unafraid.*

---

cubits   A cubit is the distance from the elbow to the end of the middle finger.

11. Leviticus 26:25, Sifra Weiss 112a

AND YOU SHALL BE DELIVERED INTO ENEMY HANDS (Lev. 26: 25). The law is that a dead body is not permitted to remain within the city of Jerusalem overnight. When they take the body out to bury it, those who bury the dead will fall into the hands of the enemy.

WHEN I BREAK YOUR STAFF OF BREAD (Lev. 26:26). This includes all substitutes for bread. TEN WOMEN SHALL BAKE YOUR BREAD IN A SINGLE OVEN (Lev. 26:26) without kindling wood. THEY SHALL DOLE OUT YOUR BREAD BY WEIGHT (Lev. 26:26) for the bread will be ruined and they will sit and weight it while it is in the oven. R. Jose the son of a Damascene woman says, "A parable. A man has an *issar* and a *perutah* in his hand and sits and tries to decide what to do with them. He says: If I buy a bit of food with it, I will not be satisfied. I shall purchase some dates. Perhaps if I eat them, I will be satisfied. Nevertheless, he eats them and is not satisfied, as it is said AND THOUGH YOU EAT, YOU SHALL NOT BE SATISFIED (Lev. 26:26)."

Another interpretation: THOUGH YOU EAT, YOU SHALL NOT BE SATISFIED. This is famine that comes as a consequence of warfare. YOU SHALL EAT THE FLESH OF YOUR SONS AND THE FLESH OF YOUR DAUGHTERS (Lev. 26:29). It was said of Doeg son of Joseph that he died and left his wife with a young son. Each year she would take his measurement and give the equivalent of his weight in gold to Heaven. But when they besieged the citadel of Jerusalem, she slaughtered him with her own hand and ate him. It is of her that Jeremiah lamented SEE O LORD, AND BEHOLD, TO WHOM YOU HAVE DONE THIS! ALAS, WOMEN EAT THEIR OWN FRUIT, THEIR NEWBORN BABES! (Lam. 2:20). The Holy Spirit replies: PRIEST AND PROPHET ARE SLAIN IN THE SANCTUARY OF THE LORD! (Lam. 2:20). This refers to Zechariah the son of Jehoiada the priest.

Another interpretation: YOU SHALL EAT THE FLESH OF YOUR SONS AND THE FLESH OF YOUR DAUGHTERS (Lev. 26:29). This teaches only that fathers will eat the flesh of their sons and daughters. What

---

11. *issar* This and the *perutah* are coins of small value.
Zechariah—a priest who was killed by the people at the behest of King Joash for prophesying against him. See 2 Chron. 24:17–22.

about children eating their fathers? The verse says ASSUREDLY, PARENTS SHALL EAT THEIR CHILDREN IN YOUR MIDST, AND CHILDREN SHALL EAT THEIR PARENTS (Ezek. 5:10).

I WILL DESTROY YOUR CULT PLACES (Lev. 26:30)—literally. AND CUT DOWN YOUR INCENSE STANDS (Lev. 26:30)—this refers to the wizards and necromancers among the people of Israel.

AND I WILL HEAP YOUR CARCASSES UPON YOUR LIFELESS FETISHES (Lev. 26:30). What are the carcasses doing upon the lifeless fetishes? Rather it refers to what happened when Elijah, of blessed memory, would go among those dying of famine. He would find one who was swollen and famished and would say to him, "My son. From what clan do you come?"

He would answer him, "From such and such a clan."

He would say to him, "How many were in the clan?"

He would answer, "Three thousand."

"How many are left?"

He would answer, "I alone."

He would say to him, "Say: Hear O Israel, the Lord is our God, the Lord is One."

Immediately he would cry out and say "Silence! One is not to mention the name of the Lord. That is not what my father taught me." What would he do? Take out his fetish, place it upon his heart, fondle it and kiss it until his stomach would burst and he and his fetish would fall to the ground. Thus it says I WILL HEAP YOUR CARCASSES UPON YOUR LIFELESS FETISHES (Lev. 26:30).

I WILL SPURN YOU (Lev. 26:30). This refers to exile. Some say, "This refers to the removal of the Divine Presence." I WILL LAY YOUR CITIES IN RUIN (Lev. 26:31). Not "city" or "cities" but YOUR CITIES—in order to include metropolises and major divisions as well.

---

dying of famine—as recorded in 1 Kings 18:2.
Say: Hear O Israel—the profession of faith also recited before death.
removal of the Divine Presence The Shekhina, which had dwelt in the Temple, removed itself from earth as a consequence of the sins of the people.

AND MAKE YOUR SANCTUARIES DESOLATE (Lev. 26:31). Not "sanctuary" or "My sanctuary" but YOUR SANCTUARIES—in order to include synagogues and houses of study as well.

AND I WILL NOT SAVOR YOUR PLEASING ODORS (Lev. 26:31)—literally. I WILL MAKE THE LAND DESOLATE (Lev. 26:32). This is actually a beneficent act so that Israel will not say: Since we have been exiled from our land, now the enemy come and takes pleasure in it, as it is said SO THAT YOUR ENEMIES WHO SETTLE IN IT SHALL BE AP-PALLED BY IT (Lev. 26:32). Even those enemies who come thereafter will take no pleasure in it.

AND I WILL SCATTER YOU AMONG THE NATIONS (Lev. 26:33). This was a severe punishment for Israel, for if people who go into exile are all together in one place, they see one another and take comfort from each other. This will not be the case with you, for in the future I will scatter you among the nations as a man scatters barley seed with a winnowing fork and you will not be close to one another, as it is said I WILL SCATTER THEM AS WITH A WINNOWING FORK THROUGH THE SETTLE-MENTS OF THE EARTH. I WILL BEREAVE, I WILL DESTROY MY PEOPLE FOR THEY WOULD NOT TURN BACK FROM THEIR WAYS (Jer. 15:7). AND I WILL UNSHEATHE THE SWORD AGAINST YOU (Lev. 26:33). The sword which has been let loose against you will not so quickly be sheathed again. It is like water which is spilled and cannot be returned to its vessels.

YOUR LAND SHALL BECOME A DESOLATION AND YOUR CIT-IES A RUIN (Lev. 26:33). This was a severe punishment for Israel, for when a man leaves his vineyard and his home knowing that he will return to them, it is as if his vineyard and his home are not destroyed. But with you that is not the case for YOUR LAND SHALL BECOME A DESOLA-TION AND YOUR CITIES A RUIN (Lev. 26:33). Why? Because you are not to return to them in the end. THEN SHALL THE LAND MAKE UP FOR ITS SABBATH YEARS (Lev. 26:34). I told you to sow for six years

---

houses of study—batei midrash, literally "houses of interpretation." Unlike synagogues, which were mainly for prayer and the reading of the Torah, these buildings were used by scholars for study. They too were a kind of sanctuary.

and let the land stay fallow for Me for one year. This was so that you should know that the earth is Mine. But you did not do so. Therefore you shall be exiled from it and it will stay fallow on its own all the years that it is indebted unto Me, as it is said THEN SHALL THE LAND MAKE UP FOR ITS SABBATH YEARS THROUGHOUT THE TIME THAT IT IS DESO-LATE (Lev. 26:34). It shall rest all the days that it is desolate.

AS FOR THOSE OF YOU WHO SURVIVE, I WILL CAST A FAINT-NESS INTO THEIR HEARTS (Lev. 26:36). It does not say "I will cast hope into their hearts," but I WILL CAST A FAINTNESS INTO THEIR HEARTS. What is that? Terror, fear, worry, trembling, and awe. THE SOUND OF A DRIVEN LEAF SHALL PUT THEM TO FLIGHT (Lev. 26:36). Said R. Joshua b. Korcha, "We were once sitting among trees when a wind came and drove the leaves against one another and we stood up and fled, shouting, 'Woe to us—horsemen are upon us!' After a while we turned around and saw that there was no one there. We sat down where we were and wept and said, 'Woe to us—that upon us has been fulfilled the verse THE SOUND OF A DRIVEN LEAF SHALL PUT THEM TO FLIGHT. FLEEING AS THOUGH FROM THE SWORD, THEY SHALL FALL THOUGH NONE PURSUES (Lev. 26:36)!—from lack of strength.' "

THEY SHALL STUMBLE OVER ONE ANOTHER (Lev. 26:37). It does not mean that they will literally stumble over one another, but that each one will stumble because of the other's sin. This teaches that all Israelites are responsible for one another.

YOU SHALL NOT BE ABLE TO STAND YOUR GROUND BEFORE YOUR ENEMIES (Lev. 26:37). This refers to the hour when Jerusalem was captured.

---

hope—reading the word with a vav, as if it came from "arach," which means hope. Rather it is to be read as "morech" without a vav, meaning fear. Another version of this midrash empha-sizes the change of person from YOU to THEIR and takes THEIR to refer to the enemy, as if the people of Israel would at least be protected there because their enemies would have some fear of them.

R. Joshua b. Korcha—who lived in the second century. The story reflects the realities of the time following the defeat of the Bar Kokhba rebellion.

BUT SHALL PERISH AMONG THE NATIONS (Lev. 26:38). R. Akiba says, "This refers to the ten tribes who were exiled to the land of the Medes."

Others say, "BUT SHALL PERISH AMONG THE NATIONS. 'Perish' means to go into exile. Could it mean literally 'perish?' When it says AND THE LAND OF YOUR ENEMIES SHALL CONSUME YOU (Lev. 26:38) we are told about actually perishing. How then shall I understand BUT SHALL PERISH AMONG THE NATIONS? 'Perish' means to go into exile."

THOSE OF YOU WHO SURVIVE SHALL BE HEARTSICK OVER THEIR INIQUITY (Lev. 26:39). It does not mean that they will be heartsick, but that their hearts will faint because of their sins and because of the sins of their fathers. But did not God promise Israel that fathers will not be judged because of children or children because of fathers, as it is said PARENTS SHALL NOT BE PUT TO DEATH FOR CHILDREN, NOR CHILDREN BE PUT TO DEATH FOR PARENTS (Deut. 24:16)? Why then is it said THEY SHALL BE SICK OVER THE INIQUITIES OF THEIR FATHERS (Lev. 26:39)? It refers to those who repeat the sins of their fathers one generation after another. Their generations will be judged for them.

AND THEY SHALL CONFESS THEIR INIQUITY AND THE INIQUITY OF THEIR FATHERS (Lev. 26:40). These are their words that follow their repentance. As soon as they confess their sins, I immediately take pity on them, as it is said AND THEY SHALL CONFESS THEIR INIQUITY AND THE INIQUITY OF THEIR FATHERS, IN THAT THEY TRESPASSED AGAINST ME, YEA, WERE HOSTILE TO ME. I IN TURN SHALL GO WITH THEM (Lev. 26:40–41).

---

one generation after another The sins of the fathers are added to the sins of the children only if the children are themselves wicked.

I IN TURN SHALL GO WITH THEM These words are detached from the phrase that follows: IN HOSTILITY (Lev. 26:41) in order to make it seem that God is promising that He will return to them. Many midrashim ignore the pauses and parse verses in a way that changes their meaning. Since the Torah has no written stops, this is considered a legitimate method of interpretation.

I IN TURN SHALL GO WITH THEM IN HOSTILITY (Lev. 26:41). They made My laws of fleeting importance in this world, so shall I make them of fleeting importance in this world.

AND HAVE REMOVED THEM INTO THE LAND OF THEIR ENE-MIES (Lev. 26:41). This is a benefit to Israel so that Israel should not say: Since we have been exiled among the nations of the world we shall follow their practices. I shall not permit them to do so. Rather I shall place My prophets over them and they will turn them back to good ways and bring them under My wings. Where is this stated? AND WHAT YOU HAVE IN MIND SHALL NEVER COME TO PASS—WHEN YOU SAY, "WE WILL BE LIKE THE NATIONS, LIKE THE FAMILIES OF THE LANDS, WORSHIPING WOOD AND STONE" (Ezek. 20:32). Rather AS I LIVE—DECLARES THE LORD GOD—I WILL REIGN OVER YOU WITH A STRONG HAND AND WITH AN OUTSTRETCHED ARM, AND WITH OVERFLOWING FURY (Ezek. 20:33). Against your will and without your acquiescence I shall impose My Kingship over you.

THEN AT LAST SHALL THEIR OBDURATE HEART HUMBLE IT-SELF (Lev. 26:41). Following their repentance they shall immediately humble their hearts in repentance. Immediately I shall take pity on them, as it is said THEN AT LAST SHALL THEIR OBDURATE HEART HUMBLE ITSELF, AND THEY SHALL ATONE FOR THEIR INIQUITY (Lev. 26:41).

THEN WILL I REMEMBER MY COVENANT WITH JACOB; ALSO MY COVENANT WITH ISAAC, AND ALSO MY COVENANT WITH ABRAHAM WILL I REMEMBER (Lev. 26:42). Why are the Patriarchs listed in reverse order? If the deeds of Abraham are not sufficient, those of Isaac will be. If the deeds of Isaac are not sufficient, those of Jacob will be. Each one of them was worthy of sustaining the entire world on his own merit. Why is "remembrance" mentioned in connection with Abraham

---

This is a benefit   God's hostility to them is for their own good. His hostility is that He will not permit them to worship idols in exile, but will send prophets who will force them back to the good way.

If the deeds of Abraham are not sufficient   In another midrash, Vayikra Rabba, the reading is: If the deeds of Jacob are not sufficient, those of Isaac will be. If the deeds of Isaac are not sufficient, the deeds of Abraham will be.

and Jacob but not Isaac? Because his ashes are seen as if they were piled up on the altar. Why is the word *af* (also) mentioned in connection with Abraham and Isaac but not Jacob? Because the progeny of Jacob's bed were wholehearted. This teaches me only about the Patriarchs. What source indicates that it was true of the Matriarchs as well? The verse contains the extra word *et*. Each et is intended to include one of the Matriarchs, as indicated by the verse THERE ABRAHAM AND HIS WIFE (v'et) SARAH WERE BURIED; THEIR ISAAC AND HIS WIFE (v'et) REBEKAH WERE BURIED; AND THERE I BURIED (et) LEAH (Gen. 49:31). How do we know that the covenant was made with the Land as well? The verse says AND I WILL REMEMBER THE LAND (Lev. 26:42).

FOR THE LAND SHALL BE FORSAKEN OF THEM, MAKING UP FOR ITS SABBATH YEARS (Lev. 26:43). I told them that the land should be sown for six years and lie fallow for Me for one year so that they should know that the earth is Mine. But they did not do so. Therefore they shall be exiled from it and it will lie fallow by itself all the *shemita* years owed to Me, as it is said FOR THE LAND SHALL BE FORSAKEN OF THEM, MAKING UP FOR ITS SABBATH YEARS BY BEING DESOLATE OF THEM, WHILE THEY ATONE FOR THEIR INIQUITY; FOR THE ABUNDANT REASON THAT THEY REJECTED MY NORMS AND SPURNED MY LAWS (Lev. 26:43). Did I requite them one for one for each and every sin? Did I not requite no more than one in a hundred of their sins before Me? What then is the meaning of FOR THE ABUNDANT REASON? FOR THE . . . REASON THAT THEY REJECTED MY NORMS refers to the laws. AND SPURNED MY LAWS refers to the laws derived by interpretation.

---

his ashes   This refers to the many midrashim that indicate that Isaac was actually sacrificed on the altar. The remembrance of his sacrifice need not be specifically mentioned because it is automatically "remembered" by God.

were wholehearted—or "perfect." Unlike Abraham who had Ishmael and Isaac who had Esau, all of Jacob's children remained faithful to God.

it was true—that the Matriarchs were equally worthy of sustaining the world and that their merit would be remembered by God.

et   This word is a grammatical form in Hebrew that appears before the direct definite object in a sentence. It has no English equivalent and cannot be translated. It appears three times in Lev. 26:42, once before each mention of "My covenant."

meaning of FOR THE ABUNDANT REASON   The Hebrew uses a form in which a word is repeated, indicating great importance. The Sages interpret it as referring to two rejections.

YET, EVEN THEN (Lev. 26:44). THEN refers to the sin committed in the wilderness. EVEN THEN refers to the sin of Baal Peor. YET, EVEN THEN refers to the sin of the following the ways of the Amorites. I WILL NOT REJECT THEM OR SPURN THEM SO AS TO DESTROY THEM (Lev. 26:44). But nothing remained to them that had not been rejected or spurned! Every gracious gift that had been given to them has been taken from them. Were it not for the Torah scroll which remains to them there would be no difference between them and the nations of the world. Rather it means I WILL NOT REJECT THEM in the days of Vespasian. OR SPURN THEM in the days of the Greeks. SO AS TO DESTROY THEM, ANNULLING MY COVENANT WITH THEM (Lev. 26:44) in the days of Haman. FOR I THE LORD AM THEIR GOD (Lev. 26:44) in the days of Gog.

How do we know that the Covenant was made with the tribes? It says I WILL REMEMBER IN THEIR FAVOR THE COVENANT WITH THE ANCIENTS WHOM I FREED FROM THE LAND OF EGYPT (Lev. 26:45). This teaches that the Covenant was made with the tribes. THESE ARE THE LAWS, NORMS, AND TEACHINGS (Lev. 26:46). LAWS—these are the laws derived by interpretation. NORMS—these are the statutes. AND TEACHINGS (Torot). This teaches that two Torahs were given to Israel, one in writing and one orally. Said R. Akiba, "Does Israel have but *two* Torahs? Was not Israel given many Torahs? THIS IS THE TORAH OF THE BURNT OFFERING (Lev. 6:2) THIS IS THE TORAH OF THE MEAL OFFERING (Lev. 6:7). THIS IS THE TO-

---

in the wilderness   The sin of the golden calf (Ex. 32).

Baal Peor—described in Num. 25:1–9 in which the Israelites committed sexual sins as part of pagan worship.

ways of the Amorites   The text has "kings of the Amorites," but this is probably a scribal error, writing "malkei" (kings) for "darkei" (ways). "Ways of the Amorites" is a common rabbinic phrase to designate all those foreign practices that the Israelites were forbidden to emulate.

Vespasian—who presided over the siege of Jerusalem and during whose reign the Temple was destroyed in 70 C.E.

Greeks—in the second century B.C.E. at the time of the Maccabean revolt.

Haman—the villain of the Book of Esther.

Gog   The apocalyptic wars of Gog and Magog are described in Ezek. 38–39.

two Torahs   The word "Torot" is in the plural. Two would be the minimum. R. Akiba interprets it to mean many more than that.

THE TORAH OF   The usual translation is "the law of" or "the ritual of." The root meaning of the word is "instruction." Since there were so many Torot, you cannot say that only two were given at Sinai.

RAH OF THE GUILT OFFERING (Lev. 7:2). THIS IS THE TORAH
OF THE SACRIFICE OF WELL-BEING (Lev. 7:11). THIS IS THE
TORAH WHEN A MAN DIES IN A TENT (Num. 19:14). THAT THE
LORD ESTABLISHED BETWEEN HIMSELF AND THE ISRAELITE
PEOPLE (Lev. 26:46). Moses merited being an intermediary between Israel
and their Father in Heaven. THROUGH MOSES ON MT. SINAI (Lev.
26:46). This teaches that the Torah, its laws, details, and explanations, were
all given through Moses at Sinai.

COMMENTARY   *The curses were seen to have been fulfilled during the
period of the Great Revolt (first century) and the subsequent Revolt of Bar
Kokhba (second century). It was of great importance to the future of Judaism and the Jewish People that the defeat be seen not as the triumph of the
superior gods of other nations, nor as the abandonment of the Jews by their
God, but as a result of their own disobedience of the Torah. They also
emphasized the Torah's message that the punishment would be concluded
by repentance and forgiveness, by a reconciliation with God. Thus although
the curses were already upon them, the blessings described earlier were yet
to come.*

---

intermediary—an interpretation based on the word BETWEEN. The laws and teachings were
not given directly by God to Israel, but came through Moses.
its laws—the method of interpretation used by the Sages had the same Divine origin as the
written Torah.

NUMBERS

1. Numbers 6.2, Sifre N. 22, 26

IF ANYONE, MAN OR A WOMAN, EXPLICITLY UTTERS A NAZ-
IRITE'S VOW, TO SET HIMSELF APART FOR THE LORD (Num.
6:2). Simeon the Righteous said, "I would never eat the guilt offering
brought by Nazirites, except once: There was one extremely handsome
youth, with beautiful eyes and curly hair, who came from the south. I asked
him, 'Whatever made you cut off your beautiful hair?'

"He said to me, 'I used to graze my flocks and would go to draw water
from the well. Looking at my reflection, my heart would tremble and seek
to cause me to perish from this world. I said [to my reflection], "O evil one!
How proud you are of that which is not yours—for all this is but dust,
worms, and corruption. I shall shave you for the sake of Heaven!"'

"Immediately I inclined my head and kissed him on his head and said
to him, 'May those like you who perform the will of God increase in Israel.
You embody that which is written IF ANYONE, MAN OR WOMAN,
EXPLICITLY UTTERS A NAZIRITE'S VOW, TO SET HIMSELF
APART FOR THE LORD (Num. 6:2).'"

COMMENTARY   *The attitude toward the Nazirite was ambivalent since
Rabbinic Judaism tended to avoid excess asceticism. This ancient tradition
concerning Simeon the Righteous, generally identified with the High Priest
Simeon of the pre-Maccabean book of Ben Sira (third century B.C.E.) sets a
high standard: The only true Nazirite is one who takes this step in order to
avoid the temptations of physical beauty and self-worship, which would
corrupt a youth. The parallel to the theme of the Greek legend of Narcissus
is too obvious to require further comment.*

2. Numbers 6:8, Sifre Zuta 242

THROUGHOUT HIS TERM AS NAZIRITE HE IS CONSECRATED TO THE LORD (Num. 6:8). Since he became a Nazirite by separating himself and by observing laws of purity, he is called "holy." Not only that, but the Scripture equates him with a prophet, as it is said AND RAISED UP PROPHETS FROM AMONG YOUR SONS AND NAZIRITES FROM AMONG YOUR YOUNG MEN (Amos 2:11).

3. Numbers 6:11, Sifre N. 30, 36

THE PRIEST SHALL OFFER ONE AS A SIN OFFERING AND THE OTHER AS A BURNT OFFERING, AND MAKE EXPIATION ON HIS BEHALF FOR HE SINNED AGAINST THE SOUL (Num. 6:11). R. Eleazar Ha-Kappar says, "Against what soul did he sin that requires him to atone? It is because he afflicted his own soul by denying himself wine. From this there is a logical deduction that if one who afflicts his soul by denying himself wine requires atonement, how much more does one who denies himself anything require atonement!" R. Ishmael says, "The Scripture is talking about a Nazirite who has become ritually unclean, as it says AND MAKE EXPIATION FOR HIM FOR THE GUILT THAT HE INCURRED THROUGH THE CORPSE (Num. 6:11)."

COMMENTARY   *The two attitudes toward the Nazirite and toward ascet-icism are found in these last two sections. On the one hand the Nazirite is praised as one who achieves holiness. In rabbinic literature holiness fre-quently indicates self-denial and separation from indulgence in sex and from idolatry. On the other hand, R. Eleazar Ha-Kappar castigates the entire prac-tice as if although the Torah permits it, it does not encourage or approve of it. He bases this on the fact that a sin offering is required. R. Ishmael dis-misses this interpretation, pointing out that the sin offering is for a Nazirite who has actually sinned through becoming ritually impure.*

---

2. *"holy"*   Holiness is associated with separation from impurity. The Nazirite takes upon himself an extra measure of such separation and is therefore entitled to the appellation "holy."

---

3. *denying himself wine*   Even though the Torah describes this as the requirement for being a Nazirite, no one is commanded to take that vow and R. Eleazar Ha-Kappar sees it is as sin.
R. Ishmael—disagrees with the previous interpretation. Becoming a Nazirite is not a sin. How-ever, if he becomes ritually unclean by contact with the dead he brings a sin offering. Other-wise, he does not.

4. Numbers 6:23, Sifre N. 39, 42

THUS SHALL YOU BLESS THE PEOPLE OF ISRAEL. SAY TO THEM (Num. 6:23). In the holy tongue. Wherever it speaks of repeating and saying using the word THUS it means: thus—in the holy tongue.

THUS SHALL YOU BLESS THE PEOPLE OF ISRAEL (Num. 6:23)—while standing. You say "while standing" but perhaps it means either while standing or while not standing. The verse says THESE SHALL STAND UPON MOUNT GERIZIM TO BLESS THE PEOPLE (Deut. 27:12). "Blessing" is stated here (Num. 6:23) and "blessing" is stated there (Deut. 27:12). Just as the blessing there is while standing, so the blessing here is while standing.

R. Nathan says, "[This verse] is not needed [for that] for we have learned elsewhere THE PRIESTS, SONS OF LEVI, SHALL COME FORWARD; FOR THE LORD YOUR GOD HAS CHOSEN THEM TO MINISTER TO HIM AND TO PRONOUNCE BLESSING IN THE NAME OF THE LORD (Deut. 21:5). Blessing is here connected to ministering. Just as ministering is performed while standing, so blessing is performed while standing."

THUS SHALL YOU BLESS THE PEOPLE OF ISRAEL (Num. 6:23) by the lifting up of hands. You say "by the lifting up of hands" but perhaps it is by the lifting up of hands and also without the lifting up of hands. The verse says AND AARON LIFTED HIS HANDS TOWARD THE PEOPLE AND BLESSED THEM (Lev. 9:22). Just as Aaron did it by the lifting up of hands, so his children shall do it by the lifting up of hands. R. Jonathan says, "In that case, just as there it is speaking about the New Moon, a com-

---

4. *the holy tongue*—Hebrew. Whenever the ceremony of the Priestly Blessing is held, the blessing is to be pronounced in Hebrew.

THUS—means using the Hebrew words exactly as they are set out here.

standing—The priests pronounce the blessing standing up.

is stated there—where the people are to stand on the mountains and the Levites pronounce the blessings and curses. This is done while standing.

ministering—performing the sacrificial service.

lifting up of hands The priests hold up their arms and stretch their hands toward the worshipers with their fingers spread out. This is said to represent the idea that the Presence of God (the *Shekhina*) peers at the people through the lattice of their fingers. See Song 2:9.

just as there—in the instance recorded in Lev. 9:22. Perhaps lifting up the hands is to be done only when the circumstances are exactly as described there.

munal offering and the High Priest, perhaps here too it would only be on the New Moon with a communal offering and by the High Priest? Therefore the verse says FOR THE LORD YOUR GOD HAS CHOSEN HIM AND HIS DESCENDANTS TO COME, OUT OF ALL YOUR TRIBES (Deut. 18:5). This connects his descendants to him. Just as he does it by the lifting up of hands, so his descendants do it by the lifting up of hands."

THUS SHALL YOU BLESS THE PEOPLE OF ISRAEL (Num. 6:23) by the specific Name of God. You say "by the specific Name of God," but perhaps it is done by a substitute. The verse says THEY SHALL PLACE MY NAME UPON THE PEOPLE OF ISRAEL (Num. 6:27). In the Temple the Specific Name is used; elsewhere, a substitute. So taught R. Josiah. R. Jonathan says, "Behold it says IN EVERY PLACE WHERE I CAUSE MY NAME TO BE MENTIONED (Ex. 20:21). This is an emasculated verse. [It should read] IN EVERY PLACE WHERE I reveal Myself to you, there you should CAUSE MY NAME TO BE MENTIONED. And where is it that I reveal Myself to you? In the Chosen House! So too you should not cause My Name to be mentioned except in the Chosen House." This was the source of the teaching: It is forbidden to mention the specific Name of God outside [the Chosen House].

THUS SHALL YOU BLESS THE PEOPLE OF ISRAEL (Num. 6:23). This teaches me only about a blessing to the men of Israel. What about a blessing for converts, women, and slaves? The verse says AND I WILL BLESS THEM (Num. 6:27). What about a blessing for the priests? The verse says AND I WILL BLESS THEM.

---

his descendants   The descendants of Aaron are mentioned in order to indicate that at all times they too must lift up hands in blessing as did Aaron.

specific Name of God   Another interpretation of the word THUS. It indicates that the exact Name, the Tetragrammaton, as written in the verses here, must be pronounced by the priests.

a substitute   The word *Adonai*, meaning "Lord," is substituted for the actual Name of God when the blessing is recited outside of the Temple.

emasculated verse—a verse that has sections missing or sections that must be provided in order to understand it properly. R. Jonathan learns the law concerning the use of God's Name from this verse rather than from the verse quoted by R. Josiah. He prefers it because it is more specific.

the men of Israel   The word translated "people" literally means "sons." Therefore it could be taken to mean only the males.

BLESS THEM   The word *THEM* includes all of these other categories in addition to the men.

THUS SHALL YOU BLESS THE PEOPLE OF ISRAEL (Num. 6:23)—face to face. You say "face to face," but perhaps it means facing the back of the people. The verse says SAY TO THEM (Num. 6:23)—face to face.

THUS SHALL YOU BLESS THE PEOPLE OF ISRAEL (Num. 6:23). Does this mean that all of those assembled must hear it or is it just among themselves? The verse says SAY TO THEM (Num. 6:23) so that the entire group of them assembled may hear it. And how do we know that a leader must tell them what to say? The verse says SAY TO THEM.

THE LORD BLESS YOU (Num. 6:24) with the blessing which is spelled out in the Torah. And thus it says BLESSED SHALL YOU BE IN THE CITY AND BLESSED SHALL YOU BE IN THE COUNTRY. BLESSED SHALL BE THE ISSUE OF YOUR WOMB . . . BLESSED SHALL BE YOUR BASKET AND YOUR KNEADING BOWL. BLESSED SHALL YOU BE IN YOUR COMINGS AND BLESSED SHALL YOU BE IN YOUR GOINGS (Deut. 28:3–6). ALL THESE BLESSINGS SHALL COME UPON YOU AND TAKE EFFECT (Deut. 28:2). When? WHEN YOU HEED THE WORD OF THE LORD YOUR GOD (Deut. 28:2).

THE LORD BLESS YOU (Num. 6:24) in your possessions. AND GUARD YOU (Num. 6:24) in your possessions.

R. Nathan says, "THE LORD BLESS YOU in your possessions AND GUARD YOU in body."

R. Isaac says, "AND GUARD YOU from the evil inclination and thus it says FOR THE LORD WILL BE YOUR TRUST; HE WILL GUARD YOUR FEET FROM BEING CAUGHT (Prov. 3:26)."

Another interpretation: AND GUARD YOU that others may not rule over you. Thus it says SEE, THE GUARDIAN OF ISRAEL NEITHER SLUMBERS NOR SLEEPS! THE LORD IS YOUR GUARDIAN, THE LORD IS YOUR PROTECTION AT YOUR RIGHT HAND. BY DAY

SAY TO THEM To speak to them you must be facing them.

among themselves—the priests.

a leader The priests do not simply recite the blessing by heart. A leader prompts them word for word. The simple meaning of SAY TO THEM is "say this to the people of Israel." The midrash interprets it to mean "someone must say the blessing to the priests," i.e., prompt them when they recite it.

THE SUN WILL NOT STRIKE YOU, NOR THE MOON BY NIGHT. THE LORD WILL GUARD YOU FROM ALL HARM; HE WILL GUARD YOUR LIFE. THE LORD WILL GUARD YOUR GOING AND COMING NOW AND FOREVER (Ps. 121:4–8).

Another interpretation: AND GUARD YOU from demons. Thus it says FOR HE WILL ORDER HIS ANGELS TO GUARD YOU WHEREVER YOU GO (Ps. 91:11).

Another interpretation: AND GUARD YOU. He will guard the covenant of your fathers for you as it says THE LORD YOUR GOD WILL GUARD WITH YOU THE GRACIOUS COVENANT THAT HE MADE ON OATH WITH YOUR FATHERS (Deut. 7:12).

Another interpretation: AND GUARD (yishmerecha) YOU. He will guard the end of days for you. Thus it says THE "DUMAH" PRONOUNCEMENT. A CALL COMES TO ME FROM SEIR: "WATCHMAN (shomer), WHAT OF THE NIGHT? WATCHMAN, WHAT OF THE NIGHT?" THE WATCHMAN REPLIED, "MORNING CAME, AND SO DID NIGHT" (Isa. 21:11).

Another interpretation: AND GUARD YOU. He will guard your soul at the hour of death. Thus it says THE LIFE OF MY LORD WILL BE BOUND UP IN THE BUNDLE OF LIFE IN THE CARE OF THE LORD (1 Sam. 25:29). I might think that this is so regardless of whether they are righteous or wicked. Therefore the verse says BUT HE WILL FLING AWAY THE LIVES OF YOUR ENEMIES AS FROM THE HOLLOW OF A SLING (1 Sam. 25:29).

Another interpretation: AND GUARD YOU. He will guard your steps from Gehenna. Thus it says HE GUARDS THE STEPS OF HIS FAITHFUL, BUT THE WICKED PERISH IN DARKNESS (1 Sam. 2:9).

Another interpretation: AND GUARD YOU. He will guard you in the world to come. Thus it says BUT THEY WHO TRUST IN THE LORD SHALL RENEW THEIR STRENGTH AS EAGLES GROW NEW PLUMES (Isa. 40:31).

---

guard the covenant   The Hebrew for guarding (sh-m-r) also means "to keep" and is frequently so translated. Here and in some of the other interpretations that is the sense of the term.

THE LORD MAKE HIS FACE TO SHINE UPON YOU (Num. 6:25).
May He grant you a shining face. R. Nathan says, "This refers to the light
of the Divine Presence as it is said ARISE, SHINE, FOR YOUR LIGHT
HAS DAWNED; THE PRESENCE OF THE LORD HAS SHONE
UPON YOU! BEHOLD! DARKNESS SHALL COVER THE EARTH,
AND THICK CLOUDS THE PEOPLES; BUT UPON YOU THE
LORD WILL SHINE AND HIS PRESENCE BE SEEN OVER YOU
(Isa. 60:1–2). MAY THE LORD BE GRACIOUS TO US AND BLESS
US; MAY HIS FACE SHINE UPON US, SELAH (Ps. 67:2). And it says
THE LORD IS GOD; HE HAS GIVEN US LIGHT (Ps. 118:27).

Another interpretation: TO SHINE (Num. 6:25). This refers to the
light of the Torah as it is said FOR THE COMMANDMENT IS A LAMP,
AND TORAH IS A LIGHT (Prov. 6:23).

AND BE GRACIOUS TO YOU (Num. 6:25). May He be gracious unto
you when you beseech Him. Thus it says I WILL BE GRACIOUS TO
WHOM I WILL BE GRACIOUS, AND SHOW COMPASSION TO
WHOM I WILL SHOW COMPASSION (Ex. 33:19).

Another interpretation: May He grant you grace in the sight of human
beings. Thus it says THE LORD WAS WITH JOSEPH: HE EX-
TENDED KINDNESS TO HIM AND GAVE HIM GRACE IN THE
SIGHT OF THE CHIEF JAILER (Gen. 39:21). And it says YET ES-
THER WON GRACE IN THE SIGHT OF ALL WHO SAW HER (Es-
ther 2:15). And it says AND GOD GRANTED DANIEL grace, KIND-
NESS AND COMPASSION IN THE SIGHT OF THE CHIEF
OFFICER (Dan. 1:9). And it says AND YOU WILL FIND GRACE AND
APPROBATION IN THE EYES OF GOD AND MAN (Prov. 3:4).

Another interpretation: AND BE GRACIOUS TO YOU (Num.
6:25)—with knowledge, understanding, enlightenment, discipline, and
wisdom.

Another interpretation: AND BE GRACIOUS TO YOU. May He be
gracious to you in the study of Torah. Thus it says SHE WILL ADORN
YOUR HEAD WITH A WREATH OF GRACE (Prov. 4:9). And it says

GRANTED DANIEL grace   The word *grace* has been added to the verse by the midrash.

FOR THEY ARE A WREATH OF GRACE UPON YOUR HEAD. A NECKLACE ABOUT YOUR THROAT (Prov. 1:9).

Another interpretation: AND BE GRACIOUS (vehuneka) TO YOU. May He be gracious to you in granting you His gifts freely (hinam). Thus it says AS THE EYES OF SLAVES FOLLOW THEIR MASTER'S HAND, AS THE EYES OF A SLAVE-GIRL FOLLOW THE HAND OF HER MISTRESS, SO OUR EYES ARE TOWARD THE LORD OUR GOD, AWAITING HIS GRACE (Ps. 123:2) and it says BE GRACIOUS TO US, O LORD! BE GRACIOUS! WE HAVE HAD MORE THAN ENOUGH OF CONTEMPT (Ps. 123:3). And it says O LORD, BE GRACIOUS TO US! IT IS TO YOU WE HAVE LOOKED (Isa. 33:2).

MAY THE LORD LIFT UP HIS COUNTENANCE UPON YOU (Num. 6:26)—when you stand and pray as it is said HE REPLIED, "VERY WELL, I HAVE ALSO LIFTED UP YOUR COUNTENANCE" (Gen. 19:21). This is a matter of logic. "If I lifted My countenance toward Lot because of Abraham My beloved, will I not lift My countenance toward you because of you and because of your ancestors?" This is what Scripture says MAY THE LORD LIFT UP HIS COUNTENANCE UPON YOU (Num. 6:26).

One verse says MAY THE LORD LIFT UP HIS COUNTENANCE UPON YOU (Num. 6:26) and another verse says AND DOES NOT LIFT UP HIS COUNTENANCE (Deut. 10:17). How can both of these verses be maintained? When Israel performs the will of God—MAY THE LORD LIFT UP HIS COUNTENANCE UPON YOU and when Israel does not perform the will of God—AND DOES NOT LIFT UP HIS COUNTENANCE. Another interpretation: Before sentence is finalized—MAY THE LORD LIFT UP HIS COUNTENANCE UPON YOU but once sentence has been finalized—AND DOES NOT LIFT UP HIS COUNTENANCE.

---

toward Lot   Lot is the subject of the verse just quoted, Gen. 19:21, in which the same phrase as that of the Priestly Blessing appears. God granted him grace only because of the merit of Abraham. The Israelites have that merit but unlike Lot they also have merit of their own.

sentence is finalized—referring to the sentence that God pronounces on a person on the Day of Atonement. God is ready to accept and be gracious and permit man to repent, but if man does not do so then the sentence is finalized and God's attitude, as it were, changes.

One verse says ALL MANKIND COMES TO YOU, YOU WHO HEAR PRAYER (Ps. 65:3) and another verse says YOU HAVE SCREENED YOURSELF OFF WITH A CLOUD THAT NO PRAYER MAY PASS THROUGH (Lam. 3:44). How can both of these passages be maintained? Before sentence is finalized—YOU WHO HEAR PRAYER but once sentence has been finalized—YOU HAVE SCREENED YOURSELF OFF WITH A CLOUD.

One verse says THE LORD IS NEAR TO ALL WHO CALL HIM, TO ALL WHO CALL HIM WITH SINCERITY (Ps. 145:18) and another verse says WHY, O LORD, DO YOU STAND ALOOF (Ps. 10:1). How can both of these verses be maintained? Before sentence is finalized—THE LORD IS NEAR TO ALL WHO CALL HIM but once sentence has been finalized—WHY, O LORD, DO YOU STAND ALOOF?

One verse says WEAL AND WOE DO NOT BEFALL AT THE WORD OF THE MOST HIGH (Lam. 3:38) and another verse says HENCE THE LORD WAS INTENT UPON BRINGING CALAMITY UPON US (Dan. 9:14). One verse says WASH YOUR HEART CLEAN OF WICKEDNESS, O JERUSALEM, THAT YOU MAY BE RESCUED (Jer. 4:14) and another verse says THOUGH YOU WASH WITH NATRON AND USE MUCH LYE, YOUR GUILT IS INGRAINED BEFORE ME (Jer. 2:22). One verse says TURN BACK, O REBELLIOUS CHILDREN (Jer. 3:22) and another verse says IF THEY TURN ASIDE, THEY WILL NOT TURN BACK (Jer. 8:4). How can both of these verses be maintained? Before sentence is finalized—TURN BACK, O REBELLIOUS CHILDREN but once sentence has been finalized—IF THEY TURN ASIDE, THEY WILL NOT TURN BACK.

One verse says SEEK THE LORD WHILE HE CAN BE FOUND (Isa. 55:6) and another verse says AS I LIVE, I WILL NOT BE SOUGHT BY YOU (Ezek. 20:3). How can both of these verses be maintained? Before sentence is finalized—SEEK THE LORD WHILE HE CAN BE FOUND but once sentence has been finalized—AS I LIVE, I WILL NOT BE SOUGHT BY YOU.

WEAL AND WOE DO NOT BEFALL   This is the interpretation of the midrash. The usual translation is "Is it not at the word of the Most High, that weal and woe befall?" The Hebrew does not make it clear if the verse is a question or a statement. The midrash chooses the latter.

One verse says FOR IT IS NOT MY DESIRE THAT ANYONE SHALL DIE (Ezek. 18:32) and another verse says FOR THE LORD WAS RESOLVED THAT THEY SHOULD DIE (1 Sam. 2:25).

One verse says MAY THE LORD LIFT UP HIS COUNTENANCE UPON YOU (Num. 6:26) and another verse says AND DOES NOT LIFT UP HIS COUNTENANCE (Deut. 10:17). How can both of these passages be maintained? MAY THE LORD LIFT UP HIS COUNTENANCE UPON YOU—in this world. AND DOES NOT LIFT UP HIS COUNTENANCE—in the world to come.

Another interpretation: MAY THE LORD LIFT UP HIS COUNTENANCE. May He remove His wrath from you.

AND GRANT YOU PEACE (Num. 6:26). When you enter—peace. When you leave—peace. Peace with all people.
R. Hananya, chief of the priests, says, "AND GRANT YOU PEACE on your household."
R. Nathan says, "This refers to the peace of the kingdom of the House of David, as it is said IN TOKEN OF ABUNDANT AUTHORITY AND OF PEACE WITHOUT LIMIT UPON DAVID'S THRONE AND KINGDOM (Isa. 9:6)."

Another interpretation: This refers to the peace of the Torah, as it is said MAY THE LORD GRANT STRENGTH TO HIS PEOPLE; MAY THE LORD BESTOW ON HIS PEOPLE PEACE (Ps. 29:11).

Great is peace. For the sake of peace [God] altered Sarah's words, as it is said THEN THE LORD SAID TO ABRAHAM, "WHY DID SARAH

THEY SHOULD DIE Although the interpretation is not stated, it is obvious that here too the one verse indicating that God does not desire anyone's death refers to the time before the sentence is finalized, the other—that He has determined that some shall die—refers to the time after sentence has been passed.

chief of the priests The position was that of the second to the High Priest.

the kingdom of the House of David—the Messianic era.

STRENGTH—frequently taken as a synonym for Torah.

altered Sarah's words In Gen. 18:12 Sarah is quoted as referring to her husband's old age. God, in telling Abraham, quotes her as referring to her own advanced age. He made this alteration in order not to cause strife between Abraham and Sarah.

LAUGH SAYING, 'SHALL I IN TRUTH BEAR A CHILD, OLD AS I AM?' " (Gen. 18:13).

Great is peace. For the sake of peace the Holy One altered [His words].

Great is peace. For the sake of peace the angel altered [his words].

Great is peace. For the sake of peace the Name written in holiness is erased by the water in order to bring peace between a man and his wife.

R. Eliezer says, "Great is peace, for the prophets placed nothing but peace in the mouths of all creatures."

R. Simeon b. Halafta says, "Great is peace, for there is no vessel which can contain a blessing but peace, as it is said MAY THE LORD GRANT STRENGTH TO HIS PEOPLE; MAY THE LORD BESTOW ON HIS PEOPLE PEACE (Ps. 29:11)."

R. Eleazar Ha-Kappar says, "Great is peace, for all blessings conclude with peace, as it is said THE LORD BLESS YOU AND GUARD YOU. THE LORD MAKE HIS FACE TO SHINE UPON YOU AND BE GRACIOUS TO YOU. THE LORD LIFT UP HIS COUNTENANCE UPON YOU AND GRANT YOU PEACE (Num. 6:24–26)."

R. Eleazar the son of R. Eleazar Ha-Kappar says, "Great is peace, for even if Israel worships idols, if there is peace among them, God says, as it were, 'Satan may not touch them!' as it is said EPHRAIM IS ADDICTED TO IMAGES—LET HIM BE (Hos. 4:17). But when they are contentious

---

the Holy One—possibly referring to the story in 1 Sam. 16 where God advises Samuel to lie to Saul so that Saul will not kill him.

the angel—who appeared to Manoah and his wife. To the wife he said YOU ARE BARREN (Judges 13:3). He did not repeat this to Manoah (Judges 13:13).

by the water   The Name of God is written on the scroll placed in water that the suspected adulteress must drink. Erasing or destroying God's Name is strictly forbidden. Why are we not only permitted but commanded to do so here? In order to clarify the woman's status and thus restore peace to their relationship. See Num. 5:23.

in the mouth of all creatures   Unclear. Possibly referring to the use of the word Peace (shalom) as the common greeting between people.

what does it say of them? THEIR HEART IS CONTENTIOUS. HE FEELS HIS GUILT (Hos. 10:2). Thus: Great is peace while contentiousness is despised."

Great is peace, for peace is needed even at the time of war, as it is said WHEN YOU APPROACH A TOWN TO ATTACK IT, YOU SHALL OFFER IT TERMS OF PEACE (Deut. 20:10). THEN I SENT MESSENGERS FROM THE WILDERNESS OF KEDEMOTH TO SIHON KING OF HESHBON WITH AN OFFER OF PEACE (Deut. 2:26). JEPHTHAH THEN SENT MESSENGERS TO THE KING OF THE AMMONITES, SAYING, "WHAT HAVE YOU AGAINST ME THAT YOU HAVE COME TO MAKE WAR ON MY COUNTRY?" THE KING OF THE AMMONITES REPLIED TO JEPHTHAH'S MESSENGERS (Judges 11:12–13). What did he say? "WHEN ISRAEL CAME FROM EGYPT, THEY SEIZED THE LAND WHICH IS MINE, FROM THE ARNON TO THE JABBOK AS FAR AS THE JORDAN. NOW, THEN, RESTORE IT PEACEABLY" (Judges 11:13).

Great is peace, for peace is needed even by the dead, as it is said AS FOR YOU, YOU SHALL GO TO YOUR FATHERS IN PEACE (Gen. 15:15). And it says YOU WILL DIE IN PEACE (Jer. 34:5).

Great is peace, for it is granted to those who return in penitence as it is said PEACE, PEACE, TO HIM THAT IS FAR OFF AND TO HIM THAT IS NEAR, SAYS THE LORD, CREATOR OF THE FRUIT OF THE LIPS (Isa. 57:19).

Great is peace, for it is bestowed as the portion of the righteous, as it is said THE RIGHTEOUS WAS TAKEN AWAY, YET HE SHALL COME TO PEACE, HE SHALL HAVE REST ON HIS COUCH WHO WALKED STRAIGHTFORWARD (Isa. 57:1–2).

Great is peace, for it is not bestowed as the portion of the wicked, as it is said THERE IS NO PEACE—SAID MY GOD—FOR THE WICKED (Isa. 57:21).

Great is peace, for it is bestowed upon those who love the Torah, as it is said THERE IS GREAT PEACE FOR THOSE WHO LOVE YOUR TORAH (Ps. 119:165).

Great is peace, for it is bestowed upon those who study Torah, as it is said AND ALL YOUR CHILDREN SHALL BE DISCIPLES OF THE LORD, AND GREAT SHALL BE THE PEACE OF YOUR CHILDREN (Isa. 54:13).

Great is peace, for it is bestowed upon the lowly, as it is said BUT THE LOWLY SHALL INHERIT THE LAND, AND DELIGHT IN ABUNDANT PEACE (Ps. 37:11).

Great is peace, for it is bestowed upon those who work righteousness, as it is said FOR THE WORK OF RIGHTEOUSNESS SHALL BE PEACE (Isa. 32:17).

Great is peace, for the name of the Holy One is designated "Peace," as it is said, SO GIDEON BUILT THERE AN ALTAR TO THE LORD AND CALLED IT THE LORD IS PEACE (Judges 6:24).

R. Hananya the Chief of the Priests says, "Great is peace for it is equal to all of the creation, as it is said I FORM LIGHT AND CREATE DARKNESS; I MAKE PEACE (Isa. 45:7)."

Great is peace, for even those who dwell on high need peace, as it is said DOMINION AND DREAD ARE HIS; HE IMPOSES PEACE IN HIS HEIGHTS (Job 25:2). It is a matter of logic. If in a place where there is no hatred and envy, enmity and malice, peace is needed, how much more is this so in a place where all of those qualities are lacking! . . .

AND I WILL BLESS THEM (Num. 6:27). In order to prevent Israel from saying, "Our blessing is dependent upon the priests," it says AND I WILL BLESS THEM. In order to prevent the priests from saying, "We shall bless Israel," it says AND I WILL BLESS THEM. I am the One who blesses

---

DISCIPLES OF THE LORD—i.e., students of God's word, the Torah. Elsewhere the second half of the verse is also interpreted as referring to those who study Torah. The word *children* is read not *banayich* but *bonayich*, meaning "those who understand," i.e., scholars.

I MAKE PEACE   The verse ends AND CREATE WOE. The Sages, however, interpreted this to mean "everything."

dwell on high—the angels.

dependent upon the priests   The priests do not "bless" the people. God gives the blessing; the priests only convey the words.

My people Israel! Thus it says INDEED, THE LORD YOUR GOD HAS BLESSED YOU IN ALL YOUR UNDERTAKINGS (Deut. 2:7). FOR THE LORD YOUR GOD WILL BLESS YOU AS HE HAS PROMISED YOU (Deut. 15:6). And it says YOU SHALL BE BLESSED ABOVE ALL PEOPLES (Deut. 7:14). And it says THE LORD WILL OPEN FOR YOU HIS BOUNTEOUS STORE, THE HEAVENS, TO PROVIDE RAIN FOR YOUR LAND IN SEASON AND TO BLESS ALL YOUR UNDERTAKINGS (Deut. 28:12). And it says I WILL FEED THEM IN GOOD GRAZING LAND (Ezek. 34:14) and it says I MYSELF WILL GRAZE MY FLOCK (Ezek. 34:15).

COMMENTARY   *This section begins by explaining the exact procedure for the Blessing of the Priests, which was pronounced daily in the Temple and also outside of it. The practice remained as a synagogue ritual even after the Temple was destroyed although in the synagogue the Name of God is not pronounced as it was in the Temple. The blessing was always considered to be of great importance and value. Small gold amulets containing it dating from the First Temple have been discovered in burial sites in Jerusalem and constitute the oldest Biblical text extant. Because of its importance, the Midrash explains each phrase and extends its meaning. This is especially true of the end of the blessing, which concludes with the word peace. The Midrash uses this as an opportunity to expound on the importance of peace in various contexts and makes it clear that of all God's blessings, peace is the most important.*

5. Numbers 9:5, Sifre N. 67, 62

AND THEY OFFERED THE PASSOVER SACRIFICE IN THE FIRST MONTH, ON THE FOURTEENTH DAY OF THE MONTH (Num. 9:5). This is said to Israel's discredit in that this was the only Passover they celebrated. Thus it says DID YOU OFFER SACRIFICE AND OBLATION TO ME THOSE FORTY YEARS IN THE WILDERNESS, O HOUSE OF ISRAEL? (Amos 5:25). R. Simeon b. Yohai says, "[True,] Israel did not bring sacrifices, but who did bring them? The tribe of Levi as it is said AND THEY OFFER YOU INCENSE TO SAVOR AND WHOLE-OFFERINGS ON YOUR ALTAR (Deut. 33:10) and it says

---

5. *only Passover they celebrated*   This is seen in the fact that no other Passover celebration is mentioned during their years of wandering.

MOSES STOOD UP IN THE GATE OF THE CAMP AND SAID, "WHOEVER IS FOR THE LORD, COME HERE!" AND ALL THE LEVITES RALLIED TO HIM (Ex. 32:26). Israel worshiped idols, but the tribe of Levi did not worship idols, as it is said YOUR PRECEPTS ALONE THEY OBSERVED (Deut. 33:9) and it says NOW, WHEREAS ALL THE PEOPLE WHO CAME OUT OF EGYPT HAD BEEN CIRCUMCISED, NONE OF THE PEOPLE BORN AFTER THE EXODUS, DURING THE DESERT WANDERINGS, HAD BEEN CIRCUMCISED (Josh. 5:5). Israel was not circumcised, but who was circumcised? The tribe of Levi as it is said AND KEPT YOUR COVENANT (Deut. 33:9).

COMMENTARY   *The Midrash wonders why the Torah bothers to mention that they offered the Passover sacrifice that year and answers that it indicates that that was the only year it was brought. The verse from Amos is then interpreted against its meaning in its context and made into a criticism of Israel for not bringing sacrifices. On the other hand, the Levites are praised for doing this and other things that Israel did not do.*

6. Numbers 9:10, Sifre N. 69, 64

WHEN ANY OF YOU OR OF YOUR POSTERITY WHO ARE DEFILED BY A CORPSE OR ARE ON A LONG JOURNEY WOULD OFFER A SACRIFICE TO THE LORD (Num. 9:10). There is a dot over the letter *hey* indicating that if he is unclean, even if it is a short journey, he does not celebrate the Passover with them.

Similarly in the verse THE LORD DECIDE BETWEEN YOU AND ME! (Gen. 16:5) there is a dot over the word ME indicating that she only told him about Hagar. There are those who say that she told him of all those who would cause dissension between him and her.

Similarly in the verse THEY SAID TO HIM, "WHERE IS YOUR WIFE, SARAH?" (Gen. 18:9) there is a dot over the words TO HIM to indicate that they did know where she was.

YOUR COVENANT—the covenant of circumcision.

---

6. *dot over the letter hey*—in the word *long*. The midrash interprets the diacritical marks as indicating that there is something different or additional to be learned from the text.

Similarly in the verse HE DID NOT KNOW WHEN SHE LAY DOWN OR WHEN SHE ROSE (Gen. 19:33) there is a dot over WHEN SHE LAY DOWN indicating that he did not know when she lay down, but did know when she rose up.

Similarly in the verse ESAU RAN TO GREET HIM. HE EMBRACED HIM AND, FALLING ON HIS NECK, HE KISSED HIM (Gen. 33:4) there is a dot over HE KISSED HIM indicating that he did not kiss him with real affection. R. Simeon b. Yohai says, "It is well known that Esau hated Jacob, but at that moment he had genuine feelings of affection and kissed him wholeheartedly."

Similarly in the verse ONE TIME, WHEN HIS BROTHERS HAD GONE TO PASTURE (et) THEIR FATHER'S FLOCK AT SHECHEM (Gen. 37:12) there is a dot over the word *et* indicating that they had gone there only in order to be by themselves.

Similarly ALL THE LEVITES WHO WERE RECORDED, WHOM AT THE LORD'S COMMAND MOSES AND AARON RECORDED BY THEIR CLANS (Num. 3:39) there is a dot over AARON to indicate that Aaron was not included in the number.

Similarly in the verse WE HAVE WROUGHT DESOLATION AT NOPHAH, WHICH IS HARD BY MEDEBA (Num. 21:30) there is a dot over it to indicate that it was thus afterward as well.

Similarly in the verse AND ONE-TENTH FOR EACH OF THE FOURTEEN LAMBS (Num. 29:15) there is a dot on TENTH to indicate that there was only one tenth.

Similarly in the verse CONCEALED ACTS CONCERN THE LORD OUR GOD; BUT WITH OVERT ACTS, IT IS FOR US AND

---

wholeheartedly   The dots are not needed to teach us something we would understand anyway, i.e., Esau's hatred for Jacob. What is unusual is that here Esau was sincere.

the word "et"—has no translation. It is a gramatical construct indicating the direct definite object.

by themselves   They did not want Joseph to follow them.

afterward   They did not really destroy the places, but only the people. Another version of this midrash says exactly the opposite.

OUR CHILDREN EVER TO APPLY ALL THE PROVISIONS OF
THIS TEACHING (Deut. 29:28) there are dots over the words FOR US
AND FOR OUR CHILDREN to indicate that you committed overt acts,
but I will reveal your concealed acts as well.

Here too the verse ON A LONG JOURNEY has a dot over it indi-
cating that if he is unclean, even if it is a short journey, he does not celebrate
the Passover with them.

COMMENTARY   *As S. Lieberman has pointed out, the diacritical marks
used in the Torah were similar to those used by the grammarians of Alexandria to indicate doubtful readings. These comments, which originated
from the school of R. Jose in the middle of the second century, sometimes
point out not a doubtful reading but a text that is unusual. They direct the
reader to consider the meaning of the word for there in something unusual
about it. Particularly interesting is the comment about Esau. His hatred of
his brother was well known, therefore it would be all too easy to understand
his kiss as suspicious and insincere. The dots tell us that in this case, he was
sincere.*

7. Numbers 10:10, Sifre N. 77, 71

YOU SHALL SOUND THE TRUMPETS OVER YOUR BURNT OF-
FERINGS AND YOUR SACRIFICES OF WELL-BEING. THEY
SHALL BE A REMINDER OF YOU BEFORE THE LORD YOUR
GOD: I THE LORD AM YOUR GOD (Num. 10:10). Why is this said?
Because from the verse IN THE SEVENTH MONTH, ON THE FIRST
DAY OF THE MONTH, YOU SHALL OBSERVE COMPLETE REST,
A SACRED OCCASION COMMEMORATED WITH LOUD BLASTS
(Lev. 23:24) we have no indication of the "kingship" [verses]. Therefore
the verse says THE LORD THEIR GOD IS WITH THEM, AND
THEIR KING'S ACCLAIM IN THEIR MIDST (Num. 23:21), referring
to "shofar" and "kingship." R. Nathan says, "The verse is not needed [for

---

7. *"kingship [verses]"*—which are recited in the prayers for the New Year, Rosh HaShannah.
Lev. 23:24 alludes to other verses recited on the themes of remembrance and the shofar but
lacks mention of kingship. Num. 23:21 supplements it.
R. Nathan—disagrees that this is the purpose of Num. 23:21. Num. 10:10 was specifically
stated in order to connect the shofar with remembrance and with the proclamation of the Lord
as God—kingship.

that purpose,] for it says YOU SHALL SOUND THE TRUMPETS (Num. 10:10) referring to the 'shofar' verses; THEY SHALL BE A REMINDER OF YOU (Num. 10:10) referring to the 'remembrance' verses; I THE LORD AM YOUR GOD (Num. 10:10) refers to 'kingship.' "

In view of this, why did the Sages prescribe "kingship" first and then "remembrance" and "shofar"? Rather it means: First proclaim Him your king, then beg Him for mercy so that you shall be remembered by Him. How? By the shofar of freedom. Shofar always indicates freedom as it is said AND IN THAT DAY, A GREAT RAM'S HORN SHALL BE SOUNDED (Isa. 27:13). But I still do not know who will sound it. The verse says MY LORD GOD SHALL SOUND THE RAM'S HORN (Zech. 9:14). But we still do not know from whence the sound will issue. That is what it says HARK, TUMULT FROM THE CITY, THUNDER FROM THE TEMPLE! IT IS THE THUNDER OF THE LORD AS HE DEALS RETRIBUTION TO HIS FOES (Isa. 66:6).

COMMENTARY   *The interpretation of the verse is connected to the liturgy for the New Year, Rosh HaShannah, which is characterized by the addition of three sets of Biblical verses to the central prayer. These verses were followed by the sounding of the shofar, the ram's horn and, eventually, were preceded and followed by special prayers. The three themes dealt with in these verses were: kingship—the proclamation of the sovereignty of God over the entire universe; remembrance—expressing God's intention to recall and fulfill the promises made to Israel; shofrot—recalling the times when the shofar sounded and God revealed Himself, as well as the prophecies indicating that yet again the shofar will sound and God will redeem Israel.*

8. Numbers 10:29, Sifre N. 78, 76

COME WITH US, AND WE WILL DO YOU GOOD; FOR THE LORD HAS SPOKEN GOOD CONCERNING ISRAEL (Num. 10:29).

"kingship" first—rather than using the order found in verse Num. 10:10: shofar, remembrance, kingship.
Rather it means   The order chosen by the Sages has a logic to it.
indicates freedom   The verse continues AND THE STRAYED WHO ARE IN THE LAND OF ASSYRIA AND THE EXPELLED WHO ARE IN THE LAND OF EGYPT SHALL COME AND WORSHIP THE LORD ON THE HOLY MOUNT IN JERUSALEM.

Until now, had God not spoken good concerning Israel? God always spoke good concerning Israel. Rather here God commands Israel to treat converts well and to act kindly toward them.

HE REPLIED TO HIM, "NO. I WILL GO. BUT I WILL GO TO MY LAND AND TO MY KINDRED" (Num. 10:30). "Neither for goods nor for land will I come. There are those who have land, but not goods; those who have goods but do not have family; but I have land, I have goods, and I have family. I am a judge in my city. If I do not go back because of my land I will go because of my possessions, and if I do not go because of my possessions, I will go because of my kindred."

HE SAID, "PLEASE DO NOT LEAVE US" (Num. 10:31). The word *please* always indicates a request. [Moses] said to him, "If you do not acquiesce in my request, I order you now to do so. The Israelites are now saying: Jethro did not convert from love but because Jethro thought that converts would receive a portion in the Land of Israel. Once he realized that they have no portion [in the Land] he left and went on his way."

Another interpretation: If you do not accept the pasture of Jericho, I command you to do so. The Israelites are now saying: Jethro did not convert from love. Jethro thought he was receiving a large gift. Once he realized that his gift was small, he left them and went his own way.

Another interpretation: You think that you are adding great glory to God, but you are only reducing the number of converts and slaves that you will bring under the wings of the Divine Presence in the future.

---

8. *commands Israel* The verse is taken to mean that God tells Israel that they should do good for converts. Jethro, the subject of this verse, is believed to have converted.

NO. I WILL GO—usually translated "I will not go." The midrash emphasizes that because of his land and kindred, mentioned at the end of the verse, he wishes to return home.

no portion Since the Land was to be apportioned among the original tribes, others who joined the people of Israel would not share this.

he left—abandoning Israel and rejecting his conversion, which was based on impure motives.

pasture of Jericho—a portion of land set aside for whatever tribe would give up land for the building of the Temple. Until then, it was to be used by Jethro's descendants.

his gift was small—the pasture of Jericho was not a large section.

adding great glory—by converting others in your own land. Coming with Israel, however, would bring greater glory to God.

INASMUCH AS YOU KNOW WHERE WE SHOULD CAMP IN THE WILDERNESS (Num. 10:31). [Moses] said to him, "If anyone else, who had not witnessed the miracles and wonders in the wilderness, were to depart and go on his way, it would be understandable. But you—who witnessed the miracles and wonders—how can you depart and go on your way? Please, do not leave us!" R. Judah says, "He said to him, 'You are he who witnessed the favor granted our ancestors in Egypt, as it is said AND THE LORD HAD DISPOSED THE EGYPTIANS FAVORABLY TOWARD THE PEOPLE (Ex. 12:36)—how can you depart and go on your way? Please, do not leave us!' "

AND CAN BE OUR EYES (Num. 10:31). Do not close the door before future converts who will say: If Jethro, the father-in-law of the king, did not accept [God], why should anyone else do so?

Another interpretation: AND CAN BE OUR EYES (Num. 10:31). We expect no less than that you should sit with us in the Sanhedrin and instruct us in the Torah!

Another interpretation: AND CAN BE OUR EYES. We expect no less than that you should enlighten our eyes in whatever matters escape our understanding. As it is said, YOU SHALL ALSO SEEK OUT FROM AMONG ALL THE PEOPLE CAPABLE MEN ... (Ex. 18:21). But was not Moses commanded these things at Sinai as it is said AND GOD SO COMMANDS YOU, YOU WILL BE ABLE TO BEAR UP (Ex. 18:23)? Why did Moses forget it? In order to give more merit to one who was already meritorious; in order to give Jethro the credit.

Another interpretation: AND CAN BE OUR EYES. You shall be as precious to us as the apple of our eyes, as it is said YOU TOO MUST LOVE THE STRANGER (Deut. 10:19); YOU SHALL NOT OPPRESS THE

---

did not accept If he leaves, it will be considered that he rejects God and does not become a convert.
forget it The words GOD SO COMMANDS YOU indicates that God had already given Moses the plan for appointing judges under him. Moses, however, forgot this so that Jethro would be able to tell it to him and thus receive credit.
meritorious—i.e., Jethro.
precious to us All strangers—i.e., converts—are to be beloved, as indicated in the verses quoted.

STRANGER (Ex. 23:9); YOU SHALL NOT WRONG A STRANGER
OR OPPRESS HIM (Ex. 22:20).

SO IF YOU COME WITH US, WE WILL EXTEND TO YOU THE
SAME BOUNTY THAT THE LORD GRANTS US (Num. 10:32). What
was the bounty granted him? They said: When Israel divided up the Land,
they set aside the pasture of Jericho which was five hundred ama by five
hundred ama and said that it would go to whoever had the Temple built in
his territory. They gave it into the care of Jonadab the Rechabite and they
benefited from it for four hundred and forty years, as it is said IN THE
FOUR HUNDRED AND EIGHTIETH YEAR AFTER THE ISRA-
ELITES LEFT THE LAND OF EGYPT, IN THE MONTH OF ZIV—
THAT IS, THE SECOND MONTH—IN THE FOURTH YEAR OF
HIS REIGN OVER ISRAEL, SOLOMON BEGAN TO BUILD THE
HOUSE OF THE LORD (1 Kings 6:1). Deducting the forty years Israel
was in the wilderness that leaves four hundred and forty years that they
benefited from it. Once the Divine Presence came to rest in the portion of
Benjamin, the Benjaminites came to claim their portion and they evacuated
the land for them, as it is said THE DESCENDANTS OF THE KENITE,
THE FATHER-IN-LAW OF MOSES, WENT UP WITH THE
JUDITES FROM THE CITY OF PALMS (Judges 1:16).

COMMENTARY   *In rabbinic tradition Jethro is the prototype of the convert, the non-Jew who witnesses the wonders of the Lord, accepts God, and
converts. His desire to return to his home rather than accompany them to
the Land of Canaan was therefore difficult to understand. Wherever the
Bible referred to the alien (ger), the Sages understood this as referring to
the convert. "Ger" became the rabbinic word for a convert.*

9. Numbers 10:35, Sifre N. 84, 80

WHEN THE ARK WAS TO SET OUT (Num. 10:35). There is a sign at
the beginning and at the end of this passage indicating that this is not its
proper place. R. Judah the Prince says, "It indicates that this is a book in its

---

ama—a cubit, the length of an arm from the elbow to the finger tip.
Jonadab the Rechabite—a descendent of Jethro.

---

9. *sign* In the Torah, this passage is set off by the inverted letter nun, which resembles
brackets.

own right." From this they derived the rule that if there is a book which has been erased but retains eighty-five letters, the number found in the section of WHEN THE ARK WAS TO SET OUT, it defiles the hands.

R. Simeon says, "There is a sign at the beginning and at the end indicating that this is not its proper place. What should have been there? THE PEOPLE TOOK TO COMPLAINING (Num. 11:1). A parable. This may be likened to people who said to a king, 'Will you not accompany us to the ruler of Acre?' He arrived at Acre, but the ruler had gone on to Tyre. He reached Tyre but he had gone on to Zidon. He reached Zidon but he had gone on to Biri. He reached Biri but he had gone on to Antioch. He reached Antioch and the people began to grumble and complain that the king had caused them to undertake such a journey, but really the king should have complained that he had undertaken such a journey because of them! Thus the Divine Presence traveled thirty-six miles that day so that Israel might enter the Land. Israel began to grumble and complain to God about the journey, but actually God should have complained that for their sakes the Divine Presence had traveled thirty-six miles so that they could enter the Land of Israel."

COMMENTARY   *The discussion here concerns another diacritical mark common in the ancient world, an inverted letter nun. There are two opinions offered here concerning the meaning of this mark: that it indicates a displacement or that it marks a separate book. Because the "book" is so brief, instead of leaving the usual spaces, marks are utilized. Those who believe that the verse is in the wrong place think that it was put there deliberately in order to separate various complaints of the people.*

MOSES WOULD SAY: ADVANCE, O LORD! (Num. 10:35). There is another verse which says ON A SIGN FROM THE LORD THEY MADE CAMP AND ON A SIGN FROM THE LORD THEY BROKE CAMP (Num. 9:23). How can both of these verses be maintained? A parable. A

---

defiles the hands—a technical term meaning that it is holy. This passage is treated as if it were a separate book and therefore defines the minimum number of letters needed to make a sacred book. If letters have faded in a scroll, but eighty-five remain, that scroll retains its sacred nature.
should have been there   The passage telling of the complaint should have immediately followed the passage about the long journey (Num. 10:33–34). The parable explains the sequence of events.
both of these verses   They contradict one another. One says that Moses told them when to travel, the other that the sign came from the Lord.

human king said to his servant, "Will you help me arise so that I can go and give an inheritance to my son?"

Another interpretation: To what may this be likened? To a human king who was traveling accompanied by his friend. When he traveled he would say, "I will not travel until my friend arrives," and when he stopped he would say, "I will not encamp until my friend arrives." Thus we can maintain both that they encamped at Moses' command and at God's command and that they journeyed at Moses' command and at God's command.

ADVANCE, O LORD! MAY YOUR ENEMIES BE SCATTERED (Num. 10:35) referring to those who were encamped. AND MAY YOUR FOES FLEE (Num. 10:35) referring to those who were pursuing them. BEFORE YOU! (Num. 10:35). They flee before You. We are nothing to them unless You are with us! When You are not with us, we are nothing to them. Thus it says UNLESS YOU GO IN THE LEAD, DO NOT MAKE US LEAVE THIS PLACE (Ex. 33:15). How do we know this? It says WHILE THEY WERE FLEEING BEFORE ISRAEL DOWN THE DESCENT FROM BETH-HORON, THE LORD HURLED HUGE STONES ON THEM FROM THE SKY (Josh. 10:11) and it says O MY GOD, MAKE THEM LIKE THISTLEDOWN, LIKE STUBBLE DRIVEN BY THE WIND. AS A FIRE BURNS A FOREST, AS FLAMES SCORCH THE HILLS (Ps. 83:14–15).

MAY YOUR FOES FLEE (Num. 10:35). Does He Who Spoke and the world came into being really have foes? Rather the verse means that if one hates Israel it is as if he hated He Who Spoke and the world came into being.

Similarly, it says IN YOUR GREAT TRIUMPH YOU BREAK YOUR OPPONENTS (Ex. 15:7). Are there really opponents of He Who Spoke and the world came into being? Rather the verse means that if one rises up against Israel it is as if he rose up against God.

Similarly it says DO NOT IGNORE THE SHOUTS OF YOUR FOES, THE DIN OF YOUR ADVERSARIES THAT ASCENDS ALL

How do we know this?—that the Lord fights against the enemy and therefore they flee from Him and not from Israel.

really have foes "Foes" implies someone who can harm you. No one can harm God, but they could harm Israel. In that way they are God's foes.

THE TIME (Ps. 74:23); SURELY YOUR ENEMIES, O LORD, SURELY YOUR ENEMIES PERISH (Ps. 92:10); THOSE WHO KEEP FAR FROM YOU PERISH (Ps. 73:27); FOR YOUR ENEMIES RAGE, YOUR FOES ASSERT THEMSELVES. THEY PLOT CRAFTILY AGAINST YOUR PEOPLE (Ps. 83:3–4); O LORD, YOU KNOW I HATE THOSE WHO HATE YOU, AND LOATHE YOUR ADVERSARIES. I FEEL A PERFECT HATRED TOWARD THEM; I COUNT THEM MY ENEMIES (Ps. 139:21–22) and it says WHOEVER TOUCHES YOU TOUCHES THE PUPIL OF HIS EYE (Zech. 2:12). R. Judah says, "It does not say "pupil of the eye," but THE PUPIL OF HIS EYE as if the verse were speaking, as it were, of Heaven. Thus Scripture uses a euphemism.

Similarly WHY MAKE OF ME YOUR TARGET, AND A BURDEN TO MYSELF? (Job 7:20). Scripture uses a euphemism.

Similarly AND PROVOKE ME STILL FURTHER AND THRUST THE BRANCH TO THEIR NOSTRILS (Ezek. 8:17). Scripture uses a euphemism.

Similarly YOU, O LORD, ARE FROM EVERLASTING; MY HOLY GOD, WE NEVER DIE (Hab. 1:12). Scripture uses a euphemism.

Similarly THEY EXCHANGED THEIR GLORY FOR THE IMAGE OF A BULL THAT FEEDS ON GRASS (Ps. 106:20). Scripture uses a euphemism.

Similarly IF YOU WOULD DEAL THUS WITH ME, KILL ME RATHER, I BEG YOU, AND LET ME SEE NO MORE OF MY WRETCHEDNESS! (Num. 11:15). Scripture uses a euphemism.

Similarly BUT MY PEOPLE HAS EXCHANGED ITS GLORY FOR WHAT CAN DO NO GOOD (Jer. 2:11). Scripture uses a euphemism.

Similarly LET HER NOT BE AS ONE DEAD, WHO EMERGES FROM HIS MOTHER'S WOMB WITH HALF HIS FLESH EATEN AWAY (Num. 12:12). Scripture uses a euphemism.

So too here. It says THE PUPIL OF HIS EYE (Zech. 2:12). R. Judah says, "It does not say 'the pupil of the eye' but THE PUPIL OF HIS EYE. The verse is speaking, as it were, of God."

---

of Heaven This verse and those that follow actually refer to God but lest they be seen as improper they were reformulated as if they did not refer to God but to someone else.
TO MYSELF—actually means "to You."
HIS MOTHER'S WOMB—really refers to the mother of Miriam, Aaron, and Moses.

If one helps Israel, it is as if he had helped He Who Spoke and the world came into being, as it is said "CURSE MEROZ!" SAID THE ANGEL OF THE LORD. "BITTERLY CURSE ITS INHABITANTS, BECAUSE THEY CAME NOT TO THE AID OF THE LORD, TO THE AID OF THE LORD AMONG THE WARRIORS" (Judges 5:23).

R. Simeon b. Eleazar says, "No other part of the body is as precious as the eye and [God] used it as a metaphor for Israel. It is like a man who is beaten about the head and seeks above all else to protect his eyes. Thus no other part of the body is as precious as the eye and [God] uses it as a metaphor for Israel. Thus it says NO, MY SON! NO, O SON OF MY WOMB! NO, O SON OF MY VOWS! (Prov. 31:2) and it says ONCE I WAS A SON TO MY FATHER, THE TENDER DARLING OF MY MOTHER (Prov. 4:3)."

R. Jose b. Eleazar says, "It is like a man who sticks his finger in his eye and gouges it. Pharaoh harmed you. What did I do to him? PHARAOH'S CHARIOTS AND HIS ARMY HE HAS CAST INTO THE SEA (Ex. 15:4).

Sisera harmed you. What did I do to him? THE STARS FOUGHT FROM HEAVEN, FROM THEIR COURSES THEY FOUGHT AGAINST SISERA (Judges 5:20).

Sennacherib harmed you. What did I do to him? THAT NIGHT AN ANGEL OF THE LORD WENT OUT AND STRUCK DOWN ONE HUNDRED AND EIGHTY-FIVE THOUSAND IN THE ASSYRIAN CAMP, AND THE FOLLOWING MORNING THEY WERE ALL DEAD CORPSES (2 Kings 19:35).

Nebuchadnezzar harmed you. What did I do to him? HE WAS DRIVEN AWAY FROM MEN, HE ATE GRASS LIKE CATTLE, AND HIS BODY WAS DRENCHED WITH THE DEW OF HEAVEN UNTIL HIS HAIR GREW LIKE EAGLE'S [FEATHERS] AND HIS NAILS LIKE [THE TALONS OF] BIRDS (Dan. 4:30).

If one helps Israel—the opposite of the case of the enemies discussed above.

R. Simeon b. Eleazar—another interpretation of the phrase APPLE OF HIS EYE.

and gouges it—yet another interpretation of Zech. 2:12. Inadvertently he injures his eye. Thus when an enemy touches Israel, God then injures that person so that the person has really caused the harm that comes upon him.

Haman harmed you. What did I do to him? AND HE HAS BEEN IMPALED ON THE STAKE FOR SCHEMING AGAINST THE JEWS (Esther 8:7).

COMMENTARY   *The special relationship between God and Israel is emphasized once again in this section. God and Israel cannot be separated. If any nation believes that by hating or harming Israel it is doing the work of God, it is mistaken. The exact opposite is the case. Any harm done to Israel brings down the wrath of God. The section concludes with a repetition of the verses indicating that God is with Israel in exile and suffers with them. This section has not been translated here since it can be found above on page 59. It is a commonplace of the midrashic literature that entire blocks will appear in many different places with only minor variations, if any. The list of euphemisms here indicates that the Sages believed that certain editorial changes had been made in the text in order to prevent misunderstandings. The Scribes were careful not to write anything about God that could be interpreted as improper.*

10. Numbers 11:9, Sifre N. 89, 90

WHEN THE DEW FELL ON THE CAMP AT NIGHT, THE MANNA WOULD FALL UPON IT (Num. 11:9). This teaches that it would come down on the door sills and the doorposts. One might think that when they ate it, it was disgusting and dirty. The verse says OVER THE SURFACE OF THE WILDERNESS LAY A FINE AND FLAKY SUBSTANCE, AS FINE AS FROST ON THE GROUND (Ex. 16:14). A coating of frost would descend first, creating a kind of tray on the earth. Then the manna would descend on that and from there would Israel gather it and eat it. That is fine as far as the underneath layer is concerned, but could not crawling things and insects lie upon the top layer? The verse states WHEN THE FALL OF DEW LIFTED (Ex. 16:14) teaching that it rested as if within a case. They would say the Shema, recite the Prayer, after which each one would go to the entrance to his house and gather enough to sustain him and his household. Afterward, the sun would heat it and it would melt.

---

10. *tray on the earth*—so that the manna would not become dirty by touching the ground.
the Shema—a collection of Biblical passages recited in the morning and the evening.
the Prayer—the basic collection of blessings that is recited three times a day: evening, morning, and afternoon.

Similarly R. Simeon said, "Why was it that the manna did not come down all together once a year? So that they should constantly turn their hearts toward their Father in Heaven. A parable. It may be likened to a king who decreed that he would give his son his allowance once a year. He would see his father only that once a year when he received his allowance. Then he decreed that he should receive his allowance daily. The son said 'Even if I see my father only when he gives me my allowance, that is enough for me.' Thus it was with Israel. If there were five males or five females in a household, a man would sit and anticipate it, saying, 'Woe unto me. Perhaps the manna will not descend tomorrow and we will die of hunger. May it be His will that it descend!' Thus their hearts would be turned toward Heaven."

Similarly R. Dostai b. Jose says, "Why did not God create hot springs in Jerusalem like those in Tiberius? So that a man should not say to his fellow, 'Let us arise and go up to Jerusalem. If we go only for one bath, that will be enough for us.' Thus the pilgrimage to Jerusalem would be performed for impure motives."

COMMENTARY   *Anachronistically, the Sages are describing the morning ritual of their time, which consisted of reciting the Shema and the Amida, the central prayer, as if it were the practice of the Israelites in the wilderness. Since one may not eat before these recitations, they assumed that the Israelites did not gather their manna until they had recited them. Many such anachronisms are found in the Midrash, including the fact that the Amida itself was composed by the Patriarchs. As for the daily gathering of the manna, they see this as yet another way to create a feeling of dependency on God. The concern is voiced that all the practices of religion, such as the pilgrimage to Jerusalem, were performed in such a way that they direct the heart of the individual toward Heaven.*

MOSES HEARD THE PEOPLE WEEPING ACCORDING TO THEIR FAMILIES (Num. 11:10). R. Nehorai used to say, "This teaches that Israel was distressed when Moses told them the laws of incest. It teaches

---

Similarly R. Dostai   It is actually not similar since here the subject is purity of motive and not awareness of dependence on God. Therefore the word *similarly* is missing in some midrash collections.

distressed   The phrase ACCORDING TO THEIR FAMILIES is taken to mean "because of family relationships now forbidden."

that men married their sister, their father's sister, or their mother's sister. When Moses told them to desist from incest they were distressed."

WEEPING ACCORDING TO THEIR FAMILIES. Since their hearts were proud of their sin, they would come together as families and speak of it publicly.

EVERY PERSON AT THE ENTRANCE OF HIS TENT (Num. 11:10). This teaches that they would wait until Moses left the house of study, sitting there and complaining.

THE LORD WAS VERY ANGRY, AND MOSES WAS DISTRESSED (Num. 11:10). Here Moses was indignant and the Holy One tried to restrain him. In the incident of the golden calf, the Holy One was indignant and Moses tried to restrain Him.

AND MOSES SAID TO THE LORD, "WHY HAVE YOU DEALT ILL WITH YOUR SERVANT, AND WHY HAVE I NOT ENJOYED YOUR FAVOR, THAT YOU LAID THE BURDEN OF ALL THIS PEOPLE UPON ME? DID I CONCEIVE ALL THIS PEOPLE, DID I BEAR THEM?" (Num. 11:11–12). When had He spoken thus to him? When He said to him BUT GO NOW, LEAD THE PEOPLE WHERE I TOLD YOU (Ex. 32:34). It is still unclear, however, until the verse says SO THE LORD SPOKE TO MOSES AND AARON AND CHARGED THEM IN REGARD TO THE ISRAELITES (Ex. 6:13). He said to them, "Know that they are stubborn and troublesome. You must be prepared for them to curse you and stone you." WHERE AM I TO GET MEAT TO GIVE TO ALL THIS PEOPLE (Num. 11:13)? Are there only one or two of them that I might deal with them?

I CANNOT CARRY ALL THIS PEOPLE BY MYSELF (Num. 11:14). [He said this] because the Holy One showed Moses all of the suffering that was to come upon them in the future. R. Simeon used to say, "A parable. It may be likened to one who was being led to his execution together with his

---

restrain Him—as in Ex. 32:10 where God says to Moses LET ME GO as if Moses were holding Him back from destroying the people.
suffering Moses could manage the work of leading Israel but he could not bear the thought that they would have to suffer in the future.

children. He said to the executioner, 'Slay me before you slay my children.' This is unlike what happened to Zedekiah, of whom it is written THE KING OF BABYLON HAD ZEDEKIAH'S SONS SLAUGHTERED BE-FORE HIS EYES . . . THEN THE EYES OF ZEDEKIAH WERE PUT OUT (Jer. 52:10–11). Thus Moses said to God, 'If that is what You are going to do to me, KILL ME RATHER, I BEG YOU (Num. 11:15). I would rather You would slay me first so that I need not witness the suffer-ings which are to come upon them in the future.' "

THEN THE LORD SAID TO MOSES, "GATHER FOR ME SEVENTY . . ." (Num. 11:16). Why is this said? Since it says I CANNOT CARRY ALL THIS PEOPLE BY MYSELF (Num. 11:14), God said to him, "I am giving you what you requested."

GATHER FOR ME (Num. 11:16). The Sanhedrin should be for My Name's sake.

Wherever it says "for Me" (li) it indicates that it will endure forever and ever.
    Concerning the priests it says AND CONSECRATE THEM TO SERVE ME (li) (Ex. 28:41).
    Concerning the Levites it says AND THE LEVITES SHALL BE MINE (li) (Num. 8:14).
    Concerning Israel it says FOR IT IS TO ME (li) THAT THE ISRA-ELITES ARE SERVANTS (Lev. 25:55).
    Concerning the Land it says FOR THE LAND IS MINE (li) (Lev. 25:23).
    Concerning the firstborn it says FOR EVERY FIRSTBORN AMONG THE ISRAELITES IS MINE (li) (Num. 8:17).
    Concerning the Temple it says AND LET THEM MAKE ME (li) A SANCTUARY (Ex. 25:8).

---

to do to me—make me witness their suffering. Some versions have "If I have found favor in Your eyes, KILL ME."
Sanhedrin—the Greek name later given to the group of elders that was said to rule the people during the period of the Second Temple and was viewed as the continuation of this group of seventy elders.
for My Name's sake The words FOR ME mean "in order to serve Me for pure motives."
endure forever and ever This is another interpretation of FOR ME. Since it is connected to God, it will endure forever.

Concerning the altar it says MAKE FOR ME (li) AN ALTAR OF EARTH (Ex. 20:21).

Concerning the oil it says THIS SHALL BE FOR AN ANOINTING OIL SACRED TO ME (li) THROUGHOUT ALL GENERATIONS (Ex. 30:31).

Concerning the kingship it says FOR I HAVE DECIDED ON ONE OF HIS SONS TO BE A KING UNTO ME (li) (1 Sam. 16:1).

Concerning the sacrifices it says IN PRESENTING TO ME (li) AT STATED TIMES (Num. 28:2).

Thus wherever it says "for Me" it indicates that it will endure forever and ever.

SEVENTY MEN (Num. 11:16). The Sanhedrin should consist of seventy members. SEVENTY MEN. They should be wise, brave, experienced, and of good account.

OF ISRAEL'S ELDERS (Num. 11:16). God honors the elders more than just once or twice. Wherever you find mention of the elders, God honors them. Thus it says GO AND ASSEMBLE THE ELDERS OF ISRAEL (Ex. 3:16).

THEN MOSES AND AARON WENT AND ASSEMBLED ALL THE ELDERS OF THE ISRAELITES (Ex. 4:29).

THEN HE SAID TO MOSES, "COME UP TO THE LORD, YOU AND AARON, NADAB AND ABIHU, AND SEVENTY ELDERS OF ISRAEL" (Ex. 24:1).

TO THE ELDERS HE SAID, "WAIT HERE FOR US UNTIL WE RETURN TO YOU." (Ex. 24:14).

ON THE EIGHTH DAY MOSES CALLED AARON AND HIS SONS, AND THE ELDERS OF ISRAEL (Lev. 9:1).

Thus wherever you find mention of the elders, God honors them. R. Simeon b. Yochai says, "How do we know that in the future God will honor the elders? As it is said THEN THE MOON SHALL BE ASHAMED, AND THE SUN SHALL BE ABASHED. FOR THE LORD OF HOSTS WILL REIGN ON MOUNT ZION AND IN JERUSALEM, AND HIS GLORY WILL BE REVEALED TO HIS ELDERS (Isa. 24:23). It does not say 'His Glory will be revealed to His angels' or 'to His prophets' but HIS GLORY WILL BE REVEALED TO HIS ELDERS. Now it is a matter of logic. If He Who Spoke and the world came into being will honor His elders in the future, how much more are human beings duty bound to honor the elders! Thus you find that God was as troubled about one elder as

He was about all of Israel, as it is said I WAS ANGRY AT MY PEOPLE, I DEFILED (hillalti) MY HERITAGE (Isa. 47:6)—that is I forgave (mahullalim) all except: UPON THE ELDER YOU MADE YOUR YOKE EXCEEDINGLY HEAVY (Isa. 47:6)."

OF WHOM YOU HAVE EXPERIENCE AS ELDERS AND OFFICERS OF THE PEOPLE (Num. 11:16). You must know if they are acceptable to Me. AS ELDERS AND OFFICERS OF THE PEOPLE. This teaches that no one is appointed to the earthly court unless he is appointed to the Heavenly court, until people praise him saying of him: That man is fit to be appointed, he is a *hasid*. It befits him to be a sage.

COMMENTARY   *The Sages considered themselves to be the heirs of the Biblical elders. Therefore they emphasize the importance of honoring and heeding the elders. The list of verses that include the word li, TO ME, is more than an exercise in semantics. By indicating that this word means that these things will endure forever, they were voicing their firm belief that the reality of the time in which they lived, after the destruction of the Temple, the loss of control over their land, and the inability to carry out many of the mitzvot that were connected to the Temple, was only temporary. All of this would be restored. The hasid (pious one), mentioned in connection with the appointment of judges, connoted the rabbinic idea of the individual who obeys the entire Torah and goes far beyond it in extending helpfulness to others.*

11. Numbers 11:21, Sifre N. 95, 94

BUT MOSES SAID, "THE PEOPLE WHO ARE WITH ME NUMBER SIX HUNDRED THOUSAND MEN (Num. 11:21)." R. Simeon b. Yochai says, "R. Akiba had one explanation for this and I have two different ones. I prefer my interpretation to that of my Teacher. He said, 'Scripture says COULD ENOUGH FLOCKS AND HERDS BE SLAUGHTERED TO SUFFICE THEM? (Num. 11:22). Even if you were to give them all the flocks and herds in the world it would not suffice for them.' And I say:

---

a hasid—a person of great piety.

---

11. *I say*   R. Akiba takes the verse literally: They would never be satisfied no matter how much I gave them. R. Simeon takes it to mean that they really have enough so that giving them more would be meaningless. They are just seeking excuses to be rebellious.

Were they complaining because they did not have flesh to eat? At the Exodus from Egypt, does it not say A MIXED MULTITUDE WENT UP WITH THEM, AND VERY MUCH LIVESTOCK, BOTH FLOCKS AND HERDS (Ex. 12:38)? Could they possibly have eaten all of that in the wilderness? The verse says THE REUBENITES AND THE GADITES OWNED CATTLE IN VERY GREAT NUMBERS (Num. 32:1). Rather they were looking for an excuse to cease following God. OR COULD ALL OF THE FISH OF THE SEA BE GATHERED FOR THEM TO SUFFICE THEM? (Num. 11:22). Even if you were to supply them with fish to eat, they would complain. Did not the well accompany them in the wilderness and supply them with great fish, more than they could use? Rather they were looking for an excuse to cease following God.

"Another interpretation: Since God showed Moses all the suffering that would come upon them in the future, Moses said to God, 'My Lord, is it fair to them to give them [what they ask] and then to slay them? Does one say to an ass: Take a bushel of barley and then we shall cut off your head! Does one say to a man: Take a bushel of gold and descend to hell!' He said to him, 'Then what do you suggest?' [Moses] said to Him, 'I shall go and pacify them.' [God] said to him, 'As long as you are here, let Me tell you— they will not listen to you.' Moses went to them and said IS THERE A LIMIT TO THE LORD'S POWER (Num. 11:23)? HE STRUCK THE ROCK AND WATERS FLOWED, STREAMS GUSHED FORTH; CAN HE NOT PROVIDE BREAD? (Ps. 78:20). They said, 'This is a compromise. He simply does not have the ability to grant our requests!' "

COMMENTARY   *A disciple would not usually contradict his master. Thus R. Simeon's remark is unusual. The dispute concerns the fact that the verse seems to indicate that Moses questioned God's ability to provide food for such a vast number of people. R. Akiba therefore interprets it to means that Moses says that no matter how much you give them, it will not be enough. R. Simeon offers two explanations: (1) Moses says they are simply being*

---

the well—described in Num. 21:17-18. The legend was that it accompanied them throughout their journey.

Another interpretation   Moses felt that there was no point in giving them so much since they were going to be punished in the future.

compromise   The water and other things He gave us are only partially satisfactory.

rebellious; (2) Moses says that there is no point in granting the request since they are to be slain in any case. That generation suffered various plagues and punishments in the wilderness.

12. Numbers 12:1, Sifre N. 99, 97

MIRIAM AND AARON SPOKE AGAINST MOSES (Num. 12:1). The word *spoke* always indicates harsh language. Thus it says THE MAN WHO IS THE LORD OF THE LAND SPOKE HARSHLY TO US (Gen. 42:30). AND THE PEOPLE SPOKE AGAINST GOD AND AGAINST MOSES (Num. 21:5). Thus the word *spoke* always indicates harsh language, while the word *said* always indicates pleading. Thus it says AND SAID, "I BEG YOU, MY FRIENDS, DO NOT COMMIT SUCH A WRONG" (Gen. 19:7) and it says AND HE SAID, "PLEASE HEAR MY WORDS" (Num. 12:6).

MIRIAM AND AARON SPOKE AGAINST MOSES. (Num. 12:1). This teaches that both of them spoke against him, but Miriam opened the discussion. Usually Miriam did not speak before Aaron unless there was some emergency. Similarly we read BUT YOU GO AND READ ALOUD THE WORDS OF THE LORD FROM THE SCROLL WHICH YOU WROTE AT MY DICTATION (Jer. 36:6). Usually Baruch did not speak before Jeremiah unless there was an emergency.

MIRIAM AND AARON SPOKE AGAINST MOSES. How did Miriam know that Moses had ceased fulfilling the mitzvah of reproduction? She noticed that Zipporah did not adorn herself with jewelry and said to her, "What has happened that you do not adorn yourself with jewelry?" She said to her, "Your brother no longer performs his husbandly duties." That is how Miriam knew and told her brother so that both of them spoke against him.

---

12. *Miriam opened the discussion*   Since her name comes first, we know that she was the first to speak. This also explains why her punishment was the more severe.

reproduction   The command given to mankind in Gen. 1:28 to have sexual relations in order to reproduce is the first mitzvah of the Torah.

jewelry—which would stimulate the husband to have relations with his wife.

R. Nathan says, "Miriam was with Zipporah when A YOUTH RAN OUT AND TOLD MOSES, SAYING 'ELDAD AND MEDAD ARE ACTING THE PROPHET IN THE CAMP!' (Num. 11:27). When Zipporah heard that she said, 'Woe to their wives!' Thus Miriam knew and told her brother so that both of them spoke against him."

It is a matter of logic. If Miriam, who did not intend to speak evil of her brother but to praise him, who did not intend to lessen Moses' fulfillment of the mitzvah of reproduction but to increase it, and who spoke of this only to herself, was punished, how much more will punishment come upon one who intends to speak evil of his fellow and not to praise him, to decrease fulfillment of the mitzvah of reproduction and not to increase it, and who speaks publicly and not merely to himself!

It is a [similar] matter of logic in regard to King Uzziah who was punished even though he did not intend to aspire to greatness for his own glory but for that of his Maker. How much more will one be punished who aspires to greatness for his own glory and not for that of his Maker!

BECAUSE OF THE CUSHITE WOMAN (Num. 12:1). Scripture informs us that whoever saw her would marvel over her beauty, as it is said THE FATHER OF MILCAH AND ISCAH (Gen. 11:29) meaning that everyone would gaze at (sachin) her. THE EGYPTIANS SAW HOW VERY BEAUTIFUL THE WOMAN WAS. PHARAOH'S COURTIERS SAW HER AND PRAISED HER TO PHARAOH (Gen. 12:14–15). R. Eliezer the son of R. Jose the Galilean says, "The name Zipporah means *zafu ureu*—'come and see' how lovely (she is)!"

R. Nathan—offers a different explanation of how Miriam came to know this intimate fact. Miriam overheard Zipporah's remark.

woe to their wives Based on Moses' behavior, she assumes that anyone who prophesies, as does her husband, does not have sexual relations.

King Uzziah Although a good king of many accomplishments, he mistakenly took it upon himself to offer incense in the Temple. His punishment was that he contracted leprosy. See 2 Chron. 26:16–21.

HOW VERY BEAUTIFUL THE WOMAN WAS This verse is speaking of Sarah. This was also the case with Zipporah.

BECAUSE OF THE CUSHITE WOMAN (Num. 12:1). Was she indeed a Cushite? Was she not a Midianite as it is said NOW THE PRIEST OF MIDIAN HAD SEVEN DAUGHTERS (Ex. 2:16)? Why then does the verse say Cushite? Rather it means that just as the skin of a Cushite is different, so Zipporah was different in that her beauty was greater than that of all other women.

Similarly it says SHIGGAION OF DAVID, WHICH HE SANG TO THE LORD, CONCERNING CUSH, A BENJAMINITE (Ps. 7:1). Was he indeed a Cushite? Rather it means that just as the skin of a Cushite is different, so Saul was different in his appearance, as it is said HE WAS A HEAD TALLER THAN ANY OF THE PEOPLE (Sam. 1 9:2).

Similarly it says TO ME, O ISRAELITES, YOU ARE JUST LIKE THE CUSHITES—DECLARES THE LORD (Amos 9:7). Were they indeed Cushites? Rather it means that just as the skin of the Cushite is different, so Israel is different from all the nations in its observance of the mitzvot.

Similarly it says EBED-MELECH THE CUSHITE, A EUNUCH WHO WAS IN THE KING'S PALACE, HEARD (Jer. 38:7). Was he indeed a Cushite? Rather it means that just as the skin of the Cushite is different, so the deeds of Baruch son of Neriah were different from those of all other members of a royal entourage.

FOR HE MARRIED A CUSHITE WOMAN (Num. 12:1). Since it says BECAUSE OF THE CUSHITE WOMAN HE HAD MARRIED (Num. 12:1) why does the verse say FOR HE MARRIED A CUSHITE WOMAN? Some women are lovely in their appearance but not in their actions or in their actions but not in their appearance, as it is said LIKE A GOLD RING IN THE SNOUT OF A PIG IS A BEAUTIFUL WOMAN BEREFT OF SENSE (Prov. 11:22), but this one is beautiful in her appearance and beautiful in her actions, therefore it says FOR HE MARRIED A CUSHITE WOMAN.

Cushite   The Cushites were Ethiopians, yet we are told that Zipporah was a Midianite. Therefore Cushite must have some other meaning.

Baruch—Jeremiah's secretary. Although it is not clear from the text, the Sages assumed that Ebed-melech was another name for Baruch. The name means "servant of the king."

THEY SAID, "HAS THE LORD SPOKEN ONLY THROUGH MO-
SES?" (Num. 12:2) "Did not the Holy One speak with the Patriarchs as
well and yet they did not desist from fulfilling the mitzvah of reproduction!"
"HAS HE NOT SPOKEN THROUGH US AS WELL?" (Num. 12:2)—
"yet we have not desisted from fulfilling the mitzvah of reproduction."
THE LORD HEARD IT (Num. 12:2). This teaches that no other human
being was present. They spoke about him only between themselves, as it is
said THE LORD HEARD IT. R. Nathan says, "They also spoke about
Moses in his presence, as it is said THE LORD HEARD IT. NOW MO-
SES WAS A VERY HUMBLE MAN (Num. 12:2–3), but Moses held himself in concerning this."

COMMENTARY   *In their interpretation of this incident, the Sages taught
that Moses had not married another woman, but that the wife referred to
was the wife taken in Midian, Zipporah. The gossip concerning her was
that Moses, because of his position of holiness, had ceased having sexual
relations with her. Although purity in sexual matters was considered a mark
of holiness, the Sages did not usually consider refraining from marital relations to be appropriate except at the specific times when this is called
for. It may be, however, that some of these interpretations did consider it
appropriate in this case. This could be based on the fact that just as the*
*Israelites were told to refrain from marital relations when they prepared to
receive the word of God at Sinai, so Moses, who was in continual contact
with God, was expected to refrain. Whether or not the criticism was correct, Miriam and Aaron were punished for it because any sort of gossip,
known as "the evil tongue," is forbidden.*

NOW MOSES WAS A VERY HUMBLE MAN (Num. 12:3). He was
humble in spirit. You say "humble in spirit," but perhaps it means humble
in body. Therefore the verse says YOU SHALL DO TO HIM AS YOU
DID TO SIHON KING OF THE AMORITES (Num. 21:34). He attacked
Sihon and killed him. He attacked Og and killed him.

Another interpretation. VERY HUMBLE (Num. 12:3). Humble in
spirit. You say "humble in spirit" but perhaps it means humble in his wealth.

---

no other human being was present   Since the verse states THE LORD HEARD IT, the implication is that no one else did.
humble in body—physically weak.
humble in wealth—poor.

Therefore the verse says MOSES HIMSELF WAS VERY GREAT IN THE LAND OF EGYPT (Ex. 11:3) and thus we find that the sapphire of which the tablets [of the Covenant] were made belonged to Moses, as it is said CARVE OUT FOR YOURSELF TWO TABLETS OF STONE LIKE THE FIRST (Deut. 10:1) and elsewhere it says THE TABLETS WERE GOD'S WORK (Ex. 32:16) and it says UNDER HIS FEET WAS THE WORK OF A PAVEMENT OF SAPPHIRE (Ex. 24:10) thus connecting one "work" to another "work." Just as the work mentioned there was of sapphire, so the work mentioned here was made of sapphire.

MORE SO THAN ANY OTHER MAN ON EARTH (Num. 12:3) but not more so than the Patriarchs. R. Jose says, "More than even the Patriarchs." If so, what is the meaning of ANY OTHER MAN? [More than ANY OTHER MAN] but not more than the ministering angels.

SUDDENLY THE LORD CALLED TO MOSES, AARON AND MIRIAM (Num. 12:4). R. Simeon b. Menasia says, "Suddenly Moses was afraid when He spoke to him suddenly."

"COME OUT, YOU THREE, TO THE TENT OF MEETING" (Num. 12:4). This teaches that all three were called simultaneously in one utterance, something which the mouth cannot describe and the ear cannot understand. Thus it says THE LORD SPOKE ALL THESE WORDS SAYING (Ex. 20:1). ONE THING GOD HAS SPOKEN; TWO THINGS HAVE I HEARD (Ps. 62:12) and it says BEHOLD, MY WORD IS LIKE FIRE—DECLARES THE LORD—AND LIKE A HAMMER THAT SHATTERS ROCK! (Jer. 23:29).

THE LORD CAME DOWN IN A PILLAR OF CLOUD, STOPPED AT THE ENTRANCE OF THE TENT (Num. 12:5). The qualities of human

---

the tablets—referring to the second set, which Moses had to carve out. The implication is that he had to provide the stone from his own possessions, and since, according to the Sages, the first set was made of sapphire, Moses had to provide sapphire. That he could do so indicated that he had great wealth.

"work" mentioned here—the tablets.

not more so than the Patriarchs The Patriarchs are not like other men and are not included in the term OTHER MAN ON EARTH. R. Jose disagrees.

If so If the phrase includes the Patriarchs, why bother to state it at all. Whom does it intend to exclude?

ALL THESE WORDS All of the Ten Pronouncements were uttered simultaneously.

beings are not like the qualities of the Holy One. When human beings go forth to war they go accompanied by many men, but when they go to make peace they are accompanied by only a few. But He Who Spoke and the world came into being is otherwise. When He goes forth to make war He goes alone, as it is said THE LORD, THE WARRIOR—LORD IS HIS NAME (Ex. 15:3) but when He comes in peace, He comes with thousands and myriads as it is said GOD'S CHARIOTS ARE MYRIADS UPON MYRIADS, THOUSANDS UPON THOUSANDS; THE LORD IS AMONG THEM AS IN SINAI IN HOLINESS (Ps. 68:18).

AND CALLED OUT, "AARON AND MIRIAM!" THE TWO OF THEM CAME FORWARD (Num. 12:5). Why did Moses not go out with them? So that Israel would not say: Moses too is included in [God's] wrath.

Another interpretation. Scripture instructs you in proper conduct. If a man wishes to speak with his fellow he should not ask him to come over to him but should draw him near by means of something that [the other] really wants and then speak to him.

Another interpretation: So that [Moses] should not hear the shame of Aaron.

Another interpretation: One does not speak the praise of a person in his presence. R. Eleazar b. Azariah says, "We find that it is proper to say part of the praise of a person in his presence, for thus we find concerning Noah as it is said FOR YOU ALONE HAVE I FOUND RIGHTEOUS BEFORE ME IN THIS GENERATION (Gen. 7:1) whereas when [Noah] was not present, He says of him NOAH WAS A RIGHTEOUS MAN; HE WAS BLAMELESS IN HIS AGE (Gen. 6:9). R. Eliezer b. R. Jose the Galilean says, "We find that it is proper to say part of the praise of He Who Spoke and the world came into being, as it is said SAY TO GOD, 'HOW AWESOME ARE YOUR DEEDS' (Ps. 66:3) and if one says only a part of the praise of He Who Spoke and the world came into being, how much more is this so concerning human beings!"

AND HE SAID, "HEAR NOW (na) THESE MY WORDS" (Num. 12:6). The word *na* always means "please." It is a matter of logic. If He Who

---

He comes with thousands—indicating that peace is more important and beloved than war. Here, God is angry and comes alone.

the praise of a person Since God was going to speak the praises of Moses to Miriam and Aaron, it was not appropriate for Moses to be there to hear it.

AWESOME—whereas in other places speaking about God, the praise is much more extended.

Spoke and the world came into being uses pleading language, certainly human beings should. R. Simeon b. Yochai says, "What does the verse HEAR NOW THESE MY WORDS mean? They tried to interrupt the words of God. God said to them, 'Wait until I am still.' How much more is it so that one man should not interrupt the words of another."

WHEN THE LORD SPEAKS THROUGH ONE OF YOU, I MAKE MYSELF KNOWN TO HIM IN A VISION (Num. 12:6). Perhaps it means "I speak with Moses as I speak with other prophets, through dreams and visions." Therefore the verse says NOT SO WITH MY SERVANT MOSES (Num. 12:7). HE IS TRUSTED THROUGHOUT MY HOUSEHOLD (Num. 12:7) aside from the ministering angels. R. Jose says, "Including the ministering angels."

WITH HIM I SPEAK MOUTH TO MOUTH (Num. 12:8). Mouth to mouth I said to him to separate himself from his wife.

MANIFESTLY (Num. 12:8). This refers to the manifestation of the word. You say that this refers to the manifestation of the word. Perhaps it refers to the manifestation of the Divine Presence? The verse says "BUT," HE SAID, "YOU CANNOT SEE MY FACE, FOR MAN MAY NOT SEE ME AND LIVE" (Ex. 33:20). R. Akiba says, "MAN—means exactly that. AND LIVE refers to the ministering angels." R. Simeon of Timneh said, "I do not intend to contradict the words of R. Akiba but to add to them. MAN—means exactly that. AND LIVE refers to the holy beasts and the ministering angels." R. Eleazar b. Jose says, "Not merely that they cannot see Him, but they do not even know His place, as it is said BLESSED IS THE PRESENCE OF THE LORD IN HIS PLACE (Ezek. 3:12). And what is the meaning of the verse FOR MAN MAY NOT SEE ME AND LIVE (Ex. 33:20)? When he is alive, he will not see Me, but at the hour of his death he will. Thus it says ALL THOSE WHO GO DOWN TO THE DUST SHALL KNEEL BEFORE HIM, EVEN HE THAT CANNOT KEEP HIS SOUL ALIVE (Ps. 22:30)."

I said to him to separate Moses is not to be blamed for his abstinence. It was God who told him to do so.
the word—personified as an emanation from God.
AND LIVE The midrash treats this not as a verb. but as a noun—"living beings." Neither man nor angels can see God.

AND NOT IN RIDDLES (Num. 12:8) Why is this said? Since it says O MORTAL, PROPOUND A RIDDLE AND RELATE AN ALLEGORY TO THE HOUSE OF ISRAEL (Ezek. 17:2) one might think that just as I speak to the prophets in riddles and allegories, so do I speak with Moses. Therefore the verse says AND NOT IN RIDDLES.

AND HE BEHOLDS THE LIKENESS OF THE LORD (Num. 12.8). This refers to the appearance of His back. You say this refers to the appearance of His back. Perhaps it refers to the appearance of His face? The verse says THEN I WILL TAKE MY HAND AWAY AND YOU WILL SEE MY BACK (Ex. 33:23). That refers to the appearance of His back. BUT MY FACE MUST NOT BE SEEN (Ex. 33:23). That refers to the appearance of His face. And it says HE UNROLLED IT BEFORE ME, AND IT WAS INSCRIBED ON BOTH THE FRONT AND THE BACK (Ezek. 2:10). But do not even ordinary people and those who are rather simple do thus? What then does the verse mean by THE FRONT AND THE BACK? THE FRONT in this world and THE BACK in the world to come. THE FRONT—the quietude of the wicked and the suffering of the righteous in this world. THE BACK—the reward of the righteous and the punishment of the wicked in the world to come. ON IT WERE WRITTEN LAMENTATIONS, UTTERANCES, AND WOES (Ezek. 2:10). LAMENTATIONS of the wicked, as it is said THIS IS A LAMENTATION, AND IT SHALL BE INTONED: THE WOMEN OF THE NATIONS SHALL INTONE IT, THEY SHALL INTONE IT OVER EGYPT AND HER MULTITUDE (Ezek. 32:16). UTTERANCES (hegeh) of the righteous, as it is said WITH THE TEN-STRINGED HARP, WITH VOICE AND LYRE (higayon) TOGETHER (Ps. 92:4). WOES of the wicked, as it is said WOE SHALL FOLLOW WOE (Ezek. 7:26).

HOW THEN DID YOU NOT SHRINK FROM SPEAKING AGAINST MY SERVANT, AGAINST MOSES (Num. 12:8). The reason that the verse says AGAINST MY SERVANT, AGAINST MOSES is to indicate that you were not speaking against Moses but against Me. A parable. This

---

ordinary people They too write on both sides of a scroll. There must therefore be some deeper meaning to the phrase in Ezekiel.

quietude of the wicked Moses was able to understand the seeming injustices of the world, which ordinary men cannot fathom.

may be likened to a human king who appointed a governor over a city and the people of that city would speak against him. The king said to them, "You did not speak against my governor, but against me! And if you say, 'I do not recognize his authority,' that is even worse than the other!"

STILL INCENSED WITH THEM, THE LORD DEPARTED (Num. 12:9). Only after He informed them of their wrongdoing did He decree their banishment. This is a matter of logic. If He Who Spoke and the world came into being did not become angry with human beings until He had informed them of their wrongdoing, certainly a human being should not be angry with his fellow until he has informed him of his wrongdoing. R. Nathan says, "Why did He first inform them of their wrongdoing and then decree their banishment? So that they should not be able to say as did Job LET ME KNOW WHAT YOU CHARGE ME WITH (Job 10:2)."

AS THE CLOUD WITHDREW FROM THE TENT (Num. 12:10). A parable. A human king said to a tutor, "Chastise my son, but chastise him only after I have left," because a father has pity on his son. It is a matter of logic. If God pities the righteous when it is a time of His anger, certainly He will pity them when it is a time of His favor, as it is said THUS SAID THE LORD: IN AN HOUR OF FAVOR I ANSWER YOU (Isa. 49:8).

THERE WAS MIRIAM LEPROUS, WITH SNOW-WHITE SCALES (Num. 12:10). This indicates that her leprosy was virulent, which teaches us how pure of skin she had been. Thus it says THE LORD SAID TO HIM FURTHER, "PUT YOUR HAND INTO YOUR BOSOM." HE PUT HIS HAND INTO HIS BOSOM; AND WHEN HE TOOK IT OUT, HIS HAND WAS LEPROUS, WITH SNOW-WHITE SCALES (Ex. 4:6), which teaches us that they were pure of skin.

AND AARON TURNED (Num. 12:10). This means that he "turned" (was healed) from his leprosy. R. Judah b. Beterah says, "In the future anyone who says that Aaron was afflicted with leprosy will have to stand judgment. If He Who Spoke and the world came into being concealed this and you reveal it, you will have to stand judgment in the future.

---

time of His anger—when God's Quality of Justice is dominant rather than His Quality of Mercy. Even then He has pity on the righteous.

and you reveal it The statement is true, but if God did not cause it to be recorded He did not want to bring shame on Aaron by making it known.

NUMBERS

"In the future anyone who says that Zelophehad was the man who gathered sticks [on the Sabbath] will have to stand judgment. If He Who spoke and the world came into being concealed this and you reveal it, you will have to stand judgment in the future.

"And in the future anyone who says that Akavya b. Mehallel was declared a heretic will have to stand judgment."

AND AARON TURNED TOWARD MIRIAM, HE SAW THAT SHE WAS LEPROUS (Num. 22:10). The verse informs us that whenever he looked at her, it would break out upon her.

AND AARON SAID TO MOSES, "O MY LORD, ACCOUNT NOT TO US THE SIN" (Num. 12:11). He said to him, "Since we sinned inadvertently, forgive us. It was not deliberate."

LET HER NOT BE AS ONE DEAD (Num. 12:12). Just as a dead body causes impurity to those within a tent, so a leper causes impurity through intercourse.

Said Aaron, "It is as if I had lost my sister! I cannot isolate her and I cannot declare her impure, nor can I purify her!" Thus we learn that Aaron held that one may not deal with the leprosy of those related to him. WHO EMERGES FROM HIS MOTHER'S WOMB (Num. 12:12). It means: from the womb of our mother—but Scripture used veiled language. WITH HALF HIS FLESH EATEN AWAY (Num. 12:12). He should have said "... half our flesh ..." as it says AFTER ALL, HE IS OUR BROTHER, OUR OWN FLESH (Gen. 37:27).

---

the man who gathered sticks The name of this man who violated the Sabbath is not mentioned in the Scripture since God did not want to reveal it. See Num. 15:32–36.
Akavya b. Mehallel—a Sage of the first century C.E. who refused to renounce his opinions when the majority disagreed with him. He was excommunicated and declared a heretic. R. Judah b. Beterah believed that this was not so.
we sinned inadvertently—intending only to cause Moses to fulfill the command to reproduce and not to spread slander about him.
so a leper causes impurity In this way, the leper may be compared to the dead.
I cannot isolate her The task of the priests, as described in Lev. 13–14, is to diagnose the disease, isolate the leper, and eventually declare that person pure again. Aaron cannot do that because a priest does not deal with his own relative. Therefore as far as he is concerned, she is AS ONE DEAD. He can do nothing for her.
veiled language The accurate description would have been considered improper language about one's mother.

SO MOSES CRIED OUT TO THE LORD, SAYING, "O GOD, PRAY HEAL HER!" (Num. 12:13) The verse wishes to teach you proper conduct. If one wants to petition for his needs, he should first say two or three words asking for favor and then petition for his needs.

TO THE LORD, SAYING (Num. 12:13). What does the verse indicate by the word *SAYING?* [Moses] said to Him, "Tell me if You will heal her or not." The Holy One responded BUT THE LORD SAID TO MOSES, "IF HER FATHER SPAT IN HER FACE, WOULD SHE NOT BEAR HER SHAME FOR SEVEN DAYS? LET HER BE SHUT OUT OF THE CAMP FOR SEVEN DAYS, AND THEN LET HER BE READMITTED (Num. 12:14–15)."

Eleazar b. Azariah says, "There are four instances in which Moses asked that the Holy One respond to his request and He did so. One instance was BUT MOSES APPEALED TO THE LORD, SAYING, 'THE ISRAELITES WOULD NOT LISTEN TO ME; HOW THEN SHOULD PHARAOH HEED ME, A MAN OF IMPEDED SPEECH' (Ex. 6:12). The word *SAYING* indicates that he said to Him, 'Tell me if You are going to redeem them or not' and the Holy One responded YOU SHALL SOON SEE WHAT I WILL DO TO PHARAOH (Ex. 6:1).

"Another instance was MOSES SPOKE TO THE LORD SAYING, 'LET THE LORD, SOURCE OF THE BREATH OF ALL FLESH, APPOINT SOMEONE OVER THE COMMUNITY' (Num. 27:15). The word *SAYING* indicates that he said to Him, 'Tell me if You are going to appoint leaders for them or not,' and God responded AND THE LORD ANSWERED MOSES, 'SINGLE OUT JOSHUA SON OF NUN' (Num. 27:18).

"Another instance is I PLEADED WITH THE LORD AT THAT TIME SAYING (Deut. 3:23). The word *SAYING* indicates that he said to Him, 'Tell me if I will enter the Land or not,' and God responded ENOUGH! (Deut. 3:26).

"So too in this verse the word *SAYING* indicates that he said, 'Tell me if You will heal her or not,' and the Holy One responded IF HER FATHER SPAT IN HER FACE (Num. 12:14)."

---

favor—throwing oneself on the mercy of God. In this case the first two Hebrew words "el na" (God—please) are seen as such an asking for favor while PRAY HEAL HER is the petition.
SAYING The word is superfluous and is interpreted as meaning that Moses asked God to "say," i.e., to answer, his question.

O GOD, PRAY HEAL HER (Num. 12:13). Why did not Moses pray [for her] at length? So that Israel should not say, "Because she is his sister he stands and prays for her at length."

Another interpretation: So that Israel should not say, "His sister is deeply afflicted and all he can do is pray at length!" Another interpretation: Is this not Moses who prays and God hears his prayer! As it says YOU WILL DECREE AND IT WILL BE FULFILLED (Job 22:28) and it says THEN, WHEN YOU CALL, THE LORD WILL ANSWER (Isa. 58:9).

R. Eliezer's disciples asked him, "How long should a man's prayer be?" He said to them, "Not longer than that of Moses as it is said I THREW MYSELF DOWN BEFORE THE LORD—EATING NO BREAD AND DRINKING NO WATER FORTY DAYS AND FORTY NIGHTS (Deut. 9:18)." "And how brief may it be?" He said to them, "Not briefer than that of Moses, as it is said O GOD, PRAY HEAL HER (Num. 12:13). There is a time to be brief and there is a time to be lengthy."

BUT THE LORD SAID TO MOSES, "IF HER FATHER SPAT IN HER FACE WOULD SHE NOT BEAR HER SHAME FOR SEVEN DAYS?" (Num. 12:14). R. Ahai b. R. Joshia says, "It is as if she were doubly chastised. Had her father, who was flesh and blood, chastised her, she would have borne her shame for seven days. If she would have done so for seven days in the case of her father, surely when chastised by He Who Spoke and the world came into being should it not be fourteen days? It is sufficient for the amount to be the same as that from which we have learned it. Just as in the case of her father it would be seven days, so in the case of He Who Spoke and the world came into being it is seven days."

LET HER BE SHUT OUT (Num. 12:14). The Holy One isolated her. The Holy One proclaimed her impure. The Holy One purified her. . . .

AFTER THAT THE PEOPLE SET OUT FROM HAZEROTH (Num. 12:16). Were there two places called Hazeroth that they journeyed from

---

Moses who prays There is no need for him to pray at length since God always responds positively to his petitions.

sufficient This is a principle of interpretation. Since we learn it from the instance of the father, which is seven days, we need not increase that amount. Other midrashim say that the time was indeed doubled but that God forgave seven days at Moses' bidding, so that her actual period of isolation was seven days.

The Holy One isolated her Although this is usually done by the priest, Aaron, her relative, was not allowed to do this. God Himself served, as it were, in place of the priest.

two places called Hazeroth—possibly based on the peculiarity of Num. 11:35, which reads lit-one and encamped in another? Rather Israel had hardly begun to travel when they heard that Miriam had been afflicted with leprosy, so they turned back and encamped there again. Therefore it says AFTER THAT THE PEOPLE SET OUT FROM HAZEROTH.

COMMENTARY   *On the one hand the tendency of the midrash is to emphasize the greatness of Moses: He is a man of wealth and power, he is a man whose humility was exceeded by that of no other human being who had ever lived. His closeness to God was unrivaled and his power of prophecy was greater than that of any other prophet. His understanding of God's ways was deeper than that of all others. Therefore speaking against him was a terrible act. It is like speaking against God. On the other hand, the motivation of Miriam, the prime mover in this, is clearly depicted as pure. She and Aaron do not shame Moses before others and intend only to chide him for what they perceive as his error in not observing the mitzvah of procreation. Their sin is termed inadvertent and the people honor Miriam by waiting for her until she has been healed and purified. God's attitude toward Miriam and Aaron is punishing but mitigated by their righteousness and His pity. He chastises them, but as a father who does so for the good of the child and does not want to be present when the punishment takes place. It is God Himself who in the end purifies her as well. The editor of this section has also taken the opportunity to use this story as an opportunity to teach proper human conduct. This motif appears several times. Thus we learn that people should not command others, but draw them near in ways that are pleasant to them, that one says only a part of the praise of a person when that person is present, that one should not interrupt when another is speaking, and that one should preface requests with words asking for favor.*

13. Numbers 15:22, Sifre N. 111, 116

IF YOU UNWITTINGLY FAIL TO OBSERVE ANY ONE OF THE COMMANDMENTS (Num. 15:22). Idolatry had been included among all the transgressions for which the community must bring a bull [as an offer-'

---

erally: KIBROTH-HATTAAVAH THE PEOPLE TRAVELED HAZEROTH. The next verse says WHEN THEY WERE IN HAZEROTH (Num. 12:1) so that the impression is given that they were in Hazeroth and then arrived at Hazeroth.

---

13. *Idolatry had been included*   In Lev. 4:1–4 only a bull is brought for failing to observe a mitzvah by mistake. Here a he-goat is also specified. This discrepency is explained as saying that here the reference is to a specific prohibition more severe than the others: idolatry.

ing], but then Scripture singled it out from the rest in order to stress its severity and to specify that [for idolatry] the community must bring a bull for a burnt offering and a he-goat for a sin offering. That was the reason for stating this section. . . .

WHICH THE LORD HAS DECLARED TO MOSES (Num. 15:22). What is the source which teaches that one who accepts idolatry rejects the Ten Pronouncements? The verse says WHICH THE LORD HAS DE-CLARED (dibber) TO MOSES (Num. 15:22) and elsewhere it says THE LORD SPOKE ALL THESE WORDS (devarim), SAYING (Ex. 20:1) ONE THING HAS GOD SPOKEN (dibber) (Ps. 62:12), BEHOLD, MY WORD (devari) IS LIKE FIRE—DECLARES THE LORD (Jer. 23:29).

What is the source which teaches that [one who accepts idolatry also rejects] all that was commanded to Moses? The verse says ANYTHING THAT THE LORD HAS ENJOINED UPON YOU THROUGH MO-SES (Num. 15:23) And whatever was commanded to the prophets? The verse says FROM THE DAY THAT THE LORD GAVE THE COM-MANDMENT (Num. 15:23). And even whatever was commanded to the Patriarchs? The verse says AND ON THROUGH THE GENERA-TIONS (Num. 15:23). And when did the Holy One begin to command the Patriarchs? As it says AND THE LORD COMMANDED THE MAN (Gen. 2:16). Scripture indicates that whoever accepts idolatry rejects the Ten Pronouncements, that which was commanded to Moses, that which was commanded to the prophets, and that which was commanded to the Patriarchs and whoever rejects idolatry accepts the entire Torah.

14. Numbers 15:30, Sifre N. 112, 120

BUT THE PERSON WHO ACTS DEFIANTLY (Num. 15:30). This re-fers to one who uses the Torah for heretical purposes as did Manasseh son of Hezekiah. HE REVILES THE LORD (Num. 15:30)—for he would sit

---

HAS DECLARED—the same Hebrew root as in the word *pronouncements*. Thus one who violates this matter that was declared, i.e., idolatry, has violated the Ten Pronouncements or Declarations.
all that was commanded to Moses—the laws that were given to Moses to transmit to the people.
THE MAN—Adam, included here as a patriarch or ancestor.

---

14. *uses the Torah for heretical purposes*—literally "reveals aspects of the Torah." His inter-pretations are false and present aspects of the Torah that are not really there.
Manasseh son of Hezekiah—described by Scripture as an idolater (2 Kings 21). Here heretical practices of a latter period are added to his sins and he becomes the archetype of the heretic.

and expound interpretations which questioned the actions of God. He said, "Had He nothing to write in the Torah except REUBEN CAME UPON SOME MANDRAKES IN THE FIELD (Gen. 30:14)? Had he nothing to write in the Torah except AND LOTAN'S SISTER WAS TIMNA (Gen. 36:22)?" Of him Scripture has written YOU ARE BUSY MALIGNING YOUR BROTHER, DEFAMING THE SON OF YOUR MOTHER. IF I FAILED TO ACT WHEN YOU DID THESE THINGS, YOU WOULD FANCY THAT I WAS LIKE YOU (Ps. 50:20–21). Lest you think that God's ways are the ways of humans it says SO I CENSURE YOU AND CONFRONT YOU WITH CHARGES (Ps. 50:21). Isaiah came and expounded AH, THOSE WHO HAUL SIN WITH CORDS OF FALSE-HOOD AND INIQUITY AS WITH CART ROPES! (Isa. 5:18). Iniquity begins as a spider's thread but in the end it becomes AS WITH CART ROPES.

Rabbi Judah the Prince says, "One should not rejoice over the sincere performance of one mitzvah but because it brings many mitzvot in its wake. And one should not fret over one transgression but because it brings many transgressions in its wake, for one mitzvah causes another and one transgression causes another." . . .

BECAUSE HE HAS SPURNED THE WORD OF THE LORD (Num. 15:31). This refers to a Sadducee. AND VIOLATED HIS COMMAND-MENT (Num. 15:31). This refers to the *apikoros*. Another interpretation: BECAUSE HE HAS SPURNED THE WORD OF THE LORD. This refers to one who uses the Torah for heretical purposes. AND VIOLATED HIS COMMANDMENT. This refers to one who violates the covenant of circumcision. This is the source of R. Eleazar of Modi'in's statement, "One who desecrates the sacred offerings and spurns the festivals and violates the covenant of our father Abraham, even though he has many mitzvot to his credit deserves to be banished from this world. If one says: I accept all of the Torah except for this matter, it is of him that the verse says BECAUSE HE HAS SPURNED THE WORD OF THE LORD. If one says: All of

---

questioned the actions of God—and made His writings, the Torah, seem absurd.

Sadducee—who rejected the traditional interpretations or Oral Torah, which, to the Pharisees, were no less the word of the Lord than the Written Torah.

apikoros—the rabbinic term for a heretic or nonbeliever, named after the followers of the Greek philosopher Epicurus, whose emphasis on worldly pleasures was disdained by the Sages.

violates the covenant of circumcision—referring to an operation performed by Jews who wished to disguise the fact that they were circumcised during the period of Hellenization in the second century B.C.E. and later.

the Torah is from the Holy One except for this matter which Moses said on his own, it is of him that the verse says BECAUSE HE HAS SPURNED THE WORD OF THE LORD."

Another interpretation: BECAUSE HE HAS SPURNED THE WORD OF THE LORD (Num. 15:31). R. Meir says, "This refers to one who learns but does not teach others." R. Nathan says, "This refers to one who can learn but does not teach." R. Nehorai says, "This refers to one who pays no attention to the teachings of the Torah." R. Ishmael says, "The verse is speaking of idolatry, as it is said BECAUSE HE HAS SPURNED THE WORD (d'var) OF THE LORD—he spurned the First Pronouncement (dibbur) which the Almighty said to Moses I AM THE LORD YOUR GOD . . . YOU SHALL HAVE NO OTHER GODS BESIDES ME (Ex. 20:2–3)."

THAT PERSON SHALL BE CUT OFF (hikaret tikeret) (Num. 15:31)—CUT OFF (hikaret) from this world and CUT OFF (tikaret) from the world to come, so taught R. Akiba. R. Ishmael said to him, "And since it also says THAT PERSON SHALL BE CUT OFF (Num. 15:30) would this indicate that there are three cuttings off from three worlds? What does the verse THAT PERSON SHALL BE CUT OFF (Num. 15:31) mean? The Torah is speaking in human language."

HE BEARS HIS GUILT (Num. 15:31). Death atones in all cases but here HE BEARS HIS GUILT, similarly to that which is said AND THEIR IN-IQUITIES UPON THEIR BONES (Ez. 32:27). Does this mean that [there is no atonement] even if he repented? The verse states when HE BEARS HIS GUILT (Num. 15:31) but not when he has repented. Thus it says IF THERE IS CORRUPTION TO HIM, THEY ARE NOT HIS CHIL-DREN; THEIR BLEMISH IS WITHIN THEM (Deut. 32:5). When the blemish is still within them they are not His children, but when the blemish is not within them they are His children.

R. Ishmael says, "Why does it say HE BEARS HIS GUILT (Num. 15:31)? Since it says VISITING THE GUILT OF THE FATHERS UPON THE CHILDREN (Ex. 20:5) one might think that the sin of idolatry will

---

three worlds Using sarcasm, R. Ishmael protests R. Akiba's system of interpretation in which grammatical forms such as a doubling of a verb are used to deduce additional meanings.

not when he has repented Since the verse says HE BEARS HIS GUILT, it indicates that he has not repented. Had he repented, here too death would have brought him atonement.

also be visited upon children unto the third and fourth generation, therefore the verse says HE BEARS HIS GUILT (Num. 15:31). The transgression is upon that person alone and is not visited upon children unto the third and fourth generation."

R. Nathan says, "It is a good sign for an individual when his sin is requited after his death. If he is not eulogized, not buried, devoured by a beast, or if rain falls upon him—these are good signs that his sin is requited after his death. Even though there is no proof, there is a hint at this in what was said, AT THAT TIME—DECLARES THE LORD—THE BONES OF THE KINGS OF JUDAH, OF ITS OFFICERS, OF THE PRIESTS, OF THE PROPHETS, AND OF THE INHABITANTS OF JERUSALEM SHALL BE TAKEN OUT OF THEIR GRAVES AND EXPOSED TO THE SUN, THE MOON, AND ALL THE HOST OF HEAVEN (Jer. 8:1–2)"

R. Simeon b. Eleazar said, "I used this [verse] to refute the books of the heretics which say that the dead are not resurrected. I said to them: It says THAT PERSON SHALL BE CUT OFF—HE BEARS HIS GUILT (Num. 15:31). And the words HE BEARS HIS GUILT can only mean that in the future he will have to account for his sins on the day of judgment."

COMMENTARY   *In these sections we see the reaction of the Sages to various heretical or anti-Pharisaic groups that existed during or after the period of the Second Temple. Idolatry and all that it involved was a major concern since Jews living in the Land of Israel were in constant contact with it. There were entire communities that were populated by non-Jews who practiced idolatry. The Mishna contains an entire section regulating the contacts between Jews and idolaters. Not without justice did the Sages believe that the rejection of idolatry was the essence of Judaism. In addition, the Pharisaic Sages prior to the destruction of the Temple in 70 C.E. were challenged by the Sadducees, who rejected all of the oral tradition, which formed the basis of Pharisaic law and belief, including the central belief in the resurrection of the dead. Certainly there were also heretical groups and individuals who held Scripture up to ridicule as does Manasseh in rabbinic legend, ques-*

---

his sin is requited after his death—something happens after his death that punishes him in this world, either a physical damage to his body or a slight to his memory and honor.

heretics—possibly the Sadducees, who did not believe in the resurrection of the dead.

in the future Since the verse first mentions his death—CUT OFF—and then speaks of his bearing HIS GUILT, this guilt must be with him after his death, thus proving that the Torah teaches about resurrection and afterlife.

tioning the importance of various passages in order to undermine belief in the Torah's Divine origin.

15. Numbers 15:39, Sifre N. 115, 128

LOOK AT IT AND RECALL ALL THE COMMANDMENTS OF THE LORD AND OBSERVE THEM, SO THAT YOU DO NOT FOLLOW YOUR HEART AND EYES IN YOUR LUSTFUL URGE (Num. 15:39).

R. Nathan says, "There is no mitzvah in the Torah that does not have a reward. The mitzvah of fringes will prove this. There was once a man who was careful to observe the mitzvah of fringes. He heard that there was a prostitute in one of the cities of the sea who charged four hundred pieces of gold. He sent her four hundred pieces of gold and arranged an assignation. When the time came, he came and sat himself at the entrance to her house. Her servant entered and said to her, 'That man who made an appointment with you is sitting at the entrance to the house.'

"She said to her, 'Let him enter.'

"When he came in she offered him seven beds of silver and one of gold and she was in the top one. There were steps of silver between them and the top one of gold. When he began to prepare for the deed, his four fringes appeared and seemed to him to be four witnesses that confronted his face. He immediately descended and sat himself upon the ground.

"She too descended and sat upon the ground and said to him, 'I swear by Rome that I shall not let you go until you tell me what defect you saw in me.'

"He said to her, 'By the Temple Service, I saw no defect in you, for in the whole world there is no beauty like yours. But there is a simple mitzvah which the Lord our God has commanded us and in connection with it wrote I, THE LORD YOUR GOD; I, THE LORD YOUR GOD twice. I, THE LORD YOUR GOD—will pay your reward in the future. I, THE LORD YOUR GOD will requite it of you in the future.'

"She said to him, 'By the Temple Service, I will not let you go until

---

15. *a reward*   All of the mitzvot are beneficial.

appeared   As he was undressing, he saw the fringes on his garment.

four witnesses   The four fringes were four witnesses that he was obligated to obey God and to refrain from this sin.

By the Temple Service   Previously she had sworn by Rome. Now she shows her appreciation of the value of Judaism.

you write your name, the name of your city, and the name of the Academy in which you study Torah.'

"He wrote his name, the name of his city, the name of his teacher, the name of the Academy in which he studied Torah. She then gave away her money, giving a third to the state, a third to the poor, and keeping a third for herself which she took with her when she went and stood in the Academy of R. Hiyya. She said to him, 'My master, convert me.'

"He said to her, 'Have you fallen in love with one of the students?' She produced the document she had in her possession.

"He said to [the student], 'Arise. You have been successful in your enterprise. That which she offered you illicitly will be offered to you legally. That is the reward [of this mitzvah] in this world and I do not know what it will be in the world to come.'"

COMMENTARY   *In order to teach that God's decrees have both an immediate effect in keeping the individual from sin and a reward that will come in the future, R. Nathan tells a morality tale that is surely a classic of its kind. Since the verse speaks of the purpose of wearing the fringes being to counteract the lustful urges of the heart and eyes, the story illustrates how this literally happened. The reward, promised in the phrase I, THE LORD YOUR GOD, follows when the beautiful woman he desired lustfully becomes his legally.*

16. Numbers 24:4, Sifre Zuta 254

Moses had three qualities which Balaam lacked.

Moses would speak to Him while standing upright, as it says BUT YOU REMAIN STANDING HERE WITH ME (Deut. 5:28). He spoke with Balaam only when he was prostrate, as it says PROSTRATE, BUT WITH EYES UNVEILED (Num. 24:4).

Moses would speak with Him mouth to mouth, as it is said WITH HIM I SPEAK MOUTH TO MOUTH (Num. 12:8) and of Balaam it says WORD OF HIM WHO HEARS GOD'S SPEECH (Num. 24:4) indicating that he did not speak with Him mouth to mouth.

Moses would speak to Him face to face, as it is said THE LORD WOULD SPEAK TO MOSES FACE TO FACE (Ex. 33:11) but with Balaam He spoke only in parables, as it is said HE TOOK UP HIS PARABLE AND SAID (Num. 24:15).

Balaam had three qualities which Moses did not have.

270

Moses did not know Who spoke to him. Balaam did know Who spoke to him as it is said WHO OBTAINS KNOWLEDGE FROM THE MOST HIGH, AND BEHOLDS VISIONS FROM THE ALMIGHTY (Num. 24:16).

Moses did not know when the Holy One would speak with him and Balaam knew what the Holy One was going to speak to him about, as it says HE OBTAINS KNOWLEDGE FROM THE MOST HIGH (Num. 24:16).

It may be likened to a king's chef who knew what was going to be served at the king's table and how much was being expended on it.

Thus Balaam knew what the Holy One was going to speak to him about. Balaam spoke to Him whenever he wanted, as it is said PROSTRATE, BUT WITH EYES UNVEILED (Num. 24:16). As soon as he would prostrate himself, He would reveal to him whatever he wanted to know. But Moses could not speak to Him whenever he wanted.

R. Simeon said, "Moses too would speak to Him whenever he wanted, as it is said WHEN MOSES WENT INTO THE TENT OF MEETING TO SPEAK WITH HIM (Num. 7:89). Whenever he wanted, he would enter and He would speak to him."

R. Eliezer the son of R. Jose the Galilean says, "It seems to me that the Divine Presence never came down to earth, as it is said FROM THE HEAVENS HE LET YOU HEAR HIS VOICE TO DISCIPLINE YOU (Deut. 4:36). YOU YOURSELVES SAW THAT I SPOKE TO YOU FROM THE VERY HEAVENS (Ex. 20:19). How then do I interpret the verse WHEN MOSES WENT INTO THE TENT OF MEETING (Num. 7:89)? It was some sort of stream of fire which would come down from heaven between the two Cherubim and would speak with him from there, as it is said BETWEEN THE TWO CHERUBIM; THUS HE SPOKE TO HIM (Num. 7:89)."

COMMENTARY   *The contrast between Moses and Balaam is drawn in many places in the Midrash, which does not deny to this prophet of the nations great ability. Contrasting verses about the two of them, they draw*

---

16. *never came down to earth*   Although Moses had to go into the Tent to speak to God, this does not mean that God was in the tent here on earth.

stream of fire   The word of God emanated as a stream of fire.

up a list of superior qualities for each. *Nevertheless, even when he seems to have a closeness to God that Moses lacks, the Sages ascribe that not to his greatness but to his lowly position. God can reveal Himself to whomever He chooses and speak through any mouth, but to Moses He gave a position of nobility, to Balaam a position of servility. On the question of God's descent to earth, whenever it comes up the Sages reiterate that it did not take place literally. They considered it a dangerous idea that would break Judaism's rather rigid division between the realm of man and the realm of God. God's word, therefore, frequently assumes the role of an emanation from Him that makes contact with man on earth.*

17. Numbers 27:1, Sifre N. 133, 176

THE DAUGHTERS OF ZELOPHEHAD... CAME FORWARD (Num. 27:1). When the daughters of Zelophehad heard that the Land was being divided among the tribes according to the males and not the females, they gathered together and took council with one another. They said, "God's compassion is not like human compassion. Humans are more compassionate toward males than females, but He Who Spoke and the world came into being is not like that. His compassion extends to both males and females. His compassion extends to every creature, as it is said WHO GIVES FOOD TO ALL FLESH, HIS STEADFAST LOVE IS ETERNAL (Ps. 136:25), WHO GIVE THE BEASTS THEIR FOOD (Ps. 147:9) and it says THE LORD IS GOOD TO ALL, AND HIS TENDER MERCY IS UPON ALL HIS WORKS (Ps. 145:9)."

OF MANESSITE FAMILY—SON OF HEPHER SON OF GILEAD SON OF MACHIR SON OF MANASSEH (Num. 27:1). The verse informs us that just as Zelophehad was a firstborn, so [his daughters] were all firstborn and it teaches us that all of them were pure daughters of the pure. A person whose deeds are not described, the child of parents whose deeds are not described, but to whom Scripture attaches praise, is a righteous person the son of a righteous person. A person whose deeds are not described, the child of parents whose deeds are not described, but to whom Scripture attaches blame, is a wicked person the son of a wicked person.

R. Nathan says, "The verse comes to teach us how great is the righ-

---

17. *all firstborn*—to different mothers.

R. Nathan—holds the view that their father was a wicked man, the anonymous "gatherer of sticks." See below p. 274. That his daughters were so righteous is a tribute to them since they had been raised by a sinner.

teousness of a righteous person who was raised by a wicked person but did not follow his path. How great is the wickedness of a wicked person who was raised by a righteous person but did not follow his path. Esau was raised by two righteous people, Isaac and Rebecca, yet he did not follow their path. Obadiah was raised by two wicked people, Ahab and Jezebel, but did not follow their path and he prophesied concerning Esau the wicked who was raised by two righteous people, Isaac and Rebecca, but did not follow their path, as it is said THE PROPHECY OF OBADIAH . . . THUS SAYS MY LORD GOD CONCERNING EDOM (Obad. 1:1)."

COMMENTARY   *There is a dispute among the rabbis concerning the character of Zelophehad. Some, such as the anonymous sage quoted above, thought him to have been a righteous man and enunciated a general principle to prove it. R. Nathan, on the other hand, seems to have considered him to have been wicked: He was the one who gathered sticks on the Sabbath. Therefore this discussion of the ancestry of these virtuous daughters only proves that genetics and environment do not determine everything. But it does take a great deal of righteousness to overcome a wicked background and a great deal of wickedness to erase a righteous background. In a playful mastery of texts, he brings opposite examples and unites them in a kind of "measure against measure" in the verse from Obadiah. The story of the daughters of Zelophehad becomes the occasion for reiterating God's mercies and stresses His mercy toward the oppressed, exemplified here by women who are not treated well by men.*

SON OF MANASSEH SON OF JOSEPH (Num. 27:1). Just as Joseph treasured the Land of Israel, so his descendants treasured the Land of Israel.

THE NAME OF THE DAUGHTERS WERE MAHLAH, NOAH, HOGLAH, MILCAH, AND TIRZAH (Num. 27:1). Lest one think that whoever comes first in the Scripture is first in importance, the verse says MAHLAH, TIRZAH, HOGLAH, MILCAH, AND NOAH, ZELOPHE-HAD'S DAUGHTERS (Num. 36:11) which teaches that they were equal to one another.

Obadiah—was thought to have been part of Ahab's court and subject to the influence of that infamous pair.

equal to one another   The fact that the order is not the same in the two verses indicates that the order of listing is not the order of importance.

THEY STOOD BEFORE MOSES, ELEAZAR THE PRIEST (Num. 27: 2). The verse informs us that they stood before them only in the fortieth year, the year in which Aaron died, as it says AARON THE PRIEST ASCENDED MOUNT HOR AT THE COMMAND OF THE LORD AND DIED THERE, IN THE FORTIETH YEAR AFTER THE ISRAELITES HAD LEFT THE LAND OF EGYPT (Num. 33:38).

BEFORE MOSES, ELEAZAR THE PRIEST (Num. 27:2). If Moses did not know, would Eleazar have known? The verse is abbreviated and was explained by the words of R. Jeshaya Abba Hanin who said in the name of R. Eleazar, "They were in the house of study so they came and stood before them."

(Sifre Zuta 317) Said R. Eleazar b. R. Simeon the priest, "Does it make sense that one who went to Moses would then go to Eleazar and to the princes and to all the assembly? They went first to the rulers of tens. They said to them: We do not know. They went to the rulers of fifties. They said to them: We do not know. They went to the rulers of hundreds. They said to them: We do not know. They went to the rulers of thousands. They said to them: We do not know. They went to Eleazar. He said to them: I do not know. Eleazar then took them and led them to Moses. How do we know that Moses also said: I do not know? The verse says MOSES BROUGHT THEIR CASE BEFORE THE LORD (Num. 27:5)."

OUR FATHER DIED IN THE WILDERNESS (Num. 27:3). R. Akiba says, "Here it says IN THE WILDERNESS and elsewhere it says IN THE WILDERNESS (Num. 15:32). Just as here it refers to Zelophehad so there it refers to Zelophehad."

---

fortieth year   Even though the story appears before the death of Aaron, the fact that it mentions that they appeared not before Aaron but before his son Eleazar indicates that it must have taken place after Aaron's death. The Sages believed that the Torah has no chronological order.

would Eleazar have known   Why did they come before Eleazar, who could not have answered their question?

verse is abbreviated—an important part of a verse is not written but must be understood and inferred.

They were in the house of study   Moses and Eleazar were together. The women did not come to inquire of Eleazar but of Moses. Eleazar just happened to be there.

and to the princes   The verse continues THE CHIEFTAINS, AND THE WHOLE ASSEMBLY (Num. 27:2). Why would they go first to the highest authority, Moses, and then to lesser and lesser authorities?

there it refers to Zelophehad   The person who gathered sticks was Zelophehad.

274

HE WAS NOT ONE OF THE FACTION (Num. 27:3) referring to those who complained. WHICH BANDED TOGETHER AGAINST THE LORD (Num. 27:3) referring to the group of spies. KORACH'S FACTION referring to Korach's band. BUT DIED FOR HIS OWN SINS (Num. 27:3)—but he did not cause others to sin with him. AND HE HAS LEFT NO SONS (Num. 27:3). For had he had a son, we would not be making this claim.

LET NOT OUR FATHER'S NAME BE LOST TO HIS CLAN (Num. 27:4). R. Judah says, "Here it says NAME and elsewhere it says NAME (Deut. 25:6). Just as there it refers to an inheritance, so here it refers to an inheritance. Just as there it refers to progeny, so here it refers to progeny."

JUST BECAUSE HE HAD NO SON (Num. 27:4). Why is this stated? Did it not say AND HE HAS LEFT NO SONS (Num. 27:3)? What does JUST BECAUSE HE HAD NO SON mean? It shows us how intelligent they were, how well they understood the laws. "If he had the daughter of a son, we would not be making this claim."

GIVE US A HOLDING AMONG OUR FATHER'S KINSMEN! (Num. 27:4) R. Nathan says, "Women are so much better than men. The men said LET US HEAD BACK FOR EGYPT (Num. 14:4) but the women said GIVE US A HOLDING AMONG OUR FATHER'S KINSMEN!"

(Sifre Zuta 316) When did they stand before Moses? At the same time that Israel said to Moses LET US HEAD BACK FOR EGYPT (Num. 14:4). Moses said to them, "All of Israel wants to return to Egypt and you want a holding in the Land of Israel!" They said, "We know that in the end all Israel will possess the Land . . ."

MOSES BROUGHT THEIR CASE BEFORE THE LORD (Num. 27:5). R. Hidka Simeon HaShikmoni said, "I had a companion who was one of R. Akiba's pupils and he said, 'Moses knew that the daughters inherited. The

---

he did not cause others to sin with him   even if he died because of the sin of gathering sticks on the Sabbath, which, unlike the other sins mentioned, involved no one else.

elsewhere it says NAME—in reference to a brother who dies childless. The surviving brother marries the widow and their child is considered the child of the deceased brother.

the daughter of a son   Had he had a son who in turn had a daughter, that daughter's claim would take precedence.

question was whether they inherit that which is potentially his or only that which he actually possessed. These laws of inheritance should really have been proclaimed by Moses, but the daughters of Zelophehad merited having it said through them. Thus we add merit to the meritorious and guilt to the guilty.' "

THE LORD SAID TO MOSES, "THE PLEA OF ZELOPHEHAD'S DAUGHTERS IS JUST" (Num. 27:6–7). The daughters of Zelophehad have a just claim, for indeed thus is it written before Me on high. Happy is the man with whom God agrees! Similarly it says THE PLEA OF THE JOSEPHITE TRIBE IS JUST (Num. 36:5). Similarly it says I PARDON, AS YOU HAVE ASKED (Num. 14:20). In the future the nations of the world will say: Happy is the man with whom God agrees!

YOU SHOULD GIVE THEM A HEREDITARY HOLDING (Num. 27: 7) referring to the portion of their father. AMONG THEIR FATHER'S KINSMEN (Num. 27:7) referring to the portion of the father's brothers. TRANSFER THEIR FATHER'S SHARE TO THEM (Num. 27:7). This informs us that the daughters of Zelophehad received three portions of the inheritance: their father's portion, their grandfather's portion, and the portion belonging to their father as a firstborn. R. Eliezer b. Jacob says, "They also received the portion of their father's brothers."

18. Numbers 27:12, Sifre N. 134, 179

THE LORD SAID TO MOSES, "ASCEND THESE HEIGHTS OF AB-ARIM" (Num. 27:12)—Mt. Nebo. This was in the portion of the Reubenites and the Gadites. When Moses entered the portion of the Reubenites and the Gadites he was overjoyed and said, "It would seem that He has lifted the ban against me—" and he began to pour out his supplications before

---

In the future—a Messianic reference. At that time others will recognize that Moses was the true prophet with whom God Himself agreed.

---

18. *lifted the ban* Since this was territory permanently occupied by the tribes of Israel, Moses thinks that it is like the Land of Israel, which he had been forbidden to enter. If God has permitted him to come here, it must mean that He no longer means to keep Moses from the Land of Israel. It was not so, however. These lands did not have the same status as the western side of the Jordan.
to pour out supplications before God—referring to Deut. 3:23: I PLEADED WITH THE LORD AT THAT TIME.

God. A parable. This may be likened to a human king who decreed that his son should not enter the entrance to the palace. He entered the gate and [the king] was following after him, the courtyard, and he was following after him, the portico, and he was following after him. But when he came to the bedroom he said to him, "My son—from here on you are prohibited from entering." Thus when Moses entered the portion of the Reubenites and the Gadites he was overjoyed and said, "It would seem that He has lifted the ban against me—" and he began to pour out his supplications before God.

It is a matter of logic. If Moses, the wisest of the wise, the greatest of the great, the father of prophets, knowing that a decree had been made against him, nevertheless did not refrain from asking for mercy, certainly others should not! As it is said I PLEADED WITH THE LORD AT THAT TIME (Deut. 3:23) with all manner of supplications . . . "O LORD (Adonai)" (Deut. 3:24). You are the Master (Adon) of every person in the world. GOD (Deut. 3:24). With justice did You create the world. YOU HAVE BEGUN (Deut. 3:24). You have begun to create an opening for Your servant when You let me enter the portion of the Reubenites and the Gadites. Another interpretation: YOU HAVE BEGUN. You have begun to show Your servant miracles and wonders, as it is said MOSES SAID, "I MUST TURN ASIDE TO LOOK" (Ex. 3:3). Another interpretation: YOU HAVE BEGUN. You have begun to revoke the oath You had written in the Torah WHOSOEVER SACRIFICES TO A GOD OTHER THAN THE LORD ALONE SHALL BE PROSCRIBED (Ex. 22:19), for Your children worshiped an idol, but when I beseeched mercy for them, You forgave them. You have begun to revoke the oath.

YOUR GREATNESS (Deut. 3:24). This refers to Your Quality of Goodness, as it is said THEREFORE, I PRAY, LET MY LORD'S FORBEARANCE BE GREAT (Num. 14:17).

AND YOUR MIGHTY HAND (Deut. 3:24). This refers to Your right hand which is proffered to every person in the world, as it is said YOUR RIGHT HAND, O LORD, GLORIOUS IN POWER, YOUR RIGHT HAND, O LORD, SHATTERS THE FOE! (Ex. 15:6) and it says BUT YOUR RIGHT HAND, YOUR ARM, AND YOUR GOODWILL, FOR YOU FAVORED THEM (Ps. 44:4) and BY MYSELF HAVE I

With justice   The Name God (Elohim) was associated by the rabbis with the Quality of Justice since the same Hebrew word means "judges."

SWORN, FROM MY MOUTH HAS ISSUED TRUTH, A WORD THAT SHALL NOT TURN BACK: TO ME EVERY KNEE SHALL BEND, EVERY TONGUE SWEAR LOYALTY (Isa. 45:23).

MIGHTY (Deut. 3:24) in that You overcome the Quality of Justice with [the Quality of] Mercy, as it is said WHO IS A GOD LIKE YOU, FORGIVING INIQUITY AND REMITTING TRANSGRESSION; WHO HAS NOT MAINTAINED HIS WRATH FOREVER AGAINST THE REMNANT OF HIS OWN PEOPLE, BECAUSE HE LOVES GRACIOUSNESS! HE WILL TAKE US BACK IN LOVE; HE WILL COVER UP OUR INIQUITIES, YOU WILL HURL ALL OUR SINS INTO THE DEPTHS OF THE SEA. YOU WILL KEEP FAITH WITH JACOB (Micah 7:18-20).

WHAT GOD IS THERE IN HEAVEN OR ON EARTH (Deut. 3: 24). For the nature of God is not like the nature of human beings. With human beings, if one is greater than another he can overrule the decrees of the other. But with You—who can do so? Thus it says HE IS ONE; WHO CAN DISSUADE HIM? WHATEVER HE DESIRES, HE DOES (Job 23:13).

R. Judah b. Babba says, "A parable. If a man is under royal prohibition, even if he gives a great deal of money it will not be lifted. But You say 'Repent and I will receive you,' as it is said I WIPE AWAY YOUR SINS LIKE A CLOUD, YOUR TRANSGRESSIONS LIKE MIST—COME BACK TO ME, FOR I REDEEM YOU (Isa. 44:22)."

Another interpretation: WHAT GOD IS THERE IN HEAVEN OR ON EARTH (Deut. 3:24). Does this imply that there is one somewhere else? The verse says KNOW THEREFORE THIS DAY AND KEEP IN MIND THAT THE LORD ALONE IS GOD IN HEAVEN ABOVE AND ON EARTH BELOW; THERE IS NO OTHER (Deut. 4:39)—not even in the reaches of space.

THAT CAN DO ACCORDING TO YOUR WORKS AND YOUR MIGHTY ACTS (Deut. 3:24). YOUR WORKS in Egypt AND YOUR MIGHTY ACTS at the Sea. Another interpretation: YOUR WORKS AND YOUR MIGHTY ACTS at the rivers of Arnon.

LET ME, I PRAY, CROSS OVER AND SEE (Deut. 3:25). The word *please* (na) always indicates a request.

---

rivers of Arnon—the stream they crossed in order to reach the territory of Sihon the Amorite king. See Deut. 2:24.

AND SEE THE GOOD LAND ON THE OTHER SIDE OF THE JORDAN (Deut. 3:25). This is what R. Judah said, "It is the Land of Canaan which is good, not the portion of the Reubenites and the Gadites."

THAT GOOD HILL COUNTRY (Deut. 3:25). This refers to Jerusalem.

AND THE LEBANON (Deut. 3:25). This refers to the Temple as it says THROW OPEN YOUR GATES, O LEBANON, AND LET FIRE CONSUME YOUR CEDARS! (Zech. 11:1) and AND LEBANON SHALL FALL IN MAJESTY (Isa. 10:34). Others say that LEBANON refers to the appointment of kings.

BUT THE LORD WAS WRATHFUL WITH ME (Deut. 3:26). This is like a man who says, "So-and-so was wrathful with me and consumed with anger against me." ON YOUR ACCOUNT (Deut. 3:26). You were the ones who caused it. Thus it says THEY PROVOKED WRATH AT THE WATERS OF MERIBAH AND MOSES SUFFERED ON THEIR ACCOUNT (Ps. 106:32). AND WOULD NOT LISTEN TO ME (Deut. 3:26)—He would not accept my prayer. R. Nathan says, "It says SEE, GOD IS MIGHTY; HE IS NOT CONTEMPTUOUS (Job. 36:5). The Holy One is not contemptuous of the prayer of the multitude, but in this instance He WOULD NOT LISTEN TO ME (Deut. 3:26)—He would not accept my prayer."

THE LORD SAID TO ME, "ENOUGH!" (Deut. 3:26). He said to him, "Moses—that is enough for you in this matter," for the righteous are not permitted to reach the point of committing serious transgression. This was the basis of R. Ishmael's saying, "The popular saying is: The load is determined by the capacity of the camel."

Another interpretation: If God did not show favoritism to Moses, the wisest of the wise, the greatest of the great, the father of prophets, how much more [does He not show favoritism] to those who divert and distort justice!

ENOUGH (rab) (Deut. 3:26). He said to him, "There is much (harbeh) which is saved away for you, much which is hidden away for you," as it is said HOW ABUNDANT (rab) IS THE GOOD THAT YOU HAVE IN

Canaan which is good   Moses was in the territory of those tribes and did not refer to it as good.
the Temple   Lebanon was taken as a reference to the Temple because the root of the word means "white" and the Temple was the place that "whitened the sins of Israel."
kings—unclear. Perhaps the majesty of kings is being compared to the cedars of Lebanon, the most majestic of trees. See Judges 9:15.

STORE FOR THOSE WHO FEAR YOU (Ps. 31:20) and it says SUCH THINGS HAD NEVER BEEN HEARD OR NOTED. NO EYE HAS SEEN (THEM), O GOD, BUT YOU, WHO ACT FOR THOSE WHO TRUST IN YOU (Isa. 64:3).

Another interpretation: ENOUGH (rab) (Deut. 3:26). He said to him, "Much (harbeh) have you toiled, much have you worked. Now, Moses, go—rest," as it is said BUT YOU, GO ON TO THE END; YOU MAY REST, AND ARISE TO YOUR DESTINY AT THE END OF THE DAYS (Dan. 12:12).

He said to Him, "If You refuse, let me enter as an ordinary man." He replied, "The king does not enter as an ordinary man."

He said to Him, "If You refuse, let me become Joshua's disciple." He replied, "The Master does not become his disciple's disciple."

He said to Him, "If You refuse, let me enter through the air or through an underground space." He replied, "YOU SHALL NOT ENTER IT (Deut. 32:52)."

He said to Him, "If You refuse, let my bones pass over the Jordan." He replied, "YOU SHALL NOT CROSS YONDER JORDAN (Deut. 3: 27)." Can the dead CROSS? Rather He replied, "Moses—even your bones shall not go across the Jordan."

NEVER SPEAK TO ME OF THIS MATTER AGAIN (Deut. 3:26). On this matter, you may speak to Me no more, but concerning anything else—your word is My command.

A parable. This may be likened to a king who issued a severe decree concerning his son. The son begged his father [to rescind it]. He said to him, "Do not beseech me on this matter, but concerning anything else— your word is my command. Just command what you will, and you shall have it."

He said to Him, "If you refuse, let me see [the Land]." He replied, "This I shall do. GO UP TO THE SUMMIT OF PISGAH (Deut. 3:27)." This verse informs us that God showed Moses distant places as if they were close, places which cannot be seen as if they were seen. Indeed, [He showed him] all that is called the Land of Israel, as it is said MOSES WENT UP FROM THE STEPPES OF MOAB TO MOUNT NEBO, TO THE SUMMIT OF PISGAH, OPPOSITE JERICHO, AND THE LORD SHOWED HIM THE WHOLE LAND: GILEAD AS FAR AS DAN; ALL NAPHTALI; THE LAND OF EPHRAIM AND MANASSEH; THE WHOLE LAND OF JUDAH AS FAR AS THE WESTERN SEA; THE NEGEB; AND THE PLAIN—THE VALLEY OF JERICHO, THE CITY OF PALM TREES—AS FAR AS ZOAR (Deut. 34:1–3).

AND THE LORD SAID TO HIM; THIS IS THE LAND (Deut. 34:
4). R. Akiba says, "This verse informs us that God showed Moses all the
areas of the Land of Israel like a table set [before him] as it is said AND
THE LORD SHOWED HIM THE WHOLE LAND (Deut. 34:1)."

R. Eliezer says, "He gave power to Moses' eyes so that he could see
from one end of the world to the other. Thus we find that the righteous can
see from one end of the world to the other, as it is said WHEN YOUR
EYES BEHOLD A KING IN HIS BEAUTY, WHEN THEY CONTEM-
PLATE THE LAND ROUND ABOUT (Isa. 33:17)." Thus you can say
that there are two 'seeing's'—one of pleasure and one of pain. "Concerning
Abraham it says RAISE YOUR EYES AND LOOK OUT FROM
WHERE YOU ARE, TO THE NORTH AND SOUTH, TO THE EAST
AND WEST, FOR I GIVE ALL THE LAND THAT YOU SEE TO
YOU AND YOUR OFFSPRING FOREVER (Gen. 13:14–15)." This is a
'seeing' of pleasure. "Concerning Moses it says ASCEND THESE
HEIGHTS OF ABARIM TO MOUNT NEBO, WHICH IS IN THE
LAND OF MOAB FACING JERICHO, AND VIEW THE LAND OF
CANAAN WHICH I AM GIVING THE ISRAELITES AS THEIR
HOLDING (Deut. 32:49). GO TO THE SUMMIT OF PISGAH AND
GAZE ABOUT, TO THE WEST, THE NORTH, THE SOUTH, AND
THE EAST. LOOK AT IT WELL, FOR YOU SHALL NOT GO
ACROSS YONDER JORDAN (Deut. 3:27)." This is a 'seeing' of pain.

"You can say that there are two 'coming forwards,' one which is for
the sake of Heaven and one which is not for the sake of Heaven. YOU
CAME FORWARD AND STOOD AT THE FOOT OF THE MOUN-
TAIN (Deut. 4:11). That is a 'coming forward' for the sake of Heaven.
THEN ALL OF YOU CAME FORWARD TO ME AND SAID, 'LET
US SEND MEN AHEAD TO EXPLORE THE LAND FOR US' (Deut.
1:22). That is a 'coming forward' which is not for the sake of Heaven."

GIVE JOSHUA HIS INSTRUCTIONS, AND IMBUE HIM WITH
STRENGTH AND COURAGE (Deut. 3:28). INSTRUCTIONS—in
matters of teaching. R. Judah says, "Instruct him concerning the Gibe-
onites." Another interpretation: INSTRUCTIONS—concerning the
difficulties, the troubles, and the quarrels.

---

in matters of teaching Joshua would follow Moses as the person instructing Israel in how to
live according to God's Torah.

FOR HE SHALL GO ACROSS AT THE HEAD OF THE PEOPLE (Deut. 3:28). This informs us that two leaders cannot be appointed for the same generation.

AND HE SHALL ALLOT TO THEM THE LAND (Deut. 3:28). This informs us that Joshua would not depart this world before giving Israel possession of the land.

THAT YOU MAY ONLY SEE (Deut. 3:28). This informs us that Moses saw with his eyes places where Joshua did not tread with his feet.

MEANWHILE WE STAYED ON IN THE VALLEY NEAR BETH-PEOR (Deut. 3:29). He said to them, "See the transgression which I transgressed, and how many pleas I made but was not forgiven; and see how many transgressions you transgressed yet God said to you, 'Repent and I will accept it.'"

R. Judah b. Babba says, "In three places where Israel committed serious transgressions God said to them 'Repent and I shall accept it.' Thus it says THE PLACE WAS NAMED MASSAH AND MERIBAH BECAUSE THE ISRAELITES QUARRELED (Ex. 17:7). And what else does it say? IF YOU WILL HEED THE LORD YOUR GOD DILIGENTLY DOING WHAT IS UPRIGHT IN HIS SIGHT . . . THEN I WILL NOT BRING UPON YOU ANY OF THE DISEASES THAT I BROUGHT UPON THE EGYPTIANS (Ex. 15:26).

"And thus it says AGAIN YOU PROVOKED THE LORD AT TABAREH, AND AT MASSAH, AND AT KIBROTH-HATTAAVAH (Deut. 9:22). And what else does it say? AND NOW, O ISRAEL, WHAT IS IT THAT THE LORD YOUR GOD DEMANDS OF YOU? (Deut. 10:12).

"Here too it says MEANWHILE WE STAYED ON IN THE VALLEY NEAR BETH-PEOR (Deut. 3:29) AND NOW, O ISRAEL, GIVE HEED TO THE LAWS (Deut. 4:1)."

WHEN YOU HAVE SEEN IT, YOU TOO SHALL BE GATHERED TO YOUR KIN, JUST AS YOUR BROTHER AARON WAS (Num. 27:

---

same generation—at the same time. Their terms of office may not overlap.

BETH-PEOR—Baal-peor where the Israelites sinned with the women of Moab (see Num. 25: 1–5). The place is mentioned in order to contrast God's forgiveness of the people after their serious transgression with His refusal to forgive Moses for much less.

13). This informs us that Moses wanted a death like Aaron's, as it is said JUST AS YOUR BROTHER AARON WAS.

FOR IN THE WILDERNESS OF ZIN, WHEN THE COMMUNITY WAS CONTENTIOUS, YOU DISOBEYED MY COMMAND TO UP-HOLD MY SANCTITY IN THEIR SIGHT BY MEANS OF WATER (Num. 27:14). R. Simeon b. Eleazar says, "Moses and Aaron died by Heavenly decree, as it is said BY FAILING TO UPHOLD MY SANCTITY AMONG THE ISRAELITE PEOPLE (Deut. 32:51). Had you sanctified Me, the time would not yet have come for you to die."

Israel had two rulers. One said, "Do not record my sin." The other said, "Record my sin." David said, "Do not record my sin," as it is said OF DAVID. A MASKIL. HAPPY IS HE WHOSE TRANSGRESSION IS FORGIVEN, WHOSE SIN IS COVERED OVER (Ps. 32:1). Moses said, "Record my sin," as it is said FOR, IN THE WILDERNESS OF ZIN, WHEN THE COMMUNITY WAS CONTENTIOUS, YOU DIS-OBEYED MY COMMAND TO UPHOLD MY SANCTITY IN THEIR SIGHT BY MEANS OF WATER (Num. 27:14).

A parable. This may be likened to two women sentenced by the court. One was sentenced for licentiousness, the other for having stolen unripe figs of the Sabbatical year. The one who stole the unripe figs of the Sabbatical year said, "I beg of you—proclaim my sin so that spectators shall not say, 'Just as that one is guilty of licentiousness, so this one is guilty of licentiousness.' " So they hung the figs around her neck and the crier called out before her "This one is being punished because of the unripe figs."

R. Eleazar of Modi'in says, "Come and see how precious the righteous are to the Holy One, for wherever their deaths are recorded, their sin is also recorded. Why is that done? So that people should not have the opportunity to say, 'They committed all kinds of licentious deeds secretly. That is why they died.' Thus the death of the sons of Aaron is recorded in four places and in each place where their death is repeated, their sin in also recorded to inform us that this was their only sin. It is a matter of logic. If God pities the righteous when He is angry with them, how much more will He do so when it is a time of favor for them! As it is said THUS SAID THE LORD:

Heavenly decree   Their deaths were not natural but decreed by God as a punishment.
pities the righteous   He shows His pity by caring for their reputations and disclosing their sins, which are less heinous than people might think.

IN AN HOUR OF FAVOR I ANSWER YOU AND ON A DAY OF SALVATION I HELP YOU (Isa. 49:8)."

MOSES SPOKE TO THE LORD, SAYING (Num. 27:15). This tells us how praiseworthy are the righteous. Even at the hour of their death, they neglect their own needs for the needs of the community.

SAYING (Num. 27:15). The word *SAYING* is used to indicate that he said to Him, "Tell me if You intend to appoint leaders for them or not," and the Holy One replied SINGLE OUT JOSHUA SON OF NUN, AN IN-SPIRED MAN, AND LAY YOUR HAND UPON HIM (Num. 27:18).

COMMENTARY   *The transgression and death of Moses are dealt with many times in the Midrash. The harshness of God's decree seems to contradict the rabbinic concept of the Quality of Mercy as dominant as well as the ever-present possibility of repentance. For this reason the Sages make it a point to emphasize that one should never despair of forgiveness and that the Quality of Mercy or Goodness overcomes that of Justice. On the one hand, it is made clear that Moses' transgression was serious enough that under no conditions would God forgive it. But it is also emphasized that his transgression was much less serious than those of the people of Israel. It is because of his stature that he is held accountable for something that might have been forgiven others. He could and should have sanctified God, but did not. In relationship to the sin of David, that of Moses is much less severe. These two men are often compared as the greatest of Israel's leaders. The sin of David, however, was truly reprehensible. Therefore he himself sought to hide it. Moses speaks of his publicly so that there should be no suspicion that he had sinned in other ways. Furthermore, the Midrash emphasizes that there were good reasons for refusing to permit Moses to enter as a leader or to bring his body there after death and that God still loved Moses and had great reward in store for him.*

19. Numbers 31:21, Sifre N. 157, 213

ELEAZAR THE PRIEST SAID TO THE TROOPS WHO HAD TAKEN PART IN THE FIGHTING, "THIS IS THE RITUAL LAW" (Num. 31:21). Because of his anger Moses erred.

---

needs of the community   Moses is concerned about future leadership for the community.

---

19. *Moses erred*   That is why the instruction is coming from Eleazar and not from Moses.

R. Eleazar b. Azariah says, "On three occasions Moses became angry and erred. Thus it says HE WAS ANGRY WITH ELEAZAR AND ITHAMAR, AARON'S REMAINING SONS, AND SAID (Lev. 10:16). What did he say? WHY DID YOU NOT EAT THE SIN OFFERING IN THE SACRED AREA? (Lev. 10:17).

Another instance is LISTEN, YOU REBELS, SHALL WE GET WATER FOR YOU OUT OF THIS ROCK? (Num. 20:10). What does it say? AND MOSES RAISED HIS HAND AND STRUCK THE ROCK TWICE WITH HIS ROD (Num. 20:11).

Here too it says MOSES BECAME ANGRY WITH THE COMMANDERS OF THE ARMY, THE OFFICERS OF THOUSANDS AND THE OFFICERS OF HUNDREDS WHO HAD COME BACK FROM THE CAMPAIGN (Num. 31:14). THIS IS THE RITUAL LAW THAT THE LORD HAS ENJOINED ON MOSES (Num. 31:21). Because of his anger Moses erred.

There are those who say that Moses gave Eleazar the priest permission to speak so that when Moses would die they would not say "When your teacher Moses was alive, you would not dare to speak. *Now* you want to speak?"

R. Josiah says, "He was simply quoting a teaching in the name of the one who had taught it. As it is said AND ESTHER REPORTED IT TO THE KING IN MORDECAI'S NAME (Esther 2:22).

COMMENTARY   *Moses is seldom spared the rod of rabbinic criticism. For all his greatness, he was a human being with human faults. Anger is the one of which they most frequently speak because it is a quality they abhorred, seeing it as leading to loss of good sense and reason. The idea of quoting someone and giving credit where credit is due was very important to them. It would, they said, using the language of hyperbole, bring redemption to the world.*

IN THE SACRED AREA   Moses criticizes Aaron for the way he offered a sacrifice, but Aaron has an explanation that Moses then accepts (Lev. 10:20). The Sages connected this with the question of whether a priest in mourning should partake of sacrifice. Aaron's two sons had just perished.

Moses gave Eleazar the priest permission   Thus Moses had not erred but had deliberately permitted Eleazar to instruct the troops in order to enhance Eleazar's authority.

one who had taught it—as the verse says HAS ENJOINED ON MOSES. Moses is not being punished. He has already taught it and Eleazar is merely quoting him.

20. Numbers 35:34, Sifre Numbers 161, 222

YOU SHALL NOT DEFILE THE LAND IN WHICH YOU LIVE IN
WHICH I MYSELF ABIDE, FOR I THE LORD ABIDE AMONG THE
ISRAELITE PEOPLE (Num. 35:34). The verse indicates that bloodshed
defiles the Land and causes the Divine Presence to remove itself.

It was bloodshed which caused the Temple to be destroyed. It once happened that two priests were running and rushing to ascend the ramp [to the
altar]. One preceded the other by four *amot*. The other took a dagger and
stabbed him in the heart. R. Zadok came and stood on the steps of the hall
and said, "Listen to me, my brothers of the house of Israel! It says IF, IN
THE LAND THAT THE LORD YOUR GOD IS GIVING YOU TO
POSSESS, SOMEONE SLAIN IS FOUND LYING IN THE OPEN,
THE IDENTITY OF THE SLAYER NOT BEING KNOWN, YOUR
ELDERS AND OFFICIALS SHALL GO OUT AND MEASURE THE
DISTANCES FROM THE CORPSE TO THE NEARBY TOWNS
(Deut. 21:1–2). Let us measure and see who should bring the heifer. Is it
the 'heichal' or the 'azarot'?" All Israel broke out in moaning and weeping.
Afterward the father of the youth came and found him in his death throes.
He said to them, "Our brothers—I am your atonement. My son is still in his
death throes and the knife is not impure." This indicates that the impurity
of knives was more important to them than bloodshed! Similarly it says
MOREOVER, MANASSEH PUT SO MANY INNOCENT PERSONS

---

20. *bloodshed defiles the Land* The previous verse states that BLOOD POLLUTES THE
LAND. This verse mentions that God abides in the land. The implication is that He will not
abide there when it is polluted by bloodshed.

to ascend the ramp In the morning, the practice was for priests to race up the ramp and the
first to reach the altar had the privilege of cleaning it of the remnants of the last sacrifices.

stabbed him—out of anger at having lost and therefore denied the privilege.

'heichal'—the section of the Temple containing the golden altar or the *'azarot'*—the main fore-
court of the Temple. When a corpse was found and the slayer was unknown, the closest city
had to bring a heifer and make confession of innocence. So in this case, a section of the Temple
itself should make expiation. Obviously that law does not apply in this case. R. Zadok is attempting to emphasize the seriousness of bloodshed and the terrible moral contamination this
has brought to the most sacred of all places.

I am your atonement Some versions read "He is your atonement." His death will atone for
the sins of the priests.

not impure Since he is not dead yet, the knife has not acquired impurity and can be used for
the sacrifice.

TO DEATH THAT HE FILLED JERUSALEM [WITH BLOOD] FROM END TO END (2 Kings 21:16). This was the source of the saying: Because of the sin of bloodshed the Divine Presence removes itself and the Temple is defiled. . . .

R. Nathan says, "Precious are the people of Israel, for wherever they were exiled, the Divine Presence was with them. They were exiled to Egypt, the Divine Presence was with them, as it is said I WAS EXILED TO YOUR FATHER'S HOUSE IN EGYPT WHEN THEY WERE SUBJECT TO THE HOUSE OF PHARAOH (1 Sam. 2:27). They were exiled to Babylonia, the Divine Presence was with them as it is said FOR YOUR SAKE I WAS SENT TO BABYLON (Isa. 43:14). They were exiled to Elam, the Divine Presence was with them, as it is said AND I WILL SET MY THRONE IN ELAM (Jer. 49:38). They were exiled to Edom, the Divine Presence was with them, as it is said WHO IS THIS COMING FROM EDOM, IN CRIMSONED GARMENTS FROM BOZRAH (Isa. 63:1). And when they return, the Divine Presence returns with them, as it is said THEN THE LORD YOUR GOD WILL RETURN YOUR CAPTIVITY, AND HAVE COMPASSION UPON YOU (Deut. 30:3). It does not say 'He shall cause them to return,' but 'The Lord your God will return.' It also says FROM LEBANON, MY BRIDE, WITH ME! TRIP DOWN FROM AMANA'S PEAK, FROM THE PEAK OF SENIR AND HERMON, FROM THE DENS OF LIONS, FROM THE HILLS OF LEOPARDS (Song 4:8)."

Rabbi Judah the Prince says, "A parable. This may be likened to a king who said to his slave, 'If you need me, I am with my son. Whenever you need me, I will be with my son.' Thus it says WHO ABIDES WITH THEM IN THE MIDST OF THEIR UNCLEANNESS (Lev. 16:16) and it says BY DEFILING MY TABERNACLE WHICH IS AMONG THEM (Lev. 15:31) and it says SO THAT THEY DO NOT DEFILE THE CAMP OF THOSE IN WHOSE MIDST I DWELL (Num. 5:3) and it says YOU SHALL NOT DEFILE THE LAND IN WHICH YOU LIVE, IN

I WAS EXILED—usually translated "I revealed Myself." The Hebrew words for "exiled" and "revealed" have a similar sound.
I WAS SENT TO BABYLON—usually translated "I send."
This may be likened to a king The parable explains the verse FOR I THE LORD ABIDE

WHICH I MYSELF ABIDE, FOR I THE LORD ABIDE AMONG THE
ISRAELITE PEOPLE (Num. 35:34)."

COMMENTARY   *The attitude of the Sages toward the Temple and the
Temple Service was one of great respect. It was one of the central pillars on
which existence itself depended. Nevertheless they, like the prophets before
them, would not hesitate to denounce abuses of its sanctity. If the priests
were guilty of bloodshed, of what value was the Temple? God Himself
would not abide within it under those conditions. R. Nathan's discussion
also reflects a theme repeated in many contexts: God's great love of Israel,
which caused Him to be with them wherever they were. The Exile of Israel
was also, as it were, the Exile of God. The redemption of Israel was also the
redemption of God.*

AMONG THE ISRAELITE PEOPLE. Israel is God's child and He is constantly with them
wherever they are.

DEUTERONOMY

1. Deuteronomy 1:3, Sifre D. 2, 10

IT WAS IN THE FORTIETH YEAR, ON THE FIRST DAY OF THE ELEVENTH MONTH, THAT MOSES SPOKE TO THE ISRAELITES (Deut. 1:3). This teaches us that he rebuked them only when he was about to die. From whom did he learn this? From Jacob who rebuked his sons only when he was about to die, as it is said AND JACOB CALLED HIS SONS AND SAID, "COME TOGETHER THAT I MAY TELL YOU WHAT IS TO BEFALL YOU IN DAYS TO COME (Gen. 49:1). REUBEN, YOU ARE MY FIRSTBORN (Gen. 49:3)." Now do we not know that Reuben was the firstborn? This teaches that he said to him, "Reuben, my son, let me tell you why I did not rebuke you all these years. It was so that you should not abandon me and attach yourself to my brother Esau."

There are four reasons why one rebukes another person only when about to die:
    —so that he will not be rebuking and constantly rebuking over and over;
    —so that the other will not be embarrassed when he sees him;
    —so that he will not bear a grudge against him;
    —so that he will depart from him in peace, for rebuke brings peace.

---

1. *rebuked them*   The midrash takes the book of Deuteronomy as a book of rebuke.

about to die   All of these words of rebuke are spoken immediately prior to Moses' death. Why did he wait so long?

the firstborn   This was mentioned as a way of saying that Jacob had wanted Reuben to retain his relationship with him and therefore refrained from saying what he was about to say now.

why I did not rebuke you   Reuben had cohabited with Jacob's concubine, Bilhah, but Jacob did not rebuke him. (See Gen. 35:22.) Only now does he denounce Reuben for this: YOU BROUGHT DISGRACE—MY COUCH HE MOUNTED (Gen. 49:4).

brings peace   After the rebuke, the two parties can make peace.

Thus you find concerning Abraham that it is said THEN ABRAHAM RE-BUKED ABIMELECH (Gen. 21:25), after which it says AND THE TWO OF THEM MAKE A PACT (Gen. 21:27).

Thus too concerning Isaac it says ISAAC SAID TO THEM, "WHY HAVE YOU COME TO ME, SEEING THAT YOU HAVE BEEN HOSTILE TO ME AND HAVE DRIVEN ME AWAY FROM YOU?" (Gen. 26:27), after which it says ISAAC THEN BADE THEM FAREWELL, AND THEY DEPARTED FROM HIM IN PEACE (Gen. 26:31).

Thus too you find that Joshua rebuked Israel only when he was about to die, as it says OR IF YOU ARE LOATH TO SERVE THE LORD, CHOOSE THIS DAY WHICH ONES YOU ARE GOING TO SERVE (Josh. 24:15), after which it says BUT THE PEOPLE REPLIED TO JOSHUA, "NO, WE WILL SERVE THE LORD!" (Josh. 24:21).

Thus too you find that Samuel rebuked Israel only when he was about to die, as it says HERE I AM! TESTIFY AGAINST ME, IN THE PRESENCE OF THE LORD AND IN THE PRESENCE OF HIS ANOINTED ONE: WHOSE OX HAVE I TAKEN, OR WHOSE ASS HAVE I TAKEN? (1 Sam. 12:3). THEY RESPONDED, "YOU HAVE NOT DEFRAUDED US"... HE SAID TO THEM, "THE LORD THEN IS WITNESS, AND HIS ANOINTED IS WITNESS TO YOUR ADMISSION THIS DAY THAT YOU HAVE FOUND NOTHING IN MY POSSESSION." THEY RESPONDED, "HE IS!" (1 Sam. 12:4–5).

Thus too you find that David rebuked his son Solomon only when he was about to die, as it says WHEN DAVID'S LIFE WAS DRAWING TO A CLOSE, HE INSTRUCTED HIS SON SOLOMON AS FOLLOWS. "I AM GOING THE WAY OF ALL THE EARTH" (1 Kings 2:1).

COMMENTARY   *Although the Sages felt that there was a duty to rebuke a person for his or her faults and misdeeds, in this passage we find a practical approach to the problem. If the rebuke will bring about problems, it is better to postpone it literally until the last moment when it may do some good. Biblical examples for this deathbed rebuke illustrate the point.*

---

concerning Abraham   In this case and the others that follow, rebuke leads to peace and better relationships.

David rebuked his son Solomon   He adjured him to obey God and follow Him, implying that Solomon had not always done so.

2. Deuteronomy 1:9, Sifre D. 9, 16

THEREUPON I SAID TO YOU (Deut. 1:9). Moses said to Israel, "I am not saying this to you on my own but from the mouth of the Holy One."

"I CANNOT BEAR THE BURDEN OF YOU BY MYSELF" (Deut. 1:9). Is it possible that Moses—the man who had taken them out of Egypt, split the sea for them, brought down the manna for them, fetched the quails for them, and performed miracles and wonders for them—could not judge Israel? Rather thus did he say to them, "THE LORD YOUR GOD HAS MULTIPLIED YOU (Deut. 1:10) upon the backs of your judges."

Similarly Solomon said, "GRANT, THEN, YOUR SERVANT AN UNDERSTANDING MIND TO JUDGE YOUR PEOPLE" (1 Kings 3:9). Is it possible that Solomon—the man of whom it was said THE LORD HAD GIVEN SOLOMON WISDOM . . . (1 Kings 5:26) and SOLOMON'S WISDOM WAS GREATER THAN THE WISDOM OF ALL THE KEDEMITES AND THAN ALL THE WISDOM OF THE EGYPTIANS. HE WAS THE WISEST OF ALL MEN: [WISER] THAN ETHAN THE EZRAHITE, AND HEMAN, CHALKOL, AND DARDA THE SONS OF MAHOL. HIS FAME SPREAD AMONG ALL THE SURROUNDING NATIONS (1 Kings 5:10–11)—could not judge them? Rather thus did he say to them, "I am not like all the other judges. A human king sits upon his tribune and sentences people to death by the sword, by strangulation, by fire, or by stoning and it makes no difference. And if the guilty party is to be fined one *sela* he may take two, if the fine is two he may take three, a *denar* he may take a *mina*. I am not like that. If I make a monetary judgment, I am as accountable as if it were a capital case." Thus it is said DO NOT ROB THE WRETCHED BECAUSE HE IS WRETCHED; DO NOT CRUSH THE POOR MAN IN THE GATE;

---

2. *upon the backs of your judges* The judge bears additional responsibility for any errors of judgment. Moses certainly was capable of judging, but he was wary of the responsibility involved.

a human king—an ordinary king not bound by the divine laws.

death by the sword The law of the Torah specifies these four different methods of execution. For each crime there is a specified mode. The judge is responsible to see to it not only that only the guilty are executed, but also that the method of execution is correct.

mina One *mina* equals 100 *denar*.

FOR THE LORD WILL TAKE UP THEIR CAUSE AND DESPOIL THOSE WHO DESPOIL THEM OF LIFE (Prov. 22:22–23).

UNTIL YOU ARE TODAY AS NUMEROUS AS THE STARS IN THE SKY (Deut. 1:10). You are as established as the day. This is the source of the teaching: There are seven groups of the righteous in paradise, one higher than the other.

The first: RIGHTEOUS MEN SHALL PRAISE YOUR NAME; THE UPRIGHT SHALL DWELL IN YOUR PRESENCE (Ps. 140:14).

The second: HAPPY IS THE MAN YOU CHOOSE AND BRING NEAR TO DWELL IN YOUR COURTS (Ps. 65:5).

The third: HAPPY ARE THOSE WHO DWELL IN YOUR HOUSE; THEY FOREVER PRAISE YOU (Ps. 84:5).

The fourth: LORD, WHO MAY SOJOURN IN YOUR TENT (Ps. 15:1).

The fifth: WHO MAY DWELL IN YOUR HOLY MOUNTAIN (Ps. 15:1)

The sixth: WHO MAY ASCEND THE MOUNTAIN OF THE LORD (Ps. 24:3).

The seventh: WHO MAY STAND IN HIS HOLY PLACE (Ps. 24:3).

R. Simeon b. Yochai says, "In the future the faces of the righteous will resemble seven joyous things: the sun, the moon, the sky, the stars, the lightning, lilies, and the menorah of the Temple.

The sun: how so? MAY ALL HIS FRIENDS BE AS THE SUN RISING IN MIGHT (Judges 5:31).

The moon: how so? BEAUTIFUL AS THE MOON (Song 6:10).

The sky? AND THE KNOWLEDGEABLE WILL BE RADIANT LIKE THE BRIGHT EXPANSE OF SKY (Dan. 12:3).

OF LIFE   The judge's life may be forfeit even for an error in a monetary case. Thus Solomon had the wisdom and capability to judge, but the responsibility was so great he felt the need to request God's help.

as the day—reading the verse "You are the day [today]."

This is the source   The comparison of Israel to the stars, which are grouped in different levels, is the source of the idea that there are different groups of the righteous.

seven groups   Both this and the subsequent discussion of seven joyous things are based on an interpretation of IN YOUR PRESENCE IS PERFECT JOY (Ps. 16:11) in which PERFECT JOY (sova semahot) is read "seven joys" (sheva semahot).

the menorah—the seven-branched candelabrum.

The stars? AND THOSE WHO LEAD THE MANY TO RIGH-
TEOUSNESS WILL BE LIKE THE STARS FOREVER AND EVER
(Dan. 12:3).

The lightning? THEY RACE LIKE STREAKS OF LIGHTNING
(Nah. 2:5).

The lilies? FOR THE LEADER; ON THE LILIES (Ps. 45:1).

To the menorah of the Temple? As it is said I SEE A MENORAH OF
GOLD AND BY IT ARE TWO OLIVE TREES, ONE ON THE
RIGHT OF THE BOWL AND ONE ON ITS LEFT (Zech. 4:3).

MAY THE LORD, THE GOD OF YOUR FATHERS, INCREASE
YOUR NUMBERS A THOUSANDFOLD (Deut. 1:11). They said to him,
"Our teacher Moses, you cannot bless us, for God has already promised
Abraham our father I WILL BESTOW MY BLESSING UPON YOU
AND MAKE YOUR DESCENDANTS AS NUMEROUS AS THE
STARS OF HEAVEN AND THE SANDS ON THE SEASHORE (Gen.
22:17), while you are setting a limit to our blessing!"

A parable. A king had many possessions. He had a young son and
needed to travel to lands beyond the sea. He said, "If I leave him in charge
of my possessions he will squander them, rather I shall appoint a guardian
for him until he grows up." When that child grew up, he said to his guardian, "Give me the silver and gold that my father left for me in your trust."
He gave him enough to sustain him from his own possessions. When the
son began to complain, he said to him, "Whatever I gave you came from my
possessions. That which your father left you is being saved for you." Thus
Moses said to Israel, "THE LORD THE GOD OF YOUR FATHERS,
INCREASE YOUR NUMBER A THOUSANDFOLD (Deut. 1:11). That
is my blessing. AND BLESS YOU AS HE PROMISED YOU (Deut. 1:11).
That is your blessing [from God.] [May you be] as the sand of the seas, as
the plants of the earth, as the fish of the sea and as the stars of the heavens
for multitude."

HOW CAN I ALONE BEAR THE TROUBLE OF YOU (Deut. 1:12).
This teaches that they were troublemakers. If one saw that the other side
was winning a lawsuit, he would say, "I have more witnesses to bring; I have
new evidence to bring. Tomorrow I will continue the case and add more

---

setting a limit Abraham was promised blessings that are unlimited. You—Moses—speak
about "a thousandfold."

judges." Thus it says THE TROUBLE OF YOU teaching that they were troublemakers.

AND THE BURDEN (Deut. 1:12). This teaches that they were *apikorsim*. If Moses went out early they would say, "Why did the son of Amram go out [so early]? Maybe things do not go well for him at home." If he went out late they would say, "Why did the son of Amram not go out [early]? What do you think! He sits there and plots and schemes against you, devising things which are worse than anything done by the house of On, as it is said AND ON SON OF PELETH—DESCENDANTS OF REUBEN—(Num. 16:1)." Thus it says AND THE BURDEN (Deut. 1:12), teaching that they were *apikorsim*.

AND THE BICKERING (Deut. 1:12). This teaches that they were litigious. They would spend a *sela* in order to win two, two to win three. Thus it says AND THE BICKERING—teaching that they were litigious.

Another interpretation: THE TROUBLE OF YOU AND THE BURDEN AND THE BICKERING (Deut. 1:12). If Moses went out early they would say, "Why did the son of Amram hurry so to go out? It is because his children and members of his household want to gather the largest pieces of the manna." If he went out late they would say, "He was eating, drinking, and sleeping." If Moses walked amongst them they would say, "He wants to make us stand up in his presence." If he walked around the side they would say, "We have this mitzvah of standing in the presence of an elder and he wants to take it from us." Moses said to them, "If I go in your midst I cannot satisfy you and if I go around the side I cannot satisfy you!"

GET YOU (habu) (Deut. 1:13). *Habu* always indicates asking advice, as it is said WHAT DO YOU ADVISE US (habu) TO DO? (2 Sam. 16:20), LET US, THEN (habu) DEAL SHREWDLY WITH THEM (Ex. 1:10).

---

apikorsim—sceptics, unbelievers who scoffed at the Sages.
house of On   The correct reference is most likely to On meaning Egypt, as in Gen. 41:50.
two to win three   They would go to court when all they could receive would be a very small profit. Some versions have it that they would go even if it would cost them more than they would receive.
make us stand up   Lev. 19:32 requires that people stand before an elder. They complain that Moses deliberately walks among them so that they will have to get up to show him respect.

MEN (Deut. 1:13). Would it even occur to us that women [would be appointed]? Why then does the verse say MEN? To indicate [MEN] of wisdom and knowledge, MEN of experience and ability.

WHO ARE WISE (Deut. 1:13). That is what Arios asked R. Jose, saying to him, "What is the definition of a 'wise man'?"

He said to him, "One who can establish his teaching."

"Perhaps that is the definition of one who is 'discerning.'"

He said to him, "The verse mentions DISCERNING (Deut. 1:13) afterward. What is the distinction between a 'wise man' and a 'discerning man'? A wise man is like a wealthy money-changer. When he is brought coins to examine, he examines them, and when he is not brought any coins, he takes out his own and examines them. A discerning man is like a poor money-changer. When he is brought coins to examine, he examines them, but when no coins are brought to him, he sits idly by."

AND KNOWN TO YOUR TRIBES (Deut. 1:13). "They should be well known to you, for when someone wraps himself in his cloak and comes and sits before me, I do not know what tribe he comes from, but you recognize him for you grew up amongst them." Therefore it is said AND KNOWN TO YOUR TRIBES. They should be well known to you.

Rabban Gamliel says, "There is never an appointment made to a court without people muttering about it and saying, 'Why should so-and-so have been appointed? Why wasn't so-and-so appointed?'" Therefore it says AND KNOWN TO YOUR TRIBES. They should be well known to you.

AND I WILL APPOINT THEM AS YOUR HEADS (Deut. 1:13). Do you think that if you appointed them they are appointed but if not, they are not appointed? The verse says AND I WILL APPOINT THEM AS YOUR HEADS. If I appointed them they are appointed, and if not they are not appointed. Do you think that if you raised them up they are exalted and if not, they are not exalted? The verse says AND I WILL APPOINT

---

women Although in the Biblical period there were women leaders such as Miriam and Hulda who were prophetesses and Deborah who was a judge, during the rabbinic period this was not so. Since it was so obvious to them that only men could be appointed judges, they wondered why the verse specified it.

Arios—a gentile who converted to Judaism.

wraps himself in his cloak The judge wore a cloak when trying a case.

If I appointed them The power of appointment was with Moses, not with the people.

THEM AS YOUR HEADS. If I raise them up they are exalted, and if not they are not exalted.

Another interpretation: If you observe their decrees YOUR HEADS will be preserved, and if not YOUR HEADS will not be preserved.

Another interpretation: Do not read it as AND I WILL APPOINT THEM (wa-'asimem) AS YOUR HEADS but "Their guilt (wa-'ashmom) is on YOUR HEADS." This teaches that the guilt of Israel rests upon the heads of their judges. Thus it says NOW, O MORTAL, I HAVE APPOINTED YOU A WATCHMAN FOR THE HOUSE OF ISRAEL; AND WHEN-EVER YOU HEAR A MESSAGE FROM MY MOUTH, YOU MUST TRANSMIT MY WARNING TO THEM. WHEN I SAY TO THE WICKED, "WICKED MAN, YOU SHALL DIE," BUT YOU HAVE NOT SPOKEN TO WARN THE WICKED MAN AGAINST HIS WAY, HE, THAT WICKED MAN, SHALL DIE FOR HIS SINS, BUT I WILL DEMAND A RECKONING FOR HIS BLOOD FROM YOU. BUT IF YOU HAVE WARNED THE WICKED MAN TO TURN BACK FROM HIS WAY, AND HE HAS NOT TURNED FROM HIS WAY, HE SHALL DIE FOR HIS OWN SINS, BUT YOU WILL HAVE SAVED YOUR LIFE (Ezek. 33:7–9).

YOU ANSWERED ME AND SAID, "WHAT YOU PROPOSE TO DO IS GOOD" (Deut. 1:14). "You should have said to me, 'Our teacher Moses, from whom is it better to learn Torah, from you or from your students or your students students? Is it not [better to learn] from you since you labored over it, as it is said AND HE WAS THERE WITH THE LORD FORTY DAYS AND FORTY NIGHTS; HE ATE NO BREAD AND DRANK NO WATER (Ex. 34:28). AND I STAYED ON THE MOUNTAIN FORTY DAYS AND FORTY NIGHTS, EATING NO BREAD AND DRINKING NO WATER (Deut. 9:9).' But I know that behind my back you say, 'Now he will appoint some eighty thousand judges over us, and if I am not appointed, my son will be, and if not my son, my son's son, and we can bring him a gift and he will distort judgment in our favor.' " Therefore

---

YOUR HEADS will be preserved   Appointing the judges as your heads means that your heads, i.e., your very lives, are dependent on your obedience to them.

upon the heads of their judges   Judges are responsible for the actions of the people. The term *judges* is here used in the sense of leaders or elders, similar to the status of the judges in the Book of Judges.

it says, YOU ANSWERED ME (Deut. 1:14). If I delayed doing it, you would say, "Do this quickly!"

SO I TOOK YOUR TRIBAL LEADERS, WISE AND EXPERIENCED MEN (Deut. 1:15). I attracted them with words. I said to them, "Happy are you. Over whom are you appointed? Over the children of Abraham, Isaac, and Jacob, human beings who are called brothers and friends, a pleasant vineyard and portion, sheep of His pasture and other terms of endearment."

WISE AND EXPERIENCED MEN (Deut. 1:15) This is one of seven qualities which Jethro specified to Moses. He found only three of them however, WISE AND EXPERIENCED MEN.

AND APPOINTED THEM HEADS OVER YOU (Deut. 1:15) so that they should be honored by you, heads of commerce, heads of business, heads of negotiations, heads of entering and leaving, coming in first and leaving last, therefore it says AND APPOINTED THEM HEADS OVER YOU so that they should be honored by you.

CHIEFS OF THOUSANDS (Deut. 1:15). If there are 1,999, one chief of a thousand is appointed. CHIEFS OF HUNDREDS (Deut. 1:15). If there are 199, one chief of a hundred is appointed. CHIEFS OF FIFTIES (Deut. 1:15). If there are 99, one chief of fifty is appointed. CHIEFS OF TENS (Deut. 1:15). If there are 19, one chief of ten is appointed.

AND OFFICIALS (Deut. 1:15). This refers to the Levites who flogged with a lash, as it is said THE LEVITICAL OFFICIALS ARE AT YOUR DISPOSAL (2 Chron. 19:11) and it says THE LEVITES WERE QUIETING THE PEOPLE, SAYING, "HUSH" (Neh. 8:11).

AT THAT TIME I CHARGED YOUR MAGISTRATES AS FOLLOWS, "HEAR OUT YOUR BROTHER AND DECIDE JUSTLY" (Deut. 1:16). I said to them, "Be patient in judgment. If a case comes before

---

If I delayed The word *answer* also has the meaning of "prompt." The verse is interpreted to mean not "You answered me," but "You prompted me," i.e., you urged me to do it quickly.
seven qualities—as listed in Ex. 18:21 and Deut. 1:13: able men, God-fearing, men of truth, spurning ill-gotten gain, men wise and discerning. "Men" is understood as a quality, as in the interpretation of the word in Deut. 1:13.
one chief A second chief is not appointed until there is another complete unit.

you once, twice, or three times, do not say 'This case has already come
before me and I decided it once, then again and even a third time,' but be
patient in judgment." This is what the men of the Great Assembly used to
say, "Be patient in judgment, raise up many disciples and make a fence
around the Torah."

AT THAT TIME . . . AS FOLLOWS (Deut. 1:16). In the past you were
independent. Now you are the servants of the community. It once happened
that R. Johanan b. Nuri and R. Eleazar Hisma were put in charge of the
Academy by Rabban Gamliel, but the students did not realize that they were
there. Toward evening they went and sat among the students. Now Rabban
Gamliel's practice was that if he came in and said "Ask what you will," it
was a sign that there was no supervisor there. If he came in and did not say,
"Ask what you will," it was a sign that there was a supervisor there. He
came in and found R. Johanan b. Nuri and R. Eleazar Hisma sitting among
the students. He said to them, "Johanan b. Nuri and Eleazar Hisma, you are
harming the community by not attempting to exercise your authority over
the community. In the past, you were independent. From now on you are
the servants of the community!"

HEAR OUT YOUR BROTHERS (Deut. 1:16). It was R. Ishmael's practice that when litigants would come before him for judgment, one of whom
was a Jew and the other a gentile, he would use either Jewish or gentile law,
whichever would vindicate the Jew. He said, "What do I care? Does not the
Torah say HEAR OUT YOUR BROTHERS?" Rabban Simeon b. Gamliel
says, "There is no need [to interpret the verse thus]. If they come to
be judged by Jewish law, judge them by Jewish law. If they come to be
judged by gentile law, judge them by gentile law AND DECIDE JUSTLY
(Deut. 1:16)."

AND DECIDE JUSTLY (Deut. 1:16). Let the righteous man come with
his just case and bring evidence. For example, a man is wrapped in his cloak

---

Great Assembly According to tradition these were the early leaders from Ezra until some time
in the second century B.C.E.
fence around the Torah—create regulations that will prevent people from violating the mitzvot
even accidentally.
in charge They were to supervise the students during their studies.
There is no need R. Ishmael understands BROTHERS to mean Jews, but there is no need to
interpret the verse as if it gives permission to ignore the rights of the non-Jew. The end of the
verse clearly requires that justice be done.

when another says, "It is mine!" A man is plowing with his heifer when another comes and says, "It is mine!" A man is in possession of his field when another comes and says, "It is mine!" A man is living in his house when another comes and says, "It is mine!" Therefore it is said AND DECIDE JUSTLY. Let the righteous man come with his just case and bring evidence.

BETWEEN ANY MAN (Deut. 1:16)—excluding a minor. This is the source of the teaching: Orphans are not subject to a lawsuit.

BETWEEN ANY MAN AND HIS FELLOW (Deut. 1:16). This teaches only about a man and another man. What about a man and a woman or a woman and a man, a nation and a family, one family and another? The verse says A MAN AND HIS FELLOW—in any instance.

OR A STRANGER (ger) (Deut. 1:16). This refers to one who piles up (oger) charges against others. He says to him, "You plowed a furrow in my field." He says, "I did not plow." "Your ox killed my ox." He says, "He did not kill it." "Your ox killed my slave." He says "He did not kill him." Thus it says OR A STRANGER. This refers to one who piles up charges against others.

Another interpretation: OR A STRANGER. This refers to his neighbor.
    Another interpretation: This refers to his best man.
    Another interpretation: This refers to the settler [on his property].

YOU SHALL NOT BE PARTIAL IN JUDGMENT (Deut. 1:17). This refers to one who is responsible for appointing judges. Perhaps you would say, "This fellow is pleasant. I shall appoint him a judge. This fellow is heroic. I shall appoint him a judge. This fellow is a leader of prayer. I shall appoint him a judge. This fellow is a Hellenist. I shall appoint him a judge." The result will be that the guilty will go free and the innocent be convicted,

---

in any instance   At first the expression ANY MAN AND HIS FELLOW is understood to refer only to two men, but the correct understanding is any other person or group.
the settler   Stranger (ger) comes from the verb *la-gur,* to live or settle.
appointing judges   Thus the verse does not mean that the judge should not be partial, but that the one who appoints judges should not be partial in his appointments, favoring those who seem to have some outwardly pleasing characteristic. Judges must be appointed only on the basis of their ability and character.
a Hellenist—he understands Greek. This too is an outward quality.

not because [the judge] is wicked, but because he is ignorant. This is considered being partial in judgment.

HEAR OUT LOW AND HIGH ALIKE (Deut. 1:17). You might say, "Well this one is poor and this one is rich. and it is a mitzvah to help the poor, I will rule in his favor and he will then be able to support himself honorably." Therefore the verse says HEAR OUT LOW AND HIGH ALIKE.

Another interpretation: HEAR OUT LOW AND HIGH ALIKE (Deut. 1:17). How can I dishonor this rich man for the sake of a *denar?* I will find him innocent and when he goes out, I shall tell him, "Pay the other, for you are really guilty." Therefore the verse says HEAR OUT LOW AND HIGH ALIKE.

FEAR NO MAN (Deut. 1:17). You might say, "I am afraid of this man lest he slay my child or set fire to my stacks of grain or cut down my trees." The verse says FEAR NO MAN, FOR JUDGMENT IS GOD'S (Deut. 1:17). Thus Jehoshaphat said HE CHARGED THE JUDGES: "CONSIDER WHAT YOU ARE DOING, FOR YOU JUDGE NOT ON BEHALF OF MAN, BUT ON BEHALF OF GOD." (2 Chron. 19:6).

AND THE MATTER THAT IS TOO DIFFICULT FOR YOU (Deut. 1:17). The Holy One said to Moses, "You think that you can judge difficult cases? By your life, I shall bring you a case that your student's student will be able to judge, but you cannot." What was that? The case of the daughters of Zelophehad. Thus it says AND MOSES BROUGHT THEIR CASE BEFORE THE LORD (Num. 27:5).

Similarly it says SAUL APPROACHED SAMUEL INSIDE THE GATE AND SAID TO HIM, "TELL ME, PLEASE, WHERE IS THE HOUSE

---

to support himself honorably   By finding in the poor man's favor, the judge thinks to help him support himself. That is an admirable goal, but justice is not to be perverted even for this.

a denar   For such a small amount of money should I shame the rich man by finding him guilty? *Therefore the verse says HEAR OUT LOW AND HIGH ALIKE*   You are not to take into consideration the honor due to the status of the rich. In a court proceeding justice must be done. Charity is separate.

judge difficult cases   Since Moses tells the others that when a case is too difficult for them they are to bring it to him, he implies that no case is too difficult for him. God will teach him otherwise.

OF THE SEER?" AND SAMUEL ANSWERED SAUL, "I AM THE SEER" (1 Sam. 9:18–19). The Holy One said to him, "You think you are the seer? I shall show you that you are not the seer." When did He do that? When He said to him FILL YOUR HORN WITH OIL AND SET OUT; I AM SENDING YOU TO JESSE THE BETHLEHEMITE, FOR I HAVE DECIDED ON ONE OF HIS SONS TO BE KING (1 Sam. 16:1). What does it say? WHEN THEY ARRIVED AND HE SAW ELIAB, HE THOUGHT: "SURELY THE LORD'S ANOINTED STANDS BEFORE HIM" (1 Sam. 16:6). Said the Holy One to him, "Did I not tell you— I am the seer! PAY NO ATTENTION TO HIS APPEARANCE OR HIS STATURE, FOR I HAVE REJECTED HIM. FOR NOT AS MAN SEES [DOES THE LORD SEE]; MAN SEES ONLY WHAT IS VISIBLE, BUT THE LORD SEES INTO THE HEART" (1 Sam. 16:7).

COMMENTARY   *This section provides the Sages with a welcome opportunity to make many observations concerning the importance of judges, their proper appointment and the way in which they are to fulfill their task. The difficulty Moses faced as a judge, according to this midrash, was not the fact that it took so much of his time, but that it required such exacting work and carried with it such a penalty if not done correctly. The justice the Torah demanded was not capricious and the judge carried on his back the entire burden of the society. Those to be appointed had to be of the highest integrity; they were not to be appointed because of any outward stature but only because of their uprightness and ability to perform the work. Since the Sages were themselves judges, the Biblical stories carried a message for them. The dispute between R. Ishmael and Rabban Simeon b. Gamliel is couched in terms of the interpretation of a verse. R. Ishmael stresses the first part in which "brothers," that is, one's fellow Israelites, are mentioned, while Rabban Simeon points out that the latter part of the verse demands that the judge decide justly, which would not be the case if the non-Jew is discriminated against. The reality reflected here is that often a case in which one litigant was not Jewish would come before them. R. Ishmael, who had personally suffered at the hands of the Romans, did not care for the rights of non-Jews. Rabban Simeon was not willing to compromise justice and his view prevailed in the codification of Jewish law.*

3. Deuteronomy 3:23, Sifre D. 26, 36

I PLEADED (ethanan) WITH THE LORD AT THAT TIME, SAYING (Deut. 3:23). This is the meaning of the verse THE POOR MAN SPEAKS

BESEECHINGLY; THE RICH MAN'S ANSWER IS HARSH (Prov. 18: 23) . . . Israel had two excellent leaders, Moses and David King of Israel. The entire world could have been sustained by their good deeds, yet they never asked God to grant them anything except as an expression of His grace (hinnam). Now if those two, who could have sustained the entire world by their good deeds, never asked God to grant them anything except as an expression of His grace, certainly anyone who is not even one thousand-thousand-thousandth or ten-thousand-ten thousandth part the disciples of their disciples should not ask Him to grant him anything except as an expression of His grace!

Another interpretation: I PLEADED WITH THE LORD (Deut. 3:23). There are nine expressions for prayer:

—cry, cry for help, moaning—these three are found in the verses: A LONG TIME AFTER THAT, THE KING OF EGYPT DIED. THE ISRAELITES WERE GROANING UNDER THE BONDAGE AND CRIED OUT; AND THEIR CRY FOR HELP FROM THE BONDAGE ROSE UP TO GOD. GOD HEARD THEIR MOANING (Ex. 2:23–24)

—anguish, calling out—these are found in the verse IN MY ANGUISH I CALLED ON THE LORD (2 Sam. 22:7)

—cry of prayer, plea—these two in the verse AS FOR YOU, DO NOT PRAY FOR THIS PEOPLE, DO NOT RAISE A CRY OF PRAYER ON THEIR BEHALF, DO NOT PLEAD WITH ME (Jer. 7:16)

—prostrating—as in the verse WHEN I LAY PROSTRATE BEFORE THE LORD (Deut. 9:25)

—prayer—as in the verse I PRAYED TO THE LORD (Deut. 9:26)

—entreating—as is the verse ISAAC ENTREATED WITH THE LORD ON BEHALF OF HIS WIFE (Gen. 25:21)

—standing—as in the verse PHINEHAS STOOD UP AND INTERVENED (Ps. 106:30)

—imploring—as in the verse BUT MOSES IMPLORED THE LORD, HIS GOD (Ex. 32:11)

—pleading—as it is said I PLEADED WITH THE LORD (Deut. 3:23)

---

3. *an expression of His grace*—literally "free."

sustained the entire world   Their merits were sufficient to warrant the continued existence of the universe.

standing (amidah)—the name of the central prayer of each service.

COMMENTARY   *The major components of Jewish liturgy were formulated during the same period as the Midrash. Consequently the same basic vocabulary, terminology, Hebrew style, and themes are found in both. The comment about Moses and David, the greatest of the leaders of Israel, is significant for an understanding of the general philosophy of prayer and of certain specific categories of prayer known as Tahanun (Pleading). It also deals with the question of the importance of good deeds. This midrash affirms that good deeds do indeed matter. They can sustain the world. Nevertheless, when coming before the Almighty with a request, one approaches God not on the basis of deserving His favor, but by appealing to His nature. Whatever God grants is a free gift, that is, an act of grace on His part. This is part of an ongoing discussion with early Christianity concerning the role of deeds in attaining God's favor. Whereas Christianity placed faith above deeds, Judaism continued to emphasize deeds. Without them, God will certainly not grant His gifts. No amount of deeds, however, can ever match His graciousness. Therefore, ultimately it is neither deeds nor faith but the grace of God, that which He grants to man freely, on which humanity must depend.*

4. Deuteronomy 3:25, Sifre D. 28, 44

LET ME, I PRAY, CROSS OVER AND SEE (Deut. 3:25). Is it possible that Moses would have begged God to let him enter the land when elsewhere it is written YOU SHALL NOT GO ACROSS YONDER JORDAN (Deut. 3:27)?

A parable. A king had two slaves. He decreed that one of them should not drink wine thirty days. [That slave] said, "He has decreed that I should not drink wine thirty days? I shall not taste it an entire year or even two years!" Why did he say this? In order to mitigate his master's words. [The king] then decreed that the other [slave] should not drink wine thirty days. [That slave] said, "Can I possibly live without wine for thirty days? I [cannot do without it] for even an hour!" Why did he say this? In order to demonstrate how precious were his master's commands. Thus Moses demonstrated how precious were God's commands by begging Him to let him enter the land. Thus it says LET ME, I PRAY, CROSS OVER AND SEE.

---

4. *begged God* It would have been impudent and inappropriate for Moses to plead for himself when God had already pronounced His judgment on the matter.

mitigate his master's words He shows contempt toward his master by indicating that the punishment means nothing to him.

THAT GOOD MOUNT AND THE LEBANON (Deut. 3:25). Everyone called it MOUNT. Abraham called it MOUNT as it is said ON THE MOUNT OF THE LORD THERE IS VISION (Gen. 22:14).

Moses called it MOUNT as it is said THAT GOOD MOUNT (Deut. 3:25).

David called it MOUNT as it is said WHO MAY ASCEND THE MOUNT OF THE LORD? (Ps. 24:3)

Isaiah called it MOUNT as it is said IN THE DAYS TO COME, THE MOUNT OF THE LORD'S HOUSE SHALL STAND FIRM ABOVE THE MOUNTAINS (Isa. 2:2).

The nations called it MOUNT as it is said AND MANY PEOPLES SHALL GO AND SHALL SAY: "COME LET US GO UP TO THE MOUNT OF THE LORD" (Isa. 2:3).

AND THE LEBANON (Deut. 3:25). What is the source which teaches that "Lebanon" always refers to the Temple? As it is said YOU ARE AS GILEAD TO ME, AS THE SUMMIT OF LEBANON (Jer. 22:6) and THE THICKETS OF THE FOREST SHALL BE HACKED AWAY WITH IRON, AND THE LEBANON TREES SHALL FALL IN THEIR MAJESTY (Isa. 10:34). Why is it called Lebanon? Because it makes the sins of Israel white (malbin) as it is said BE YOUR SINS LIKE CRIMSON, THEY SHALL TURN SNOW-WHITE (yalbinu) (Isa. 1:18).

BUT THE LORD WAS WRATHFUL (yit'abber) WITH ME ON YOUR ACCOUNT AND WOULD NOT LISTEN TO ME (Deut. 3:26). R. Eliezer says, "He was filled with wrath against me." R. Joshua says, "Like a woman who cannot speak because of the pangs of pregnancy (ubbrah)." ON YOUR ACCOUNT (Deut. 3:26) because of you this was done to me. AND WOULD NOT LISTEN TO ME (Deut. 3:26) and would not accept my prayer.

THE LORD SAID TO ME, "ENOUGH (rab)" (Deut. 3:26). He said to him, "Moses, if a man makes a vow, to whom does he turn to be released

---

Everyone called it MOUNT   The midrash identified "mount" with Mount Moriah, i.e., the Temple Mount in Jerusalem.

because of you—and not because of something Moses had done.

to be released   If a man made a vow and then wished to be released of the obligation to observe it, he had to turn to his rabbi to arrange a ceremony to annul it.

from it? Is it not to his master (rabo)? Do you not have to obey the decision of your Master (rabcha)?"

Another interpretation: THE LORD SAID TO ME, "ENOUGH" (Deut. 3:26). He said to him, "Moses, you must be an example to all judges, for they will say, 'If in the case of Moses—the wisest of the wise, the greatest of the great—[God] was not partial in judgment, in that it was decreed that he not enter the Land because he had said LISTEN YOU REBELS (Num. 20:10), surely this will be the case with anyone who diverts or distorts justice.' "

If Moses, who was told ENOUGH. NEVER SPEAK TO ME OF THIS MATTER AGAIN! (Deut. 3:26) did not refrain from pleading for mercy before the Holy One, how much more should this be the case with the rest of humankind.

If Hezekiah, who was told SET YOUR AFFAIRS IN ORDER, FOR YOU ARE GOING TO DIE; YOU WILL NOT GET WELL (2 Kings 20:1), did not refrain from pleading for mercy before the Holy One because he believed that even if a sharp sword is upon a person's neck, one should not refrain from [asking for] mercy, as it is said THEREUPON HEZE-KIAH TURNED HIS FACE TO THE WALL AND PRAYED TO THE LORD (Isa. 38:2), how much more should this be the case with the rest of Israel.

Another interpretation: THE LORD SAID TO ME, "ENOUGH" (Deut. 3:26). He said to him, "Moses, there is so much stored up for you in the world-to-come!" It is like a person who says to his friend, "I have so much stored up for you. Do not shame me."

Another interpretation: THE LORD SAID TO ME, "ENOUGH." It is like a person who says to his friend, "So-and-so has gone beyond the limits in his treatment of so-and-so."

NEVER SPEAK TO ME OF THIS MATTER AGAIN! GO UP TO THE SUMMIT OF PISGAH (Deut. 3:26–27). This was the source of R. Eliezar

---

your Master   God is Moses' Master, i.e., his Rabbi. The verse then means not "enough" but is God's statement to Moses that he must obey Him because He is his Master.

an example   Again the verse is understood as "You are a master" in the sense of an example for others.

Do not shame me   Do not make it appear to others that I am giving you nothing.

b. Jacob's teaching, "One prayer is more effective than a hundred good deeds, for with all of Moses' good deeds he had never been told GO UP and now, on this matter, he is told GO UP AND GAZE ABOUT, TO THE WEST (Deut. 3:27)."

This is the source of the teaching:

Those who are outside of the Land should turn toward the Land of Israel when they rise to pray, as it is said AND THEY PRAY TO YOU IN THE DIRECTION OF THEIR LAND (1 Kings 8:48).

Those who are in the Land of Israel should turn toward Jerusalem when they rise to pray, as it is said AND THEY PRAY TO YOU IN THE DIRECTION OF THE CITY (2 Chron. 6:34).

Those who are in Jerusalem should turn toward the Temple when they rise to pray as it is said TO PRAY TOWARD THIS HOUSE (2 Chron. 6:32).

Those who are within the Temple should direct their hearts toward the Holy of Holies when they rise to pray, as it is said AND THEN THEY PRAY TOWARD THIS PLACE (2 Chron. 6:26).

Thus those who are in the north face the south, those in the south face the north, those in the east face the west, those in the west face the east so that all Israel is praying toward one place!

AND GAZE ABOUT (Deut. 3:27). A parable. A king decreed that his son should not enter his bedchamber. When he entered the palace, the king drew him in and welcomed him. When he entered the dining room, he drew him in and spoke to him. When he started to enter the bedchamber, he said to him, "From here onward you are forbidden to enter." Thus Moses said to the Holy One, "All I can claim of the Land of Israel is just the width of the Jordan, these fifty cubits." [God] said to him LOOK AT IT WELL, FOR YOU SHALL NOT GO ACROSS (Deut. 3:27).

GIVE JOSHUA HIS INSTRUCTIONS (Deut. 3:28). "Instruction" always means imbuing with zeal, as it says THEN MOSES CALLED

One prayer is more effective Moses' plea to God results in God's granting him the possibility of seeing the Land of Israel, which is understood here as a favor to Moses, mitigating his punishment.

this is the source of the teaching: Those who are outside The fact that Moses, who is in Transjordan, on the east bank of the river, is commanded to face toward the west, is understood as instructing all outside the Land to face toward it when praying.

JOSHUA, AND SAID TO HIM IN THE SIGHT OF ALL ISRAEL: BE STRONG AND RESOLUTE (Deut. 31:7). BE STRONG in Torah AND RESOLUTE in good deeds.

FOR HE SHALL GO ACROSS AT THE HEAD OF THIS PEOPLE (Deut. 3:28). If he goes across ahead of them, they will go across, and if not they will not go across. AND HE SHALL ALLOT TO THEM THE LAND (Deut. 3:28). If he allots it, it will be allotted to them and if not, it will not be allotted. Thus you find that when they went to wage war against Ai, thirty six righteous men fell, as it is said THE MEN OF AI KILLED ABOUT THIRTY-SIX OF THEM, PURSUING THEM (Josh. 7:5). JOSHUA THEREUPON RENT HIS CLOTHES. HE AND THE ELDERS OF ISRAEL LAY UNTIL EVENING WITH THEIR FACES TO THE GROUND IN FRONT OF THE ARK OF THE LORD . . . "AH, LORD GOD!" CRIED JOSHUA. "WHY DID YOU LEAD THIS PEOPLE ACROSS THE JORDAN. O LORD, WHAT CAN I SAY AFTER ISRAEL HAS TURNED TAIL BEFORE ITS ENEMIES?" (Josh. 7:6–8). BUT THE LORD ANSWERED JOSHUA: "ARISE! WHY DO YOU LIE PROSTRATE? (Josh. 7:10). Is this not what I said to your master Moses from the start: If he goes across ahead of them, they will go across, and if not, they will not go across. If he allots it, it will be allotted to them and if not, it will not be allotted. You sent them but you did not go after them!"

COMMENTARY   *Interpretations and legends concerning the tragic fate of Moses are intertwined with comments concerning the Temple and prayer. A series of verses in which the word* mount *appears connects the Temple Mount with the mount on which Abraham offered up his son Isaac and then reminds us that this same mount will be the scene of the final establishment of God's kingdom in the end of days. The rule that all prayer is directed toward the Temple is connected to Moses' prayer.*

5. Deuteronomy 6:4, Sifre D. 31, 49

HEAR, O ISRAEL! THE LORD IS OUR GOD, THE LORD IS ONE (Deut. 6:4). Why is this said? Because it says SPEAK TO THE CHIL-

---

5. *Why is this said?* Why is the section addressed to Israel, another name for Jacob, rather than to the children of Abraham or Isaac? The first answer is that there is a general rule that speaking was to be done to the children of Israel. The legend that follows explains why.

DREN OF ISRAEL (Ex. 25:2). It does not say "Speak to the children of Abraham," or "Speak to the children of Isaac," but SPEAK TO THE CHILDREN OF ISRAEL.

Our father Jacob merited having the word [of God] directed to his children because our father Jacob worried throughout his lifetime, thinking "Woe is me! Perhaps unworthy children will come from me as they did from my fathers! . . . Ishmael came from Abraham; Esau came from Isaac. But as for me—let no unworthy children come from me as they did from my fathers!"

This too is the meaning of the verses JACOB THEN MADE A VOW, SAYING, "IF GOD REMAINS WITH ME, IF HE PROTECTS ME ON THIS JOURNEY THAT I AM MAKING, AND GIVES ME BREAD TO EAT AND CLOTHING TO WEAR, AND I RETURN SAFE TO MY FATHER'S HOUSE—THE LORD SHALL BE MY GOD" (Gen. 28:20–21). Could you possibly imagine that our father Jacob would say: IF HE . . . GIVES ME BREAD TO EAT AND CLOTHING TO WEAR . . . THE LORD SHALL BE MY GOD and if not, He shall not be my God? The verse really means AND I RETURN SAFE TO MY FATHER'S HOUSE—THE LORD SHALL BE MY GOD—in any case. What then does the verse THE LORD SHALL BE MY GOD really mean? "May He then cause His Name to rest upon me so that no unworthy children may not come from me at any time."

Thus too it says WHILE ISRAEL STAYED IN THAT LAND, REUBEN WENT AND LAY WITH BILHAH, HIS FATHER'S CONCUBINE; AND ISRAEL HEARD (Gen. 35:22). When Jacob heard this, he was shocked and thought, "Woe unto me! Perhaps unworthy ones have emerged among my children!" But the Holy One assured him that Reuben had repented, as it is said NOW THE SONS OF JACOB WERE TWELVE IN

He shall not be my God The simple reading of the text seems to indicate that Jacob is making his worship of the Lord conditional on what God does for him when he is in exile. The midrash rejects this.

really means If the Lord is his God is any case, there is no reason to state it. The real meaning is that it is a request on Jacob's part: through all of this, may "the Lord be my God" by making certain that I will have no children who are unworthy and who do not accept Him.

When Jacob heard this The force of ISRAEL HEARD is that he questioned the righteousness of his son Reuben and feared that his children were not worthy.

repented Once Reuben repented, he could be counted again in the number. All twelve were worthy.

NUMBER (Gen. 35:22). Did we not know that they were twelve? Rather this indicates that he was informed by the Holy One that Reuben had repented. We are taught Reuben fasted all his life, as it is said THEN THEY SAT DOWN TO A MEAL (Gen. 37:25). Could you possibly imagine that the brothers would sit down to a meal without their eldest brother? Therefore this teaches us that he fasted all his life. Eventually Moses accepted his repentance, as it is said MAY REUBEN LIVE AND NOT DIE (Deut. 33:6).

Thus too we find that when our father Jacob was about to depart this world, he called his children to him and reproved each one individually, as it is said AND JACOB CALLED HIS SONS . . . REUBEN, YOU ARE MY FIRSTBORN . . . SIMEON AND LEVI ARE A PAIR . . . YOU, O JUDAH, YOUR BROTHERS SHALL PRAISE . . . (Gen. 49:1,3,5,8). After he reproved each one individually, he called them all together. He said to them, "Do you have any doubts within your hearts about He Who Spoke and the world came into being?"

They said to him, "HEAR, O ISRAEL our father. Just as there are no doubts in your heart about He Who Spoke and the world came into being, thus there are no doubts within our hearts about He Who Spoke and the world came into being. Rather THE LORD IS OUR GOD, THE LORD IS ONE (Deut. 6:4)."

Therefore it says THEN ISRAEL BOWED AT THE HEAD OF THE BED (Gen. 47:31). Now did he really bow at the head of the bed? Rather he gave thanks and praise that no unworthy children had come from him. Some say that THEN ISRAEL BOWED AT THE HEAD OF THE BED (Gen. 47:31) means that he gave thanks that Reuben had repented.

Another interpretation: He said "Blessed is the Name of His glorious Majesty for ever and ever!" The Holy One said to him, "Jacob, all your life you wanted this—that your children should recite the Shema morning and evening."

Moses accepted his repentance   When Moses blessed the people before his death, he proclaimed that Reuben would live, i.e., had been accepted back by God because of his act of repentance.
Rather THE LORD IS OUR GOD   We, the sons of Jacob, accept the Lord as our God.
the head of the bed   The bed symbolizes the issue of his bed, his children. The second interpretation takes the word *head* to refer to Reuben, the firstborn of the bed.
the Shema—the three paragraphs from the Torah that are recited twice daily, morning and evening: Deut. 6:4–9, Deut. 9:13–21, and Num. 15:37–41. The title derives from the first word of the first verse: HEAR (shema), O ISRAEL.

DEUTERONOMY

COMMENTARY   *In this rather complex midrash, the liturgical recitation of the Shema, which includes a response not found in the Bible (Blessed is the Name of His glorious Majesty forever and ever!) is given a novel interpretation. Whereas in the Biblical context it is Moses who speaks to the people of Israel and instructs them concerning the nature of the Lord and the duty of loving Him, the Sages create a legend concerning the patriarch Jacob whose other name was Israel. It is Jacob who is addressed by his sons who assure Father Israel that they accept the One God, to which Jacob responds "Blessed is the Name..." Woven into the midrash are interpretations of other verses, all of which are intended to prove the original thesis that unlike his father and grandfather, Jacob had no unworthy children. In view of the fact that the people of Israel trace themselves to Jacob and his sons, while some of the nations consider themselves descendants of either Abraham's other son or Isaac's, this has theological implications as well.*

HEAR, O ISRAEL (Deut. 6:4). This was the source of the teaching: If one recited the Shema but cannot hear it himself, he has not fulfilled his obligation.

THE LORD IS OUR GOD (Deut. 6:4). Why is this said? Does it not say THE LORD IS ONE (Deut. 6:4)? What then is the meaning of OUR GOD (Deut. 4:6)? His Name rests especially upon us.

Similarly it says THREE TIME A YEAR ALL YOUR MALES SHALL APPEAR BEFORE THE SOVEREIGN LORD, THE GOD OF ISRAEL (Ex. 34:23). Why do I need the words THE GOD OF ISRAEL when it says THE SOVEREIGN LORD? His Name rests especially upon Israel.

Similarly it says THUS SAID THE LORD OF HOSTS, THE GOD OF ISRAEL (Jer. 32:14). Why do I need the words THE GOD OF ISRAEL when it says elsewhere BEHOLD I AM THE LORD, THE GOD OF ALL FLESH. IS ANYTHING TOO WONDROUS FOR ME? (Jer. 32:27). His Name rests especially upon Israel.

Similarly it says PAY HEED, MY PEOPLE, AND I WILL SPEAK,

---

fulfilled his obligation—of reciting the Shema.
Does it not say THE LORD IS ONE   If there is only one God, obviously He is also OUR GOD and there is no need to state it.
rests especially upon us   The phrase indicates that although He is the sole God and therefore the God of all, He has a special relationship and connection to Israel.

310

O ISRAEL, AND I WILL ARRAIGN YOU. I AM GOD, YOUR GOD (Ps. 50:7). My Name rests especially upon you.

Another interpretation: THE LORD IS OUR GOD (Deut. 6:4)—over us. THE LORD IS ONE (Deut. 6:4) over all humankind.

THE LORD IS OUR GOD in this world. THE LORD IS ONE in the world-to-come. Thus it says AND THE LORD SHALL BE KING OVER ALL THE EARTH; IN THAT DAY SHALL THE LORD BE ONE AND HIS NAME ONE (Zech. 14:9).

YOU SHALL LOVE THE LORD YOUR GOD (Deut. 6:5). Perform [the mitzvot] out of love. [Scripture] distinguished between one who performs out of love and one who performs out of fear. The reward of him who performs out of love is doubled and redoubled. When it says FEAR THE LORD YOUR GOD AND SERVE HIM (Deut. 10:20) we see that if one [serves] another because of fear, if the master becomes dependent upon him, he will simply leave him. You, however, should perform out of love.

Only in regard to God is there love where there is fear and fear where there is love.

Another interpretation: YOU SHALL LOVE THE LORD YOUR GOD. Make Him beloved to all humanity as did Abraham your father in the matter referred to in the verse AND THE SOULS THEY MADE IN HARAN (Gen. 12:5). Is it not so that if all humankind were to band together to create one gnat and endow it with a soul, it could not do so? Rather this verse teaches that our father Abraham converted people and brought them under the wings of the Divine Presence.

WITH ALL YOUR HEART (Deut. 6:5). With both your inclinations, the inclination to good and the inclination to evil.

---

if the master becomes dependent upon him   If the master loses his power and comes, instead, to need the slave, the slave no longer fears him and will not continue to serve him since he does so only because of coercion.

only in regard to God   Since both love and fear are commanded in the Torah, even though fear is the inferior motive, both must be needed. This makes the case of God different from that of human beings whom we either love or fear.

brought them under the wings of the Divine Presence—an expression meaning to convert to Judaism.

both your inclinations   There are two similar Hebrew words for "heart." One is written with one letter "bet," the other with two. In this verse the word with two letter bets is used. The interpretation is that this indicates that we are to love with two sections of the heart, i.e., our two basic inclinations.

Another interpretation: WITH ALL YOUR HEART. With all the heart that is within you. Your heart should not be divided in regard to God.

AND WITH ALL YOUR SOUL (Deut. 6:5). Even if He takes your soul. Thus it says IT IS FOR YOUR SAKE THAT WE ARE SLAIN ALL DAY LONG, THAT WE ARE REGARDED AS SHEEP TO BE SLAUGH-TERED (Ps. 44:23). R. Simeon b. Menasya says, "Can a man be killed daily? Rather the Holy One ascribes it to the righteous as if they were slain daily."

Simeon b. Azzai says, "WITH ALL YOUR SOUL (Deut. 6:5). Love Him until the soul is wrung from you."

R. Eliezer says, "If it says WITH ALL YOUR SOUL why does it add WITH ALL YOUR MIGHT (Deut. 6:5)? And if it says WITH ALL YOUR MIGHT, why does it say WITH ALL YOUR SOUL? For those whose bodies are more precious to them than their wealth, it says WITH ALL YOUR SOUL. For those whose wealth is more precious than their bodies, it says WITH ALL YOUR MIGHT."

R. Akiba says, "If it says WITH ALL YOUR SOUL, logic dictates that [you must love Him] WITH ALL YOUR MIGHT! What, then, does Scripture mean by WITH ALL YOUR MIGHT (meod)? Whatever measure (middah) He metes out to you, whether a measure of goodness or of punishment—(love Him)."

Similarly David says, I RAISE THE CUP OF DELIVERANCE AND INVOKE THE NAME OF THE LORD (Ps. 116:13); I CAME UPON TROUBLE AND SORROW AND I INVOKED THE NAME OF THE LORD (Ps. 116:3-4).

So too Job says THE LORD HAS GIVEN, AND THE LORD HAS TAKEN AWAY; BLESSED BE THE NAME OF THE LORD (Job 1:21)—for both the measure of goodness and the measure of punishment. What did his wife say to him? "YOU STILL KEEP YOUR INTEGRITY! BLASPHEME GOD AND DIE!" (Job 2:9). What did he reply? "TALK AS ONE OF THE SHAMELESS WOMEN TALKS! SHOULD WE AC-

---

heart that is within you   Dividing the Hebrew word for "your heart"—"levavecha"—into two words yields "lev becha," "the heart within you."

be divided   To have a divided heart means to have doubts.

R. Akiba—believes that since logic infers that if we are commanded to love God with our very lives, surely we are commanded to love Him with our possessions, the words WITH ALL YOUR MIGHT must refer not to possessions, but to something else.

TALK AS ONE OF THE SHAMELESS WOMEN TALKS—usually translated as a rebuke: "You talk like the shameless women talk." The midrash transforms it into a request by Job that his wife should be no worse than the women of the flood, the shameless women, who did not complain when punishment came upon them.

CEPT ONLY GOOD FROM GOD AND NOT ACCEPT EVIL? (Job 2:10) The people of the generation of the flood were vile during good times, but when punishment came upon them, they accepted it—whether they liked it or not. Is this not a matter of logic: If one who is vile during good times behaves well when punishment comes upon him, should not we, who are pleasant during good times, be pleasant when punishment comes upon us?" That is what he meant when he said "TALK AS ONE OF THE SHAMELESS WOMEN TALKS!" (Job 2:10). . . .

Furthermore, one should rejoice in chastisement more than in prosperity, for if a man is prosperous all his life, his sins are not forgiven. What causes forgiveness of sin? Chastisement.

R. Eliezer b. Jacob says, "It says FOR WHOM THE LORD LOVES, HE CHASTISES AS A FATHER THE SON WHOM HE FAVORS (Prov. 3:12). What causes the son to be favored by his father? Chastisement."

R. Meir says, "It says KNOW IN YOUR HEART THAT THE LORD YOUR GOD CHASTISES YOU JUST AS A MAN CHASTISES HIS SON (Deut. 8:5). You and your heart know what you have done and that the chastisement I have brought upon you does not measure up to the deeds you have done."

R. Jose b. R. Judah says, "Precious are chastisements for the name of God rests upon those who suffer, as it is said THE LORD YOUR GOD CHASTISES YOU (Deut. 8:5)."

R. Nathan b. R. Joseph says, "Just as a covenant is made concerning the Land so is a covenant made concerning chastisement, as it is said THE LORD YOUR GOD CHASTISES YOU (Deut. 8:5) and it says FOR THE LORD YOUR GOD IS BRINGING YOU INTO A GOOD LAND (Deut. 8:7)."

R. Simeon b. Yohai says, "Precious are chastisements for three wonderful gifts which all the nations of the world are anxious to have were given to Israel—and they were given only through chastisement. They are: Torah, the Land of Israel, and the world-to-come.

"What source teaches about Torah? FOR LEARNING WISDOM AND CHASTISEMENT (Prov. 1:2) and it says HAPPY IS THE MAN WHOM YOU CHASTISE, O LORD, THE MAN YOU INSTRUCT IN YOUR TORAH (Ps. 94:12).

---

chastisement—suffering.

"What about the Land of Israel? THE LORD YOUR GOD CHAS-
TISES YOU ... FOR THE LORD YOUR GOD IS BRINGING YOU
INTO A GOOD LAND (Deut. 8:5;7).

"The world-to-come? FOR THE COMMANDMENT IS A LAMP,
THE TEACHING IS A LIGHT, AND THE WAY TO LIFE IS THE
REBUKE THAT CHASTISES (Prov. 6:23). What is the way which brings
a man to the world-to-come? Chastisement."

R. Nehemiah says, "Precious are chastisements for just as the sacrifices
bring favor, so chastisement brings favor. Concerning sacrifices it says
THAT IT MAY BE FAVORABLE (nirzah) IN HIS BEHALF, IN EXPI-
ATION FOR HIM (Lev. 1:4). Concerning chastisement it says WHILE
THEY ATONE (yirzu) FOR THEIR INIQUITY (Lev. 26:43). Further-
more, chastisements bring favor even more than sacrifices, for sacrifices
involve money while chastisements involve the body. Thus it says SKIN
FOR SKIN—ALL THAT A MAN HAS HE WILL GIVE UP FOR HIS
LIFE (Job 2:4)."

Once R. Eliezer was ill and R. Tarphon, R. Joshua, R. Eleazar b. Azariah, and R. Akiba came to visit him.

R. Tarphon said to him, "My Master, you are more precious to Israel
than the orb of the sun, for the orb of the sun enlightens this world and you
enlighten this world and the world-to-come."

R. Joshua said to him, "My Master, you are more precious to Israel
than the gift of rain, for rain bestows life in this world and you bestow life
in this world and in the world-to-come."

R. Eleazar b. Azariah said to him, "My Master, you are more precious
to Israel than father and mother, for father and mother bring one into this
world and you bring people into this world and into the world-to-come."

R. Akiba said to him, "My Master, precious are chastisements."

R. Eliezer said to his disciples, "Prop me up." R. Eliezer sat up and said
to him, "Speak, Akiba."

[Akiba] said to him, "Behold it says MANASSEH WAS TWELVE
YEARS OLD WHEN HE BECAME KING, AND HE REIGNED
FIFTY-FIVE YEARS IN JERUSALEM. HE DID WHAT WAS DIS-
PLEASING TO THE LORD (2 Chron. 33:1–2) and it says THESE TOO
ARE PROVERBS OF SOLOMON, WHICH THE MEN OF KING
HEZEKIAH OF JUDAH COPIED (Prov. 25:1). Could you possibly imag-

---

the body The verse from Job demonstrates that it is easier to give up money or possessions
than one's body. A sacrifice is nothing more than one's possession, while suffering involve
one's body. Therefore it is an even more effective means of attaining favor.

314

ine that Hezekiah taught Torah to all Israel but did not teach Torah to his son Manasseh? But none of the instruction he gave him and none of the effort he invested in him had any effect—only chastisements as it is said THE LORD SPOKE TO MANASSEH AND HIS PEOPLE, BUT THEY WOULD NOT PAY HEED, SO THE LORD BROUGHT AGAINST THEM THE OFFICERS OF THE ARMY OF THE KING OF AS-SYRIA, WHO TOOK MANASSEH CAPTIVE IN MANACLES, BOUND HIM IN FETTERS, AND LED HIM OFF TO BABYLON. IN HIS DISTRESS, HE ENTREATED THE LORD HIS GOD AND HUMBLED HIMSELF GREATLY BEFORE THE GOD OF HIS FATHERS. HE PRAYED TO HIM, AND HE GRANTED HIS PRAYER, HEARD HIS PLEA, AND RETURNED HIM TO JERU-SALEM TO HIS KINGDOM (2 Chron. 33:10–13). Thus—precious are chastisements."

COMMENTARY   *This extended discussion investigates the role of love in the service of God. In contrast to fear, it endures at all times. We are, however, commanded to fear God as well. Usually fear and love cancel one another out, but in the case of God both apply. Nevertheless love is the higher motive and receives the greater reward. Love must be wholehearted and may also be interpreted as meaning to cause others to love God, that is, to bring them to worship Him as a part of the people of Israel. This is illustrated by the well-known midrash that Abraham "made souls" in the sense that he and Sarah converted all with whom they came in contact in Haran and then brought them with them on the journey to Canaan. The various phrases of the verse are interpreted as referring to the readiness to sacrifice many things, worldly possessions and even life itself. R. Akiba ingeniously connects the word might to the word measure on the basis of their similar sound and thus concludes that loving with all one's might means being ready to love God regardless of the "measure" he metes out, be it prosperity or suffering, and proves his point through examples from David and Job. Human suffering or chastisement is the heart of the theological dilemma of the monotheistic faith. If there is only one Power and that Power is the embodiment of goodness and morality, how may we account for suffering that comes upon the righteous individual? How did Israel explain the suffering that came upon it during the period of the first few centuries C.E., suffering that was all too intense? While this section may not give a satisfactory philosophical answer, it asserts that chastisements are not to be considered a sign of disfavor, but a means of coming closer to God and of attaining His favors. R. Eliezer is not comforted in his illness by the praise of his disciples, but R. Akiba interests and comforts him by insisting that suffering is precious to God. This alone gives it meaning.*

R. Meir says, "It says YOU MUST LOVE THE LORD YOUR GOD WITH ALL YOUR HEART (Deut. 6:5). Love him with all your heart as did your father Abraham, of whom it is said BUT YOU, ISRAEL, MY SERVANT, JACOB, WHOM I HAVE CHOSEN, SEED OF ABRAHAM WHO LOVES ME (Isa. 41:8)."

AND WITH ALL YOUR SOUL (Deut. 6:5)—as did Isaac who bound himself upon the altar as it is said AND ABRAHAM PICKED UP HIS KNIFE TO SLAY HIS SON (Gen. 22:10).

AND WITH ALL YOUR MIGHT (meodecha) (Deut. 6:5). Give thanks (modeh) unto Him as did your father Jacob as it is said I AM UNWORTHY OF ALL THE KINDNESS THAT YOU HAVE SO STEADFASTLY SHOWN YOUR SERVANT: WITH MY STAFF ALONE I CROSSED THIS JORDAN, AND NOW I HAVE BECOME TWO CAMPS (Gen. 32:11).

TAKE TO HEART THESE WORDS WITH WHICH I CHARGE YOU THIS DAY (Deut. 6:6). Rabbi Judah the Prince says, "Why is this said? When it says YOU MUST LOVE THE LORD WITH ALL YOUR HEART (Deut. 6:6) I am not informed how I should love God, therefore the verse says TAKE TO HEART THESE WORDS WHICH I CHARGE YOU THIS DAY (Deut. 6:6). If you put these words upon your heart, you will recognize He Who Spoke and the world came into being and you will cleave to His ways."

WHICH I CHARGE YOU THIS DAY (Deut. 6:6). You should not regard these words as some antiquated edict to which no one pays any attention, but as a new edict which everyone runs to read.

TAKE TO HEART (Deut. 6:6). This was the source of R. Josiah's teaching: One must bind his inclination with an oath, for thus we find that in every instance the righteous bind their inclination with an oath.

---

antiquated edict   Edicts were posted in writing in the town square. If one remained there a long time, no one paid any attention to it. The twice-daily proclamation of the Shema should be recited each time as if it were being heard for the first time.

inclination—referring to the two inclinations of human beings: the good inclination and the evil inclination. By taking an oath to do no evil, the righteous bind themselves by oath not to follow their evil inclination. With the wicked, the opposite is the case. Although the heart is the source of the inclinations, the specific connection to the verse is unclear. Material may be missing.

Concerning Abraham it says I SWEAR TO THE LORD, GOD MOST HIGH, CREATOR OF HEAVEN AND EARTH, THAT I WILL NOT TAKE SO MUCH AS A THREAD OR A SANDAL STRAP, OR ANYTHING THAT IS YOURS (Gen. 14:22–23).

Concerning Boaz it says I WILL REDEEM YOU MYSELF, AS THE LORD LIVES! LIE DOWN UNTIL MORNING (Ruth 3:13).

Concerning David it says AND DAVID WENT ON, "AS THE LORD LIVES, THE LORD HIMSELF WILL STRIKE HIM DOWN, OR HIS TIME WILL COME AND HE WILL DIE, OR HE WILL GO DOWN TO BATTLE AND PERISH" (1 Sam. 26:10).

Concerning Elisha it says AS THE LORD LIVES, WHOM I SERVE, I WILL NOT ACCEPT ANYTHING (2 Kings 5:16).

Just as the righteous bind their inclination in order to prevent [evil actions], so do the wicked bind their inclination in order to do [evil], as it is said AS THE LORD LIVES, I WILL RUN AFTER HIM AND GET SOMETHING FROM HIM (2 Kings 5:20).

IMPRESS THEM (shinantam) UPON YOUR CHILDREN (Deut. 6:7). They should be so finely honed in your mouth that when someone asks you about some matter, you will not stutter but be able to answer immediately. Thus it says SAY TO WISDOM, "YOU ARE MY SISTER," AND CALL UNDERSTANDING A KINSWOMAN (Prov. 7:4) and it says BIND THEM ON YOUR FINGERS; WRITE THEM ON THE TABLET OF YOUR MIND (Prov. 7:3) and it says YOUR ARROWS ARE SHARPENED (shenunim) (Ps. 45:6). What is the reward for this? THEY PIERCE THE BREAST OF THE KING'S ENEMIES; PEOPLE FALL AT YOUR FEET (Ps. 45:6). And it says LIKE ARROWS IN THE HAND OF A WARRIOR ARE SONS BORN TO A MAN IN HIS YOUTH (Ps. 127:4). What is said of them? HAPPY IS THE MAN WHO FILLS HIS QUIVER WITH THEM; THEY SHALL NOT BE PUT TO SHAME WHEN THEY CONTEND WITH THE ENEMY IN THE GATE (Ps. 127:5). . . .

UPON YOUR CHILDREN (Deut. 6:7)—your disciples. Thus we find that the disciples are always called "children," as it is said CHILDREN OF THE PROPHETS AT BETHEL CAME OUT TO ELISHA (2 Kings 2:

---

finely honed—sharp. The Hebrew word *shinantem* (impress them) also means to sharpen, as in Ps. 45:6 quoted below.

3). Were they really children of the prophets? Were they not disciples of the prophets? This teaches us that disciples are always called "children."

Thus it says THE CHILDREN OF THE PROPHETS WHO WERE AT JERICHO CAME OVER TO ELISHA (2 Kings 2:5). Were they children of the prophets? Were they not disciples of the prophets? Thus we find that disciples are called "children."

Thus we find that Hezekiah, king of Judah, taught all of the Torah to Israel and called them "children," as it is said NOW, MY SONS, DO NOT BE SLACK (2 Chron. 29:11).

Just as disciples are called "children," so the teacher is called "father," as it is said ELISHA SAW IT, AND HE CRIED OUT, "OH, FATHER, FATHER! ISRAEL'S CHARIOTS AND HORSEMEN!" (2 Kings 2:12). And it says ELISHA HAD BEEN STRICKEN WITH THE ILLNESS OF WHICH HE WAS TO DIE, AND KING JOASH OF ISRAEL WENT DOWN TO SEE HIM. HE WEPT OVER HIM AND CRIED, "FA-THER, FATHER! ISRAEL'S CHARIOTS AND HORSEMEN!" (2 Kings 13:14).

RECITE THEM (Deut. 6:5). Make them the essence [of your concern] and not merely incidental. They should be the exclusive subject of your discussions. Other matters should not be mixed with them, as some do. Lest you say "Now that I have studied the wisdom of Israel, I will go and study the wisdom of the nations," the verse says TO WALK IN THEM (Lev. 18: 4)—and not to be quit of them. Thus it says THEY WILL BE YOURS ALONE, OTHERS HAVING NO PART WITH YOU (Prov. 5:17) and WHEN YOU WALK IT WILL LEAD YOU; WHEN YOU LIE DOWN IT WILL WATCH OVER YOU; AND WHEN YOU ARE AWAKE IT WILL TALK WITH YOU (Prov. 6:22).

WHEN YOU WALK IT WILL LEAD YOU (Prov. 6:22)—in this world.

WHEN YOU LIE DOWN IT WILL WATCH OVER YOU (Prov. 6:22)—at the time of death.

AND WHEN YOU ARE AWAKE (Prov. 6:22)—in the days of the Messiah.

IT WILL TALK WITH YOU (Prov. 6:22)—in the world-to-come.

COMMENTARY   *These verses, which are part of the daily recitation of the Shema, are understood as emphasizing the importance of the study of*

ELISHA SAW IT—the chariot taking Elijah, his teacher, to heaven.

Torah. Those who teach Torah are given the status of a parent and their pupils are then called their "children." This midrash reflects the actual relationship between the Master and his disciples during the Tannaitic period (100 B.C.E.–200 C.E.). The Master was attended by his disciples who traveled with him, tended to his needs, and later transmitted his words and the incidents of his life. The obligations of the disciple to his Master were at least as great as those due a parent. The study of Torah is one of the central value-concepts of the Midrash. Here the demands for study are taken to the extreme—to the exclusion of study of any other material at all. The reality, however, was quite otherwise. In the most prominent rabbinic families Greek language and wisdom were studied and, as S. Lieberman has demonstrated in Hellenism and Jewish Palestine, the rabbis were well acquainted with this material. These statements, then, may be seen either as intended to emphasize the study of Torah and discourage the masses from undertaking other study, or as the statements of those rabbis, such as R. Simeon b. Yochai, who evidenced antagonism toward anything—including work— that would rob time from study of Torah.

6. Deuteronomy 11:10, Sifre D. 37, 69

FOR THE LAND WHICH YOU ARE ABOUT TO INVADE AND OCCUPY IS NOT LIKE THE LAND OF EGYPT FROM WHICH YOU HAVE COME (Deut. 11:10). This was said in order to pacify Israel when they left Egypt, for they said, "Perhaps the land to which we are going is not as beautiful as this land!" God said to them "FOR THE LAND WHICH YOU ARE ABOUT TO INVADE AND OCCUPY IS NOT LIKE THE LAND OF EGYPT." This teaches that the Land of Israel is superior to it.

Does that verse speak in praise of the Land of Israel or in praise of the Land of Egypt? The verse says NOW HEBRON WAS FOUNDED SEVEN YEARS BEFORE ZOAN OF EGYPT (Num. 13:22). What was Zoan? The royal city, as we see from the verse THOUGH HIS PRINCES ARE PRES-

---

6. *does that verse speak in praise* The verse simply states that the Land of Israel is not like the Land of Egypt. Can you infer from this that Israel is better than Egypt? Perhaps it is the other way around.

Zoan—the city of Tanis, which was Egypt's capital city during David's reign.

ENT IN ZOAN (Isa. 30:4). What was Hebron? The refuse of the Land of Israel, as we see from the verse SARAH DIED IN KIRIATH-ARBA—NOW HEBRON—THEN ABRAHAM ROSE FROM BESIDE HIS DEAD, AND SPOKE TO THE CHILDREN OF HETH, SAYING, "I AM A RESIDENT ALIEN AMONG YOU; SELL ME A BURIAL SITE AMONG YOU" (Gen. 23:2-4). It is a matter of logic: If Hebron, the refuse of the Land of Israel, is superior to the best of Egypt, which is the best of all lands, certainly the verse must be speaking in praise of the Land of Israel!

Should you say, "But the one who built this did not build that!" the verse says THE DESCENDANTS OF HAM: CUSH, MITZRAIM, PUT, AND CANAAN (Gen. 10:6). Ham, who built the one, also built the other. Would he have built the ugly one before the beautiful one? Rather he first built the beautiful one and then the ugly one.

A parable. A man built two great rooms, a beautiful one and an ugly one. He does not first build the ugly one and then the beautiful one, rather he builds the beautiful one and then uses the refuse from the first to build the ugly one afterward. Thus since Hebron was built first it was the more beautiful.

Thus you find that it is God's way that whatever is more precious comes first.

Torah, which is the most precious of all, was created before all else, as it is said THE LORD CREATED ME AT THE BEGINNING OF HIS COURSE, AS THE FIRST OF HIS WORKS OF OLD. IN THE DISTANT PAST WAS I FASHIONED, AT THE BEGINNING, AT THE ORIGIN OF EARTH (Prov. 8:22-23).

The refuse of the Land of Israel It was not good for anything except burials. The printed texts quote Gen. 35:27, which does not fit well in the context. The two verses have similar phrases and since manuscripts quote only a few words or letters, it was not unusual for an incorrect verse to be inserted.

If Hebron—which was the least of the Land of Israel, was built first, it was superior to Zoan. The supposition is that whatever was built first was better.

did not build that If two places are built by two different people, the older is not necessarily the better.

Ham—the father of both Mitzraim (Egypt) and Canaan built both cities. Surely he built the better one (Hebron) first.

DEUTERONOMY

The Temple, which is the most precious of all, was created before all else, as it is said O THRONE OF GLORY EXALTED FROM OF OLD, OUR SACRED SHRINE (Jer. 17:12).

The Land of Israel, which is the most precious of all, was created before all else, as it is said HE HAD NOT YET MADE EARTH AND FIELDS OR THE WORLD'S FIRST CLUMPS OF CLAY (Prov. 8:26). . . .

R. Simeon b. Yohai says, "WORLD means the Land of Israel, as it is said PLAYING WITH THE WORLD, HIS LAND (Prov. 8:31). Why is it called "world" (tebel)? Because it is enriched (metubellet) with everything. Every land has something which no other land has and the other lands have something that land does not have, but the Land of Israel lacks nothing, as it is said WHERE YOU WILL LACK NOTHING (Deut. 8:9)."

Another interpretation: Why is it called "world" (tebel)? Because of the spice (tebel) which is within it. Which spice is that? Torah, as it is said THERE IS NO TORAH AMONG THE NATIONS (Lam. 2:9). From this we deduce that the Torah is in the Land of Israel.

Thus you find that when Sannacherib came to entice Israel, what did he say to them? UNTIL I COME AND TAKE YOU AWAY TO A LAND LIKE YOUR OWN (2 Kings 18:32). He did not say "to a land more beautiful than your own," but TO A LAND LIKE YOUR OWN. Now this is a matter of logic. If one who came to praise his own land dared not speak disparagingly of the Land of Israel, certainly the verse must be speaking in praise of the Land of Israel.

R. Simeon b. Yohai says, "That man was a fool and did not know how to entice. A Parable. A man wants to betroth a woman. If he says to her, 'Your father is a king and I am a king; your father is wealthy and I am wealthy; your father gives you meat and fish to eat and old wine to drink and

---

The Temple—referring to the idea of the preexisting Heavenly Temple, which existed even before the creation of the world.

The Land of Israel According to the traditions of the Sages, Jerusalem is the navel of the world. All Creation began with the Land of Israel.

Why is it called "world"? Why is the Land of Israel called "world"?

THERE IS NO TORAH AMONG THE NATIONS The verse is actually HER KINGS AND HER LEADERS ARE AMONG THE NATIONS; TORAH IS NO MORE (Lam. 2:9). By changing the punctuation, the Sages achieved this new reading. Biblical texts are written without punctuation, thus making this easy to do.

when Sannacherib came—returning to the question about the praise of the Land of Israel.

I will give you meat and fish to eat and old wine to drink,' that is no entice-ment. What should he say to her? 'Your father is a commoner, but I am a king; your father is poor but I am wealthy; your father gives you greens and beans to eat, but I will give you meat and fish; your father gives you new wine, but I will give you old wine to drink; your father takes you to the bath on foot, but I shall take you there in a litter.' " Now this is a matter of logic. If one who came to praise his own land dared not speak disparagingly of the Land of Israel, certainly the verse must be speaking in praise of the Land of Israel.

It says SIDONIANS CALL HERMON SIRION, AND THE AMORITES CALL IT SENIR (Deut. 3:9) and elsewhere it says AS FAR AS MOUNT SION, THAT IS, HERMON (Deut. 4:48). Thus we see that it has four different names. What need can anyone possible have for so many? Four kingdoms were fighting over it. Each one said, "It shall be called by my name!" This is a matter of logic. If four kingdoms fought over the most insignificant of all the mountains of Israel, certainly the verse must be speak-ing in praise of the Land of Israel.

Similarly it says DANNAH, KIRIATH-SANNAH—THAT IS, DEBIR (Josh. 15:49) and elsewhere it says THE NAME OF DEBIR WAS FOR-MERLY KIRIATH-SEPHER (Josh. 15:15). Thus we see that it has three different names. What need can anyone possibly have for so many? Three kingdoms were fighting over it. Each one said, "It shall be called by my name!" This is a matter of logic. If three kingdoms fought over the most insignificant of all the cities of Israel, certainly the verse must be speaking in praise of the Land of Israel.

Similarly it says ASCEND THESE HEIGHTS OF ABARIM, MOUNT NEBO (Deut. 32:49) and elsewhere it says GO UP TO THE SUMMIT OF PISGAH (Deut. 3:27). Thus we see that it has three different names. What need can anyone possibly have for so many? Three kingdoms were fighting over it. Each one said, "It shall be called by my name!" This is a matter of logic. If three kingdoms fought over the most insignificant of the mountains of the Land of Israel, certainly the verse must be speaking in praise of the Land of Israel.

If four kingdoms fought over the most insignificant of all the mountains of Israel This would surely prove that the Land of Israel is a superior land.

It says I GAVE YOU A DESIRABLE LAND—THE FAIREST HERITAGE OF ALL THE NATIONS (Jer. 3:19). A land filled with magnificent fortifications for kings and governments, for any king or government which does not possess [a fortification] in the Land of Israel says, "I have accomplished nothing!" . . . It is the same as is currently done in Rome. Any king or government which does not possess [a portion] in Rome says, "I have accomplished nothing!" . . .

A DESIRABLE (zevi) LAND (Jer. 3:19). Just as the deer (zevi) is swifter of foot than any wild or domestic animal, so the fruits of the Land of Israel are swifter to grow than all the fruits of other lands.

Another interpretation: Just as the hide of the deer, when separated from the flesh, cannot contain it, so the Land of Israel cannot contain its fruits [when Israel observes the Torah].

Just as the flesh of the deer is easier to digest than that of any other animal or beast, so the fruit of the Land of Israel is easier to digest than that of all other lands. If they are easy to digest, does this mean that they are not rich? The verse says A LAND FLOWING WITH MILK AND HONEY (Deut. 11:9)—rich as milk and sweet as honey. Thus it says LET ME SING FOR MY BELOVED, A SONG OF MY LOVER ABOUT HIS VINEYARD. MY BELOVED HAD A VINEYARD ON A FRUITFUL HILL (be-keren ben shemen) (Isa. 5:1). Just as the horn (keren) is the highest part of the ox, so the land of Israel is the highest of the lands. Perhaps it means that just as the horn is the refuse of the ox, so the Land of Israel is the refuse of all the lands. Therefore the verse says A FRUITFUL HILL (be-keren ben shemen). The Land of Israel is rich (shemenah).

This teaches that whatever is higher is of greater excellence. Since the Land of Israel is the highest of all, it is also the most excellent of all, as it is said LET US BY ALL MEANS GO UP, AND WE SHALL GAIN POSSESSION OF IT (Num. 13:30). THEY WENT UP AND SCOUTED THE LAND (Num. 13:21). THEY WENT UP INTO THE NEGEB (Num. 13:22). THEY WENT UP FROM EGYPT (Gen. 45:25).

The Temple, which is the highest of all, is of greater excellence, as it is said YOU SHALL ARISE AND GO UP TO THE PLACE WHICH

---

magnificent fortifications—probably based on the similarity between the words *zevi* (desirable) and *zava* (army).

cannot contain it   The hide shrivels up.

The Land of Israel is rich—and therefore cannot be considered refuse.

This teaches that whatever is higher   The reference to the horn of the ox in Isa. 5:1 teaches that the highest part is the best.

THE LORD YOUR GOD HAS CHOSEN (Deut. 17:8). AND THE MANY PEOPLES SHALL GO AND SHALL SAY: "COME, LET US GO UP TO THE MOUNT OF THE LORD" (Isa. 2:3). FOR THE DAY IS COMING WHEN WATCHMEN SHALL PROCLAIM ON THE HEIGHTS OF EPHRAIM: COME, LET US GO UP TO ZION, TO THE LORD OUR GOD! (Jer. 31:6).

COMMENTARY *This is a part of a long section on the topic of the praise of the Land of Israel. Many different ideas and midrashim were put together in order to create a paean of praise to the Land, and this at a time when the Land had undergone warfare and was in an impoverished state. Thus the physical and social reality stood in stark contrast to the Biblical descriptions of the wonderful land and its prosperity. The Midrash did not solve that problem by logic but by asserting that all the Biblical descriptions were correct and even going beyond them in praise of the Land. The people of Israel were to keep before them at the most difficult time the vision of what the Land was "really" like so that in the eyes of faith it would retain its luster. Undoubtedly this was also intended to help stem the tide of those who considered leaving because of the difficult conditions. Note the beautiful structure of the section. It begins with a series of proofs that the Biblical verse comparing Israel to Egypt means to indicate that the Land of Israel is superior to Egypt; it then asserts that the Land of Israel is the most precious and the most ancient of all and brings in subthemes of the Temple and the Torah, both of which are connected to the Land. It asserts that kingdoms fight over it because of its preciousness, that it contains everything that is rich and good, and concludes by bringing a chorus of verses, all of which contain the words going up, which serves as a crescendo to uplift the spirit.*

7. Deuteronomy 11:10, Sifre D. 38, 74

Once R. Eliezer, R. Joshua, and R. Zadok were reclining at the wedding feast of the son of Rabban Gamliel. Rabban Gamliel mixed a cup [of wine] for R. Eliezer, but the latter did not want to take it from him. R. Joshua, however, took it. R. Eliezer said to him, "What is this, Joshua? Is it proper that we recline and permit Gamliel son of Rabbi to stand and serve us?"

---

7. *mixed a cup of wine* Wine was served by mixing water with essence.
Rabban Gamliel—their superior.
son of Rabbi—an honorific title.

R. Joshua answered him, "Let him serve us. After all, Abraham, the greatest man in the world, served the ministering angels when he thought that they were idol-worshiping Arabs, as it is said LOOKING UP, HE SAW THREE MEN STANDING NEAR HIM... HE SAID, MY LORDS, IF IT PLEASE YOU... LET ME FETCH A MORSEL OF BREAD (Gen. 18:2–5). This is a matter of logic: If Abraham, the greatest man in the world, served ministering angels when he thought that they were idol-worshiping Arabs, shall not Gamliel son of Rabbi serve us?"

R. Zadok said to them, "You have abandoned the honor of God to busy yourselves with the honor of human beings! If He Who Spoke and the world came into being causes the wind to blow, brings up clouds, causes rain to fall, raises up plants, and thus sets a table before each and every one, shall not Gamliel son of Rabbi serve us?"

COMMENTARY   *Here we have another example of the way in which interpretation of Scripture took place in the most informal of settings, in this case a wedding feast, and then became part of the transmitted tradition. The tale is intended, however, not merely to interpret the story of Abraham but to teach proper conduct and attitudes, to inculcate the value-concept of proper treatment of strangers, and to emphasize the aspect of God as provider for all.*

8. Deuteronomy 11:13, Sifre D. 41, 85

MOSES SUMMONED ALL THE ISRAELITES AND SAID TO THEM: HEAR, O ISRAEL, THE LAWS AND NORMS THAT I PROCLAIM TO YOU THIS DAY! STUDY THEM AND OBSERVE THEM FAITHFULLY! (Deut. 5:1). Once R. Tarfon, R. Akiba, and R. Jose the Galilean were reclining at Bet Aris in Lod when this question was asked of them: Which is greater, study or performance?

R. Tarphon said, "Performance is greater."

R. Akiba said, "Study is greater."

---

thought they were idol-worshiping Arabs   The verse calls them MEN indicating that Abraham had no idea that they were angels. Therefore his treatment of them must be seen as his normal way of attending to passers-by.

honor of God   God's honor is greater than that of man. If we wish to talk about giving up honor to an inferior, let us speak about God rather than Abraham.

---

8. *Bet Aris*—a village near the city of Lod (Lydda).

They all agreed that study is greater because it leads to performance.

R. Jose the Galilean said, "Study is greater for it preceded the dough offering by forty years, tithes by fifty-four years, Sabbatical years by sixty-one years, and Jubilees by one hundred and three years. Just as punishment for neglect of study is greater than punishment for neglect of performance, so greater reward is given for study than for performance, as it is said AND TEACH THEM TO YOUR CHILDREN—RECITING THEM (Deut. 11:19) after which it says TO THE END THAT YOU AND YOUR CHILDREN MAY ENDURE (Deut. 11:21) [while concerning performance] it says HE GAVE THEM THE LAND OF NATIONS; THEY INHERITED THE WEALTH OF PEOPLES, THAT THEY MIGHT KEEP HIS LAWS AND OBSERVE HIS TEACHINGS (Ps. 105:44–45).

COMMENTARY   *Religions are frequently based on performance, which can become a kind of behavioralism. If Judaism is replete with actions that must be performed or avoided (the traditional number is 613), then religious achievement could be measured in the number of these that are fulfilled. By stressing study these Sages indicate both that study is itself a value and a way of following God and that study alone leads to performance that is meaningful. That is the meaning of the compromise formula. Performance is a dead end. Study, on the other hand, leads to performance, establishes and enriches it.*

9. Deuteronomy 11:15, Sifre D. 43, 94

It once happened that Rabban Gamliel, R. Joshua, R. Eleazar b. Azariah, and R. Akiba were approaching the city of Rome. When they were one hundred and twenty miles away they heard the murmuring of the great metropolis. They began weeping, but R. Akiba laughed.

They said to him, "Akiba—why is it that we weep but you laugh?!"

He said to them, "As for you—why did you weep?"

They said to him, "Should we not weep when these pagans who sacrifice to idols and bow down to images dwell in security, peace, and serenity

---

preceded the dough offering by forty years   This could not be offered until they reached the Land of Israel. Study began once there was a revelation at Sinai.

tithes—were not practiced until the Land had been conquered and divided among the tribes fourteen years later. So too with the other practices mentioned.

while the House which is our God's footstool has become a burnt ruin and a refuge for wild beasts?"

He said to them, "That is exactly why I laughed! If this is what [God] grants to those who anger Him, how much more will He grant to those who fulfill His will!"

Another time they were going up to Jerusalem. When they came to Mt. Scopus, they rent their garments. When they came to the Temple Mount and saw a jackal running out of the Holy of Holies, they began weeping but R. Akiba laughed.

They said to him, "Akiba, you never fail to astonish us. Here we are weeping and you are laughing!"

He said to them, "As for you, why do you weep?"

They said to him, "Should we not weep when a jackal runs out of the place of which it is written ANY OUTSIDER WHO ENCROACHES SHALL BE PUT TO DEATH (Num. 1:51)? We are the living embodiment of the verses BECAUSE OF THIS OUR HEARTS ARE SICK, BECAUSE OF THESE OUR EYES ARE DIMMED: BECAUSE OF MOUNT ZION, WHICH LIES DESOLATE; JACKALS PROWL OVER IT (Lam. 5:17–18)!"

He said to them, "That is exactly why I laughed. It says AND CALL RELIABLE WITNESSES, THE PRIEST URIAH AND ZECHARIAH SON OF JEBERECHIAH, TO WITNESS FOR ME (Isa. 8:2). Now what does Uriah have to do with Zechariah? What did Uriah say? ZION SHALL BE PLOWED AS A FIELD, JERUSALEM SHALL BECOME HEAPS OF RUINS AND THE TEMPLE MOUNT A SHRINE IN THE WOODS (Jer. 26:18). And what did Zechariah say? THUS SAID THE LORD OF HOSTS: THERE SHALL YET BE OLD MEN AND WOMEN IN THE SQUARES OF JERUSALEM, EACH WITH STAFF IN HAND BECAUSE OF THEIR GREAT AGE. AND THE SQUARES

---

9. *our God's footstool*—the Temple.

those who anger Him—the Romans.

those who fulfill His will—the people of Israel. Thus there is reason for hope.

going up to Jerusalem Jews could no longer live there. They went for the purpose of mourning over the ruins of the Temple.

rent their garments—an act of mourning performed when seeing the ruins of the Temple, which were visible from Mt. Scopus.

Uriah Jer. 26:20 records that another prophet named Uriah prophesied the same things as Jeremiah.

OF THE CITY SHALL BE CROWDED WITH BOYS AND GIRLS PLAYING IN THE SQUARES (Zech. 8:4). God says, 'These are My two witnesses. If the words of Uriah are fulfilled, so shall the words of Zechariah be fulfilled, but if the words of Uriah are not fulfilled, so the words of Zechariah shall not be fulfilled.' I rejoiced that the words of Uriah have finally been fulfilled, for in the future the words of Zechariah will be fulfilled!"

Thus did they say to him, "Akiba, you have comforted us."

COMMENTARY   *These poignant tales, whatever their legendary aspects, reflect the historical reality of the end of the first century and the beginning of the second century C.E. when Sages were sent on missions to Rome both to meet with Roman officials on affairs of the Jewish community in the Land of Israel and to confer with their fellow Jews who dwelt in Rome. These stories also capture the feeling of despair that even the Sages felt when seeing the might of Rome, the pagan giant that had been able to successfully destroy the Temple without coming to harm. The figure of Akiba looms above the others as the man of deep hope and conviction whose faith proved well founded in the long run.*

10. Deuteronomy 11:22, Sifre D. 49, 114

WALKING IN ALL HIS WAYS (Deut. 11:22). This refers to the ways of God: THE LORD! THE LORD!—A GOD COMPASSIONATE AND GRACIOUS (Ex. 34:6). It says BUT EVERYONE WHO IS CALLED BY THE NAME OF THE LORD SHALL ESCAPE (Joel 3:5). Now how is it possible for a person to be called by the Name of God? Rather—

as God is called "compassionate," so should you be compassionate;

as the Holy One is called "gracious," so should you be gracious—as it is said THE LORD IS GRACIOUS (hanun) AND COMPASSIONATE (Ps. 145:8) and grants His favors freely (hinam);

as God is called "righteous," as it is said FOR THE LORD IS RIGHTEOUS; HE LOVES RIGHTEOUS DEEDS (Ps. 11:7)—so should you be righteous;

as God is called "kind" as it is said FOR I AM KIND—DECLARES THE LORD (Jer. 3:12)—so should you be kind;

therefore it says BUT EVERYONE WHO IS CALLED BY THE NAME OF THE LORD SHALL ESCAPE (Joel 3:5) and EVERYONE THAT IS CALLED BY MY NAME (Isa. 43:7) and THE LORD MADE EVERYTHING FOR HIS PURPOSE (Prov. 16:4).

AND HOLDING FAST TO HIM (Deut. 11:22). How is it possible for a person to ascend on high and hold fast to fire? For is it not said elsewhere FOR THE LORD YOUR GOD IS A CONSUMING FIRE (Deut. 4:24) AND HIS THRONE WAS TONGUES OF FLAME: ITS WHEELS WERE BLAZING FIRE (Dan. 7:9)? Rather—hold fast to the Sages and their disciples and I will consider it as if you had ascended on high and received [the Torah] there—and not as if you had ascended and received it in peace but as if you had done battle to receive it. Thus it says YOU ASCENDED ON HIGH, HAVING TAKEN CAPTIVES (Ps. 68:19).

Those who expound *haggadot* say, "Do you want to come to know He Who Spoke and the world came into being? Learn *haggadot*—for by doing that you will come to know He Who Spoke and the world came into being and hold fast to His ways."

COMMENTARY   *The concept of the Imitation of God is expounded in these passages. God has no "life" in the ordinary sense of that term, therefore one cannot be asked to live as He does, but He does have ways or attributes. One who wishes to be like God, as it were, to cling to Him, to be associated with His Name, may do so by performing the deeds that are attributed to Him: compassion, righteousness, and kindness. The way in which this can be best achieved is by heeding the Sages and their teachings. Mysticism was also rife during this same period of time and literature survives describing the mystic voyage to attain the Presence of God, a voyage fraught with danger. This midrash may be cautioning the untrained individual against dabbling in such practices, assuring him that attending the Sages carries the same reward as mystic practices. Of a similar nature is the advice that the best way to come to an understanding and a closeness to God is through the study of the sayings and teaching of the Sages, the nonlegal interpretations, parables, and legends known as *haggadah*.*

11. Deuteronomy 31:14, Sifre D. 304, 323

THE LORD SAID TO MOSES: THE TIME IS DRAWING NEAR FOR YOU TO DIE (Deut. 31:14). R. Simeon b. Yohai says, "Blessed is the

---

10. *hold fast to fire* Since God is described as fire, holding fast to Him means holding onto fire, an obvious impossibility.

done battle—as Moses did, according to the legends, going through the dangers of fire and water to receive the Torah.

haggadot—the nonlegal portions of the tradition.

truthful Judge, the Master of all that happens, before whom there is no corruption or favoritism. Thus it says TRUST NO FRIEND, RELY ON NO INTIMATE (Micah 7:5)."

Moses replied to the Holy One, "Master of the universe, since I depart this world with great agony, show me a trustworthy man who will take charge of Israel so that I can take leave of them in peace." Thus it says WHO SHALL GO OUT BEFORE THEM AND COME IN BEFORE THEM (Num. 27:17).

[This anticipates what is written] WE HAVE A LITTLE SISTER WHOSE BREASTS ARE NOT YET FORMED (Song 8:8)—four kingdoms will rule over Israel, and [Israel] will have no wise or understanding leader. This will be in the days of Ahab, king of Israel, and Jehoshaphat, king of Judah, when ALL ISRAEL IS SCATTERED OVER THE HILLS LIKE SHEEP WITHOUT A SHEPHERD (1 Kings 22:17)—SO THAT THE LORD'S COMMUNITY MAY NOT BE LIKE SHEEP THAT HAVE NO SHEPHERD (Num. 27:17).

AND THE LORD ANSWERED MOSES, "SINGLE OUT JOSHUA SON OF NUN" (Num. 27:18). "SINGLE OUT someone as heroic as yourself." The Holy One answers Moses and says to him, "Give Joshua a spokesman and let him propound questions, expound and convey instructions during your lifetime, so that when you depart this world Israel will not say to him 'During the lifetime of your master, you did not dare speak—and now you speak?' "

Others say: He raised him up from the ground and sat him between his knees. Moses and Israel would lift up their heads to hear Joshua's words. What would he say? "Blessed is the Lord who gave Torah to Israel through Moses our teacher." Thus did Joshua speak.

R. Nathan says, "Moses was deeply saddened that none of his sons was appointed. The Holy One said to him, 'Why should you be so sad that none of your sons were appointed? Are not Aaron's children like your own? The

---

11. *truthful Judge*—or the faithful Judge, i.e., God. This is the formula that is recited on hearing of a death or of any calamity. It indicates that one accepts God's judgment. Here it is the acceptance of the justice of God's decree against Moses.

TRUST NO FRIEND The friend here is God. He will not play favorites. All men, even Moses, must die.

WE HAVE A LITTLE SISTER Moses fears that after his death the situation will be like that alluded to in this verse: a people without leadership.

man whom I shall appoint over Israel will have to go and stand at Eleazar's doorway.' A parable. This may be likened to a human king whose son was not fit to rule. He took the kingship from him and gave it to the son of a friend. He said to him, 'Even though I have conferred greatness upon you, go and stand at the doorway of my son.' Thus the Holy One said to Joshua, 'Even though I have conferred greatness upon you, go and stand at the doorway of Eleazar,' as it is said BUT HE SHALL STAND BEFORE ELEAZAR THE PRIEST (Num. 27:21).

"At that time Moses recovered his strength and would encourage Joshua in the sight of all Israel, as it is said THEN MOSES CALLED JOSHUA AND SAID TO HIM IN THE SIGHT OF ALL ISRAEL: BE STRONG AND RESOLUTE (Deut. 31:7). He said to him, 'This people that I am giving you are still as young kids. They are infants. Do not be overly strict with them about their actions, for even their Master was not strict with them about their actions. Thus it says I FELL IN LOVE WITH ISRAEL WHEN HE WAS STILL A CHILD (Hos. 11:1).' "

R. Nehemiah says, "[He said,] 'I am not permitted to, but had I permission I would bring them in to dwell near the tents of the shepherds.' " ...

It is told of Rabban Johanan b. Zakkai that he was once riding on an ass followed by his disciples when he saw a young woman collecting grains of barley from under the feet of animals belonging to Arabs. When she saw Rabban Johanan b. Zakkai she covered herself with her hair and stood before him.

She said to him, "My Master, give me provisions."

He said to her, "Whose daughter are you?"

She said to him, "The daughter of Nakdimon b. Gurion am I." She

---

Eleazar's doorway—the High Priest, son of Aaron. Since Joshua, the new leader, would have to consult with Moses' kin, Eleazar, Moses could be consoled that his own sons did not inherit his position.

young kids This section is based on the verse IF YOU DO NOT KNOW, O FAIREST OF WOMEN, GO FOLLOW THE TRACKS OF THE SHEEP, AND GRAZE YOUR KIDS BY THE TENTS OF THE SHEPHERDS (Song 1:8). Joshua is the shepherd, Israel the kids, while the tents of the shepherds refer to the places in the Land of Israel where the patriarchs dwelt.

covered herself with her hair—an indication of her poverty. Her garments did not cover her properly nor did she have the headcovering worn by married women.

Nakdimon—a man whose great wealth was legendary. At one point he had enough food to feed the entire population.

continued, "Do you not remember, my Master, that you signed my wedding contract?"

Rabban Johanan b. Zakkai said to his disciples, "I did indeed sign this woman's wedding contract and I read in it that one million gold *dinar* were to be paid her by her father-in-law's family and her own family. When [her family] went to worship at the Temple Mount, fine woolen carpets were spread out under their feet. Thus would they enter, worship, and return to their homes in great joy. All my life I sought to understand the verse IF YOU DO NOT KNOW, O FAIREST OF WOMEN, GO FOLLOW THE TRACKS OF THE SHEEP, AND GRAZE YOUR KIDS BY THE TENTS OF THE SHEPHERDS (Song 1:8). Read not "gediyotayich"— YOUR KIDS—but "geviyotayich"—your bodies! When Israel fulfills the will of God no nation or kingdom can rule over them, but when Israel does not fulfill the will of God, He delivers them into the hand of a lowly nation. Not even into the hands of a lowly nation, but under the feet of animals belonging to a lowly nation!"

COMMENTARY   *In the hands of the Sages the appointment of Joshua as Moses' successor takes on the coloring of their own practices. Moses, who was given the title "Rabbenu" (our Master) in rabbinic literature, is like an elder Sage who wishes to confer authority on a younger disciple. He gives him a spokesman, someone with a loud voice who will convey his words to the assembled group. He raises him from the ground. When the Sages assembled, the Master sat above them while the students literally sat at their feet. Whatever the Master said was repeated by a special person whose job it was to repeat the Master's words in a loud voice. The quotation from Song 1:8 brings up a poignant story in which the same verse was quoted by Rabban Johanan b. Zakkai. The story probably takes place around the year 70 C.E. when famine devastated the people. Even the wealthiest were reduced to begging for food. THE FAIREST OF WOMEN is interpreted as both this one young woman and the whole people of Israel. IF YOU DO NOT KNOW means: If you, Israel, do not know enough to follow God's ways, you will then FOLLOW THE TRACKS OF THE SHEEP, follow after animals in order to forage for food and GRAZE YOUR KIDS—try to feed your bodies by getting food from THE SHEPHERDS—the Arabs to whom the animals belong. Rabban Johanan b. Zakkai, who was smuggled out of Jerusalem in a coffin and persuaded Vespasian to grant him and other Sages a safe haven in the coastal town of Jabneh, was the outstanding spiritual figure of the time and an opponent of the revolt whose results, he rightly predicted, would be catastrophic.*

In one year three righteous people died—Moses, Aaron, and Miriam—and after Moses died, Israel had no more pleasure, as it is said BUT I LOST THE THREE SHEPHERDS IN ONE MONTH (Zech. 11:8). Did they die in one month? Was it not one year that they all died? It is as it is said THE WELL WHICH THE CHIEFTAINS DUG, WHICH THE NOBLES OF THE PEOPLE STARTED (Num. 21:18)—indicating that after Miriam died, the well ceased but then was restored through the merit of Moses and Aaron. Aaron died and the pillar of cloud ceased as well, and both of them were restored through the merit of Moses. Moses died, and all three disappeared and never returned. At that time Israel was scattered and devoid of all gifts.

[When Aaron died] all Israel gathered before Moses and said to him, "Where is your brother Aaron?"

He said to them, "He has been hidden away for the world to come."

They did not believe him and said to him, "We know that you are cruel. Could it be that he said something improper to you and you decreed that he should die?"

What did the Holy One do? He brought Aaron's bier and suspended it in the heavens. The Holy One stood and eulogized him while the ministering angels responded after Him. What did they say? PROPER RULINGS WERE IN HIS MOUTH, AND NOTHING PERVERSE WAS ON HIS LIPS. HE SERVED ME WITH COMPLETE LOYALTY AND HELD THE MANY BACK FROM INIQUITY (Mal. 2:6).

At that time the Holy One said to the Angel of Death, "Go and bring Me the soul of Moses."

He went and stood before him and said to him, "Moses—give me your soul."

He said to him, "Where I sit, you have no right to stand—and you dare say to me 'Give me your soul!?' " He rebuked him and he left crestfallen.

THE WELL WHICH THE CHIEFTAINS DUG   The Hebrew text has Ps. 47:10, which also contains the words "the chieftains" but which is inappropriate here.

all three   The third gift was the manna. Since all three gifts disappeared at once, it was as if Israel had lost all three of her leaders in one month. This is the interpretation of the verse from Zechariah.

and eulogized him   God eulogizes Aaron and demonstrates to the people that Moses was not responsible for Aaron's disappearance.

The Angel of Death went and reported to the Mighty One. Once again the Holy One said to him, "Go and bring Me his soul."

He went to [Moses'] place to seek him, but could not find him. He went to the Sea and said to it, "Moses—have you seen him?"

[The Sea] responded, "Since the day when he caused Israel to pass through me, I have not seen him."

He went to the mountains and hills and said to them, "Moses—have you seen him?"

They responded, "Since the day when Israel received the Torah on Mount Sinai, we have not seen him."

He went to Gehenna and said to her, "Moses—have you seen him?"

She replied, "His name have I heard; him I have not seen."

He went to the ministering angels and said to them, "Moses—have you seen him?"

They responded, "Go to humankind."

He went to Israel and said to them, "Moses—have you seen him?"

They responded, "God has known his way and has hidden him away for the world-to-come and no creature knows his whereabouts." As it is said HE BURIED HIM IN THE VALLEY IN THE LAND OF MOAB, NEAR BETH-PEOR; AND NO ONE KNOWS HIS BURIAL PLACE TO THIS DAY (Deut. 34:6).

Upon the death of Moses, Joshua wept, wailed, and mourned over him with great bitterness and said, "My father, my father! My master, my master! My father—who raised me. My master—who taught me Torah." And he went on mourning him for a long time until finally the Holy One said to him, "Joshua—how long do you intend to go on mourning? Did his death affect only you? Did it not affect Me most of all? For from the day of his death there has been great mourning before Me, as it is said MY LORD GOD OF HOSTS SUMMONED ON THAT DAY TO WEEPING AND LA-MENTING, TO TONSURING AND GIRDING WITH SACK-CLOTH (Isa. 22:12). He has been assured that he has a place in the world-

---

Gehenna—the nether world, a place of punishment named after a valley near Jerusalem where children were offered to Molech (2 Chron. 28:3, 33:6) and which later became a garbage dump (2 Kings 23:10).

hidden him away   The souls of the righteous are stored at the throne of God until the time of the resurrection of the dead.

to-come." Thus it is said THE LORD SAID TO MOSES: YOU ARE SOON TO LIE WITH YOUR FATHERS AND ARISE (Deut. 31:16).

COMMENTARY   *The deaths of the great leaders are expounded upon here. The tale of God's defense of Moses is most ingenious. For all his greatness, Moses was not beloved by the people. He was perceived by them as harsh and cruel. Although the Torah does indeed depict Moses as the leader who speaks sharply to the people, even while defending them before God, this midrash and many like it pick up on the frequent disharmony between Moses and the people and make it the basis for this dramatic confrontation. From a literary point of view, the story told here of the death of Moses is even more masterful and is full of poignancy. In order to emphasize the greatness of Moses, the dread Angel of Death is made a figure of fun. He cannot stand against Moses' rebuke and after that, he cannot even locate his intended victim. Death's search gives the midrash the opportunity to take us on a journey back through the important places in Moses' career, thus reminding us of his greatness. In the end, it is God alone, and not His messenger, who can take the soul of such a person. And it is God who mourns him more than does any human being.*

12. Deuteronomy 32:1, Sifre D. 306, 328

GIVE EAR, O HEAVENS, LET ME SPEAK (Deut. 32:1). R. Meir says, "When Israel was worthy, they gave witness to themselves, as it is said THEREUPON JOSHUA SAID TO THE PEOPLE, 'YOU ARE WITNESSES AGAINST YOURSELVES THAT YOU HAVE BY YOUR OWN ACT CHOSEN TO SERVE THE LORD' (Josh. 24:22). When they corrupted themselves, as it is said EPHRAIM SURROUNDS ME WITH DECEIT, THE HOUSE OF ISRAEL WITH GUILE (Hos. 12:1), He called upon the tribes of Judah and Benjamin to witness against them, as it is said NOW, THEN, DWELLERS OF JERUSALEM AND MEN OF JUDAH, YOU BE THE JUDGES BETWEEN ME AND MY VINEYARD: WHAT MORE COULD HAVE BEEN DONE FOR MY VINEYARD? (Isa. 5:3–4).

AND ARISE   The verse actually reads: YOU ARE SOON TO LIE WITH YOUR FATHERS. THIS PEOPLE WILL ARISE. . . . The Midrash has created new meaning by attaching the Hebrew word meaning "will arise" to the previous words.

"When the tribes of Judah and Benjamin were corrupted, as it is said JUDAH HAS BROKEN FAITH (Mal. 2:11), He called upon the prophets to witness against them, as it is said THE LORD WARNED ISRAEL AND JUDAH BY EVERY PROPHET (2 Kings 17:13).

"When they rebuked the prophets, as it is said BUT THEY MOCKED THE MESSENGERS OF GOD AND DISDAINED HIS WORDS AND TAUNTED HIS PROPHETS (2 Chron. 36:16), He called upon the heavens to witness against them, as it is said I CALL HEAVEN AND EARTH TO WITNESS AGAINST YOU THIS DAY (Deut. 4:26).

"When they corrupted the heavens, as it is said DON'T YOU SEE WHAT THEY ARE DOING IN THE TOWNS OF JUDAH AND IN THE STREETS OF JERUSALEM? THE CHILDREN GATHER STICKS, THE FATHERS BUILD THE FIRE, AND THE MOTHERS KNEAD DOUGH, TO MAKE CAKES FOR THE QUEEN OF HEAVEN (Jer. 7:17–18), He called upon the earth to witness against them, as it is said HEAR, O EARTH! I AM GOING TO BRING DISASTER UPON THIS PEOPLE (Jer. 6:19).

"When they corrupted the earth, as it is said THE ALTARS OF THESE ARE ALSO LIKE STONE HEAPS UPON A PLOWED FIELD (Hos. 12:12), He called upon the roads to witness against them, as it is said THUS SAID THE LORD: STAND BY THE ROADS AND CONSIDER (Jer. 6:16).

"When they corrupted the roads, as it is said YOU BUILT YOUR MOUND AT EVERY CROSSROAD (Ezek. 16:25), He called upon the nations to witness against them, as it is said HEAR WELL, O NATIONS, AND KNOW, O COMMUNITY, WHAT IS IN STORE FOR THEM (Jer. 6:18).

"When they corrupted the nations, as it is said THEY MINGLED WITH THE NATIONS AND LEARNED THEIR WAYS (Ps. 106:35), He called upon the mountains to witness against them, as it is said HEAR, YOU MOUNTAINS, THE CASE OF THE LORD—YOU FIRM FOUNDATIONS OF THE EARTH! FOR THE LORD HAS A CASE AGAINST HIS PEOPLE, HE HAS A SUIT AGAINST ISRAEL (Micah 6:2).

"When they corrupted the mountains, as it is said THEY SACRIFICE ON THE MOUNTAINTOPS (Hos. 4:13), He called upon the animals to witness against them, as it is said AN OX KNOWS ITS OWNER, AN ASS ITS MASTER'S CRIB: ISRAEL DOES NOT KNOW, MY PEOPLE TAKES NO THOUGHT (Isa. 1:3).

"When they corrupted the animals, as it is said THEY EXCHANGED

THEIR GLORY FOR THE IMAGE OF A BULL THAT FEEDS ON GRASS (Ps. 106:20), He called upon the fowl to witness against them, as it is said EVEN THE STORK IN THE SKY KNOWS HER SEASONS, AND THE TURTLEDOVE, SWIFT AND CRANE KEEP THE TIME OF THEIR COMING; BUT MY PEOPLE PAY NO HEED TO THE LAW OF THE LORD (Jer. 8:7).

"When they corrupted the animals, the beasts, and the fowl, as it is said I ENTERED AND LOOKED, AND THERE WERE DETESTABLE FORMS OF CREEPING THINGS AND BEASTS (Ezek. 8:10), He called upon the fish to witness against them, as it is said OR SPEAK TO THE EARTH, IT WILL TEACH YOU; THE FISH OF THE SEA, THEY WILL INFORM YOU (Job 12:8).

"When they corrupted the fish, as it is said YOU HAVE MADE MANKIND LIKE THE FISH OF THE SEA (Hab. 1:14), He called upon the ant to witness against them, as it is said LAZYBONES, GO TO THE ANT; STUDY ITS WAYS AND LEARN (Prov. 6:6)."

R. Simeon b. Eleazar says, "How humiliating it is for that man to have to learn from the ant! If he were to learn and act accordingly, it would be humiliating enough, but here he should have learned from its ways and did not even do so!"

In the future the Congregation of Israel will say to the Holy One, "Master of the Universe, the witnesses against me still exist!" As it is said I CALL HEAVEN AND EARTH TO WITNESS AGAINST YOU THIS DAY (Deut. 30:19).

He says to her, "Behold—I make them disappear," as it is said FOR BEHOLD! I AM CREATING A NEW HEAVEN AND A NEW EARTH (Isa. 65:17).

She says to Him, "Master of the Universe, when I see the places where I acted corruptly I am ashamed," as it is said LOOK AT YOUR DEEDS IN THE VALLEY (Jer. 2:23).

He says to her, "Behold—I make them disappear," as it is said LET EVERY VALLEY BE RAISED (Isa. 40:4).

She says to Him, "Master of the Universe, my name still exists."

He says to her, "Behold—I will make it disappear," as it is said AND YOU SHALL BE CALLED BY A NEW NAME (Isa. 62:2).

---

12. *did not even do so*—as indicated by the continuation in Prov. 6:9: HOW LONG WILL YOU LIE THERE, LAZYBONES? This is a separate interpretation of the verse in Proverbs, which has no connection to its usage above.

337

She says to Him, "Master of the Universe, my name is still connected to the Baalim."

He says to her, "Behold I will make it disappear." As it is said FOR I WILL REMOVE THE NAMES OF THE BAALIM FROM HER MOUTH (Hos. 2:19).

She says to Him, "Master of the Universe, nevertheless members of my house will continue to make mention of it."

He says to her, "AND THEY SHALL NEVERMORE BE MENTIONED BY NAME (Hos. 2:19)."

Again on the morrow—in the future—she will say to Him, "Master of the Universe, You have written IF A MAN DIVORCES HIS WIFE, AND SHE LEAVES HIM AND MARRIES ANOTHER MAN, CAN HE EVER GO BACK TO HER? (Jer. 3:1)."

He says to her, "Did I not write A MAN—and has it not been said elsewhere FOR I AM GOD, NOT MAN (Hos. 11:9)?" Another interpretation. [He says to her], "Have you been divorced from Me, O House of Israel? Is it not written elsewhere WHERE IS THE BILL OF DIVORCE OF YOUR MOTHER WHOM I DISMISSED? AND WHICH OF MY CREDITORS WAS IT TO WHOM I SOLD YOU OFF? (Isa. 50:1)"

Another interpretation: GIVE EAR, O HEAVENS (Deut. 32:1). A parable. A king handed his son over to the care of a tutor who was to guard him. The son thought, "Does my father really think that handing me over to a tutor will be effective? I will merely wait until he has eaten, drunk, and fallen asleep and then I will go and do whatever I want." His father said to him, "I have handed you over to the tutor with strict instructions that he is never to budge from you." Thus Moses said to Israel, "Do you think that you can escape from under the wings of the Divine Presence or remove yourself from the earth? Furthermore, the heavens themselves record [your every deed], as it is said HEAVEN WILL EXPOSE HIS INIQUITY (Job 20:27). How do we know that the earth also is aware [of your every deed]? As it is said EARTH WILL RISE AGAINST HIM (Job 20:27)."

In the future the Congregation of Israel will stand before God for judgment and will say to Him, "Master of the Universe, I do not know who has re-

---

NOT MAN—therefore even if God and Israel have been divorced, God can and will take Israel back.

buffed whom and who changed his attitude toward whom. Did Israel rebuff God? Did God change His attitude toward Israel?" When it says THEN THE HEAVENS PROCLAIMED HIS RIGHTEOUSNESS (Ps. 50:6) it is clear that Israel rebuffed God and God did not change His attitude toward Israel. Thus it says FOR I AM THE LORD—I HAVE NOT CHANGED (Mal. 3:6).

Another interpretation: GIVE EAR, O HEAVENS (Deut. 32:1). R. Judah says, "A parable. A king had two deputies in the city to whom he entrusted his possessions and gave control of his son. He said to them, 'As long as my son acts in accord with my wishes, indulge him in luxury, and let him eat and drink whatever he wants. But if my son does not act in accord with my wishes, he gets nothing from me!' Thus when Israel acts according to God's wishes, what does it say of them? THE LORD WILL OPEN FOR YOU HIS BOUNTEOUS STORE, THE HEAVENS (Deut. 28:12) but when they do not act in accord with God's wishes what does it say of them? THE LORD'S ANGER WILL FLAME UP AGAINST YOU, AND HE WILL SHUT UP THE SKIES SO THAT THERE WILL BE NO RAIN AND THE GROUND WILL NOT YIELD ITS PRODUCE (Deut. 11:17)."

Another interpretation: GIVE EAR, O HEAVENS (Deut. 32:1). R. Nehemiah says, "A parable. A king had a son who fell into depravity. [The king] began to complain about him to his brothers, to his friends, to his neighbors, and to his relatives. He did not stop complaining and finally said, 'Heaven and earth! To whom can I complain about you except to these!' Thus it says GIVE EAR, O HEAVENS, LET ME SPEAK; LET THE EARTH HEAR THE WORDS I UTTER! (Deut. 32:1)."

Another interpretation: GIVE EAR, O HEAVENS (Deut. 32:1). R. Judah says, "Even these are not sufficient for the righteous, for they enlarge the world in which they live. When Israel acts in accord with the wishes of God, what does it say of them? THE LORD WILL OPEN FOR YOU HIS BOUNTEOUS STORE, THE HEAVENS (Deut. 28:12). 'Opening'

Israel rebuffed God   Since the heavens proclaim God's righteousness, it is clear that He did not abandon Israel.

two deputies—symbolizing Heaven and earth. Just as they give the king's son food and drink or withhold it when he is undeserving, so Heaven and earth dispense or withhold rain and food depending on Israel's conduct.

enlarge—improve.

always means 'enlarging,' as it is said AND HE OPENED HER WOMB (Gen. 29:31). Nor are they sufficient for the wicked, for they narrow the world in which they live. When Israel does not act in accord with the wishes of God, what does it say of them? FOR THE LORD'S ANGER WILL FLARE UP AGAINST YOU, AND HE WILL SHUT UP THE SKIES (Deut. 11:17). 'Shutting up' always means 'narrowing,' as it is said FOR THE LORD HAD CLOSED FAST EVERY WOMB (Gen. 20:18)."

Another interpretation: GIVE EAR, O HEAVENS, LET ME SPEAK (Deut. 32:1). The Holy One said to Moses, "Say to Israel: Look at the heavens which I created to serve you. Have they changed their ways? Has the orb of the sun said, 'I will no longer arise in the east and illumine the whole earth?' Rather it is as it is said THE SUN RISES AND THE SUN SETS (Eccl. 1:5). Not only that, but it rejoices to act in accord with My wishes, as it is said THE SUN IS LIKE A GROOM COMING FORTH FROM HIS CHAMBER, LIKE A HERO EAGER TO RUN HIS COURSE (Ps. 19:5–6)."

LET THE EARTH HEAR THE WORDS I UTTER (Deut. 32:1). "Look at the earth which I created to serve you. Has it changed its ways? Have you sown seed in it and it has not grown? Have you sown wheat and barley has sprung up? Has your cow said, 'I will not thresh or plough today'? Has your ass said, 'I will not carry a burden or walk today'? Concerning the Sea it says SHOULD YOU NOT REVERE ME—SAYS THE LORD—SHOULD YOU NOT TREMBLE BEFORE ME, WHO SET THE SAND AS BOUNDARY TO THE SEA (Jer. 5:22). Since I decreed [its boundaries], has it changed its ways? Has it said, 'I will arise and flood the world'? Rather it says WHEN I MADE BREAKERS MY LIMIT FOR IT, AND SET UP ITS BAR AND DOORS, AND SAID 'YOU MAY COME SO FAR AND NO FARTHER; HERE YOUR SURGING WAVES WILL STOP' (Job 38:10–11). Not only that, but it is troubled and knows not what to do, as it is said THOUGH ITS WAVES TOSS, THEY CANNOT PREVAIL (Jer. 5:22). Is this not a matter of logic: If these things, which do not benefit from reward nor suffer from punishment, which, if they do well, are not rewarded and if they sin they are not punished, which have no concern for sons or daughters, do not change their ways, you—who do receive reward when you do well and are punished when you sin, who

---

changed their ways—depart from the natural course of conduct that God decreed when He created them.

care for your sons and your daughters—how much more should you not change your ways!"

Another interpretation: GIVE EAR, O HEAVENS (Deut. 32:1). R. Benaiah would say, "When a man is found guilty, it is the witnesses who first raise their hands against him as it is said LET THE HANDS OF THE WITNESSES BE THE FIRST AGAINST HIM (Deut. 17:7) and then others join in, as it is said AND THE HANDS OF THE REST OF THE PEOPLE THEREAFTER (Deut. 17:7). Thus when Israel does not act in accord with the wishes of God, what does it say of them? FOR THE LORD'S ANGER WILL FLARE UP AGAINST YOU, AND HE WILL SHUT UP THE SKIES (Deut. 11:17) and afterward other punishments come upon them, as it is said AND YOU WILL SOON PERISH (Deut. 11:17). But when Israel acts in accord with the wishes of God, what does it say of them? IN THAT DAY, I WILL RESPOND—DECLARES THE LORD—I WILL RESPOND TO THE SKY (Hos. 2:23) and I WILL SOW HER IN THE LAND AS MY OWN (Hos. 2:25)."

Another interpretation: GIVE EAR, O HEAVENS (Deut. 32:1). R. Judah b. Hananiah would say, "When Moses said GIVE EAR, O HEAVENS, LET ME SPEAK (Deut. 32:1), the heavens and the heavens of heavens stood still. When he said LET THE EARTH HEAR THE WORDS I UTTER (Deut. 32:1) the earth and all upon it stood still. If this astounds you, consider what is said of Joshua: HE SAID IN THE PRESENCE OF THE ISRAELITES: 'STAND STILL, O SUN, AT GIBEON, O MOON, IN THE VALLEY OF AIJALON!' AND THE SUN STOOD STILL AND THE MOON HALTED . . . NEITHER BEFORE NOR SINCE HAS THERE EVER BEEN SUCH A DAY (Josh. 10:12–14). Thus we learn that the righteous have command over the entire world."

Another interpretation: GIVE EAR, O HEAVENS (Deut. 32:1). Since Moses was close to the heavens, he said GIVE EAR, O HEAVENS. Since he was far from the earth, he said LET THE EARTH HEAR THE WORDS I UTTER (Deut. 32:1). Isaiah came and added HEAR, O HEAVENS (Isa. 1:2) since he was far from the heavens and AND GIVE EAR, O EARTH (Isa. 1:2) since he was close to the earth. . . . The Sages say, "It is not that

---

It is not that   The reason that Isaiah used the opposite expressions from Moses when addressing Heaven and earth is not because he was far from Heaven and close to earth while Moses was close to Heaven and far from earth but in order to make the two witnesses, Heaven and earth, equal in their testimony.

but rather that if the testimony of witnesses is identical, the testimony stands, and if not, it does not stand. Thus had Moses said GIVE EAR, O HEAVENS the heavens would have said 'We only heard through "giving ear" '; had he only said LET THE EARTH HEAR, the earth would have said, 'We only heard by "hearing" '; therefore Isaiah came and added HEAR, O HEAVENS AND GIVE EAR, O EARTH (Isa. 1:2) thus ascribing 'giving ear' and 'hearing' to the heavens and 'giving ear' and 'hearing' to the earth."

Another interpretation: GIVE EAR, O HEAVENS, LET ME SPEAK (Deut. 32:1)—because the Torah was given from the heavens, as it is said YOU YOURSELVES SAW THAT I SPOKE TO YOU FROM THE VERY HEAVENS (Ex. 20:19). LET THE EARTH HEAR THE WORDS I UTTER (Deut. 32:1)—because the Israelites stood upon it when they said ALL THAT THE LORD HAS SPOKEN WE WILL DO AND OBEY (Ex. 24:7).

Another interpretation: GIVE EAR, O HEAVENS (Deut. 32:1)—that Israel had not fulfilled the mitzvot given her concerning the heavens. And which are they? The intercalation of the year and the determination of the months, as it is said LET THERE BE LIGHTS IN THE EXPANSE OF THE HEAVENS TO SEPARATE DAY FROM NIGHT; THEY SHALL SERVE AS SIGNS FOR THE SET TIMES—THE DAYS AND THE YEARS (Gen. 1:14). LET THE EARTH HEAR (Deut. 32:1)—that they had not fulfilled the mitzvot given to them concerning the earth. And which are they? Gleanings, forgotten sheaves, the corners of the field, heave offering, tithes, Sabbatical years, and Jubilee years.

Another interpretation: GIVE EAR, O HEAVENS (Deut. 32:1)—that they had not fulfilled all the mitzvot given to them from the heavens. LET THE

---

intercalation of the year   An additional month is added to the year in order to bring the months and the seasons into proper relationship. This is needed since the Hebrew calendar is based on the moon and not on the sun.

determination of the months   This is done by observing the heavens in order to site the new moon.

Gleanings, forgotten sheaves, the corners of the field—all of which must be left for the poor when the earth is harvested.

given to them from the heavens   Some came directly from Heaven, as the Ten Pronouncements. Others were given through Moses on earth during the years of their wandering.

EARTH HEAR THE WORDS I UTTER (Deut. 32:1)—that they had not fulfilled all the mitzvot given to them on earth. Moses called two witnesses that will exist forever and ever to testify against Israel, as it is said I CALL HEAVEN AND EARTH TO WITNESS AGAINST YOU THIS DAY (Deut. 30:19) and the Holy One brought the Song to testify against them, as it is said THEREFORE WRITE DOWN THIS SONG (Deut. 31:19). We do not know whose testimony will endure, that of the Holy One or that of Moses. When it says THIS SONG SHALL CONFRONT THEM AS A WITNESS (Deut. 31:21) we know that it is [the testimony] of the Holy One which will outlast that of Moses, while that of Moses will not outlast [the testimony] of the Holy One. Why then did Moses call two witnesses that will exist forever and ever to testify against Israel? He said, "I am but flesh and blood. Tomorrow I will die. If Israel wishes to say: We never received the Torah, who will contradict her?" Therefore he called two witnesses that will exist forever and ever to testify against her.

The Holy One brought the Song to testify against them. He said, "The Song will testify against them from below and I will testify against them from above." How do we know that God is called a witness? As it is said BUT I WILL STEP FORWARD TO CONTEND AGAINST YOU, AND I WILL ACT AS A RELENTLESS WITNESS (Mal. 3:5). And I AM HE WHO KNOWS AND BEARS WITNESS—DECLARES THE LORD (Jer. 29:23) and LET MY LORD GOD BE WITNESS AGAINST YOU—MY LORD FROM HIS HOLY ABODE (Micah 1:2).
MAY MY DISCOURSE COME DOWN AS THE RAIN (Deut. 32:2). MY DISCOURSE means words of Torah, as it is said FOR I HAVE GIVEN YOU GOOD DISCOURSE; DO NOT FORSAKE MY TORAH (Prov. 4:2). And it says ACCEPT MY DISCIPLINE RATHER THAN SILVER (Prov. 8:10) and "discipline" always means words of Torah, as it is said MY SON, HEED THE DISCIPLINE OF YOUR FATHER, AND DO NOT FORSAKE THE TORAH OF YOUR MOTHER (Prov. 1:8). And it says HEED DISCIPLINE AND BECOME WISE; DO NOT SPURN IT (Prov. 8:33) and HOLD FAST TO DISCIPLINE; DO NOT LET GO; KEEP IT; IT IS YOUR LIFE (Prov. 4:13). It also says TAKE

---

the Song—the Torah, which will be the eternal witness.
Why then did Moses call two witnesses If God's witness, the Torah, would endure forever, what need was there for Moses to invoke Heaven and earth to testify about Israel? The answer is that they might deny ever having received the Torah. In that case Heaven and earth will then testify that they did receive it.

WORDS WITH YOU AND RETURN TO THE LORD (Hos. 14:3) and WORDS always means words of Torah, as it is said THE LORD SPOKE THESE WORDS TO YOUR WHOLE CONGREGATION AT THE MOUNTAIN (Deut. 5:19).

AS THE RAIN (Deut. 32:2). Just as the rain endures forever, so words of Torah endure forever. But is it possible that just as the rain causes some to rejoice and some to be distressed—for if one's tank is full of wine and one's threshing floor [full of grain] he will be distressed—thus words of Torah [cause some to rejoice and some to be distressed]? The verse says MY SPEECH DISTILL AS THE DEW (Deut. 32:2). Just as the entire world rejoices over dew, thus the entire world rejoices over words of Torah.

LIKE SHOWERS ON YOUNG GROWTH (Deut. 32:2). Just as showers come down upon the young growth and cause it to spring up and grow, so words of Torah cause you to spring up and grow. Thus it says HUG HER TO YOU AND SHE WILL EXALT YOU (Prov. 4:8). LIKE DROPLETS ON THE GRASS (Deut. 32:2). Just as the droplets come down on the grass and adorn it and enhance it, so words of Torah adorn you and enhance you, as it is said FOR THEY ARE A GRACEFUL WREATH UPON YOUR HEAD, A NECKLACE ABOUT YOUR THROAT (Prov. 1:9) and SHE WILL ADORN YOUR HEAD WITH A GRACEFUL WREATH; CROWN YOU WITH A GLORIOUS DIADEM (Prov. 4:9).

Another interpretation: MAY MY DISCOURSE COME DOWN AS THE RAIN (Deut. 32:2). One should always gather words of Torah into general rules. As you gather them into general rules, should you also dispense them as general rules? The verse says MAY MY DISCOURSE COME DOWN (ya-arof) AS THE RAIN. "Ya-arof" is a Canaanite term. One does not say "Break this *sela* for me but "arof" this *sela* for me. Thus one should gather words of Torah into general rules, but break them up and dispense them like the drops of dew—not like the drops of rain which are large but like the drops of dew which are small.

LIKE SHOWERS ON THE YOUNG GROWTH (Deut. 32:2). Just as the showers come down upon the young growth and permeate it thoroughly

---

Canaanite term—Phoenician meaning to change or break money into smaller components.

so that it does not become wormy, so one should permeate words of Torah thoroughly in order not to forget them. Thus R. Jacob b. R. Hanilai said to Rabbi Judah the Prince, "Come let us permeate some laws so that they will not become rusty." LIKE DROPLETS ON THE GRASS (Deut. 32:2). Just as these droplets come down upon the grass, cleanse them and perfume them, so one should perfume words of Torah and study them over and over again.

Another interpretation: MAY MY DISCOURSE COME DOWN (ya-arof) AS THE RAIN (Deut. 32:2). R. Eliezer b. R. Jose the Galilean says, " 'Ya-arof' always means killing, as it is said THERE IN THE WADI THEY SHALL BREAK THE NECK (we-arfu) OF THE HEIFER (Deut. 21:4). Just as the heifer atones for the shedding of blood, so words of Torah atone for all transgressions." LIKE SHOWERS (se irim) ON YOUNG GROWTH (Deut. 32:2). Just as se irim (goats) atone for sins, so do words of Torah atone for sins. LIKE DROPLETS ON THE GRASS (Deut. 32: 2). Just as the droplets are pure and cover everything, so do words of Torah cover all sin and transgression.

Another interpretation: MAY MY DISCOURSE COME DOWN AS THE RAIN (Deut. 32:2). The Sages say, "Moses said to Israel, 'Perhaps you do not know how much I suffered for the Torah, how much effort I put into it, how much I toiled for it'—as it is said AND HE WAS THERE WITH THE LORD FORTY DAYS AND FORTY NIGHTS; HE ATE NO BREAD AND DRANK NO WATER (Ex. 34:28) and AND I STAYED ON THE MOUNTAIN FORTY DAYS AND FORTY NIGHTS, EATING NO BREAD AND DRINKING NO WATER (Deut. 9:9)—'I went among the angels, among the beasts, among the fiery angels—any one of whom can destroy the world and all it inhabitants by fire—' as it is said FIERY ANGELS STOOD IN ATTENDANCE OF HIM (Isa. 6: 2)—'I gave my life for it, I gave my blood for it. Just as I learned it through suffering, so should you learn it through suffering.' Perhaps just as you learn it by suffering, so you should teach it by suffering? The verse says MY SPEECH DISTILL (tizzal) AS THE DEW (Deut. 32:2)—think of it as something sold cheaply (zol), like three or four *seah* of wheat for a *sela*."

---

permeate words of Torah—study Torah thoroughly, investigating the smallest details.
teach it by suffering—make it difficult or expensive to acquire.
wheat for a sela This is a reasonable market price. So too Torah should not be difficult to acquire.

LIKE SHOWERS (se'irim) ON YOUNG GRASS (Deut. 32:2). When one goes to study Torah, it leaps upon him at first like a *se'ir*—*se'ir* always means a satyr, as it is said WILDCATS SHALL MEET HYENAS, SATYRS SHALL GREET EACH OTHER (Isa. 34:14) and THERE SATYRS SHALL DANCE (Isa. 13:21).

Another interpretation. MAY MY DISCOURSE COME DOWN AS THE RAIN (Deut. 32:2). R. Benaiah used to say, "If you have occupied yourself with words of Torah for their own sake, words of Torah come alive for you, as it is said THEY ARE LIFE TO HIM WHO FINDS THEM (Prov. 4:22). But if you do not occupy yourself with words of Torah for their own sake, they will slay you, as it is said MAY MY DISCOURSE COME DOWN (ya-arof) AS THE RAIN (Deut. 32:2) and *arifah* always means killing, as it is said THERE, IN THE WADI, THEY SHALL BREAK THE NECK (we-orfu) OF THE HEIFER (Deut. 21:4) and it says FOR MANY ARE THOSE SHE HAS STRUCK DEAD, AND NUMEROUS ARE HER VICTIMS (Prov. 7:26)."

Another interpretation: MAY MY DISCOURSE COME DOWN AS THE RAIN (Deut. 32:2). R. Dostai b. Judah says, "If you gather the words of Torah together as water is gathered into a cistern, in the end you will benefit from your studies, as it is said DRINK WATER FROM YOUR OWN CISTERN (Prov. 5:15). But if you gather words of Torah as rain is gathered in ditches, pits, and caves, in the end you will irrigate and water others as well, as it is said RUNNING WATER FROM YOUR OWN WELL (Prov. 5:15) and it says YOUR SPRINGS WILL GUSH FORTH IN STREAMS IN THE PUBLIC SQUARES (Prov. 5:16)."

Another interpretation: MAY MY DISCOURSE COME DOWN AS THE RAIN (Deut. 32:2). R. Meir used to say, "Always gather words of Torah into rules, for if you gather them as specific details, they will wear you out and you will not know what to do. A parable. A man went to Caesarea and needed a hundred or two hundred *zuz* for expenses. If he takes them as individual pieces, they would wear him out and he would not know what to do. But if he consolidates them into *selaim*, he can then change them and spend them wherever he wants. Similarly, if one goes to the market in Bet

---

leaps upon him   At the beginning, it is a difficult undertaking.
for their own sake—and not for some ulterior or self-serving motive.

Ilias and needs a hundred *minas* or two myriads for expenses, if he takes them as *selaim*, they will wear him out and he will not know what to do, but if he consolidates them into golden *denars*, he can change them and spend them wherever he wants."

Another interpretation: MAY MY DISCOURSE COME DOWN AS THE RAIN (Deut. 32:2). Just as the rain comes down upon fruit trees and gives each one its own flavor according to its nature—the vine, the olive tree, the fig tree, each one according to its nature—so it is with words of Torah. Although they are basically one, they contain Scripture, Mishna, Talmud, *halachot*, and *haggadot*.

LIKE SHOWERS ON THE YOUNG GROWTH (Deut. 32:2). Just as these showers come down on the young growth and cause them to grow— some of them red, some green, some black, and some white, so it is with the words of Torah. Some men [who study it] are wise, some are worthy, some are righteous, and some are pious.

Another interpretation: Just as with the rain, you cannot anticipate it, as it says MEANWHILE THE SKY GREW BLACK WITH CLOUDS; THERE WAS WIND, AND A HEAVY DOWNPOUR FELL (1 Kings 18:45), so with the disciples of the wise. You do not know what their character is until they teach interpretations, *halachot* and *haggadot* or until they are appointed leaders of the community. . . .

COMMENTARY   *Since Moses' words are words of Torah, this midrash interprets these verses describing his discourse as descriptions of Torah and takes the opportunity to make many different comments on the worth of Torah, the effect of studying it, and the methodology of study and teaching.*

---

a hundred minas—worth 10,000 shekels.

two myriads—worth 20,000 shekels.

so it is with words of Torah—not in the narrow sense of Scripture, but in the larger meaning of Jewish religious teaching, which includes Bible and rabbinic teaching.

Mishna—Rabbinic teaching. The other terms then detail three different types: Talmud means midrash, i.e., interpretation of Scripture; *halachot* are laws and *haggadot* are legendary material or discussions not connected to scriptural verses.

cannot anticipate it   In the previous verse in 1 Kings 18:43, rain is not anticipated. It comes up suddenly.

disciples of the wise—the students of the Sages.

*This includes the creation of general rules that make it easier to understand
and remember, by teaching Torah in small amounts so that it is more easily
absorbed. The description of Moses going to receive the Torah is of particular interest. It reflects early mystical texts in which Moses does not merely
go to the top of Mount Sinai, but takes a mystical journey into heaven, a
journey that is fraught with danger since it requires him to pass through the
realms of beasts and fire that guard the place of the Holy.*

FOR THE NAME OF THE LORD I PROCLAIM (Deut. 32:3). We find
that Moses did not make mention of the Name of the Holy One until he had
first uttered twenty-one words. From whom did he learn this? From the
ministering angels, for the ministering angels mention the Name of God
only after saying the threefold "holy," as it is said AND ONE WOULD
CALL TO THE OTHER, "HOLY, HOLY, HOLY! THE LORD OF
HOSTS!" (Isa. 6:3). Said Moses, "It is enough for me to be seven times as
modest as the ministering angels." It is a matter of logic: If Moses, who was
the wisest of the wise, the greatest of the great, and the father of the prophets did not make mention of the Name of God until he had first uttered
twenty-one words, how much more must we be cautious about mentioning
the Name of God for no reason.

R. Simeon b. Yohai says, "How do we know that one should not say 'For the
Lord—a burnt offering,' 'For the Lord—a meal offering,' 'For the Lord—an
offering of well-being,' but 'A burnt offering for the Lord,' 'A meal offering
for the Lord,' 'An offering of well-being for the Lord'? The verse says AN
OFFERING OF CATTLE TO THE LORD (Lev. 1:2). Is this not a matter
of logic: If in connection with that which is consecrated to Heaven, the
Holy One said, 'Do not place My Name upon it until it has been consecrated,' how much more must we be cautious about mentioning the Name
of God for no reason or in a place of shame?"

FOR THE NAME OF THE LORD I PROCLAIM (Deut. 32:3). R. Jose
says, "How do we know that when those who lead the service in the syna-

---

twenty-one words   There are twenty-one Hebrew words in Deut. 32:1–3 before the Name of
the Lord is mentioned.
seven times—seven times the three words of the angels, which precede God's Name, thus
twenty-one words.
modest—or cautious.
consecrated to Heaven—the various sacrifices.

gogue say 'Bless the Lord—the Blessed One—' the rest should respond "Blessed is the Lord—the Blessed One—to all eternity'? As it is said FOR THE NAME OF THE LORD I PROCLAIM; ASCRIBE GREATNESS TO OUR GOD! (Deut. 32:3)." R. Nehorai said to him, "By Heaven, that is the way it is in battle—the rank and file begin and the heroes take the triumph!"

How do we know that one does not recite the invitation to the Grace After Meals when there are fewer than three people? As it is said FOR THE NAME OF THE LORD I PROCLAIM; ASCRIBE GREATNESS TO OUR GOD! (Deut. 32:3).

How do we know that one should reply "Amen" upon hearing a blessing? As it is said FOR THE NAME OF THE LORD I PROCLAIM; ASCRIBE GREATNESS TO OUR GOD!

How do we know that we should recite "Blessed is the Name of His Glorious Majesty for all eternity"? As it is said FOR THE NAME OF THE LORD I PROCLAIM.

How do we know that when people recite the words "Blessed be His great Name" others reply "forever and ever"? As it is said ASCRIBE GREATNESS TO OUR GOD!

COMMENTARY   *This verse is taken by the Midrash as a warrant for many different prayer formulas. Both at the reading of the Torah and prior to the recitation of the Shema, the leader calls on the congregation to bless God, to which they respond with a blessing. Similarly the Grace After Meals begins with the leader calling on others to bless God, which they then do.*

Bless the Lord—the Blessed One   This formula of blessing is used before reading from the Torah. Later it also became the introduction to the recitation of the Shema in the morning and the evening service.

the heroes take the triumph   The ones who come last and complete the battle are more important. So those who answer the blessing are considered more important than the person who says the blessing.

three people   In order to begin the Grace with an introductory call to recite the prayer there must be at least two people to answer the invitation. This is derived from the fact that the Hebrew verb for ASCRIBE is in the plural.

Blessed is the Name . . .   This is said quietly after the recitation of the first line of the Shema in which God's Name is "proclaimed": HEAR, O ISRAEL, THE LORD IS OUR GOD, THE LORD IS ONE (Deut. 6:4). This may also refer to the practice in the Temple of replying thus on the Day of Atonement when the High Priest called out the Name of the Lord as part of the ritual.

Blessed be His great Name   The text gives the Hebrew version of the well-known Aramaic prayer, the Kaddish.

THE ROCK (tzur)! (Deut. 32:4). The Artist (tzayar)—for He formed (tzar) the world first and then formed (yatzar) man in it, as it is said THE LORD GOD FORMED (yitzar) MAN FROM THE DUST OF THE EARTH (Gen. 2:7).

HIS DEEDS ARE PERFECT (Deut. 32:4). His workmanship is perfect in regard to all creatures and no one has a right to complain in any way. No one can consider things and say, "If only I had three eyes! If only I had three hands! If only I had three feet! If only I walked on my head! If only my face were turned the other way!—how nice it would be for me!" The verse says YEA, ALL HIS WAYS ARE JUST (Deut. 32:4). He judges all creatures and gives them what is appropriate for them.

A FAITHFUL GOD (Deut. 32:4). He had faith in the world He was to create. NEVER FALSE (Deut. 32:4). He created human beings to be righteous and not to be wicked. Thus it is said BUT, SEE, THIS I DID FIND: GOD MADE MEN UPRIGHT BUT THEY HAVE ENGAGED IN TOO MUCH REASONING (Eccl. 7:29). TRUE AND UPRIGHT IS HE (Deut. 32:4). He conducts Himself uprightly with all creatures.

Another interpretation: THE ROCK! (Deut. 32:4). The Powerful One. HIS DEEDS ARE PERFECT (Deut. 32:4). His workmanship is perfect in regard to all creatures and no one has a right to complain in any way. No one can consider things and say, "Why were the people of the generation of the flood swept away by water? Why were the people of the Tower scattered from one end of the world to the other? Why were the people of Sodom swept away by fire and brimstone? Why was Aaron given the priesthood? Why was David given the kingship? Why were Korah and his followers swallowed up by the earth? The verse says YEA, ALL HIS WAYS ARE JUST (Deut. 32:4). He judges all creatures and gives them what is appropriate for them."

A FAITHFUL GOD (Deut. 32:4). He keeps His trust. NEVER FALSE (Deut. 32:4). He collects that which is His at the end. The ways of the Holy One are not like the ways of human beings. When a human being entrusts a purse of two hundred [shekels] to someone to whom he owes a *manah*, when he comes to collect it, that person will say to him, "I am deducting the *manah* you owe me. Take the rest." So too if a workman owes his employer a *denar*, when he comes to collect his wages, that man will say to him, "I am deducting the *denar* you owe me. Take the rest." But He Who Spoke and the world came into being is not like that. Rather He is A FAITHFUL GOD (Deut. 32:4). He keeps His trust. NEVER FALSE (Deut. 32:4). He collects that which is His at the end. TRUE AND UPRIGHT IS HE (Deut. 32:4) as it is said FOR THE LORD IS RIGHTEOUS; HE LOVES RIGHTEOUS DEEDS (Ps. 11:7).

Another interpretation. THE ROCK! (Deut. 32:4). The Powerful One. HIS WAYS ARE PERFECT (Deut. 32:4). The work of all creatures is complete before Him—giving reward to the righteous and dispensing punishment to the wicked. Neither takes anything with them in this world. How do we know that the righteous take nothing that is theirs in this world? As it is said HOW ABUNDANT IS THE GOOD THAT YOU HAVE IN STORE FOR THOSE WHO FEAR YOU (Ps. 31:20). And how do we know that the wicked take nothing that is theirs in this world? As it is said LO, I HAVE IT ALL PUT AWAY, SEALED UP IN MY STOREHOUSES, TO BE MY VENGEANCE AND RECOMPENSE (Deut. 32:34–35). When will both receive their due? YEA, ALL HIS WAYS ARE JUST (Deut. 32:4)—on the morrow when He sits in judgment upon His throne of justice. He judges each one and gives him what is appropriate to him.

A FAITHFUL GOD (Deut. 32:4). Just as He grants the perfectly righteous a reward in the world-to-come for any mitzvah he performed in this world, so He grants the perfectly wicked a reward in this world for the slightest mitzvah he has performed in this world.

Just as He punishes the perfectly wicked in the world-to-come for the transgressions he has committed in this world, so He punishes the perfectly righteous in this world for the slightest transgression he has performed in this world.

NEVER FALSE (Deut. 32:4). When a man departs this world, all of his deeds are spread out before him and say to him, "Thus did you do on such-and-such a day, and thus did you do on such-and-such a day. Do you accept this?" And he says, "Yes," and they say to him, "Sign!" as it is said THE HAND OF EVERY MAN SHALL SIGN IT, THAT ALL MEN MAY KNOW HIS DOINGS (Job 37:7). TRUE AND UPRIGHT IS HE (Deut.

---

for the slightest mitzvah The prosperity of the wicked in this world is their reward for any good thing they have done. Thus they will receive no reward in the world to come.

32:4). [Each man] then acknowledges the justice of God's judgment and says, "Well have I been judged." Thus it says YOU ARE JUST IN YOUR SENTENCE, AND RIGHT IN YOUR JUDGMENT (Ps. 51:6).

Another interpretation: THE ROCK!—HIS DEEDS ARE PERFECT (Deut. 32:4). When they apprehended R. Hanina b. Teradion, they decreed that he was to be burned together with his Scroll [of the Torah]. They said to him, "It has been decreed that you are to be burned together with your Scroll." He proclaimed this verse: THE ROCK! HIS DEEDS ARE PERFECT.

They said to his wife, "It was been decreed that your husband is to be burned, and you to be executed." She proclaimed this verse: A FAITHFUL GOD, NEVER FALSE (Deut. 32:4).

They said to his daughter, "It has been decreed that your father is to be burned, your mother to be executed and you are to be assigned [disgraceful] work." She proclaimed this verse: WONDROUS IN PURPOSE AND MIGHTY IN DEED, WHOSE EYES OBSERVE ALL THE WAYS OF MEN, SO AS TO REPAY EVERY MAN ACCORDING TO HIS WAYS, AND WITH THE PROPER FRUIT OF HIS DEEDS! (Jer. 32:19).

Said R. Judah the Prince, "How great are these righteous ones—at the hour of their tribulation three such appropriate verses—of which there are no better in all of Scripture!—came to them enabling them to acknowledge the justice of God's judgment." These three directed their hearts and acknowledged the justice of God's judgment upon them.

A philosopher protested to the Prefect and said to him, "Sir, do not boast that you have burned the Torah—for it returns from whence it came, unto its Father's house." He said to him, "Tomorrow your fate will be the same as theirs!" He said to him, "You have given me good tidings—that tomorrow my portion will be with them in the world-to-come."

Another interpretation: THE ROCK!—HIS DEEDS ARE PERFECT (Deut. 32:4). When Moses descended from Mount Sinai, all Israel crowded around him and said to him, "Moses—tell us: What is justice like in

---

apprehended R. Hanina   He was the only one of the Sages to consistently defy the Hadrianic decree against teaching Torah during the second century C.E.
executed—by the sword.
work   She was to be consigned to a brothel.
philosopher—a gentile who was a member of the governor's council.

[Heaven] above?" He said to them, "I tell you, not only does He not justify the guilty or condemn the righteous, but He does not even exchange one thing for the other. A FAITHFUL GOD, NEVER FALSE (Deut. 32:4)."

COMMENTARY   *This tale of martyrdom takes place during the Hadrianic persecutions. The emphasis here is on the act of Sanctifying God's Name even at the moment of death and of publicly proclaiming His righteousness. The practice of finding appropriate sayings or verses in order to justify God's actions is recorded as early as the Book of Maccabees. Eventually the verse HEAR O ISRAEL, THE LORD IS OUR GOD, THE LORD IS ONE (Deut. 6:4) was accepted as the verse to recite before martyrdom. The Sages are constantly concerned with the justification of the ways of God. In this section they reiterate their belief that God is the perfect craftsman, that there is no cause for complaint either about the way in which He created the world and its creatures, including man, or about His moral judgments. Human beings receive their rewards and punishment in this world and in the world-to-come, balancing out what would be perceived otherwise as injustice. One is to proclaim God as the righteous judge both in regard to His actions toward the person and toward others.*

IS CORRUPTION HIS? NO. THE BLEMISH IS HIS CHILDREN'S (Deut. 32:5), Even though they are full of blemishes, they are called "children." So taught R. Meir, as it is said THE BLEMISH IS HIS CHILDREN'S. R. Judah says, "They are not blemished, as it is said NO BLEMISH IS HIS CHILDREN'S."

Thus it says BROOD OF EVILDOERS! DEPRAVED CHILDREN! (Isa. 1:4). If they are called "children" when they are depraved, how much more would this be so if they were not depraved!

Similarly THEY ARE WISE AT DOING WRONG (Jer. 4:22). If they are called "wise" when they do wrong, how much more would this be so if they were doing good! Similarly THEY ARE FOOLISH CHILDREN (Jer. 4:22). If they are called "children" when they are foolish, how much more would this be so if they were wise!

Similarly THEY WILL COME TO YOU IN CROWDS AND SIT BEFORE YOU AS MY PEOPLE AND WILL HEAR YOUR WORDS

NO BLEMISH IS HIS CHILDREN'S   By parsing the verse differently, attaching the negative to the first rather than the last section, R. Judah obtains a meaning opposite to that of R. Meir. *when they are depraved*—following R. Meir's interpretation.

(Ezek. 33:31). Does this mean that they will then obey them? The verse says BUT WILL NOT OBEY THEM (Ezek. 33:31). This is a matter of logic. If they are called MY PEOPLE when they hear but do not obey, how much more would this be true if they were to hear and obey!

They said in the name of Abba Hedores, "Israel corrupted itself by violating every prohibition in the Torah." Why? In order not to give the wicked an excuse to say: When we sin, we trouble Him. To what may this be likened? To one who is being taken out to be crucified. His father weeps and his mother prostrates herself before him in grief. Each one says, "Woe unto me!" But it is really experienced only by the one going to be crucified. Thus it says WOE TO THEM! FOR ILL HAVE THEY SERVED THEM-SELVES (Isa. 3:9).

THAT CROOKED AND TWISTED GENERATION (Deut. 32:5). Moses said to Israel, "You are crooked and perverse and you are going straight to the fire!" To what may this be likened? To one who had a crooked staff which he gave to an artisan to fix. He fixes it by fire, and if that does not help, he tries to fix it in a wood press. If that does not work, he chips at it with an adze and casts it into the fire. Thus it says I WILL BLOW UPON YOU WITH THE FIRE OF MY WRATH; AND I WILL DELIVER YOU INTO THE HANDS OF BARBARIANS, CRAFTSMEN OF CORRUPTION (Ezek. 21:36).

Another interpretation: Moses said to Israel, "I have measured out to you the same measure with which you measured," as it is said WITH THE PURE YOU ACT IN PURITY, AND WITH THE PERVERSE YOU ARE TWISTED (2 Sam. 22:27). THAT CROOKED AND TWISTED GENERATION (Deut. 32:5).

DO YOU THUS REQUITE THE LORD? (Deut. 32:6). A parable. It may be likened to one who stood in the forum and insulted a senator. The by-standers said to him, "Fool! You are insulting a senator? If he wished to

---

Israel corrupted itself   This is another interpretation of Deut. 32:5, reading it as if it said "They corrupted themselves with every 'No,' "—by violating every prohibition.
Why?   Why is God so patient, permitting Israel to sin so much?
really experienced   Any real "woe" is experienced only by the one who sinned and is therefore being punished. The sinner does not harm God.

strike you, to tear your garment or to send you to prison, could you prevent it? If he were a centurion, who is even more important, how much more would this be so, and if he were a consul, who is even more important, how much more would this be so!"

Another interpretation: DO YOU THUS REQUITE THE LORD? (Deut. 32:6). A parable. This may be likened to one who stood in the forum and insulted his own father. The bystanders said to him, "Fool! Whom are you insulting? Is it not your own father? Consider all that he has done for you. If you did not honor him before, you certainly should do so now lest he will all his possessions to others!" Thus Moses said to Israel, "If you do not recall all of the miracles and wonders the Holy One performed for you in Egypt, at least think of all the favors He has in store for you in the world-to-come!"

O DULL AND WITLESS PEOPLE (Deut. 32:6). DULL in the past. AND WITLESS in the future. Similarly ISRAEL DOES NOT KNOW, MY PEOPLE TAKES NO THOUGHT (Isa. 1:3) ISRAEL DOES NOT KNOW in the past. MY PEOPLE TAKES NO THOUGHT in the future. What caused Israel to be dull and foolish? They did not acquire wisdom through Torah. Thus it says THEIR CORD IS PULLED UP AND THEY DIE, AND NOT WITH WISDOM (Job 4:21).

IS HE NOT THE FATHER WHO CREATED YOU? (Deut. 32:6). Simeon b. Halafta says, "If the weaker is above and the stronger underneath who wins? Can you defeat him? This is certainly so if the stronger is above and the weaker underneath! Thus it says KEEP YOUR MOUTH FROM BEING RASH, AND LET NOT YOUR THROAT BE QUICK TO BRING FORTH SPEECH BEFORE GOD. FOR GOD IS IN HEAVEN AND YOU ARE ON EARTH (Eccl. 5:1)."

IS HE NOT THE FATHER WHO CREATED (konecha) YOU? (Deut. 32:6). Moses said to Israel, "You are precious to Him. You are His possession (kinyan) and not His inheritance. A parable. A person inherited ten

---

if the weaker is above In a wrestling contest, the stronger will win even if he is underneath.
GOD IS IN HEAVEN He is not only stronger, but also above. It is certainly foolish to contend with Him.
His possession—that which He made for Himself.
not His inheritance—that which He merely acquired, which would be much less important to Him.

fields from his father and then went and purchased (kanah) one field from his own funds. He preferred that one to all of those he had inherited from his father. Similarly, a person inherited ten palaces from his father and then went and purchased one palace from his own funds. He preferred that one to all of those he had inherited from his father. Thus Moses said to Israel, "You are precious to Him. You are His possession and not His inheritance."

WHO CREATED (konecha) YOU. This is one of three things called God's possession (kinyan).

Torah is called God's possession, as it is said THE LORD ACQUIRED ME (kanani) at the beginning of His course (Prov. 8:22).

Israel is called God's possession, as it is said IS HE NOT THE FATHER WHO CREATED (konekha) YOU (Deut. 32:6).

The Temple is called God's possession, as it is said THE MOUNTAIN HIS RIGHT HAND HAD ACQUIRED (kanta) (Ps. 78:54).

COMMENTARY   *The theme of God's relationship to Israel is dealt with once again in this section. Is Israel blemished and corrupt or pure and blameless? The answer to this question is predicated on the interpretation of the problematic verse Deuteronomy 32:5. Where is the word NO to be placed? With the first half of the verse or with the second? If with the first, then Israel is blemished. If with the second, Israel is not blemished. Even those, like R. Meir, who believe that Israel is blemished, then go out of their way to state that this verse and many others indicate that even when they are corrupted, God still looks on them as His children and calls them "wise." The section, after exhorting Israel to realize how foolish their actions have been (the result of lack of wisdom through Torah), then affirms the preciousness of Israel to God. Together with the Temple and the Torah, they are His most precious personal possessions. At a time when others were asserting that God had rejected Israel, this was a powerful affirmation of the ancient relationship.*

13. Deuteronomy 32:7, Sifre D. 310, 350

REMEMBER THE DAYS OF OLD (Deut. 32:7). He said to them, "Remember what I did to the earlier generations—what I did to the people of

---

God's possession—or God's special creation.

the generation of the flood, what I did to the people of the generation of the dispersion, and what I did to the people of Sodom.

CONSIDER THE YEARS OF EACH GENERATION (Deut. 32:7). There is no generation in which there are not people like those of the generation of the flood or the people of Sodom. Nevertheless, each individual is judged according to his actions.

ASK YOUR FATHER, HE WILL INFORM YOU (Deut. 32:7). This refers to the prophets, as in the verse ELISHA SAW IT, AND HE CRIED OUT, "O FATHER, FATHER! ISRAEL'S CHARIOTS AND HORSEMEN!" (2 Kings 2:12). YOUR ELDERS, THEY WILL TELL YOU (Deut. 32:7). This refers to the elders, as in the verse GATHER FOR ME SEVENTY OF ISRAEL'S ELDERS (Num. 11:16).

Another interpretation: REMEMBER THE DAYS OF OLD (Deut. 32:7). He said to them, "Whenever the Holy One brings sufferings upon you, remember all the good things and consolations He is going to grant you in the world-to-come."

CONSIDER THE YEARS OF EACH GENERATION (Deut. 32:7). This refers to the generation of the Messiah, which will last for three generations, as it is said LET THEM FEAR YOU AS LONG AS THE SUN SHINES, WHILE THE MOON LASTS, GENERATION UPON GENERATIONS (Ps. 72:5).

---

13. *dispersion*—the generation of the Tower of Babel whose punishment was that they were dispersed throughout the world. See Gen. 11:1–9.

according to his actions—whereas at the earlier time, the entire generation was punished.

FATHER, FATHER! Elisha is referring to his teacher, the prophet Elijah.

the elders—the members of the Sanhedrin.

the good things The first interpretation was that this verse is a warning that God may punish you as He did the earlier generations. This interpretation is that the verse is a consolation. If you are suffering now, remember that as He did good things in the past, so will He do them again in the future.

three generations—based on the Hebrew for GENERATION UPON GENERATIONS (Ps. 72:5), the first being singular, the second plural (a minimum of two), thus implying a total of three generations.

ASK YOUR FATHER, HE WILL INFORM YOU (Deut. 32:7). On the morrow, Israel will hear and see as if from the mouth of the Holy One Himself, as it is said YOUR EARS WILL HEED THE COMMAND FROM BEHIND YOU (Isa. 30:21). YOUR GUIDE WILL NO MORE BE IGNORED, BUT YOUR EYES WILL WATCH YOUR GUIDE (Isa. 30:20).

YOUR ELDERS, THEY WILL TELL YOU (Deut. 32:7)—what I showed the elders at the mountain, as it is said THEN HE SAID TO MOSES, "COME UP TO THE LORD, YOU AND AARON, NADAB AND ABIHU, AND SEVENTY ELDERS OF ISRAEL" (Ex. 24:1).

WHEN THE MOST HIGH GAVE NATIONS THEIR HOMES (Deut. 32:8). Before the appearance of Abraham, the Holy One would judge the world according to His Quality of Harshness, as it were. When the people of the flood sinned, He swept them away like sparks in water. When the people of the tower sinned, He scattered them from one end of the world to the other. When the people of Sodom sinned, He swept them away with brimstone and fire. But once Abraham appeared in the world, he was privileged to endure the sufferings which began to occur, as it is said THERE WAS A FAMINE IN THE LAND. AND ABRAM WENT DOWN TO EGYPT (Gen. 12:10). And should you inquire, "Why was there suffering?" the answer is: because of the preciousness of Israel. HE FIXED THE BOUNDARIES OF PEOPLES IN RELATION TO ISRAEL'S NUMBERS (Deut. 32:8).

COMMENTARY   *The obvious difference between the way in which God judged and punished wicked generations at the beginning of history, as related in Genesis, and the reality of life at their time caused the Sages to reflect on God's ways. They offer here two different explanations. One is that God now judges the individual as an individual rather than an entire generation. The other is that the appearance of Abraham was a watershed in*

---

the mouth of the Holy One   Now you have to rely on what past generations tell you. Soon God Himself will reveal His plans to you.

endure the sufferings   The implication is that since the appearance of Abraham the world has been governed by God's Quality of Mercy, rather than His Quality of Harshness or Justice. The suffering, however, now came on Abraham and his descendants. They were the suffering servant referred to in Isa. 42.

human history. Prior to his time God's attribute of justice predominated. Afterward, His Quality of Mercy was uppermost and somehow the suffering that Abraham and the people of Israel had to endure was seen as a compensation for this and as a sign of God's love for them. This idea has obvious similarities to the prophet Isaiah's doctrine of the suffering servant. Certain Gnostic sects claimed that the Hebrew Scriptures represented a God of cruelty while there was also a God of love who was revealed in other writings such as those of the Christians. Jewish doctrine reaffirms that there is only one God, but this God has two Qualities, one of which is Justice, the other Mercy. Since the time of Abraham, the first Hebrew, God has governed through mercy. There are many comments in the midrashic interpretation to the Song of Moses (Deut. 32) that seek to explain and justify the suffering of Israel, which was so intense at that time. In every instance the Sages sought to combat the Roman claim that they were more powerful than the God of Israel and the Christian claim that God had punished and abandoned Israel. Even if God had punished them, it was not because of His love of the Romans, who were considered the Kingdom of Evil, but because of their own sins. Most important, He had not abandoned them and would not do so. Even suffering could be seen as a sign of love and they would remain His children forever.

Another interpretation: WHEN THE MOST HIGH GAVE NATIONS THEIR HOMES (Deut. 32:8). When the Holy One apportioned territory to each nation, He fixed their boundaries so that they would not be mixed. He sent the children of Gomer to Gomer, the children of Magog to Magog, the children of Media to Media, the children of Javan to Javan, the children of Tubal to Tubal. He fixed the boundaries of the nations so that they should not enter the Land of Israel. HE FIXED THE BOUNDARIES OF PEOPLES IN RELATION TO ISRAEL'S NUMBERS (Deut. 32:8).

Another interpretation: WHEN THE MOST HIGH GAVE NATIONS THEIR HOMES (Deut. 32:8). When the Holy One gave the Torah to Israel, He stood watching and observing, as it is said WHEN HE STANDS, HE MAKES THE EARTH SHAKE, WHEN HE GLANCES, HE MAKES NATIONS TREMBLE (Hab. 3:6). There was no nation, however, worthy to accept the Torah except Israel. HE FIXED THE BOUNDARIES OF THE PEOPLES IN RELATION TO ISRAEL'S NUMBERS (Deut. 32:8).

Javan—Greece.

Another interpretation: WHEN THE MOST HIGH GAVE NATIONS THEIR HOMES (Deut. 32:8). When the Holy One apportioned territory to each nation, He made Gehenna their portion, as it is said ASSYRIA IS THERE WITH ALL HER COMPANY, THEIR GRAVES ROUND ABOUT, ALL OF THEM SLAIN, FELLED BY THE SWORD. THEIR GRAVES SET IN THE FARTHEST REACHES OF THE PIT (Ezek 32:22–23). ALL THE PRINCES OF THE NORTH AND ALL THE SI DONIANS ARE THERE, WHO WENT DOWN IN DISGRACI (Ezek. 32:30). EDOM IS THERE, HER KINGS AND ALL HER CHIEF-TAINS (Ezek. 32:29). And should you inquire, "Who took all of their wealth and glory?" the answer is, "Israel." HE FIXED THE BOUND-ARIES OF THE PEOPLES IN RELATION TO ISRAEL'S NUMBERS (Deut. 32:8).

Another interpretation: WHEN THE MOST HIGH GAVE NATIONS THEIR HOMES (Deut. 32:8). When the Holy One bestowed homes upon the sin-fearing and the worthy among the nations. AND SET THE DIVI-SIONS OF MAN (Deut. 32:8). This refers to the generation of the dispersion, as it is said AND FROM THERE THE LORD SCATTERED THEM OVER THE FACE OF THE WHOLE EARTH (Gen. 11:9).

HE FIXED THE BOUNDARIES OF PEOPLES (Deut. 32:8). R. Eliezer b. R. Jose the Galilean says, "It says THERE ARE SIXTY QUEENS, AND EIGHTY CONCUBINES (Song 6:8). Sixty and eighty make one hundred and forty. When our ancestors descended into Egypt there were only seventy of them, as it is said YOUR ANCESTORS WENT DOWN TO EGYPT SEVENTY PERSONS IN ALL (Deut. 10:22). Then it says THE BOUNDARIES OF PEOPLES (Deut. 32:8). It does not say 'the boundary of nations' but THE BOUNDARIES OF NATIONS. The nations were awarded a portion twice that of Israel."

BUT THE LORD'S PORTION IS HIS PEOPLE (Deut. 32:9). A parable. A king had a field which he gave to tenants. The tenants began stealing from it, so he took it away from them and gave it to their children. When they began to act worse than their fathers, he took it from them and gave it to their children, but they began to act even worse than the others. A son was

---

the sin-fearing and the worthy   God gave territory to the nations because there are worthy people among them.

born to him, so he said to them, "Get out of my property. You have no business there. Give me back my portion so that I may repossess it." Thus when our father Abraham came into the world, unworthy children—Ishmael and the children of Keturah—issued from him. When Isaac came into the world, unworthy children issued from him—Esau and all the princes of Edom, who were even worse than their predecessors. But when Jacob came into the world, no unworthy children issued from him. All of his children were worthy, as it says JACOB WAS A PERFECT MAN, WHO STAYED IN CAMP (Gen. 25:27). When did God repossess His portion? Beginning with Jacob, as it says BUT THE LORD'S PORTION IS HIS PEOPLE, JACOB HIS OWN ALLOTMENT (Deut. 32:9) and it says FOR THE LORD HAS CHOSEN JACOB FOR HIMSELF (Ps. 135:4).

Nevertheless the matter remains uncertain. Did the Holy One choose Jacob or did Jacob choose the Holy One? The verse says ISRAEL, AS HIS TREASURED POSSESSION (Ps. 135:4). Nevertheless the matter still remains uncertain and we do not know if the Holy One chose Israel as His treasured possession or if Israel chose the Holy One. The verse says THE LORD YOUR GOD CHOSE YOU FROM AMONG ALL OTHER PEOPLES ON EARTH TO BE HIS TREASURED PEOPLE (Deut. 14: 2). And how do we know that Jacob also chose the Lord? As it is said NOT LIKE THESE IS THE PORTION OF JACOB (Jer. 10:16). . . .

COMMENTARY   *Both here and in many other sections, the Midrash emphasizes the righteousness of all of Jacob's children in contrast to the sinfulness of some of the descendants of both Abraham and Isaac. This too may be part of the polemic of the Sages, defending the status of Israel against Christian doctrines. Since the "repossession," that is, the chosenness, begins only with Jacob, it excludes all others, even those who can claim descent from Abraham or Isaac. The people of Israel alone were and remain His treasured possession. God chose them and they also chose God.*

HE FOUND HIM IN A DESERT REGION (Deut. 32:10). This refers to Abraham. A parable. A king went out with his troops into the desert. His

---

PERFECT MAN—The Hebrew, usually translated "a mild man," also has the meaning of complete. The implication is that there was no defect in his progeny. See above page 308.
remains uncertain Was the initiative for making Jacob and Israel God's portion God's or Jacob's?
A king went out In this parable, the king represents Abraham and the brave man is God, who rescued Abraham from persecution in the desert, the land of the Chaldeans.

troops deserted him in a place where there were marauders, wandering soldiers, and robbers and went on their own way. One brave man remained loyal to him and said to him, "My lord King, do not be discouraged or afraid of anything. By your life! I will not leave you until I have safely returned you to your palace where you can rest peacefully on your own bed." Just as it is said I AM THE LORD WHO BROUGHT YOU OUT FROM UR OF THE CHALDEANS TO GIVE YOU THIS LAND AS A POSSESSION (Gen. 15:7).

HE ENGIRDED HIM (Deut. 32:10) as it says THE LORD SAID TO ABRAM, "GO FORTH FROM YOUR NATIVE LAND" (Gen. 12:1).

WATCHED OVER HIM (Deut. 32:10). Before Abraham appeared in this world, The Holy One was, as it were, king of the heavens alone, as it is said THE LORD, THE GOD OF HEAVEN, WHO TOOK ME FROM MY FATHER'S HOUSE (Gen. 24:7). But once Abraham had appeared in this world, he made Him king over heaven and earth, as it is said AND I WILL MAKE YOU SWEAR BY THE LORD, THE GOD OF HEAVEN AND THE GOD OF EARTH (Gen. 24:3). GUARDING HIM AS THE PUPIL OF HIS EYE (Deut. 32:10). Had the Holy One asked Abraham for the pupil of his eye, he would have given it to Him. Not only the pupil of his eye, but even that which is most precious of all—his very life, as it is said TAKE YOUR SON, YOUR ONLY ONE, ISAAC (Gen. 22:2). Now, was it not well known that he was his only son? Rather this refers to (Abraham's) life which is called "only one" as it is said SAVE MY LIFE FROM THE SWORD, MY ONLY ONE FROM THE CLUTCHES OF A DOG (Ps. 22:21).

Another interpretation: HE FOUND HIM IN A DESERT REGION (Deut. 32:10). This refers to Israel, as it is said I FOUND ISRAEL AS GRAPES IN THE DESERT (Hos. 9:10).

IN AN EMPTY HOWLING WASTE (Deut. 32:10). In a place full of troubles, a place of marauders, wandering soldiers, and robbers.

[Abraham's] life   The phrase YOUR ONLY ONE is superfluous if referring to Isaac. Therefore it is interpreted as referring to Abraham's own life. He was commanded to offer that up as well as offering Isaac and he was willing to do so.

HE ENGIRDED HIM (Deut. 32:10) before Mount Sinai, as it is said YOU SHALL SET BOUNDS FOR THE PEOPLE ROUND ABOUT (Ex. 19: 12). WATCHED OVER HIM (Deut. 32:10) by means of the Ten Pronouncements. This teaches us that when the Pronouncement went out of the mouth of the Holy One, Israel could see it and became enlightened by it and knew whatever interpretations, *halachot*, logical deductions, and analogies were in it.

GUARDING HIM AS THE PUPIL OF HIS EYE (Deut. 32:10). They went backward twelve miles and forward twelve miles at each Pronouncement, yet they were not afraid of the thunder or the lightning.

Another interpretation: HE FOUND HIM IN A DESERT REGION (Deut. 32:10). Everything was found and supplied for them in the desert. The well arose for them, the manna descended for them, the quail was found for them, the clouds of glory surrounded them.

IN AN EMPTY HOWLING WILDERNESS (Deut. 32:10). In a place full of troubles, a place of marauders, wandering soldiers, and robbers. HE ENGIRDED HIM (Deut. 32:10) with banners, three on the north, three on the south, three on the east, and three on the west.

WATCHED OVER HIM (Deut. 32:10) in regard to the two gifts. If anyone from among the nations tried to take a handful of manna, he emerged empty-handed—to take water from the well, he emerged empty-handed.

GUARDING HIM AS THE PUPIL OF HIS EYE (Deut. 32:10) as in the verse ADVANCE, O LORD! MAY YOUR ENEMIES BE SCATTERED, AND MAY YOUR FOES FLEE BEFORE YOU! (Num. 10:35).

---

halachot—the laws.

logical deductions, and analogies These rabbinic methods for the interpretation of Scripture were included in the revelation at Sinai. The visible Pronouncement, i.e., the word of God, taught Israel not only of the words of the Torah, but also of all that was to be derived from it.

backward twelve miles The force of the Revelation was such as to cause them to move back and forward like a tremendous wave. Nevertheless, God guarded them and they were not afraid.

with banners—the standards of the tribes who encamped thus around Tent of Meeting. See Num. 2.

Another interpretation: HE FOUND HIM IN A DESERT REGION (Deut. 32:10). This refers to the future, as it is said ASSUREDLY, I WILL SPEAK COAXINGLY TO HER AND LEAD HER THROUGH THE DESERT AND SPEAK TO HER TENDERLY (Hos. 2:16).

IN AN EMPTY HOWLING WASTE (Deut. 32:10). This refers to the four kingdoms, as it is said WHO LED YOU THROUGH THE GREAT AND TERRIBLE DESERT (Deut. 8:15).

HE ENGIRDED HIM (Deut. 32:10) with elders.
WATCHED OVER HIM (Deut. 32:10) with prophets.
GUARDED HIM AS THE PUPIL OF HIS EYE (Deut. 32:10) guarding them from the evil spirits so that they should not injure them, as it is said WHOSOEVER TOUCHES YOU TOUCHES THE PUPIL OF HIS OWN EYE (Zech. 2:12).

THE LORD ALONE DID GUIDE HIM (Deut. 32:12). The Holy One said to them, "Just as you sat alone in this world and derived no pleasure from the nations, thus shall I set you alone in the future and none of the nations will derive pleasure from you!"

NO ALIEN GOD AT HIS SIDE (Deut. 32:12). None of the princes of the nations shall be permitted to come and rule over them, as it is said WHEN I GO OFF, THE PRINCE OF GREECE WILL COME IN (Dan. 10:20). HOWEVER, THE PRINCE OF THE PERSIAN KINGDOM OPPOSED ME (Dan. 10:13). HOWEVER, I WILL TELL YOU WHAT IS RECORDED IN THE BOOK OF TRUTH (Dan. 10:21).

Another interpretation: THE LORD ALONE DID GUIDE HIM (Deut. 32:12). In the future I shall give you possessions from one end of the world to the other. Thus it says FROM THE EASTERN BORDER TO THE WESTERN BORDER: ASHER—ONE (Ezek. 48:2). FROM THE

---

the future The previous interpretations of the verse saw it as a description of events in history. This one sees it as a prediction of the coming time of redemption.
the four kingdoms Zech. 6:1 was interpreted to indicate that Israel would be attacked by four kingdoms.
LED YOU—in Hebrew *molichecha*, which is similar to the word for kingdoms, *malchuyot*.
princes of the nations The divine beings, angels, assigned to guard each nation will not be at HIS SIDE, i.e., Israel's side.

EASTERN BORDER TO THE WESTERN BORDER: REUBEN—ONE (Ezek. 48:6). FROM THE EASTERN BORDER TO THE WESTERN BORDER: JUDAH—ONE (Ezek. 48:7). What is the meaning of ASHER—ONE; REUBEN—ONE; JUDAH—ONE? That in the future Israel will encompass an area stretching from east to west in length, and twenty-five thousand rods, or seventy-five miles, in width.

NO ALIEN GOD AT HIS SIDE (Deut. 32:12). There shall be no idolaters among you. Thus it says ASSUREDLY, BY THIS ALONE SHALL JACOB'S SIN BE PURGED AWAY (Isa. 27:9).

Another interpretation: THE LORD ALONE DID GUIDE HIM (Deut. 32:12). In the future, I shall sit you among pleasure in the world.

NO ALIEN GOD AT HIS SIDE (Deut. 32:12). There will be none among you engaged in fruitless matters, as it is said LET ABUNDANT (pisat) GRAIN BE IN THE LAND (Ps. 72:16). The wheat will yield handfuls (pissah) of cakes. LET HIS CROPS RUSTLE LIKE THE FOREST OF LEBANON (Ps. 72:16). The stalks of wheat will rustle against one another, so that their fine grain will sift down to the earth. You will be able to come and take handfuls of it, enough to sustain yourself. . . .

HE SET HIM ATOP THE HIGHLANDS (Deut. 32:13). This refers to the Temple, which was higher than all the world as it is said YOU SHALL PROMPTLY GO UP TO THE PLACE WHICH THE LORD YOUR GOD HAS CHOSEN (Deut. 17:8). And it says AND THE MANY PEOPLES SHALL GO AND SHALL SAY: "COME, LET US GO UP TO THE MOUNT OF THE LORD" (Isa. 2:3).

TO FEAST ON THE YIELD OF THE EARTH (Deut. 32:13). This refers to the baskets of first-fruits.

HE FED HIM HONEY FROM THE CRAG, AND OIL FROM THE FLINTY ROCK (Deut. 32:13). This refers to the libations of oil.

CURD OF KINE AND MILK OF FLOCKS; WITH THE BEST OF LAMBS AND RAMS (Deut. 32:14). This refers to sin offerings, burnt

---

first fruits—which were brought as a offering to the Temple. Every part of the verse is now interpreted as referring to Temple offerings.

offerings, offerings of well-being, thanksgiving and guilt offerings, and those of lesser sanctity.

WITH THE VERY FINEST WHEAT (Deut. 32:14). This refers to the offerings of fine flour.

AND FOAMING GRAPE-BLOOD WAS YOUR DRINK (Deut. 32:14). This refers to the libations of wine.

Another interpretation: HE SET HIM ATOP THE HIGHLANDS (Deut. 32:13). This refers to the Torah, as it is said THE LORD CREATED ME AT THE BEGINNING OF HIS COURSE (Prov. 8:22).

TO FEAST ON THE YIELD OF THE EARTH (Deut. 32:13). This refers to Scripture.

HE FED HIM HONEY FROM THE CRAG (Deut. 32:13). This refers to Mishna.

AND OIL FROM THE FLINTY ROCK (Deut. 32:13). This refers to Talmud.

CURD OF KINE AND MILK OF FLOCKS; WITH THE BEST OF LAMBS AND RAMS (Deut. 32:14). This refers to logical inferences, analogies, rules, and answers.

WITH THE VERY FINEST WHEAT (Deut. 32:14). This refers to *halachot*, which are the essence of Torah.

AND FOAMING GRAPE-BLOOD WAS YOUR DRINK (Deut. 32:14). This refers to *haggadot*, which attract man's heart like wine.

CREATED ME—wisdom, equated with Torah. In this interpretation all the phrases of the verse refer to varieties of Torah.
Mishna—rabbinic teaching.
Talmud—teaching derived from Biblical texts.
logical inferences—hermenutical methods of interpretation.
halachot—traditional laws.
haggadot—the legends, parables, and nonlegal interpretations that were easily comprehended and very attractive to people.

Another interpretation: HE SET HIM ATOP THE HIGHLANDS (Deut. 32:13). This refers to the world. . . .

TO FEAST ON THE YIELD OF THE EARTH (Deut. 32:13). This refers to the four kingdoms, as it is said WILD BOARS GNAW AT IT, AND CREATURES OF THE FIELD FEED ON IT (Ps. 80:14).

HE FED HIM HONEY FROM THE CRAG AND OIL FROM THE FLINTY ROCK (Deut. 32:13). This refers to the oppressors who have taken possession of the Land of Israel and from whom it is as difficult to extract a *perutah* as from a flinty rock. On the morrow Israel will inherit their possessions and take pleasure from them as from oil and honey.

CURD OF KINE (Deut. 32:14). This refers to their consuls and generals.
AND MILK OF FLOCKS (Deut. 32:14). This refers to their colonels.
AND RAMS (Deut. 2:14). This refers to their centurions.
BULLS OF BASHAN (Deut. 32:14). This refers to the privileged soldiers who pick [food] from between their teeth (ben shinayim).
AND HE-GOATS (Deut. 32:14). This refers to their senators.
WITH THE VERY FINEST WHEAT (Deut. 32:14). This refers to their noble ladies.
AND FOAMING GRAPE-BLOOD WAS YOUR DRINK (Deut. 32:14). On the morrow Israel will inherit their possessions and take pleasure from them as from oil and honey.

COMMENTARY   *The fact that Deuteronomy 32:10 says FOUND HIM, without specifying to whom that refers, provides an opportunity for various Sages to interpret it in reference to different people or groups. The editor puts these together with no attempt to determine if one interpretation is better than another, illustrating what Kadushin called the "indeterminacy of belief." Thus it may refer to Abraham and every section of the verse can refer to some event in Abraham's life. Or it may refer to Israel, in which case the verse refers to events such as the theophany at Sinai. On the other hand the details may refer to the wandering in the desert. Yet another interpretation is offered in which the point of reference is not Israel in the past, but Israel in the future, providing Messianic and apocalyptic visions. Similarly HIGHLANDS in Deuteronomy 32:13 is undefined and is then*

---

perutah—a very small coin of little value.

variously interpreted as the Temple, the Torah, or the world, meaning the current status of the people of Israel. Thus the Midrash applies the ancient prophecies to the situation of the Jews at their own time and to the prospects for the future. The interpretations here are an exact description of the situation in the Land of Israel in the second century C.E. They also include the vision of the future when the privileged Romans would lose all and Israel would inherit all of their goods.

14. Deuteronomy 32:26, Sifre D. 323, 370

I THOUGHT I WOULD REDUCE THEM TO NAUGHT (afahem) (Deut. 32:26). I thought in My anger, "Where are they (api ayeh hem)?" I WOULD MAKE THEIR MEMORY CEASE AMONG MEN. WERE IT NOT (Deut. 32:26–27). I thought, "They shall not endure in this world," but what shall I do to them? WERE IT NOT FOR THE LORD, WHO WAS ON OUR SIDE WHEN MEN ASSAILED US (Ps. 124:2).

Another interpretation: I THOUGHT I WOULD REDUCE THEM TO NAUGHT, I WOULD MAKE THEIR MEMORY CEASE AMONG MEN. WERE IT NOT (Deut. 32:26–27)—they shall not endure in this world, but what shall I do to them? WERE IT NOT THAT THE LORD OF HOSTS LEFT US SOME SURVIVORS (Isa. 1:9).

Another interpretation: I THOUGHT I WOULD REDUCE THEM TO NAUGHT . . . WERE IT NOT (Deut. 32:26–27) as it is said HE WOULD HAVE DESTROYED THEM WERE IT NOT FOR MOSES HIS CHOSEN ONE WHO CONFRONTED HIM IN THE BREACH TO AVERT HIS DESTRUCTIVE WRATH (Ps. 106:23). . . .

THEIR ENEMIES WHO MIGHT MISJUDGE (yenakru) (Deut. 32:27). When Israel is in distress the nations of the world distance themselves (menakkerim) from them and act as if they never knew them. Thus we find that when they tried to flee to the north, they would not take them in but handed them over, as it is written in the verse THUS SAID THE LORD: FOR THREE TRANSGRESSIONS OF TYRE, FOR FOUR, I WILL NOT REVOKE IT: BECAUSE THEY HANDED OVER AN ENTIRE POPULATION TO EDOM (Amos 1:9). They tried to flee to the south, but they handed them over, as it is said THUS SAID THE LORD: FOR THREE TRANSGRESSIONS OF GAZA, FOR FOUR, I WILL NOT REVOKE IT: BECAUSE THEY EXILED AN ENTIRE POPULA-TION, WHICH THEY DELIVERED TO EDOM (Amos 1:6). They tried to flee to the east, but they handed them over, as it is said THUS SAID THE LORD: FOR THREE TRANSGRESSIONS OF DAMASCUS, FOR FOUR, I WILL NOT REVOKE IT (Amos 1:3). They tried to flee to the west, but they handed them over, as it is said THE BURDEN UPON THE WEST. IN THE SCRUB, IN THE WEST, YOU WILL LODGE, O CARAVANS OF THE DEDANITES! (Isa. 21:13).

But when Israel prospers, the nations of the world flatter them and act as if they were brothers. Thus Esau said to Jacob I HAVE ENOUGH, MY BROTHER; LET WHAT YOU HAVE REMAIN YOURS (Gen. 33:9). Thus Hiram said to Solomon "MY BROTHER," HE SAID, "WHAT SORT OF TOWNS ARE THESE YOU HAVE GIVEN ME?" (1 Kings 9:13).

AND SAY, "OUR OWN HAND HAS PREVAILED" (Deut. 32:27) as those fools who said "BY OUR MIGHT WE HAVE CAPTURED KAR-NAIM" (Amos 6:13).

FOR THEY ARE A FOLK VOID OF SENSE (Deut. 32:28). R. Judah interpreted this in reference to Israel. R. Nehemiah interpreted it in reference to the nations of the world.

R. Judah interpreted it in reference to Israel: Israel voided the good counsel He had given them, and "counsel" always means Torah, as it is said MINE ARE COUNSEL AND RESOURCEFULNESS (Prov. 8:14).

LACKING IN ALL DISCERNMENT (Deut. 32:28). Not one of them would consider and say, "Just the other day one of us could rout a thousand men of the nations, and two put ten thousand to flight and now one man of the nations routs a thousand of us and two put ten thousand to flight." UNLESS THEIR ROCK HAD SOLD THEM (Deut. 32:30).

R. Nehemiah interpreted it in reference to the nations: The nations have voided the seven mitzvot which I gave them.

LACKING IN ALL DISCERNMENT (Deut. 32:28). Not one of them would consider and say, "Now one of us routs a thousand Israelites, and two put ten thousand to flight. In the days of the Messiah, one Israelite

---

14. *in reference to Israel* The FOLK VOID OF SENSE is Israel.
voided the seven mitzvot The nations of the world are the FOLK DEVOID OF SENSE. This can be seen in that they do not observe the seven basic regulations governing decent human conduct that, according to rabbinic tradition, were given to the children of Noah after the flood.

will rout a thousand of us and two will put then thousand to flight." UN-LESS THEIR ROCK HAD SOLD THEM (Deut. 32:30).

It once happened during the Judean revolt, that a mounted decurion pursued an Israelite to kill him, but he did not overtake him. Before [the decurion] caught him, a serpent emerged and stung the Israelite on the heel. The Israelite said to him, "Do not think to boast that 'Because we are mighty they have been delivered into our hands—' UNLESS THEIR ROCK HAD SOLD THEM (Deut. 32:30)!"

WERE THEY WISE, THEY WOULD THINK UPON (yaskilu) THIS (Deut. 32:29). If Israel would only look upon (histaklu) the Torah which I gave them, no nation or kingdom could rule over them. THIS always means Torah, as it is said THIS IS THE TORAH THAT MOSES SET BEFORE THE ISRAELITES (Deut. 4:44).

Another interpretation: WERE THEY WISE, THEY WOULD THINK UPON THIS (Deut. 32:29). If Israel would only look upon what their father Jacob said to them, no nation or kingdom could rule over them. What did he say to them? "Accept the Kingship of Heaven upon yourselves, vie with one another in reverence for Heaven and act toward one another with loving-kindness."

HOW COULD ONE HAVE ROUTED A THOUSAND (Deut. 32:30). If you have not fulfilled the Torah, how do you expect Me to fulfill the promise you requested that one of you should rout a thousand men from the nations? OR TWO PUT TEN THOUSAND TO FLIGHT (Deut. 32:30) but now one from the nations routs a thousand of you and two of them put ten thousand to flight.

UNLESS THEIR ROCK HAD SOLD THEM, THE LORD HAD GIVEN THEM UP (Deut. 32:30). I will not give you up Myself, but have others do it. It once happened that in Judea flies gave them up. . . .

Judean revolt—probably referring to the Bar Kokhba rebellion in the second century C.E.
decurion—an officer in charge of ten horsemen.
look upon—or "consider."
but have others do it—as if the verse read "The Lord has not given them up."
flies gave them up—an obscure reference.

FOR THEIR ROCK IS NOT LIKE OUR ROCK (Deut. 32:31). The power which You give them is not like the power You give us. When you give us power, we act toward them according to the Quality of Mercy, but when you give them power, they act toward us according to the Quality of Cruelty. They slay us, burn us, and crucify us.

OUR ENEMIES BEING JUDGES (Deut. 32:31). In the Torah You wrote that an enemy may not judge or testify—THOUGH HE WAS NOT AN ENEMY OF HIS (Num. 35:23). Only then may he testify. AND DID NOT SEEK HIS HARM (Num. 35:23). Only then may he judge. And now You appoint our enemies witnesses and judges over us!

AH! THE VINE FOR THEM IS FROM SODOM (Deut. 32:32). R. Judah interprets this in reference to Israel. R. Nehemiah interprets it in reference to the nations of the world.

R. Judah says, "Are you of the vine of Sodom or the vineyards of Gomorrah? Are you not rather a sacred vineyard, as it is said I PLANTED YOU WITH NOBLE VINES, ALL WITH CHOICEST SEED (Jer. 2:21).

"THE GRAPES FOR THEM ARE POISON (Deut. 32:32). You are the children of Primal Adam upon whom and upon whose descendants after him I decreed death until the end of all generations.

"A BITTER GROWTH THEIR CLUSTERS (Deut. 32:32). The gall of the great among you is spread out in them like a cluster, and 'cluster' always means a large [bunch], as it is said THERE IS NOT A CLUSTER TO EAT, NOT A RIPE FIG I COULD DESIRE (Micah 7:1).

"THEIR WINE IS THE VENOM OF ASPS (Deut. 32:33). You envenomed the pious and God-fearing among you like asps. THE PITILESS POISON (rosh) OF VIPERS (Deut. 32:33). Your leaders (roshim) became like vipers who are pitiless."

Another interpretation: THEIR WINE IS THE VENOM OF ASPS (Deut. 32:33). You envenomed the patient and sin-fearing among you like asps. . . .

R. Nehemiah interprets it in reference to the nations of the world. "You are certainly like the vine of Sodom and the vineyards of Gomorrah. . . . You are the disciples of the primal serpent that caused Adam and Eve to go astray.

"A BITTER GROWTH THEIR CLUSTERS (Deut. 32:32). The gall of the great among you is spread out in them like a serpent."

371

COMMENTARY   *The Midrash frequently gives alternative interpretations to the same verse. Here various verses are applied either to Israel or to the nations. In either case, however, the Sages are unanimous in contending that the change in fortunes of the Israelites, in which they are not able to defeat the Romans, is due not to the might or the merit of the Romans, but to God, who has "sold them." The cruelty of the Romans is graphically described and contrasted to the mercy of the Israelites who, even when they have the power, never slay and crucify as they do. The Israelites could avoid the bitterness of their fate if they would live according to God's Torah. Then no nation could rule over them.*

15. Deuteronomy 32:36, Sifre D. 326, 377

FOR THE LORD WILL JUDGE HIS PEOPLE (Deut. 32:36). When the Holy One judges the nations, He rejoices, but when He judges His people He regrets it, as it were, as it is said FOR THE LORD WILL JUDGE HIS PEOPLE AND REPENT HIMSELF CONCERNING HIS SERVANTS (Deut. 32:36). "Repent" always means "regret," as it is said FOR I REPENT THAT I MADE THEM (Gen. 6:8). I REPENT THAT I MADE SAUL KING (1 Sam. 15:11).

WHEN HE SEES THAT THEIR MIGHT IS GONE (Deut. 32:36). When He sees that they go into captivity after their destruction. Another interpretation: WHEN HE SEES—that they despair of redemption. Another interpretation: THAT THEIR MIGHT IS GONE, AND NEITHER BOND NOR FREE IS LEFT (Deut. 32:36). When He sees that there is no one who has a coin in his pocket, as it is said WHEN THE BREAKING OF THE POWER OF THE HOLY PEOPLE COMES TO AN END, THEN SHALL ALL THESE THINGS BE FULFILLED (Dan. 12:7).

Another interpretation: WHEN HE SEES THAT THEIR MIGHT IS GONE (Deut. 32:36). When He sees that they have no one to ask for mercy

---

15. *the nations*   HIS PEOPLE (Deut. 32:36) is taken to mean the nations since HIS SERVANTS in the second half of the verse refers to Israel. He judges the nations gladly, but when He has to judge His servants, Israel, He regrets it.

to ask for mercy   They have no great leader who can intercede with God as did the great leaders of the past; Moses, Aaron, and Phinehas.

upon them as did Moses, as it is said HE WOULD HAVE DESTROYED THEM HAD NOT MOSES HIS CHOSEN ONE CONFRONTED HIM IN THE BREACH TO AVERT HIS DESTRUCTIVE WRATH (Ps. 106:23).

Another interpretation: WHEN HE SEES THAT THEIR MIGHT IS GONE (Deut. 32:36). When He sees that they have no one to ask for mercy upon them as did Aaron, as it is said HE STOOD BETWEEN THE DEAD AND THE LIVING UNTIL THE PLAGUE WAS CHECKED (Num. 17:13).

Another interpretation: WHEN HE SEES THAT THEIR MIGHT IS GONE (Deut. 32:36). When he sees that they have no one to ask for mercy upon them as did Phinehas, as it is said PHINEHAS STEPPED FORWARD AND INTERVENED AND THE PLAGUE CEASED (Ps. 106:30).

Another interpretation: WHEN HE SEES THAT THEIR MIGHT IS GONE AND NEITHER BOND NOR FREE IS LEFT—

> none locked up,
> none free,
> none to help Israel.

HE WILL SAY: WHERE ARE THEIR GODS (Deut. 32:37) . . . R. Judah says, "In the future Israel will say to the nations of the world, 'Where are your counsels and your generals?' "

WHO ATE THE FAT OF THEIR OFFERINGS (Deut. 32:38)—to whom we used to give *opsonia, donativa,* and *alaria*—LET THEM RISE UP AND HELP YOU (Deut. 32:38). It does not actually say "let them rise up and let them help you," but "let them rise up and let *him* help you." R. Nehemiah says, "This refers to the wicked Titus, the son of Vespasian's

---

where are your counsels The day will come when the enemy will cease to rule and will no longer have leaders who can harm Israel.

opsonia, donativa, and alaria—three allowances given Roman soldiers: food, money awarded on special occasions, and money used to purchase salt.

let him help you Although the vocalized Hebrew text reads both verbs as plural, the second verb (help) is actually spelled in the singular. Therefore the subject would be one person and not many. It refers, then, to Titus, who considered himself a god, but will be punished for his impiety.

Titus—the emperor of Rome 79–81 C.E., who destroyed the Temple in 70 C.E.

Vespasian's wife—but not of Vespasian, therefore a bastard.

wife, who entered the Holy of Holies, and cut the two curtains with his sword and said, 'If He is God—let Him come and stop me!' WHO ATE THE FAT OF THEIR OFFERINGS (Deut. 32:38). [Titus] said, 'Moses misled them when he told them to build for themselves an altar and offer up sacrifices and pour out libations, as it is said YOU SHALL OFFER ONE LAMB IN THE MORNING, AND THE OTHER LAMB YOU SHALL OFFER AT TWILIGHT (Num. 28:4).' "

LET THEM RISE UP TO YOUR HELP AND LET THEM BE A SHIELD UNTO YOU! (Deut. 32:38). The Holy One is willing to forgive anything, but desecration of His Name He will requite immediately.

SEE, THEN, THAT I, I AM HE (Deut. 32:39). This is a refutation of those who claim that there is no Power in heaven. One may refute those who say that there are two Powers in heaven by saying, "Does it not also say THERE IS NO GOD BESIDES ME? (Deut. 32:39)." On the question of whether or not He has the ability to kill, to give life, to punish, or to bestow benefit, the verse says SEE, THEN, THAT I, I AM HE . . . I DEAL DEATH AND GIVE LIFE (Deut. 32:39) and it says THIS SAID THE LORD, THE KING OF ISRAEL, THEIR REDEEMER, THE LORD OF HOSTS: I AM THE FIRST AND I AM THE LAST, AND THERE IS NO GOD BUT ME (Isa. 44:6).

Another interpretation: I DEAL DEATH AND GIVE LIFE (Deut. 32:39). This is one of four assurances He gave them which hint at the resurrection of the dead:

> I DEAL DEATH AND GIVE LIFE;
> MAY I DIE THE DEATH OF THE UPRIGHT, MAY MY FATE BE LIKE THEIRS (Num. 23:10);
> MAY REUBEN LIVE AND NOT DIE (Deut. 33:6);
> IN TWO DAYS HE WILL MAKE US WHOLE AGAIN; ON THE THIRD DAY HE WILL RAISE US UP (Hos. 6:2).

I might think that these refer to the death of one person and the life of

---

curtains—which separated the Holy of Holies from the rest of the structure. No one but the High Priest was allowed to enter therein.

Moses misled them Finding no statue within and not immediately struck down for his desecration, Titus assumes that Israel has no god to whom to offer all their sacrifices. It was all Moses' plot.

another, therefore the verse says I WOUNDED AND I WILL HEAL (Deut. 32:39). Just as the wound and the healing refer to one and the same person, so death and life refer to one and the same person.

NONE CAN DELIVER FROM MY HAND (Deut. 32:39). Fathers cannot deliver their sons. Abraham could not deliver Ishmael and Isaac could not deliver Esau. This indicates only that fathers cannot deliver their sons. What about brothers delivering brothers? The verse says A BROTHER CANNOT REDEEM A MAN (Ps. 49:8). Isaac cannot deliver Ishmael and Jacob cannot deliver Esau. Even if a man were to give all the wealth in the world, he cannot attain atonement, as it is said A BROTHER CANNOT REDEEM A MAN, OR PAY HIS RANSOM TO GOD; THE PRICE OF LIFE IS TOO HIGH (Ps. 49:8–9). When a man sins against [life], there is no payment [which is sufficient].

COMMENTARY   *As in the sections above, here too the verses are applied to the Roman persecution of the Jews. The helplessness of their situation is summed up in one bitter line: None locked up, none free, none to help Israel. The story of Titus's desecration of the Sanctuary is found in various places. Here the emphasis is on his declaration that since there is no god found there (i.e., no idol), the entire religion of Israel is a farce. This desecration of God's Name, the opposite of the rabbinic value of the Sanctification of God's Name, is unforgivable. There are many places here where attempts are made to refute those who negate the beliefs of the Sages. This ranges from those who deny the existence of God to those who believe that there are two gods and also includes a disputation with the Sadducean opponents of the Sages. This is found in a discussion of the power of God to resurrect the dead. This rabbinic concept was a dogma of the Pharisees and bitterly opposed by the Sadducees. The Sages constantly attempted to find Biblical proof for it, since the Sadducees accepted only the Bible and not tradition or "Oral Torah" as authoritative. This attempt led to interpretations that are far from the simple meaning of the text.*

---

to one and the same person—and in that order, thus indicating that after death comes life— resurrection.

cannot deliver their sons The piety and merit of a father will not save a wicked son from punishment.

against [life] There is no payment that can be made that will atone for the taking of human life.

16. Deuteronomy 32:43, Sifre D. 333, 382

O NATIONS, ACCLAIM HIS PEOPLE! (Deut. 32:43). On the morrow, when the Holy One brings redemption to Israel, the nations of the world will rage against Him, nor will this be the first time, for they have raged before as indicated by the verse THE PEOPLE HAVE HEARD; THEY ARE ENRAGED (Ex. 15:14).

Another interpretation: O NATIONS, ACCLAIM HIS PEOPLE! (Deut. 32:43). In the future the nations of the world will praise Israel, as it is said O NATIONS, ACCLAIM HIS PEOPLE!

The heavens too will [praise Israel], as it is said SHOUT, O HEAVENS, FOR THE LORD HAS ACTED; SHOUT ALOUD, O DEPTHS OF THE EARTH! (Isa. 44:23). What about the mountains and the hills? It says BEFORE YOU, MOUNT AND HILL SHALL SHOUT ALOUD (Isa. 55:12). The trees will also do so, as it is said AND ALL THE TREES OF THE FIELD SHALL CLAP THEIR HANDS (Isa. 55:12). The patriarchs and matriarchs will also [praise], as it is said LET *SELA'S* INHABITANTS SHOUT, CALL OUT FROM THE PEAKS OF THE MOUNTAINS (Isa. 42:11).

FOR HE'LL AVENGE THE BLOOD OF HIS SERVANTS, WREAK VENGEANCE ON HIS FOES (Deut. 32:43). There will be two acts of vengeance: vengeance for the blood and vengeance for the violence. How do we know that whatever violence the nations of the world perpetrated against Israel is considered as if they had shed innocent blood? As it is said I WILL GATHER ALL THE NATIONS AND BRING THEM DOWN TO THE VALLEY OF JEHOSHAPHAT. THERE I WILL CONTEND WITH THEM OVER MY VERY OWN PEOPLE, ISRAEL (Joel 4:2). EGYPT SHALL BE A DESOLATION, AND EDOM A DESOLATE WASTE, BECAUSE OF THE OUTRAGE TO THE PEOPLE OF JUDAH, IN WHOSE LAND THEY SHED THE BLOOD OF THE INNOCENT (Joel 4:19).

AND MAKE EXPIATION FOR THE LAND OF HIS PEOPLE (Deut. 32:43). How do we know that when Israel is slain by the nations, it brings

---

16. *SELA'S INHABITANTS* "Sela" means a rock. It is taken to refer to those who dwell within the rocky earth, i.e., the dead.

them expiation in the world-to-come? As it is said A PSALM OF ASAPH. O GOD, HEATHENS HAVE ENTERED YOUR DOMAIN, DEFILED YOUR HOLY TEMPLE, AND TURNED JERUSALEM INTO RUINS. THEY HAVE LEFT YOUR SERVANTS' CORPSES AS FOOD FOR THE FOWL OF HEAVEN, AND THE FLESH OF YOUR FAITHFUL FOR THE WILD BEASTS. THEIR BLOOD WAS SHED LIKE WA-TER AROUND JERUSALEM (Ps. 79:1-3).

Another interpretation: AND MAKE EXPIATION FOR THE LAND OF HIS PEOPLE (Deut. 32:43). How do we know that the descent of the wicked to Gehenna makes expiation for them? As it is said I GIVE EGYPT AS A RANSOM FOR YOU, ETHIOPIA AND SABA IN EXCHANGE FOR YOU. BECAUSE YOU ARE PRECIOUS TO ME, AND HON-ORED AND I LOVE YOU, I GIVE MEN IN EXCHANGE FOR YOU AND PEOPLES IN YOUR STEAD (Isa. 43:3-4).

R. Meir used to say, "The Land of Israel makes expiation for all those who dwell therein, as it is said AND NONE WHO LIVES THERE SHALL SAY, 'I AM SICK'; IT SHALL BE INHABITED BY FOLK WHOSE SIN HAS BEEN FORGIVEN (Isa. 33:24)." Nevertheless, the matter is still unclear. Are their iniquities forgiven upon it or do they suffer their iniquities upon it? When it says AND MAKE EXPIATION FOR THE LAND OF HIS PEOPLE (Deut. 32:43) it indicates that their iniquities are forgiven upon it. Thus R. Meir used to say, "Whoever dwells in the Land of Israel, recites the Shema morning and evening and speaks the Holy Tongue is assured of the world to come."

You may well say: How great is this Song! It contains references to the present, the past, and the future as well as to this world and the world-to-come!

COMMENTARY   *As the last line in this section indicates, the midrashic interpretation of the Song of Moses applied it to the current situation and*

---

it brings them expiation   This may be based on the fact that after they are slain they are called FAITHFUL, in Hebrew *hasid*, sometimes translated "pious" or even "saint," a title indicating that such a person has been granted expiation.
suffer their iniquities upon it   The word FORGIVEN could possibly mean "tolerated," in which case they would not be being forgiven, but working out their sin there.
this Song—the Song of Moses in Deut. 32, which has been expounded here.

377

found in it a prediction of what would happen on the morrow, in the future when God would judge the nations and bring about the Messianic age and the world-to-come. The vision of the future is one of God's vengeance on the nations and of Israel's redemption and inheritance of the world-to-come, which will cause all, even her enemies, to shout her praises. One can well imagine that these words served the people as a consolation during those difficult days.

17. Deuteronomy 32:48, Sifre D. 337, 386

THAT VERY DAY THE LORD SPOKE TO MOSES (Deut. 32:48). Three times the expression THAT VERY DAY is used:

THAT VERY DAY NOAH AND NOAH'S SONS, SHEM, HAM, AND JEPHET, WENT INTO THE ARK (Gen. 7:13). This teaches us that the people of Noah's generation said, "By our oath, if we see him [try to enter the ark], we will not let him go. Furthermore, we will take picks and axes and wreck his ark over him!" Said the Holy One, "Behold I will bring him into the ark at high noon! Let anyone who objects try to do something about it!"

And why is the expression THAT VERY DAY used in reference to Egypt? FOR ON THAT VERY DAY I BROUGHT YOUR RANKS OUT OF THE LAND OF EGYPT (Ex. 12:17). The Egyptians said, "By our oath, if we see them [try to leave], we will not let them go. Furthermore, we will take our swords and cutlasses and kill them!" Said the Holy One, "Behold I will take them out at high noon! Let anyone who objects try to do something about it!"

And why is the expression THAT VERY DAY used here (Deut. 32:48)? The Israelites said, "By our oath, if we see [Moses trying to leave us], we will not let him go. The man who brought us out of Egypt, split the sea for us, brought down the manna for us, fetched the quail for us, and performed miracles and wonders for us! We will not let him go!" Said the Holy One, "Behold I will bring him into the cave at high noon! Let anyone who objects try to do something about it!" Thus it says THAT VERY DAY THE LORD SPOKE TO MOSES SAYING (Deut. 32:48).

---

17. *at high noon* The words *VERY DAY* can mean something that is bright, the height of the day.

into the cave—on the mountain where Moses is to die.

ASCEND THESE HEIGHTS OF ABARIM (Deut. 32:49). It is an elevation for you, not a degradation.

THESE HEIGHTS OF ABARIM. They have four names: the heights of Abarim, Mount Nebo, Mount Hor, and Top of Pisgah. Why is it called Mount Nebo? Because in it are buried three prophets (nebi-im) whose deaths were not the result of sin, namely Moses, Aaron, and Miriam.

WHICH IS IN THE LAND OF MOAB (Deut. 32:49). This teaches that He revealed to him the dynasty of kings who would spring from Ruth the Moabitess.

FACING JERICHO (Deut. 32:49). This teaches that He revealed to him the dynasty of prophets who would spring from Rahab the harlot. AND VIEW THE LAND OF CANAAN (Deut. 32:49). R. Eliezer says, "The finger of the Holy One became Moses' guide and pointed out to him all the borders of the Land of Israel: thus far the territory of Ephraim—thus far the territory of Mennaseh—." R. Joshua says, "Moses saw it all by himself. How was this possible? [God] gave power to Moses' eyes so that he could see from one end of the world to the other."

YOU SHALL DIE ON THE MOUNTAIN THAT YOU ARE ABOUT TO ASCEND (Deut. 32:50). [Moses] said to Him, "Master of the universe, why must I die? Would it not be better for people to say 'Moses is good' out of personal experience rather than from rumor? Would it not be better for people to say 'This is Moses who took us out of Egypt, split the sea for us, brought us down the manna for us, and wrought miracles and wonders for us' than 'Moses was like that and did such-and-such?' "

[God] replied, "Enough, Moses. It is My decree which applies equally to all human beings," as it is said THIS IS THE TORAH: WHEN A MAN DIES IN A TENT (Num. 19:14) and THIS IS THE TORAH OF A MAN, O LORD GOD (2 Sam. 7:19).

---

an elevation Since Moses is told ASCEND—go up—this indicates that he is not being punished, but exalted.

three prophets Miriam actually died and was buried at Kadesh (Num. 20:1). The midrash assumes that she too was buried at Mt. Nebo because of her importance and her sinless status.

dynasty of prophets According to rabbinic tradition, Rahab of Jericho converted and was the ancestress of many prophets, including Jeremiah.

A MAN DIES—any man and every man is subject to death, including Moses, the greatest of men.

The ministering angels said to the Holy One, "Master of the universe! Why did primal Adam die?"

[God] replied, "Because he did not carry out My commands."

They said to Him, "But Moses did carry out Your commands!"

[God] replied, "It is My decree which applies equally to all human beings," as it is said THIS IS THE TORAH WHEN A MAN DIES IN A TENT (Num. 19:14).

AND SHALL BE GATHERED TO YOUR KIN (Deut. 32:50)—to Abraham, Isaac, and Jacob; to Amram and Kohath; to Miriam and your brother Aaron.

AS YOUR BROTHER AARON DIED (Deut. 32:50). This was the death that you desired.

How do we know that Moses desired the same death as Aaron? When the Holy One said to him, "TAKE AARON AND HIS SON ELEAZAR AND BRING THEM TO MOUNT HOR. DIVEST AARON OF HIS GARMENTS" (Num. 20:25–26), [Moses] took the priestly garments from him and put them on to Eleazar one by one.

[Moses] said to [Aaron], "Go into the cave," and he went in.

"Lie down upon the couch," and he did so.

"Stretch out your arms," and he did so.

"Stretch out your legs," and he did so.

"Close your mouth," and he did so.

"Close your eyes," and he did so.

At that time Moses said, "Happy is the man who dies in this manner." Thus it is said AS YOUR BROTHER AARON DIED (Deut. 32:50). This was the death that you desired.

FOR YOU BROKE FAITH WITH ME (Deut. 32:51). You caused [Israel] to break faith with Me. BY FAILING TO UPHOLD MY SANCTITY AMONG THE ISRAELITE PEOPLE (Deut. 32:51). You caused [Israel] not to sanctify My Name.

YOU DISOBEYED MY COMMAND (Num. 27:14). You caused them to disobey Me. The Holy One said to Moses, "Did I not say to you WHAT

---

the death that you desired   The phrase AS YOUR BROTHER AARON DIED does not mean simply that Aaron died and so will you, but that you will die in the same way that Aaron died, quietly at the hand of God, something Moses desired.

IS THAT IN YOUR HAND? . . . CAST IT ON THE GROUND (Ex. 4:2–3)? And you cast it. If you did not hesitate to perform those signs with your own hands, why did you hesitate in this simple task?"

How do we know that Moses did not depart this world until the Holy One enveloped him in His wings? As it is said THEREFORE YOU SHALL NOT LEAD THIS CONGREGATION INTO THE LAND THAT I HAVE GIVEN THEM (Num. 20:12).

YOU MAY VIEW THE LAND FROM A DISTANCE, BUT YOU SHALL NOT ENTER IT (Deut. 32:52). Here it says BUT YOU SHALL NOT ENTER IT and elsewhere it says BUT YOU SHALL NOT CROSS THERE (Deut. 34:4). It is impossible to say BUT YOU SHALL NOT CROSS THERE when it already says BUT YOU SHALL NOT ENTER IT (Deut. 32:52) and it is impossible to say BUT YOU SHALL NOT EN-TER IT when elsewhere it says BUT YOU SHALL NOT CROSS THERE (Deut. 34:4). [This indicates] that Moses said to the Holy One, "If I cannot enter [the Land] as a king, let me enter as a commoner. If I cannot enter alive, let me enter dead." The Holy One replied "BUT YOU SHALL NOT CROSS THERE (Deut. 34:4)—

> not as a king,
> not as a commoner,
> not alive,
> and not dead!"

COMMENTARY *The various legends concerning the death of Moses are scattered throughout these midrashic books. Among the themes that are prominent in this section are the love of the people for Moses; Moses' desire to reach the Land of Israel; and the fact that the death of Moses was a necessity. This is seen not so much as a punishment—one startling comment even denies that he, Aaron, and Miriam had really sinned—but because he was a human being and nothing more. All human beings die. It is difficult not to see this as a comment on Christian belief. So too underlying the discussion of the sin of Adam that resulted in his death seems to be the*

---

this simple task—speaking to the stone in order to obtain water. See Num. 20:8.
enveloped him in His wings—an expression used to mean being gathered unto God at the time of death. The connection to the verse is unclear.
let me enter dead If he wished his body to be taken across, the verse NOT CROSS THERE would apply.

assertion that the death of Adam and the death of all men is the result of their individual sins and not some primal sin that affects all. If there was any sin connected to Moses it was that he had an opportunity to sanctify God's Name and did not do so. The absoluteness of the Divine decree is empha-sized in the poetic line with which the section ends, words that, in the He-brew and even in the translation, ring with the inevitability of the tolling of a bell: not as a king, not as a commoner, not alive, and not dead!

18. Deuteronomy 33:2, Sifre D. 343, 394

HE SAID: THE LORD CAME FROM SINAI (Deut. 33:2). This verse indicates that when Moses began to speak, he did not speak of the needs of Israel until he had first spoken the praise of God.

A parable. An advocate hired by a certain person to speak on his behalf stood upon the podium. He did not speak of the needs of his client until he had first spoken the praises of the king.

> "Happy is the world because he is its king!
> Happy is the world because he is its judge!
> The sun shines on us because of him!
> The moon shines on us because of him!"

Others joined him in this praise, after which he began to speak of the needs of his client. When he finished, he concluded by again speaking the praises of the king.

Thus Moses our teacher did not speak of the needs of Israel until he had spoken the praise of God, as it is said HE SAID: THE LORD CAME FROM SINAI (Deut. 33:2). Only then did he speak of the needs of Israel, as it is said THEN HE BECAME KING IN JESHURUN, WHEN THE HEADS OF THE PEOPLE ASSEMBLED, THE TRIBES OF ISRAEL TOGETHER. MAY REUBEN LIVE AND NOT DIE (Deut. 33:5-6). When he finished, he concluded by again speaking the praises of God: O JESHURUN, THERE IS NONE LIKE GOD (Deut. 33:26).

---

18. *when Moses began to speak* This verse is the opening of Moses' farewell blessing in which he talks about the future of each of the tribes. It begins, however, with a prologue that speaks about God.

the praises of the king—who is sitting in judgment.

So too David the King began with the praise of God, as it is said HAL-LELUJAH. SING TO THE LORD A NEW SONG (Ps. 149:1). Only then did he speak the praise of Israel FOR THE LORD DELIGHTS IN HIS PEOPLE (Ps. 150:4). When he finished, he concluded by again speaking the praises of God: HALLELUJAH. PRAISE GOD IN HIS SANCTUARY (Ps. 150:1).

So too Solomon his son began with the praise of God: THERE IS NO GOD LIKE YOU IN THE HEAVENS AND ON THE EARTH, YOU WHO STEADFASTLY MAINTAIN THE COVENANT WITH YOUR SERVANTS (2 Chron. 6:14). Only then did he speak of the needs of Israel: SO, TOO, IF THERE IS A FAMINE IN THE LAND (2 Chron. 6:28). When he finished, he concluded by again speaking the praises of God: ADVANCE, O LORD GOD, TO YOUR RESTING-PLACE, YOU AND YOUR MIGHTY ARK (2 Chron. 6:41).

So too the Eighteen Benedictions which the early prophets instituted for Israel to recite in daily prayer begin not with the needs of Israel but with the praise of God:

> The great, mighty and awesome God!
> You are holy and Your name is awesome!

After that:

> Liberator of the imprisoned
> Healer of the sick!

And then:

> We thankfully acknowledge You!

COMMENTARY   *The Midrash explains the structure of the central prayer of every service, the Eighteen Benedictions (also called the Amida), by analogy to the blessing of Moses and to the actual pattern used in the ancient world when petitioning a ruler. There is first a description of the glory of*

Eighteen Benedictions—the central prayer recited at each service.

the early prophets—possibly referring to Abraham, Isaac, and Jacob. There is a tradition that Abraham inaugurated the morning prayer, Isaac the afternoon prayer, and Jacob the evening prayer.

Liberator of the imprisoned—phrases from the prayer that are considered to be petitions.

the ruler. Only then is the request presented. At the conclusion, the ruler is praised again. So too the prayer describes and praises God both at the beginning and at the conclusion, while petitions, even those implied by the mention of those actions of God that are desired, are found only in the middle section.

Another interpretation: HE SAID: THE LORD CAME FROM SINAI (Deut. 33:1). When the Holy One revealed Himself in order to give Torah to Israel, He revealed Himself not only to Israel but to all of the nations. . . .

Thus it was with every nation. He asked them all if they would accept the Torah, as it is said ALL THE KINGS OF THE EARTH SHALL PRAISE YOU, O LORD, FOR THEY HAVE HEARD THE WORDS YOU SPOKE (Ps. 138:4). Could this mean that they heard and accepted? The verse says IN ANGER AND WRATH WILL I WREAK RETRIBUTION ON THE NATIONS THAT HAVE NOT OBEYED (Micah 5:14). And if it were not bad enough that they did not obey, they did not even observe the seven mitzvot which the children of Noah had accepted upon themselves, but cast them off. When the Holy One saw this, He gave them to Israel as well. A parable. A man took his ass and his dog to the threshing floor. He loaded the ass with a *letek* of grain and the dog with three *seah*. The ass went along but the dog began to pant, so he took one *seah* from him and put it on the ass, and then the second and the third. Thus Israel accepted the Torah, its explanations and detailed laws, and (God) took away from the children of Noah those seven mitzvot and Israel came and accepted them. Thus it says THE LORD CAME FROM SINAI; HE SHONE UPON THEM FROM SEIR (Deut. 33:2).

Another interpretation: HE SHONE UPON THEM FROM SEIR (Deut. 33:2). When the Holy One comes to punish Seir in the future, He will cause the entire earth and all its inhabitants to tremble as He caused it to tremble

---

seven mitzvot—the seven Noachide laws: prohibitions of idolatry, blasphemy, sexual sins, theft, eating the limbs of a living animal, and the obligation to establish a just legal system.

FROM SEIR—Edom. Why was God coming from Seir? He had been there offering the Torah to the nations. Not only did they not accept it, but seeing the way in which the gentiles were not observing the Noachide laws, He took them away and gave them to Israel. On the refusal of the nations to accept the Torah see above page 146.

to punish Seir Seir or Edom is synonymous with Rome. Edom, meaning "red," is used as a description of Esau. Rome's color was also red—the imperial purple. Rome will be destroyed.

384

at the giving of the Torah, as it is said O LORD, WHEN YOU CAME FORTH FROM SEIR, ADVANCED FROM THE COUNTRY OF EDOM, THE EARTH TREMBLED; THE HEAVENS DRIPPED, YEA, THE CLOUDS DRIPPED WATER (Judges 5:4) and THEN HIS BROTHER EMERGED, HOLDING ON TO THE HEEL OF ESAU; SO THEY NAMED HIM JACOB (Gen. 25:26). The Holy One said to them, "No nation or people shall come between you."

A parable. A king wanted to give one of his sons a gift but was afraid of his [son's] brothers, friends, and relatives. What did the son do? He adorned himself and arranged his hair, whereupon the king said, "To you shall I give this gift." Thus when our father Abraham appeared in the world, unworthy children issued from him, Ishmael and the sons of Keturah who were even worse than [the generations] before them. Isaac also had unworthy children, Esau and all the princes of Edom, who were even worse than those before them, but none of Jacob's children were unworthy, all of them were worthy, as it is said BUT JACOB WAS A PERFECT MAN, WHO STAYED IN CAMP (Gen. 25:27). Said the Holy One to him, "To you shall I give the Torah," therefore it says THE LORD CAME FROM SINAI; HE SHONE UPON THEM FROM SEIR (Deut. 33:2).

Another interpretation. THE LORD CAME FROM SINAI (Deut. 33:2). When the Holy One revealed Himself to give the Torah, He caused all of the world and its inhabitants to tremble, as it is said THE VOICE OF THE LORD IS OVER THE WATERS . . . THE VOICE OF THE LORD IS POWER (Ps. 29:3–4).

At that time all the nations gathered together with Balaam and said to him, "It seems as if the Holy One is about to destroy the world with water!"

He said to them, "THE LORD GRANTS STRENGTH TO HIS PEOPLE (Ps. 29:11)"—and STRENGTH always refers to Torah, as it is said WITH HIM ARE STRENGTH AND RESOURCEFULNESS (Job 12:16).

---

come between you After the destruction of Rome, there will be no other nation that will rule over Israel. That will be the beginning of the Messianic era.

adorned himself He did everything to make himself pleasing. So Jacob was pleasing because of the worthiness of all his children.

PERFECT MAN—usually translated "mild." See above page 361.

THE LORD GRANTS STRENGTH Balaam replies that the commotion they perceive in the natural world is not because God is destroying the world, but because He is giving the Torah to Israel.

They said to Him, "If that is the case, MAY THE LORD BESTOW ON HIS PEOPLE WELL-BEING (Ps. 29:11)."

HE APPEARED FROM MOUNT PARAN (Deut. 33:2). Four times does He appear:

the first time was in Egypt, as it is said GIVE EAR, O SHEPHERD OF ISRAEL WHO LEADS JOSEPH LIKE A FLOCK! APPEAR, YOU WHO ARE ENTHRONED ON THE CHERUBIM (Ps. 80:2);

the second time was at the giving of the Torah, as it is said HE APPEARED FROM MOUNT PARAN (Deut. 33:2);

the third will be in the days of Gog and Magog, as it is said GOD OF RETRIBUTION, LORD, GOD OF RETRIBUTION, APPEAR! (Ps. 94:1);

the fourth will be in the days of the Messiah, as it is said FROM ZION, PERFECT IN BEAUTY, GOD APPEARED (Ps. 50:2).

AND APPROACHED FROM MIRIADS HOLY (Deut. 33:2). Human beings do not act the same way as does the Holy One. When a human being makes a wedding celebration for his son, he displays all of his treasures and everything he owns, but He Who Spoke and the world came into being is not like that. Rather AND APPROACHED FROM MIRIADS HOLY and not "from *all* the miriads holy."

Another interpretation: AND APPROACHED FROM MIRIADS HOLY (Deut. 33:2). When a human king holds court in his palace, among those present are people who are handsomer than he, more praiseworthy than he, stronger than he, but that is not the case with He Who Spoke and the world came into being. AND APPROACHED (ata) FROM MIRIADS HOLY— He is outstanding (ot) among the miriads holy.

When He revealed Himself at the sea, they recognized Him immediately, as it is said THIS IS MY GOD AND I WILL ENSHRINE HIM, THE GOD OF MY FATHER AND I WILL EXALT HIM (Ex. 15:2). . . .

Gog and Magog—the period of warfare and turmoil prior to the final judgment and redemption.
miriads holy Although this may be a place name, the midrash understands it to refer to the ministering angels. Only some of them came with God; He did not display His entire entourage.
they recognized Him immediately The word *this* indicates that they saw Him and pointed to Him. They did not mistake any of the angels for God. See above page 104.

A FIERY LAW FOR THEM FROM HIS RIGHT (Deut. 33:2). When the Pronouncement emerged from the mouth of the Holy One, it emerged from the right of the Holy One to the left of Israel and encircled the camp of Israel twelve miles in every direction, after which it would return by the right of Israel to the left of the Holy One, and the Holy One would seize it with His right hand and engrave it upon the tablet. His voice would reach from one end of the world to the other, as it is said THE VOICE OF THE LORD KINDLES FLAMES OF FIRE (Ps. 29:7).

A FIERY LAW FOR THEM FROM HIS RIGHT (Deut. 33:2). This informs us that words of Torah may be compared to fire:

just as fire comes from heaven, so do words of Torah come from heaven, as it is said YOU YOURSELVES SAW THAT I SPOKE TO YOU FROM THE VERY HEAVENS (Ex. 20:19);

just as fire [bestows] life upon the world, so words of Torah [bestow] life upon the world.

just as fire warms one who draws close to it, but one far away is chilled, so it is with words of Torah—when a man occupies himself with them, they give him life, but when he withdraws from them, they cause his death;

just as fire is used in this world and in the world-to-come, so words of Torah are used in this world and in the world-to-come;

just as fire leaves a mark on the body of one who uses it, so words of Torah leave a mark on the body of one who uses them;

just as fire causes people to recognize those who work with it, so words of Torah cause the disciples of the wise to be recognized by their manner of walking, their speech, and their outer dress.

A FIERY LAW FOR THEM. Were it not for the law given with it, no man could withstand it.

LOVER, INDEED, OF THE PEOPLE (Deut. 33:3). This teaches that God loved Israel in a way that He did not love any other nations or kingdoms.

---

life upon the world—or possibly "life eternal."

leaves a mark The study of Torah transfigures a person.

law given with it—the normal ways of conducting oneself. Torah is too powerful by itself and must be combined with work and worldly occupation. Thus FIERY means Torah and LAW means normal life. Both are needed.

THEIR HALLOWED ARE ALL IN YOUR HAND (Deut. 33:3). This refers to the leaders of Israel who gave their lives for Israel.

Of Moses it is written AND YET, IF YOU WOULD ONLY FORGIVE THEIR SIN! IF NOT, ERASE ME FROM THE RECORD WHICH YOU HAVE WRITTEN! (Ex. 32:32).

Of David it is written WAS IT NOT I ALONE WHO ORDERED THE NUMBERING OF THE PEOPLE? I ALONE AM GUILTY, AND HAVE CAUSED SEVERE HARM; BUT THESE SHEEP, WHAT HAVE THEY DONE? O LORD MY GOD, LET YOUR HAND FALL UPON ME AND MY FATHER'S HOUSE, AND LET NOT YOUR PEOPLE BE PLAGUED! (1 Chron. 21:17).

THEY SIT AT YOUR FEET (Deut. 33:3).

> Even though they are persecuted;
> even though they are smitten;
> even though they are despised.

ACCEPTING YOUR PRONOUNCEMENTS (Deut. 33:3)—accepting them upon themselves and saying ALL THAT THE LORD HAS SPOKEN WE WILL DO AND OBEY (Ex. 24:7).

Another interpretation: LOVER, INDEED, OF THE PEOPLE (Deut. 33:3). This teaches that the Holy One did not dispense love to the nations of the world as He did to Israel. This is demonstrated by the law which was taught: That which is stolen from a non-Jew is permitted, but that stolen from an Israelite is forbidden.

It once happened that the government dispatched two officials, with instructions to go and pretend to be Jews in order to investigate the nature of the Torah. They went to Rabban Gamliel at Usha, studied Bible, Mishna, midrash, *halachot*, and *haggadot*. When they were about to depart, they said

---

gave their lives   IN YOUR HAND means with God in death. The leaders were willing to die for Israel.

they are persecuted   This refers not to Moses and David, but to the leaders at that time who remained true to God regardless of the hardships.

Mishna—rabbinic teaching.

midrash—teachings connected to verses.

halachot—traditional laws.

haggadot—nonlegal material such as legends.

to [the Sages], "The entire Torah is fine and praiseworthy with the exception of this one teaching of yours that that which is stolen from a non-Jew is permitted, but that stolen from an Israelite is forbidden! Nevertheless we will not reveal this to the government."

COMMENTARY   *The ferocity with which the worth of the Torah and its exclusive connection to Israel is described in many of these interpretations can be well understood in light of the times in which they were written. Challenged on all sides, the right of existence of Israel could be justified only if the Torah were of eternal worth and could not be superseded. The story of the Roman investigators may well reflect historical fact. Before permitting the Jews to conduct their own courts according to the rules of the Torah, the Romans wished to investigate its contents. Other rabbinic sources indicate that as a result of this incident, Rabban Gamliel prohibited property stolen from non-Jews. R. Akiba is also recorded as stating that stealing from the non-Jew was even more serious than stealing from Jews since it also involved desecration of God's Name.*

19. Deuteronomy 34:5, Sifre Deuteronomy 357, 427

SO MOSES DIED THERE (Deut. 34:5). Is it possible that Moses died and wrote SO MOSES DIED THERE? Rather Moses wrote everything up to this point, and from here on Joshua wrote the rest.

R. Meir objected, "Scripture itself says MOSES WROTE DOWN THIS TORAH AND GAVE IT TO THE PRIESTS (Deut. 31:9)! Is it possible that Moses gave the Torah while it was lacking even one letter? Rather this teaches that Moses would write whatever the Holy One told him. This is similar to what we are told in the verse THEN BARUCH

---

not reveal this   These officials were investigating the function of these courts, which governed the Jewish community during the early second century C.E. Therefore treatment of non-Jews was not important. The Talmud records, however, that as a result property stolen from non-Jews was then declared forbidden.

19. *BARUCH*—Jeremiah's scribe. He wrote whatever Jeremiah told him to write. So Moses simply wrote whatever God told him to write, including the story of his own death. Another version adds that he wrote it with tears in his eyes.

ANSWERED THEM, 'HE WOULD DICTATE ALL THOSE WORDS TO ME, AND I WOULD WRITE THEM DOWN IN THE SCROLL IN INK' (Jer. 36:18)."

R. Eliezar says, "A divine voice went out from the midst of the camp twelve miles in every direction and proclaimed, 'Moses is dead!' This is evident from the verse SO MOSES DIED (vaymat Moshe) THERE (Deut. 34:5)—'Woe! Moses is dead (vay - met Moshe)!' "

How do we know that forgiveness went forth from the grave of Moses to the graves of the ancestors? Here it says SO MOSES DIED THERE and elsewhere it says THERE ABRAHAM AND HIS WIFE SARAH WERE BURIED (Gen. 49:31).

Some say that Moses never died but stands and serves on high. Here it says THERE (Deut. 34:5) and elsewhere it says AND HE WAS THERE WITH THE LORD (Ex. 34:28).

COMMENTARY   *The controversy concerning the last verses of Deuteronomy reflects differing conceptions of the nature of the Torah itself. To the school of R. Ishmael, who took a more natural and human view, there was no problem in considering the possibility that at one point the Torah could have lacked certain verses. To R. Akiba and his followers, however, such a thing was inconceivable. Their mystic concept of the Torah as predating the very creation of the world called for an entirely different attitude. The remark concerning Moses serving on high sounds very much like an assertion that he who is at the side of God is not the one the Christians describe, but Moses, the supreme prophet of Israel.*

THE SERVANT OF THE LORD (Deut. 34:5). Scripture speaks not in deprecation of Moses but in praise of him. Thus we find that the early prophets are called servants, as it is said INDEED, MY LORD GOD DOES NOTHING WITHOUT HAVING REVEALED HIS PURPOSE TO HIS SERVANTS THE PROPHETS (Amos 3:7).

AT THE COMMAND OF THE LORD (Deut. 34:5). When God takes the souls of the righteous, He does so with gentleness.

A parable. It may be compared to a trustworthy person in a city. Everyone entrusted their valuables to him. When someone would come to take what belonged to him, this person would take it out and give it to him since he knew exactly where everything was. But if his son, his servant, or his messenger had to find it, they would turn things upside down because they did not know where things were. Thus it is that when God takes the souls of the righteous, He does so with gentleness, but when He takes the souls of the wicked, He entrusts that task to merciless and ruthless angels who drag those souls along. Thus it says A RUTHLESS MESSENGER WILL BE SENT AGAINST HIM (Prov. 17:11) and THEIR SOULS DIE TREMBLING (Job 36:14).

HE BURIED HIM IN THE VALLEY (Deut. 34:6). If it says IN THE VALLEY, why does it say IN THE LAND OF MOAB (Deut. 34:6) and if it says IN THE LAND OF MOAB, why does it say IN THE VALLEY? This indicates that Moses died in the portion of Reuben but was buried in the field which was the portion of Gad.

AND NO MAN KNOWS HIS BURIAL PLACE TO THIS DAY (Deut. 34:6). Some say that Moses himself did not know his burial place, as it is said AND NO MAN KNOWS HIS BURIAL PLACE and MAN always means Moses, as it is said NOW MOSES WAS A VERY HUMBLE MAN (Num. 12:3).

The imperial house of Caesar once sent two commissioners with instructions to find the burial place of Moses. They went and stood up above and saw it down below, so they went down below but then they saw it up above! They split up, some going above and some below at the same time, and those up above saw it below and those down below saw it up above! Thus is it said AND NO MAN KNOWS HIS BURIAL PLACE (Deut. 34:6).

MOSES WAS A HUNDRED AND TWENTY YEARS OLD (Deut. 34:7). He was one of four who died at the age of one hundred and twenty. They were: Moses, Hillel the Elder, Rabban Johanan b. Zakkai, and R. Akiba.

DIE TREMBLING   The usual translation is THEY DIE IN THEIR YOUTH. The Hebrew word *noar* also has the meaning of shaking or trembling. Unlike the righteous, who died quietly because God takes their souls gently, the wicked die trembling.

Hillel the Elder—perhaps the greatest Sage of all. He came to Jerusalem from Babylonia and became the head of the Pharisaic community in the first century B.C.E.

Rabban Johanan b. Zakkai   Following the defeat at the hands of the Romans and the destruction of the Temple in the year 70 C.E., he headed the Academy at Jabneh, which became the supreme body of the Jewish people.

R. Akiba—flourished in the second half of the first century C.E. and the beginning of the second century. He was an ignorant shepherd who began to study only as an adult and became the leading teacher and founder of methodology of interpretation. He was martyred during the Hadrianic persecution.

Moses was in Egypt forty years, in Midian forty years, and led Israel forty years.

Hillel the Elder was forty years old when he came up from Babylonia, served the Sages forty years, and led Israel for forty years.

Rabban Johanan b. Zakkai was a merchant for forty years, served the Sages forty years, and led Israel for forty years.

R. Akiba was forty years old when he began to study Torah, served the Sages forty years, and led Israel forty years.

There are six pairs who lived the same number of years:
Rebekah and Kohath,
Levi and Amram,
Joseph and Joshua,
Samuel and Solomon,
Moses and Hillel the Elder,
and Rabban Johanan b. Zakkai and R. Akiba.

HIS EYES WERE UNDIMMED (Deut. 34:7). This teaches that the eyes of the dead are dimmed. AND HIS VIGOR WAS UNABATED (Deut. 34:7). R. Eliezar b. Jacob says, "Read it not AND HIS VIGOR WAS UN-ABATED but 'and his vigor is unabated'—even now! If anyone were to touch the flesh of Moses, its vigor would spring forth in all directions."

AND THE ISRAELITES BEWAILED MOSES (Deut. 34:8)—one day. THE DAYS CAME TO AN END (Deut. 34:8)—two days. OF WAILING IN MOURNING FOR MOSES (Deut. 34:8)—three days. What then were the THIRTY DAYS (Deut. 34:8)? This teaches that they bewailed him thirty days prior to his death.

How do we know that the period of naziriteship is thirty days? Here it says DAYS and elsewhere it says THROUGHOUT HIS DAYS AS A NAZIRITE (Num. 6:4). Just as the DAYS here are thirty, so the days there refer to thirty days.

---

are dimmed   Moses was the exception. That is why it is specifically mentioned that HIS EYES WERE UNDIMMED.

three days   The intense period of mourning in Jewish law is the first three days.

prior to his death   When informed that Moses was to die, the Israelites bewailed him for thirty days.

NOW JOSHUA SON OF NUN WAS FILLED WITH THE SPIRIT OF WISDOM (Deut. 34:9). Why? BECAUSE MOSES HAD LAID HIS HANDS UPON HIM (Deut. 34:9). AND THE ISRAELITES HEEDED HIM (Deut. 34:9)—there is no greater heeding than this—DOING AS THE LORD HAD COMMANDED MOSES (Deut. 34:9)—but they had not yet begun to revere him, as it says ON THAT DAY THE LORD EX-ALTED JOSHUA IN THE SIGHT OF ALL ISRAEL, SO THAT THEY REVERED HIM ALL THE DAYS AS THEY HAD REVERED MOSES (Josh. 4:14). At that time they began to revere him.

NEVER AGAIN DID THERE ARISE IN ISRAEL A PROPHET LIKE MOSES (Deut. 34:10). None arose in Israel, but one did arise among the nations of the world. Who was that? Balaam son of Beor. . . .
WHOM THE LORD KNEW FACE TO FACE (Deut. 34:10). Why is this said? Since it says OH, LET ME BEHOLD YOUR PRESENCE (Ex. 33:18)—[God] said to him, "In this world which is likened to a face, you may not see it, as it is said YOU CANNOT SEE MY FACE (Ex. 33:20). But you will see it in the world-to-come, which is likened to the back, as it is said THEN I WILL TAKE MY HAND AWAY AND YOU WILL SEE MY BACK (Ex. 33:23). When did He show it to him? When he was near death. Thus we learn that the dead do see [God's glory]."

FOR THE VARIOUS SIGNS AND PORTENTS THAT THE LORD SENT HIM TO DISPLAY IN THE LAND OF EGYPT, AGAINST PHARAOH AND ALL HIS COURTIERS AND HIS WHOLE COUN-TRY (Deut. 34:11). [He was sent] personally to the land of Egypt, to Pha-raoh and to his courtiers. AND FOR ALL THE GREAT MIGHT (Deut. 34:12). This refers to the death of the firstborn.
AND AWESOME POWER (Deut. 34:12). This refers to the splitting of the Sea of Reeds.

R. Eliezer says, "FOR THE VARIOUS SIGNS AND PORTENTS (Deut. 34:11). How do we know that this refers to the events at Mount Sinai as well? The verse says AND FOR ALL THE GREAT MIGHT (Deut. 34:12).

Balaam son of Beor On Balaam and Moses see above page 270.
[sent] personally Moses was sent to each of these three. Thus he had three specific tasks to undertake in his mission.

"What about the events in the wilderness? The verse says AND AWE-SOME POWER (Deut. 34:12).

"What about the breaking of the tablets? Elsewhere it says SMASH-ING THEM BEFORE YOUR EYES (Deut. 9:17) and here it says THAT MOSES DISPLAYED BEFORE THE EYES OF ALL ISRAEL (Deut. 34:11)."

COMMENTARY   *The attitude of the Midrash toward the death of Moses understandably vacillates between emphasizing that Moses was a human be-ing who had to die like all others and following the lead of Scripture in emphasizing his uniqueness. It is, after all, God Himself who tends to his death and burial and it is the Torah that first creates the mystery of the unknown grave. The rabbinic imagination seized on all of this and enhanced it manyfold. The comparison drawn between Moses and the three great Sages—Hillel, Rabban Johanan n. Zakkai, and R. Akiba—emphasizes the Pharisaic assertion that their authority came through Moses and that their Sages were continuing the work he had begun.*

II.
INTERPRETATION OF LEGAL PORTIONS—HALAKHA

EXODUS

1. Exodus 13:9, Mekhilta Pisha 17, I 150

AND THIS SHALL SERVE YOU AS A SIGN ON YOUR HAND (Ex. 13:9). One scroll containing four sections. Logic would dictate that since the Torah says "put phylacteries on your head, put phylacteries on your hand," that just as the one on the head has four scrolls so the one on the hand should have four scrolls. Therefore the verse says AND THIS SHALL SERVE YOU AS A SIGN ON YOUR HAND indicating one scroll containing four sections.

Is it possible that just as the one on the hand has one scroll so the one on the head should have only one scroll? Logic would dictate that since the Torah says "put phylacteries on your hand, put phylacteries on your head," that just as the one on the hand has one section, so the one on the head should have one section. Therefore the verse says SYMBOL (Ex. 13:16), SYMBOL (Deut. 6:8), and SYMBOLS (Deut. 11:18), thus indicating that there are four symbols!

Perhaps, then, one should make four pouches with four sections each? The verse says AS A REMINDER BETWEEN YOUR EYES (Ex. 13:9) indicating one pouch containing the four sections.

---

1. *One scroll*—one piece of parchment on which four sections from the Torah are written. Since the verse says A SIGN it indicates one sign, i.e., one scroll.

phylacteries—two pouches, one for the head and one for the hand, containing parchment scrolls on which are written four sections from the Torah: Ex. 13:1–10; Ex. 13:11–16; Deut. 6:4–9; Deut. 11:13–21.

four scrolls In the pouch bound to the head, each of the four sections is written on a separate small scroll.

four symbols The word *symbol* appears twice in the singular and once in the plural, indicating four symbols, i.e., four separate scrolls for that of the head.

ON YOUR HAND. On the upper part of the arm. You say this means the upper part of the arm. Perhaps it means literally the hand? Logic dictates that since the Torah says "put phylacteries on your head, put phylacteries on your hand," that just as the one on the head is on the upper part of the head, so the one on the hand must be on the upper part of the arm.

You say this means the upper part of the arm. Perhaps it means literally the hand? The verse says AND THIS SHALL SERVE YOU AS A SIGN (Ex. 13:9). It is a sign FOR YOU and not a sign for others.

R. Isaac says, "On the upper part of the arm or literally the hand itself? The verse says THEREFORE IMPRESS THESE MY WORDS UPON YOUR VERY HEART (Deut. 11:18) indicating that it must be opposite the heart. What is opposite the heart? The upper part of the arm."

ON YOUR HAND. This is the left arm. You say that this is the left arm. Perhaps it is the right arm? [There is a verse which,] although not proof, is at least an indication: MY OWN HAND FOUNDED THE EARTH, MY RIGHT HAND SPREAD OUT THE SKIES (Isa. 48:13). And it says HER HAND REACHED FOR THE TENT PIN, HER RIGHT HAND FOR THE WORKMEN'S HAMMER (Judges 5:26). Thus the word *hand* always indicates the left hand.

R. Nathan says, "BIND THEM ... INSCRIBE THEM (Deut. 6:8–9). Just as one inscribes with the right hand, so one binds with the right hand."

Abba Jose says, "We have found that the right hand is called 'hand.' [There is a verse which] although not proof, is at least an indication: BUT ISRAEL STRETCHED OUT HIS RIGHT HAND AND LAID IT ON EPHRAIM'S HEAD, THOUGH HE WAS THE YOUNGER, AND HIS LEFT HAND ON MANASSEH'S HEAD ... SO HE TOOK HOLD OF HIS FATHER'S HAND (Gen. 48:14–17). Why then does the verse say ON YOUR HAND? To indicate that the left-handed man should put it upon his right arm."

AND THIS SHALL SERVE YOU AS A SIGN ON YOUR HAND AND AS A REMINDER BETWEEN YOUR EYES (Ex. 13:9). Whenever the

---

a sign FOR YOU—and not for others. Therefore it need not be where others can see it (the hand) but where you alone can see it on the upper arm.

R. Isaac—finds the source of the teaching in a different verse.

always indicates the left hand Since these verses specifically mention the right hand, the word *hand* by itself must mean the other one, the left hand.

the right hand is called "hand"—and not the left hand exclusively.

phylactery of the hand is on the hand, place the phylactery of the head upon the head. This is the source of the teaching that the [proper performance of the] mitzvah of phylacteries is that one first puts on the one of the hand and then that of the head, and when removing them, first removes that of the head and then that of the arm.

BETWEEN YOUR EYES on the upper part of the head. You say this means on the upper part of the head. Perhaps it means literally BETWEEN YOUR EYES? The verse says YOU ARE THE CHILDREN OF THE LORD YOUR GOD. YOU SHALL NOT GASH YOURSELVES OR SHAVE BETWEEN YOUR EYES (Deut. 14:1). Just as BETWEEN YOUR EYES there means on the upper part of the head, so BETWEEN YOUR EYES (Ex. 13:9) here means on the upper part of the head.

R. Judah says, "Since the Torah says 'put phylacteries on your hand, put phylacteries on your head,' just as the hand means a place that may become impure through leprosy, so the head means a place which may become impure through leprosy."

IN ORDER THAT THE TEACHINGS OF THE LORD MAY BE IN YOUR MOUTH (Ex. 13:9). Why is this said? Since it said AND THIS SHALL SERVE YOU AS A SIGN (Ex. 13:9) I might have thought that women are included. Logic dictates that since the *mezuzah* is a positive mitzvah and phylacteries are a positive mitzvah, and we know that *mezuzah* is observed by woman as well as by men, I might have thought that phylacteries are to be observed by women as well as by men. Therefore the verse says IN ORDER THAT THE TEACHINGS OF THE LORD MAY BE IN YOUR MOUTH to indicate that [the mitzvah of phylacteries] is obligatory only upon one who is obligated to study the Torah. This is the source of the teaching: Everyone is obligated to put on phylacteries except women and slaves.

BETWEEN YOUR EYES there—in the verse from Deut. Shaving must refer to the upper part where the hair grows and not literally between the eyes.

mezuzah A parchment on which are written Deut. 6:4–9 and 11:13–21, which is placed in a case and affixed to the doorpost of a room.

obligated to study This is an obligation of men, not women. By connecting phylacteries and study, they conclude that women are not obligated to observe phylacteries.

Michal the daughter of Kushi used to put on phylacteries. Jonah's wife used to make the pilgrimage. Tabi the slave of Rabban Gamliel used to put on phylacteries.

AS A REMINDER BETWEEN YOUR EYES—IN ORDER THAT THE TEACHINGS OF THE LORD MAY BE IN YOUR MOUTH (Ex. 13:9). This is the source of the teaching that if one puts on phylacteries it is as if he is reading the Torah, and if one is reading the Torah he need not put on phylacteries.

YOU SHALL KEEP THIS INSTITUTION AT ITS SET TIME (Ex. 13:10). Why is this said? Since it says AND THIS SHALL SERVE YOU AS A SIGN ON YOUR HAND (Ex. 13:9), I might have thought that minors are included. Logic dictates that since the *mezuzah* is a positive mitzvah and phylacteries are a positive mitzvah, and we know that *mezuzah* is observed by minors as well as by adults, I might have thought that phylacteries are to be observed by minors as well as by adults. Therefore the verse says YOU SHALL KEEP THIS INSTITUTION (Ex. 13:10) to indicate that phylacteries are observed only by one who knows how to KEEP them. This is the source of the teaching: Any minor who knows how to properly keep phylacteries may have phylacteries made for him.

YOU SHALL KEEP THIS INSTITUTION. This refers to the institution of phylacteries. You say that this refers to the institution of phylacteries. Perhaps it refers to the institution of all the mitzvot. You must say that it refers to that which is under discussion, namely phylacteries.

FROM DAYS TO DAYS (Ex. 13:10). Why is this said? Since it says AND THIS SHALL SERVE YOU AS A SIGN (Ex. 13:9), I might have thought that night time was to be included. Logic dictates that since *mezuzah* is a

---

Michal the daughter of Kushi—David's wife, the daughter of Saul, whom the Sages called "Kushi" on the basis of Ps. 7:1. The midrashic legends considered her to have been a particularly pious woman who put on phylacteries even though not obligated to do so.
the pilgrimage—to the Temple in Jerusalem three times a year. This too was not obligatory for women.
Tabi—a non-Jewish slave who was renowned for his piety. These are all examples of mitzvot performed by people who were not required to do so, but were permitted to do so.
if one is reading the Torah At that time he is doing that which the phylacteries symbolize. The ancient practice was that phylacteries were worn by many of the Sages during the entire day.

positive mitzvah and phylacteries are a positive mitzvah and we know that *mezuzah* is observed both night and day, so phylacteries should be worn both night and day. Therefore the verse says FROM DAYS TO DAYS (Ex. 13:10)—you wear them during the day but not at night.

Another interpretation: FROM DAYS TO DAYS. Why is this said? Since it says AND THIS SHALL SERVE YOU AS A SIGN (Ex. 13:9), I might have thought that Sabbaths and Holy Days were to be included. Logic dictates that since *mezuzah* is a positive mitzvah and phylacteries are a positive mitzvah and we know that *mezuzah* is observed on the Sabbath and Holy Days, so phylacteries should be worn on the Sabbath and Holy Days. Therefore the verse says FROM DAYS TO DAYS (Ex. 13:10) excluding the Sabbath and Holy Days. As R. Josiah says . . . "There are days when you wear them and days when you do not, thus excluding the Sabbath and Holy Days."

R. Isaac says, "Since the Sabbath is called A SIGN (Ex. 31:17) and phylacteries are called A SIGN (Ex. 13:9) there is no need for a sign within a sign. Perhaps there should be a sign within a sign? You must say that the Sabbath, which is called a sign and A COVENANT (Ex. 31:16), sets aside phylacteries which are only called a sign."

R. Eliezer says, "Since the Sabbath is called A SIGN (Ex. 31:17) and phylacteries are called A SIGN (Ex. 13:9), there is no need for a sign within a sign. Perhaps there should be a sign within a sign? You must say that the Sabbath, which is punishable by extinction or death at the hands of a court, sets aside phylacteries which is not punishable by extinction or death at the hands of a court."

Another interpretation: FROM DAYS TO DAYS (Ex. 13:10). This indicates that a man should examine his phylacteries once in twelve months. Here it says FROM DAYS TO DAYS and elsewhere it says IT MAY BE REDEEMED UNTIL A YEAR HAS ELAPSED SINCE ITS SALE, THE REDEMPTION PERIOD SHALL BE FOR DAYS (Lev. 25:29). Just as the DAYS there refers to a period no less that twelve months, so the DAYS here refers to a period no less than twelve months. So taught the School of

---

mezuzah is observed both night and day   It is permanently affixed to the doorpost.
FROM DAYS TO DAYS   The purpose of this phrase is to exclude the mistaken conclusion that phylacteries should be worn at night.
extinction—death at the hands of Heaven and not by a human court.

Hillel. The School of Shammai says, "There is no need for him to even examine them." Shammai the Elder says, "These are the phylacteries of my mother's father."

COMMENTARY   *The regulations concerning phylacteries were developed during the rabbinic period. Phylacteries (in Hebrew tefillin) consist of two containers into which selected passages from the Torah are placed. These are then worn upon the upper arm and on the forehead. The general practice today is to wear them only during the morning prayers, but in the rabbinic period many Sages wore them during the entire day. Then the containers were soft leather pouches, whereas today they are hard leather boxes. The straps with which they are fastened are wound seven times on the arm, a sacred number in Judaism, and are also wound around the fingers in such as way as to suggest a marriage ring. The verses from the prophet that are recited when placing them on the fingers reinforce this image: I WILL ESPOUSE YOU FOREVER: I WILL ESPOUSE YOU WITH RIGHTEOUSNESS AND JUSTICE, AND WITH GOODNESS AND MERCY, AND I WILL ESPOUSE YOU WITH FAITHFULNESS. THEN YOU SHALL KNOW THE LORD (Hos. 2:21–22). The phylacteries serve as signs of love, devotion, and dedication to God and as acceptance of His kingship. The exact way in which they are made, used, and placed is detailed in this section of the Midrash.*

2. Exodus 21:2, Mekhilta Nezikin 1, III 5

WHEN YOU ACQUIRE A HEBREW SLAVE, HE SHALL SERVE SIX YEARS (Ex. 21:2). Since it states IF HE LACKS THE MEANS, HE SHALL BE SOLD FOR HIS THEFT (Ex. 22:2), I might think that if HE SHALL BE SOLD FOR HIS THEFT it is forever, therefore the verse says HE SHALL SERVE SIX YEARS (Ex. 21:2). This informs us that he is to serve for six years and go free in the seventh.

---

examine his phylacteries—check them to make certain that the writing and the condition of the parchment are such that they are proper for use.
phylacteries of my mother's father—therefore quite old, but still needing no examination.

---

2. *it is forever* Since that verse carries no specific time or limitation, we might think that there is no time limitation on slavery. The other verse, however, does mention a specific number of years and applies to all situations.

HE SHALL SERVE SIX YEARS (Ex. 21:2). I might think that this includes all kinds of service, therefore the verse says DO NOT SUBJECT HIM TO THE TREATMENT OF A SLAVE (Lev. 25:39). This was the source of the teaching: He shall not wash [his master's] feet for him, nor put on his shoes for him, carry his things to the bath house for him, support his hips when he ascends stairs, carry him in a litter or a chaise or a sedan chair as do slaves, as it is said BUT AS FOR YOUR ISRAELITE BROTHERS, NO ONE SHALL RULE RUTHLESSLY OVER THE OTHER (Lev. 25:46). But he may demand such service from his son or his disciple.

HE SHALL SERVE SIX YEARS. I might think that this means both service which is humiliating and that which is not, therefore the verse says HE SHALL REMAIN UNDER YOU AS A HIRED OR BOUND LABORER (Lev. 25:40). Just as you have no right to make A HIRED LABORER deviate from his usual work, so you have no right to make a Hebrew slave deviate from his usual work. This was the source of the teaching: His master may not make him do work in which he must serve the public such as caring for a well, a bath attendant, a barber, a tailor, a butcher, or a baker. R. Jose says, "If this was his specific trade, he may perform it, but his master may not make him change his usual work for any of these." AS A HIRED OR BOUND LABORER. Just as a hired laborer works only during the day and not at night, so a Hebrew slave works during the day but not at night. R. Jose says, "It all depends upon what his trade is."

IN THE SEVENTH YEAR HE SHALL BE FREED (Ex. 21:2). This means the seventh year of his purchase. You say that it means the seventh year of his purchase, but perhaps it means the seventh calendar year? The verse says HE SHALL SERVE SIX YEARS (Ex. 21:2)—indicating that the seventh year is that of his purchase and not the seventh calendar year.

HE SHALL BE FREED (Ex. 21:2). Why is this stated? Since it says WHEN YOU SET HIM FREE (Deut. 15:13) I might think that the master must write him a writ of emancipation, therefore the verse says HE SHALL

---

the seventh calendar year—the cycle of seven years, which was counted to determine the Sabbatical year.

of his purchase   He must serve until the seventh year after he became a slave and is not freed during the Sabbatical year if it comes before that.

a writ of emancipation   The fact that the verse says SET HIM FREE might be thought to mean that his emancipation is dependent on his master's taking a legal step to free him. That is not the case. He automatically becomes a free man when the period of time is over.

BE FREED (Ex. 21:2). Perhaps [the slave] must give him money in order to be freed? The verse says WITHOUT PAYMENT (Ex. 21:2).

COMMENTARY   *The Sages interpreted the rules of indentured servitude in such as way as to mitigate its harshness. At one point they said "He who acquires a slave acquires a master" since so much had to be done for the slave. This passage requires people to respect the dignity of their slaves and severely limits the type of work a slave can be required to do. A child or a disciple, often compared to a child in regard to his teacher, is required to do servile things from which a slave is exempt. The following section continues this trend, demonstrating that even the slave who was to serve "for life" was to be freed at the Jubilee year.*

3. Exodus 21:6, Mekhilta Nezikin 2, III 17

AND HE SHALL THEN REMAIN HIS SLAVE FOR LIFE (Ex. 21:6). Until the Jubilee year. For one could have reasoned that if money, which has the power to acquire anything, can acquire a slave for no more than six years, surely piercing, which acquires nothing but slaves, should not have the power to acquire the slave for more than six years! What then is the meaning of FOR LIFE? Until the Jubilee year. Perhaps we should interpret FOR LIFE literally? Therefore the verse says IT SHALL BE A JUBILEE FOR YOU; EACH OF YOU SHALL RETURN TO HIS HOLD-ING AND EACH OF YOU SHALL RETURN TO HIS FAMILY (Lev. 25:10).

R. Judah the Prince says, "Come and see that 'for life' always means for fifty years, as it is said AND HE SHALL THEN REMAIN HIS SLAVE FOR LIFE. Until the Jubilee year. How so? With the Jubilee year he goes free; with the death of his master he goes free."

---

3. *Until the Jubilee year*   The slave who does not wish to go free at the end of six years goes free at the next Jubilee year, the year that marks the end of seven cycles of seven Sabbatical years, regardless of when that is.

piercing—of the ear. The slave who wished to continue to serve had his ear pierced as a sign of his continuing slavery. See Ex. 21:5.

SHALL RETURN TO HIS FAMILY   Everyone, including the so-called slave for life, must return to his family. Therefore "for life" cannot be taken literally.

for fifty years   Since the verse in Leviticus indicates that the slave goes free at the Jubilee, the maximum he can serve would be fifty years.

HE SHALL THEN REMAIN HIS SLAVE (Ex. 21:6). He shall serve him, but not his son. For one could have reasoned that if in the case of a slave who serves six years, where Scripture releases him after a short period, he must serve both him and his son, surely in the case of the slave whose ear is pierced, where Scripture delays his release, he must serve both him and his son! Therefore the verse says HIS SLAVE. He shall serve *him*, but not his son. This was the source of the teaching: A Hebrew slave shall serve the son but not the daughter. The slave whose ear has been pierced and the female Hebrew slave shall serve neither the son nor the daughter.

4. Exodus 21:18, Mekhilta Nezikin 6, III 51

WHEN MEN QUARREL AND ONE STRIKES THE OTHER WITH STONE OR FIST, AND HE DOES NOT DIE BUT HAS TO TAKE TO HIS BED—IF HE THEN GETS UP AND WALKS OUTDOORS UPON HIS STAFF, THE ASSAILANT SHALL GO UNPUNISHED, EXCEPT THAT HE MUST PAY FOR HIS IDLENESS AND HIS CURE (Ex. 21:18-19). Why was this section stated? When it says EYE FOR EYE (Ex. 21:24) we know nothing about payment for idleness or healing. Therefore the verse says WHEN MEN QUARREL...IF HE THEN GETS UP AND WALKS OUTDOORS...HE MUST PAY FOR HIS IDLENESS AND HIS CURE. This verse comes to teach us about those matters which are missing from the other.

WHEN MEN QUARREL (Ex. 21:18). This teaches me only about men. What about women? R. Ishmael used to say, "Since all the laws of damages in the Torah are silent about this, when in one case Scripture specifies clearly that women are as liable as men in this matter, the intention is to apply this to all cases of damages in the Torah so that in all of them women are as liable as men."

R. Josiah says, "WHEN A MAN OR WOMAN COMMITS ANY WRONG (Num. 5:6). Why is this stated? When it says WHEN A MAN

He shall serve him   Since the verse says HIS SLAVE, it indicates that he serves him only and is not inherited by the master's son.

---

4. *EYE FOR EYE*   According to rabbinic interpretation, this indicated the basic payment that was to be made for injury. It was not to be taken literally. It does not, however, indicate other payments for idleness and healing. Therefore a second verse is required.
when in one case—that referred to by R. Josiah which appears in Num. 5:6.

OPENS A PIT (Ex. 21:33) I know only that a man is liable. What about a woman? Therefore the verse says WHEN A MAN OR A WOMAN (Num. 5:6) in order to make women equal to men in regard to all the laws of damages in the Torah."

R. Jonathan says, "We have no need for this. Does it not state elsewhere THE ONE RESPONSIBLE FOR THE PIT MUST MAKE RESTITUTION (Ex. 21:34); THE ONE WHO STARTED THE FIRE MUST MAKE RESTITUTION (Ex. 22:5)? Why then does it say WHEN A MAN OR WOMAN (Num. 5:6)? In order to teach the matter which is under discussion there."

COMMENTARY   *The Sages sometimes dispute a legal ruling and take sides regarding whether an action is permitted or prohibited. Other times, however, they are in agreement concerning the actual law but dispute the method of arriving at the ruling. In this case all are agreed that women are liable for damages. R. Ishmael and R. Josiah learn this from Numbers 5:6, which they apply as a general rule to all cases. R. Jonathan learns the general rule from Exodus 21:34 and 22:5.*

5. Exodus 21:19, Mekhilta Nezikin 9, III 53

IF HE THEN GETS UP AND WALKS (Ex. 21:19). I might think that this means inside the house. Therefore the verse says OUTDOORS (Ex. 21:19). I might think that as long as it is OUTDOORS, it applies even if he is withering away. Therefore the verse says GETS UP AND WALKS OUTDOORS UPON HIS STAFF (Ex. 21:19)—in a state of health.

This is one of three things in the Torah that R. Ishmael expounded figuratively. A similar one was IF THE SUN HAS RISEN UPON HIM (Ex. 22:2). Does the sun rise only upon him? Does it not rise upon the entire

---

We have no need for this   We do not need the verse Num. 5:6 in order to teach us that women are equal to men in laws of damages. We learn it from the verses cited by R. Jonathan.
THE ONE RESPONSIBLE—whether it be a man or a woman.
the matter which is under discussion—namely, that both men and women must confess and make restitution when they commit a wrong.

---

5. *in a state of health*   The verse is not to be taken literally. It does not matter where or how he walks, but that he be healthy.
only upon him   The reference is to a thief who breaks in at night. If one kills him, he is not guilty. But if he kills him after the sun rises, he is guilty.

world! But as the sun comes in peace to the world, so if it is known that [the thief] left him in peace, and he nevertheless killed him, he is guilty.

Similarly AND THEY SHALL SPREAD OUT THE CLOTH (Deut. 22:17). They must make the matter as clear as a cloth.

So in our verse UPON HIS STAFF means in a state of health.

COMMENTARY   *R. Ishmael's approach to the interpretation of Biblical texts was quite different from that of his colleague R. Akiba. Akiba's insistence that the each word, each letter, each mark in the Torah could be utilized for interpretive purposes led to rulings far removed from the simple meaning of the text. Ishmael held that the language used by the Torah was human language, but because of that he also thought that some expressions were to be taken figuratively. Thus, paradoxically, in some instances his more rationalist view led him to understandings that were far removed from the simple meaning. As this paragraph indicates, however, there were only a few such passages. In general the Sages were cautious of using allegorical methods of expounding Scripture since it was all too liable to lead to readings in which the actual meaning and the specific requirements for observance would be seen as mere poetical metaphors. This differentiated them both from such Jewish interpreters as Philo of Alexandria, who often used symbolic or allegorical interpretations, and some of the early Church Fathers, who also favored such interpretations.*

6. Exodus 21:23, Mekhilta Nezikin 8, III 67

THE PENALTY SHALL BE LIFE FOR LIFE (Ex. 21:23). He must pay life for life and not monetary compensation for life. Another interpretation: THE PENALTY SHALL BE LIFE FOR LIFE. He must pay life and not life and monetary compensation.

---

left him in peace   According to R. Ishmael the reference to the sun is figurative. It does not mean that the sun has risen, but that just as the sun is peaceful, so the thief intended no bodily harm.

make the matter as clear as a cloth   R. Ishmael interprets the verse to mean that the question of the woman's virginity must be made completely clear and not that a sheet with bloodstains must be displayed.

---

6. *THE PENALTY*   The case under discussion is a pregnant woman injured during a fight between two men. If injury other than miscarriage ensues, a penalty is exacted.

pay life for life   If the woman dies, the man responsible must die.

R. Judah the Prince says, "THE PENALTY SHALL BE LIFE FOR
LIFE—monetary compensation." You say "monetary compensation," but
perhaps it means execution? You can reason thus: Here the expression "laid
upon" (Ex. 21:22) is used and there the expression "laid upon" (Ex. 21:30)
is used. Just as the "laid upon" there refers to monetary compensation, so
the "laid upon" here refers to monetary compensation.

EYE FOR EYE (Ex. 21:23)—monetary compensation. You say "monetary
compensation," but perhaps it literally means "an eye?" R. Ishmael used to
say, "It says HE WHO KILLS A BEAST SHALL MAKE RESTITUTION
FOR IT; BUT HE WHO KILLS A HUMAN BEING SHALL BE PUT
TO DEATH (Lev. 24:21). The Scripture makes a connection between injuries to a human being and injuries to a beast and between injuries to a beast
and injuries to a human being. Just as there is monetary compensation for
injuries to a beast, so there is monetary compensation for injuries to a
human being."

R. Isaac says, "It says IF RANSOM IS LAID UPON HIM, HE MUST
PAY WHATEVER IS LAID UPON HIM TO REDEEM HIS LIFE (Ex.
21:30). This is a matter of logic. If only monetary compensation is paid in a
case where capital punishment is imposed, is it not logical that here, where
there is no capital punishment, only monetary compensation is required?"

R. Eleazar says, "EYE FOR EYE. I might think that he pays monetary
compensation whether it was done deliberately or not. Therefore the Scripture singles out the case of one who deliberately inflicted a wound and states
that the compensation there is the actual infliction of a wound, as it is said
IF ANYONE MAIMS HIS FELLOW, AS HE HAS DONE SO SHALL

"laid upon" there In Ex. 21:30 the expression refers to a goring ox and clearly means a fine.
On this basis R. Judah believes that here too the expression "life for life" is not literal, but
means a fine, as do the other expressions—"eye for eye," etc., in Ex. 21:24-5. The reference
may then be to the unborn fetus.

makes a connection The purpose of speaking about animals and beasts in one verse is to teach
that just as when a beast is injured there is payment, so when a person is injured there is
payment.

capital punishment is imposed The verse concerns the owner of a dangerous ox that killed a
person and says that it is possible for the owner of the animal to redeem his life by paying a
ransom. Thus even though he really should be executed he is permitted to live if he gives a
ransom. That is more serious than our case of mere injury. Surely, then, monetary compensation is intended here and not actual injury to the guilty person.

only monetary compensation This is an opinion that differs from that of R. Eleazar. For inadvertent injury nothing would be paid.

R. Eleazar—the only one of the sages who believed that the Torah was to be taken literally.

IT BE DONE TO HIM (Lev. 24:19). This is the general rule. EYE FOR
EYE (Lev. 24:20) is a specific statement. In the case of a general rule followed by a specific statement, the general rule contains nothing more than
what is in the specific statement."

COMMENTARY   *This section is part of a discussion of the famous or infamous lex talionis. The question was: Are we to take this phrase literally or
to understand it as indicating punishment that is equal to the crime, but
not necessarily of the same kind? Using various principles of interpretation
different authorities justify their decision that it does not mean literal physical punishment. One Sage takes the position that it was literal at least in
certain cases. This selection demonstrates the use of complex rules of interpretation in order to determine the correct interpretation of Biblical law.
These principles developed over the centuries. The most famous sets of
rules were those developed by Hillel in the first century B.C.E. and the much
more complex set developed by R. Ishmael at the end of the first century C.E.
Similar rules were used by Greek grammarians to determine the meaning of
documents such as the writings of Homer.*

7. Exodus 21:37, Mekhilta Nezikin 12, III 99

WHEN A MAN STEALS AN OX OR A SHEEP, AND SLAUGHTERS
IT OR SELLS IT, HE SHALL PAY FIVE OXEN FOR THE OX (Ex.
21:37)—four in addition to the one he stole. AND FOUR SHEEP FOR
THE SHEEP (Ex. 21:37)—three plus the one he stole. R. Meir says,
"Come and see how precious labor is to He Who Spoke and the world came
into being! Because the ox performs labor, one must pay fivefold for it, but
for the sheep, which does not perform labor, one must pay only fourfold!"

Rabban Johanan b. Zakkai says, "God is concerned with human dignity. For an ox which walks by itself, one pays fivefold. But for a sheep
which [the thief] must carry on his back, he pays only fourfold!"

COMMENTARY   *In this selection the problem addressed is not the application of a law, but its meaning. Although some of the Sages declared that*

---

the specific statement—indicates actual infliction but only when it was done intentionally.
of the same kind—but not identical with the specific case mentioned.

---

7. *must carry on his back*   The thief has to carry the sheep when he steals it while the ox is led
and goes on its own. Because of this extra work, he pays a smaller fine for the sheep.

certain ritual laws could not be understood rationally but must be accepted as decrees of the Almighty, the general tendency was to find moral and ethical reasons for the mitzvot. Here two Sages offer their interpretation of the fact that the compensation required for the theft of various animals differed. Both agree that the value underlying the ruling is the worth and dignity of labor, but one sees it in the labor of the animal, the other in the effort that was required of the thief. The implication is clear. If a thief is given consideration for his effort and labor, certainly this is so in the case of honest labor.

8. Exodus 22:1, Mekhilta Nezikin 13, III 101

IF THE THIEF IS SEIZED WHILE TUNNELING AND HE IS BEATEN TO DEATH, THERE IS NO BLOODGUILT IN HIS CASE (Ex. 22:1). What exactly is this case? There is doubt if he intended merely to steal or if he intended to kill. You say, "There is doubt if he intended merely to steal or if he intended to kill," but is it not rather that there is doubt if he intended to steal or not? You must say that if, in the case of one who definitely came to steal, one who kills him is guilty, certainly in the case where there is a doubt if he came to steal or not, one would be guilty for killing him. Therefore you cannot possibly accept the second explanation but must interpret it the first way, namely that there is doubt if he intended merely to steal or if he intended to kill.

From this you can reason that if, in the case of the shedding of blood which contaminates the earth and causes the Divine Presence to remove itself from the world, the doubt is disregarded [in order to possibly save his life], certainly in the case of actually saving a life the doubt is to be disregarded.

---

8. *merely to steal or if he intended to kill* Was the thief intending to kill while perpetrating the theft or had he no such intention? Since there is a doubt, the thief may be killed to protect one's life. Otherwise there is no justification for killing the thief and the killer would be liable to execution.

shedding of blood—the blood of the thief.

disregarded The doubt is set aside and one kills the thief, even though he may not have intended to kill. Saving one's own life thus is permitted even in doubtful circumstances.

actually saving a life—which must be done even if it involves the desecration of the Sabbath. If the case is one in which there is a doubt as to whether or not it is really necessary to do this on the Sabbath, one must nevertheless do it. The doubt does not set aside the imperative to save someone else's life.

IF THE SUN HAS RISEN UPON HIM, THERE IS BLOODGUILT IN HIS CASE (Ex. 22:2). R. Ishmael says, "Does the sun rise only upon him? Does it not rise upon the entire world? Rather it means that just as the sun comes to the world in peace, so if it is known that he came toward him in peace and he nevertheless killed him, he is guilty." You say that this is the meaning of the verse, but may it not be that it intends to distinguish between night and day, to tell you that if he killed him during the day he is guilty, but if he killed him at night he is not guilty? The verse says BUT YOU SHALL DO NOTHING TO THE GIRL. THE GIRL IS NOT GUILTY OF A CAPITAL OFFENSE, FOR THE CASE IS LIKE THAT OF A MAN ATTACKING ANOTHER AND MURDERING HIM (Deut. 22:26). Now what have we learned about the murderer from this? This is a case of something which was intended to illuminate but is itself illuminated. Just as in this case there is no distinction between night and day, so in our case there is no distinction between night and day. Just as here, if he anticipates his action and kills him first, he is not guilty, so there if she anticipated his action and killed him first, she is not guilty. Just as there, if there was someone who could protect her from him but nevertheless she killed him she is guilty, so here if there was someone who could have protected him but nevertheless he killed him, he is guilty.

COMMENTARY   *The first explanations of Exodus 22:2 are based on the principle of kal vahomer—logical reasoning or inference from minor to major. R. Ishmael offers his allegorical interpretation. This is disputed but Ishmael rebuts this by bringing another case from the Torah to which it can be compared.*

R. Ishmael See above, page 406 where this is one of three cases in which he interpreted the Torah in a figurative rather than a literal fashion. It means that if you know he came with peaceful intentions, you may not kill him with impunity. Here we are given R. Ishmael's reasoning.

between night and day—understanding the Torah literally.

THE GIRL If an engaged girl was raped in open country and no one could come to her rescue or know about it, the girl is not guilty as she would be had she consented or not cried out in the city.

is itself illuminated The murderer was mentioned here in order to help us understand the case of rape, but it turns out that the verse helps up to understand something about murder as well. According to R. Ishmael, we learn from the case of rape that there is no distinction between night and day and therefore there is no such distinction in the case of the thief either. Thus the verse is to be understood figuratively.

9. Exodus 22:20, Mekhilta Nezikin 18, III 137

YOU SHALL NOT WRONG A STRANGER OR OPPRESS HIM, FOR YOU WERE STRANGERS IN THE LAND OF EGYPT (Ex. 22:20). Do not wrong him verbally and do not oppress him financially. Do not say to him, "Only yesterday you were worshiping Bel, Kores, or Nebo! Until now pork was spewing from between your teeth, and you dare stand up and speak against me!" What is the source which teaches that if you wrong him, he may also wrong you? As it is said YOU SHALL NOT WRONG A STRANGER OR OPPRESS HIM, FOR YOU WERE STRANGERS IN THE LAND OF EGYPT. This was the source of R. Nathan's saying: Do not reproach another with a fault which is your own.

Beloved are converts for He constantly warns us about mistreating them. YOU SHALL NOT WRONG A STRANGER (Ex. 22:20). YOU MUST LOVE THE STRANGER, FOR YOU WERE STRANGERS IN THE LAND OF EGYPT (Deut. 10:19). YOU SHALL NOT OPPRESS A STRANGER, FOR YOU KNOW THE FEELINGS OF THE STRANGER, HAVING YOURSELVES BEEN STRANGERS IN THE LAND OF EGYPT (Ex. 23:9).
    R. Eliezer says, "It is because the convert has an evil disposition that Scripture is constantly warning us about them."
    R. Simeon b. Yohai says, "It says BUT MAY HIS FRIENDS BE AS THE SUN RISING IN MIGHT! (Judges 5:31). Now who is greater, he who loves the king or he whom the king loves? Surely it is he whom the king loves. And it is written AND LOVES THE STRANGER, PROVIDING HIM WITH FOOD AND CLOTHING (Deut. 10:18)."

Beloved are converts, for He constantly refers to them in the same terms He uses to refer to Israel.
    Israel is called "slaves," as it is said FOR IT IS TO ME THAT THE ISRAELITES ARE SLAVES; THEY ARE MY SLAVES, WHOM I FREED FROM THE LAND OF EGYPT, I THE LORD YOUR GOD

---

9. *STRANGER*   In Hebrew "ger," which, in the rabbinic period, came to mean a convert.
worshiping Bel   The convert is not to be reminded of his previous idolatrous beliefs or actions in order not to shame him.
may also wrong you   You too are vulnerable, since your status is the same as his. Your past also contains things of which you would not want to be reminded.
R. Eliezer   Unlike the other sages here, his attitude is negative toward converts. The warnings are because of the bad character of the convert.

(Lev. 25:55)—and converts are called "slaves," as it is said AND TO LOVE THE NAME OF THE LORD, TO BE HIS SLAVES (Isa. 56:6).

Israel is called "servants," as it is said WHILE YOU SHALL BE CALLED "PRIESTS OF THE LORD," AND TERMED "SERVANTS OF OUR GOD" (Isa. 61:6)—and converts are called "servants," as it is said AS FOR THE FOREIGNERS WHO ATTACH THEMSELVES TO THE LORD TO SERVE HIM (Isa. 56:6).

Israel is called "friends," as it is said BUT YOU, ISRAEL, MY SERVANT, JACOB, WHOM I HAVE CHOSEN, SEED OF ABRAHAM MY FRIEND (Isa. 41:8)—and converts are called "friends," as it is said THE STRANGER, THE FRIEND (Deut. 10:18).

Covenant is mentioned in connection to Israel, as it is said THUS SHALL MY COVENANT BE MARKED IN YOUR FLESH AS AN EVERLASTING PACT (Gen. 17:13)—and covenant is mentioned in connection to converts, as it is said AND WHO HOLD FAST TO MY COVENANT (Isa. 56:6).

Acceptance is mentioned in connection to Israel, as it is said, TO WIN ACCEPTANCE FOR THEM BEFORE THE LORD (Ex. 28:38)—and acceptance is mentioned in connection to converts, as it is said THEIR BURNT OFFERINGS AND SACRIFICES SHALL BE ACCEPTED ON MY ALTAR; FOR MY HOUSE SHALL BE CALLED A HOUSE OF PRAYER FOR ALL PEOPLES (Isa. 56:7).

Guarding is mentioned in connection to Israel, as it is said SEE, THE GUARDIAN OF ISRAEL NEITHER SLUMBERS NOR SLEEPS! (Ps. 121:4)—and guarding is mentioned in connection to converts, as it is said THE LORD WATCHES OVER THE STRANGER (Ps. 146:9).

Abraham called himself a convert (ger), as it is said I AM A STRANGER (ger) AND A RESIDENT AMONG YOU (Gen. 23:4).

David called himself a convert (ger), as it is said I AM ONLY A STRANGER (ger) IN THE LAND (Ps. 119:19) and FOR WE ARE STRANGERS (gerim) WITH YOU, MERE TRANSIENTS LIKE OUR FATHERS; OUR DAYS ON EARTH ARE LIKE A SHADOW, WITH NOTHING IN PROSPECT (1 Chron. 29:15) and FOR LIKE ALL MY FOREBEARS I AM A STRANGER (ger), RESIDENT WITH YOU (Ps. 39:13).

THE STRANGER, THE FRIEND—usually translated "loves the stranger."
the days and years   Abraham's age is taken into account in the reward he will receive for circumcision.

Beloved are converts for our father Abraham was not circumcised until the age of ninety-nine, for had he been circumcised at age twenty or thirty, only those under the age of thirty could have been converted, therefore God postponed it for him until he reached the age of ninety-nine in order not to bar the door before prospective converts, and also in order to reward the days and years and to increase the reward of those who perform His will, fulfilling what is said THE LORD DESIRES HIS [SERVANT'S] VINDI-CATION, [THEREFORE] HE ENLARGES AND GLORIFIES HIS TORAH (Isa. 42:21).

You also find that [converts] are one of the four groups which respond to He Who Spoke and the world came into being:

ONE SHALL SAY, "I AM THE LORD'S" (Isa. 44:5)—"I belong entirely to the Lord, Let no sin be mixed with me;"

ANOTHER SHALL USE THE NAME "JACOB" (Isa. 44:5)—these are the righteous converts;

ANOTHER SHALL MARK HIS ARM "THE LORD'S" (Isa. 44:5)—these are those who repent;

AND ADOPT THE NAME "ISRAEL" (Isa. 44:5)—these are those who revere Heaven.

COMMENTARY   *Throughout the Midrash, the Biblical "stranger" is understood to mean a convert. This section is typical of the positive attitude toward converts displayed throughout early midrash. The one negative remark is lost in the plethora of enthusiastic praise intended to indicate that the convert is equal to the Israelite born to the covenant. During the period prior to and following the rise of Christianity, Judaism was a missionary religion and competed successfully with its daughter among the population of the pagan world. The reference here to circumcision is a reflection of that competition as well, since the question of requiring or not requiring circumcision of the flesh was a matter of debate both between the two religions and within early Christianity. Here the Midrash asserts its importance and claims that Abraham's circumcision at an advanced age not only resulted in great reward for him but also served deliberately as God's sign to all that this was a requirement for joining His chosen flock and could be performed at any age.*

[converts] *are one of the four groups*   Converts are one of the groups singled out for praise by Isaiah.

revere Heaven—but are not official converts.

10. Exodus 23:2, Mekhilta Kaspa 2, III 161

DO NOT SIDE WITH THE MULTITUDE TO DO WRONG (Ex. 23:2). This indicates that although you should not side with them to do wrong, you should side with them to do good. How so? If twelve vote to acquit and eleven to convict—he is acquitted. If thirteen vote to convict and ten to acquit—he is convicted. If eleven vote to acquit and twelve to convict, I might think that he is convicted, therefore the verse says AND DO NOT GIVE PERVERSE TESTIMONY IN A DISPUTE BY LEANING TO-WARD THE MULTITUDE (Ex. 23:2). The Torah says that one is sentenced to death by witnesses and one is sentenced to death by majority vote. Just as in the case of witnesses, two are required, so in the case of the majority vote, two are required. If eleven vote to acquit and eleven vote to convict and one says, "I do not know," we have here a warning to the judge that he should incline only toward the side of innocence. This is the meaning of the verse which says AND DO NOT GIVE PERVERSE TESTIMONY IN A DISPUTE BY LEANING TOWARD THE MULTITUDE.

NOR MUST YOU SHOW DEFERENCE TO A POOR MAN IN HIS DISPUTE (Ex. 23:3). Why is this stated? When it says DO NOT FAVOR THE POOR OR SHOW DEFERENCE TO THE RICH (Lev. 19:15) I only know these specific prohibitions. What about the opposite? Therefore the verse says NOR MUST YOU SHOW DEFERENCE TO A POOR MAN IN HIS DISPUTE (Ex. 23:3). Abba Hanin says in the name of R. Eliezer, "This verse is referring to the laws of gleaning, the forgotten sheaf and the corners of the field."

COMMENTARY   *The discussion of the number of votes needed to convict is in reference to capital cases. Monetary disputes were brought before courts of three judges while capital cases, because of the seriousness and irreversibility of the penalty, were tried before courts of twenty-three judges. The codes of law specify many measures to make conviction difficult. Among them is the law connected to Exodus 23:2, which requires that a simple majority is not enough for conviction. There must always be a minimum majority of two. The principle cited that one should incline only*

---

10. *DO NOT GIVE PERVERSE TESTIMONY*   The verb is singular, taken as warning that one person's vote is not enough to incline the vote toward conviction.
laws of gleaning—the equitable distribution of the gifts to the poor, which are described in Lev. 19:9–10; Lev. 23:22; Deut. 24:19–22.

toward the side of innocence was applied in many instances. The result was
that conviction was extremely difficult to achieve.

11. Exodus 23:6, Mekhilta Kaspa 3, III 168

YOU SHALL NOT PERVERT JUSTICE FOR YOUR NEEDY IN
THEIR DISPUTES (Ex. 23:6). Why is this stated? When it says NOR
MUST YOU SHOW DEFERENCE TO A POOR MAN IN HIS DIS-
PUTE (Ex. 23:3) I only know about the poor. What about the extremely
needy? Therefore the verse says YOU SHALL NOT PERVERT JUS-
TICE FOR YOUR NEEDY IN THEIR DISPUTES (Ex. 23:6). Abba
Hanin says in the name of R. Eliezer, "This verse is referring to the laws of
gleaning, the forgotten sheaf and the corners of the field."

If a wicked person and a worthy person appear before you for judgment,
you must not say, "Since he is a wicked person, I shall pervert the judgment
against him." That is the meaning of the verse YOU SHALL NOT PER-
VERT THE RIGHTS OF YOUR NEEDY IN THEIR DISPUTES (Ex.
23:6)—meaning one who is "needy" in mitzvot.

KEEP FAR FROM A FALSE CHARGE (Ex. 23:7). This is a warning
against speaking slander.
    Another interpretation: KEEP FAR FROM A FALSE CHARGE. This
is a warning to a judge not to permit an ignorant person to sit in judgment
with him.
    Another interpretation: He should not permit advocates to stand by

---

11. *FOR YOUR NEEDY*—Usually translated YOU SHALL NOT SUBVERT THE
RIGHTS OF YOUR NEEDY but understood by the Midrash as if it were saying not to deviate
from strict justice in order to help the needy.
extremely needy If we had only Ex. 23:3 I might think that it was forbidden to favor the poor,
but permitted to favor the destitute.
"needy" in mitzvot—lacking in mitzvot, wicked. Just because one has the reputation of being a
wicked person, the judge is not to disregard the law in order to convict him. The case must be
judged fairly on its merits.
slander—literally "the evil tongue," speaking evil of anyone.
not to permit In some cases two judges chosen by the parties chose the third judge. If they
choose an ignorant person as the third, they will render a false judgment.
advocates The judges must reach an independent judgment on the basis of the testimony of
the litigants and the witnesses alone, uninfluenced by the opinions of others.

him, as it is said THE CASE OF BOTH PARTIES SHALL COME BE-
FORE THE JUDGE (Ex. 22:8).

R. Nathan says, "KEEP FAR FROM A FALSE CHARGE (Ex. 23:7).
This is a warning to separate oneself from heresy. Thus it says NOW, I
FIND WOMAN MORE BITTER THAN DEATH (Eccl. 7:26) and it says
BUT THE KING SHALL REJOICE IN GOD; ALL WHO SWEAR BY
HIM SHALL EXULT AND THE MOUTH OF LIARS IS STOPPED
(Ps. 63:12)."

Another interpretation: KEEP FAR FROM A FALSE CHARGE (Ex.
23:7). If one fellow is sitting and properly expounding laws, and another
hears him and says, "I shall dispute and disprove this and then restructure it
so that I may be called a Sage," of him it is said KEEP FAR FROM A FALSE
CHARGE. This one is a speaker of falsehoods.

DO NOT BRING DEATH ON THE INNOCENT AND THE RIGH-
TEOUS (Ex. 23:7). If there is one witness who testifies that that person
was worshiping the sun and another who testifies that that person was worshiping the moon, I might think that these two may be combined in order to
convict him. Therefore the verse says DO NOT BRING DEATH ON
THE INNOCENT AND THE RIGHTEOUS.

If they saw someone pursuing another in order to slay him, with a
sword in his hand—and they say to him, "You should know that he is a
member of the covenant and the Torah says WHOEVER SHEDS THE
BLOOD OF MAN, BY MAN SHALL HIS BLOOD BE SHED (Gen.
9:6)," and he says to them, "I know that," after which the witnesses lose
sight of him, but after a while they find the other person slain, gasping his
last, and the dripping sword in the hand of the slayer—I might think that he
is guilty. Therefore the verse says DO NOT BRING DEATH ON THE
INNOCENT AND THE RIGHTEOUS (Ex. 23:6).

---

heresy—which is falsehood about God.

WOMAN MORE BITTER   Evil women were taken as the personification of heresy.

expounding laws—in the Academy, not in a court.

combined   Since two witnesses are needed for conviction, one might wish to consider the
testimony of both of them as valid. This cannot be done, however, since each one testifies to a
different offense. Even if both are true, you do not have two witnesses to any one offense.

and they say to him—thus giving him warning. There must be prior warning against committing
a crime before one can be convicted of it.

that he is guilty—that he can be convicted and executed. This is not possible, however, unless
there are two witnesses to the actual deed.

Simeon b. Shetah once put to death a false witness who schemed against his fellow. R. Judah b. Tabbai said to him, "May I never see the consolation if you have not shed innocent blood! The Torah says that one may be executed only upon the testimony of witnesses and [that it may happen] that one will be executed upon the testimony of false witnesses who scheme against him. Just as there must be two witnesses, so there must be two scheming witnesses in order to make one guilty of being a scheming witness."

It once happened that Judah b. Tabbai entered a ruin and found there a man slain, gasping his last, and the sword dripping blood in the hand of the slayer. Judah b. Tabbai said to him, "May [punishment] come upon me if it was not either you or I who killed him! But what can I do, for the Torah has said that A CASE CAN BE VALID ONLY ON THE TESTIMONY OF TWO WITNESSES OR MORE (Deut. 19:15). Be He Who Knows, He Who is the Master of Thoughts, He will requite punishment from that man!" The man had not even managed to leave the place when a serpent bit him and he died.

DO NOT BRING DEATH ON THE INNOCENT (Ex. 23:7). If, after one was convicted by the court, evidence was found in his favor, I might think that he stands convicted. Therefore the verse says DO NOT BRING DEATH ON THE INNOCENT. Has he emerged from your court as he emerged from Mine? The verse says FOR I WILL NOT ACQUIT THE WRONGDOER (Ex. 23:7).

DO NOT BRING DEATH ON . . . THE VINDICATED (Ex. 23:7). If, after one was acquitted by the court, evidence was found against him, I

---

schemed against his fellow   The law of false witnesses is found in Deut. 19:19–21. According to the Sages this means that these are witnesses who are found to be lying on the basis of testimony of others that they were elsewhere when the crime took place and could not have witnessed it.

two scheming witnesses   Unless there were two who schemed their testimony would have had no effect since two witnesses are required. Therefore if only one witness was shown to be a scheming witness, he is not to be put to death. Therefore Simeon b. Shetah should not have executed the false witness.

he stands convicted—and therefore the case cannot be reopened to consider new favorable evidence.

THE INNOCENT   If he is actually innocent, even if you have declared him guilty, he must be given another chance.

from Mine   In God's court, he is innocent. Therefore you must reopen the case.

THE VINDICATED—usually translated "the righteous." The Hebrew word, *zadik*, means either righteous or innocent in a law case.

might think that he should be returned for trial. Therefore the verse says DO NOT BRING DEATH ON ... THE VINDICATED. Has he emerged vindicated from My court as he emerged from yours? The Torah says FOR I WILL NOT ACQUIT THE WRONGDOER. If in regard to the Quality of Punishment which is the lesser, the Torah says FOR I WILL NOT ACQUIT THE WRONGDOER, how much more is this so in regard to the Quality of Goodness which is the greater!

DO NOT TAKE BRIBES (Ex. 23:8). One might say, "I shall take money, but I will not pervert justice," therefore the verse says FOR BRIBES BLIND THE EYES OF THE WISE (Deut. 16:19). It is a matter of logic. If in the case of one who takes bribes but did not intend to pervert justice the Torah says FOR BRIBES BLIND THE EYES, how much more is this so in regard to one who takes them in order to pervert justice!

FOR BRIBES BLIND THE EYES OF THE WISE—in matters of Torah. You say "in matters of Torah," but perhaps it means literally THE WISE. The verse says FOR BRIBES BLIND THE CLEAR-SIGHTED (Ex. 23:8). This refers to those who are clear-minded, who, on the basis of their own judgment, can discern between the pure and the impure. This is the source of the teaching: Whoever takes money and perverts justice will not depart this world until his eyes lose their sight. R. Nathan says, ". . . until one of these three things happens: his mind will become confused in matters of Torah and he will declare the pure impure and the impure, pure; or he will become dependent upon others; or his eyesight will diminish."

COMMENTARY   *As in the previous section, here too the Midrash emphasizes the importance of justice, free from prejudice, bribery, or ulterior motives on the part of the judges. Here too we see the way in which the law*

---

returned for trial   Even if there is new evidence, once declared innocent, he cannot be retried. There is no double jeopardy.

vindicated from My court   God's justice, however, will prevail over him regardless of his escaping human justice.

Quality of Punishment—God's Quality of Justice, as opposed to His Quality of Mercy.

which is the greater   Since God's mercy is more powerful than His justice, one may expect that if He sees to it that punishment comes on those who deserve it, He will certainly bring reward and goodness to those who are innocent and deserving.

clear-minded—i.e., to general wisdom. These are the wise. Therefore the verse that speaks of THE WISE is referring to the Sages, who are wise in Torah.

This is the source   The verse in Deuteronomy is the source of the idea that the eyes of the corrupt will lose their sight.

was skewed toward acquittal in capital cases. No amount of circumstantial evidence, even the dripping sword (the equivalent of today's smoking gun) could convict in a case leading to execution. The Sages, however, were convinced that God's court was more capable than theirs and His justice more effective.

12. Exodus 31:12, Mekhilta Shabbata 1, III 197

AND THE LORD SPOKE TO MOSES (Ex. 31:12)—not through an angel and not through a messenger.

NEVERTHELESS YOU MUST KEEP MY SABBATHS (Ex. 31:13). Why is this stated? When it says YOU SHALL NOT DO ANY WORK (Ex. 20:10) I only know of those things which are considered actual work. What about *shebut*? The verse says NEVERTHELESS YOU MUST KEEP MY SABBATHS—in order to include *shebut*.

R. Ishmael, R. Eleazar b. Azariah, and R. Akiba were once walking along the way and Levi the netmaker and Ishmael the son of R. Eleazar b. Azariah were following them. This question was asked of them: What is the source which teaches that saving a life takes precedence over the Sabbath?

R. Ishmael replied, "IF THE THIEF IS SEIZED WHILE TUNNELING AND HE IS BEATEN TO DEATH, THERE IS NO BLOOD-GUILT IN HIS CASE (Ex. 22:1). There is doubt here if he intended merely to steal or [if he intended] to kill. From this you can reason that if [in this doubtful case] the shedding of blood, which contaminates the earth and causes the Divine Presence to remove itself from the world, takes precedence over the Sabbath, surely saving a life takes precedence over the Sabbath."

R. Eleazar b. Azariah replied, "If circumcision, which involves only

---

12. *shebut*—a term meaning "resting" or "desisting." This is the category of actions that the Sages prohibited on the Sabbath even though they were not strictly included in the categories of prohibited work. They are actions that resemble the prohibited activities, seem contrary to the spirit of the Sabbath, or might bring one to actual desecration of the Sabbath.

there is doubt Nevertheless the thief was killed because even in doubtful cases one has the right to defend his own life. Since the reference in the Torah does not specify weekday or Sabbath, the assumption is that it could be done on the Sabbath as well. See also the discussion on page 406.

circumcision—is to be performed on the eighth day of the child's life, even if it is the Sabbath.

one part of a person's body, takes precedence over the Sabbath, surely this would be so concerning the entire body!" They said to him, "According to your reasoning, since this is so only in cases of certainty, so too here it would be so only in cases of certainty."

R. Akiba says, "If punishment of a murderer takes precedence over the Temple service, which takes precedence over the Sabbath, surely saving a life takes precedence over the Sabbath!"

R. Jose the Galilean says, "When it says NEVERTHELESS, YOU MUST KEEP MY SABBATHS (Ex. 31:13), the word NEVERTHELESS makes a distinction: there are Sabbaths upon which you rest and there are Sabbaths upon which you do not rest."

R. Simeon b. Menasiah says, "It says YOU SHALL KEEP THE SAB-BATH, FOR IT IS HOLY TO YOU (Ex. 31:14). TO YOU is the Sabbath given over, and you are not given over to the Sabbath."

R. Nathan says, "It says THE ISRAELITE PEOPLE SHALL KEEP THE SABBATH, OBSERVING THE SABBATH THROUGHOUT THE GENERATIONS AS A COVENANT FOR ALL TIME (Ex. 31:16). Desecrate one Sabbath for him so that he may observe many Sabbaths."

FOR THIS IS A SIGN BETWEEN ME AND YOU (Ex. 31:13)—and not between Me and the nations of the world. . . .

FOR IT IS HOLY FOR YOU (Ex. 31:14). This informs us that the Sabbath adds holiness to Israel. "Why is so-and-so's store closed?" "Because he observes the Sabbath." "Why is so-and-so not engaging in work?" "Because he is observing the Sabbath. He is testifying that He Who Spoke and the world came into being created His world in six days and rested upon the

---

only in cases of certainty   If there is some doubt as to the time, for example, if the birth occurred at twilight and we are not certain if the Sabbath is the eighth day or not, the circumcision is not held on the Sabbath. This might imply that in cases of doubtful saving of life as well, the Sabbath takes precedence. That is not the case.

over the Temple service   The murderer could be taken from the very altar of the Temple. See Ex. 21:14.

upon which you do not rest—because you must do prohibited work in order to save a life.

given over to the Sabbath   The Sabbath does not take precedence over your life or the life of others.

desecrate one Sabbath—by saving someone's life.

FOR YOU—seems to be an unnecessary phrase. It indicates that the observance of the Sabbath adds to Israel's holiness.

seventh." Thus it says MY WITNESSES ARE YOU—DECLARES THE LORD (Isa. 43:10).

COMMENTARY   *Although the Sabbath originated in the Bible, many of the specific rules of its observance, often quite technical, were formulated by the Sages. The question under discussion here is a general one. What may be done to save a life on the Sabbath? The answer was "Anything." The situation in which this matter is discussed is interesting. Discussions of this sort were not confined to formal sessions in the Academy but might and did take place wherever and whenever groups of Sages were together. Note also that in this case there is no disagreement concerning the regulation. The question was to find the Biblical source of something that was taken for granted and each Sage has his own method of doing so. If, as in the case of R. Eleazar b. Azariah, his answer is found lacking, the others do not hesitate to demonstrate its weakness. It should be noted that the answer "TO YOU is the Sabbath given over, and you are not given over to the Sabbath," which is even broader than the question under discussion, is identical with that found in Mark 2:27. This, of course, does not imply that the application of this formulation was the same.*

13. Exodus 35:1, Mekhilta Shabbata 2, III 205

MOSES THEN CONVOKED THE WHOLE ISRAELITE COMMUNITY AND SAID TO THEM: THESE ARE THE THINGS THAT THE LORD HAS COMMANDED YOU TO DO: ON SIX DAYS WORK MAY BE DONE, BUT ON THE SEVENTH DAY YOU SHALL HAVE A SABBATH OF COMPLETE REST (Ex. 35:1–2). Why is this section said? When it says AND LET THEM MAKE ME A SANCTUARY (Ex. 25:8) I might think that this means that they were to do so both on the Sabbath and on weekdays. How then would I apply the verse HE WHO PROFANES IT SHALL BE PUT TO DEATH (Ex. 31:14)? In regard to all work except that of building the Sanctuary. If it applies to the work of building the Sanctuary, how would I apply the verse AND LET THEM MAKE ME A SANCTUARY (Ex. 25:8)? On all other days except the Sabbath. Perhaps that includes the Sabbath. Logic would dictate that if the Temple Service, which can be done only when preparations are made,

---

13. *to do so*—to construct the Sanctuary both on weekdays and on the Sabbath.
the Temple Service—took place on the Sabbath, even though it involved many activities otherwise forbidden on the Sabbath.

takes precedence over the Sabbath, surely the preparations themselves, without which no Temple service can take place, should take precedence over the Sabbath! This would include such things as repairing on the Sabbath the horn of the altar which has broken off or the knife which has become defective. The verse says THEN MOSES CONVOKED (Ex. 35:1) indicating that these things can be done on the weekday, but not on the Sabbath.

AND SAID TO THEM: THESE ARE THE THINGS (Ex. 35:1). R. Judah the Prince says, "This includes the thirty-nine main categories of work which Moses gave to them orally."

BUT THE SEVENTH DAY SHALL BE HOLY TO YOU (Ex. 35:2) Israel should not say, "Since the performance of work is permissible within the Temple, it should also be permissible elsewhere. Therefore the verse says BUT THE SEVENTH DAY SHALL BE HOLY TO YOU—it is HOLY TO YOU but it is profane to God. . . ."

YOU SHALL KINDLE NO FIRE THROUGHOUT YOUR SETTLEMENTS ON THE SABBATH DAY (Ex. 35:3). [Perhaps] one is not permitted to kindle a light or to put things away to be kept warm or to make himself a fire for the Sabbath on the eve of the Sabbath. The verse says YOU SHALL KINDLE NO FIRE THROUGHOUT YOUR SETTLEMENTS ON THE SABBATH DAY—you may not kindle fire ON THE SABBATH DAY but you may kindle fire on the eve of the Sabbath for the Sabbath.

COMMENTARY   *As the Sages themselves noted, the Scriptural references to the work prohibited or permitted on the Sabbath are virtually nonexistent. The laws of the Sabbath are likened to a mountain that hangs by a hair. In order to clarify matters, the Sages outlined thirty-nine categories of prohibited work, everything else being permitted. These categories covered the basic methods of human creation, creation of food, of clothing, of build-*

---

the thirty-nine main categories   Rabbinic law outlined thirty-nine types of work that were forbidden on the Sabbath.

profane to God   God is not bound by the Sabbath. The Temple is God's territory. Within it, activities forbidden elsewhere on the Sabbath may be performed.

on the eve of the Sabbath   The verse is ambiguous and could be understood to mean that no fire should be allowed to burn on the Sabbath even if kindled before it.

for the Sabbath—to burn on the Sabbath day.

ings and utensils, and of written scrolls. They then connected these with the Sanctuary, either with the building of the Sanctuary—which was forbidden on the Sabbath, regardless of that structure's importance—or with the service of the Temple, which was permitted on the Sabbath since it was specifically commanded by the Torah and was considered God's realm as opposed to the realm of humankind. Obviously many of these regulations were matters of dispute between the Pharisees and other groups. One such dispute concerned the use of fire. Since the Torah says not to kindle it, does this mean that there was to be no fire at all on the Sabbath day? There were—and are—sects that interpreted it thus. The Sages, however, understood it to mean that on the Sabbath fire was not to be started or touched, but fires previously lit could be permitted to burn. The Sages made it a practice to light fires before the Sabbath so that there would be light and warmth on that day, to prevent it from becoming a gloomy time. They even went so far as to proclaim the lighting of such lamps a mitzvah, to be performed by the women of the household accompanied by the recitation of a special blessing.

LEVITICUS

1. Leviticus 1:4, Sifra Finkelstein 19

SPEAK TO THE SONS OF ISRAEL . . . HE SHALL LAY HIS HAND UPON THE HEAD OF THE BURNT OFFERING (Lev. 1:2–4). Israelites lay their hands but gentiles do not lay their hands. Now which is more inclusive, "waving" or "laying on"? Waving is more inclusive than laying on for waving is performed both for animate and inanimate offerings, while laying on is performed only for animate offerings. Certainly if we exclude [gentiles] from waving, which is more inclusive, we shall exclude them from laying on, which is less inclusive! So you say, but is waving more inclusive than laying on or is laying on more inclusive than waving? For laying on is performed by all the partners while waving is not performed by all the partners. If we exclude [gentiles] from waving, which is less inclusive, shall we exclude them from laying on, which is more inclusive?

Thus since waving has some requirements which laying on does not have and laying on has some which waving does not have, the verse must tell us explicitly SPEAK TO THE SONS OF ISRAEL . . . HE

---

1. *gentiles*—who send an offering to the Temple.

waving An offering was presented before the Lord by an action of waving. See, for example, Lev. 14:12.

inanimate offerings—such as the first sheaf of the harvest (Lev. 23:11).

partners—when an offering is brought by more than one person.

exclude [gentiles] from "waving" The Sages had determined on the basis of their interpretation of Lev. 7:29 that gentiles were not to perform the act of waving.

more inclusive—since all the partners perform it but do not perform waving. Therefore perhaps gentiles should be permitted to lay their hands on the sacrifice.

the verse must tell us Since logic is of no help in this matter, since the question of which action is more inclusive may be argued either way, the verse specifies that laying on of hands is intended only for those who belong to the people Israel, thus excluding gentiles.

425

SHALL LAY HIS HAND. Israelites lay their hands but gentiles do not lay their hands.

THE SONS OF ISRAEL (Lev. 1:2)—lay their hands but the daughters of Israel do not lay their hands. R. Jose and R. Simeon say, "It is optional for women to lay on their hands." R. Jose said, "Abba Eleazar said to me, 'We had a calf for a well-being offering which we brought to the Women's Court and women laid their hands upon it.' " Is laying on performed in the Women's Court? Rather that was done in order to give the women pleasure.

Is it possible that laying on is not performed [by women] for burnt offerings since they do not require waving, but only for offerings of well-being since they do require waving? The verse says AND SAY TO THEM (Lev. 1:2)—thus including all matters which are under discussion. Just as [women] do not lay their hands on burnt offerings, so they do not lay their hands on offerings of well-being.

ANY MAN (Lev. 1:2)—thus including converts. OF YOU (Lev. 1:2)—thus excluding apostates. Why interpret it thus—ANY MAN—thus including converts. OF YOU—thus excluding apostates? After the verse has included, it excludes. The verse says THE SONS OF ISRAEL (Lev. 1:2). Just as the Israelites have accepted the covenant, so converts accept the covenant, excluding apostates who do not accept the covenant.

Perhaps one would reason: The Israelites are children of those who accepted the covenant and so too apostates are children of those who accepted the covenant, thus excluding converts who are not children of those who accepted the covenant. Therefore the verse says OF YOU—now. Therefore you must say that just as the Israelites accepted the covenant, so converts have accepted the covenant, excluding apostates who do not accept the covenant. Thus it says THE SACRIFICE OF THE WICKED MAN

---

optional Women are not required to do so, but are permitted to.

Women's Court—The section at the east of the Temple Court, so called because women were not permitted to go beyond it.

pleasure—but the act was not a fulfillment of the mitzvah of laying on the hands.

converts Proselytes, i.e., non-Jews who have become Jews, are specifically included in the laying on of hands by the words ANY MAN.

has included The words ANY MAN are intended to include some group.

it excludes The words OF YOU exclude someone. Who is excluded?

apostates—are excluded since they do not resemble the people of Israel in having accepted the Covenant. On the contrary, they reject it.

THE WICKED MAN—the apostate.

IS AN ABOMINATION, THE MORE SO AS HE OFFERS IT IN DE-
PRAVITY (Prov. 21:27).

ANY MAN . . . HE PRESENTS (Lev. 1:2). Does this mean that he is required to do so? The verse says WHEN HE PRESENTS (Lev. 1:2)—indicating that it is optional.

AN OFFERING TO THE LORD (Lev. 1:2). The sanctification of it must
precede the offering of it. So taught R. Judah. R. Simeon said, "What source
teaches that a man should not say, 'To the Lord—a burnt offering; to the
Lord—a meal offering; to the Lord—an offering of well-being,' but rather
he should say, 'A burnt offering to the Lord; a meal offering to the Lord'?
The verse says AN OFFERING TO THE LORD. From this we may infer
that if one who is about to sanctify [an offering] is nevertheless told by the
Torah not to place the Name of the Lord upon the offering, certainly one is
not to mention the Name of Heaven for no reason!"

THE LORD (Lev. 1:2). Wherever an offering is mentioned, the Name
LORD appears in order not to give sectarians any support.

COMMENTARY   *The Sages gave scrupulous attention to each word and
even to the order in which words appear. In determining the law they used
a combination of logic and Biblical authority, preferring wherever possible
to find a Scriptural basis for their practices.*

2. Leviticus 12:3, Sifra Weiss 58a

ON THE EIGHTH DAY THE FLESH OF HIS FORESKIN SHALL BE
CIRCUMCISED (Lev. 12:3). Does this mean any time, either day or night?
DAY means daytime and not at night. This informs me that if the child is
circumcised on the eighth day it must be during the daytime. What indicates
that the child who is circumcised on the ninth, tenth, or eleventh day, or at

The sanctification of it—the declaration that this offering is dedicated to God.
the Name of the Lord—the specific name, known as the Tetragrammaton, which was unique to
the God of Israel.
sectarians—such as those who believe in two gods. If any name could be used, it might imply
that each name represented a different deity.

---

2. *ninth, tenth* A circumcision may be postponed for reasons of health. In that case, must it
be performed only during the daytime?

any other time, must be circumcised during the daytime? The verse says
ON THE ... DAY.

A disciple once said to R. Akiba, "One wants to say so, but it seems to
me that since it says SHE SHALL BE UNCLEAN SEVEN DAYS (Lev.
12:2) and then ON THE EIGHTH DAY (Lev. 12:3), one might think that
we have here fifteen days—seven and eight! Therefore the verse says ON
THE ... DAY." R. Akiba said to him, "You have dived into deep waters
and brought up a shard in your hand. Does it not say elsewhere AT
THE AGE OF EIGHT DAYS, EVERY MALE AMONG YOU
THROUGHOUT THE GENERATIONS SHALL BE CIRCUMCISED
(Gen. 17:12)?"

ON THE ... DAY (Lev. 12:3) indicates that any time during the daylight
is proper for circumcision. Nevertheless, those who are zealous perform
mitzvot as quickly as they can, as it is said SO EARLY NEXT MORNING,
ABRAHAM SADDLED HIS ASS (Gen. 22:3).

ON THE EIGHTH DAY THE FLESH OF HIS FORESKIN SHALL BE
CIRCUMCISED (Lev. 12:3)—even if it is the Sabbath. How then is HE
WHO PROFANES IT SHALL BE PUT TO DEATH (Ex. 31:14) to be
applied? It refers to all other acts of work except for circumcision. Perhaps
I should apply HE WHO PROFANES IT SHALL BE PUT TO DEATH
to circumcision as well, in which case how would I apply ON THE
EIGHTH DAY (Lev. 12:3)? To all days except the Sabbath. Therefore the
verse says ON THE EIGHTH DAY—even if it is the Sabbath.

THE FLESH OF HIS FORESKIN SHALL BE CIRCUMCISED (Lev.
12:3)—even if there is a discoloration there. How then is IN CASES OF A

The verse says ON THE ... DAY   In Hebrew the literal order is "On the day the eighth."
Thus "On the day" stands by itself and is taken to mean: during the daytime—whatever day it
is performed.
A disciple   His view is that ON THE ... DAY does not mean during the daytime but is needed
to teach that the circumcision must take place on the eighth day. It is required because of the
possible confusion caused by these verses, which might be interpreted to mean that the eighth
day is eight days after the seven-day period of the mother's ritual impurity following the birth.
a shard—something valueless. You have made a great effort for nothing.
Does it not say elsewhere   Your teaching is not valid since we have another verse that teaches
specifically that the period of time is eight days. Therefore this one is not needed for that
purpose and can be used to teach that circumcision must always be performed in the daytime.
HE WHO PROFANES IT—the Sabbath. Does this not mean that even circumcision does not
supersede the Sabbath?
THE FLESH   This is an extra word that teaches that the circumcision is to be performed
even if there is a discoloration.

SCALY AFFECTION BE MOST CAREFUL (Deut. 24:8) to be applied? It refers to everything except for circumcision. Perhaps I should apply IN THE CASE OF A SCALY AFFECTION BE MOST CAREFUL to circumcision as well, in which case how would I apply THE FLESH OF HIS FORESKIN SHALL BE CIRCUMCISED (Lev. 12:3)? When there is no discoloration there. Therefore the verse says THE FLESH—even when there is a discoloration there.

HIS FORESKIN (Lev. 12:3)—when there is definitely a foreskin this takes precedence over the Sabbath, but if it is doubtful, it does not take precedence over the Sabbath.

HIS FORESKIN—when there is definitely a foreskin this takes precedence over the Sabbath, but the case of an *androgynous* does not take precedence over the Sabbath. R. Judah says, "The case of an *androgynous* does take precedence over the Sabbath and one is even liable for the penalty of extinction because of it."

HIS FORESKIN—the foreskin takes precedence over the Sabbath, but the case of a child born at twilight does not take precedence over the Sabbath.
    The foreskin takes precedence over the Sabbath, but a child born circumcised does not take precedence over the Sabbath—for the School of Shammai said that in such a case a drop of blood must be let so that there should be blood of the covenant, while the School of Hillel says that it is not necessary. R. Simeon b. Eleazar says, "The Schools of Shammai and Hillel did not dispute whether or not a child born circumcised requires the letting of a drop of blood as blood of the covenant, since that is really a case of the

---

this takes precedence—or "sets aside" the Sabbath, permitting something to be done that would usually be considered a desecration of the Sabbath.

androgynous   A Greek word referring to one who has both male and female characteristics. Since there is a doubt as to the need to perform a circumcision, the Sabbath takes precedence.

born at twilight   If the child is born Friday evening at a time when there is a question if it is still Friday or if the Sabbath has already begun, or Saturday evening at a time when it may still be the Sabbath or not, the circumcision is performed on Friday (in the first case) or Sunday (in the second case) and the Sabbath is not set aside.

blood of the covenant   Circumcision is the sign of the Covenant between God and Israel, and is called the "covenant of Abraham." The School of Shammai believes that even if a child is born without a foreskin, a drop of blood must be let to indicate that the child has been admitted to the covenant but it need not be done on the Sabbath.

foreskin being pressed down. What was their dispute? The case of a convert who was already circumcised. The School of Shammai said that a drop of blood must be let as blood of the covenant, while the School of Hillel says that it is not necessary."

3. Leviticus 14:34, Sifra Weiss 72b

WHEN YOU ENTER (Lev. 14:34). Could this be from the time you enter the other side of the Jordan? The verse says THE LAND (Lev. 14:34)—the special Land. Could this be the land of Moab and Ammon? The verse says WHICH I GIVE YOU (Lev. 14:34) and not Moab and Ammon. AS A POSSESSION (Lev. 14:34)—only when you have conquered it. What is the source which teaches that if they conquered it but had not divided it up, or had divided it up according to families but not according to specific family heads, so that each individual did not know what belonged to him, it is not yet subject to the law of plagues? The verse says THE OWNER OF THE HOUSE SHALL COME (Lev. 14:35)—only when each individual knows what belongs to him.

AND I INFLICT AN ERUPTIVE PLAGUE (Lev. 14:34). R. Judah said, "This was meant to inform them that such plagues **would** come upon them." R. Simeon said, "AND I INFLICT AN ERUPTIVE PLAGUE—excluding those caused by supernatural forces. UPON A HOUSE IN THE LAND YOU POSSESS (Lev. 14:34)—excluding a house built upon ships or rafts upon four beams, but including one built upon a tree or upon pillars."

YOU POSSESS (Lev. 14:34). That which you possess is rendered impure by plagues, but Jerusalem is not rendered impure by plagues. R. Judah said,

---

pressed down—so that it appears as if there is no foreskin, but it really exists. Therefore blood must be let according to both schools.
convert The ruling of later Jewish law, although disputed by some, is that such a convert must have the blood of the covenant let.

---

3. *could this be*—the application of the law of plagues.
the other side of the Jordan—where some of the tribes did settle. Nevertheless, it was not to be considered within the Holy Land.
supernatural forces—explained in the Talmud as caused by evil spirits. The emphasis is on the word *I*—things inflicted by God and not by evil spirits. This differs from R. Judah's interpretation.
built upon ships—because it is not IN THE LAND.
Jerusalem That city was not possessed by any individual or tribe, but belonged to the entire nation. Therefore this law did not apply.

"I have not heard of any exclusion except that of the Temple." R. Ishmael says, "YOU POSSESS—that which you possess is rendered impure by these plagues, but the lands of the nations are not rendered impure by them. And just as their lands are not rendered impure by these plagues, so their garments are not rendered impure by them."

THE OWNER OF THE HOUSE (Lev. 14:35) may not send a messenger. Is this so even if he is old or ill? The verse says SHALL COME AND TELL THE PRIEST (Lev. 14:35). The priest shall then investigate exactly how the plague came upon the house. SAYING (Lev. 14:35). The priest shall speak pressing words to him: "My son, the eruptive plague always comes as a result of the evil tongue. IN CASE OF AN ERUPTIVE PLAGUE BE MOST CAREFUL . . . REMEMBER WHAT THE LORD YOUR GOD DID TO MIRIAM ON THE JOURNEY AFTER YOU LEFT EGYPT (Deut. 24:8–9). What is the connection between these things? It teaches us that the eruptive plague always comes as a result of the evil tongue. This is a matter of logic: If this happened to Miriam who did not speak thus in the presence of Moses, how much more will it happen to one who speaks against his fellow in his presence!"

R. Simeon b. Eleazar says, "Plagues also come as a result of arrogance as we see in the case of Uzziah: WHEN HE WAS STRONG, HE GREW SO ARROGANT HE ACTED CORRUPTLY: HE TRESPASSED AGAINST HIS GOD BY ENTERING THE TEMPLE OF THE LORD TO OFFER INCENSE ON THE INCENSE ALTAR. THE PRIEST AZARIAH, WITH EIGHTY OTHER BRAVE PRIESTS OF THE LORD, FOLLOWED HIM IN AND, CONFRONTING KING UZ-ZIAH, SAID TO HIM, 'IT IS NOT FOR YOU, UZZIAH, TO OFFER INCENSE TO THE LORD, BUT FOR THE AARONITE PRIESTS. . . .' UZZIAH, HOLDING THE CENSER AND READY TO BURN INCENSE, GOT ANGRY, BUT AS HE GOT ANGRY WITH THE PRIESTS, LEPROSY BROKE OUT ON HIS FOREHEAD . . .

---

the Temple—alone belonged to everyone. The rest of Jerusalem did belong to individuals and was therefore subject to this law.

their garments—referring to Lev. 13:47 where laws of eruptions on clothing are found.

old or ill In those cases someone else may come and inform the priest of the plague.

evil tongue—gossip or slander. This was Miriam's sin for which she was punished with leprosy. See Num. 12.

in the presence of Moses Miriam spoke about Moses to Aaron, when neither Moses nor anyone else was present. Nevertheless she was punished.

FOR THE LORD HAD STRUCK HIM WITH A PLAGUE. KING UZ-
ZIAH WAS A LEPER UNTIL THE DAY OF HIS DEATH (2 Chron.
26:16–21)."

COMMENTARY   *In this rather simple form of midrash the phrases are
interspersed with the rabbinic interpretation of the verse. The presence of
comments of a moral nature, such as those concerning Miriam and Uzziah,
demonstrates that there is no strict distinction between law and lore in
Midrash.*

4. Leviticus 16:29, Sifra Weiss 82b

AND THIS SHALL BE TO YOU A LAW FOR ALL TIME: IN THE
SEVENTH MONTH ON THE TENTH DAY OF THE MONTH (Lev.
16:29). AND THIS SHALL BE TO YOU—and not to others. A LAW
FOR ALL TIME (olam)—concerning the Everlasting (olamim) House. IN
THE SEVENTH MONTH. Could this mean the entire month? The verse
says ON THE TENTH DAY OF THE MONTH.

YOU SHALL AFFLICT YOUR SOULS (Lev. 16:29). Could this mean
that one should seat oneself in the heat and in the cold in order to make
oneself uncomfortable? . . . YOU SHALL AFFLICT YOUR SOULS—
affliction which will affect your souls. What is that? Eating and drinking.
They said in the name of R. Ishmael, "YOU SHALL AFFLICT YOUR
SOULS is stated here and HE AFFLICTED YOU AND SUBJECTED
YOU TO HUNGER (Deut. 8:3) is stated elsewhere. Just as the 'affliction'
stated there is hunger, so the 'affliction' stated here is hunger."

AND YOU SHALL DO NO MANNER OF WORK (Lev. 16:29). Does
this mean that one should not trim vegetables, arrange couches, or wash
cups? We reason thus: "Work" is stated here and work is stated elsewhere
in regard to the work of the Sanctuary (Ex. 31:3). Just as the work stated in
regard to the Sanctuary is skillful work, so the work stated here is skillful
work. Perhaps it means that just as the work stated in regard to the Sanctuary

---

4. *Everlasting (olamim) House*—the Temple. Thus the verse is speaking of a law "for the
Temple," where these ceremonies took place.
which will affect your souls—something that can affect the soul, i.e., life itself.
skillful work   The definition of work is a technical one as expounded by Jewish law.

was finished work, so the work stated here must be finished work such as not writing on a scroll, not weaving a garment, or not winnowing. How do we know that one may not write two letters, weave two meshes in a sieve or a winnow? The verse says not merely "work" but NO MANNER OF WORK, thus including all of this.

This teaches me about work which is optional. What about work which is in connection with a mitzvah? What indicates that one may not write two letters in sacred scrolls, phylacteries, or *mezuzot* or make two stitches in the breeches or the curtains? The verse says not merely "work" but NO MANNER OF WORK, thus including all of this.

This teaches me only about work which carries with it the penalty of extinction. What about work which does not carry with it the penalty of extinction? What indicates that one may not write one letter, make one stitch, weave one mesh in a sieve or a winnow? The verse says not merely "work" but NO MANNER OF WORK, thus including all of this.

This teaches me only about work which is of the same category of work which carries with it the punishment of extinction. What about work which is not of the same category of work which carries with it the punishment of extinction? What indicates that one may not climb a tree, ride on the back of an animal, sail on the water, clap hands, stamp feet, or dance? The verse says IT SHALL BE A SABBATH OF COMPLETE REST (Lev. 16:31) indicating *shebut*.

This teaches me only about *shebut* which is optional. What about *shebut* which is in connection with a mitzvah? What indicates that one is not to

---

finished work—work that has completed the creation of a specific thing.

write two letters   These are the minimum amounts that come under the definition of work. This is less than a finished product but is nevertheless forbidden.

work which is optional—things one does for oneself as opposed to that which is done in connection with what God commands, the observance of mitzvot.

phylacteries—or *tefillin*, small boxes or pouches containing scrolls with excerpts from the Torah, which are bound on the arm and the head.

mezuzot—containers in which are placed scrolls with excerpts from the Torah. They are then affixed to each doorway.

the breeches—the sacred garments of the priests.

curtains—of the Sanctuary.

extinction—punishment by God rather than at the hands of a human court.

write one letter   This is below the amount that warrants extinction. Is it also forbidden?

shebut—actions forbidden on the Sabbath or, in this case, on the Day of Atonement, which are not part of the categories of forbidden work derived from the Torah. While of lesser severity, they are nevertheless prohibited.

dedicate something—to the Sanctuary.

dedicate something, make valuations, proscribe goods, give *terumah* or tithes, betroth, divorce, annul a marriage, or perform *haliza,* nor redeem fruits of the fourth year or second tithe? The verse says IT SHALL BE A SABBATH OF COMPLETE REST (Lev. 16:31) indicating *shebut.*

NEITHER THE CITIZEN NOR THE ALIEN WHO RESIDES AMONG YOU (Lev. 16:29). CITIZEN indicates the citizens. THE CITIZEN includes the wives of citizens. ALIEN indicates the convert. THE ALIEN includes the wives of converts. AMONG YOU includes women and slaves.

COMMENTARY   *Many midrashim are concerned with elucidating the exact meaning of Biblical prohibitions or practices. Here the Scripture commands the observance of the Day of Atonement and requires affliction of the soul, but does not specify what that means. Similarly it forbids work, without defining work. By comparing one verse to another in which the same word appears, the Sages define these terms. By pointing to words that seem extraneous they include various categories about which there could be a question. It is likely that in many such instances the prohibitions were already accepted and in effect. The attempt is to strengthen them by finding some way of attaching these practices to Biblical verses.*

5. Leviticus 19:11, Sifra Weiss 88b

YOU SHALL NOT STEAL; YOU SHALL NOT DEAL DECEITFULLY OR FALSELY ONE MAN WITH ANOTHER (Lev. 19:11). This teaches me only about one man and another man. What about a man and a woman? The verse says WITH ANOTHER—any other person. YOU SHALL NOT STEAL; YOU SHALL NOT DEAL DECEITFULLY OR FALSELY ONE MAN WITH ANOTHER. YOU SHALL

---

valuations—for a gift to the Sanctuary, as explained in Lev. 27:1.

proscribe goods—for the sake of the Sanctuary. See Lev. 27:28.

terumah—a portion of the produce set aside for the priests.

annul a marriage A woman betrothed by her father while she was a minor may refuse this marriage when she reaches maturity.

haliza—the ceremony in which a man whose brother died childless permits the widow to marry someone else. See Deut. 25:9.

fruits of the fourth year Only after four years is the fruit of a tree permitted to be eaten. See Lev. 19:23-25.

citizens—those born into the people of Israel.

NOT SWEAR FALSELY BY MY NAME (Lev. 19:11–12). Thus if you steal, you will be led to deceive, to swear falsely, and eventually to swear falsely by My Name.

YOU SHALL NOT SWEAR FALSELY BY MY NAME (Lev. 19:12). Why is this stated? Since it says YOU SHALL NOT SWEAR FALSELY BY THE NAME OF THE LORD YOUR GOD (Ex. 20:7) we might have thought that one is guilty of this only if one uses the Unique Name. What indicates that all of the various designations of God are to be included [in this prohibition]? The verse says BY MY NAME (Lev. 19:12)—any name that I have. PROFANING THE NAME OF YOUR GOD (Lev. 19:12). This teaches that a false oath profanes the Name of God.

Another interpretation. PROFANING (hilalta). You will become fair game (hullin) for wild beasts and animals. Thus it says THAT IS WHY A CURSE CONSUMES THE EARTH, AND ITS INHABITANTS PAY THE PENALTY; THAT IS WHY EARTH'S DWELLERS HAVE DWINDLED, AND FEW MEN ARE LEFT (Isa. 24:6).

YOU SHALL NOT COERCE YOUR NEIGHBOR (Lev. 19:13). Does this mean that one is not even permitted to say, "So-and-so is a hero," when he is not; "So-and-so is wise," when he is not; "So-and-so is wealthy," when he is not? The verse says YOU SHALL NOT COMMIT ROBBERY (Lev. 19:13). Just as robbery is characterized as connected with monetary affairs, so "coercion" is characterized as connected with monetary affairs. What is specifically intended? Suppression of the wages of a hired laborer. THE WAGES OF A LABORER SHALL NOT REMAIN WITH YOU UNTIL MORNING (Lev. 19:13). This teaches me only about the wages for the services of a man. What about wages for the services of an animal or implements? What about the fee paid for use of lands? The verse says THE WAGES—of anything.

UNTIL MORNING. One is not guilty of transgressing this until the first morning. Is one guilty even if he did not come and demand his wages?

---

5. *the Unique Name*—the Tetragrammaton.

a hero   The meaning of this is unclear. Some have interpreted it as if they were reading the word *coerce* (ta-ashok) as if it were "desire" (tahshok), in which case it would mean that one who is not a hero should not envy the fact that another is a hero, and so forth. More likely is the possibility that it means that one may not hurt (coerce) his neighbor by giving him false information about others, telling him that so-and-so is a hero, when he really is not. In any case, it is agreed that this is not the meaning of the verse.

monetary affairs   The coercion referred to is not verbal but financial.

The verse says WITH YOU. I said WITH YOU only to indicate that it must be for your benefit. Is one guilty if he has deposited it with a storekeeper or a moneychanger? The verse says WITH YOU—it must remain with you for your benefit.

THE WAGES OF A LABORER SHALL NOT REMAIN WITH YOU UNTIL MORNING. This teaches that the wages of a day laborer may be collected all night. What source teaches that the night laborer may collect all day? The verse says YOU MUST PAY HIM HIS WAGES ON THE SAME DAY, BEFORE THE SUN SETS (Deut. 24:15).

YOU SHALL NOT INSULT THE DEAF (Lev. 19:14). This teaches me only about the deaf. What about including all human beings? The verse says YOU SHALL NOT INSULT A CHIEFTAIN AMONG YOUR PEOPLE (Ex. 22:27). In that case, why mention the deaf? The deaf is characterized as one who is alive, thus excluding the dead, who is not alive.

OR PLACE A STUMBLING BLOCK BEFORE THE BLIND (Lev. 19:14)—before one who is "blind" about a certain thing. If someone comes to you and says, "Is the daughter of this person permitted to be married to a priest?" do not say to him, "She is permitted," when you know that she is forbidden.

If someone comes to you for advice, do not give him advice which is not correct. Do not say to him, "Go out early in the morning," so that robbers will assault him. "Go out at noon," so that he will be overcome by the heat. Do not say to him, "Sell your field and buy an ass," so that you can craftily take it from him. You may say, "Well, I'm only giving him good advice!" but this is a matter for one's conscience, as it is said YOU SHALL FEAR YOUR GOD: I AM THE LORD (Lev. 19:14).

I said—God speaking through the Torah.

your benefit—or by your choice rather than that of the wage earner.

A CHIEFTAIN A prohibition exists against insulting or cursing both a deaf man and a chieftain. The difference between them is great and indicates that you may not insult anyone in the entire spectrum.

"blind"—not physically, but in the sense that he does not know something and may be easily deceived.

married to a priest For example, priests are not to marry divorcees.

good advice—as if to say, "I really meant well." How can anyone know what your intentions really were?

YOU SHALL NOT RENDER AN UNFAIR DECISION (Lev. 19:15).
This teaches that a judge who perverts justice is called "unfair," "detested," "abominable," "proscribed," and "abhorrent." He causes five things to happen:

> he renders the earth unclean;
> he profanes the Name of God;
> he causes the Divine Presence to depart;
> he brings Israel down by the sword;
> he exiles Israel from its Land.

DO NOT FAVOR THE POOR (Lev. 19:15). Do not say, "This man is poor, and since both I and this wealthy man are duty bound to provide for him, I will find in his favor and in that way we will provide for him in an honorable way." Therefore it says DO NOT FAVOR THE POOR.

OR SHOW DEFERENCE TO THE RICH (Lev. 19:15). Do not say, "He is a wealthy man from a good family. I do not want to shame him and see his embarrassment. How can I embarrass him?" Therefore it says NOR SHOW DEFERENCE TO THE RICH.

JUDGE YOUR NEIGHBOR FAIRLY (Lev. 19:15). One [of the litigants] should not be permitted to speak as much as he wants while you tell the other "Be brief!"

One should not stand while the other sits. R. Judah said, "I have heard that if they want to permit both of them to sit, they may do so. What is forbidden is for one of them to stand while the other sits."

Another interpretation: JUDGE YOUR NEIGHBOR FAIRLY. Judge each man by the scale of merit.

---

is called These terms have probably been taken from the following verses: FOR ANYONE WHO DOES THOSE THINGS, EVERYONE WHO DEALS DISHONESTLY, IS *ABHORRENT* TO THE LORD YOUR GOD (Deut. 25:16). YOU MUST REJECT IT AS *ABOMINABLE* AND ABHORRENT, FOR IT IS *PROSCRIBED* (Deut. 7:26). EVERY ABHORRENT ACT THAT THE LORD *DETESTS* (Deut. 12:31).

to provide for him The duty of giving charity and helping the poor is incumbent upon all. The other party to the case is a wealthy man who also has the obligation of giving charity to this poor person.

in his favor—in favor of the poor man, not because he is in the right but in order to force the wealthy man to pay him something and thus give him charity.

scale of merit—give him the benefit of the doubt.

DO NOT GO ABOUT AS A TALEBEARER (rachil) AMONG YOUR PEOPLE (Lev. 19:16). Do not speak gently (rach) to this one and harsh to that one.

Another interpretation: Do not be like a peddler (rochel) who loads his things and goes on his way.

R. Nehemiah said, "The procedure of judges is that the litigants stand before them. They listen to their arguments and then send them out while they discuss the matter. When they have come to a conclusion, they bring them back in and the senior judge says, 'So-and-so: you are vindicated. So-and-so: you are liable.'" How do we know that when they go out one of the judges should not say, "I was in your favor, but my colleagues were against you. What could I do since they outnumbered me?" Therefore it says DO NOT GO ABOUT AS A TALEBEARER AMONG YOUR PEOPLE. And thus it says ONE WHO GOES ABOUT AS A TALEBEARER GIVES AWAY SECRETS, BUT A TRUSTWORTHY SOUL KEEPS A CONFIDENCE (Prov. 11:13).

What is the source which teaches that if one has evidence, he is not permitted to keep silent? The verse says DO NOT STAND UPON THE BLOOD OF YOUR NEIGHBOR (Lev. 19:16).

What source teaches that if you see someone drowning in the river, being attacked by robbers or a wild beast, you must rescue him? The verse says DO NOT STAND UPON THE BLOOD OF YOUR NEIGHBOR.

What source teaches that if one is pursuing his fellow to kill him, or pursuing a male or a betrothed woman, you must rescue [the pursuer] even at the cost of his life? The verse says DO NOT STAND UPON THE BLOOD OF YOUR NEIGHBOR.

YOU SHALL NOT HATE YOUR KINSMAN IN YOUR HEART (Lev. 19:17). Could this mean: Do not curse him, do not strike him, do not slap him? The verse says IN YOUR HEART.

---

speak gently   The Sages connect this verse with the previous matter under discussion, a case heard by a court.

pursuing a male—to commit homosexual rape.

rescue [the pursuer]   You must rescue the pursuer from the sin he wants to commit, even if this means killing him.

IN YOUR HEART   The prohibition is not against overt acts, which are also prohibited elsewhere, but against an attitude and a feeling.

YOU SHALL SURELY REPROVE YOUR NEIGHBOR (Lev. 19:17). What is the source which teaches that if you have reproved someone four or five times, you should do so yet again? The verse says YOU SHALL SURELY REPROVE. Is this so even if when you reprove him, his face becomes distorted? The verse says BUT INCUR NO GUILT BECAUSE OF HIM (Lev. 19:17).

R. Tarphon said, "By the Temple Service! I doubt if there is anyone in this generation who is worthy enough to reprove!"

R. Eleazar b. Azariah said, "By the Temple Service! I doubt if there is anyone in this generation who is capable of receiving reproof!"

R. Akiba said, "By the Temple Service! I doubt if there is anyone in this generation who knows how to reprove others!"

R. Johanan b. Nuri said, "I call heaven and earth to testify for me that four or five times Akiba was reproved by Rabban Gamliel in Jabneh because of me—for I complained against him—but it was done in such a way that his love for me only increased."

YOU SHALL NOT TAKE VENGEANCE (Lev. 19:18). How far does vengeance extend? A said to B, "Lend me your sickle," but B would not lend it to him. The next day B said to A, "Lend me your spade," and A said to B, "I will not lend it to you just as you would not lend me your sickle!" This is what is meant when it says YOU SHALL NOT TAKE VENGEANCE.

OR BEAR A GRUDGE (Lev. 19:18). How far does bearing a grudge extend? A said to B, "Lend me your spade," but B would not lend it to him. The next day B said to A, "Lend me your sickle," and A said to B, "Here it is. I am not like you who would not lend me your spade!" This is what is meant when it says OR BEAR A GRUDGE.

YOU SHALL NOT TAKE VENGEANCE OR BEAR A GRUDGE AGAINST YOUR KINSFOLK (Lev. 19:18)—but you may take vengeance or bear a grudge against others.

LOVE YOUR NEIGHBOR AS YOURSELF (Lev. 19:18). R. Akiba says, "This is the great principle of the Torah." Ben Azzai says, "THIS IS THE

SURELY REPROVE   The Hebrew form repeats the word *reprove* twice, indicating that the action must be repeated as often as necessary.

his face becomes distorted   If he looks as if he will become ill or faint, for example, because of what you are telling him.

R. Johanan b. Nuri—a supervisor in the Academy.

BOOK OF THE GENERATIONS OF ADAM (Gen. 5:1), an even greater principle!"

COMMENTARY   *As in other legal sections, here too the Sages are concerned with the definition of terms. For example, when Scripture forbids coercion, the Sages wish to define coercion. Similarly the terms vengeance and grudge are given specific definitions. In some cases, the Sages show a tendency to extend the meaning of a law beyond the specific and most narrow interpretation. Thus "placing a stumbling block before the blind" is extended to mean not only the physically blind, but anyone who is prevented from clearly understanding something. The stumbling block need not be physical either, but includes bad advice. The brief discussion of LOVE YOUR NEIGHBOR reflects a matter of great importance. R. Akiba chooses that verse as the basic one underlying all of the legislation of the Torah. Whatever is done is a method of implementing that or of inculcating it. Ben Azzai is concerned lest this verse be interpreted too narrowly. Who is meant by "neighbor?" This term is usually interpreted to indicate a member of the people of Israel. The verse he chooses, therefore, teaches that the Torah is concerned with all human beings, since it tells the story of the descendants of Adam, the father of all.*

6. Leviticus 19:35, Sifra Weiss 91a

YOU SHALL DO NO UNRIGHTEOUSNESS IN JUDGMENT (Lev. 19:35). This cannot be referring to justice, for that has already been dealt with. What then is meant by YOU SHALL DO NO UNRIGHTEOUSNESS IN JUDGMENT? It means in LENGTH, WEIGHT, AND CAPACITY (Lev. 19:35). This indicates that one who measures is also called a judge. For if he falsifies the measurement he is called "unfair," "detested," "abominable," "proscribed," and "abhorrent." He causes five things to happen:

> he renders the earth unclean;
> he profanes the Name of God;
> he causes the Divine Presence to depart;

---

6. *been dealt with*   Justice in court proceedings was dealt with in Lev. 19:15. See the comments of the rabbis to that verse. Therefore the reference here must be to something else.
he is called   The same terms and the same dire consequences are ascribed to the merchant with false measures as were applied above to the corrupt judge.

he brings Israel down by the sword;
he exiles Israel from its Land.

LENGTH means measurement of land.
WEIGHT means a proper balance.
CAPACITY means the large crest. Some say it means a small liquid mea-
sure. Some say that it means the strike [for leveling].
YOU SHALL HAVE AN HONEST BALANCE (Lev. 19:36). Adjust the
balance well.
HONEST WEIGHTS (Lev. 19:36). Adjust the weights well.
AN HONEST EPHAH (Lev. 19:36). Adjust the *ephot* well.
AND AN HONEST HIN (Lev. 19:36). Adjust the *hin* well.

R. Jose b. R. Judah says, "The *hin* is really included in the *ephah* and it
says AN HONEST EPHAH. Why then does it say AND AN HONEST
HIN? Your 'no' should be honest and your 'yes' (hin) should be honest."

YOU SHALL HAVE AN HONEST BALANCE (Lev. 19:36). Appoint a
market commissioner. This verse was the source of the teaching: Every
thirty days the wholesale dealer must clean his weight; the householder—
every twelve months. R. Simeon b. Gamliel said, "It is just the opposite."
The storekeeper must clean his weights once a week and clean his scales
after every usage. R. Simeon b. Gamliel said, "Under what conditions does
this apply? When selling items which are moist. When the produce is dry,
he need not [clean them every time.]" He must let the scale be tipped by a
handbreadth. If he gives an exact weight, then he must give the following

---

the large crest   A measure that had a large lip. None of these methods of measurements may be
used in such a way as to deceive.
ephot—a dry measure.
hin—a liquid measure.
The hin is really included   Since other measures are included in the *ephah*, why mention them?
your 'yes'—a play on words. *Hin* is a measure, but *hin* or *hen* means yes in Aramaic, the common
spoken language of the time.
market commissioner—*agranamos*, someone who will supervise the honesty of marketing practices.
householder—one who sells his own products, but does not have a regular store.
moist—or liquid. Then he must wipe off the weights and implements frequently because this
matter will stick and produce a false measurement.
the scale be tipped   The scale should be slightly tipped so that the customer receives a bit more
than the exact amount.
an exact weight   If the scale is set exactly, then one must give more than the exact weight since
the customer knows the usual practice and expects it.

extras: one tenth in the case of liquids and one twentieth in the case of dry produce.

I AM THE LORD YOUR GOD WHO BROUGHT YOU OUT OF THE LAND OF EGYPT (Lev. 19:36). I brought you out of the Land of Egypt on this condition—that you observe the mitzvot of just measures. Whoever acknowledges the mitzvah of just measures acknowledges the Exodus from Egypt. Whoever denies the mitzvah of just measures denies the Exodus from Egypt.

I AM THE LORD (Lev. 19:37). I can be depended upon to reward [you].

COMMENTARY   *The general statements made in Scripture in regard to honesty in business were translated into very specific terms appropriate to the business practices of the rabbinic period. Once again we find moral exhortations included since the law was not merely legal regulations but was seen as part of the Covenantal relationship between God and the people of Israel. Thus the discussion of just weights and inspection of scales concludes with a general exhortation of far-reaching moral impact. The midrash teaches that the Exodus took place only on condition that Israel uphold the laws of honest and ethical business practice. The entire meaning of the Exodus is denied and vitiated by one who breaks these regulations, regardless of what such a person professes to believe. No less than the dishonest judge, the dishonest merchant will cause the downfall of Israel and its exile.*

SAY FURTHER TO THE ISRAELITE PEOPLE (Lev. 20:2). AND TO THE ISRAELITE PEOPLE SPEAK THUS (Lev. 24:15). SPEAK TO THE ISRAELITE PEOPLE (Lev. 18:2). COMMAND THE ISRAELITE PEOPLE (Lev. 24:2). YOU SHALL FURTHER INSTRUCT THE ISRAELITES (Ex. 27:20). R. Jose says, "The Torah speaks in human language, using many different expressions. Each one must be expounded. (Thus in the verse ANY MAN AMONG THE ISRAELITES, OR AMONG THE STRANGERS RESIDING IN ISRAEL (Lev. 20:2).) ISRAELITES means the Israelite men. STRANGERS means converts. THE STRANGERS includes the wives of converts. IN ISRAEL includes their

---

acknowledges   The Hebrew contains a play on words: acknowledge—"modeh"; measures—"midot."

human language   Usually this expression means that the language of the Torah is to be understood as human language is understood, without taking into account every word or difference of expression. Here it seems to mean the opposite.

wives and slaves." If so, why does it say ANY MAN? To include gentiles who violate the laws of forbidden sexual relationships. If committed with gentiles, they are to be judged by the laws of the nations. If with Israelites, they are to be judged by the laws of Israel.

WHO GIVES ANY OF HIS OFFSPRING TO MOLECH (Lev. 20:2)—not one who gives his offspring to something else. WHO GIVES ANY OF HIS OFFSPRING TO MOLECH. Why is this said? Since it says DO NOT ALLOW ANY OF YOUR OFFSPRING TO BE OFFERED UP TO MOLECH (Lev. 18:21) I might think that he is guilty if he makes him pass through but does not deliver him, therefore the verse says WHO GIVES ANY OF HIS OFFSPRING (Lev. 20:2). I might think that he is guilty if he delivers him but does not make him pass through. The verse says DO NOT ALLOW ANY OF YOUR OFFSPRING TO BE OFFERED UP (Lev. 18:21). I might think that he is guilty if he delivers him up to be offered to Molech but not by fire. The verse says LET NO ONE BE FOUND AMONG YOU WHO OFFERS UP HIS SON OR DAUGHTER TO THE FIRE OR WHO IS AN AUGUR (Deut. 18:10). The use of the word *offer* in both verses links them together. Just as in the one (Lev. 18:21) the "offering" is to Molech, so in the other (Deut. 18:10) the "offering" is to Molech. And just as the offering in the one (Deut. 18:10) is by fire, so the offering in the other (Lev. 18:10) is by fire. Thus we find that the prohibition is against delivering and offering him up to Molech by fire.

SHALL BE PUT TO DEATH (Lev. 20:2)—by the court. What source teaches that if the court is unable to affect punishment, the people of the land should assist it? The verse says THE PEOPLE OF THE LAND SHALL PELT HIM WITH STONE (Lev. 20:2). Another interpretation. PEOPLE OF THE LAND—the people for whose sake the Land was created. Rabban Gamliel says, "The people who are destined to inherit this Land as a result of these practices."

　　PELT HIM—*him* but not his garments.

---

gentiles　Non-Jews are bound by the Noachide laws, of which this is one. Beginning with Lev. 20:10 these relationships are spelled out. The word *man* thus indicates all men.

deliver him—to the priests of Molech who perform the fire ceremony. The Rabbis in the Talmud (Sanhedrin 64b) described this as walking toward the idol on a pile of bricks surrounded on both sides by fire or leaping above a pit of flames.

the people for whose sake—the people of Israel.

destined to inherit　The Israelites are being given possession of the Land because the previous inhabitants did these practices.

not his garments　He was to be naked at the time of execution.

WITH STONE. This teaches that if he dies as the result of one stone, that is sufficient.

AND I WILL SET MY FACE (panai) (Lev. 20:3). I will free Myself (poneh) from all other matters in order to deal with him.

AGAINST THAT MAN (Lev. 20:3)—and not against the populace.

THAT—but not one who was coerced or who did it unwittingly or in error.

AND WILL CUT HIM OFF FROM AMONG HIS PEOPLE (Lev. 20:3)—and all will be well with his people.

BECAUSE HE GAVE OF HIS OFFSPRING TO MOLECH (Lev. 20:3). Why is this said? Since it says LET NO ONE BE FOUND AMONG YOU WHO CONSIGNS HIS SON OR DAUGHTER TO THE FIRE (Deut. 18:10) I only know about his son or daughter. What about the son of his son or of his daughter? The verse says BECAUSE HE GAVE OF HIS OFFSPRING TO MOLECH (Lev. 20:3). This teaches me only about his legitimate offspring. What about his illegitimate offspring? The verse says WHEN HE GIVES OF HIS OFFSPRING TO MOLECH—any offspring he may have.

AND SO DEFILED MY SANCTUARY AND PROFANED MY HOLY NAME (Lev. 20:3). This teaches that he defiles the Sanctuary, profanes the Name of God, causes the Divine Presence to remove itself, causes Israel to fall by the sword and to be exiled from its Land.

AND IF THE PEOPLE OF THE LAND SHOULD SURELY SHUT THEIR EYES (Lev. 20:4). How do we know that if they shut their eyes to one such thing, they will shut their eyes to many things? The verse says SURELY SHUT. How do we know that if one court shuts its eyes, many courts will come to shut their eyes? The verse says SURELY SHUT. How

---

STONE The Hebrew word, although usually taken to mean many stones, is actually in the singular. Thus one stone is sufficient if it kills him.

HIS OFFSPRING The term includes not only his children, but those who are born to his children as well. All are his offspring.

SURELY SHUT The Hebrew repeats the root word and could be read: He shuts—they will shut. The first ignoring of evil will cause others to ignore it.

do we know that if a lesser Sanhedrin shuts its eyes, the Great Sanhedrin will come to shut its eyes and the power of capital punishment will be taken from it? The verse says SURELY SHUT.

AND IF THE PEOPLE OF THE LAND SHOULD SURELY SHUT THEIR EYES TO THAT MAN WHEN HE GIVES OF HIS OFFSPRING TO MOLECH, AND SHOULD NOT PUT HIM TO DEATH (Lev. 20:4)—in any way that they wish to put him to death.

I MYSELF WILL SET MY FACE AGAINST THAT MAN AND HIS KIN (Lev. 20:5). . . . Why is this said? R. Simeon said, "What sin did his kin commit? This teaches you, rather, that wherever there is a customs collector in a family, they are all customs collectors. Wherever there is a robber, they are all robbers because they cover up for him."

AND WILL CUT HIM OFF (Lev. 20:5). Why is this said? Since it is said AND HIS KIN (Lev. 20:5) I might think that his family too would suffer the punishment of extinction. Therefore the verse says HIM. He will suffer extinction but his family will not suffer extinction but only chastisements.

AND WILL CUT HIM OFF . . . AND ALL WHO FOLLOW HIM IN GOING ASTRAY AFTER MOLECH (Lev. 20:5). This includes all types of idolatry.

CUT OFF FROM AMONG THEIR PEOPLE (Lev. 20:5)—and all will be well with their people.

7. Leviticus 23:5, Sifra Weiss 100a

IN THE FIRST MONTH, ON THE FOURTEENTH DAY OF THE MONTH, AT TWILIGHT THERE SHALL BE A PASSOVER OFFER-

---

Sanhedrin—the Greek term for a court. There were different numbers of members in these courts. The lesser ones had three members and dealt with monetary matters. A larger one had twenty-three and dealt with capital cases. The largest was the Sanhedrin of seventy-one, which alone could deal with the condemnation of a tribe, a false prophet or high priest, and other matters that affected the entire community. After the destruction of the Temple, capital punishment could no longer be administered.

customs collectors—or "publicans." These officials of the Roman government were considered to be without legitimate authority and no better than thieves.

extinction—death at the hands of Heaven, not by a human court.

ING TO THE LORD (Lev. 23:5). Could this mean after dark? The verse says DAY. If it says DAY, could this mean any time after the second hour? The verse says AT TWILIGHT. Just as TWILIGHT is characterized as a time when the day wanes, so DAY means a time when the day wanes, namely six hours and thereafter. And although it cannot be used as proof of this, there is a hint in the verse: "UP! WE WILL ATTACK AT NOON." "ALAS FOR US! FOR DAY IS DECLINING, THE SHADOWS OF EVENING GROW LONG" (Jer. 6:4).

AND ON THE FIFTEENTH DAY OF THAT MONTH THE LORD'S FEAST OF UNLEAVENED BREAD (Lev. 23:6). That day requires unleavened bread and the Feast of Tabernacles does not require unleavened bread. Would logic not dictate that if this day, which does not require a tabernacle, requires unleavened bread, the one which does require a tabernacle must surely require unleavened bread as well? The verse says THAT. THAT ... FEAST OF UNLEAVENED BREAD requires unleavened bread, but the Festival of Tabernacles does not require unleavened bread.

THE FEAST OF UNLEAVENED BREAD FOR THE LORD—FOR SEVEN DAYS YOU SHALL EAT UNLEAVENED BREAD (Lev. 23:6). Why is this stated? Since it says YOU SHALL EAT UNLEAVENED BREAD SIX DAYS, AND ON THE SEVENTH DAY YOU SHALL HOLD A SOLEMN GATHERING FOR THE LORD YOUR GOD (Deut. 16:8). The seventh day was part of the general rule but has

---

7. *after dark* Is the Passover sacrifice to be brought after dark, which would be the fifteenth of the month since the day begins after sunset?

second hour—of daylight. The daytime hours are divided into twelve. Two hours would be in the morning.

six hours—noon, the beginning of the second half of the day, which would fit the definition of the time when the day begins to wane.

That day On the first day of the Passover holiday one is required to eat unleavened bread, but not on Tabernacles.

a tabernacle—the special harvest hut with a roof of leaves or branches, called a *sukkah*, which is constructed for that festival. Requiring a tabernacle is seen as making the day of extra importance. Therefore the logic is that since it has more requirements than Passover, it should include that which Passover requires, the unleavened bread.

The verse says THAT This word seems to indicate something specific since it is really redundant. It teaches that no matter what logic might say, only THAT time requires unleavened bread.

the general rule—of eating the unleavened bread. The contrast between two verses, one of which mentions seven days of eating it and the other that mentions only six teaches that on the seventh day it is optional and furthermore that it is actually optional all the days of the holiday.

been singled out. Why? In order to draw the analogy that just as eating unleavened bread on the seventh day is optional, so is it optional on all of the days. Is the first evening also optional? The verse says ON THE FIFTEENTH DAY OF THE MONTH ... YOU SHALL EAT UN-LEAVENED BREAD (Lev. 23:6). Scripture determines that it is required.

This teaches us only about the time when the Temple was in existence. What about now when there is no Temple? The verse says AT EVENING YOU SHALL EAT UNLEAVENED BREAD (Ex. 12:18).

If this is so, why does it say FOR SEVEN DAYS YOU SHALL EAT UN-LEAVENED BREAD (Lev. 23:6)? One may eat unleavened bread for seven days and fulfill the requirements for observance of Passover. This is not the case in regard to the choice flour and unleavened wafers of the Nazirite which may not be eaten for the period of seven days. . . .

WHEN YOU ENTER (Lev. 23:10). Could this mean: when you arrive at the other side of the Jordan? The verse says THE LAND (Lev. 23:10) which has been specified. Could this mean: when you reach Ammon and Moab? The verse says WHICH I AM GIVING YOU (Lev. 23:10)—YOU and not Ammon and Moab. AND YOU REAP ITS HARVEST (Lev. 23:10) at the very beginning of all harvesting. Does this include irrigated fields and the plain? The verse says YOUR HARVEST (Lev. 23:10)—the harvest of all of you, have I stated, and not that of irrigated fields and the plain. HARVEST—and not of legumes. HARVEST—and not unripe corn. R. Judah says, "If one began to reap before it reached a third of its growth,

---

it is required   On the basis of this specific verse the Sages determined that the eating of un-leavened bread is required only on the first evening of Passover. At other times it is optional.

there is no Temple   The categorical statement indicates that this requirement is to be followed regardless of anything else, whether there is a Temple or not.

of the Nazirite—as described in Num. 6:13–20. What he brings must be consumed that day alone.

the other side of the Jordan—the eastern bank of the Jordan, which was inhabited by some tribes of Israel, but was not within the borders of the Land that God had promised the Israelites.

Ammon and Moab   See Deut. 2:16–19. These lands were not given to the Israelites.

irrigated fields   The corn that grew there was considered inferior, not usable for the Omer ceremony (bringing the first sheaf: in Hebrew "Omer") and could be harvested earlier. It may also have been that it ripened earlier and had to be harvested earlier.

of all of you—the time when everyone begins to harvest, not the earlier time when the irrigated fields and the plain are ready.

began to reap it—before the Omer had been offered. The offering of the Omer was brought on the second day of the Passover festival, after which new grain was permitted.

he may reap it and feed it to cattle, animals, and fowl and it is exempt from *leket,* the forgotten sheaf, and *peah* but liable for the tithe." R. Simeon says, "Even if one began to reap after it reached a third of its growth, he may reap it and feed it to cattle, animals, and fowl and it is exempt from *leket,* the forgotten sheaf, and *peah* but liable for the tithe."

AND YOU REAP ITS HARVEST, YOU SHALL BRING THE FIRST SHEAF OF YOUR HARVEST TO THE PRIEST (Lev. 23:10). The mitzvah of reaping does not apply to the priest.

HE SHALL WAVE THE SHEAF BEFORE THE LORD (Lev. 23:11). The sheaf has three designations: "Sheaf," "*shibolim,*" and "sheaf of waving." All of them refer to that which is called sheaf. AS YOUR WILL (Lev. 23:11). People are not to be forced to do this against their will. ON THE DAY AFTER THE SABBATH (Lev. 23:11). On the day after the festival it shall be waved. THE PRIEST SHALL WAVE IT (Lev. 23:11). This is the fundamental rule which indicates that all instances of waving are to be done by the priest. ON THE DAY . . . YOU SHALL OFFER.

YOU SHALL . . . WAVE THE SHEAF . . . (Lev. 23:12) even if there is no lamb. ON THE DAY THAT YOU WAVE THE SHEAF (Lev. 23:12). Waving is done only during the day. AS A BURNT OFFERING TO THE LORD A LAMB OF THE FIRST YEAR WITHOUT BLEMISH (Lev. 23:12). The year referred to is not the calendar year. . . .

---

leket—the sheaves that were accidentally dropped during harvesting and belonged to the poor. See Lev. 19:9.

peah—the section of the field that was not to be harvested but left for the poor. See Lev. 19:9 and 23:22.

after it reached a third of its growth   R. Simeon believes that even then it is only unripe corn, unfit for humans but usable for animal fodder and may be harvested as such.

the priest   When the Land was divided, none was given to the family of priests. Therefore the regulations pertaining to agriculture do not apply to them.

shibolim—ears of grain as in Ruth 2:2.

the day after the festival—the day after the first day of Passover, which was a festival day on which work was forbidden. Since it also requires the cessation of work, it could be termed "Sabbath."

be waved   The act of moving an offering back and forth was performed as part of many rituals. The fact that it was always to be performed by the priests is derived from this verse.

even if there is no lamb   The two mitzvot, the offering of the sheaf and the offering of the lamb, are independent of one another.

not the calendar year   The year referred to is the age of the animal and has no connection to any specific year on the calendar.

UNTIL THAT VERY DAY, UNTIL YOU HAVE BROUGHT THE
OFFERING OF YOUR GOD, YOU SHALL EAT NO BREAD OR
PARCHED GRAIN OR FRESH EARS (Lev. 23:14). This refers to bringing the sheaf. Perhaps it refers to bringing the lamb. See what is written
elsewhere YOU SHALL BRING (Lev. 23:9). Just as there "bringing" refers to the sheaf, so here "bringing" refers to the sheaf.

As soon as the sheaf was brought, one would find the markets of Jerusalem
filled with flour of parched grain—not in accord with the will of the Sages.
So taught R. Meir. R. Judah says, "They acted in accord with the will of the
Sages. Once the sheaf has been brought, the new produce is immediately
permissible. And for those far away, it is permissible from noon on." When
the Temple was destroyed, R. Johanan b. Zakkai decreed that it was forbidden the entire day of the waving. Said R. Judah, "Is it not forbidden according to the Torah, as it is said UNTIL THAT VERY DAY (Lev.
23:14)? Why was it permitted from noon on for those far away? Because
they knew that the court was never derelict in this matter."

IT IS A LAW FOR ALL TIME (Lev. 23:14)—for the House which is
for all time. THROUGHOUT THE GENERATIONS (Lev. 23:14)—this
should be practiced for all generations. IN ALL YOUR SETTLEMENTS
(Lev. 23:14). Both within the Land and outside of it. Said R. Simeon, "There

---

refers to bringing the sheaf   The verse speaks about an offering without specifying what it is.

R. *Meir*—believes that since the harvesting and preparation must have taken place before the
bringing of the Omer, people might have eaten this new produce as well. Therefore the Sages
did not approve.

R. *Judah*—does not fear that people will have eaten it since they respect the law of bringing the
Omer.

far away   They cannot know for certain when the Omer was brought. Nevertheless, it would
certainly have been done by noon time.

When the Temple was destroyed—the sheaf was no longer brought as an offering. Therefore a
decree was made that the new grain was not to be used that entire day.

according to the Torah   R. Judah understands that by UNTIL the verse means that the new
grain is prohibited the entire day or UNTIL YOU HAVE BROUGHT THE OFFERING.
Thus when there was such an offering, the bringing of it permitted the new grain. When there
is no offering because the Temple does not exist, the entire day is forbidden. There was no
need, therefore, for Rabban Johanan b. Zakkai to make a new ruling. It was already implicit in
the Torah itself.

from noon   Since only the bringing of the Omer permitted the eating on that day, why were
those far away permitted to eat after noon? How could they be certain that the Omer had been
brought? The answer is that they knew the court always did this with dispatch.

the House which is for all time—the Temple.

are three things which are dependent upon the land, but which are practiced both within the Land and outside of it: new grain, fourth-year products, and the law of diverse seeds. The new grain is forbidden everywhere by the Torah. Fourth-year products are a traditional law. Diverse seeds is an enactment of the Scribes.

YOU SHALL COUNT FOR YOURSELVES (Lev. 23:15). Each individual must do so. FROM THE DAY AFTER THE SABBATH (Lev. 23:15). From the day after the festival. Might it not mean the day after the weekly Sabbath commemorating the creation? R. Jose b. R. Judah said, "When it says UNTIL THE DAY AFTER THE SEVENTH SABBATH YOU SHALL COUNT FIFTY DAYS (Lev. 23:16) it means that no more than fifty days are to elapse. If it meant the weekly Sabbath commemorating the creation, there would be times when they would be fifty-one, fifty-two, fifty-three, fifty-four, fifty-five, or fifty-six days!" What then is the meaning of FROM THE DAY AFTER THE SABBATH (Lev. 23:15)? The day after the festival.

R. Judah b. Beterah says, "FROM THE DAY AFTER THE SAB-BATH. From the day after the festival. Might it not mean the weekly Sabbath commemorating the creation? When it says YOU SHALL COUNT FOR YOURSELF SEVEN WEEKS (Deut. 16:9) it indicates counting which is dependent upon the court, thus eliminating the weekly Sabbath

---

dependent upon the land—practices that have to do with agriculture. Most such things apply only to the Land of Israel. These three things are the exception.

fourth-year products   According to Lev. 19:23, the fruit of trees may not be eaten until the fourth year.

diverse seeds   One may not sow the field with more than one type of seed. See Lev. 19:19.

a traditional law—a regulation passed on orally through the generations.

an enactment of the Scribes   In addition to interpreting the laws as they appear in Scripture, the Sages also enacted certain regulations. Thus each of these three items is forbidden to Jews wherever they live, but the source of the prohibition is different in each case.

Each individual   FOR YOURSELVES means that each person must perform this act.

the festival—the first day of Passover.

the weekly Sabbath—in which case the counting would begin from the Sunday that occurs during the Passover holiday, which could be anytime during the week depending on the day on which Passover happened to begin that year.

or fifty-six days—from the second day of the festival until the end of the counting.

dependent upon the court—in that the court determines the date of the beginning of the month and therefore the beginning of the festival and the day when the counting would begin. Therefore you must COUNT FOR YOURSELVES—the counting is determined by what you, the court, decide.

eliminating the weekly Sabbath   That cannot be the meaning of the verse since the counting of days from Sabbath to Sabbath is dependent on no court, but only on the ongoing cycle of weeks.

commemorating the creation which is not dependent upon the court but which may be counted by anyone."

R. Jose says, "FROM THE DAY AFTER THE SABBATH. From the day after the festival. Might it not mean the weekly Sabbath commemorating the creation? Does it say 'From the day after the Sabbath during Passover?' Does it not say merely FROM THE DAY AFTER THE SABBATH? Now the entire year is full of Sabbaths. How could one possibly figure out which Sabbath was meant? It says here THE DAY AFTER THE SABBATH and later it says THE DAY AFTER THE . . . SABBATH (Lev. 23:16). Just as the DAY AFTER THE SABBATH there is referring to a festival and the beginning of a festival, so THE DAY AFTER THE SABBATH here is referring to a festival and the beginning of a festival."

R. Simeon b. Eleazar says, "One verse says SIX DAYS YOU SHALL EAT UNLEAVENED BREAD (Deut. 16:8) and another verse says YOU SHALL EAT UNLEAVENED BREAD FOR SEVEN DAYS (Lev. 23:6). How can both of these verses be upheld? The reference is to a kind of unleavened bread which cannot be eaten for the full seven days. That made from the new wheat can be eaten only six days. How, then, do I understand THE DAY AFTER THE SABBATH? The day after the festival."

FROM THE DAY YOU BRING . . . YOU SHALL COUNT (Lev. 23:15-16). May one reap, count, and bring whenever he wants? The verse says START TO COUNT THE SEVEN WEEKS WHEN THE SICKLE IS FIRST PUT TO THE STANDING GRAIN (Deut. 16:9). May one reap, count, and bring whenever he wants? The verse says FROM THE DAY YOU BRING . . . YOU SHALL COUNT (Lev. 22:15-16). May one reap, count, and bring during the day? The verse says YOU SHALL KEEP COUNT (UNTIL) SEVEN FULL WEEKS HAVE ELAPSED (Lev. 23:15). When are they FULL? When evening begins. May one reap at night, count at night, and bring at night? The verse says FROM . . . THE DAY THAT YOU BRING (Lev. 23:15). The bringing must be during the day. Since the bringing must be during the day, how could reaping and counting be at night? YOU SHALL COUNT FIFTY DAYS UNTIL THE DAY AFTER THE SEVENTH SABBATH (Lev. 23:16). This is what R.

---

during Passover Since the Torah does not specify that, the word *Sabbath* could mean any Sabbath anytime during the year. Clearly this is absurd and impossible.

only six days Since the Omer is not brought until the second day of Passover, the new grain could not be eaten on the first day of Passover but only on the last six days. This explains the difference between the two verses. Seven days refers to the old grain, six days to the new.

Simeon b. R. Judah said: The entire counting must be no more than fifty days. YOU SHALL COUNT FIFTY DAYS. May one count fifty and then sanctify the fifty-first? The verse says SEVEN FULL WEEKS (Lev. 23:15). If they are to be SEVEN FULL WEEKS, may we count forty-eight and sanctify the forty-ninth? The verse says COUNT FIFTY DAYS. How is this done? One counts forty-nine days and sanctifies the fiftieth day just as in done with the Jubilee.

AND YOU SHALL BRING AN OFFERING OF NEW GRAIN TO THE LORD (Lev. 23:16). It shall be new for all grain offerings. This refers only to wheat. How do we know about barley as well? When it says ON THE DAY OF THE FIRST FRUITS, YOUR FEAST OF WEEKS, WHEN YOU BRING AN OFFERING OF NEW GRAIN TO THE LORD (Num. 28:26)—if it is not referring to an offering of wheat, it refers to an offering of barley.

COMMENTARY   *The discussion here of the meaning of the word "Sabbath" in Lev. 23:15 is academic in that none of the Pharisaic sages held that it referred to the weekly Sabbath. They all agreed that it referred to the first day of the Passover festival. There had been such a dispute, however, between the Pharisees and the Sadducees. The Sadducean position was that Sabbath here meant the first weekly Sabbath after the start of Passover. This dispute was actually based upon the question of the date and the significance of the holiday of Pentecost (Shavuot) which came at the conclusion of the period of counting. In the Scripture that holiday is described as agricultural. The Pharisees believed that it was also the commemoration of the theophany at Sinai, the day of the "giving of the Torah." Since it is difficult if not impossible to have an anniversary of something if there is no fixed date, it was important for them to assign a specific date to the beginning of the period of counting so that there would be a specific date for Pentecost as*

---

sanctify the fifty-first   Perhaps one counts for fifty and then declares the next day a holiday.
SEVEN FULL WEEKS—and no more. Therefore count only forty-nine days.
sanctify the forty-ninth   Perhaps one only counts forty-eight days and declares the holiday on the forty-ninth.
COUNT FIFTY DAYS   This is more than seven full weeks. It must therefore mean that one counts forty-nine days—up to the fiftieth day—and sanctifies the fiftieth.
as is done with the Jubilee   The fiftieth year, the Jubilee, as described in Lev. 25:8–9, is arrived at by counting forty-nine full years. The fiftieth year is then sanctified as the Jubilee year. The same method is followed here in regard to the forty-nine and fifty days.

well. The Sadducees, of course, did not accept the oral tradition concerning the celebration of Pentecost.

8. Leviticus 23:23, Sifra Weiss 101b

SPEAK TO THE ISRAELITE PEOPLE THUS: IN THE SEVENTH MONTH, ON THE FIRST DAY OF THE MONTH, YOU SHALL OBSERVE COMPLETE REST, A SACRED OCCASION (Lev. 23:24). You have A SACRED OCCASION, but the nations do not have A SACRED OCCASION. Perhaps when it says THE ISRAELITE PEOPLE it means only THE ISRAELITE PEOPLE, in which case what is the source which includes converts and slaves? The verse says IT SHALL BE FOR YOU (Lev. 23:24).

YOU SHALL OBSERVE COMPLETE REST, A SACRED OCCASION COMMEMORATED WITH LOUD BLASTS (Lev. 23:24). R. Eliezer says, "COMPLETE REST refers to the sanctification of the day. A SACRED OCCASION refers to sanctifying Him." R. Akiba said to him, "The meaning of COMPLETE REST is cessation of work, for the section began with the first cessation. Rather COMMEMORATED refers to the remembrance verses, LOUD BLASTS to the shofrot verses and SACRED OCCASION to the sanctification of the day. What is the source which teaches that we should say the kingship verses with [the sanctification of the day]? The verse says I AM THE LORD YOUR GOD ... IN THE SEVENTH MONTH (Lev. 23:22–23)." R. Jose b. R. Judah says, "What is the meaning of the verse THEY SHALL BE A REMINDER OF YOU BEFORE THE LORD YOUR GOD: I AM THE LORD YOUR GOD (Num. 10:10)? The purpose of I AM THE LORD YOUR GOD is to serve as the fundamental principle that wherever there are remembrances, kingship must be placed nearby."

---

8. *only the ISRAELITE PEOPLE*—those born into the people.

sanctification of the day This is the prayer proclaiming that the day is sacred that is recited as part of the Amida, the central prayer of each service on the festival.

sanctifying Him—referring to the prayer in the Amida that proclaims that God is holy.

the first cessation The first holy day mentioned in this list, which begins in Lev. 23:3, is the Sabbath, which is the first cessation from work.

remembrance verses R. Akiba interprets the sections of this verse as referring to the three special sets of Biblical verses referring to God's remembrance, to the shofar (the horn which is sounded), and to the Kingship of God.

453

What is the order of the blessings?

    The blessing of the patriarchs is recited,
    —that of powers
    —the sanctification of God, including the kingship verses
    —the shofar is not sounded
    —the sanctification of the day and the shofar is sounded
    —the remembrance verses and the shofar is sounded

    —the shofar verses and the shofar is sounded
    —the blessing of the Temple service is said
    —the acknowledgment
    —and the blessing of the priests. So taught R. Johanan b. Nuri.

    R. Akiba said to him, "If the shofar is not sounded after the kingship verses, why are they included at all? Rather it should be as follows:
    —the blessing of the patriarchs is recited
    —that of powers
    —the sanctification of God
    —the sanctification of the day, including the kingship verses and the shofar is sounded
    —the remembrance verses and the shofar is sounded
    —the shofar verses and the shofar is sounded
    —the blessing of the Temple service is said
    —the acknowledgment
    —and the blessing of the priests."

    R. Judah the Prince says, "If one says the kingship verses with the sanctification of the day, what do we find? That the blessing which is the fourth on other occasions is also the fourth here."
    Rabban Simeon b. Gamliel said, "Recite the sanctification of the day with the remembrance verses. In that way the blessing which is fourth on other occasions is also fourth here."

---

the order of the blessings—recited in the New Year's Amida. What follows is a list of titles of each blessing.

the remembrance verses   This is not included in the texts, but appears everywhere else where this section is quoted.

If the shofar is not sounded   The verses really serve as an introduction to the shofar.

fourth on other occasions   The blessing of the sanctification of the day is the fourth blessing of the Amida on every Sabbath and Holy Day.

LEVITICUS

When they sanctified the year in Usha, Rabban Simeon b. R. Johanan b. Beroka led the prayer on the first day according to the order of R. Johanan b. Nuri. Rabban Simeon b. Gamliel said, "That is not the custom we followed in Jabneh." On the second day Hananiah b. R. Jose the Galilean led the prayer according to the order of R. Akiba. Rabban Simeon b. Gamliel said, "That is the way we did it in Jabneh."

COMMENTARY   *The sounding of the shofar accompanied by verses connected to the three main themes of the New Year (Rosh HaShannah) seems to be the most ancient part of the liturgy for that day. The complete liturgy had not been standardized by the time of the compilation of these midrashim. Different systems existed for integrating the shofar sounding and verses into the framework of the central prayer of the service, the Amida, without adding additional blessings. The main difference between the two systems described here is that R. Johanan b. Nuri adds the kingship verses to the third blessing, the sanctification of God, without a shofar blast to follow it, while R. Akiba places them together with the fourth blessing, the sanctification of the day, followed by the sound of the shofar. It was R. Akiba's system that prevailed.*

How do we know that the shofar is used? The verse says THEN YOU SHALL SOUND THE SHOFAR LOUD; IN THE SEVENTH MONTH, ON THE TENTH DAY OF THE MONTH—THE DAY OF ATONEMENT (Lev. 25:9). The only reason it says THE SEVENTH MONTH is to indicate that the LOUD BLASTS (Lev. 23:24) in the seventh month are made thus. Just as there the shofar is used, so at the New Year, the shofar is used. How do we know that a plain blast comes first? The verse says THEN YOU SHALL SOUND THE SHOFAR LOUD (Lev. 25:9). And how do we know that a plain blast comes last? The verse says YOU SHALL HAVE THE SHOFAR SOUNDED (Lev. 25:9). This

---

Usha—a town in Galilee that was the cite of the Academy of the Sages in about 140 C.E. after the Bar Kokhba rebellion.

Jabneh—the earlier site of the Academy founded by R. Johanan b. Zakkai after the fall of Jerusalem in 70 C.E.

that the shofar is used The verse only speaks of LOUD BLASTS but does not specify what instrument to use.

in the seventh month Although Lev. 25:9 is speaking of the Day of Atonement, the phrase *seventh month* indicates that on all occasions during the seventh month when there is a blast, it is to be made on the shofar.

plain blast—the sound known as *tekiah*, which is a long, level blast.

455

only indicates what is done at the Jubilee proclamation. What about the New Year? The verse says YOU SHALL SOUND THE SHOFAR LOUD IN THE SEVENTH MONTH, ON THE TENTH DAY OF THE MONTH—THE DAY OF ATONEMENT (Lev. 25:9). The only reason it says THE SEVENTH MONTH is to indicate that the LOUD BLASTS of the entire seventh month are to be like that. Just as here there is a plain blast first and last, so at the New Year there is a plain blast first and last. How do we know that what is said about the Jubilee applies to the New Year and that what is said about the New Year applies to the Jubilee? In both cases the expression THE SEVENTH MONTH is used in order to create this juxtaposition.

And how do we know that there are to be three groups of three sounds each? The verse says YOU SHALL SOUND THE SHOFAR LOUD (Lev. 25:9); COMMEMORATED BY LOUD BLASTS . . . A SACRED OCCASION (Lev. 23:24) A DAY WHEN THE SHOFAR IS SOUNDED (Num. 29:1). This teaches that there are three groups of three sounds each.

What is the order of the blasts? Tekiah—Teruah—Tekiah. Tekiah—Teruah—Tekiah—three blasts for a total of nine. The length of the Tekiah is that of the Teruah and that of the Teruah is three times that of the Shebarim. The size of the shofar is merely that it be enough to make the blasts.

COMMENTARY   *The text here does not give the complete details of the sounding of the shofar. There are three types of sounds: the Tekiah, which is one prolonged blast; the Shebarim, which is a blast broken into three sections; and the Tekiah, which is a series of short, staccato sounds. Although the number of blasts was later expanded in Jewish usage, our text and all the early texts speak of the number nine, three times three. The blessings of the Amida are also nine, although no reason has even been given for this particular number.*

IT SHALL BE A SACRED OCCASION FOR YOU: YOU SHALL PRACTICE SELF-DENIAL . . . YOU SHALL DO NO WORK THROUGHOUT THAT DAY . . . FOR IT IS A DAY OF ATONEMENT FOR YOU ON WHICH EXPIATION IS MADE ON YOUR BEHALF (Lev. 23:27–28). This indicates only that the Day of Atonement

---

at the Jubilee proclamation   The verse actually is referring to the proclamation of the Jubilee year, which was done by sounding the shofar at the conclusion of the Day of Atonement.

atones only if one makes it A SACRED OCCASION, practices self-denial, and does not work on it. What is the source which teaches that even if one did not make it a sacred occasion, practice self-denial, and refrain from work it still atones? The verse says IT IS THE DAY OF ATONEMENT. It can do so. This indicates only that the Day of Atonement atones when there are sacrifices and goats. What is the source which teaches that even if there are no sacrifices or goats it atones? The verse says IT IS THE DAY OF ATONEMENT. Is it possible that it atones both for those who repent and for those who do not repent? This is a matter of logic. The sin offering and the guilt offering atone. The Day of Atonement atones. Just as the sin offering and the guilt offering atone only for those who repent, so the Day of Atonement atones only for those who repent. But can you say this when the sin offering and the guilt offering do not atone for the deliberate transgression as they do for the inadvertent one while the Day of Atonement does atone for the deliberate transgression as well as for the inadvertent one? Since it atones both for deliberate transgressions and inadvertent ones, perhaps it atones for both those who repent and those who do not! Therefore the verse says BUT (Lev. 23:27)—to indicate that it atones only for those who repent.

YOU SHALL DO NO WORK ON THAT DAY (Lev. 23:28). This is the warning against work. AND WHOEVER DOES ANY WORK THROUGHOUT THAT DAY, I WILL CAUSE THAT PERSON TO PERISH FROM AMONG HIS PEOPLE (Lev. 23:30). This is the punishment for working. INDEED, ANY PERSON WHO DOES NOT PRACTICE SELF-DENIAL THROUGHOUT THAT DAY SHALL BE CUT OFF FROM HIS KIN (Lev. 23:29). This is the punishment for not practicing self-denial. I WILL CAUSE THAT PERSON TO PERISH (Lev. 23:30). Why is this stated? Whenever it speaks of being cut off, we do not know what exactly it means. I WILL CAUSE THAT PERSON TO PERISH teaches us that being cut off means to perish.

---

even if one did not make it a sacred occasion   This extreme view seems to accord with that of R. Judah the Prince quoted in the Talmud, Shabuot 13a, that the Day of Atonement atones automatically.

sacrifices and goats   Atonement is achieved if the Temple Service is performed, even if individuals did not observe all the regulations.

atones only for those who repent   This more limited opinion of the atonement power of the day is ascribed in the Talmud to R. Judah.

to perish—at the hands of Heaven, not by a human court.

What is the source which teaches us that on the Day of Atonement eating, drinking, bathing, anointing, sexual intercourse, and the wearing of shoes are forbidden? The verse says COMPLETE REST (Lev. 23:24)—cessation of work. Is it possible then that on the weekly Sabbath commemorating creation these things would also be forbidden? The verse says YOU SHALL OBSERVE COMPLETE REST (Lev. 23:24). YOU SHALL PRACTICE SELF-DENIAL (Lev. 23:27). On this day these things are forbidden, but not on the weekly Sabbath commemorating creation.

AND YOU SHALL PRACTICE SELF-DENIAL ON THE NINTH DAY (Lev. 23:32). Is it possible that one should begin to practice self-denial on the ninth of the month? The verse says ON THE NINTH DAY OF THE MONTH AT EVENING (Lev. 23:32). If it is AT EVENING, perhaps it begins when it is dark. The verse says AND YOU SHALL PRACTICE SELF-DENIAL ON THE NINTH DAY (Lev. 23:32). How is that to be done? By beginning to practice self-denial while it is still daylight, for one is to add from the weekday to the sacred time. This teaches me only about the time preceding the day. What about after it? The verse says FROM EVENING TO EVENING (Lev. 23:32). This teaches me only about the Day of Atonement. What about the weekly Sabbath commemorating the creation? The verse says YOU SHALL OBSERVE THIS YOUR SABBATH (Lev. 23:32). What about the festivals? The verse says YOUR SABBATH (Lev. 23:32). Thus any time one is to observe a cessation from work, one is to add time both before it and after.

COMMENTARY   *The efficacy of the Day of Atonement in bringing about reconciliation and reacceptance by God was especially important following the destruction of the Temple. Since the Scriptural description includes the sacrificial rite and the ritual of the goats as an integral part of the day, the Sages here stress that the Day of Atonement itself, even without those rituals, which could no longer be practiced, brought atonement. They were*

---

the weekly Sabbath—is also referred to as a time of complete rest. Therefore the prohibitions are not derived from that but from the phrase *self-denial*, which occurs only in connection with the Day of Atonement, not the Sabbath.

self-denial on the ninth of the month   The verse could mean that the prohibitions begin on the ninth rather than on the tenth of the month. AT EVENING means that it is the tenth, the day that begins at evening.

when it is dark—which would be only on the tenth of the month yet the first does say to PRACTICE SELF-DENIAL ON THE NINTH DAY, which would have to be before dark.

add from the weekday   A brief period of time before dark is added.

cautious to warn, however, that rituals are not magic and that the perfor-mance of the rites of that day, that is, fasting and abstinence, was effective only where repentance had taken place. There is no automatic way of at-taining atonement or salvation, they stress. The Day of Atonement is nec-essary but not sufficient without the moral and spiritual aspects that go with it.

9. Leviticus 25:17, Sifra Weiss 107b

DO NOT WRONG ONE ANOTHER (Lev. 25:17). This is referring to verbal wrongs. Perhaps it means monetary wrongs? When it says DO NOT WRONG YOUR BROTHER (Lev. 25:14) that refers to monetary wrongs. How then shall I understand DO NOT WRONG ONE AN-OTHER (Lev. 25:17)? It is referring to verbal wrongs.

In what way? If one had repented, you should not say to him, "Re-member your former actions!"

To the child of converts one should not say, "Remember the actions of your ancestors!"

To one who has just buried his son who was killed by soldiers, one should not say what Job's "friends" said to him: IS NOT YOUR PIETY YOUR CONFIDENCE, YOUR INTEGRITY YOUR HOPE? THINK NOW, WHAT INNOCENT MAN EVER PERISHED? WHERE HAVE THE UPRIGHT BEEN DESTROYED? (Job 4:6–7).

If one sees mule-drivers looking for a place to buy grain or wine, do not say to them, "Go to so-and-so" when that person never sold wheat in his life.

R. Judah says, "He should also not look at something and ask how much it costs when he has no intention of purchasing it."

You may say, "I'm only giving him good advice," but this is really a matter for one's conscience, as it says BUT FEAR YOUR GOD (Lev. 25:17).

YOU SHALL OBSERVE MY LAWS AND FAITHFULLY KEEP MY NORMS AND YOU SHALL OBSERVE THEM (Lev. 25:18) indicating that both laws and norms must be observed and kept. THAT YOU MAY LIVE UPON THE LAND (Lev. 25:18) and not be exiled. IN SECURITY (Lev. 25:18) and not be scattered. THE LAND SHALL YIELD ITS

---

9. *a matter for one's conscience* Nothing can be proven in a court of law, but the fear of God should prevent you from doing any of these things.

FRUIT AND YOU SHALL EAT YOUR FILL (Lev. 25:19). A man will eat much and be satisfied, so said R. Judah. Rabban Simeon b. Gamliel says, "That does not seem to be so much of a blessing. What does YOU SHALL EAT YOUR FILL really mean? That you will be able to eat much and not have indigestion." Another interpretation: YOU SHALL EAT YOUR FILL. There should be nothing missing from his table. There should be no wrong in him. AND YOU SHALL LIVE UPON IT IN SECURITY (Lev. 25:19) and not be scattered or fearful upon it, nor exiled from it.

---

so much of a blessing   Whenever one eats much, one is satisfied. What is so special about that?

NUMBERS

1. Numbers 5:5, Sifre Numbers 2, 4

THE LORD SPOKE TO MOSES, SAYING: SPEAK TO THE ISRA-
ELITES: WHEN A MAN OR WOMAN COMMITS ANY WRONG
TOWARD A FELLOW MAN (Num. 5:5–6). Why is this section stated?
Since it says WHEN A PERSON SINS AND COMMITS A TRESPASS
AGAINST THE LORD BY DEALING DECEITFULLY WITH HIS
FELLOW IN THE MATTER OF A DEPOSIT OR AN INVEST-
MENT, OR THROUGH ROBBERY; OR IF HE HAS INTIMIDATED
HIS FELLOW; OR IF HE HAS FOUND SOMETHING LOST AND
LIED ABOUT IT AND SWORN FALSELY (Lev. 5:21–22)—nowhere
in the Torah have we heard a prohibition of stealing from a convert. The
verse says WHEN A MAN OR WOMAN COMMITS ANY WRONG
TOWARD A FELLOW MAN THUS BREAKING FAITH WITH THE
LORD (Num. 5:6). Thus Scripture comes to teach that if one steals from a
convert, swears to him and then [the convert] dies, he must pay the principle
and an additional fifth to the priest and a guilt offering to the altar.

This is a principle of the Torah: Any section which is stated in one
place but in which something is missing is repeated elsewhere only because
of that which was missing.

R. Akiba says, "Wherever the word *saying* is found it requires an
interpretation."

---

1. *stealing from a convert* Since the verse says HIS FELLOW this could mean someone born
into the people of Israel, excluding the convert.

[*the convert*] *dies*—and leaves no heirs. Nevertheless the money must be repaid since by stating
A MAN OR WOMAN the verse includes converts.

R. Akiba—does not accept the earlier principle taught by R. Ishmael, from whom he frequently
differed. He learns the same rule, however, from the extra word *saying*.

461

2. Numbers 5:11, Sifre Numbers 7, 10

THE LORD SPOKE TO MOSES, SAYING: SPEAK TO THE ISRA-
ELITE PEOPLE AND SAY TO THEM: IF ANY MAN'S WIFE HAS
GONE ASTRAY (Num. 5:11–12). Why is this section stated? Since it says
A MAN TAKES A WIFE AND POSSESSES HER. SHE FAILS TO
PLEASE HIM BECAUSE HE FINDS SOMETHING OBNOXIOUS
ABOUT HER, AND HE WRITES HER A BILL OF DIVORCEMENT
(Deut. 24:1) we have heard only that when he has witnesses and has warned
her she receives a bill of divorcement from him. We have not heard, how-
ever, what is done when there is a doubt as to whether or not she committed
adultery. The verse says IF ANY MAN'S WIFE HAS GONE ASTRAY
(Num. 5:12). Scripture obligates her to drink the bitter waters. That is why
this section is stated.

IF ANY MAN'S WIFE HAS GONE ASTRAY (Num. 5:12). Scripture
speaks of one who is suitable to be his wife, thus eliminating a widow married to a high priest, a divorcee, or a *halutza* married to a regular priest.
Akabya b. Mehallel added: also a freedwoman and the wife of a convert.
They said to him, "There was a freedwoman in Jerusalem named Carcemit
and Shemaya and Abtalyon make her drink it." Thus did he reply, "They
made her drink something like it." They excommunicated him and he died
while still under the ban and the court ordered that his bier be stoned.

AND BROKEN FAITH WITH HIM (Num. 5:12). Does this mean that
she broke faith in carnal matters or in money matters? When it says IN
THAT A MAN HAS HAD CARNAL RELATIONS WITH HER (Num.

---

2. *has witnesses*—to her adultery. Some authorities held that the term *obnoxious* refers to sexual
misconduct. Others interpreted it to mean anything she did that was displeasing.
bill of divorcement This section reflects the attitude of the School of Shammai that the only
cause for divorce is proven adultery. What can be done if nothing can be proven?
suitable to be his wife The examples that follow are marriages that are legal after the fact but
prohibited a priori. In these cases, the woman may not be made to drink.
halutza—a woman whose husband died childless and whose brother-in-law refused to marry
her. See Deut. 25:5–10.
something like it—or possibly "they made her drink as an example," i.e., even though she was
not required to do so, they did not want other women of her category to follow her actions.
excommunicated him Akabya was excommunicated for not accepting the opinion of the Sages.
In other places, it is categorically denied that this was so.

5:13) we know that it means that she broke faith in carnal matters and not in money matters.

AND BROKEN FAITH WITH HIM. Wherever the words BROKEN FAITH occur drunkenness is always indicated. Thus it says BUT THEY BROKE FAITH WITH THE GOD OF THEIR FATHERS BY GOING ASTRAY AFTER THE GODS OF THE PEOPLES OF THE LAND (1 Chron. 5:25). And it says THE ISRAELITES, HOWEVER, BROKE FAITH WITH THE PROSCRIPTION (Josh. 7:1). And it says SAUL DIED FROM HAVING BROKEN FAITH AGAINST THE LORD (1 Chron. 10:13). And concerning Uzziah the king of Judah it says GET OUT OF THE SANCTUARY, FOR YOU HAVE BROKEN FAITH (2 Chron. 26:18). Here it says AND BROKEN FAITH WITH HIM (Num. 5:12), indicating that wherever the words BROKEN FAITH occur drunkenness is always indicated.

IN THAT A MAN HAD CARNAL RELATIONS (Num. 5:13) excluding a minor since he is not A MAN. . . .

HIDDEN FROM THE EYES OF HER HUSBAND (Num. 5:13). This excludes a blind man.

HIDDEN FROM THE EYES OF HER HUSBAND. And not when the husband saw it and covered it up. Thus if her husband knew about it he has no right to complain against her and force her to drink it.

AND SHE KEEPS SECRET AND HAS DEFILED HER SELF (Num. 5:13). There are no witnesses to the defilement but there are witnesses to keeping secret. Or is the case that there are no witnesses to either the defilement or the keeping secret? If that were so, she would be permitted to her husband! Therefore you must say that it is the first possibility and not the second. SHE KEEPS SECRET—there are no witnesses to the defilement but there are witnesses to keeping secret.

---

and not in money matters   The only reason that a woman can be made to drink the bitter waters is suspicion of adultery.
a blind man   Since the verse speaks of her husband's eyes, a blind husband is excluded. He cannot make her drink.
covered it up—interpreting the verse not as physical blindness, but as pretending not to know.
keeping secret   She spends time in a secreted place with another man. There are witnesses to this fact, even though there are none who witnessed sexual relations between the two.

SHE KEEPS SECRET. But we do not know for how long she is secreted. AND HAS DEFILED HERSELF. Keeping secret long enough to be defiled. According to R. Ishmael that is long enough to walk around a date-palm. R. Eliezer says, "Long enough to mix a cup [of wine]." R. Joshua says, "Long enough to drink it." Ben Azzai says, "Long enough to boil an egg." R. Akiba says, "Long enough to swallow it." R. Judah b. Beterah says, "Long enough to swallow three eggs, one after the other."

AND THERE IS NO WITNESS AGAINST HER (Num. 5:13). Scripture speaks of two witnesses. Or does it speak of only one witness? The verse says A SINGLE WITNESS MAY NOT VALIDATE AGAINST A PERSON ANY GUILT OR BLAME (Deut. 19:15). The only reason this verse says SINGLE is to indicate that this is the basic rule for all verses in which the word *witness* appears: It always means two unless Scripture were to specify SINGLE.

HERSELF WITHOUT BEING FORCED (Num. 5:13). This eliminates a woman who was raped whether she is from an Israelite or the priestly tribe. If in a lighter case of defilement, rape was considered the same as consensual intercourse in regard to the priesthood, certainly in the case of the Sotah, which is much more serious, rape would be considered the same as consensual intercourse in regard to the priesthood.

BUT A FIT OF JEALOUSLY COMES OVER HIM AND HE IS WROUGHT UP ABOUT HIS WIFE (Num. 5:14). According to R. Ishmael this means that he may do this if he wishes. R. Eliezer says, "It is mandatory upon him."

---

to be defiled—by having sexual relations.

two witnesses The Hebrew word is in the singular. Therefore it must be proven that more than one witness is needed.

who was raped A woman who was raped is not made to drink, only one who is suspected of willingly having relations with another man.

lighter case of defilement—such as a convert who may not marry a priest because of the suspicion that she may have been a prostitute. This is so even if she converted as a child, even though such intercourse with a minor is always considered rape.

in regard to the priesthood Such a woman would not be made to drink, but her husband, a priest, could no longer have relations with her.

he may do this A husband is permitted but not required to make his wife drink the waters when he has reason to be suspicious. R. Eliezer disagrees.

OR IF A FIT OF JEALOUSLY COMES OVER ONE AND HE IS WROUGHT UP ABOUT HIS WIFE ALTHOUGH SHE HAS NOT DEFILED HERSELF (Num. 5:14). R. Akiba says, "Why is 'defiled' written three times? It is to indicate that she is defiled for her husband, defiled for her paramour, and defiled for eating the priestly portion."

R. Ishmael says, "We do not need this verse to teach us that. If in the case of a divorced woman, which is of lesser severity since she is permitted to return to her divorced husband if he is an Israelite, she is unfit for priestly marriage, certainly in the case of the Sotah, which is of much greater severity, it is only logical that she is unfit for priestly marriage. Why then does the verse say SHE HAS DEFILED HERSELF . . . SHE HAS NOT DEFILED HERSELF (Num. 5:14)? If she is defiled, why should he not make her drink, and if she is pure, why should he make her drink? Rather the verse comes to teach you that we never make a woman drink unless there is a doubt."

THE MAN SHALL BRING HIS WIFE TO THE PRIEST (Num. 5:15). According to the Torah, the man himself brings his wife to the priest. The [Sages], however, said that two sages are sent with him on the way to make certain that he does not have relations with her.

R. Judah the Prince says, "Her husband may be trusted concerning her. We know this from logical inference: if in the case of a woman during her period, when the husband is liable to extinction for having relations with her, he is nevertheless trusted concerning her, certainly in the case of the Sotah, when the husband is not liable to extinction for having relations with her, should not her husband be trusted concerning her?" They said to him,

---

three times   The word occurs three times in Num. 5:13–14.

defiled   She is forbidden to have relations with her husband and with her paramour and, if she is entitled to eat the priestly portion, she may no longer do so.

to return to her divorced husband   As long as she never married anyone else, she can remarry her divorced husband.

the Sotah—the woman under suspicion of adultery.

unfit for priestly marriage   As the Talmud points out, R. Akiba is talking about eating the priestly portion and R. Ishmael answers him with a statement about marrying a priest. The Talmud assumes that Akiba also mentioned priestly marriage and that there was a dispute between the two as to whether another Biblical reference was needed to deduce that.

why should he not make her drink   The reading in the Talmud is: If she is defiled, why should she drink? If she is pure, why should he make her drink? The conclusion is the same: She drinks only when there is a doubt.

during her period   The Torah forbids sexual relations between husband and wife during the menstrual period. See Lev. 15:19.

extinction—death at the hands of Heaven.

"Exactly! Since he is not liable for extinction if he has relations with her, her husband certainly cannot be trusted concerning her!"

Another interpretation: How can you say this when in the case of a woman during her period, she is permitted to him after being forbidden to him, while with the Sotah, she is not permitted again after being forbidden?

Another interpretation: The men of Israel are suspect concerning the Sotah but not concerning the woman during her period. . . .

AND HE SHALL BRING AS AN OFFERING FOR HER ONE-TENTH OF AN EPHAH OF BARLEY FLOUR (Num. 5:15). Why is this stated? Since the meal offering for one who transgressed is brought because of a transgression and this offering is brought because of a transgression, I would assume that just as that offering is fine flour, so this one should be fine flour. Therefore the verse says FLOUR.

BARLEY (Num. 5:15). Why is this stated? Since the meal offering for one who transgressed is brought because of a transgression and this offering is brought because of a transgression, I would assume that just as that offering is wheat, so this should be wheat. Therefore the verse says BARLEY. Rabban Gamliel says, "If the Scribes will permit, I shall explain this as an allegory. It appears that since her actions are those of an animal, so her offering is food fit for an animal."

NO OIL SHALL BE POURED UPON IT AND NO FRANKINCENSE SHALL BE LAID ON IT (Num. 5:15). This informs us that if he put oil upon it he transgressed a negative prohibition. As he transgresses concerning oil, so it is with frankincense. One could say that he transgresses concerning oil because there is no way for him to take it back, but with frankincense, he does not transgress since he can take it back. The verse says NO OIL SHALL BE POURED UPON IT AND NO FRANKINCENSE SHALL BE LAID ON IT, informing you that if he poured oil and frankin-

---

certainly cannot be trusted It is the threat of extinction that keeps him from sinning. Since there is no such threat in the case of the Sotah, he cannot be trusted.

How can you say this—that the husband can be trusted not to have relations with her.

that offering is fine flour As described in Lev. 5:11, such an offering consisted of choice flour in contrast to this one.

fit for an animal—barley, an inferior grain, rather than wheat.

cense on it he violated a negative prohibition. Why? We are told the reason for it: FOR IT IS A MEAL OFFERING OF JEALOUSY (Num. 5:15).

A MEAL OFFERING OF JEALOUSY (Num. 5:15). This indicates two jealousies: Both the husband and the paramour are jealous. There is jealousy both here below and in heaven above.

A MEAL OFFERING OF REMEMBRANCE (Num. 5:15). I understand from this both merit and guilt. The verse says WHICH RECALLS WRONGDOING (Num. 5:15). All "remembrances" in the Torah are for good, but this one is for punishment. So taught R. Tarphon.
　　R. Akiba said, "This one is also for good as it is said BUT IF THE WOMAN HAS NOT DEFILED HERSELF (Num. 5:28)."
　　[When it says WHICH RECALLS WRONGDOING (Num. 5:15)] I know only about recalling wrongdoing. How do I know about recalling merit? The verse says A MEAL OFFERING OF REMEMBRANCE (Num. 5:15)—no matter what the case.
　　R. Ishmael says, "A MEAL OFFERING OF REMEMBRANCE is the general statement. WHICH RECALLS WRONGDOING is a detail. In the case of a general statement followed by a detail, the general statement is held to contain only that which is in the detail. . . ."

If she was defiled, punishment comes upon her immediately. But if she has merit, the merit suspends her [punishment] for three months, long enough for pregnancy to be recognized. So taught Abba Jose b. Hannan. R. Eleazar b. Isaac, a man of Darom, says, "Nine months, as it is said SHE SHALL BE

---

the reason for it　Since jealousy and suspicion are the cause of this offering, it should not have the fine anointments of oil and frankincense that accompany other offerings brought as symbols of joy and thanksgiving.

two jealousies　Since the Hebrew is a plural word we know that more than one person is jealous.

"remembrances" in the Torah are for good　When the Torah says that God remembered or visited, it always indicates that He is about to fulfill a promise and bring about good things. This seems to be the exception.

R. Ishmael—disagrees with R. Akiba.

only that which is in the detail　Therefore the "remembrance" would be for wrongdoing and not for merit.

long enough for pregnancy to be recognized　The reward for the woman who was not guilty is that she will conceive. This would be seen three months later. If she is guilty but has some merit, she will not be punished until three months have elapsed. If it took longer, neither the reward nor the punishment would be seen to be happening.

UNHARMED AND ABLE TO RETAIN SEED (Num. 5:28). Just as SEED indicates nine months, so merit is nine months." R. Ishmael says, "Twelve months. Even though there is no proof, there is a hint in the verse 'THEREFORE, O KING, MAY MY ADVICE BE ACCEPTABLE TO YOU: REDEEM YOUR SINS BY BENEFICENCE AND YOUR INIQUITIES BY GENEROSITY TO THE POOR; THEN YOUR SERENITY MAY BE EXTENDED.' TWELVE MONTHS LATER (Dan. 4:24–26)."

R. Simeon b. Yochai says, "Merit does not suspend the bitter waters, for if you were to say that merit suspends the bitter accursed waters you would diminish the power of the water for all who have to drink it and slander all the pure women who drank, for people would say: They were all defiled, but merit suspended it!"

R. Judah the Prince says, "I shall decide this. If she is pure, she will die a natural death, but if she is defiled, then she will eventually die SO THAT HER BELLY SHALL DISTEND AND HER THIGH SHALL SAG (Num. 5:27)."

R. Simeon b. Yochai says, "And who will inform all of those attending her that she will eventually die SO THAT HER BELLY SHALL DISTEND AND HER THIGH SHALL SAG? Rather as soon as she drinks it her face turns green and her eyes bulge and she stiffens up and they say 'Quickly—take her out!' so that she should not defile the Temple court."

THE PRIEST SHALL BRING HER FORWARD (Num. 5:16). This is the source of the teaching: Two suspected women are not given the drink at the same time.

AND HAVE HER STAND (Num. 5:16). Neither a male nor female slave is to stand with her since her heart will feel strengthened by them.

BEFORE THE LORD (Num. 5:16)—at the Gate of Nicanor. This is the source of the teaching: The head of the [Priestly] watch would stand the

---

she will eventually die—the unnatural death. No matter how long it takes, by the manner of her death, her guilt will be evident. According to this opinion, merit may postpone the punishment.
two suspected women Since the verse uses the singular HER, we know that this ceremony is performed individually.
her heart will feel strengthened Since she will not wish to be shamed before them, she will be obdurate and not admit her guilt.
the Gate of Nicanor—which was opposite the Holy of Holies.

impure at the Gate of Nicanor since that was where they gave the Sotah the drink.

THE PRIEST SHALL TAKE SACRAL WATER (Num. 5:17). SACRAL means that it was sanctified in a vessel, namely the water of the laver. IN AN EARTHEN VESSEL (Num. 5:17). This informs us that other vessels could not substitute for the earthen vessels. . . .

AND, TAKING SOME OF THE EARTH THAT IS ON THE FLOOR OF THE TABERNACLE (Num. 5:17). Scripture informs us that if there was no earth there, they had to take earth from somewhere else and put it there since the place sanctifies it. Isi b. Akabia says, "This indicates that the earth of the Eternal House is included as well." Isi b. Menachem says, "If in the case of one who is impure, with a minor impurity, the Temple is considered the same as the Tabernacle, certainly that is so in the case of the Sotah which is of much greater severity. What then does the verse mean by TAKING SOME OF THE EARTH THAT IS ON THE FLOOR OF THE TABERNACLE? [He must not take it from a pile]."

Since it says SOME OF THE EARTH FROM THE FIRE OF CLEANS-ING SHALL BE TAKEN FOR THE UNCLEAN PERSON (Num. 19:17)—EARTH is mentioned here (Num. 5:17) and EARTH is mentioned elsewhere (Num. 19:17). Just as EARTH here means earth which is on the surface of the water, so EARTH there means earth which is on the surface of the water. Just as there, if the earth was placed there before the water, the obligation has been fulfilled, so here if the earth is placed there before the water, the obligation is fulfilled.

---

the laver—the large basin containing water that was in the Temple court. See Ex. 38:8.

and put it there   The Hebrew reads "the earth that will be," implying that if the earth is not there, it is to be placed there.

the same as the Tabernacle   The description in the Torah is of the Sanctuary, the Tabernacle, which was erected in the wilderness. The Temple eventually built in Jerusalem was quite different. Nevertheless, the instructions for purification or other ceremonies in the one had to be followed in the other. In this case this might mean bringing earth into the Temple since the Temple floor was not of earth as it was in the Tabernacle.

from a pile   This is not found in the text, but is supplied from the parallel in the Talmud.

EARTH is mentioned elsewhere   The section referred to tells of the use of the ashes of a red heifer mixed in water in order to purify one who has come in contact with the dead. The Hebrew word used there for "ashes" and the word used here for "earth" is the same. Therefore, the two sections are compared to one another.

THE PRIEST SHALL PUT IT INTO THE WATER (Num. 5:17). It must be visible. The Torah indicates that there are three things which must be visible: the ashes of the red heifer, the earth of the water of the Sotah, and the spittle of *Halizah*. R. Ishmael says, "The blood of the bird must also be visible."

AND THE PRIEST SHALL MAKE THE WOMAN STAND BEFORE THE LORD (Num. 5:18). He makes her stand now at the conclusion in the same place he made her stand at the beginning.

AND HE SHALL LOOSEN THE HAIR OF THE WOMAN'S HEAD (Num. 5:18). In order to perform the mitzvah of loosening the hair, the priest turns toward her back and loosens it. So taught R. Ishmael. Another interpretation: This teaches that the daughters of Israel cover their hair. Even though there is no proof, there is a hint of this from the verse TAMAR PUT DUST ON HER HEAD (2 Sam. 13:19).

R. Judah says, "If her bosom was beautiful, he would not uncover it. If her hair was beautiful, he would not uncover it. If she was dressed in white, she is dressed in black. If she was dressed in black and that was becoming to her, they strip her of it and dress her in something which is ugly. If she had golden ornaments, necklaces, nose rings or rings, they are taken from her in order to make her obnoxious."

R. Johanan b. Baroka says, "The daughters of Israel are not to be made more obnoxious than the Torah specifies, rather BEFORE THE LORD AND HE SHALL LOOSEN THE HAIR OF THE WOMAN'S HEAD (Num. 5:18) [indicating that] a linen cloth was hung between her and the people. The priest turned toward her back and loosened her hair in order to perform the mitzvah of loosening her hair."

They said to him, "As she had no concern for the honor of God, so we have no concern for her honor. Rather she has made herself obnoxious in all of these things. Whoever wants to see her may do so, except for her male or female slaves since her heart is haughty because of them. Men and

---

Halizah The ceremony in which the brother of a husband who died childless refuses to marry the widow. As part of the ceremony, he must spit on her. See Deut. 25:5–10.

blood of the bird—which was used in purifying the leper. See Lev. 14:6.

in the same place—the Gate of Nicanor.

cover their hair If it were not covered, there would be no need to loosen it. The hair is not loose because it is bound in a head covering.

than the Torah specifies None of these things described here are done to her except those that are specifically mentioned in the Torah such as loosening the hair.

women, those familiar with her and those strange to her, are all permitted to see her, as it is said AND ALL THE WOMEN SHALL TAKE WARNING NOT TO IMITATE YOUR WANTONNESS (Ezek. 23:48)."

AND PLACE UPON HER HANDS (Num. 5:18). Abba Hanin says in the name of R. Eliezer, "in order to weary her so that she will recant. This is a matter of logic: If God is so considerate of those who defy His will, how much more will He be considerate of those who perform His will."

AND IN THE PRIEST'S HANDS SHALL BE THE WATER OF BITTERNESS THAT INDUCES THE SPELL (Num. 5:18). The verse informs us that the water does not become bitter until it is in the hands of the priest. Another interpretation: It is called bitter because of its eventual effect. It embitters the body and reveals the transgression.

THE PRIEST SHALL ADJURE THE WOMAN (Num. 5:19). The priest adjures her. She does not adjure herself. We might have reasoned that since "adjure" is mentioned here and "adjure" is mentioned elsewhere (Lev. 5:4), just as the adjure there is done by the person himself, so here she should adjure herself. Therefore the verse says THE PRIEST SHALL ADJURE THE WOMAN. The priest adjures her. She does not adjure herself.

SAYING TO HER (Num. 5:19) in any language that she understands. So taught R. Josiah. We might have reasoned that if in the case of the *Yebama*, which is of lesser severity, other languages may not be used in place of the holy tongue, certainly in the case of the Sotah, which is of greater severity, other languages may not be used in place of the holy tongue. Therefore the verse says SAYING TO HER—in any language that she understands. So taught R. Josiah.

R. Ishmael says, "We do not need this verse for that since elsewhere it says AND THE WOMAN SHALL SAY, 'AMEN, AMEN!' (Num. 5:22). If she does not understand, how can she say 'AMEN AMEN?' " Perhaps

---

considerate—in attempting to bring her to confession and thus spare her the punishment of the ordeal.

adjures her—makes her take an oath.

is done by the person himself The reference is to one who takes an oath for any purpose.

Yebama—the childless widow referred to in Deut. 25:5–10. There the declarations are to be made in Hebrew.

Perhaps—when she says "Amen."

she is only [responding] to the curse? When it says MAY THE LORD MAKE YOU A CURSE AND AN IMPRECATION AMONG YOUR PEOPLE (Num. 5:21) we see that the imprecation is meant as well. Why then does the verse say SAYING TO HER (Num. 5:19)? To teach the priest the correct procedure for adjuring.

IF NO MAN HAS LAIN WITH YOU (Num. 5:19). This teaches that he speaks first in her favor. He says to her, "Wine has a powerful effect. Levity has a powerful effect. Youth has a powerful effect. Many others before you have been swept away. Do not cause the Great Name written in holiness to be obliterated by the water!"

He expounds for her many incidents in the ancient Writings such as THAT WHICH WISE MEN HAVE TRANSMITTED FROM THEIR FATHERS, AND HAVE NOT WITHHELD (Job 15:18) and they relate things to her which neither she nor all her father's household are worthy to hear.

R. Ishmael says, "He begins by explaining to her the effect that the bitter waters will have. He says to her, 'My daughter, let me tell you what these bitter waters resemble. They are like a dry medicinal drug which is placed upon healthy flesh and does no harm, but if it finds a wound, it begins to penetrate. So too if you are pure, you have no reason to hesitate to drink—[BE IMMUNE TO HARM FROM THIS WATER OF BITTERNESS THAT INDUCES THE SPELL (Num. 5:19)]. But if you are defiled [MAY THIS WATER . . . ENTER YOUR BODY, CAUSING THE BELLY TO DISTEND AND THE THIGH TO SAG (Num. 5:22)].' "

BUT IF YOU HAVE GONE ASTRAY (Num. 5:20). This teaches me only about normal intercourse. What about other forms? The verse says AND HAVE DEFILED YOURSELF (Num. 5:20).

---

responding to the curse—which is in a language she understands. If "Amen" referred only to that, it would not imply that the oath or imprecation must also be in a language that she understands.

correct procedure Since, according to R. Ishmael, the verse in question is not needed to teach that the language need not be Hebrew, it must have another purpose. That purpose is to teach the correct procedure.

in her favor—bringing up the possibility that she may not be guilty. Then he continues that if she is guilty, there have been others before her and she should admit it.

IF SOME MAN HAS LAIN WITH YOU (Num. 5:20). This includes a eunuch. OTHER THAN YOUR HUSBAND (Num. 5:20). This includes the wife of a eunuch. He may make a condition concerning anything.

HERE THE PRIEST SHALL ADMINISTER THE CURSE OF ADJU-RATION TO THE WOMAN (Num. 5:21). From this we draw conclusions concerning all the adjurations in the Torah. Since adjurations are mentioned many times in the Torah with no further elaboration, and in this one there is the elaboration that it is to be both an oath and a curse, we conclude that all the adjurations in the Torah are to be both an oath and a curse. Since adjurations are mentioned many times in the Torah with no further elaboration, and in this one there is the elaboration that the specific Name of God is to be used, we conclude that all the adjurations in the Torah use the specific Name of God.

MAY THE LORD MAKE YOU A CURSE AND AN IMPRECATION AMONG YOUR PEOPLE (Num. 5:21) . . . but all will be well with your people. AMONG YOUR PEOPLE. This distinguishes between one who disgraces himself in a place where he is known and one who disgraces himself in a place where he is not known.

AS THE LORD CAUSES YOUR THIGH TO SAG AND YOUR BELLY TO DISTEND MAY THIS WATER THAT INDUCES THE SPELL ENTER YOUR BODY, CAUSING THE BELLY TO DISTEND AND THE THIGH TO SAG (Num. 5:21–22). R. Jose the Galilean says, "This refers to the belly and the thigh of the paramour." You say that this refers to the belly and the thigh of the paramour, but perhaps it refers to her belly and her thigh? When it says HER BELLY SHALL DISTEND AND

---

the wife of a eunuch Some sources indicate that this means the opposite: If her husband was a eunuch and did not have intercourse with her, she may not be made to drink. The reading here seems to indicate that even then, she may be made to drink.

anything—or possibly anyone. This may be referring to the eunuch or, as in other sources, either to the fact that sexual contact other than normal intercourse is forbidden or that even if she was only engaged and therefore had not had intercourse with her husband, he could still make her drink if he suspected that she had done so with another man.

the specific Name—the Tetragrammaton.

where he is not known—which, while still a sin, is less disgraceful.

of the paramour Since this verse would be otherwise redundant, it is interpreted to apply not to the woman but to her lover. He too is punished.

HER THIGH SHALL SAG (Num. 5:27) this refers to the belly and the thigh of the adulterous woman. To what, then, does THE BELLY TO DISTEND AND THE THIGH TO SAG (Num. 5:22) refer? This refers to the belly and the thigh of the paramour. The verse informs us that just as she is punished, so is he punished. This is a matter of logic. If the Quality of Punishment, which is the lesser, affects one's fellow, certainly the Quality of Goodness will affect one's fellow!

AND THE WOMAN SHALL SAY, "AMEN, AMEN!" (Num. 5:22). "Amen" that I was not defiled and "Amen" that I will not be defiled. So taught R. Meir, but the Sages do not agree. Rather it means "Amen" that I was not defiled, and if I was defiled may it come upon me. "Amen" in regard to this specific man and "Amen" in regard to any other man.

"Amen" if she be engaged and "Amen" if she be betrothed.

"Amen" if she is awaiting the ceremony of *yibum* and "Amen" if she has already gone through it. This is the rule: In any case where she would be forbidden to him should she have intercourse at that time, he can make a condition with her. . . .

THE PRIEST SHALL WRITE DOWN THESE CURSES (Num. 5:23). I might think that all the curses in the Torah are to be written down, therefore it says THESE CURSES.

THE PRIEST (Num. 5:23). Why is this stated? I might have reasoned that since it says "writing" here and it says "writing" elsewhere (Deut. 24:1), just as the "writing" there can be done by any person, so the "writing" here could be done by any person. Therefore the verse says THE PRIEST.

IN A SCROLL AND HE SHALL RUB IT OFF (Num. 5:23). Something that can be rubbed off. This was the source of the teaching: The writing is done not on a tablet, not on paper and not on a hide but on a scroll, as it is said IN A SCROLL; and he does not write with gum ink and not with vitriol

---

specific man—concerning whom her husband warned her.

engaged Marriage has two stages, which were originally separated by some period of time. The first was the engagement, after which the woman was forbidden to any other man. The second was the betrothal, after which they were permitted to live together.

a condition with her Even though according to the law, she might not have to drink if this happened before she was actually married or had gone through *yibum*, such a condition can be made and she would have to.

writing elsewhere—in the case of writing a bill of divorcement.

ink, but with plain ink as it is said AND HE SHALL RUB IT OFF INTO THE WATER OF BITTERNESS (Num. 5:23). Writing which can be rubbed off.

This is a matter of logic. If God said, "A scroll written in sanctity may be rubbed off in order to create peace between man and wife," certainly the scrolls of the heretics, which create enmity, hatred, and envy, and informers may certainly be rubbed off and erased from the world!

R. Ishmael says, "How should one proceed in regard to the books of the heretics? Cut out the Names of God and burn the rest."

R. Akiba says, "He should burn the entire thing since it was not written in holiness!"

AND HE SHALL RUB IT OFF INTO THE WATER OF BITTERNESS (Num. 5:23). This informs us that the writing turns the water bitter. . . .

HER BELLY SHALL DISTEND AND HER THIGH SHALL SAG (Num. 5:27). This teaches me only about her belly and her thigh. What about the other parts of her body? The verse says THE SPELL-INDUCING WATER SHALL ENTER INTO HER (Num. 5:27). Since it says SHALL ENTER INTO HER, why does it say HER BELLY SHALL DISTEND AND HER THIGH SHALL SAG? That part which was the first to sin is the first to be punished.

Similarly it says ALL EXISTENCE ON EARTH WAS BLOTTED OUT—MAN, CATTLE, CREEPING THINGS, AND BIRDS OF THE SKY (Gen. 7:23). The first to sin is the first to be punished.

Similarly it says AND THE PEOPLE WHO WERE AT THE ENTRANCE OF THE HOUSE, YOUNG AND OLD, THEY STRUCK WITH BLINDING LIGHT, SO THAT THEY WERE HELPLESS TO FIND THE ENTRANCE (Gen. 19:11). The first to sin are the first to be punished.

Similarly it says I WILL ASSERT MY AUTHORITY AGAINST PHARAOH AND ALL HIS HOST (Ex. 14:4). Since Pharaoh was the first to sin, he was the first to be punished.

Similarly it says PUT THE INHABITANTS OF THAT TOWN TO

---

scrolls of the heretics—which contain the Name of God. It is forbidden to erase that Name, but if the Name may be erased in the case of the Sotah, certainly these books may be destroyed even if that involves erasing the Name. The reference is to Christian books and reflects the enmity felt at the early period of Christianity when it was perceived as a heretical group that broke off from Judaism.

THE SWORD AND PUT ITS CATTLE TO THE SWORD (Deut. 14:16). The first to sin are the first to be punished.

So it is here. HER BELLY SHALL DISTEND AND HER THIGH SHALL SAG (Num. 5:27). That part which was the first to sin is the first to be punished. This is a matter of logic. If in the case of the Quality of Punishment, which is the lesser, the part which was the first to sin was the first to be punished, certainly this will be so in the case of the Quality of Goodness, which is the greater!

AND THE WOMAN SHALL BECOME A CURSE (Num. 5:27). They will use her as a curse: May what happened to so-and-so happen to you! They will use her as an oath: May what happened to so-and-so happen to you! Thus it says YOU SHALL LEAVE BEHIND A NAME BY WHICH MY CHOSEN ONES SHALL CURSE (Isa. 65:15). Thus we learn that the wicked become an oath for the righteous. What about the righteous being a blessing for the wicked? As it is said NATIONS SHALL BLESS THEMSELVES BY YOU AND PRAISE THEMSELVES BY YOU (Jer. 4:2). And it says ALL THE FAMILIES OF THE EARTH SHALL BLESS THEMSELVES BY YOU AND YOUR DESCENDANTS (Gen. 28:14). And it says SO HE BLESSED THEM THAT DAY, SAYING, "BY YOU SHALL ISRAEL INVOKE BLESSINGS" (Gen. 48:20).

BUT IF THE WOMAN HAS NOT DEFILED HERSELF AND IS PURE (Num. 5:28). R. Ishmael says, "Is there anyone defiled whom Scripture terms pure? What then does the verse BUT IF THE WOMAN HAS NOT DEFILED HERSELF AND IS PURE really mean? The verse informs us that because of the bad name she acquired, she was forbidden to her husband."

R. Simeon b. Yohai says, "Let it not enter your mind that any merit will suspend the effect of the bitter waters—unless THE WOMAN HAS NOT DEFILED HERSELF AND IS PURE. . . ."

---

she was forbidden   Once she is accused, she may no longer have relations with her husband. In the case of a woman who was not defiled, the reason for that was the bad reputation she acquired by defying her husband's order forbidding her to be secreted with a certain man.

BUT IF THE WOMAN HAS NOT DEFILED HERSELF AND IS PURE. She is pure for her husband, pure for the accused paramour, and pure to eat the priestly dues. SHE SHALL BE CLEARED (Num. 5:28) both from the curse and from the adjuration.

AND ABLE TO RETAIN SEED (Num. 5:28). If she was barren, she will become pregnant. So taught R. Akiba. R. Ishmael said to him, "In that case, let all barren women go and corrupt themselves so that they can become pregnant! Any woman who sits idly by loses. Rather what does the verse SHE SHALL BE CLEARED AND ABLE TO RETAIN SEED mean? If previously she had given birth with difficulty, now she will do so with ease. If previously she had borne females, now she will bear males. If previously she had borne one, now she will bear two; dark children—light children; short children—tall children."

Another interpretation: SHE SHALL BE CLEARED AND ABLE TO RETAIN SEED. This excludes the barren woman and one who is not fit to give birth. . . .

THE WOMAN SHALL BE MADE TO STAND BEFORE THE LORD AND THE PRIEST SHALL CARRY OUT ALL THIS RITUAL WITH HER. THE MAN SHALL BE CLEAR OF GUILT (Num. 5:30–31). If he does this to her he SHALL BE CLEAR OF GUILT. But if he does not do this to her, he shall not be clear of guilt.

THE MAN SHALL BE CLEAR OF GUILT (Num. 5:31). He should not say: Woe unto me, but I have slain a daughter of Israel; woe unto me for I have disgraced a daughter of Israel; woe unto me that I had relations with one who was impure. Therefore it says THE MAN SHALL BE CLEAR OF GUILT.

Simeon b. Azzai says, "The verse is speaking about the case of a woman who was pure. Since she brought herself to this state, she will not totally

---

pure for her husband Once she has been proven pure by her emergence unscathed from the ordeal, she is once more permitted to her husband.

for the accused paramour Should she become free to marry, she could marry him.

excludes the barren woman—from having to perform the ordeal.

brought herself to this state—by defying his order that she not secrete herself with a certain man. Therefore, even if she emerges as innocent, he need not feel guilt for causing her to go through this ceremony.

escape punishment. Therefore it says THE MAN SHALL BE CLEAR OF GUILT; BUT THAT WOMAN SHALL SUFFER FOR HER GUILT (Num. 5:31)."

R. Akiba says, "The verse comes to teach you that in the end she will die and her belly shall distend and her thigh will fall. Why does it say THE MAN SHALL BE CLEAR OF GUILT; BUT THAT WOMAN SHALL SUFFER FOR HER GUILT? Unlike that which is written I WILL NOT PUNISH THEIR DAUGHTERS FOR FORNICATING NOR THEIR DAUGHTERS-IN-LAW FOR COMMITTING ADULTERY; FOR THEY THEMSELVES TURN ASIDE WITH WHORES AND SACRIFICE WITH PROSTITUTES, AND A PEOPLE THAT IS WITHOUT SENSE MUST STUMBLE (Hos. 4:14). He said to them, 'Since you run after prostitution, the water will not test your wives.' Therefore it says THE MAN SHALL BE CLEAR OF GUILT—his guilt."

COMMENTARY   *This section is an excellent example of the way in which the Sages were able to restructure Biblical laws through interpretation. Sometimes this is done in order to mitigate practices that might seem unfair. Can a husband simply bring a wife to this ordeal because of whatever whim he may have? The requirement of witnesses, for example, means that the husband's rights are limited. There must be reasonable suspicion. So too the implication that the paramour will also suffer and that the ordeal will not be effective if husbands are unfaithful adds a new dimension to an ancient practice. Of course this section was written in this form when the entire institution was no longer in effect. Rabbinic tradition states that it was abolished immediately prior to the destruction of the Temple (70 C.E.) when disorder and immorality were rife in the society. Although we cannot be certain if the teachings here had been in effect prior to the destruction of the Temple, it seems reasonable to assume that at least some of these post-Biblical reinterpretations had been incorporated into practice by then. Note also the tendency to explain the details of the ceremony as symbolic: The offering is like that of animals because of her animal behavior, the parts of her body that sinned first are punished first—as well as the tendency to use sections in order to teach values: The Name of God may be erased in order to bring about a marriage reconciliation.*

---

his guilt   If he is free of guilt, the waters will test her. If not, they will be ineffective.

3. Numbers 15:37, Sifre Numbers 115, 124

THE LORD SPOKE TO MOSES, SAYING: SPEAK TO THE ISRA-ELITE PEOPLE AND INSTRUCT THEM TO MAKE FOR THEM-SELVES FRINGES (Num. 15:37–38). Women were included in this. R. Simeon exempts women from fringes because women are exempt from any positive mitzvah which is time-dependent. This is the general rule: R. Simeon said, "Any positive mitzvah which is time-dependent is observed by men but not by women; by those who are qualified, and not by those who are disqualified." R. Judah b. Babba says, "The Sages specifically exempted a woman's veil from fringes, nor would they require them upon their cloaks except that their husbands sometimes wrap themselves in them."

TO MAKE FOR THEMSELVES FRINGES (Num. 15:38). FRINGES means something which hangs over, of any length. The Elders of the School of Shammai and the Elders of the School of Hillel once went into the upper chamber of Jonathan b. Beterah and said, "There is no specific measurement for fringes." Similarly they said, "There is no specific measurement for the *lulav*."

TO MAKE FOR THEMSELVES FRINGES. I might think that one can make it of one single thread, therefore the verse says YOU SHALL MAKE TWISTED CORDS ON THE FOUR CORNERS OF THE GARMENT WITH WHICH YOU COVER YOURSELF (Deut. 22:12). You make it from many twisted cords, no less than three. So said the School of Hillel. The School of Shammai says, "Three of wool and the fourth—blue." The law is according to the School of Shammai.

---

3. *women were included*—in the requirement to wear fringes on their garments.

time-dependent—which must be performed at a very specific time. The fringes are worn only during the day and not at night. Therefore R. Simeon disagrees with the anonymous statement and exempts women. There were, however, many exceptions to this general rule.

disqualified—possibly referring to slaves. The reason may be that just as a woman's time was not her own, so too a slave's time was controlled by others.

specifically exempted A woman's garment was exempted specifically and not merely because of the general rule concerning time.

their cloaks—do require them not because of the woman, but because her husband may wear it.

specific measurement It may be any length.

three of wool—white, undyed wool.

In what instance is this so? At the beginning, but as for remainders and stubs, whatever amount there is will do.

TO MAKE FOR THEMSELVES FRINGES (Num. 15:38). I might think that one can make it entirely of fringes. Therefore the verse says TWISTED CORDS (Deut. 22:12). I might think that one can make it entirely of twisted cords. Therefore the verse says FRINGES (Num. 15:38). How is this done? Twisted cords come out of the corners and fringes from the twisted cords.

ON THE CORNERS OF THEIR GARMENTS (Num. 15:38). I might think that garments with three, five, six, seven, or eight corners are included. Therefore the verse says ON THE FOUR CORNERS OF THE GARMENT (Deut. 22:12). This excludes garments with three, five, six, seven, or eight corners. However, while excluding those, the verse includes other coverings. The verse says WITH WHICH YOU COVER YOUR-SELF (Deut. 22:12). I might think that a sleeping garment is also included. Therefore the verse says LOOK AT IT (Num. 15:39) indicating that which is worn during the day and not at night, but if it is intended for both day time and night time use, fringes are required. It would seem that both sleeping garments and garments worn by the blind are excluded. The verse says THAT SHALL BE YOUR FRINGE (Num. 15:39)—in all instances.

LET THEM ATTACH A CORD OF BLUE TO THE FRINGE AT EACH CORNER (Num. 15:38). Why is this stated? Since it says TO MAKE FOR THEMSELVES FRINGES (Num. 15:38) I might think that they are to be made of raw wool. When it says LET THEM ATTACH A CORD OF BLUE TO THE FRINGE AT EACH CORNER (Num. 15:38) [I understand that it refers to] something which is spun and twisted. I know only that the cord of blue is spun and twisted. What about the white ones? You reason thus: Since the Torah says "place a blue cord and place white ones," it must mean that just as the blue is spun and twisted, so the

---

at the beginning This refers back to the discussion of their length.

remainders When the fringes are worn out, they need not be of any prescribed length.

Twisted cords come out The section attached to the garment has threads twisted together. However after that, the threads hang down individually.

in all instances These garments are included in the requirement for fringes. The blind man may not see them, but others will.

white are spun and woven. . . . The absence of any of the four fringes renders them invalid for they are one mitzvah. R. Ishmael says, "They are four mitzvot."

R. Simeon b. Eleazar says, "Why is it called 'tekelet' (blue)? Because the firstborn of the Egyptians were destroyed (nitkalu) as it says IN THE MIDDLE OF THE NIGHT THE LORD STRUCK DOWN ALL THE FIRSTBORN IN THE LAND OF EGYPT (Ex. 12:29)." Another interpretation: because the Egyptians were destroyed (kalu) at the Sea.

Another interpretation: Why are they called "tzitzit" (fringes)? Because God peered (hetzitz) at the houses of our ancestors in Egypt, as it is said HARK! MY BELOVED! THERE HE COMES, LEAPING OVER THE MOUNTAINS, BOUNDING OVER HILLS. MY BELOVED IS LIKE A GAZELLE OR LIKE A YOUNG STAG. THERE HE STANDS BEHIND OUR WALL, GAZING THROUGH THE WINDOW, PEERING THROUGH THE LATTICE (Song 2:8–9).

R. Hananya b. Antiganos says, "What does it say of anyone who fulfills the mitzvah of fringes? IN THOSE DAYS, TEN MEN FROM NATIONS OF EVERY TONGUE WILL TAKE HOLD—THEY WILL TAKE HOLD OF EVERY JEW BY A CORNER OF HIS CLOAK (Zech. 8:23). And what does it say of anyone who negates the mitzvah of fringes? SO THAT IT SEIZES THE CORNERS OF THE EARTH AND SHAKES THE WICKED OUT OF IT (Job 38:13)."

R. Meir says, "It does not say 'Look at them' but LOOK AT IT (Num. 15:39). The verse informs us that anyone who fulfills the mitzvah of fringes is considered as if he experiences the face of the Divine Presence.

For the blue resembles the sea;

the sea resembles the sky;

the sky resembles the Throne of Glory, as it is said ABOVE THE EXPANSE OVER THEIR HEADS WAS THE SEMBLANCE OF A THRONE, IN APPEARANCE LIKE SAPPHIRE (Ezek. 1:26)."

---

four mitzvot   Each one is a specific mitzvah and the absence of one does not invalidate all the others.

the mitzvah of fringes   Since they are attached to the corners of garments, any reference to corners is taken to mean the fringes.

look at them   Since fringes are in the plural, the verse should have told us to look at them, not at IT in the singular.

the face of the Divine Presence—is the IT one really looks at, not the fringes.

LOOK AT IT AND RECALL ALL THE COMMANDMENTS OF THE LORD AND OBSERVE THEM (Num. 15:39). This refers to the paragraph HEAR, O ISRAEL (Deut. 6:4–9). You say that this refers to the paragraph HEAR, O ISRAEL. Perhaps it refers to the paragraph IF, THEN, YOU OBEY (Deut. 11:13–21). Let us see which paragraph contains both the acceptance of the kingship of Heaven and the elimination of idolatry. The obvious conclusion is: HEAR, O ISRAEL. Should HEAR, O ISRAEL precede IF, THEN, YOU OBEY or should IF, THEN, YOU OBEY precede HEAR, O ISRAEL? The obvious conclusion is that the section which contains both the acceptance of the Kingship of Heaven and the elimination of idolatry must precede IF, THEN, YOU OBEY which contains only [the command] to instruct. Should the paragraph concerning the fringes (Num. 15:37–41) precede IF, THEN, YOU OBEY? The obvious conclusion is that the paragraph which is recited both during the day and at night precedes the section concerning the fringes which is recited only during the day. In that case, perhaps we should recite all three in the evening as we do in the morning? The verse says LOOK AT IT (Num. 15:39) [which is possible] during the day but not at night. R. Simeon b. Yohai says, "HEAR, O IS-RAEL, which commands that we study, precedes IF, THEN, YOU OBEY, which commands that we instruct, which in turn precedes the paragraph concerning fringes, which commands performance [of the mitzvot], for Torah was given in order to study, instruct and perform."

LOOK AT IT (Num. 15:39). The verse informs us that if one fulfills the mitzvah of the fringes, he is considered as if he had fulfilled all of the mitzvot. It is a matter of logic: If one who fulfills the mitzvah of the fringes is considered as if he fulfilled all of the mitzvot, how much greater [will be the reward] of one who does fulfill all of the mitzvot of the Torah!

COMMENTARY   *The Biblical injunction concerning fringes was fulfilled during the Second Temple period by placing fringes on the corners of all four-cornered garments worn by men. Some Sages also required this of*

RECALL ALL THE COMMANDMENTS   This is interpreted to mean that by reciting the section of HEAR, O ISRAEL, one recalls them all.

precede—referring to the ritual recitation of these sections morning and evening known as *k'riyat Sh'ma*, "the recitation (or reading) of Hear, O Israel."

only during the day   This paragraph was recited only in the morning and not at night since fringes are worn only during the day.

fulfilled all of the mitzvot   Because of the singular IT the implication is that the entire unit, i.e., all of the mitzvot, has been fulfilled.

482

women. One of the fringes was colored a deep blue, similar to the royal purple, and symbolized the Presence of God, the Supreme King. The paragraph in which this mitzvah is found, the section under discussion here, was included in the morning recitation of the Shema as the third and final paragraph, but not in the evening Shema because the fringes themselves were not worn at night. Only much later was this practice changed.

4. Numbers 35:9, Sifre Numbers 159, 215

THE LORD SPOKE FURTHER TO MOSES: SPEAK TO THE ISRAELITE PEOPLE AND SAY TO THEM: WHEN YOU CROSS THE JORDAN INTO THE LAND OF CANAAN (Num. 35:9). Why was this section stated? Since it says THEN MOSES SET ASIDE THREE CITIES ON THE EAST SIDE OF THE JORDAN (Deut. 4:41) I only know that Moses set aside three cities on the far side of the Jordan. How do we know that Moses commanded Joshua to set aside three cities of refuge for them? The verse says WHEN YOU CROSS THE JORDAN INTO THE LAND OF CANAAN, YOU SHALL PROVIDE YOURSELVES WITH PLACES TO SERVE YOU AS CITIES OF REFUGE (Num. 35:10–11). The verse is referring to the time after conquering and settling the Land. You say that it is referring to the time after conquering and settling the Land. Perhaps it means immediately upon their entering the Land? Therefore the verse says WHEN THE LORD YOUR GOD HAS CUT DOWN THE NATIONS (Deut. 19:1). The verse is referring to the time after conquering and settling the Land.

WHEN YOU CROSS THE JORDAN INTO THE LAND OF CANAAN (Num. 35:9). This was the source of R. Judah's teaching: The Jordan is not part of the Land of Canaan. R. Simeon b. Yohai says, "It says AT THE JORDAN—JERICHO (Num. 26:3). Just as Jericho is part of the Land of Canaan, so the Jordan is part of the Land of Canaan."

YOU SHALL PROVIDE YOURSELVES (Num. 35:11). The word *provide* always means to have ready. CITIES (Num. 35:11). I might think that this means metropolises, therefore the verse says CITIES. If it means cities,

---

4. *commanded Joshua* In addition to the cities Moses had set aside, he told Joshua to set aside these others when they would arrive in Canaan.

not part of the Land of Canaan If it were, the verse would not say that you cross it in order to arrive in Canaan.

I might think it means even villages. Therefore the verse says CITIES. What does this mean? It indicates that there were markets and storage for provisions.

TO WHICH A MANSLAYER MAY FLEE (Num. 35:11). I might think that this includes any manslayer. The verse says WHO HAS KILLED A PERSON UNINTENTIONALLY (Num. 35:11). Since it says WHO KILLED A PERSON, I might think that this includes one who smote his father and mother. The verse says A MANSLAYER ... WHO KILLED A PERSON (Num. 35:11). I have only spoken of A MANSLAYER ... WHO KILLED A PERSON, excluding one who smote his father and mother. He is not exiled.

THE CITIES SHALL SERVE YOU AS A REFUGE FROM THE AVENGER (Num. 35:12). Why is this stated? Since it says AND THE BLOOD-AVENGER KILLS THE MANSLAYER, THERE IS NO BLOOD-GUILT ON HIS ACCOUNT (Num. 35:27) I might think that he may simply kill him on his own. Therefore the verse says SO THAT THE MANSLAYER MAY NOT DIE UNLESS HE HAS STOOD TRIAL BEFORE THE ASSEMBLY (Num. 35:12).

THE TOWNS THAT YOU THUS ASSIGN SHALL BE SIX CITIES OF REFUGE IN ALL (Num. 35:13) including those mentioned elsewhere. You say "including those mentioned elsewhere." Perhaps it means in addition to those mentioned elsewhere. The verse says THREE CITIES SHALL BE SET ASIDE BEYOND THE JORDAN, AND THE OTHER THREE SHALL BE SET ASIDE IN THE LAND OF CANAAN (Num. 35:14). What then does the verse THE TOWNS THAT YOU THUS ASSIGN SHALL BE SIX CITIES OF REFUGE IN ALL mean? Including those mentioned elsewhere.

THREE CITIES SHALL BE SET ASIDE BEYOND THE JORDAN (Num. 35:14). They are BEZER, IN THE WILDERNESS IN THE TA-

---

smote his father and mother In Ex. 21:15 we are told that one who does this is to be put to death. However parents are not in the category of mere persons. Therefore he is not exiled to a city of refuge but executed. The Mishna takes the opposite view.

BEFORE THE ASSEMBLY There must be a trial before the blood-avenger can execute one guilty of deliberate murder.

those mentioned elsewhere—referring to Deut. 4:41.

BLELAND, BELONGING TO THE REUBENITES; RAMOTH, IN GILEAD, BELONGING TO THE GADITES; AND GOLAR, IN BASHAN, BELONGING TO THE MANASSITES (Deut. 4:43). And opposite them were three others in the Land of Canaan as it is said SO THEY SET ASIDE KEDESH IN THE HILL COUNTRY OF NAPHTALI IN GALILEE, SHECHEM IN THE HILL COUNTRY OF EPHRAIM, AND KIRIATH-ARBA—THAT IS, HEBRON—IN THE HILL COUNTRY OF JUDAH (Josh. 20:7). This teaches us that the two and a half tribes on the far side of the Jordan were equal to the nine and a half tribes in the Land of Canaan. Incidentally we learn that most shedders of blood were in the land of Gilead. THEY SHALL SERVE AS CITIES OF REFUGE (Num. 35:14). This teaches me only that they take in people from within the Land. What about those from outside the Land? The verse says THEY SHALL SERVE (Num. 35:14).

THESE SIX CITIES SHALL SERVE THE ISRAELITES (Num. 35:15). This teaches me only about Israelites. What about converts? The verse says AND THE STRANGER (Num. 35:15). What about the alien resident? The verse says THE ALIEN IN YOUR MIDST (Num. 35:15). Perhaps as the convert is sent into exile because of an Israelite, so an Israelite is sent into exile because of a convert? You have said that if an Israelite killed him he is not liable. Certainly then he would not be sent into exile. Rather when an Israelite killed him he is not killed, and if he killed an Israelite he is killed.

---

were equal Since they were given as many cities of refuge as all the other tribes, they must have been equal to them in importance.

in the land of Gilead—the land on the far side of the Jordan. The fact that as many cities were needed for the two-and-a-half tribes there as for all the rest of the tribes indicates not that they were as important as the others but that there was more bloodshed there than elsewhere. In the Talmud this is connected to Hos. 6:8—GILEAD IS A CITY OF EVILDOERS, TRACKED UP WITH BLOOD.

THE STRANGER—always understood by the Sages to refer to one who converted to Judaism as opposed to "Israelite" or "citizen," which refers to one born an Israelite.

alien resident—a non-Jew who resides permanently in the Land of Israel and has accepted the seven Noahide mitzvot.

because of a convert—for inadvertently causing the death of a convert.

Israelite killed him—deliberately.

he is not liable Although the murder is forbidden, the court cannot punish him, but he is to be punished by God for his deed.

Israelite killed him—the convert. This passage is problematic. In the Mishna and Talmud the discussion is entirely of the resident alien and not the convert. It has been suggested that here too it is the alien who is intended. In Hebrew, convert is *"ger"* and resident alien is *"ger toshav."*

THESE SIX CITIES SHALL SERVE . . . FOR REFUGE (Num. 35:15). Why is this stated? When it says THREE CITIES SHALL BE SET ASIDE BEYOND THE JORDAN (Num. 35:14) I might think that when those three are set aside they immediately accept [those sent into exile]. The verse says THESE SIX CITIES SHALL SERVE . . . FOR REFUGE (Num. 35: 15). This verse informs us that no city was to accept them until all six had been set aside.

ANYONE, HOWEVER, WHO STRIKES ANOTHER WITH AN IRON OBJECT SO THAT DEATH RESULTS IS A MURDERER (Num. 35:16). Why is this stated? Since it says IF HE STRUCK HIM WITH A STONE IN THE HAND THAT COULD CAUSE DEATH AND DEATH RESULTED (Num. 35:17) and SIMILARLY, IF THE OB-JECT WITH WHICH HE STRUCK HIM WAS A WEAPON OF WOOD IN THE HAND THAT COULD CAUSE DEATH, AND DEATH RESULTED (Num. 35:18) I know only that he is guilty if he struck him with these implements. What about an iron tool? The verse says ANYONE, HOWEVER, WHO STRIKES ANOTHER WITH AN IRON OBJECT SO THAT DEATH RESULTS IS A MURDERER (Num. 35:16). Even without this I could have reasoned that if one who killed another with stone or wood is guilty, certainly one who killed another with an iron object is guilty. If you reasoned thus, however, you would be punishing on the basis of logical deduction. Therefore it says ANYONE, HOWEVER, WHO STRIKES ANOTHER WITH AN IRON OBJECT SO THAT DEATH RESULTS IS A MURDERER; THE MURDERER MUST BE PUT TO DEATH (Num. 35:16) to teach you that one is not punished on the basis of logical deduction.

Perhaps I would think that just as the stone had to be something which fills the hand, so the iron must be something which fills the hand. The Holy One knows, however, that iron can kill in small quantities, therefore the term IN THE HAND is not stated here. If it is no more than a needle or even a hook, that is considered an iron object which renders him guilty. What about if he pelted him with metal balls or bars? The verse says A

---

punishing on the basis of logical deduction You would execute on the basis of deduction and reasoning rather than on the basis of a specific verse or ordinance in the Torah. The Sages would not permit execution on the basis of deduction alone without Scriptural basis. Therefore this verse is needed to indicate that death as a result of an iron object is also murder.
fills the hand—as the verse says WITH A STONE IN THE HAND (Num. 35:17).

MURDERER; THE MURDERER MUST BE PUT TO DEATH (Num. 35:17)—in all instances.

IF HE STRUCK HIM WITH A STONE IN THE HAND THAT COULD CAUSE DEATH, AND DEATH RESULTED, HE IS A MURDERER; THE MURDERER MUST BE PUT TO DEATH (Num. 35:17). Why is this stated? Since it says WHEN MEN QUARREL AND ONE STRIKES THE OTHER WITH STONE OR FIST (Ex. 21:18) I might think that if he strikes him with anything, whether or not it is capable of causing death, he is liable. Therefore the verse says IF HE STRUCK HIM WITH A STONE IN THE HAND THAT COULD CAUSE DEATH. The verse informs us that he is not liable unless he struck him with something which is capable of causing death. I might think that [he is guilty] even if [he struck him] on a place which is not one which causes death. The verse says IF, HOWEVER, A MAN WHO IS HIS NEIGHBOR'S ENEMY LIES IN WAIT FOR HIM AND SETS UPON HIM AND STRIKES HIM A FATAL BLOW (Deut. 19:11). This verse indicates that he is not liable unless he strikes him with an object which is capable of causing death on a place which causes death. I know only that he is liable if he killed him with a stone. What if he rolls stones or pillars upon him? The verse says HE IS A MURDERER; THE MURDERER MUST BE PUT TO DEATH (Num. 35:17)—in all instances.

SIMILARLY, IF THE OBJECT WITH WHICH HE STRUCK HIM WAS A WEAPON OF WOOD IN THE HAND THAT COULD CAUSE DEATH, AND DEATH RESULTED, HE IS A MURDERER (Num. 35:18). Why is this stated? Since it says WHEN A MAN STRIKES HIS SLAVE, MALE OR FEMALE, WITH A ROD, AND HE DIES THERE AND THEN, HE MUST BE AVENGED (Ex. 21:20) I might think that if he strikes him with anything, whether or not it is capable of causing death, he is liable. Therefore the verse says SIMILARLY, IF THE OBJECT WITH WHICH HE STRUCK HIM WAS A WEAPON OF WOOD IN THE HAND THAT COULD CAUSE DEATH, AND DEATH RESULTED, HE IS A MURDERER (Num. 35:18). This verse indicates that he is not liable unless he strikes him with an object which is

---

with an object which is capable of causing death The attempt is to differentiate between one who intended to cause death and is to be executed and one who caused death through carelessness and should be sent into exile. If the weapon would not usually cause death or the place he hit him was not one that would usually prove fatal, then it was not deliberate.

capable of causing death. I might think that he is guilty even if [he struck him] on a place which is not capable of causing death. The verse says IF, HOWEVER, A MAN WHO IS HIS NEIGHBOR'S ENEMY LIES IN WAIT FOR HIM AND SETS UPON HIM AND STRIKES HIM A FATAL BLOW (Deut. 19:11). The verse informs us that he is not liable unless he strikes him with an object which is capable of causing death in a place which is capable of causing death. Thus we know only that he is liable if he killed him with a wooden weapon. What about if he hurled beams and poles upon him? The verse says HE IS A MURDERER; THE MURDERER MUST BE PUT TO DEATH (Num. 35:18)—in all instances.

THE BLOOD-AVENGER HIMSELF SHALL PUT THE MURDERER TO DEATH (Num. 35:19). Why is this stated? Since it says ANYONE, HOWEVER, WHO STRIKES ANOTHER WITH AN IRON OBJECT SO THAT DEATH RESULTS (Num. 35:16); IF HE STRUCK HIM WITH A STONE IN THE HAND THAT COULD CAUSE DEATH (Num. 35:17); SIMILARLY, IF THE OBJECT WITH WHICH HE STRUCK HIM WAS A WEAPON OF WOOD IN THE HAND (Num. 35:18) I know only that he is liable if he killed him with any of these objects. What about any other objects? You could reason that there is a basic principle underlying the three: Stone is not like wood and wood is not like stone and neither of them is like iron nor is iron like either of them. That which all three have in common is that they can kill a person and if they do, it is a mitzvah for the blood-avenger to kill him. Similarly, if he kills him with any object which is capable of killing, it is a mitzvah for the blood-avenger to kill him. Therefore it says THE BLOOD-AVENGER HIMSELF SHALL PUT THE MURDERER TO DEATH (Num. 35:19). . . .

OR IF HE STRUCK HIM WITH HIS HAND IN ENMITY AND DEATH RESULTED (Num. 35:21). Why is this said? Since it says ANYONE, HOWEVER, WHO STRIKES ANOTHER WITH AN IRON OBJECT (Num. 35:16); IF HE STRUCK HIM WITH A STONE IN THE HAND (Num. 35:17); SIMILARLY IF THE OBJECT WITH WHICH HE STRUCK HIM WAS A WEAPON OF WOOD IN THE HAND (Num. 35:18) I only know that he is liable if he killed him with

---

WITH HIS HAND   If the killer is his enemy, as the verse says IN ENMITY, then he is guilty of deliberate murder and is executed no matter how he killed the person.

any of these objects. What about pulling him, pushing him, strangling him, kicking him, or crushing him? The verse says WITH HIS HAND (Num. 35:21)—in all instances.

THE BLOOD-AVENGER SHALL PUT THE MURDERER TO DEATH (Num. 35:21). Why is this stated? Does it not state elsewhere THE BLOOD-AVENGER HIMSELF SHALL PUT THE MURDERER TO DEATH UPON ENCOUNTER. IT IS HE WHO SHALL PUT HIM TO DEATH (Num. 35:19)? Why then does it say THE BLOOD-AVENGER SHALL PUT THE MURDERER TO DEATH (Num. 35:21)? It might be that this applies only to the case where one has a blood-avenger. What about where one has no blood-avenger? The verse says THE BLOOD-AVENGER (Num. 35:21)—in all instances.

BUT IF HE PUSHED HIM WITHOUT MALICE AFORETHOUGHT (Num. 35:22). This excludes an enemy. OR HURLED ANY OBJECT AT HIM UNINTENTIONALLY (Num. 35:22). He did not trap him or intend to harm him.

OR WITHOUT SEEING DROPPED UPON HIM ANY DEADLY OBJECT OF STONE (Num. 35:23). This includes the blind or one who throws something at night. R. Judah says "WITHOUT SEEING (Num. 35:23) excludes the blind man." THOUGH HE WAS NOT AN ENEMY OF HIS AND DID NOT SEEK HIS HARM (Num. 35:23). Issi b. Akabia says, "Thus that which is strict for him is also lenient, and that which is lenient is strict. You cannot condemn him to death for he may have killed him inadvertently. Nor can you condemn him to exile, for he may have killed him intentionally!"

THOUGH HE WAS NOT HIS ENEMY AND DID NOT SEEK HIS HARM (Num. 35:23). This is intended to disqualify enemies from sitting

---

has no blood-avenger—no close relative whose task it is to avenge him. This superfluous verse indicates that in that case someone else performs the execution.

excludes an enemy The assumption is that if there was enmity, the killing was deliberate.

Issi b. Akabia—believes that the fact that the man was AN ENEMY does not make him automatically guilty. What it does, however, is to deny him the possibility of seeking sanctuary in the city of refuge. Thus the blood-avenger can kill him if he finds him. On the one hand, then, this view is lenient in not sending him into exile, but it is strict or harsh in denying him protection.

in judgment. This teaches me only about enemies, what about relatives? The verse says BETWEEN THE SLAYER AND THE BLOOD-AVENGER (Num. 35:24). This teaches me only that enemies and relatives are disqualified as judges, what about being witnesses? You may reason thus: Since the Torah says "execute by means of judges," "execute by means of witnesses," just as enemies and relatives are disqualified as judges, so enemies and relatives are disqualified as witnesses. Another manner of reasoning: If enemies and relatives are disqualified as judges who do not determine the outcome, should not enemies and relatives be disqualified as witnesses who do determine the outcome?

This teaches me only about a murderer. What about others who are condemned to death? The verse says IN SUCH CASES (Num. 35:24). This teaches me only about an Israelite. What about converts? The verse says IN SUCH CASES. This teaches me only about capital cases. What about monetary cases? The verse says IN SUCH CASES. Perhaps just as capital cases are judged by a court of twenty-three, so monetary cases must be judged by a court of twenty-three? The verse says SUCH. SUCH cases are judged by a court of twenty-three but monetary cases are not judged by a court of twenty-three. It says THE CASE OF BOTH PARTIES SHALL COME BEFORE THE JUDGES (Ex. 22:8).

And how do we know that capital cases are judged by a court of twenty-three? The verse says THE ASSEMBLY SHALL DECIDE (Num. 35:24)—this is ten. THE ASSEMBLY SHALL PROTECT (Num. 35:25)—this is ten. What about the other three? You reason thus: Since the Torah said "condemn to death by the mouths of witnesses," "condemn to death by the inclination of judges," just as we need two witnesses, so we

---

determine the outcome That which really determines if one is guilty or innocent is the testimony of witnesses. Judges only hand down a verdict based on testimony.

What about others Are enemies or relatives disqualified in these cases as well?

so monetary cases If the expression IN SUCH CASES puts monetary cases on a par with capital cases in regard to the disqualification of enemies and relatives, perhaps it also equates them in regard to the number of judges required.

BEFORE THE JUDGES JUDGES is plural, indicating two. A third was added to avoid an even number. Thus monetary cases require three, not twenty-three.

this is ten The word *assembly* refers to a group of ten since it is used to refer to the ten men who gave an evil report about the Land. See Num. 14:27. Since the word appears here twice, we have a total of twenty.

need two judges. Since a court may not be an even number, one more must be added. Thus the other three. . . .

THE ASSEMBLY SHALL PROTECT THE MANSLAYER (Num. 35:25). From this we reason that a person who killed someone, either unintentionally or intentionally, goes to the city of refuge and the court sends messengers to bring him from there. If he is guilty, he is executed. If he is not guilty, he is set free. If he is liable to exile, he is returned to that place, as it is said AND THE ASSEMBLY SHALL RESTORE HIM TO THE CITY OF REFUGE (Num. 35:25).

AND THERE HE SHALL REMAIN UNTIL THE DEATH OF THE HIGH PRIEST (Num. 35:25). R. Meir says, "A murderer shortens the life of man and a high priest lengthens the life of man. It is not right that he who shortens the life of man should be [free in the lifetime of] he who lengthens the life of man."

Rabbi Judah the Prince says, "A murderer contaminates the earth and causes the Divine Presence to depart. The High Priest causes the Divine Presence to rest upon man and upon the earth. It is not right that he who contaminates the earth and causes the Divine Presence to depart should [be free in the lifetime of] he who causes the Divine Presence to rest upon man and upon the earth."

BUT IF THE MANSLAYER EVER GOES OUTSIDE (Num. 35:26). R. Eleazar b. Azariah said, "If in the case of the Quality of Punishment, which is the lesser, a person who takes one step renders himself guilty, how much more is it so that the Quality of Goodness, which is the greater [permits one to gain merit]!"

COMMENTARY   *Comparing various verses, both in this section and in Deuteronomy, the midrash gives the definition of a murderer and a murder weapon. It also defines in greater detail the circumstances under which the*

---

two judges We need a majority of two to convict.

liable to exile Exile is not a means of saving him, but a punishment for unintentional but careless killing.

lengthens the life of man—by helping him achieve atonement and harmony with God.

takes one step If he merely steps out of the city of refuge, the avenger is permitted to kill him.

how much more—will one gain merit for even one step taken to perform good actions.

killing is considered unintentional. According to the Sages, an unintentional manslayer went into exile not merely to protect his life from the blood-avenger, which appears to be the main Biblical motive, but as a punishment for manslaughter. They differentiate between intentional and unintentional killing. The murderer is to be executed—not by the avenger but by the court. He who killed totally unintentionally, that is, accidentally, is freed. He who killed because of carelessness receives a punishment: exile. He too is considered one who "contaminates the earth" with blood and brings about the exile of God.

DEUTERONOMY

1. Deuteronomy 6:7, Sifre Deuteronomy 34, 60

IMPRESS THEM (shinantam) (Deut. 6:7). These sections are to be recited daily (shinun) while CONSECRATE TO ME EVERY FIRSTBORN (Ex. 13:2) and AND WHEN THE LORD HAS BROUGHT YOU (Ex. 13:11) are not recited daily. You might have reasoned that since THE LORD SPOKE (Num. 15:37), which is not contained in the phylacteries, is recited daily, CONSECRATE TO ME and AND WHEN THE LORD HAS BROUGHT YOU, which are contained in the phylacteries, should surely be recited daily! Therefore the verse says IMPRESS THEM (shinantam)—these are recited daily (shinun) while CONSECRATE TO ME and AND WHEN THE LORD HAS BROUGHT YOU are not recited daily.

Nevertheless I might say that if THE LORD SPOKE (Num. 15:37), which is preceded by many other mitzvot, is recited daily, the Ten Pronouncements, which are not preceded by any other mitzvot, should surely be recited daily! This is a matter of logic. If CONSECRATE TO ME EVERY FIRSTBORN (Ex. 13:2) and AND WHEN THE LORD HAS BROUGHT YOU (Ex. 13:11), which are contained in the phylacteries, are not recited daily, surely the Ten Pronouncements, which are not contained in the phylacteries, should not be recited daily! But THE LORD SPOKE

---

1. *recited daily*—as a part of the recitation of the Shema.

not recited daily Those sections not to be recited. Ex. 13:2 and 13:11 are not part of the Shema, but are included in the parchments in the phylacteries.

should surely be recited daily If a section that is not important enough to be included in the phylacteries is important enough to be in the Shema, surely those sections that are in the phylacteries should also be recited in the Shema.

not preceded by any other mitzvot The Ten Pronouncements are the beginning of the Covenant and of God's requirement that Israel fulfill mitzvot.

THE LORD SPOKE could prove Since this section is recited daily even though it is not in the phylacteries, that could serve as proof that the Ten Pronouncements should be recited daily even if they are not in the phylacteries.

(Num. 15:37) could prove that even though the Ten Pronouncements are not contained in the phylacteries, they should be recited daily. Therefore the verse says IMPRESS THEM (shinantam) UPON YOUR CHILDREN (Deut. 6:7)—these are recited daily, but the Ten Pronouncements are not recited daily.

COMMENTARY   *Two sets of Biblical passages became of special importance in Jewish worship, the three paragraphs of the Shema that are recited daily and the four passages that are written on scrolls and placed within the phylacteries worn during morning prayer. The first two sections of the Shema are the last two sections in the phylacteries, but the third section of the Shema is not in them and the first two sections in the phylacteries are not contained in the Shema. Thus some parts are both "recited daily," that is, contained in the Shema, and contained in the phylacteries and some are in only one or the other. The discussion in this section attempts to use logic to determine what sections are used when and finally concludes that the reason cannot be found by logical deduction but only in the words of the texts themselves. Of course this is reasoning after the fact since these practices had become accepted in that form long before these midrashim were expounded. The discussion of the Ten Pronouncements reflects the fact that originally they had been recited daily, as seems only appropriate for such an important section of the Torah. The recitation was eliminated in order to combat the teaching of heretical groups that the Ten Pronouncements were the only part of the Torah that actually had Divine origin. The identification of these heretical groups is still a matter of conjecture, although some have suggested that the reference is to early Christian groups.*

2. Deuteronomy 6:7, Sifre Deuteronomy 34, 62

WHEN YOU LIE DOWN (Deut. 6:7). You might think that this applies even if you lie down in the middle of the day. AND WHEN YOU GET UP (Deut. 6:7). You might think that this applies even if you get up in the middle of the night, therefore the verse says WHEN YOU STAY AT

---

the verse says IMPRESS THEM   This word from the Biblical verse is intended to teach that these sections alone are to be "impressed," i.e., recited, and no others—not even the Ten Pronouncements.

---

2. *that this applies*—that you are to recite the Shema whenever you lie down, even in the middle of the day.

HOME AND WHEN YOU ARE GOING ON THE WAY (Deut. 6:7)—
the Torah is using common forms of speech.

R. Ishmael was once reclining and expounding and R. Eleazar b. Azariah
was standing up. The time came for reciting the Shema. R. Ishmael got up
and R. Eleazar b. Azariah reclined.

R. Ishmael said to him, "What is this, Eleazar?"

He said to him, "Ishmael my brother, they once said to someone: Why
do you grow your beard long? and he replied: as a protest to those who shave
theirs off."

[R. Ishmael] said to him, "You reclined to fulfill the teaching of the
School of Shammai and I got up to fulfill the teaching of the School of
Hillel."

Another possible reason was so that it should not become obligatory,
since the School of Shammai taught that one must recline in the evening to
recite it and in the morning, one must get up.

BIND THEM (ukeshartam) (Deut. 6:8). These sections are to be contained
in the phylacteries (keshirah) while THE LORD SPOKE (Num. 15:37) is
not contained in the phylacteries. You might have reasoned that if CONSE-
CRATE TO ME EVERY FIRSTBORN (Ex. 13:2) and AND WHEN
THE LORD HAS BROUGHT YOU (Ex. 13:11), which are not recited daily, are contained in the phylacteries, THE LORD SPOKE (Num.
15:37) which is recited daily should surely be contained in the phylacteries.
Therefore the verse says BIND THEM (Deut. 6:8)—these are contained in
the phylacteries while THE LORD SPOKE (Num. 15:37) is not contained
in the phylacteries.

---

common forms of speech Surely one is not to recite the Shema whenever at home or going on
the way. Therefore all of those phrases are not to be understood literally.

The time came Since it was evening, R. Eleazar, following the teaching of Shammai, deliberately reclined. R. Ishmael, a Hillelite, who was reclining, could have remained that way but
stood up either in protest or to make it clear that he followed Hillel.

as a protest R. Eleazar may be implying that R. Ishmael's action was no more than a protest
against his reclining.

it should not become obligatory Had others seen both of them reclining at the evening Shema,
they might have thought that everyone agreed on this practice.

THE LORD SPOKE which is recited daily—as part of the Shema.

should surely be contained in the phylacteries If sections not in the Shema are in the phylacteries, should not this section, which is in the Shema, be in them as well?

the verse says BIND THEM—indicating that these words alone, and not THE LORD SPOKE,
are to be in the phylacteries. The argumentation is similar to that above.

Nevertheless I might say that if CONSECRATE TO ME (Ex. 13:2) and AND WHEN THE LORD HAS BROUGHT YOU (Ex. 13:11), which are preceded by many mitzvot, are contained in the phylacteries, the Ten Pronouncements, which are not preceded by any other mitzvot, should surely be contained in the phylacteries! This is a matter of logic. If THE LORD SPOKE (Num. 15:37), which is recited daily, is not contained in the phylacteries, surely the Ten Pronouncements, which are not recited daily, should not be contained in the phylacteries. But CONSECRATE TO ME (Ex. 13:2) and AND WHEN THE LORD HAS BROUGHT YOU (Ex. 13:11) could prove that although the Ten Pronouncements are not recited daily, they should be contained in the phylacteries. Therefore the verse says BIND THEM (Deut. 6:8)—these are contained in the phylacteries but the Ten Pronouncements are not contained in the phylacteries. . . .

Beloved is Israel, for the Scripture has surrounded them with mitzvot—
  phylacteries on their heads,
  phylacteries on their arms,
  mezuzot on their doorway
  and fringes on their garments.
Of them David said I PRAISE YOU SEVEN TIMES EACH DAY FOR YOUR JUST RULES (Ps. 119:164). When he entered the bathhouse and saw himself naked, he said, "Woe unto me for I am naked of mitzvot!" But when he saw the mark of circumcision he uttered praise of it, as it is said FOR THE LEADER; ON THE EIGHTH. A PSALM OF DAVID. (Ps. 12:1)

A parable. A human king said to his wife, "Adorn yourself with all of your jewelry so that you may be desirable to me." Thus the Holy One said to Israel, "My children, be marked by the mitzvot so that you shall be desirable to me." Thus does it say YOU ARE BEAUTIFUL, MY DARLING, AS TIRZAH (Song 6:4). You are beautiful when you are desirable (razui) to Me.

---

mezuzot—containers affixed to the door in which there is a scroll with the Shema written on it.
fringes See Num. 15:37.
naked of mitzvot—wearing none of these special signs or garments.
ON THE EIGHTH Circumcision takes place on the eighth day. This psalm, therefore, is understood as David's praise of circumcision.

COMMENTARY   *The discussion of the passages on the phylacteries is the mirror image of the discussion in the previous section concerning the daily recitation of the Shema. The concluding paragraphs are a poetic summary of the rabbinic attitude toward the major daily "action-symbols" of Judaism, in the phrase of Louis Finkelstein, which keep the observant Jew constantly aware of the Divine Presence and of one's obligations and relationship to Him. The comparison to the adornment of jewelry, which is found in several places, is particularly apt.*

3. Deuteronomy 15:1, Sifre Deuteronomy 111, 171

AT THE END OF EVERY SEVEN YEARS YOU SHALL PRACTICE REMISSION OF DEBTS (Deut. 15:1). May one do this at either the beginning or the end of the year? One must reason that here it says END and elsewhere it says END—(Deut. 31:10). Just as END there clearly means the end of the year and not the beginning, so END here means the end and not the beginning.

YOU SHALL PRACTICE REMISSION OF DEBTS . . . SHALL REMIT (Deut. 15:1–2). As long as [land] remission is in force, [debt] remission is in force.

SEVEN YEARS (Deut. 15:1). Could this mean a different period of seven years for each one? You must reason that seven years is stated in regard to both land and loans. Just as the seven years in the case of land is the same for everyone, so the seven years in regard to loans is the same for everyone.

You could reason exactly the opposite. Seven years is the period for a Hebrew slave and seven years is the period for a loan. Just as the seven years in regard to the Hebrew slave is different for each one, so the seven years in regard to loans is different for each one! Let us see in which case there is the

---

3. *elsewhere it says END*—in a verse concerning the Tabernacle holiday. That comes at the end of the crop year, not the beginning. Therefore here too END means the end of the year.

[debt] remission is in force   The double mention of remission indicates that there are two kinds: that of land and that of debts. Only when both are in force are they practiced. Land remission ceased with the destruction of the Temple.

a different period   Is the period of time seven years from the time that the loan was taken, in which case would it be a different period for everyone, or a fixed cycle of seven years?

for a Hebrew slave   The seven years of slavery are a different period for each slave, starting when he begins to serve.

greater resemblance. Let us learn of something which is not connected to the Jubilee from something else which is not connected to the Jubilee, in which case the matter of a Hebrew slave, which is connected to the Jubilee, is not relevant. Or should we say the opposite: Let us learn of something which is practiced both in the Land and out of it from something which is practiced both in the Land and out of it, in which case release of land, which is practiced only in the Land, is not relevant. The verse mentions SEVEN YEARS twice in order to indicate an analogy: Just as SEVEN YEARS in the case of land is the same for everyone, so the SEVEN YEARS in the case of loans is the same for everyone.

R. Jose the Galilean says, "It says THE SEVENTH YEAR, THE YEAR OF REMISSION, IS APPROACHING (Deut. 15:9). If the period of seven years is different in each case, how could it be said that it IS APPROACH-ING? From this we deduce that it is the same for everyone."

Is it possible that the remission of loans was practiced in the wilderness? The verse says YOU SHALL PRACTICE THE REMISSION OF DEBTS . . . SHALL REMIT (Deut. 15:1–2). Or does YOU SHALL PRACTICE THE REMISSION OF DEBTS . . . SHALL REMIT indicate that in the Land of Israel, where you practice remission of land, you practice remission of loans, but outside the Land, where you do not practice re-mission of land, you do not practice remission of loans? The verse says FOR THE REMISSION PROCLAIMED IS OF THE LORD (Deut. 15:2)— both in the Land and outside of it.

THIS SHALL BE THE NATURE OF THE REMISSION (Deut. 15:2). This was the source of the teaching: If one repays his debt during the sev-

---

SEVEN YEARS twice   Since logic alone could lead to differing conclusions of equal merit, we take our clue from the repetition of the words "seven years." Every seven years the land was to lie fallow and every seven years loans are forgiven. It is a uniform period for everyone.

it IS APPROACHING   This phrase indicates that a specific year called "the seventh year" is approaching. Therefore it is one year for everyone and not a different period for each person.

in the wilderness   The verse, in the future tense and with the double mention of *release*, is taken to mean that in the future, when they reach the Land where land remission will be practiced, then loan remission will also be practiced.

both in the Land and outside of it   This verse informs us that even though the practice of remission did not start until they reached the Land, once they reached it loan remission was practiced outside the Land as well.

enth year, he should be told, "It is remitted." If he says to him, "Nevertheless . . ." he may accept it from him since it is said THIS SHALL BE THE NATURE OF THE REMISSION.

The Sabbatical year remits loans, but the Jubilee year does not remit loans. One might have reasoned: If the Sabbatical year, which does not release slaves, remits loans, certainly the Jubilee year, which does release slaves, must remit loans! Therefore the verse says THIS SHALL BE THE NATURE OF THE REMISSION (Deut. 15:2)—the Sabbatical year remits loans, but the Jubilee year does not remit loans.

We might also reason in regard to slaves, that if the Jubilee year, which does not remit loans, releases slaves, surely the Sabbatical year, which remits loans, should release slaves. Therefore the verse says IN THIS YEAR OF JUBILEE (Lev. 25:13). The Sabbatical year remits loans and the Jubilee year releases slaves.

EACH CREDITOR SHALL REMIT (Deut. 15:2). We might think that this applies to stolen property and to deposits as well, therefore the verse says THAT WHICH HE HAS LENT (Deut. 15:2). We might think that THAT WHICH HE HAS LENT applies to the wages of a hired laborer or store debts, therefore the verse says THAT HE CLAIMS FROM HIS NEIGHBOR (Deut. 15:2). Since in any case eventually we are going to include all of these, why does it state THAT WHICH HE HAS LENT? To indicate that just as THAT WHICH HE HAS LENT is an obligation, so all of them are obligations.

---

he should be told The Hebrew word for THE NATURE is *devar*, which literally means "word." From this they learn that if someone offers to repay his debt, he should be told "It is remitted." As long as he says it, thus fulfilling the *devar* (word), it is permissible to accept the offered payment.

the Jubilee year—the fiftieth year is the year following the seventh Sabbatical year in a cycle. On it slaves are released, including those who took on themselves perpetual slavery.

should release slaves—but the Sabbatical year does not release slaves.

The Sabbatical year remits loans Since logic alone cannot determine correct practice, the various verses specify what is to be done: Loans are remitted in the Sabbatical year and slaves in the Jubilee year.

eventually we are going to include all of these The law, as codified in the Mishna, does include these in the categories of loans that are forgiven. Why, then, should the verses exclude them?

HE SHALL NOT DUN (Deut. 15:2). This imposes a prohibition. HIS NEIGHBOR (Deut. 15:2)—excluding others. OR KINSMAN (Deut. 15:2)—excluding the resident alien. FOR THE REMISSION PRO-CLAIMED IS OF THE LORD (Deut. 15:2)—both in the Land and outside of it.

YOU MAY DUN THE FOREIGNER (Deut. 15:3). This is a positive mitzvah. WHATEVER IS DUE YOU FROM YOUR KINSMEN (Deut. 15:3) and not whatever is in your hand of your brother's. From this we learn that a loan secured by a pledge need not be remitted.

FROM YOUR KINSMEN YOU MUST REMIT (Deut. 15:3)—but not bonds which have been handed over to the court. It was on this basis that Hillel instituted the *prosbul*. He did this in order to restore order to society, for he saw that people refrained from giving loans to one another and thus violated what the Torah said. Therefore he instituted the *prosbul*. This is the text of the *prosbul:* I declare to you, so-and-so and so-and-so, judges in such-and-such a place, that I shall collect whatever debts are owed to me at whatever time I so desire. The judges or the witnesses then sign below.

COMMENTARY   *Several legislative changes were promulgated by the Sages for the purpose of "giving order to society," that is, permitting life to continue in a proper and just way. The most prominent of these was the prosbul instituted by Hillel the Elder in the first century B.C.E. The prosbul, the name of which is an abreviation of a Greek phrase meaning "before the court," was instituted by him because the conditions of life had changed so that commerce could not continue if the Biblical laws of release were to be observed. Therefore Hillel found it necessary to change the legal practice in order to preserve the Torah's intent of creating a just society.*

THERE SHALL BE NO NEEDY AMONG YOU (Deut. 15:4). Later it says FOR THERE WILL NEVER CEASE TO BE NEEDY ONES IN

---

of your brother's—belonging to your brother.

on this basis Since the verse indicates that you have to return something but the court does not, Hillel had a basis for his innovation.

prosbul A legal document that made the debt enforceable by the court.

what the Torah said—BEWARE LEST YOU HARBOR THE BASE THOUGHT, "THE SEVENTH YEAR IS APPROACHING," SO THAT YOU ARE MEAN TO YOUR NEEDY KINSMAN AND GIVE HIM NOTHING (Deut. 15:9).

YOUR LAND (Deut. 15:11). When you do God's will, needy ones will be found only among others, but when you do not do God's will, needy ones will be found among you.

IF ONLY YOU HEAR THE LORD YOUR GOD (Deut. 15:5). This was the source of the teaching: If a man hears a little, he will be made to hear a great deal. If a man hears teachings of Torah, he will be made to hear teachings of the Scribes. AND TAKE CARE TO KEEP ALL THIS MITZVAH (Deut. 15:5)—a minor mitzvah should be as precious to you as a major one. . . .

DO NOT HARDEN YOUR HEART (Deut. 15:7). There are people who agonize over whether to give or not. AND SHUT YOUR HAND (Deut. 15:7). There are those who first extend their hand, but then shut it again. AGAINST YOUR NEEDY KINSMAN (Deut. 15:7). If you fail to give to him, you will end up taking from him. How do we know that if one has opened [his hand] once, he must continue to open it—even a hundred times? The verse says RATHER, YOU MUST OPEN YOUR HAND TO HIM AND LEND HIM SUFFICIENT FOR WHATEVER HE NEEDS (Deut. 15:8)

RATHER YOU MUST OPEN (Deut. 15:8). Open a conversation with him. If he is embarrassed, say to him, "Do you need a loan?" This was the source of the teaching: Charity is best given as a loan. LEND HIM SUFFICIENT FOR WHATEVER HE NEEDS (Deut. 15:8). You should first give him a loan and then ask him for a deposit, so taught R. Judah. The Sages say, "Say to him: bring a deposit—in order to encourage him."

WHATEVER HE NEEDS (Deut. 15:8). You are not commanded to make him rich. IN WHATEVER HE LACKS (Deut. 15:8). It once happened that Hillel the Elder gave a poor man from a good family a horse to exercise on and a servant to take care of him. And in the upper Galilee, it once

---

a minor mitzvah—usually defined as something that requires no expenditure. It may also refer to either the difficulty involved in observing it or the punishment connected to it.

a hundred times The Hebrew for MUST OPEN contains a repetition of the root word "to open." Thus you must be prepared to open your hand more than once.

a horse to exercise on For a man from a wealthy family, something that might seem extravagant is considered basic. The phrase *he lacks* means that the individual may have a lack that might not seem important to someone else.

happened that a guest was served a pound of meat a day. HE LACKS (lo) (Deut. 15:8)—this includes his wife, as in the verse I WILL MAKE HIM (lo) A FITTING HELPER (Gen. 2:18).

BEWARE LEST (Deut. 15:9). Be careful not to withold mercy. For whoever witholds mercy is compared to transgressors and to those who cast off the yoke of Heaven, as it is said BASE THOUGHT (beliya-al) (Deut. 15:9)—without a yoke (beli ol). Another interpretation: BEWARE LEST (Deut. 15:9). BEWARE is a prohibition. LEST is also a prohibition.

LEST YOU HARBOR THE BASE THOUGHT (Deut. 15:9). This is known as idolatry, for here it says BASE and elsewhere it says THAT SOME BASE FELLOWS FROM AMONG YOU (Deut. 13:14). Just as those BASE FELLOWS are guilty of idolatry, so anyone with these BASE THOUGHTS is guilty of idolatry.

"THE SEVENTH YEAR, THE YEAR OF REMISSION, IS AP-PROACHING" (Deut. 15:9). This is what R. Jose the Galilean said, "If the period of seven years is different in each case, how could it be said that it IS APPROACHING? From this we deduce that it is the same for everyone."

SO THAT YOU ARE MEAN TO YOUR NEEDY KINSMAN AND GIVE HIM NOTHING. IF HE CRIES OUT TO THE LORD AGAINST YOU (Deut. 15:9). Could it be that it is a mitzvah *not* to cry out? The verse says CRIES OUT. Could it be that it is a mitzvah to cry out? The verse says AND HE NOT CRY OUT AGAINST YOU (Deut. 24:15). Could it be that if he cries out against you YOU WILL INCUR GUILT (Deut. 15:9), and if not you will not incur guilt? The verse says YOU WILL INCUR GUILT—in any case. If that is so, why does it say IF HE CRIES OUT TO THE LORD AGAINST YOU (Deut. 15:9)? "If he cries out, I will be more swift to punish you than if he does not cry out."

How do you know that if you have given once, you must continue to give him even a hundred times? The verse says GIVE TO HIM READILY (Deut. 15:10).

---

includes his wife   Her needs must also be met.
the yoke of Heaven—the acceptance of the Kingship of God.
are guilty of idolatry   In Deut. 13:14 the discussion is of those who lead others into idolatry.
more swift to punish   The poor man may decide whether or not to cry out. God will punish you in either case, but if he does cry out, the punishment will be more immediate.

HIM (Deut. 15:10)—just between you and him. This was the source of the teaching: There was a Chamber of Secrets in Jerusalem. FOR IN RETURN (Deut. 15:10). If one intends to give and then gives, he receives the reward for the intention and for the deed. If he intends to give but is unable to do so, he receives the reward for the intention but not for the deed.

If he did not intend to give, but tells others to do so, he receives a reward for that, as it is said FOR IN RETURN FOR THIS THING (Deut. 15:10).

If he does not intend to give and does not tell others to do so, but comforts [the poor man] with kind words, how do we know that he receives a reward? The verse says FOR IN RETURN FOR THIS THING THE LORD YOUR GOD WILL BLESS YOU IN ALL YOUR EFFORTS (Deut. 15:10).

4. Deuteronomy 15:15, Sifre Deuteronomy 120, 179

ALWAYS REMEMBER THAT YOU WERE SLAVES IN THE LAND OF EGYPT (Deut. 15:15). Just as I repeatedly supplied your needs in Egypt, so you should repeatedly supply the needs [of your slave]. Just as I gave you generously in Egypt, so should you give generously [to your slave].

Thus it says THERE ARE WINGS OF A DOVE SHEATHED IN SILVER (Ps. 68:14)—this refers to the spoils of Egypt.

ITS PINIONS IN FINE GOLD (Ps. 68:14)—this refers to the spoil at the Sea.

WE WILL ADD WREATHS OF GOLD (Song 1:11)—this refers to the spoil at the Sea.

TO YOUR SPANGLES OF SILVER (Song 1:11)—this refers to the spoils of Egypt.

THEREFORE I ENJOIN THIS COMMANDMENT UPON YOU TO-DAY (Deut. 15:15). The ear is pierced during the daytime and not at night.

Chamber of Secrets—a place where people secretly brought their contributions and the poor could simply go and take what they needed.

THIS THING The Hebrew word means either a thing or a word, hence telling others or even having the intention to give receives a reward.

---

4. *the spoils of Egypt* The spoil is what God gave generously to Israel.

The ear is pierced The slave who refuses to leave at the end of six years has his ear pierced and remains in servitude.

BUT SHOULD HE SAY TO YOU, "I DO NOT WANT TO LEAVE YOU" (Deut. 15:16). Is saying it once enough? The verse says BUT IF THE SLAVE DECLARES (Ex. 21:5)—he must say it and repeat it. If he said it during the six years but did not repeat it at the end of the six years, he does not have his ear pierced, as it is said I DO NOT WISH TO BE FREED (Deut. 21:5)—he must say it at the time when he is being freed. If he said it at the end of six years but had not said it during the six years, he does not have his ear pierced, as it is said BUT IF THE SLAVE DE-CLARES (Ex. 21:5)—he must say it while he is still a slave.

FOR HE LOVES YOU (Deut. 15:16). Since it says elsewhere I LOVE MY MASTER (Ex. 21:5) do I not know that he loves his master? From here we learn that if he loves his master but his master does not love him, or if his master loves him but he does not love his master, he does not have his ear pierced, as it is said BECAUSE HE LOVES YOU (Deut. 15:16). If he has a wife and children but his master does not have a wife and children, he does not have his ear pierced, as it is said FOR HE LOVES YOU AND YOUR HOUSEHOLD (Deut. 15:16). AND IS HAPPY WITH YOU (Deut. 15:16)—thus if he is ill or his master is ill, he does not have his ear pierced.

YOU SHALL TAKE AN AWL (Deut. 15:17). How do we know that it is permitted to use a thorn, a sliver of glass, or a splinter of reed? As it is said YOU SHALL TAKE. So taught R. Jose son of R. Judah.

Rabbi Judah the Prince says, "AN AWL—since an awl is made of metal, I must conclude that only metal instruments may be used."

This was the source of R. Ishmael's teaching: In three instances the *halakha* circumvents the Scripture:

The Torah says HE SHALL POUR OUT ITS BLOOD AND COVER IT WITH EARTH (Lev. 17:13) and the *halakha* says—he may cover it with anything that grows plants.

The Torah says AND HE WRITES HER A BILL OF DIVORCE-

---

and repeat it   In Hebrew the words *the slave declares* contains a repetition of the root *to declare*, hence he must say it twice.

he does not have his ear pierced   He does not remain a slave.

his master does not love him   The phrase FOR HE LOVES YOU seems extraneous. Its meaning is that there is a mutuality between the slave and his master. If this does not exist, he is not permitted to remain in slavery.

the halakha—the practices determined by the Sages as normative.

cover it   The blood from an animal or bird is to be covered.

MENT (Deut. 24:1) and the *halakha* says—he may write it upon anything which was separated from the ground;

The Torah says AN AWL (Deut. 15:17) and the *halakha* says—with anything.

R. Judah the Prince says, "TO THE DOOR OR THE DOORPOST (Ex. 21:6)—which is in an upright position."

AN AWL (Deut. 15:17) This means the large awl.

YOU SHALL TAKE AN AWL (Deut. 15:17). I might think that this is done privately. The verse says HIS MASTER SHALL TAKE HIM BEFORE THE JUDGES (Ex. 21:6)—to the judges, so that he may convey this to the sellers. AN AWL (Deut. 15:17)—anything that will make a sign.

COMMENTARY   *Slavery—in the case of Israelites, more properly indentured servitude—continued to exist, but rabbinic law tended to make the conditions such that it was more difficult to be a master and less difficult to be a slave. In this section we see that the Torah's provision that a slave could extend his service beyond seven years was surrounded with regulations that made it more difficult to carry this out. His intention would have to be very clear and very determined before it could be done. It is interesting that R. Ishmael felt that the power of traditional law, halakha, was such that it could extend certain areas of the Torah in ways that contradicted the specific provisions of the Torah.*

5. Deuteronomy 21:1, Sifre Deuteronomy 205, 240

IF SOMEONE SLAIN IS FOUND (Deut. 21:1)—but not when this occurs frequently. This is the source of the teaching: When murderers increased, the law of the breaking of the heifer's neck was abolished. This was when

---

judges   The Hebrew word is *elohim*, which usually means God but is sometimes taken to refer to human judges.

---

5. *When murderers increased*—at the end of the period of the Second Temple at the time of Rabban Johanan b. Zakkai, c.70 C.E.

the breaking of the heifer's neck   In order to atone for the blood of an innocent victim whose body in found in an empty place belonging to no one, the elders of the nearest settlement conduct this ceremony.

Eliezer b. Dinai and Tehina b. Perishah appeared. Originally called son of Perishah, he was later renamed "son of the murderer."

AND THEY SHALL PRONOUNCE THIS DECLARATION (Deut. 21:7) in the holy tongue. "OUR HANDS DID NOT SHED THIS BLOOD" (Deut. 21:7). Would it ever occur to us that the elders of the court were shedders of blood? Rather it means: He did not come to us only to be sent away without food. We did not see him and let him go on his way with no escort.

"ABSOLVE, O LORD, YOUR PEOPLE ISRAEL" (Deut. 21:8). When it says WHOM YOU REDEEMED (Deut. 21:8) it teaches that this absolution was for those who left Egypt. ABSOLVE, O LORD, YOUR PEOPLE refers to those who are alive. WHOM YOU REDEEMED refers to the dead. This informs us that the dead too are in need of absolution. We also learn that whoever sheds blood is a sinner as far back as the time of those who left Egypt. WHOM YOU REDEEMED. It was for this that You redeemed them—so that there would not be any shedders of blood among us. Another interpretation: You redeemed us on condition that should we sin, You will absolve us. Says the Holy Spirit, "As long as you follow this law, the blood will be absolved for you."

THUS YOU WILL REMOVE (Deut. 21:9). Remove evildoers from Israel.

COMMENTARY   *The Biblical law concerning a dead body that is found in the field receives a sensitive interpretation at the hands of the Sages who emphasize the importance of preventing bloodshed and extend responsibility to taking adequate precautions to prevent anything happening to a person leaving a city. Just as other laws, such as that of the Sotah, were abolished during the period prior to the destruction of the Temple in 70 C.E., so this law was abolished. The chaotic conditions brought about by the various Zealot groups caused many deaths. The Sages, who opposed the actions of*

---

the holy tongue—Hebrew.

the elders of the court   The declaration is made by them. Who would even suspect them of the murder?

on condition that should we sin   The Covenant included the provision for the absolution of sins, since God knew in advance that sin would occur and gave Israel the means of overcoming its effects.

506

the Zealots, termed them "murderers." When society loses control, there is no point in rituals of absolution.

6. Deuteronomy 26:3, Sifre Deuteronomy 299, 318

YOU SHALL GO TO THE PRIEST IN CHARGE AT THAT TIME AND SAY TO HIM (Deut. 26:3). Be not an ingrate. "I ACKNOWLEDGE THIS DAY BEFORE THE LORD YOUR GOD THAT I HAVE ENTERED" (Deut. 26:3). You recite this only once a year, and not twice.

"THAT I HAVE ENTERED THE LAND WHICH THE LORD SWORE TO OUR FATHERS" (Deut. 26:3). This excludes converts. "TO GIVE US" (Deut. 26:3). This excludes slaves. R. Simeon says, "This excludes the other side of the Jordan which you took on your own."

THE PRIEST SHALL TAKE THE BASKET FROM YOUR HAND (Deut. 26:4). This was the source of the teaching: The rich bring their first fruits in vase-shaped baskets of silver and gold, while the poor may bring theirs in wicker baskets of peeled willow. Both the baskets and the first fruits are given to the priests in order to increase the number of gifts given to the priests.

FROM YOUR HAND (Deut. 26:4). This teaches that they require waving, so taught R. Eliezer b. Jacob.

AND SET IT DOWN IN FRONT OF THE ALTAR OF THE LORD YOUR GOD (Deut. 26:4). When the altar exists, first fruits are brought, but when there is no altar, there are no first fruits.

---

6. *once a year*   The matter under discussion is the ceremony of the first fruits. Once a year, each land owner was to bring his first fruits to the Temple and make this declaration.

excludes converts—since they cannot call those who received the Land "our fathers." The law, as determined by Maimonides and others, however, was that since the convert is considered a descendant of Abraham he may make the declaration.

the other side of the Jordan—Transjordan. Although occupied by two-and-a-half tribes (Num. 32), this area was not considered a part of the Land that God promised and allocated to the tribes but something they took on their own.

waving   Certain offerings were moved up and down symbolically before being given at the altar.

AND SET IT DOWN. This is the source of the teaching: If they were stolen or lost, one is required to replace them. If they became unclean while in the Temple Court, one scatters them and need not make the declaration.

YOU SHALL THEN RESPOND AND SAY (Deut. 26:5). "Responding" is stated here and "responding" is stated elsewhere (Deut. 27:14). Just as the "responding" there is in the holy tongue, so the "responding" here is in the holy tongue. This is the source of the teaching: At first whoever knew how to make the declaration did so, while those who did not know how had it recited to them. When people refrained from bringing [first fruits because of that,] they decreed that the declaration should be recited both to those who knew and to those who did not know. For this they relied on the verse YOU SHALL RESPOND. "Response" always means that one recites at the prompting of others.

AND SAY BEFORE THE LORD YOUR GOD: MY FATHER WAS A FUGITIVE (obed) ARAMEAN (Deut. 26:5). This teaches us that Jacob went to Aram assuming that he would perish (l'abed) and Laban is considered as if he had destroyed him (ibdo).

HE WENT DOWN TO EGYPT (Deut. 26:5). You might think that he went down there in order to assume the crown of kingship for himself. The verse says AND SOJOURNED THERE (Deut. 26:5). Does this mean with great numbers? The verse says WITH MEAGER NUMBERS (Deut. 26:5) as is explained in the verse YOUR ANCESTORS WENT DOWN TO EGYPT SEVENTY PERSONS IN ALL (Deut. 10:22).

BUT THERE HE BECAME A GREAT NATION (Deut. 26:5). This teaches that Israel was distinguishable there.

"responding" is stated elsewhere—in reference to the ceremony of curses, which was held before they entered the Land.

refrained from bringing Those who did not know how to recite the declaration were embarrassed.

be recited both to those who knew Since everyone was prompted as to what to do, there would be no embarrassment for those who did not know it.

Laban Laban was an Aramean. This interpretation assumes that he is referred to in this verse and translates it as "An Aramean was destroying my father," my father being Jacob.

AND SOJOURNED THERE Sojourning means a temporary stay of a stranger. It could not be applied to one who wanted to control the kingdom.

distinguishable They were different from the Egyptians and therefore could be discerned to be a nation.

AND HE SAW OUR PLIGHT (Deut. 26:7) as it is said SEE THE BIRTHSTOOL (Ex. 1:16).

OUR MISERY (Deut. 26:7) as it is said EVERY BOY THAT IS BORN YOU SHALL THROW INTO THE NILE BUT LET EVERY GIRL LIVE (Ex. 1:22).

[AND OUR OPPRESSION (Deut. 26:7). This refers to terrible oppression as it is said I HAVE SEEN HOW THE EGYPTIANS OPPRESS THEM (Ex. 3:9).

THE LORD FREED US FROM EGYPT (Deut. 26:8)—not by means of an angel;

> not by means of a seraph;
> not by means of a messenger;
> but the Holy One Himself in all His glory [freed us],

as it is said FOR THAT NIGHT I WILL GO THROUGH THE LAND OF EGYPT AND I WILL STRIKE DOWN EVERY FIRSTBORN IN THE LAND OF EGYPT, BOTH MAN AND BEAST; AND I WILL METE OUT PUNISHMENTS TO ALL THE GODS OF EGYPT, I THE LORD (Ex. 12:12).

> I WILL GO THROUGH THE LAND OF EGYPT—
> I and not an angel;
> AND I WILL STRIKE DOWN EVERY FIRSTBORN—
> I and not a seraph;
> AND I WILL METE OUT PUNISHMENTS TO ALL
> THE GODS OF EGYPT—I and not a messenger;
> I THE LORD—I am He; there is none other.

BY A MIGHTY HAND (Deut. 26:8). This refers to the pestilence, as it is said THEN THE HAND OF THE LORD WILL STRIKE YOUR LIVE-

---

BIRTHSTOOL The birthstool was symbolic of their plight since the midwives were to see if the infant being born was a boy or a girl and kill all the boys.
AND OUR OPPRESSION This section in parentheses is not found in the received texts, which simply state "etc." It is found, however, in the text of the Passover Haggadah.

STOCK IN THE FIELDS—THE HORSES, THE ASSES, THE CAM-ELS, THE CATTLE, AND THE SHEEP—WITH A VERY SEVERE PESTILENCE (Ex. 9:3).

BY AN OUTSTRETCHED ARM (Deut. 26:8). This refers to the sword, as it is said WITH A DRAWN SWORD IN HIS HAND DIRECTED AGAINST JERUSALEM (1 Chron. 21:16).

AND AWESOME POWER (Deut. 26:8). This refers to the revelation of the Divine Presence, as it is said OR HAS ANY GOD VENTURED TO GO AND TAKE FOR HIMSELF ONE NATION FROM THE MIDST OF ANOTHER BY PRODIGIOUS ACTS, BY SIGNS AND POR-TENTS, BY A MIGHTY HAND AND OUTSTRETCHED ARM AND AWESOME POWER, AS THE LORD YOUR GOD DID FOR YOU IN EGYPT BEFORE YOUR VERY EYES? (Deut. 4:34).

AND BY SIGNS (Deut. 26:8). This refers to the rod, as it is said AND TAKE WITH YOU THIS ROD, WITH WHICH YOU SHALL PER-FORM THE SIGNS (Ex. 4:17).

AND PORTENTS (Deut. 26:8). This refers to the blood, as it is said I WILL SET PORTENTS IN THE SKY AND ON EARTH: BLOOD AND FIRE AND PILLARS OF SMOKE (Joel 3:3).
Another interpretation:

> BY A MIGHTY HAND (Deut. 26:8)—two;
> BY AN OUTSTRETCHED ARM (Deut. 26:8)—two;
> AND AWESOME POWER (Deut. 26:8)—two;
> AND BY SIGNS (Deut. 26:8)—two;
> AND PORTENTS (Deut. 26:8)—two.

These are the ten plagues which the Holy One brought upon the Egyptians in Egypt. They are: blood, frogs, vermin, swarms of insects, pestilence, boils, hail, locusts, darkness, the slaying of the firstborn.]
R. Judah supplied a mnemonic device [for the plagues]: DZK ADSH B'HB.

---

two Each phrase indicates two plagues, some because there are two words, some because of the plural usage.
mnemonic device He took the first Hebrew letter for each of the ten plagues and put them into three words that have no meaning but could be more easily remembered.

HE BROUGHT US TO THIS PLACE (Deut. 26:9). This refers to the Temple. Perhaps it refers to the Land of Israel? When it says AND GAVE US THIS LAND (Deut. 26:9) it is clear that this is the reference to the Land of Israel. What then does AND BROUGHT US TO THIS PLACE mean? Because we come to this place, He gives us this Land.

A LAND FLOWING WITH MILK AND HONEY (Deut. 26:9). Here it says A LAND FLOWING WITH MILK AND HONEY and elsewhere it says A LAND FLOWING WITH MILK AND HONEY (Ex. 13:5). Just as A LAND FLOWING WITH MILK AND HONEY there refers to the five nations, so A LAND FLOWING WITH MILK AND HONEY here refers to the five nations. R. Jose the Galilean said, "First fruits are not brought from the other side of the Jordan, for it is not FLOWING WITH MILK AND HONEY."

> AND NOW (Deut. 26:10)—immediately.
> BEHOLD (Deut. 26:10)—with rejoicing.
> I BRING (Deut. 26:10)—of my own.

THE FIRST FRUITS OF THE SOIL (Deut. 26:10). This was the source of the teaching: When a man goes into his field and sees a ripened fig, a ripened cluster, a ripened pomegranate, he should tie it with a reed string and say "These are first fruits."

WHICH YOU, O LORD, HAVE GIVEN ME (Deut. 26:10). This was the source of the teaching: A guardian, a slave, an agent, a woman, a person of doubtful sex, or an *androgynous* may bring [first fruit], but they do not make the declaration since they cannot say WHICH YOU, O LORD, HAVE GIVEN ME.

YOU SHALL LEAVE THEM BEFORE THE LORD YOUR GOD AND BOW LOW BEFORE THE LORD YOUR GOD (Deut. 26:10). This teaches that they are set down twice, once when the declaration is recited and once when the bringer bows down.

Because we come to this place Because we come to the Temple and worship God, we are enabled to possess the Land.

the five nations—enumerated in Ex. 13:5: the Canaanites, the Hittites, the Amorites, the Hivites, and the Jebusites.

tie it with a reed string—thus designating it to be brought to the Temple.

androgynous—a person with characteristics of both sexes.

AND YOU SHALL ENJOY (Deut. 26:11) with all kinds of enjoyments.
ALL THE BOUNTY (Deut. 26:11)—this refers to the Song.
THAT THE LORD YOUR GOD HAS BESTOWED UPON YOU
AND YOUR HOUSEHOLD (Deut. 26:11). This teaches that a man may
bring first fruits from the holdings of his wife and recite the declaration.
TOGETHER WITH THE LEVITE AND THE STRANGER IN
YOUR MIDST (Deut. 26:11). This is the source of the teaching: Israelites
and bastards may recite the declaration, but converts and freed slaves may
not do so since they have no portion in the Land.

COMMENTARY   *The declaration made when bringing the first fruits to
the Temple is one of the few liturgical texts in the Torah. The Sages here
formulate the ways in which it was to be recited when the Temple existed.
In addition, they interpreted the declaration, explaining every phrase. They
particularly emphasized the personal intervention of God, denying any role
for anyone other than the Holy One in the redemption from Egypt, even
though this goes against the plain sense of Scripture. Is this a protest against
the role of an intermediary in the process of redemption, which was insisted
on by early Christianity? The Sages also made the Biblical text of the declaration together with their interpretation of it the central feature of the Passover night recitation, the Haggadah. These few verses became the required
minimum for the telling of the story of the Exodus.*

---

the Song—Psalm 30, which was recited when the procession reached the Temple court.

RABBINIC AUTHORITIES
BY GENERATIONS

The term *Tannaim* refers to those Sages after Hillel and Shammai (first century B.C.E.) until the time of R. Judah the Prince (third century C.E.). They are divided into generations as follows:

T (Tanna) I—period prior to the destruction (70 C.E.) and immediately following

T II—period after the destruction (c.90–110 C.E.)

T III—period prior to the Bar Kochba rebellion (c.110–135)

T IV—period after the rebellion (c.135–175 C.E.)

T V—period of Judah the Prince (c.175–early third century)

There are many Sages who cannot be classified simply because we know too little about them. In such cases, the name appears with no generation listed. A few authorities belong to an even earlier period. These are the so called pairs, groups of two leaders who headed the Pharisaic Academy in the centuries before the Common Era.

Abba Hanin T III–IV
Abba Hedores
Abba Jose b. Dostai T IV
Abba Joseph of Mahoz
Abba Saul T III–IV
Absalom the Elder
Abtalyon—"pairs" 1st century
   B.C.E.
Aha T IV or V
Ahai b. Josiah
Akabya b. Mehallel T I
Akiba T III

Ben Azzai T III
Ben Zoma T III
Benaiah T V

Dosa T I
Dostai b. Jose
Dostai b. Judah T V

Eleazar b. Ahbai
Eleazar b. Azariah T III
Eleazar b. Isaac T III

Eleazar b. Jose T IV
Eleazar b. Jose the Galilean T V
Eleazar b. Judah of Kfar Tota
  T III
Eleazar b. Simeon T V
Eleazar ha-Kappar T V
Eleazar Hisma T III
Eleazar of Modi'in T III
Eliezer T II
Eliezer b. Jacob 1 T II
          2 T IV

(Rabban) Gamliel T II

Hanania Chief of the Priests T I
Hanania b. Antigonos T III
Hanania b. Gamliel T IV
Hanania b. Halnisi
Hanina b. Teradion T III
Hanina nephew of R. Joshua
  T III
Hidka Simeon HaShikmoni
  T IV
Hiyya b. Nachmani T IV

Isaac T IV
Ishmael T III
Isi b. Akabia
Isi b. Menachem

Jacob b. Hanilai T V
Jeshaya Abba Hanin
Johanan b. Baroka T III
Johanan b. Nuri T III
(Rabban) Johanan b. Zakkai T I
Jonathan T IV
Jonathan b. Beterah
Jose T IV
Jose b. R. Joseph T IV
Jose b. R. Judah T V
Jose the Galilean T III

Jose son of a woman from
  Damascus T III–IV
Joshua T II
Joshua b. Korha T IV
Josiah T IV
Judah b. Babba T III
Judah b. Beterah 1. T I
                  2. T III
Judah b. Hananiah
Judah (b. Ilai) T IV
Judah b. Lakish T V
Judah b. Tabbai—"pairs" 1st
  century B.C.E.
Judah the Prince T V

Matya b. Heresh T III–IV
Meir T IV

Nathan T IV
Nehemiah T IV
Nehorai T IV

Shemaya—"pairs" 1st century
  B.C.E.
Simai—end of Tannaitic,
  beginning of Amoraic period
Simeon b. Eleazar T V
(Rabban) Simeon b. Gamliel
  1st—T I, 2nd—T IV
Simeon b. Johanan b. Beroka
Simeon b. Judah T V
Simeon b. Menasia T V
Simeon b. Shetah—"pairs" 1st
  century B.C.E.
Simeon b. Yohai T IV
Simeon of Kitron
Simeon of Timneh T III

Tarphon T III

Zadok T I
Zerika Amora III

SELECTED
BIBLIOGRAPHY

A. PRIMARY TEXTS: TRANSLATIONS AND COMMENTARIES

The Fathers According to Rabbi Nathan, Judith Goldin (New Haven, 1955)
Mekilta de-Rabbi Ishmael, Jacob Z. Lauterbach (Philadelphia, 1949)
Sifra. The Rabbinic Commentary on Leviticus. Jacob Neusner (1985)
Sifre to Numbers, Jacob Neusner (Atlanta, 1986)
Sifre. A Tannaitic Commentary on the Book of Deuteronomy, Reuven Hammer (New Haven, 1986)

B. STUDIES OF PORTIONS OF PRIMARY TEXTS

H. W. Basser, *Midrashic Interpretations of the Song of Moses* (New York, 1984)
Judah Goldin, *The Song at the Sea* (New Haven, 1971)
Max Kadushin, *A Conceptual Approach to the Mekilta* (New York, 1969)

C. ANTHOLOGIES OF MIDRASH

H. N. Bialik and Y. H. Ravnitzky, *The Book of Legends* (New York, 1992)
Louis Ginzberg, *Legends of the Jews* (Philadelphia, 1954)
Louis Ginzberg, *Legends of the Bible* (New York, 1956)
Nahum Glatzer, *Hammer on the Rocks, A Midrash Reader* (New York, 1956)
Gary G. Porton, *Understanding Rabbinic Midrash* (Hoboken, 1985)

D. STUDIES OF MIDRASH

Daniel Boyarin, *Intertextuality and the Reading of Midrash* (Bloomington, 1990)

SELECTED BIBLIOGRAPHY

Michael Fishbane, *The Garments of Torah* (Bloomington, 1989)

Steven D. Fraade, *From Tradition to Commentary* (Albany, 1991)

Louis Ginzberg, *On Jewish Law and Lore* (Philadelphia, 1955)

Judah Goldin, *Studies in Midrash and Related Literature* (Philadelphia, 1988)

David Weiss Halivni, *Midrash, Mishnah, and Gemara* (Cambridge, 1986)

Geoffrey H. Hartman and Sanford Budick, eds., *Midrash and Literature* (New Haven, 1986)

Max Kadushin, *The Rabbinic Mind* (New York, 1952)

Saul Lieberman, *Hellenism in Jewish Palestine* (New York, 1962)

Solomon Schechter, *Some Aspects of Rabbinic Theology* (New York, 1936)

Ephraim Urbach, *The Sages: Their Concepts and Beliefs* (Jerusalem, 1975)

Burton L. Visotzky, *Reading the Bible* (New York, 1991)

E. INTRODUCTIONS TO MIDRASH

Jacob Neusner, *What is Midrash?* (Philadelphia, 1987)

Jacob Neusner, *Invitation to Midrash* (San Fransisco, 1988)

INDEX TO PREFACE
AND INTRODUCTION

INDEX OF RABBINIC
AUTHORITIES

INDEX OF RABBINIC AUTHORITIES

INDEX TO TEXT

Other Volumes in this Series

Francis and Clare • THE COMPLETE WORKS

Gregory Palamas • THE TRIADS

Pietists • SELECTED WRITINGS

The Shakers • TWO CENTURIES OF SPIRITUAL REFLECTION

Zohar • THE BOOK OF ENLIGHTENMENT

Luis de León • THE NAMES OF CHRIST

Quaker Spirituality • SELECTED WRITINGS

Emanuel Swedenborg • THE UNIVERSAL HUMAN AND SOUL-BODY INTERACTION

Augustine of Hippo • SELECTED WRITINGS

Safed Spirituality • RULES OF MYSTICAL PIETY, THE BEGINNING OF WISDOM

Maximus Confessor • SELECTED WRITINGS

John Cassian • CONFERENCES

Johannes Tauler • SERMONS

John Ruusbroec • THE SPIRITUAL ESPOUSALS AND OTHER WORKS

Ibn 'Abbād of Ronda • LETTERS ON THE SŪFĪ PATH

Angelus Silesius • THE CHERUBINIC WANDERER

The Early Kabbalah •

Meister Eckhart • TEACHER AND PREACHER

John of the Cross • SELECTED WRITINGS

Pseudo-Dionysius • THE COMPLETE WORKS

Bernard of Clairvaux • SELECTED WORKS

Devotio Moderna • BASIC WRITINGS

The Pursuit of Wisdom • AND OTHER WORKS BY THE AUTHOR OF THE CLOUD OF UNKNOWING

Richard Rolle • THE ENGLISH WRITINGS

Francis de Sales, Jane de Chantal • LETTERS OF SPIRITUAL DIRECTION

Albert and Thomas • SELECTED WRITINGS

Robert Bellarmine • SPIRITUAL WRITINGS

Nicodemos of the Holy Mountain • A HANDBOOK OF SPIRITUAL COUNSEL

Henry Suso • THE EXEMPLAR, WITH TWO GERMAN SERMONS

Bérulle and the French School • SELECTED WRITINGS

The Talmud • SELECTED WRITINGS

Ephrem the Syrian • HYMNS

Hildegard of Bingen • SCIVIAS

Birgitta of Sweden • LIFE AND SELECTED REVELATIONS

John Donne • SELECTIONS FROM *DIVINE POEMS,* SERMONS, *DEVOTIONS AND PRAYERS*

Jeremy Taylor • SELECTED WORKS

Walter Hilton • *SCALE OF PERFECTION*

Ignatius of Loyola • *SPIRITUAL EXERCISES* AND SELECTED WORKS

Anchoritic Spirituality • *ANCRENE WISSE* AND ASSOCIATED WORKS

Nizam ad-din Awliya • *MORALS FOR THE HEART*

Pseudo-Macarius • THE FIFTY SPIRITUAL HOMILIES AND THE *GREAT LETTER*

Gertrude of Helfta • *THE HERALD OF DIVINE LOVE*

Angela of Foligno • COMPLETE WORKS

Margaret Ebner • MAJOR WORKS

Marguerite Porete • *THE MIRROR OF SIMPLE SOULS*

John Henry Newman • SELECTED SERMONS

Early Anabaptist Spirituality • SELECTED WRITINGS

Elijah Benamozegh • ISRAEL AND HUMANITY